Win32
System Services
THE HEART OF WINDOWS® 98
AND WINDOWS® 2000

ISBN 0-13-022557-6

9 780130 225573

90000

PRENTICE HALL PTR MICROSOFT® TECHNOLOGIES SERIES

NETWORKING

- Microsoft Technology: Networking, Concepts, Tools
Woodard, Gattuccio, Brain

- NT Network Programming Toolkit
Murphy

- Building COM Applications with Internet Explorer
Loveman

- Understanding DCOM
Rubin, Brain

- Web Database Development for Windows Platforms
Gutierrez

PROGRAMMING

- Windows Script Host
Aitken

- The Windows 2000 Device Driver Book, Second Edition
Baker, Lozano

- Win32 System Services: The Heart of Windows 2000 and Windows 98, Third Edition
Brain, Reeves

- Programming the WIN32 API and UNIX System Services
Merusi

- Windows CE 3.0: Application Programming
Grattan, Brain

- The Visual Basic Style Guide
Patrick

- Windows Shell Programming
Seely

- Windows Installer Complete
Easter

- Windows 2000 Web Applications Developer's Guide
Yager

- Developing Windows Solutions with Office 2000 Components and VBA
Aitken

- Multithreaded Programming with Win32
Pham, Garg

- Developing Professional Applications for Windows 98 and NT Using MFC, Third Edition
Brain, Lovette

- Introduction to Windows 98 Programming
Murray, Pappas

- The COM and COM+ Programming Primer
Gordon

- Understanding and Programming COM+: A Practical Guide to Windows 2000 DNA
Oberg

- Distributed COM Application Development Using Visual C++ 6.0
Maloney

- Distributed COM Application Development Using Visual Basic 6.0
Maloney

- The Essence of COM, Third Edition
Platt

- COM-CORBA Interoperability
Geraghty, Joyce, Moriarty, Noone

- MFC Programming in C++ with the Standard Template Libraries
Murray, Pappas

- Introduction to MFC Programming with Visual C++
Jones

- Visual C++ Templates
Murray, Pappas

- Visual Basic Object and Component Handbook
Vogel

- Visual Basic 6: Error Coding and Layering
Gill

- ADO Programming in Visual Basic 6
Holzner

- Visual Basic 6: Design, Specification, and Objects
Hollis

- ASP/MTS/ADSI Web Security
Harrison

BACKOFFICE

- BizTalk: Implementing Business-To-Business E-Commerce
Kobielus

- Designing Enterprise Solutions with Microsoft Technologies
Kemp, Kemp, Goncalves

- Microsoft Site Server 3.0 Commerce Edition
Libertone, Scoppa

- Building Microsoft SQL Server 7 Web Sites
Byrne

- Optimizing SQL Server 7
Schneider, Goncalves

ADMINISTRATION

- Microsoft SQL Server 2000 Optimization Guide
Fields

- Windows 2000 Cluster Server Guidebook
Libertone

PRENTICE HALL SERIES ON MICROSOFT® TECHNOLOGIES

Win32 System Services

THE HEART OF WINDOWS® 98 AND WINDOWS® 2000

Marshall Brain

Ron Reeves

Prentice Hall PTR, Upper Saddle River, NJ 07458
www.phptr.com

Library of Congress Cataloging-in-Publication Data Available

Acquisitions Editor: Mike Meehan
Production Editor: Rose Kernan
Cover Design: Nina Scuderi
Cover Design Director: Jerry Votta
Manufacturing Manager: Maura Zaldivar
Marketing Manager: Debby van Dijk

 © 2001 by PrenticeHall PTR
Prentice-Hall, Inc.
Upper Saddle River, NJ 07458

Prentice Hall books are widely used by corporations and government agencies for training, marketing, and resale.

The publisher offers discounts on this book when ordered in bulk quantities.
For more information, contact Corporate Sales Department, phone: 800-382-3419;
fax: 201-236-7141; e-mail: corpsales@prenhall.com
or write: Prentice Hall PTR
        Corporate Sales Department
        One Lake Street
        Upper Saddle River, NJ 07458

Printed in the United States of America
10   9   8   7   6   5   4   3   2   1

ISBN 0-13-022557-6

Prentice-Hall International (UK) Limited, *London*
Prentice-Hall of Australia Pty. Limited, *Sydney*
Prentice-Hall Canada Inc., *Toronto*
Prentice-Hall Hispanoamericana, S.A., *Mexico*
Prentice-Hall of India Private Limited, *New Delhi*
Prentice-Hall of Japan, Inc., *Tokyo*
Pearson Education Asia Pte. Ltd.
Editora Prentice-Hall do Brasil, Ltda., *Rio de Janeiro*

CONTENTS

The Win32 system services are the innovative, cutting-edge capabilities that make Windows 2000 and Windows 98 interesting and exciting. Amid all of the media attention surrounding Windows 2000 and 98, you have probably heard and read about many of the modern capabilities that these operating systems contain:

- Processes and threads
- Synchronization
- Remote Procedure Calls (RPCs) and DCOM (Distributed COM)
- Event logging
- Network communications
- TCP/IP network communications
- File mapping and Active Directory
- Interprocess and Interprocessor communication
- Compressed file access
- Network drive- and printer-sharing
- Serial communications
- Services (background processing like UNIX daemons)
- Object and file security

The goal of this book is to show you how to use all of these different services in your own applications. This book contains hundreds of concise, clear, and easy-to-understand example programs and explanations. The examples show you how to access the system services listed above, as well as many others. You can use these examples directly, to understand the concepts. You can also drop the sample code into your own programs and then extend it to give your applications new and useful features.

By learning about the many and varied system services available inside of Windows 2000 and 98, you can make your programs much more interesting to the user. For example, if you learn about threads and then add multiple threads to your applications, the user gets a much smoother interface (see Chapter 6). Your program will also take advantage of multiple processors on machines that have them. If you add network support to your applications, the user is able to access network resources that are unavailable on a single machine (see Chapter 8). If you add modem support, you can use it to let the user dial into a remote system (see Chapter 11). Or you might use a modem to let the user dial a support line or registration system for a product that your company sells.

The goal of this book is to give you a thorough and clear understanding of the system services so that you can take advantage of all of the capabilities that Windows has to offer.

Audience

This book is designed for two types of people. If you are a devoted connoisseur or student of programming, the study of the system functions is interesting in its own right. It's fun to see what functions are available, and to try to think of ways to exploit those capabilities. One way to use this book is to simply browse through it and see what is possible. You can work with the examples and extend them in ways that you find enjoyable.

If, on the other hand, you are a programmer with a deadline, enjoyable entertainment is probably not your goal. You may have looked at the huge number of functions in the Windows API and found it discouraging. Where do you start? What you need is a set of useful examples and clear explanations that quickly solve your specific problems. You will find this book useful because it organizes concepts logically and provides the material that you need to master a specific topic very quickly.

If you are migrating from another operating system to Windows, this book will help you to quickly map your existing knowledge into the Windows framework. See Chapter 1 for a list of the 121 most common programming questions in Windows, as well as for the locations of the sections that contain the answers.

Organization

This book is organized by functional categories. For example, Chapter 2 talks about all of the functions that pertain to file input/output and file handling. Chapter 3 deals with disk drives. Chapter 4 discusses directories. Chapter 5 talks about the next-generation directory services, known as Active Directory in Windows 2000. Chapter 6 talks about processes and threads. You will find that each chapter starts with a general overview of the topic, followed by sections that describe and give examples for subsets of functions.

In many chapters you will find integrating examples that combine different capabilities from several chapters to create larger applications. Many of these larger examples form complete applications that you can use as starting points for new projects of your own.

Philosophy

Several principles guide the content of this book. The first principle is the most important and is therefore used throughout: it is *simplicity*. There is nothing worse than looking up a function, only to find that its example is embedded within sample code that takes three days to comprehend because it is 28 pages long. In all cases a function is first demonstrated in code that is as simple as possible so that you can extract the essence of each one very quickly. They may then be integrated into larger examples. In many cases you will look at the example code and say to yourself, "This is easy!" That is exactly the intent. If the book makes everything look simple and easy for you, then it has accomplished its goal.

The second principle driving this book is the idea of functional *families*. Functions in the 32-bit API very rarely exist on their own—it is far more common to find small collections of functions that relate very closely to one another. For example, the **ReadFile** function reads from a file, but you must open the file with **CreateFile** before you can read from it and then remember to close it with **CloseHandle** afterwards (see Chapter 2). These functions belong to a family. In this book you will generally find small groupings of functions described as logical units.

The third principle in this book is that of *currency*. The Windows API has been around for some time, and when you look at it you will find that there is a certain amount of layering. The documentation will often say things like, "this function is retained for compatibility with version 1.8, but has been superseded by function xyz." This book deals only with the current functions, and leaves the superseded ones to die in peace.

The last principle guiding this book is *independence*. Each chapter in this book is as stand-alone as possible, so that you can jump around in the book as you please. In cases where material from other chapters is important, you will find references to the related sections.

Prerequisites and Languages

This book makes no assumptions about your former knowledge of systems programming in Windows or in any other system. Its only real assumption is that you know C and/or C++. You will find that the example code can be divided into two categories:

1. Text examples that run in "console mode." These programs run from the MS-DOS prompt, accept keyboard input, and produce text output. They form the vast majority of the code in this book because they are

simple. These programs are C++– compatible, but the only elements really being used from C++ are the I/O stream libraries.

2. "Windows" programs that use the Windows GUI. These programs use C++ and the Microsoft Foundation Class library (MFC). The book Visual C++: Developing Professional Applications for Windows 98 and NT using MFC, by Marshall Brain and Lance Lovette (ISBN 0-13-085121-3), describes how to create programs with MFC, and will be useful as a tool to help you understand these examples if you are not already familiar with MFC. You can develop C-language Windows programs using only the Win32 API. However, the Visual C++ tools make low-level Win32 programming easier. But to take advantage of the Visual C++ and MFC tools, you should have a good grasp of the underlying Win32 API

If you are a C programmer with no C++ experience, you will have no trouble understanding the console programs. The only unusual thing you will see is code that looks like this:

```
char s[100];
// Prompt the user
cout << "Enter a line of text: ";
// Read a line of text from the user
cin.getline(s,100);
// Echo the user's input to stdout
cout << s << endl;
```

This code declares a character string **s**, and then uses "cout <<" to output a prompt to the user. The "cin.getline" statement reads a line of text from the user. The final "cout" statement echoes the line. The book Visual C++: Developing Professional Applications in Windows 95 and NT using MFC, by Marshall Brain and Lance Lovette (ISBN 0-13-305145-5), contains an extensive C++ appendix to help you get started with the language if you are interested. It will also help you understand the MFC code.

The Diskette and the On-line Index

The diskette included with this book contains the source code for all of the examples in the book, as well as the source and data for an on-line indexing program. The index is broken down by sections and includes every word found in the manuscript.

To use the index, follow the directions in the README file on the disk to compile the program. When you run the index, you will see a display that contains an edit area, three buttons (Help, Search and Quit), and a list area. Any words that you type in the edit area are used to search for appropriate sections. For example, if you want to find out how to create a DLL entry point, you would type "DLL entry point" in the edit area. Press the "Search" button to begin the search. The index program will list all sections that contain all three of those words. Enter as many words as you like to home in on what you want. Word matching is exact and case-insensitive. If a word does not appear in the book, the program will tell you.

There are many cases where an exact match does not work well. For example, there may be a section that contains "thread" and "create" but not "creating" and "threads," so if you enter the line "creating threads" on the edit line you get no matches. You can use the "*" wild card character at the end of a word to solve this problem. For example, by entering "creat*" the system will use OR to gather together all words with the root "creat" ("create," "creates," "creation," etc.). You may want to get in the habit of using the wild card character at the end of all words: "creat* thread*," for example. This often yields more helpful results.

If an obvious word seems to be missing from the index, try to find it in the book to make sure you are spelling it correctly. For example, "resize" is spelled "re-size" in the book, and you need to spell it the same way.

Contents of the Book

Each chapter in this book talks about a different service in the 32-bit API. Chapter 1 contains a list of the 121 most common questions about the system services, and it will help you to quickly find material that interests you. The list below summarizes the different chapters in the book to help you with browsing.

- Chapter 1 is an introduction. It contains a list of the 121 most common programming questions about the Windows system services. This list will serve as a good road map for you. The chapter also contains general information that is useful throughout the book.
- Chapter 2 discusses files. It shows you how to open, read, and write files, how to read from compressed files, how to map files into memory, and so on. The 32-bit API contains quite a few interesting file capabilities.
- Chapter 3 introduces the drive structure of Windows. You will learn how to query the drives on your local machine, as well as how to query and connect to drives on the network.
- Chapter 4 discusses the directory structure. It shows you how to create and traverse directory trees.
- Chapter 5 talks about the next-generation directory structure of Windows 2000. It shows you how to create and use this new directory capability. It also gives suggestions on when to use this active-directory capability.

- Chapter 6 offers a complete introduction to processes and threads in the Windows environment. You will see how to multi-thread your own applications, as well as MFC applications. There is also a discussion of processes, interprocess communication, and inheritance.
- Chapter 7 discusses Windows synchronization mechanisms. Critical sections, mutexes, semaphores and events help you write multi-threaded code that does not step on itself. The chapter introduces you to general synchronization principles and bugs, and shows solutions to a number of standard problems. It also shows you how to incorporate synchronization mechanisms into an MFC program without stalling its event loop.
- Chapter 8 talks about network communications. Windows contains two different native technologies for communicating over a network: mailslots and named pipes. Windows also supports UPD and TCP packets on TCP/IP networks. The latter capabilities let you intercommunicate with UNIX and other TCP/IP machines. The chapter includes a complete introduction to network principles and terminology.
- Chapter 9 intoduces Remote Procedure Calls, or RPCs. An RPC lets you make a function call that is transmitted over a network and executed on another machine. This chapter contains a complete introduction to the hows and whys of RPCs, as well as design principles to keep in mind when creating client/server systems with RPCs. It contains examples of auto, implicit, explicit, and context binding, and also shows how to incorporate RPCs into MFC programs.
- Chapter 10 discusses Distributed COM (DCOM). This chapter shows how DCOM objects are created and distributed to create a distributed network.
- Chapter 11 talks about communications ports in Windows systems. It shows you how to access both the serial and parallel ports, and demonstrates a simple terminal emulator and bulletin board system.
- Chapter 12 discusses Windows 2000 services. These are background processes that start at boot time and run regardless of who is logged in, just like daemons in UNIX. This chapter shows you how to create your own services and install them in NT's service manager. It also shows you how to place RPC servers into services so they run continuously.
- Chapter 13 offers a complete introduction to the Windows 2000 security system. This system is uniform across all NT objects, so you will learn how to secure files, registry keys, pipes, semaphores, and so on. It teaches you everything you need to know to create and modify access control lists and security descriptors.

- Chapter 14 discusses consoles, which you will use when you want to create text-based programs in Windows. For example, if you want to create a terminal emulator, consoles offer an easy way to handle the keyboard input and character output for the emulator.
- Chapter 15 talks about Microsoft Management Console (MMC). It will demonstrate the possibilities, and methods for using ATL (Active Template Library) to do Snap-ins.
- Chapter 16 shows you how to access system information, and how to log users off and shut down or reboot the system. For example, this chapter shows you how to determine how many CPUs a system contains, or how many buttons there are on the mouse.
- Chapter 17 shows you how to modularize your programs using dynamic link libraries (DLLs). Windows can be thought of as an extensible operating system because of DLLs. A programmer can easily add capabilities that others can use by creating a DLL and publishing its interface. Windows itself places much of its functionality in DLLs.
- Chapter 18 discusses some of the basics of the Component Object Model (COM). This will prepare us for the discussion in Chapter 19, of COM+ and Windows 2000.
- Chapter 19 discusses the new COM+ and Windows 2000. This will prepare us for the discussion about Windows 2000 Distributed Network Architecture (DNA), which follows this chapter.
- Chapter 20 discusses Windows 2000 Distributed Network Architecture (DNA). It covers the possibilities and gives a three-tiered architecture example.
- Chapter 21 contains short discussions and examples on six miscellaneous topics: the registry, the event log, the Windows time model, error handling, structured exception handling, and the memory model.
- Appendix A shows you how to compile the different types of code found in the book.
- Appendix B contains information on contacting the authors via E-mail to ask questions and obtain free supplements and updates to this book.

Contacting the Author: Questions, Comments, and Version Changes

One thing about Microsoft is that it never stands still for very long. Its compilers and libraries are constantly changing. One of the goals for this book is that its code be as compatible as possible with existing and future releases of

Microsoft compiler products. Another goal is to give you "investment-grade" knowledge—knowledge that does not lose its value over time, and that is transferable between as many different platforms as possible.

As things change, however, you need a way to get updates and corrections. You may also have questions, comments or suggestions for improving this book. If so, we would like to hear from you. You can use our free E-mail information server to get updates and supplements to this book. You can also send questions and comments via E-mail or U.S. mail. Please see Appendix B for instructions.

Acknowledgments

Marshall Brain would like to sincerely thank Shay Woodard for his effort on the previous edition of this book. Shay developed quite a few of the early-version example programs that you will find here, including most of the code in Chapters 6, 8, 9, and 21.

This book would not exist were it not for Mike Meehan. Also, author Ron Reeves would like to thank his associate and friend Robert J. Oberg for recommending him to Mike Meehan to author this version of the book.

A group of high-intensity systems programmers helped on the previous version of this book by providing technical proofing skills. Marshall Brain would like to thank Michael S. Yoder, Lida Chen, T. Ramjee, Richard P. Basch, Kevin Hanrahan, Tony Morris, Vladimir Svirsky, Jasmine Ved, Ben Rosenbaum and Paul Horan for their help.

Marshall Brain would like to also thank Leigh Ann Brain for being his wife, and for her tremendous support, patience, and back rubs.

Ron Reeves would like to thank his wonderful and supportive wife Paulette Marie Reeves for her many years of love and devotion.

Introduction

The advanced system services in the 32-bit API are the heart of Windows 2000 and Windows 98. You may have heard or read about many of them while learning about and experimenting with Windows 2000 and 98: function calls that execute over the network, multi-threading, standardized and heterogeneous network communications, the advanced C2 security system of Windows 2000, and so on. These are the cutting-edge capabilities that make both Windows 2000 and Windows 98 unique and interesting. The goal of this book is to show you how to use all of the Windows system services in your own applications.

The purpose of this chapter is to act as a road map and introduction. It also discusses several concepts that are of general interest because they are used constantly throughout the book. You may want to briefly scan this chapter now to see what is available, and then come back to specific sections as you need them.

1.1 One Hundred and Twenty-One Questions About Windows 2000 and 98

Many programmers coming to Windows 2000 and Windows 98 have questions about it. This section contains 121 of the most common system-programming questions, and information about where to look to find the answers. Use this list as a map for the rest of the book. These questions start with the most common and move toward the exotic.

1.1.1 General

1. How do I compile code on a Windows system? See Section 1.2 and Appendix A.

2. What are objects and handles? Why do they exist? See Section 1.5.

3. Why do there seem to be so many bugs in the 32-bit API? See Section 1.7.

1.1.2 File Operations

4. How do I read from and write to a file? See Sections 2.3 and 2.7.

5. How do I read and write a large quantity of data in a way that does not stall out my user interface? See Section 7.5 (overlapped I/O) or Chapter 6 (threads).

6. How do I move, copy, and delete files from within a program? See Section 2.5.

7. How do I call for the movement of a file, but postpone the actual move operation until the next time the system reboots because the file is currently in use? See Section 2.5.

8. How do I create a temporary file? See Section 2.6.

9. How do I create a temporary file that automatically deletes itself when the program is finished using it? See Section 2.7.

10. How do I map a file into memory to drastically improve read/write performance? See Section 2.11.

11. How do I read compressed files without decompressing them? See Section 2.10.

12. How do I uncompress a compressed file from within an application? See Section 2.10.

13. How do I tune system performance while reading certain files? For example, I have to read a large file from beginning to end, and it is flushing out the disk cache. How do I prevent that? See Section 2.7.

14. How do I access file information such as the size of the file, the last change date, and the attribute bits? See Section 2.4.

15. How do I lock whole files or individual records for exclusive or read-only access? See Section 2.9.

1.1.3 Drive Operations

16. How do I find out if a certain disk drive is mounted locally or over the network? See Section 3.3.

17. How do I find out which file system (FAT, HPFS, NTFS, etc.) a volume was formatted with? See Section 3.2.

18. How do I find out how much free space is available on a drive? See Section 3.4.

19. How do I determine which of the 26 drive letters are currently attached to a drive? See Section 3.5.

20. How do I change the volume label of a drive from within an application? See Section 3.6.

21. How can I create a list of all of the machines on the network? See Section 3.7.

22. How do I loop through all of the machines on the network and list all of the printers and drives they are currently sharing? See Section 3.7.

23. How do I form or cancel a connection to a remote drive or printer? See Section 3.7.

1.1.4 Directory Operations

24. How do I create and delete directories? See Section 4.2.

25. How do I set the current directory or find out the current directory? See Section 4.3.

26. How do I search the PATH and system directories for a file? See Section 4.4.

27. How do I search a directory for a file? See Section 4.5.

28. How do I recursively traverse all of the directories on a drive? See Section 4.5.

29. How do I detect changes to files and directories? For example, if a new file is added to a directory, is there an easy way to detect that immediately? See Section 4.7.

1.1.5 Active Directory—Answers Are in Section 5.4

30. How does a workstation discover its site?

31. How does a workstation find a directory server?

32. How do I log on?

33. What happens to access control lists on domain resources after migration?

34. What happens to ACLs when I delete a domain?

35. What happens to local groups?

36. When is the global catalog searched?

37. Do I have to use Microsoft's DNS service?

38. What are the advantages of using Microsoft's DNS service?

39. What happens to DHCP?

40. What happens to WINS?

1.1.6 Processes and Threads

41. How do I multi-thread an application? What does that mean? What is a thread? See Chapter 6.

42. How do I design an application so that it runs lengthy operations in the background rather than making the user wait? For example, my application has to recalculate an aerodynamic model and I do not want the user interface to hang for half an hour during the computation. See Chapter 6.

43. How can I take advantage of multiple threads to simplify the design of simulations that contain many separate and interacting entities? See Chapter 6.

44. How do I create separate threads that can handle high-priority events successfully without monopolizing the CPU? See Section 6.7.

45. How does the scheduling and priority system work? See Section 6.7.

46. How do I multi-thread an application so that it takes maximum advantage of multiple-CPU architectures in Windows 2000? See Section 6.5.

47. How do I launch a new separate and independent process from within an application? See Section 6.9.

48. How can I let two separate processes share data? For example, I want to be able to run an application that controls a service, so the application needs to be able to talk to the service. See Section 6.11.

49. How can I create a new process that inherits handles from its parent? See Section 6.10.

50. How do I assign local storage to each thread in a multi-threaded application? See Section 6.6.

51. How do I add multiple threads to an MFC program? See Section 6.4.

1.1.7 Synchronization

52. Why does Windows contain so many different synchronization mechanisms? Semaphores, Critical section, Mutexes—what good are they? See Chapter 7.

53. How do I guarantee that two threads do not access the same resource at the same time? See Chapter 7.

54. I have a multi-threaded program that occasionally locks up for no apparent reason. What is causing this problem? See Section 7.3.

55. How do I integrate synchronization mechanisms into an MFC program without shutting down the event loop? See Section 7.7.

1.1.8 Network Communications

56. How can I create an application that can talk with other copies of the same application, or other different applications, on the network? See Chapter 8.

57. How do I broadcast information on the network so that all of the machines on the network see it? See Section 8.3.

58. How do I create point-to-point network connections between two Windows machines? See Section 8.4.

59. How do I create client/server architectures? What code and techniques are necessary to create the server and the client? See Section 8.5.

60. How do I communicate with UNIX and other TCP/IP machines using UDP and TCP packets? See Section 8.6.

61. How do I read and write to the same pipe in a multi-threaded application? See Section 8.5.

1.1.9 Remote Procedure Calls

62. How do I use Remote Procedure Calls? What is a Remote Procedure Call? See Chapter 9.

63. How do I design a program so that it effectively uses Remote Procedure Calls? How do I know when and when not to use RPCs? See Section 9.3.

64. How do I create client/server architectures using RPCs? See Chapter 9.

65. How do I create an IDL file and use the MIDL compiler? See Chapter 9.

66. How do I create an RPC server in Windows? See Section 9.5.

67. What is the RPC name server? How do I register an RPC server that I create with the name server? See Sections 9.6 and 9.8.

68. How do I create an RPC server that runs on its host machine all of the time, starting when the host boots? See Section 12.11 and Chapter 12.

69. How do I call an RPC from an RPC client program? See Chapter 9.

70. Can an RPC client on a Windows machine access an RPC server on a UNIX machine? What about the reverse? See Section 9.8.

71. What is the difference between automatic and manual binding in RPCs? See Chapter 9.

1.1.10 Serial Communications

72. How do I use communications ports in Windows? I want to create a BBS or a terminal emulator. See Chapter 14.

73. How do I send and receive characters from a communications port? See Section 11.4.

74. How do I set communications parameters like baud rate and parity on a communications port? See Section 11.4.

75. How do I manage different flow control policies on a communications port? See Section 11.6.

76. How do I easily communicate with other Telnet servers on the network? See Section 11.7.

1.1.11 Windows 2000 Services

77. How do I run an application in the background under Windows 2000, starting when the machine boots and regardless of who is logged on? For example, I need to run a background data-logging program in my lab, but I don't want to tie up the entire machine. See Chapter 12.

78. How do I integrate a service into the Services applet of the Windows 2000 Control Panel? See Section 12.5.

79. How do I create multiple service threads that share global variables? See Section 12.7.

80. How can a service communicate with the user? See Section 12.5.

1.1.12 Security

81. How does the Windows 2000 security system work? See Chapter 13.

82. How do I change the security attributes on a file from within one of my applications? See Sections 13.4 and 13.8.

83. How do I secure a named pipe so that only certain users on the network can access it? See Sections 13.4 and 13.9.

84. How do I un-secure a named pipe so that any user can access it? See Section 13.9.

85. How do I create a named pipe server than any user on the network can access, but preserve security at the same time? Is there a way for a named pipe server to impersonate a connected user? See Section 13.9.

86. How do I access the auditing features of the security system so that accesses to certain objects get logged in the event viewer? See Section 13.2.

87. What are ACL, DACL, SACL, SID, and ACE? See Section 13.3.

88. How do I modify existing security descriptors? See Section 13.8.

89. How do I set the system time or shut down the system? Even though I'm the Windows 2000 administrator, the system functions for these operations fail when I run the code. See Section 13.7.

90. What is a privilege? How do I enable and disable privileges? See Section 13.7.

1.1.13 Consoles

91. How do I port a text program (for example, a program based on the curses library in UNIX or a vt-100 terminal emulator) over to Windows? See Chapter 14.

92. How do I access keystrokes from the keyboard one character at a time (raw input) in a console program? See Section 14.4.

93. How do I add streaming text output to a normal Windows or MFC program to help with debugging? See Section 14.3.

1.1.14 System Functions

94. How do I find out the number of buttons on the mouse? See Section 16.2.

95. How do I find out the screen width and height? See Section 16.2.

96. How do I get and set system colors? See Section 16.2.

97. How do I find out the number of processors in the machine? See Section 16.1.

98. How do I find out the machine's name on the network? See Section 16.2.

99. How do I find out what version of Windows is currently running? See Section 16.2.

100. How do I get and set environment variable information? See Section 16.3.

101. How do I shut down the system or log off the current user? How do I shut down remote machines on the network? See Section 16.4.

1.1.15 Dynamic Link Libraries

102. What is a Dynamic Link Library? What are the advantages of DLLs? See Chapter 17.

103. How do I create, compile, and load a DLL? See Sections 17.3 and 17.4.

104. What is the difference between run-time and load-time linking? What are the advantages of each approach? See Section 17.5.

105. How do I distribute a DLL so that other programmers can use it? See Chapter 17.

106. What is a DLL entry point? How can I use one to improve memory management? See Section 17.6.

107. How do I create global and dynamic variables that are shared or private inside a DLL? See Section 17.7.

1.1.16 Miscellaneous

108. What is the registry? See Section 21.1.

109. Where is the best place to store configuration information for my application? See Section 21.1.

110. How do I add a new key to the registry? See Section 21.1.

111. How do I read and write registry values? See Section 21.1.

112. How do I store events from my own applications in the event log? See Section 21.2.

113. How do I determine which events belong in the event log? See Section 21.2.

114. How do I create strings for my event log messages? See Section 21.2.

115. How do I get and set the current system time? See Section 21.3.

116. How do I find out what time zone the current machine is in? See Section 21.3.

117. How do I allocate and free memory at the system level? See Section 21.4.

118. How can I play sounds other than a simple beep during errors? See Section 21.6.

119. When creating my own libraries, how can I make their functions conform to Windows' GetLastError format? See Section 21.6.

120. What is structured exception handling? How can I use it in my programs? See Section 21.5.

121. How do I contact the author? See Appendix B.

1.2 Compiling Code

This book contains hundreds of listings. You will find that these listings break down into four different categories:

1. Pure console programs that read and write text data
2. GUI programs using the 32-bit API

3. GUI programs using MFC

4. Other programs: DLL code, RPC code, and so on

Appendix A contains information on compiling the first three types of code. The fourth type is covered when the code appears. For example, Chapter 9 on RPCs contains makefiles for using the MIDL compiler and for compiling RPC programs.

1.3 Terminology

Windows, like UNIX or VMS, is a complete operating system. When you use this operating system, you refer to it as "Windows 2000," or "Windows 98," or generically as "Windows," and leave it at that. When you program for the system, you are programming for Windows as well. More specifically, however, you are using the "Win32 API" (Application Programmer Interface), also known as "the 32-bit API." In this book, programming for "Windows," "Win32," and "the 32-bit API" are equivalent, and you will find them used interchangeably.

The 32-bit API is huge. It contains thousands of functions broken up into hundreds of categories. It is a comprehensive, all-encompassing programmer interface to the many capabilities provided by the Windows operating system. The API is the same whether you are using Windows 2000 or Windows 98. However, a number of functions will report "not implemented" errors in Windows 98 because they are not supported. See Section 1.8 for a description of the differences between Windows 98 and Windows 2000.

The 32-bit API is so called to distinguish it from the older 16-bit API used by standard Windows 3.1 running on top of MS-DOS. The 16-bit API contains all of the Windows and Graphics functions found in the 32-bit API (that is why most older Windows programs port to Windows 2000 and 95 so easily), but the 16-bit API does not have any of the system services found in the 32-bit API. The 32-bit API also includes a number of operations normally found in the standard C libraries, in an attempt to centralize things. For example, the 32-bit API includes functions to move, zero, and copy blocks of memory (see Section 21.4).

Win32s is a subset of the 32-bit API. It runs on DOS machines, and provides a way to execute Win32 applications in the older Windows environment. Win32s is missing about half of the system services. For example, it does not support threads, services, event logging, or RPCs, etc. You can call these functions in Win32s, but they will return error codes.

This book deals with the system services of the 32-bit API. The system services are the core of the operating system. They give you access to the modern capabilities that make the 32-bit versions of Windows interesting:

- Processes and threads
- Synchronization
- Remote Procedure Calls (RPCs)
- Event logging
- Network communications
- TCP/IP networking with UNIX and other machines
- File mapping
- Interprocess communication
- Compressed file access
- Network drive and printer sharing
- Serial communications
- Services (background processing like UNIX daemons)
- Object and file security

The other two major sections of the API are the Graphics Device Interface (GDI) for drawing and printing, and the Window Management functions for creating GUIs. Both of these sections are encapsulated by MFC, which is described below. Because of MFC, you generally do not access either of these sections directly when creating Windows applications in C++.

You will generally write and compile your Win32 programs using either "the Microsoft Win32 SDK" or Visual C++. The SDK is a command-line environment, while Visual C++ is a graphical environment.

Visual C++ (but not the SDK) ships with a C++ class library called the Microsoft Foundation Class library, or MFC. MFC makes the creation of GUI programs much easier. It encapsulates all of the window-management and GDI functions available in the 32-bit API. Another book in this series is called "Visual C++: Developing Professional Applications for Windows 98 and Windows 2000 using MFC," and it covers MFC programming in detail. Many of the system-services examples in this book show you how to apply the concepts to MFC code. For example, Chapter 6 contains examples that show you how to multi-thread MFC programs. Chapter 7 shows you how to handle semaphores, mutexes, and events in MFC code, and Chapter 9 applies RPCs to an MFC program.

1.4 Error Handling

Most functions in the 32-bit API return error status in two different ways. Many functions return the first indication of an error in the return value for the function. For example, the **RemoveDirectory** function in Chapter 4 is typical:

RemoveDirectory	*Removes an empty directory*

```
BOOL RemoveDirectory(
    LPTSTR dirName)
```

DirName	Name/path of the directory to remove
Returns TRUE on success	

The **RemoveDirectory** function returns a boolean value that is TRUE if the function was successful and FALSE otherwise. Other functions return a specific value to indicate an error:

OpenService	*Opens a connection to the specified service*

```
SC_HANDLE OpenService(
    SC_HANDLE scm,
    LPCTSTR name,
    DWORD access)
```

scm	A handle to the SCM from **OpenSCManager**
name	The name of the service used internally
access	The desired access
Returns a handle to the service or NULL on error	

The **OpenService** function returns 0 when something goes wrong. A typical use of the **GetLastError** function is shown below:

```
success = RemoveDirectory(s);
if (!success)
    cout << "Error code = " << GetLastError()
        << endl;
```

GetLastError	*Returns the error code of the most recent error*

```
DWORD GetLastError(VOID)
```

Returns the error code of the last error

When the return value indicates an error, you can obtain a numeric error code identifying the exact problem by calling the **GetLastError** function. **GetLastError** returns an integer that you can look up in the "Error Codes" section of the API help file (see Section 1.6). For example, in the example above the error value might be five. When you look up that value in the Error Codes section, you will find that it translates to "Access Denied," which means that the file system's security features will not allow you to delete the specified directory.

1.5 Handles and Objects

Windows uses the concepts of a handle and an *object* throughout the system services. An object is owned by the operating system and represents a system resource. For example, a thread is represented as an object. The operating system stores all information about the thread in the thread's object. The object is opaque to the programmer.

A handle points to an object. It is possible to create a single object and refer to it with several different handles. You can think of the handles as pointers that let you access the object.

The 32-bit API defines the following "kernel objects." All of them return a handle when they are created or opened:

Object	Function	Chapter
Access tokens	OpenProcessToken	Chapter 13
	CloseHandle	
Console	CreateConsoleScreenBuffer	Chapter 14
	CloseHandle	
Console device	GetStdHandle	Chapter 14
	CloseHandle	
Communication port	CreateFile	Chapter 11
	CloseHandle	
Event	CreateEvent	Chapter 7
	CloseHandle	
Event log	OpenEventLog	Chapter 21
	CloseEventLog	
File	CreateFile	Chapter 2
	CloseHandle	
File change	FindFirstChangeNotification	Chapter 7
	FindCloseChangeNotification	
File mapping	CreateFile	Chapter 2
	CloseHandle	
Find file	FindFirstFile	Chapter 4
	FindClose	
Mailslot	CreateMailslot	Chapter 8
	CloseHandle	
Mutex	CreateMutex	Chapter 7
	CloseHandle	

Object	Function	Chapter
Named pipe	CreateNamedPipe	Chapter 8
	CloseHandle	
Pipe	CreatePipe	
	CloseHandle	
Process	CreateProcess	Chapter 6
	CloseHandle	
Semaphore	CreateSemaphore	Chapter 7
	CloseHandle	
Thread	CreateThread	Chapter 6
	CloseHandle	

Of these objects, some are global. For example, there is one instance of the event log and any process can open a handle to it. Some are private. For example, a Find File handle is private to the process that opens it. Others can be shared among processes:

- Process
- Thread
- File
- File mapping
- Event
- Semaphore
- Mutex
- Named pipe
- Mailslot
- Communication device

For example, one thread or process might create a semaphore, and other processes and threads can open handles to it so that they can all use it for synchronization. The single semaphore object is shared by the all of the processes and threads. It is also possible to duplicate and inherit (Chapter 7) handles to these objects.

Most objects that return a handle can be secured using the Windows 2000 security system. See Chapter 13 for a complete list and details. Security is a primary reason for this "object" model. The other reason for it is that it adds a level of abstraction to the operating system, which keeps programmers from knowing too much. A HANDLE is a generic 32-bit pointer. It tells you, as a programmer, nothing about the object it points to, so you are unable to get into the low-level structures and code directly to them. This allows the operating system to change over time without its designers having to worry about code that breaks the rules.

If you want to open a file and access it through the 32-bit API, you use the **CreateFile** function (see Chapter 2) as shown below:

Listing 1.1   *An API-level program that reads from a file and writes to it*

```cpp
// file3.cpp

#include <windows.h>
#include <iostream.h>

void main()
{
    HANDLE fileHandle;
    BOOL success;
    char s[10];
    DWORD numRead;
    char filename[MAX_PATH];

    // get the file name
    cout << "Enter filename: ";
    cin >> filename;

    // Open the file
    fileHandle = CreateFile(filename, GENERIC_READ,
        0, 0, OPEN_EXISTING, 0, 0);
    if (fileHandle == INVALID_HANDLE_VALUE)
    {
        cout << "Error number " << GetLastError()
            << " occured on file open." << endl;
        return;
    }

    // Read from file until eof, writing to stdout
    do
    {
        success = ReadFile(fileHandle, s, 1,
            &numRead, 0);
        s[numRead] = 0;
        cout << s;
    }
    while (numRead>0 && success);

    // Close the file
    CloseHandle(fileHandle);
}
```

Note that the call to **CreateFile** returns a HANDLE to the variable **fileHandle**. This variable points to a *file object* that talks to the actual file on the disk. The file object in this case remembers the state of the file. For example, it remembers where the file pointer is in the file. The code in Listing 1.1 uses the **fileHandle** in the call to **ReadFile** to read from the file, and then again in the call to **CloseHandle** to close the file.

As another example, let's say that you want to use a mutex object (see Chapter 7) to control access to a global resource. The program calls **Create-Mutex** to create a mutex object, and the function returns a handle to the object. The object is owned by the operating system and remembers the state of the mutex, while the handle lets your program reference the object to query and change the state using functions like **WaitForSingleObject** and **Release-Mutex** (see Chapter 7). When you create the mutex you can give it a name.

Now another program can call **OpenMutex** with that same name. The process will receive a handle that refers to the same operating system object. It can query the mutex and change its state, so now the two programs can synchronize their behavior using the single mutex object managed by the operating system. Once *both* processes close their handles to the object, the operating system deletes the object.

For more information on objects and handles, see Chapters 7 and 13, and the "Handles and Objects" section in the documentation. See the following section for a discussion on the documentation.

1.6 Using the Microsoft Documentation

The 32-bit API comes with quite a bit of documentation. It is available both on-line and on paper. On paper it is referred to as the Win32 Programmer's Reference books (five volumes). On-line it is in a help file named api32.hlp. The on-line version is generally much easier to use, because of both the hypertext links and the Search button (especially the NEAR capability), which lets you find any word in the entire file instantly.

The goal of this book is not to duplicate the information already available in these references. That would be impossible. Here, the goal is to help you see how to use the functions available in the API to solve problems. Therefore, this book is full of concise, easy-to-understand example code and explanations that help you understand how to use the capabilities of the 32-bit API in your own programs.

You should use Microsoft's 32-bit API documentation as a supplement to this book. When you are working through an example, look up each function or structure in the API documentation so that you can see what all the parameters and members actually do. See Section 1.7 for an explanation of why this can be important. The explanations in the on-line help file are generally quite clear, and will make sense in the context of the example. Click over to some of the related structures and functions to read about them as well. You can rapidly master the API this way.

1.7 Bugs in the 32-Bit API

Occasionally you will write a new Windows program, and it simply will not work the way you expect it to work. You will write the program and run it, and it will crash. You will look at the code and diddle with it a little bit, and the problem will remain. After 15 minutes, your response to this improbability is going to be, "Wow, I found a bug in the 32-bit API. I can't believe that they don't test this stuff more carefully." At dinner that night you will rail at your spouse about the inept programmers at Microsoft.

That is the natural human reaction. However, I'd say that in 99.9% of cases, the problem lies in your code rather than in the API. In many cases, the problem lies in your perception of how you *think* the code should work, even though the documentation clearly states otherwise and you skipped over or missed that part.

To let you see just how easy it is to create problems when working with the API, let me show you five of my own bugs. These bugs all arose while developing the sample code for this book. You, of course, won't make mistakes this stupid, but they demonstrate some of the possibilities. In each one of the five cases, it seemed at first that there was a mysterious and unknown bug somewhere deep in the bowels of the API, but it later turned out to be a stupid mistake on my part.

1. In Listing 6.2, the original code did not contain the keyword **volatile**. The program worked fine as long as there was a call to **Sleep** or some other API function inside the thread function, but as soon as I removed the call to **Sleep**, **count** remained resolutely at zero. However, if I turned on debugging, the code worked just fine. Obviously there was a bug in the thread-handling portion of the API causing **count**'s faulty behavior. However, it turned out to be compiler optimizations that caused the **count** variable to get placed in a register. Adding the **volatile** keyword turns off those optimizations, so the code works fine.

2. When developing the inheritance example in Listings 6.13 and 6.14, it seemed to be impossible to get the child process to inherit anything. I would run the code, and the child would display an "invalid handle" error every time. In some cases, the behavior was even more bizarre: The child process would get created over and over again, even though there are no loops anywhere in the code. Obviously there was a bug in the handle-inheriting portion of the API. However, it turned out that I was passing the **sa** parameter to **CreateProcess** as the last parameter rather than as the fourth. Changing the erroneous parameter list eliminated the problem. The **sa** parameter *is* last in the call to **CreateNamedPipe**, but not to **CreateProcess**.

3. In the multi-threaded client program shown in Listing 8.11, the code simply refused to handle the incoming pipe data correctly. Either the incoming data was ignored completely, or the program would read one piece of data and then stop, or, if the overlapped structures were made global, the program would work with one client but then mysteriously and continuously loop in the server whenever a second client connected. Obviously it was a serious bug in the way overlapped I/O works with named pipes. However, it turned out that I was not creating the events and placing them in the overlapped structures to properly initialize them. I was thinking that because I didn't use the events anywhere in the code, I did not need to create them. Once I created the events correctly, the code worked just fine.

4. In the bounded buffer example using semaphores in Listing 7.8, the first version I created just would not work at all. It would terminate immediately, or run a little and die, without any hint of an error message. Nothing seemed to be wrong—it just would up and die for no apparent reason. Obviously the semaphore portion of the API was seriously flawed, or the mixing of two different synchronization mechanisms led to internal interactions that rendered the entire API inoperable. However, it turned out that I was placing the two thread handles into `handles[1]` and `handles[2]` rather than into `handles[0]` and `handles[1]`. Fixing that minor problem had a wonderful effect on the code.

5. I worked on the simple **push** and **pop** functions in Chapter 7 very early in my Windows career. I happen to like synchronization problems and I wanted to try out critical sections. The test code would run a tiny bit and then hang. I'd run it again and it would hang again. Every now and then it worked fine, but then it would hang again in the next test. Nothing seemed to fix the problem. I tried everything, but adding in the critical sections just destroyed the ability of the program to execute. Obviously the critical section portion of the API was totally flawed. Apparently Microsoft had added it at the last minute and never bothered to test it. However, it turned out that I had forgotten to place a call to **LeaveCriticalSection** before the first return in the **pop** function, so the code could not proceed if that branch got executed. Adding the function call solved the problem.

As you can see, I make my fair share of mistakes, just like everybody else. For the record, let me state that I have written and helped test thousands and thousands and thousands of lines of Windows code, and I have seen many hundreds of "mysterious API bugs." However, I have *never* seen one that did not go away once the programmer wrote the code correctly. It's something to keep in mind when one of your programs is misbehaving. Read the manual, and look carefully at your code. The bug is in there somewhere, staring back at you.

1.8 Differences Between Windows 98 and Windows 2000

Windows 2000 and Windows 98 are very similar at the API level. In fact, a good way to think about Windows 98 is to think of it as "Windows 2000 Lite." Windows 98 does most of the things that Windows 2000 can do, but there are several capabilities that Windows 2000 has that Windows 98 lacks. In particular, Windows 98 is missing parts of Windows 2000 security system (Chapter 13), Windows 2000 services (Chapter 12), and some Windows 2000 network functionality (Chapter 8). A good way to understand these differences is to compare Windows 2000, Windows 98, and Windows 3.1 and see how they evolved from one another.

Windows 3.1 and Windows for Workgroups 3.1 were built on top of MS-DOS, the Microsoft operating system for PC-class machines. This layering is a liability because MS-DOS is primitive by today's standards. MS-DOS has a very simple file system with limited features and no security. MS-DOS offers none of the capabilities the user would expect to find in a "real" operating system—features such as virtual memory, multiple processes, interprocess communication, and so on. Windows 3.1 takes care of some of these problems itself as best it can. For example, it offers a good memory management system and cooperative multi-tasking. But because it is built on DOS, the system is fragile, and the file management facilities are poor. The system is also permanently attached to PC-compatible hardware. There is really no easy way to move it to other platforms.

Windows 2000 is Microsoft's answer to these problems. It is a complete and modern operating system built from the ground up as a total solution to workstation computing. Windows 2000 offers everything you would expect to find in a modern operating system:

- 32-bit instructions and memory addressing: Like any other modern workstation operating system, Windows 2000 uses a 32-bit numeric and address format. Unlike older DOS and Windows machines, memory addressing is "flat," so you can create arrays as large as you like in memory.
- Preemptive multi-tasking (processes and threads): Microsoft Windows 3.1 uses *cooperative multi-tasking*, in which applications yield the processor to one another at each application's discretion. Windows 2000 instead uses *preemptive multi-tasking*. Under this system the OS automatically allocates CPU time to each application (called a *process*). Because the OS, rather than the individual applications, is in control of CPU time slices, the system is extremely stable and

robust. In addition, Windows 2000 applications can divide themselves up into separate *threads* of execution. An application might do this in order to perform a lengthy calculation in the background without affecting the user interface. The OS can schedule threads independently.

- Symmetric Multi-processing: A Windows 2000 machine can contain more than one CPU. In a multi-processor machine, Windows 2000 will allocate different threads to different CPUs to take full advantage of all CPU power available. In addition, Windows 2000 is itself multi-threaded, and its different threads can run on separate processors.
- Multiple platforms (Intel, MIPS, Alpha, etc.): Windows 2000 is designed to run on a variety of processor architectures. Unlike UNIX, which looks different depending on whose hardware it is running on, Windows 2000 looks exactly the same to both the user and the programmer, no matter which sort of architecture is running it.
- Remote procedure calls: Windows 2000 supports OSF-style Remote Procedure Calls (RPCs), which can be used to easily build client/server applications that run efficiently on a network.
- Total network support (TCP/IP, NetBEUI, etc.): Windows 2000 is designed to run on a network, and supports a native format for communication with other Windows 2000 machines as well as machines running TCP/IP protocols.
- C2 certified security: When using the Windows 2000 File System (NTFS), Windows 2000 creates a secure system. All users must log in with an account name and password. Files and directories on the disk are protected by access control lists (ACLs). Applications are isolated from one another in memory so that the crash of one does not affect any of the others.

Microsoft has covered all of the power in Windows 2000 with the familiar Windows-type interfaces found in the other Windows products. This decision means that anyone familiar with previous versions of Windows can use Windows 2000 very quickly. From an administrative standpoint, Windows 2000 contains many new features. Windows 2000 attempts to completely separate use of the system from administration of the system so that users do not have to waste their time on administrative tasks. A user may "own" the machine on his or her desktop, but that does not mean that the user wants to spend time backing up the hard disks, installing software, or configuring the network. Those administrative tasks are better left to a trained administrator. Windows 2000 therefore provides separate administrative tools that allow remote access. For example, if a machine is sitting on a network in a large company, an administrator can attach to the machine over the network to update software, change accounts, and so on. Windows 98 contains very little in the way of administrative features.

From a programmer's standpoint, Windows 2000 uses the Win32 API, which contains a wealth of advanced operating system services. These services are the subject of this book.

Windows 98 contains most of the API features of Windows 2000. The Win32 API in Windows 2000 and Windows 98 are identical, and Windows 98 therefore uses the same process and thread model, the same file-access functions, the same network-access functions, and so on. Most of the differences between Windows 2000 and Windows 98 are omissions. Certain features were removed from Windows 98 to improve its performance on low-end hardware. The list below summarizes these differences:

- Symmetric Multi-processing: Windows 98 works only on single-CPU hardware architectures.
- Multiple platforms: Windows 98 currently runs only on Intel hardware.
- C2 certified security: Windows 98 contains only part of Windows 2000's advanced security features.

You will learn about other, more subtle differences in the process of reading this book.

In general, you can think of Windows 2000 as a complete workstation operating system intended for use in corporate, university, and engineering environments. Windows 98 is a lower-end product intended more for home and small-business applications.

Files

*F*ile access is one of the most basic services provided by any operating system. For example, the word DOS, which has become something of a generic term for an operating system in many circles, stands for Disk Operating System. The "Disk" portion of the name demonstrates how important files are in the grand scheme of things.

This chapter discusses file access. It shows you how to open and close files, how to read from and write to them, and how to gather information about files in Windows 2000 and Windows 98. Many of the functions discussed here are duplicated or combined in higher-level libraries. For example, when you use **fprintf** in C or **ofstream** in C++ you indirectly access many of these functions. The **CFile** class in MFC also uses these functions extensively to provide a high-level interface. Because of these high-level libraries, you may have little or no need to work at the API level when you begin programming in Windows and want to open a file or two.

In many cases, however, it is beneficial to drop down to the API level to access files. Generally, you do this because you want to take advantage of a feature not exposed in the high-level implementation. A good example is the Windows 2000 security options, discussed in Chapter 13. The only way to access security features in one of your programs is to work at the API level when opening the file.

Compatibility Note: All of the code in this chapter works identically in both Windows 2000 and Windows 98, with only one minor exception noted for the **MoveFileEx** *function in Section 2.5.*

2.1 The Possibilities

Files are important in Windows because many different objects are accessed using the file routines. Certain techniques are used in the 32-bit API to open a file, read from it and write to it, and close the file. The API uses identical techniques to work with communications ports (Chapter 11), named pipes, and mailslots on the network (Chapter 8). Therefore, understanding how to work with files is central to understanding many communications task in Windows.

Files are quite interesting in Windows because of all the different capabilities built into the 32-bit API for working with them. For example:

- As you would expect, you can open, read, and write files. (See Sections 2.3 and 2.7.)
- You can also open and read compressed files *without decompressing them*. (See Section 2.10). If you happen to have a file type that is very large and that compresses very well, you can work with it in its compressed form and save quite a bit of disk space.
- You can open files and read and write them asynchronously. (See Section 7.5.) This *overlapping* technique makes it possible to perform background I/O tasks without necessarily multi-threading your application. Overlapped I/O is also the basis for multi-threaded access to a named pipe, as discussed in Section 8.5.
- You can access a great deal of status information about files through the 32-bit API. (See Section 2.4.)
- You can map files into the virtual memory system to significantly improve their performance. (See Section 2.10.) This technique is also used for high-speed interprocess communication (See file mapping in Section 6.11.)
- You can lock files or individual records of files. (See Section 2.9.)

A topic like file access that would be mundane in many other operating systems has a good bit of variety and interest in the 32-bit API.

Directories and disk drives are closely related to files, and are discussed in detail in the following two chapters. File security is covered in Chapter 13.

2.2 Overview

A file, in the strictest sense of the word, is a set of sectors on a disk, identified under a unique file name. In many systems and languages, at least at a low level, you treat a file just that way—you can actually read off buffered or un-buffered sectors of information in sector-sized chunks. Most programming languages and operating systems also offer a character-based (as well as a structure-based) abstraction that allows you to deal with information at a more natural level.

In the 32-bit API, you think of a file as a collection of bytes. This is identical to the low-level access paradigm provided by UNIX. You can seek to any byte offset and read a block of bytes of any size. If you want to work at a higher level of abstraction—for example, thinking of the file as a set of text lines—you use the libraries in a language like C or C++ to handle the abstraction for you. One of the nice things about the low-level file-access functions in the API is that they are fairly easy to understand and use.

Figure 2.1 shows two ways that you will access files in Windows. Files typically contain either text, or binary data in the form of structures stored directly onto the disk. You can use the **ReadFile** and **WriteFile** functions to access these characters or structures. If you have ever used the **fread** and **fwrite** functions in <stdio.h> you will find the use of these API functions very similar.

These same **ReadFile** and **WriteFile** functions appear throughout the API in a variety of roles. You will use them, for example, to read from and write to communication ports and the network. In these applications you will also be able to think of the data in terms of single characters or structures.

A number of functions in the API allow you to gather information about a file once you open it. For example, given an open file, you can determine its size, type, creation times, and so on. You can also use the API functions to move, copy, and delete files.

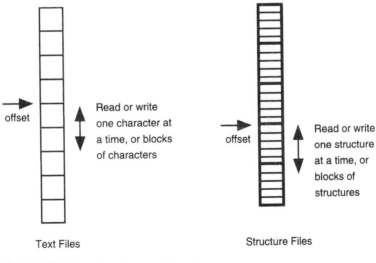

Text Files   Structure Files

| Figure 2.1 | *Text files and files of structures* |

2.3 Opening and Reading from a File

Let's say that you want to write a program that performs the simplest possible file operation: you want to open a file, read from it, and write its contents to the screen. The easiest way to do this is to use the I/O library that ships with C or C++. Listings 2.1 and 2.2 demonstrate a simple file-reading program in straight C, and then in C++. To learn how to compile this code, see Appendix A.

Listing 2.1   *A C program that reads from a file and writes its contents to the screen*

```
// file1.cpp

#include <windows.h>
#include <stdio.h>

void main()
{
   char filename[MAX_PATH];
   char c;
   FILE *f;

   // get file name
   printf("Enter filename: ");
   gets(filename);

   // open the file
   f = fopen(filename, "r");
   if (f)
      // read until eof
      while ((c = fgetc(f)) != EOF)
         printf("%c",c);

   // close the file
   fclose(f);
}
```

Listing 2.2   *A C++ program that reads from a file and writes its contents to the screen*

```
// file2.cpp

#include <windows.h>
#include <iostream.h>
#include <fstream.h>

void main()
```

```
{
    char filename[MAX_PATH];
    char c;

    // get the file name
    cout << "Enter filename: ";
    cin >> filename;

    // open the file
    ifstream infile(filename);
    if (infile)
        // read until eof
        while (infile.get(c))
            cout << c;

    // close the file
    infile.close();
}
```

In both of these simple programs, the code requests a file name from the user, opens the file, and reads characters from the file until it reaches the end of the file. Each character appears on the screen.

If you want to perform this same task at the level of the API, then you need to learn about three different functions: **CreateFile**, **ReadFile**, and **CloseHandle**. Accessing the file at the API level follows the same general pattern seen in Listings 2.1 and 2.2, as shown in Listing 2.3. The program gets a file name, opens the file, reads until EOF, and then closes the file.

Listing 2.3   *An API-level program that reads from and writes to a file*

```
// file3.cpp

#include <windows.h>
#include <iostream.h>

void main()
{
    HANDLE fileHandle;
    BOOL success;
    char s[10];
    DWORD numRead;
    char filename[1000];

    // get the file name
    cout << "Enter filename: ";
    cin >> filename;

    // Open the file
    fileHandle = CreateFile(filename, GENERIC_READ,
```

```
              0, 0, OPEN_EXISTING, 0, 0);
      if (fileHandle == INVALID_HANDLE_VALUE)
      {
         cout << "Error number " << GetLastError()
            << " occured on file open." << endl;
         return;
      }

      // Read from file until eof, writing to stdout
      Do
      {
         success = ReadFile(fileHandle, s, 1,
            &numRead, 0);
         s[numRead] = 0;
         cout << s;
      }
      while (numRead>0 && success);

      // Close the file
      CloseHandle(fileHandle);
   }
```

The **CreateFile** function opens a file for read and/or write access. We
will see in later chapters that this same function also opens mail slots, named
pipes, communication ports, and so on. It is also dealt with in more detail in
Section 2.7.

CreateFile   *Opens a file, named pipe, mailslot, or communications port*

```
HANDLE CreateFile(
   LPCTSTR name,
   DWORD accessMode,
   DWORD shareMode,
   LPSECURITY_ATTRIBUTES securityAttributes,
   DWORD create,
   DWORD attributes,
   HANDLE templateFile)
```

name	Name of the file to open
accessMode	Read/Write mode
shareMode	The way the file should be shared
securityAttributes	Address of a security structure. See Chapter 13
create	The way the file should be created
attributes	Settings for file attribute bits and flags
templateFile	File containing extended attributes

Returns a handle on success, or INVALID_HANDLE_VALUE

In Listing 2.3, the CreateFile function accepts the name of the file, a GENERIC_READ access mode that stipulates that the file will be used in a read-only mode, a share mode that prevents any other process from opening the file, and an OPEN_EXISTING creation mode that specifies that the file already exists. The call uses no security information, no attributes, and no template. The function returns either a handle to the file object that it opened, or an error value to indicate an error. If an error occurs, you can use the **GetLastError** function to retrieve an error code (see Section 1.3).

Once the file is open, the **ReadFile** function reads data from it one character at a time. **ReadFile** is a generic block-reading function. You pass it a buffer and the number of bytes for it to read, and the function retrieves the specified number of bytes from the file starting at the current offset. Listing 2.3 requests blocks of size one byte.

ReadFile   *Reads bytes from the specified file*

```
BOOL ReadFile(
    HANDLE file,
    LPVOID buffer,
    DWORD requestedBytes,
    LPDWORD actualBytes,
    LPOVERLAPPED overlapped)
```

file	File handle created with **CreateFile**
buffer	Buffer to hold the read bytes
requestedBytes	The number of bytes desired
actualBytes	The number of bytes actually placed in the buffer
overlapped	Pointer to overlapped structure. See Section 7.5

Returns TRUE on success

In Listing 2.3, the code reads the file one character at a time until **ReadFile** indicates end-of-file. The **CloseHandle** function closes the file once the operations on it are complete.

CloseHandle   *Closes an open handle*

```
BOOL CloseHandle(

                    HANDLE object)
```

object	The handle to close

Returns TRUE on success

Section 2.7 deals with the topic of file access in much more detail. In this section, the goal has been to show that file access at the API level is not much different from normal file access techniques that you already understand.

2.4 Getting and Setting File Information

The API contains several functions that are useful for retrieving file information. For example, you can find out when a file was last modified, how its attribute bits are currently set, and the size of the file. The following sections detail the different capabilities that are available. Several of these functions require an open file handle rather than the file's name. See the previous section or Section 2.7 for details on the **CreateFile** function.

2.4.1 Getting the File Times

The **GetFileTime** function retrieves three different pieces of time information from an open file: the Creation time, the Last Access time, and the Last Write time. The FAT file system supports only the last write time, but NTFS and HPFS support all three.

GetFileTime	*Get file time information*

```
BOOL GetFileTime(
    HANDLE file,
    LPFILETIME creationTime,
    LPFILETIME lastAccessTime,
    LPFILETIME lastWriteTime)
```

File	Handle to a file from **CreateFile**
creationTime	Time of file creation
lastAccessTime	Time of last file access
lastWriteTime	Time of last file write
Returns TRUE on success	

In Listing 2.4, the **CreateFile** function opens the requested file name. **GetFileTime** uses the handle that it returns to access the file times, and then passes the last write time up to the **ShowTime** function to dump the time to stdout.

Listing 2.4   *Retrieving the file time*

```
// filetime.cpp

#include <windows.h>
#include <iostream.h>

void ShowTime(FILETIME t)
// Dumps the t to stdout
```

```
{
    FILETIME ft;
    SYSTEMTIME st;

    FileTimeToLocalFileTime(&t, &ft);
    FileTimeToSystemTime(&ft, &st);
    cout << st.wMonth << "/" << st.wDay
        << "/" << st.wYear << "    " << st.wHour
        << ":" << st.wMinute << endl;
}

void main()
{
    HANDLE fileHandle;
    char filename[MAX_PATH];
    FILETIME create, lastWrite, lastAccess;
    BOOL success;
    FILETIME ft;
    SYSTEMTIME st;

    // get the file name
    cout << "Enter filename: ";
    cin >> filename;

    // open the file
    fileHandle = CreateFile(filename, GENERIC_READ,
        FILE_SHARE_WRITE,
        0, OPEN_EXISTING, 0, 0);
    if (fileHandle == INVALID_HANDLE_VALUE)
    {
        cout << "Error number " << GetLastError()
            << endl;
        return;
    }
    else
    {
        // get the file times
        success = GetFileTime( fileHandle, &create,
            &lastAccess, &lastWrite);
        cout << "Last write time: ";
        ShowTime(lastWrite);
        // the other two won't work in FAT systems
    }
    CloseHandle(fileHandle);
}
```

FILETIME is a structure that contains two 32-bit values. The 64 bits together represent the number of 100-nanosecond time increments that have passed since January 1, 1601. The **FileTimeToLocalTime** and **FileTime-**

ToSystemTime functions convert the 64-bit value to local time and then to a form suitable for output—see Chapter 21 for details.

2.4.2 Getting File Size

The **GetFileSize** function returns the size of the file in bytes, or 0xFFFFFFFF if there is an error. In the FAT file system the largest file size possible can be represented in less than 32 bits, but NTFS is a 64-bit file system and **GetFile-Size** therefore returns 64 bits of size information if you request it. Since the Windows 2000 File System can accommodate single volumes that span multiple drives, it is not unreasonable to expect to occasionally find files larger than 4 gigabytes, although they are quite rare now. There is currently no easy way to deal with integers larger than 32 bits, but Microsoft provides a library called "largeint" (see \mstools\h\largeint.h) that does help.

GetFileSize   *Returns a 64-bit size value for the file*

```
DWORD GetFileSize(
    HANDLE file,
    LPDWORD fileSizeHigh)
```

file   Handle to an open file from **CreateFile**

fileSizeHigh   High order 32-bits of size (pass address)

Returns the low-order 32 bits of the file size, or 0xFFFFFFFF

The low-order 32 bits of size information come from the return value, while the high-order 32 bits come from the **fileSizeHigh** parameter when you pass in a pointer to a DWORD. You can also pass in NULL for this parameter if you are not interested in receiving the high-order 32 bits of information. Listing 2.5 shows how to access the information.

Listing 2.5   *Obtaining the size of a file*

```cpp
// filesize.cpp

#include <windows.h>
#include <iostream.h>

void main()
{
    HANDLE fileHandle;
    char filename[1000];
    DWORD sizeLo, sizeHi;

    // get file name
    cout << "Enter filename: ";
    cin >> filename;
```

```
// open the file
fileHandle = CreateFile(filename, GENERIC_READ,
   FILE_SHARE_WRITE, 0, OPEN_EXISTING, 0, 0);
if (fileHandle == INVALID_HANDLE_VALUE)
{
   cout << "Error number " << GetLastError()
      << endl;
   return;
}

// report file size
else
{
   sizeLo = GetFileSize(fileHandle, &sizeHi);
   cout << "Size (low 32 bits)  = " << sizeLo
      << endl;
   cout << "Size (high 32 bits) = " << sizeHi
      << endl;
}
CloseHandle(fileHandle);
}
```

2.4.3 Getting File Attributes

Files have attribute bits associated with them, which hold special information about the file. You can view the attributes from the File Manager by selecting a file and then choosing the **Properties** option in the **File** menu. Inside a program you can examine attribute bits with the **GetFileAttributes** function.

GetFileAttributes   *Gets the attribute bits for a file*

```
DWORD GetFileAttributes(
   LPTSTR fileName)
```

Filename   The name of the file

Returns the attribute bits in a DWORD, or 0xFFFFFFFF on error.

Listing 2.6 demonstrates how to acquire and examine the attribute bits. The system returns not only the four standard bits seen in the File Manager (archive, read only, system, and hidden), but also bits indicating that the file name is actually a directory, as well as a temporary status bit to mark temporary files.

Listing 2.6   *Retrieving the file attributes*

```
// fileattr.cpp

#include <windows.h>
#include <iostream.h>
```

| Listing 2.6 | *Retrieving the file attributes (continued)* |

```cpp
void ShowAttributes(DWORD attributes)
// Shows the file attributes on stdout
{
    if (attributes & FILE_ATTRIBUTE_ARCHIVE)
        cout << "   archive\n";
    if (attributes & FILE_ATTRIBUTE_DIRECTORY)
        cout << "   directory\n";
    if (attributes & FILE_ATTRIBUTE_HIDDEN)
        cout << "   hidden\n";
    if (attributes & FILE_ATTRIBUTE_NORMAL)
        cout << "   normal\n";
    if (attributes & FILE_ATTRIBUTE_READONLY)
        cout << "   read only\n";
    if (attributes & FILE_ATTRIBUTE_SYSTEM)
        cout << "   system\n";
    if (attributes & FILE_ATTRIBUTE_TEMPORARY)
        cout << "   temporary\n";
}

void main()
{
    char filename[MAX_PATH];
    DWORD attributes;

    cout << "Enter filename: ";
    cin >> filename;
    attributes = GetFileAttributes(filename);
    ShowAttributes(attributes);
}
```

It is also possible to set file attributes using the **SetFileAttributes** function. This function accepts a file name and one or more attribute constants, and returns a Boolean value indicating success or failure.

SetFileAttributes	*Sets file attributes*

```cpp
BOOL SetFileAttributes(
    LPTSTR fileName,
    DWORD attributes)
```

Filename	The name of the file
attributes	One or more attributes

Returns TRUE on success

The same attribute constants seen in the **ShowAttributes** function of Listing 2.6 are available. For example, you might set a file as hidden and read-only with the following statement:

```
success = SetFileAttributes("xxx",
    FILE_ATTRIBUTE_HIDDEN
    FILE_ATTRIBUTE_READONLY);
```

Generally those are the only two attributes you will want to set. The other bits, for example, the directory bit, are set automatically by system calls when appropriate, and should not be altered.

Another way to set attribute bits is during file creation. See Section 2.7.

2.4.4 Getting All File Information

The APIs contains a function named **GetFileInformationByHandle** that returns all of the information described in the previous three sections in one call. It is useful when you want to access or display all information about a file in one call.

GetFileInformationByHandle   *Retrieves all file information*

```
BOOL GetFileInformationByHandle(
    HANDLE file,
    LPBY_HANDLE_FILE_INFORMATION fileInformation)
```

File	Handle to an open file from **CreateFile**
fileInformation	Information about the file
Returns TRUE on success	

The information comes back in a structure that contains the attributes, size, and time data discussed in the previous sections, along with volume, index, and link information not available anywhere else. The volume serial number is a unique number assigned to the volume when it was formatted. The file index is a unique identifier attached to the file while it is open. Listing 2.7 demonstrates the process.

Listing 2.7 *Retrieving file information*

```
// fileinfo.cpp

#include <windows.h>
#include <iostream.h>

void ShowAttributes(DWORD attributes)
```

Listing 2.7   *Retrieving file information (continued)*

```
{
   if (attributes & FILE_ATTRIBUTE_ARCHIVE)
       cout << "   archive\n";
   if (attributes & FILE_ATTRIBUTE_DIRECTORY)
       cout << "   directory\n";
   if (attributes & FILE_ATTRIBUTE_HIDDEN)
       cout << "   hidden\n";
   if (attributes & FILE_ATTRIBUTE_NORMAL)
       cout << "   normal\n";
   if (attributes & FILE_ATTRIBUTE_READONLY)
       cout << "   read only\n";
   if (attributes & FILE_ATTRIBUTE_SYSTEM)
       cout << "   system\n";
   if (attributes & FILE_ATTRIBUTE_TEMPORARY)
       cout << "   temporary\n";
}

void ShowTime(FILETIME t)
{
   FILETIME ft;
   SYSTEMTIME st;

   FileTimeToLocalFileTime(&t, &ft);
   FileTimeToSystemTime(&ft, &st);
   cout << st.wMonth << "/" << st.wDay
       << "/" << st.wYear << "   " << st.wHour
       << ":" << st.wMinute << endl;
}

void main()
{
   char filename[MAX_PATH];
   HANDLE fileHandle;
   BOOL success;
   BY_HANDLE_FILE_INFORMATION info;

   cout << "Enter filename: ";
   cin >> filename;
   fileHandle = CreateFile(filename, GENERIC_READ,
       FILE_SHARE_WRITE, 0, OPEN_EXISTING, 0, 0);
   if (fileHandle == INVALID_HANDLE_VALUE)
   {
       cout << "Error number " << GetLastError()
           << endl;
       return;
   }
   else
   {
       success =
```

```
        GetFileInformationByHandle(fileHandle,
        &info);
    if (success)
    {
        ShowAttributes(info.dwFileAttributes);
        cout << "Last write time: ";
        ShowTime(info.ftLastWriteTime);
        cout << "Volume serial number: "
            << info.dwVolumeSerialNumber << endl;
        cout << "File size: " << info.nFileSizeLow
            << endl;
        cout << "Number of links: "
            << info.nNumberOfLinks << endl;

        cout << "High index: "
            << info.nFileIndexHigh << endl;
        cout << "Low index = "
            << info.nFileIndexLow << endl;
    }
  }
}
```

The index information, combined with the volume serial number for the drive, forms a unique identifier for the file. The number of links is useful only on file systems that support symbolic links.

2.4.5 Getting the File Path

The **GetFullPathName** function is simply a convenience. It appends the requested file name to the current path to form a complete path name. However, it does no checking on the resulting path name to ensure that it is valid.

GetFullPathName	*Concatenates a file name to the current path*
```DWORD GetFullPathName(LPCTSTR fileName, DWORD bufferSize, LPTSTR buffer, LPTSTR filePart)```	
fileName	The name of the file
bufferSize	Size of buffer for resulting path name
buffer	Buffer for the resulting path name
filePart	Pointer to the file name in the buffer
Returns the length of the full path name, or 0 on error	

Listing 2.8 shows how to use the **GetFullPathName** function and then display its output to stdout.

> **Listing 2.8**   *Creating a complete path name for a file*

```
// filepath.cpp

#include <windows.h>
#include <iostream.h>

const int BUFFSIZE = 1000;

void main()
{
   char filename[1000];
   DWORD pathSize;
   char pathBuffer[BUFFSIZE];
   char *address;

   cout << "Enter filename: ";
   cin >> filename;
   pathSize = GetFullPathName(filename, BUFFSIZE,
      pathBuffer, &address);
   if (pathSize < BUFFSIZE)
      pathBuffer[pathSize] = 0;
   Else
      pathBuffer[0] = 0;
   cout << pathBuffer << endl;
   cout << address << endl;
}
```

2.5 File Operations

The APIs provides three functions for the common file operations of moving, copying, and deleting files. You can use these functions inside your programs to duplicate the functionality of the command-line equivalents.

The **CopyFile** function copies the source file to the destination file name. If an error occurs during the copy, **GetLastError** contains the error code (see Sections 1.4 and 21.6).

CopyFile   *Copies a file*

```
BOOL CopyFile(
   LPTSTR sourceFile,
   LPTSTR destFile,
   BOOL existFail)
```

sourceFile	File name for the source file
destFile	File name for the destination
existFail	Determines if an existing destination file should be preserved

Returns TRUE on success

The **existFail** parameter controls the behavior of the function when the destination file name already exists. If you set it to TRUE, the function fails when the destination file name already exists. When set to FALSE, the function overwrites an existing file. Listing 2.9 demonstrates the use of this function.

Listing 2.9   *Copying files*

```
// copyfile.cpp

#include <windows.h>
#include <iostream.h>

void main()
{
   char sourceFilename[MAX_PATH];
   char destFilename[MAX_PATH];
   BOOL success;

   cout << "Enter source filename: ";
   cin >> sourceFilename;
   cout << "Enter destination filename: ";
   cin >> destFilename;
   success = CopyFile(sourceFilename, destFilename,
      TRUE);
   if (!success)
      cout << "Error code = " << GetLastError();
   else
      cout << "success\n";
}
```

The APIs supports both a simple and an enhanced move function. The simple version moves a file from one name to another on a single volume. It simply changes the pointers in the directory structure, so it is fast. However, it does not allow movement across volumes or between different drive letters. The enhanced version allows files to move across volumes by copying and then deleting the original file, and it can also protect existing files or delay movement. Listing 2.10 demonstrates the **MoveFileEx** function.

MoveFileEx	*Moves files on or between volumes*

```
BOOL MoveFileEx(
    LPTSTR sourceFile,
    LPTSTR destFile,
    DWORD flags)
```

sourceFile	Source file name
destFile	Destination file name
Flags	Flags that control how the move is performed

Returns TRUE on success

The flags can be set to either MOVEFILE_REPLACE_EXISTING, MOVE-FILE_COPY_ALLOWED, or MOVEFILE_DELAY_UNTIL_RE-BOOT. The first option lets you control whether or not the function deletes an existing destination file during the move. The second determines whether cross-volume moves are allowed. The third works only in Windows 2000. It sets up for the move but does not actually perform it until the very beginning of the next reboot. This is handy for moving operating system files and other files that are open (and therefore immobile) when the move request is made.

Listing 2.10   *Moving a file.*

```
// movxfile.cpp

#include <windows.h>
#include <iostream.h>

void main()
{
    char sourceFilename[MAX_PATH];
    char destFilename[MAX_PATH];
    BOOL success;

    cout << "Enter source filename: ";
    cin >> sourceFilename;
    cout << "Enter destination filename: ";
    cin >> destFilename;
    success = MoveFileEx(sourceFilename,
        destFilename, 0);
    if (!success)
        cout << "Error code = " << GetLastError();
    else
        cout << "success\n";
}
```

The **DeleteFile** function deletes an existing file, provided that it is not open. It accepts the name of the file and deletes it immediately.

DeleteFile   *Deletes a file*

```
BOOL DeleteFile(
   LPTSTR fileName)
```

fileName   Name of the file to delete

Returns TRUE on success

If the return value is FALSE, use the **GetLastError** function to retrieve the error code, as shown in Listing 2.11.

Listing 2.11   *Deleting a file*

```
// delfile.cpp

#include <windows.h>
#include <iostream.h>

void main()
{
   char filename[MAX_PATH];
   BOOL success;

   cout << "Enter filename: ";
   cin >> filename;
   success = DeleteFile(filename);
   if (success)
      cout << "success\n";
   else
      cout << "Error number: " << GetLastError();
}
```

2.6 Temporary Files

The APIs contains two functions that make it easy to create temporary files. The first function retrieves the path to the Windows temporary directory, while the second creates a unique temporary file in that directory.

GetTempPath   *Returns the path to the temp directory*

```
DWORD GetTempPath(
   DWORD bufferSize,
   LPTSTR buffer)
```

bufferSize	Maximum size of the buffer
Buffer	The buffer that holds the path

Returns the number of characters placed in the buffer or, if greater than **bufferSize**, the required size of the buffer

---

GetTempFileName	*Returns the name and path of a unique temp file*

```
UINT GetTempFileName(
   LPCTSTR path,
   LPCTSTR prefix,
   UINT unique,
   LPTSTR tempFile)
```

path	The path for the new temporary file
prefix	The prefix used on the new file name
unique	A number, either zero or unique
tempFile	Buffer to hold the new name, at least MAX_PATH long

Returns the unique number used in the name, or 0 on error

You can specify a prefix of up to three characters that the function will place at the beginning of the new file name. An application might use the same prefix on all temporary files so that it can easily clean them up later. The **unique** number can be either zero or a number of your choosing. If it is zero, the system will pick a number that generates a unique file name. When **unique** is zero, the system automatically creates the new file in the temporary directory and closes it. When you supply a non-zero value for **unique**, you should create the new temporary file with **CreateFile**.

Listing 2.12   *Creating a temp file*

```
// tempfile.cpp

#include <windows.h>
#include <iostream.h>

const int BUFFSIZE = 1000;

void main()
{
   DWORD pathSize;
   char pathBuffer[BUFFSIZE];
   char tempFilename[MAX_PATH];
   UINT uniqueNum;
```

```
pathSize = GetTempPath( BUFFSIZE, pathBuffer);
if (pathSize < BUFFSIZE)
   pathBuffer[pathSize] = 0;
else
   pathBuffer[0] = 0;
cout << pathBuffer << endl;

uniqueNum = GetTempFileName(pathBuffer, "smp",
   0, tempFilename);
cout << tempFilename << endl;
cout << hex << uniqueNum << endl;
}
```

In Listing 2.12, the system requests the name of the temp directory, and then uses it to create a new temporary file. The program outputs the new file name. Since **unique** is zero in this code, you can also look in the temp directory and see that the new file exists.

See also the FILE_FLAG_DELETE_ON_CLOSE option in Section 2.7.

2.7 File Reading and Writing

Section 2.3 briefly introduced simple file reading using **CreateFile**, **ReadFile**, and **CloseHandle**. In this section we will examine file seeking, reading, and writing in more detail, and look at the **CreateFile** function more carefully. The operations here are all synchronous, so they block until complete. Section 2.8 discusses asynchronous file operations.

Listing 2.3 contains a program that performs a simple file read, designed for a text file or a file of bytes. Listing 2.13 demonstrates a file-write operation that writes structures to a new file.

Listing 2.13   *Writing structures to a file*

```
// filewrit.cpp

#include <windows.h>
#include <iostream.h>

typedef struct
{
   int a, b, c;
} data;

void main()
{
   HANDLE fileHandle;
```

Listing 2.13   *Writing structures to a file. (continued)*

```
BOOL success;
DWORD numWrite;
char filename[MAX_PATH];
int x;
data dataRec;

// get the file name
cout << "Enter filename: ";
cin >> filename;

// Open the file
fileHandle = CreateFile(filename, GENERIC_WRITE,
    0, 0, CREATE_NEW, 0, 0);
if (fileHandle == INVALID_HANDLE_VALUE)
{
    cout << "Error number " <<
        GetLastError() << endl;
    return;
}

// write 10 structures to the file
x = 0;
do
{
    dataRec.a = dataRec.b = dataRec.c = x;
    success = WriteFile(fileHandle, &dataRec,
        sizeof(data), &numWrite, 0);
}
while ((x++ < 10) && success);

// Close the file
CloseHandle(fileHandle);
}
```

The **WriteFile** function is similar to the **ReadFile** function, writing the specified number of bytes to disk. The function does not care what the bytes represent, so you can use it to write text or structures. In Listing 2.13, the program writes one structure's set of bytes in a single operation, and repeats the operation ten times.

WriteFile   *Writes a block of bytes to a file*

```
BOOL WriteFile(
    HANDLE fileHandle,
    CONST VOID *buffer,
    DWORD bytesToWrite,
```

```
   LPDWORD bytesWritten,
   LPOVERLAPPED overlapped)
```

fileHandle	Handle to a file created by **CreateFile**
buffer	Data to write
bytesToWrite	The number of bytes to write
bytesWritten	The number of bytes actually written
overlapped	Overlapped structure. See Section 6.5.

Returns TRUE on success

Listings 2.3 and 2.13 both use the **CreateFile** function in its simplest configuration. For example, in Listing 2.13, the GENERIC_WRITE constant signals that we need write access to the file, and the CREATE_NEW constant indicates that the system should create a new file rather than overwrite an existing one (if the file name already exists, the function fails). However, **CreateFile** has many other capabilities.

CreateFile   *Opens a file*

```
HANDLE CreateFile(
   LPCTSTR name,
   DWORD accessMode,
   DWORD shareMode,
   LPSECURITY_ATTRIBUTES securityAttributes,
   DWORD create,
   DWORD attributes,
   HANDLE templateFile)
```

Name	Name of the file to open
AccessMode	Read/Write mode
ShareMode	The way the file should be shared
securityAttributes	Address of a security structure. See Chapter 13
Create	The way the file should be created
attributes	Settings for normal file attribute bits
templateFile	File containing extended attributes

Returns a handle to the file, or INVALID_HANDLE_VALUE on failure

---

When using the **CreateFile** function, you have control over several different things:

1. The read and write mode
2. The way the file will be shared
3. A variety of attributes and performance hints

You can also send the function security attributes, as discussed in detail in Chapter 10.

The second parameter passed to **CreateFile** controls read and write access. You can pass in any of the following three combinations:

GENERIC_READ	Read only
GENERIC_WRITE	Write only
GENERIC_READ | GENERIC_WRITE	Read/write

Generally you use the third option when you plan to open a file of structures that you will read and modify simultaneously. You use GENERIC_READ when you want read-only access, and GENERIC_WRITE when you need write-only access.

The third parameter passed to **CreateFile** controls the share mode of the file. You control access to the entire file using this parameter. The following four variations are possible:

0	exclusive use of the file
FILE_SHARE_READ	read-share from the file
FILE_SHARE_WRITE	write-share the file
FILE_SHARE_READ | FILE_SHARE_WRITE	open access

If you pass 0 to the **shareMode** parameter, then the entire file is locked while you have it open. Any other process attempting to open the file will receive a share violation. The remaining options grant increasing levels of access to other processes. Alternately, you can lock individual byte ranges as discussed in Section 2.9.

The **security** parameter is discussed in Chapter 13.

The **create** parameter controls the failure behavior of **CreateFile** during creation. Any of the following options is possible:

CREATE_NEW	Create a new file. Fails if file name exists
CREATE_ALWAYS	Create a new file. Destroys any existing file
OPEN_EXISTING	Opens an existing file. Fails if file not found
OPEN_ALWAYS	Creates a file if one does not exist, or opens the existing file
TRUNCATE_EXISTING	Deletes the contents of the file if it exists. Fails if it does not exist

The **attributes** parameter lets you set the file attributes, and it also lets you tell the system your intended use of the file so that you can improve overall system performance. You can OR together non-conflicting combinations of the following constants as needed in an application:

FILE_ATTRIBUTE_ARCHIVE	Mark file for backup
FILE_ATTRIBUTE_NORMAL	Default

FILE_ATTRIBUTE_HIDDEN	Mark file as hidden
FILE_ATTRIBUTE_READONLY	Mark file as read only
FILE_ATTRIBUTE_SYSTEM	Mark file for OS use only
FILE_ATTRIBUTE_TEMPORARY	Mark file as temporary
FILE_FLAG_WRITE_THROUGH	Write through cache to disk
FILE_FLAG_OVERLAPPED	See Section 8.5
FILE_FLAG_NO_BUFFERING	Use no cache on this file
FILE_FLAG_RANDOM_ACCESS	File will be accessed randomly
FILE_FLAG_SEQUENTIAL_SCAN	File will be accessed sequentially
FILE_FLAG_DELETE_ON_CLOSE	Delete file when closed
FILE_FLAG_BACKUP_SEMANTICS	Create as backup file
FILE_FLAG_POSIX_SEMANTICS	Follow POSIX naming rules

Many of the flag options are hints that you give to help the operating system improve its overall performance. For example, if you know you are opening a 10-meg file that you will read from beginning to end and never use again, then it is a waste for the operating system to cache any of it. You should therefore use the FILE_FLAG_NO_BUFFERING and FILE_FLAG_SE-QUENTIAL_SCAN options. If you are creating a temporary file that you want to delete when you close it, you can let the OS do it automatically using the FILE_ FLAG_DELETE_ON_CLOSE and FILE_ATTRIBUTE_TEMPORARY flags. See the API documentation for details on all of these different options. You can set file attributes at creation or change them later, as shown in Section 2.4.3.

It is possible to read from or write to a file either sequentially or at random byte offsets in the file. You typically use random offsets when the file contains a set of structures. The **SetFilePointer** function moves the file pointer to the indicated position.

SetFilePointer *Moves the file pointer*

```
DWORD SetFilePointer(
  HANDLE fileHandle,
  LONG distance,
  PLONG distanceHigh,
  DWORD method)
```

fileHandle	Handle created by **CreateFile**
distance	Distance to move pointer (low 32 bits)
distanceHigh	Pointer to distance to move pointer (high 32 bits), or NULL
method	FILE_BEGIN, FILE_CURRENT, or FILE_END

Returns the new location of the file pointer, or 0xFFFFFFFF on error

---

The new file position can move a certain distance relative to the beginning of the file, the end of the file, or the current position. Positive values move forward, and negative values move backward. The program fragment in Listing 2.14 demonstrates a program that seeks through a file in 1,000 byte hops and extracts 10 bytes at a time.

Listing 2.14   *Code fragment demonstrating the use of the SetFilePointer function*

```
do
{
    success = ReadFile(fileHandle, s, 10,
        &numRead, 0);
    s[numRead] = 0;
    cout << s << endl;
    SetFilePointer(fileHandle, 1000, 0,
        FILE_CURRENT);
}
while (numRead>0 && success);
```

It is also common to store fixed-size structures in a file and to seek randomly to a specific structure. In many cases you will lock the structure while you are accessing it. See Section 2.9 for an example.

2.8 Asynchronous File Operations

The APIs supports an asynchronous form of file access that allows you to start an I/O operation and then proceed with other activities while the operation completes in the background. The technique is referred to as *overlapped I/O*. It exists in Windows for two reasons:

1. Overlapped I/O lets you create the impression of multi-threading without actually implementing a separate thread. In certain situations this makes the code more compact, or lets you handle asynchronous file I/O more easily than a second thread would.

2. Overlapped I/O makes it possible for separate threads in a single program to manipulate the same file object simultaneously. With overlapped I/O, each thread can keep track of its file position independently of other threads, and this lets threads simultaneously access the same pipe, file, etc.

Asynchronous operations can be extremely useful when you want to perform multiple file operations on the same file handle simultaneously. For example, in Section 8.5.2, a single-named pipe is read in one thread and written in another. Overlapped I/O is the only way to handle this situation.

See Chapter 7 for a complete description of events and overlapped I/O.

2.9 File Locking

When we discussed the **CreateFile** function in Section 2.7, you saw that its third parameter controls the accessibility of an open file to other processes. For example, if you specify FILE_SHARE_READ when you open a file with **CreateFile**, then other processes can open the file for read access but not for write access. You can also open a file so that no other process can access it at all, by passing a zero in for the share mode.

While this file-wide access control scheme is appropriate in many cases, there are many others where it is simply too general. For example, you may have a file of structures available on a server. It might contain employee records, and there may be many users on the network who need to simultaneously access the file to retrieve or modify employee information. The file-wide access control system implemented by **CreateFile** has a granularity that is too coarse for this sort of activity. What you want is the ability to lock individual records while they are in use, and to then free them up when the user has finished with them. See Figure 2.2.

Process 1 needs read access to this record

Process 2 needs exclusive write access to this record

Process 4 needs to read from this record as well

Processes 3 and 5 need read access to this record

File of employee records

Figure 2.2   *Many users may need access to different parts of the same file. File locking lets each user lock just the part they need*

The APIs offers two different functions, **LockFile** and **LockFileEx**, to implement this functionality.

LockFile   *Locks a range of bytes*

```
BOOL LockFile(
   HANDLE fileHandle,
   DWORD fileOffsetLow,
   DWORD fileOffsetHigh,
   DWORD lockLow,
   DWORD lockHigh)
```

fileHandle	Handle to the file to lock
fileOffsetLow	Offset to start of locked section (low-order 32 bits)
fileOffsetHigh	Offset to start of locked section (high-order 32 bits)
lockLow	Number of bytes to lock (low-order 32 bits)
lockHigh	Number of bytes to lock (high-order 32 bits)
Returns TRUE on success	

UnlockFile   *Unlocks a locked range of bytes*

```
BOOL UnlockFile(
   HANDLE fileHandle,
   DWORD fileOffsetLow,
   DWORD fileOffsetHigh,
   DWORD unlockLow,
   DWORD unlockHigh)
```

fileHandle	Handle to the file to lock
fileOffsetLow	Offset to start of locked section (low-order 32 bits)
fileOffsetHigh	Offset to start of locked section (high-order 32 bits)
unlockLow	Number of bytes to unlock (low-order 32 bits)
unlockHigh	Number of bytes to unlock (high-order 32 bits)
Returns TRUE on success	

LockFileEx   *Locks a range of bytes*

```
BOOL LockFileEx(
   HANDLE fileHandle,
   DWORD flags,
   DWORD reserved,
   DWORD numBytesLow,
   DWORD numBytesHigh,
   LPOVERLAPPED overlapped)
```

fileHandle	Handle to file created by **CreateFile**

flags	Access flags
reserved	Must be zero
numBytesLow	Number of bytes to lock (low-order 32 bits)
numBytesHigh	Number of bytes to lock (high-order 32 bits)
overlapped	Structure containing starting address of block

Returns TRUE on success

UnlockFileEx	*Unlocks a locked range of bytes*

```
BOOL UnlockFileEx(
    HANDLE file,
    DWORD reserved,
    DWORD numBytesLow,
    DWORD numBytesHigh,
    LPOVERLAPPED overlapped)
```

fileHandle	Handle to file created by **CreateFile**
flags	Access flags
reserved	Must be zero
numBytesLow	Number of bytes to lock (low-order 32 bits)
numBytesHigh	Number of bytes to lock (high-order 32 bits)
overlapped	Structure containing starting address of block

Returns TRUE on success

The **LockFileEx** function is slightly more bothersome to use because you have to create an OVERLAPPED structure (see Section 7.5) and place into it the starting address of the block that you want to lock (the rest of the fields in the structure are unused). However, **LockFileEx** offers more control over the locking process and is therefore preferred in many cases.

Listing 2.15 contains code that demonstrates how to lock a structure in a file using the **LockFile** function. The program assumes the existence of a data file created by Listing 2.13, and locks record three in the file. The program then waits for the user to press return to unlock the record and continue.

Listing 2.15   *Locking a record with LockFile. Use Listing 2.13 to create the file*

```
// filelck1.cpp

#include <windows.h>
#include <iostream.h>

typedef struct
```

Listing 2.15   *Locking a record with LockFile. Use Listing 2.13 to create the file (continued)*

```
{
    int a, b, c;
} data;

void main()
{
    HANDLE fileHandle;
    BOOL success;
    char filename[MAX_PATH];
    char s[100];

    // get the file name
    cout << "Enter filename: ";
    cin.getline(filename, 100);

    // Open the file
    fileHandle = CreateFile(filename, GENERIC_READ,
        FILE_SHARE_READ,
        0, OPEN_EXISTING, 0, 0);
    if (fileHandle == INVALID_HANDLE_VALUE)
    {
        cout << "Error number " << GetLastError()
            << endl;
        return;
    }

    // Lock record 3, wait, and unlock
    success = LockFile(fileHandle, sizeof(data) * 2,
        0, sizeof(data), 0);
    if (!success)
        cout << "Lock error = " << GetLastError()
            << endl;
    cout << "Press return to continue: ";
    cin.getline(s, 100);
    UnlockFile(fileHandle, sizeof(data) * 2,
        0, sizeof(data), 0);

    // Close the file
    CloseHandle(fileHandle);
}
```

Listing 2.15 shows how easy it is to lock and later unlock a range of bytes. You can see the effect of the lock by running a second instance of the program in a separate command shell. Run Listing 2.15, and then, while it has the record locked, open a second command shell and run Listing 2.15 again. Since the first instance of the program has locked record three, the second instance of the program will fail with a lock violation—two programs cannot lock the same block simultaneously. Similarly, Windows will not allow any other process to read or write to the locked range.

The **LockFile** function forms an exclusive lock—no other process can read or write any part of the locked block until the program releases it with **UnlockFile**. Generally you will want to lock a range of bytes for the absolute minimum amount of time possible so that all other processes can access the record when they need it.

The **LockFileEx** function does the same thing as **LockFile**, but gives you more control over the process. In the **flags** parameter, you can use one of the following four combinations of flags:

```
0
LOCKFILE_FAIL_IMMEDIATELY
LOCKFILE_EXCLUSIVE_LOCK
LOCKFILE_FAIL_IMMEDIATELY | LOCKFILE_EXCLUSIVE_LOCK
```

The LOCKFILE_FAIL_IMMEDIATELY flag controls the behavior of the function when it tries to lock a range of bytes that already has been locked by another process. If this flag is specified, then **LockFileEx** returns immediately with a lock violation. On the other hand, if it is not specified, then **LockFileEx** will wait for the requested block to become available. It will then lock the block and return. This process is demonstrated by Listing 2.16.

Listing 2.16   *Using the LockFileEx function in its waiting mode*

```cpp
// filelck2.cpp

#include <windows.h>
#include <iostream.h>

typedef struct
{
    int a, b, c;
} data;

void main()
{
    HANDLE fileHandle;
    BOOL success;
    DWORD numRead;
    char filename[MAX_PATH];
    data dataRec;
    OVERLAPPED overlap;

    // get the file name
    cout << "Enter filename: ";
    cin >> filename;
```

Listing 2.16   *Using the LockFileEx function in its waiting mode (continued)*

```
// Open the file
fileHandle = CreateFile(filename, GENERIC_READ,
    FILE_SHARE_READ,
    0, OPEN_EXISTING, 0, 0);
if (fileHandle == INVALID_HANDLE_VALUE)
{
    cout << "Error number " << GetLastError()
        << endl;
    return;
}

// Seek and Read from the file until eof
overlap.Offset = 0;
overlap.OffsetHigh = 0;
do
{
    LockFileEx(fileHandle, 0, 0, sizeof(data), 0,
        &overlap);
    success = ReadFile(fileHandle, &dataRec,
        sizeof(dataRec), &numRead, 0);
    if (!success)
        cout << "Last error = " << GetLastError()
            << endl;
    else
        cout << "Data = " << dataRec.a << endl;
    UnlockFileEx(fileHandle, 0, sizeof(data), 0,
        &overlap);
    overlap.Offset += sizeof(data);
}
while (numRead>0 && success);

// Close the file
CloseHandle(fileHandle);
}
```

To demonstrate Listing 2.16, you should run 2.15 in one shell, and then 2.16 in another. Listing 2.16 tries to read through a file sequentially and output the data it finds. Since Listing 2.15 locks record three, Listing 2.16 will stall when it tries to lock record three. The **LockFileEx** function will not return until you press the return key in the instance of Listing 2.15. Then 2.16 will continue and read until end-of-file.

Now, modify Listing 2.16 so that the **LockFileEx** function uses the LOCKFILE_FAIL_IMMEDIATELY flag. Run Listings 2.15 and 2.16 again. When Listing 2.16 hits record three, it will fail, and then the **ReadFile** function will fail as well. You can detect the failure in **LockFileEx** by looking at its return value and **GetLastError**, or detect it in **ReadFile** as shown in Listing 2.16.

The LOCKFILE_EXCLUSIVE_LOCK flag controls whether a locked block has an exclusive lock just like the one formed by **LockFile**, or a more permissive write lock. A write lock prevents other processes from writing to the block in question, but does allow them to read from it. This mode is very common, especially in situations like the employee-record example discussed earlier. One process may lock a record because the user needs to modify it, but that should not necessarily exclude other users or processes from reading the record.

2.10 Compressed Files

The 32-bit APIs have a small extension library that works with compressed files. The compress command creates a compressed file that you can either decompress to a new file during your application's execution, or read from directly, without decompressing it at all. See Figure 2.3. Certain types of files compress very efficiently. For example, many different types of bitmap files compress at a 90% level or better, and most text files achieve a 50% compression factor. The

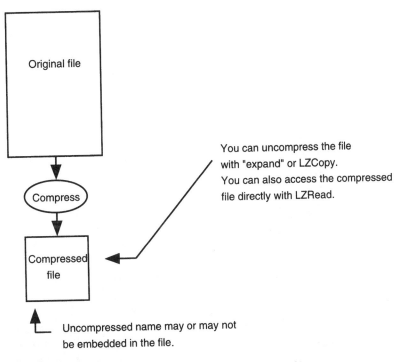

Figure 2.3   *Creating and accessing a compressed file*

ability to read compressed files directly allows you to keep certain files in a compressed format to save disk space.

In order to test the compressed file facility, you need a file to compress. The code in Listing 2.17 is a very simple C++ program that creates a text file containing 10,000 lines of data. You can adjust the size of the file to suit your taste. The 10,000-line file requires about 238K of disk space.

Listing 2.17   *Creates a large text file for testing purposes*

```cpp
// lztest.cpp

#include <windows.h>
#include <iostream.h>
#include <fstream.h>

void main()
{
    char filename[MAX_PATH];
    int x;

    cout << "Enter filename: ";
    cin >> filename;
    ofstream f(filename);
    if (f)
        for (x=0; x<10000; x++)
            f << "This is test line " << x << endl;
    f.close();
}
```

Assume that you name the file xxx.txt. You can compress this file to a new file named xxx.lz using the `compress` command:

```
compress xxx.txt xxx.lz
```

This file compressed from 238K in xxx.txt down to 42K in xxx.lz, a compression ratio of 83%. [For the sake of comparison, pkzip compressed it to 38K, or 84%, and was somewhat faster.] The main reason for the high compression ratio is the large amount of redundant data in the file. The `compress` command also has a `/r` option that embeds the original name of the file in the compressed file. The command that you use on the command line to uncompress a file is called `expand`.

The code in Listing 2.18 shows how to access a compressed file directly using the **LZOpenFile**, **LZSeek**, **LZRead**, and **LZClose** functions. Note that you must include the file `lz32.lib` in the list of link libraries in order for the code to compile.

LZOpenFile   *Opens a compressed file for reading*

```
INT LZOpenFile(
   LPTSTR fileName,
   LPOFSTRUCT openBuf,
   WORD style)
```

fileName	The name of the file to open
openBuf	A pointer to a structure **LZOpenFile** loads with file information
style	One or more bit constants that control file access

Returns an integer value identifying the file, or a negative value indicating the error code

---

LZSeek   *Seeks to a position in an lz file*

```
LONG LZSeek(
   INT fileHandle,
   LONG offset,
   INT origin)
```

fileHandle	Handle returned by **LZOpenFile**
offset	Byte offset into the file
origin	Reference point for offset: from beginning, end, or current.

Returns the offset of the file pointer, or a negative error code

---

LZRead   *Reads from an lz file*

```
INT LZRead(
   INT fileHandle,
   LPSTR buffer,
   INT count)
```

fileHandle	Handle returned by **LZOpenFile**
buffer	Buffer to place data into
count	Number of bytes to read

Returns the number of bytes read, or a negative error code

LZClose   *Closes an lz file*

```
VOID LZClose(
   INT fileHandle)
```

fileHandle	Handle returned by **LZOpenFile**

Returns nothing

It is important to recognize that the file handles returned by **LZ-FileOpen** can be used only by other **LZ** commands, as shown in the example program. Also note that the **info** parameter returned by **LZOpenFile** contains several pieces of information that may or may not be useful to you. See the documentation for details.

In Listing 2.18, the compressed file is a text file, but it can be any type of file that you can access at a byte level. The code in Listing 2.18 opens the file, seeks to the position 100,000 in the file, and then reads and displays 20 bytes from the file.

Listing 2.18   *Reading from a compressed file*

```cpp
// lzread.cpp

#include <windows.h>
#include <iostream.h>
#include <stdio.h>

void main()
{
    char filename[MAX_PATH];
    OFSTRUCT info;
    INT fileHandle;
    LONG seekResult;
    INT readResult;
    char buffer[10];
    int x;

    cout << "Enter filename: ";
    cin >> filename;
    fileHandle = LZOpenFile(filename,
        &info, OF_READ);
    if (fileHandle < 0)
    {
        cout << "Source error = " << fileHandle
            << endl;
        return;
    }
    seekResult = LZSeek(fileHandle, 100000, 0);
    cout << "Seek result = " << seekResult << endl;
    for (x=0; x < 20; x++)
    {
        readResult = LZRead(fileHandle, buffer, 1);
        if (readResult >= 0)
            buffer[readResult] = 0;
        else
            buffer[0] = 0;
        cout << readResult << " " << buffer << endl;
    }
```

```
    cout << endl;
    LZClose(fileHandle);
}
```

A fundamental question to ask at this point concerns performance. Although the capability shown in Listing 2.18 seems ideal, it is worthless if it takes 10 seconds to access each byte. If you do some tests on your own, you will probably find the following:

1. Sequential read speed on a compressed file is nearly indistinguishable from a normal file read.
2. Seeking and reading in a forward direction gives similarly good performance.
3. Backward seeking is a problem. When you seek from the end of the file toward the beginning, performance degrades by a factor of 50 or more compared to a normal file seek and read.

For example, the file created by Listing 2.17 contains 238K bytes. Write a program to seek to position 230,000, read 10 bytes, then to seek to position 229,000, read 10 bytes, and so on, decrementing the file position by 1,000 each time until the beginning of the file is reached. Doing this with **SetFilePosition** and **ReadFile**, as shown in Listing 2.14, returns an almost instantaneous response. Using **LZSeek** and **LZRead**, however, will take quite a while. If you need to do random or backward seeks in a file, you should test the **LZ** functions on some sample data first to make sure that the program's performance will be acceptable to your users. An important factor in the performance measurements that you make is the speed of your CPU.

The **LZCopy** function lets you copy a file from one place to another. If the file is compressed, it is expanded during the copy to its full size at the destination. Listing 2.19 demonstrates how to use the **LZCopy** command.

LZCopy *Copies a compressed file and expands it in the process*

```
LONG LZCopy(
    INT sourceFile,
    INT destFile)
```

sourceFile	Handle of the source file
destFile	Handle of the destination file

Returns the size of the expanded file, or a negative error code

Listing 2.19   *Copying a compressed file*

```cpp
// lzcopy.cpp

#include <windows.h>
#include <iostream.h>
#include <stdio.h>

void main()
{
    char sourceFilename[MAX_PATH];
    char destFilename[MAX_PATH];
    OFSTRUCT sourceInfo, destInfo;
    INT sourceHandle, destHandle;
    // get source and dest file names
    cout << "Enter source filename: ";
    cin >> sourceFilename;
    cout << "Enter destination filename: ";
    cin >> destFilename;

    // open both files
    sourceHandle = LZOpenFile(sourceFilename,
        &sourceInfo, OF_READ);
    if (sourceHandle < 0)
    {
        cout << "Source error = " << sourceHandle
            << endl;
        return;
    }
    destHandle = LZOpenFile(destFilename, &destInfo,
        OF_CREATE);
    if (destHandle < 0)
    {
        cout << "Dest error = " << destHandle
            << endl;
        return;
    }

    // perform the copy and close the files
    cout << "Result of copy = ";
    cout << LZCopy(sourceHandle, destHandle)
        << endl;
    LZClose(sourceHandle);
    LZClose(destHandle);
}
```

You can also use the **GetExpandedName** function to retrieve the name of the compressed file. If the original compression used the /r option, then the compressed file contains its original file name, and you can extract and use this name for the destination.

GetExpandedName   *Retrieves the name from a compressed file*

```
INT GetExpandedName(
    LPSTR source,
    LPTSTR buffer)
```

source   The name of the compressed file

buffer   The buffer in which to place the name

Returns 1 on success or LZERROR_BADVALUE on failure

You should make the buffer big enough to hold the file name (see Section 3.2 for information on obtaining the maximum file name length for a file system). On success, the **GetExpandedName** function returns TRUE. If the file is not compressed, or if it was not compressed with the /r option, the function returns LZERROR_BADVALUE.

2.11 File Mapping

The 32-bit APIs provides a feature called *file mapping,* which allows you to map a file directly into the virtual memory space of an application. We will see in Chapter 6 that this capability is often used to implement interprocess communication schemes, but the technique is also useful for simplifying or speeding file access.

You can map a file for either read-only or read-write access. Once mapped, you access the file by address (using array or pointer syntax) rather than using file access functions such as **ReadFile** or **WriteFile** (see also **ReadProcessMemory** and **WriteProcessMemory**). When used in read-write mode, the technique is especially useful because it gives you total control over when data gets flushed to disk.

For example, say that you need to access data in a file and you know that you will make a large number of writes to the file in rapid succession. Also imagine that, for performance reasons, you cannot afford the time it takes to perform all of those writes. Typically you would solve this problem by reading the file to an array, accessing the array, and then writing the array back to disk. File mapping does this automatically—it maps the file into memory for you. In addition, as discussed in Chapter 6, you can share the memory image among multiple processes, and the image will remain coherent to all viewers on a single machine.

Listing 2.20 shows how to use file mapping in read-only mode.

Listing 2.20   *Reading from a mapped file*

```cpp
// mapfile.cpp

#include <windows.h>
#include <iostream.h>

void main()
{
    HANDLE fileHandle;
    char filename[MAX_PATH];
    HANDLE mapFileHandle;
    char *mapView;

    // get the file name
    cout << "Enter filename: ";
    cin >> filename;

    // open the file
    fileHandle = CreateFile(filename,
        GENERIC_READ, 0,
        0, OPEN_EXISTING, 0, 0);
    if (fileHandle == INVALID_HANDLE_VALUE)
    {
        cout << "Error number " << GetLastError()
            << endl;
        return;
    }

    // create the mapping
    mapFileHandle = CreateFileMapping(
        fileHandle, 0, PAGE_READONLY,
        0, 0, "mapfile");
    if (mapFileHandle <= 0)
    {
        cout << "Mapping error "
            << GetLastError() << endl;
        return;
    }

    // map the file to an address
    mapView = (char *)
        MapViewOfFile(mapFileHandle,
        FILE_MAP_READ, 0, 0, 0);

    // dump the file
    cout << mapView;

    // clean up
    if (!UnmapViewOfFile(mapView))
```

```
        cout << "problem unmapping\n";
    CloseHandle(mapFileHandle);
    CloseHandle(fileHandle);
}
```

The program in Listing 2.20 begins by asking the user for a file name and opening the file with **CreateFile**, using the techniques described in Section 2.7. It then calls the **CreateFileMapping** function to create the mapping. This step determines the size of the mapping as well as its data, and gives the mapping a name so that other processes can view the same object. In this simple example the name "mapfile" is never used again, but in interprocess communication, other processes can open the same mapping by using that name.

CreateFileMapping   *Creates and names a mapping*

```
HANDLE CreateFileMapping(
    HANDLE fileHandle,
    LPSECURITY_ATTRIBUTES security,
    DWORD protect,
    DWORD sizeHigh,
    DWORD sizeLow,
    LPTSTR mapName)
```

fileHandle	Handle to the file, or 0xFFFFFFFF for a memory block
security	Security attributes. See Chapter 10
protect	Access protection (read-only vs. read-write)
sizeHigh	Maximum size of the mapping, high 32 bits
sizeLow	Maximum size of the mapping, low 32 bits
mapName	Name of the mapping

Returns a handle to the mapping or 0 on error

In Listing 2.20, the protection is set to read-only, and the size is set to the current file size by setting **sizeLow** and **sizeHigh** to zero.

The **MapViewOfFile** function actually loads the file data into the memory space of the process, and returns the new address of the data. In Listing 2.20, **mapView** is declared as a pointer to a character so that the data can be thought of as text. You can declare **mapView** to be of any type. For example, if the file contains a set of structures, let **mapView** be a pointer to that type of structure.

MapViewOfFile   *Loads a file mapping into memory*

```
LPVOID MapViewOfFile(
    HANDLE mapHandle,
    DWORD access,
    DWORD offsetHigh,
    DWORD offsetLow,
    DWORD number)
```

mapHandle	Handle to the mapping
access	Type of access (read-only, read-write, etc.)
offsetHigh	Offset into the file, high 32 bits
offsetLow	Offset into the file, low 32 bits
number	Number of bytes to map

Returns the starting address of the view, or 0 on error

In Listing 2.20, the code maps the entire file with read-only access. Once mapped, **mapView** points to the address of the mapping, and you use it just like any other pointer or array. If you load a text file with this program, the **cout** statement writes the entire file to stdout, as shown. Once you have finished with the file, use **UnmapViewOfFile** to unload the memory and write any changes back to the original file. No changes were made here, but the next example makes use of this feature.

UnmapViewOfFile   *Releases the view and writes changes back to the file*

```
BOOL UnmapViewOfFile(
    LPVOID address)
```

address	Address of the mapping

Returns TRUE on success

Listing 2.21 shows a second example of file mapping. Here the program opens the mapped file for read-write access and then writes to the file. The changes are flushed to disk only when the program calls **UnmapViewOfFile**.

Listing 2.21   *Reading and writing a mapped file*

```
// mapfilew.cpp

#include <windows.h>
#include <iostream.h>

void main()
```

```
{
    HANDLE fileHandle;
    char filename[MAX_PATH];
    HANDLE mapFileHandle;
    char *mapView;
    int i;

    // get the name of a file
    cout << "Enter filename: ";
    cin >> filename;

    // open the file
    fileHandle = CreateFile(filename,
        GENERIC_READ | GENERIC_WRITE, 0,
        0, OPEN_EXISTING, 0, 0);
    if (fileHandle == INVALID_HANDLE_VALUE)
    {
        cout << "Error number " << GetLastError()
            << endl;
        return;
    }

    // create the mapping
    mapFileHandle = CreateFileMapping(fileHandle, 0,
        PAGE_READWRITE, 0, 0, "mapfile");
    if (mapFileHandle <= 0)
    {
        cout << "Mapping error " << GetLastError()
            << endl;
        return;
    }

    // map the view to an address
    mapView = (char *) MapViewOfFile(mapFileHandle,
        FILE_MAP_WRITE, 0, 0, 0);

    // show the file
    cout << mapView;

    // modify the file
    for (i=0; i<20; i++)
        mapView[i] = 'x';

    // clean up
    if (!UnmapViewOfFile(mapView))
        cout << "problem unmapping\n";
    CloseHandle(mapFileHandle);
    CloseHandle(fileHandle);
}
```

In Listing 2.21, **mapView** is treated like an array when the program writes characters to the mapping. The changes to the mapping get flushed to disk when the program calls **UnmapViewOfFile**. Alternatively, you can force file writes with the **FlushViewOfFile** function.

FlushViewOfFile	*Flushes changes in the view to disk*

`BOOL FlushViewOfFile(`
`   LPVOID address,`
`   DWORD number)`	

address	The base address of the bytes to flush
number	The number of bytes to flush
Returns TRUE on success	

When using **FlushViewOfFile**, you generally flush the entire file. The system is smart enough to write back to disk only those memory pages that actually contain modified data.

2.12 Conclusion

This chapter presents many of the individual concepts involved in handling and manipulating files. In Windows, file access is quite interesting because of all of the different techniques available in the APIs: normal file I/O, overlapped I/O, compressed files, file mapping, and so on.

The **CreateFile**, **ReadFile**, and **WriteFile** concepts discussed in this chapter apply not only to files, but also to several other I/O channels. For example, these same functions appear in Chapters 8, 11, and 14.

Chapter 7 discusses synchronization and contains several sections that discuss overlapped and extended overlapped I/O in detail. Section 6.11 discusses interprocess communication, and file mapping can be a very useful technique.

Chapters 3 and 4 show you how to access disk drives and directories. These concepts are important to the discussion of files because drives and directories hold the files that you access. Chapter 5 looks at the next-generation file management for distributed systems Active Directory.

See Chapter 13 for information on securing files.

Drives

One of the neat things about studying operating systems is that they are built by people. *That may or may not continue to be true in the future. If we ever come to the point where it is not true, OSs will probably become a lot more consistent, but somewhat more boring.*

Since people design and build operating systems, operating systems are by their very nature quirky. People who are involved in an operating system early in its life have quite a bit of say in how the overall system ultimately works and what it includes. Their viewpoints and prejudices tend to influence both the user environment and the programmer environment. These originators therefore contribute to a system's quirkiness far more than the legions of programmers who come along after the OS has become a standard.

You can easily see the effect of the originators in the user interface for UNIX. The creators of UNIX favored commands that are short and rich, so UNIX has commands like "ls," which lists files. It has a short and obscure name and 20 different options. Another very good example can be found in the "vi" editor that comes with every copy of UNIX. Vi is possibly the quirkiest editor ever built, is wildly frustrating to any new user, and takes hours and hours to master. But it will exist forever because it became part of the UNIX operating system early in its life.

Windows comes with its own historical quirks, because it has a very interesting pedigree. Windows comes from Windows 3.1, which is built on top of MS-DOS, which originally borrowed almost its entire interface from a system called CP/M. It is easy to imagine that CP/M was designed almost completely by a guy in a garage working on an early 8-bit microprocessor. Perhaps that is a slight exaggeration, but it is probably not far from the truth. That guy has had an invisible effect on a great many things in Windows.

One of the most obvious things born of this heritage, the subject of this chapter, is the way Windows handles disk drives using *drive letters*. It comes straight out of CP/M. Drive letters are not a bad way to handle disk drives. However, people moving over from UNIX will find the concept bothersome because the UNIX scheme is somewhat more elegant. In UNIX, every drive on a system is *mounted* into a single directory tree. You might have 10 different physical drives on your UNIX machine, along with six connected over the network, but your view of those drives in UNIX is a single, homogeneous tree.

In MS-DOS, every drive—or *volume*—has a letter. This usually holds true in Windows, although Windows 2000 does allow multiple drives to connect together in *volume sets* or *stripe sets* that let single volumes contain many separate physical drives. Nonetheless, every Windows machine has a drive letter for each floppy drive, one or more drive letters for its hard disks, separate drive letters for things such as CD-ROM and cartridge drives, and then more letters for every drive mounted from the network. This configuration is shown in Figure 3.1.

Since there are only 26 letters in the English alphabet, a machine can have at most 26 separate volumes.

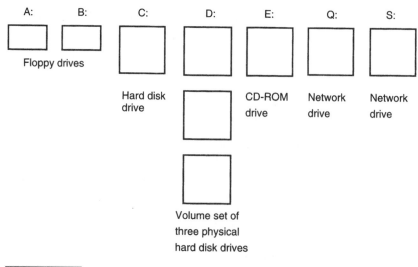

Figure 3.1   *Drive letters on a typical Windows machine*

The 32-bit APIs for Windows gives you several functions that you can use to access information about individual drives. You use these functions to find, for example, the maximum size and free space on a drive. Windows also contains a set of **WNet** functions that let you find and connect to network drives and printers shared by other machines.

Compatibility Note: All of the code in this chapter works identically in both Windows 2000 and Windows 98.

3.1 The Possibilities

The 32-bit APIs for Windows gives you several functions that you can use to access information about individual drives. You use these functions to find, for example:

- The maximum size and free space on a drive
- The type of the drive (network drive, CD-ROM drive, and so on)
- The file system used when the drive was formatted

Windows also contains a set of **WNet** functions that lets you find and connect to network drives and printers shared by other machines. With these functions you can:

- Enumerate all the domains on the network
- Enumerate all the machines in each domain
- Enumerate all the drives and printers on each machine
- Connect to any drive on the network
- Disconnect from any drive

All the connection options seen by a user in the File Manager are implemented using the **WNet** functions.

3.2 Getting Volume Information

You can obtain information about any volume available locally on your machine or mounted over the network using the **GetVolumeInformation** function. Listing 3.1 demonstrates this function.

Listing 3.1   *Results of the GetVolumeInformation function*

```
// drvgvi.cpp

#include <windows.h>
#include <iostream.h>
```

| Listing 3.1 | *Results of the GetVolumeInformation function (continued)* |

```
void main()
{
    BOOL success;
    char volumeName[MAX_PATH];
    DWORD volumeSerialNumber;
    DWORD maxNameLength;
    DWORD fileSystemFlags;
    char systemName[MAX_PATH];

    // get the volume information for drive C
    success = GetVolumeInformation("c:\\",
        volumeName, MAX_PATH,
        &volumeSerialNumber,
        &maxNameLength,
        &fileSystemFlags,
        systemName, MAX_PATH);

    // output information
    cout << "Volume name: " << volumeName << endl;
    cout << "Volume serial number: "
        << volumeSerialNumber << endl;

    cout << "File system type: " << systemName
        << endl;
    cout << "Maximum file name length:"
        << maxNameLength << endl;

    cout << "File system characteristics: \n";
    if (fileSystemFlags & FS_CASE_IS_PRESERVED)
        cout << "    Case is preserved\n";
    else
        cout << "    Case is not preserved\n";

    if (fileSystemFlags & FS_CASE_SENSITIVE)
        cout << "    Case sensitive\n";
    else
        cout << "    Not case sensitive\n";

    if (fileSystemFlags & FS_UNICODE_STORED_ON_DISK)
        cout << "    Unicode stored\n";
    else
        cout << "    Unicode not stored\n";
}
```

GetVolumeInformation   *Returns information about a drive*

```
BOOL GetVolumeInformation(
    LPTSTR rootName,
    LPTSTR volumeName,
```

```
DWORD volumeNameSize,
LPDWORD volumeSerialNumber,
LPDWORD maximumNameLength,
LPDWORD fileSystemFlags,
LPTSTR fileSystemName,
DWORD fileSystemNameSize)
```

RootName	The name of the logical drive
VolumeName	The name of the volume
VolumeNameSize	Size of the volume name
VolumeSerialNumber	Volume serial number
MaxNameLength	Maximum length of any file name
FileSystemFlags	Information flags for the file system
FileSystemName	Name of the file system (FAT, NTFS, and so on)
FileSystemNameSize	Size of the file system name
Returns TRUE on success	

As you can see in Listing 3.1, the **GetVolumeInformation** function returns the volume name and serial number, along with the type of file system used on the volume (FAT, NTFS, HPFS, or other) and the length of the maximum file name for the file system in use on that volume. The function also returns a flag word that gives you characteristics of the file system such as case sensitivity. The following flags are defined:

FS_CASE_IS_PRESERVED	The file system saves the case of characters when it stores file names on the disk
FS_CASE_SENSITIVE	The file system distinguishes uppercase and lowercase characters in file names
FS_UNICODE_STORED_ON_DISK	File names support unicode

3.3 Getting Drive Types

You can use the **GetDriveType** function to determine the type of any drive connected to your system. Listing 3.2 shows you how to use this function.

Listing 3.2   *Checking the drive type with the GetDriveType function*

```
// drvtype.cpp

#include <windows.h>
#include <iostream.h>
```

Listing 3.2   *Checking the drive type with the GetDriveType function (continued)*

```
void main()
{
    UINT driveType;

    // Get the drive type for drive C
    driveType = GetDriveType("c:\\");
    switch (driveType)
    {
      case 0:
          cout << "error\n";
          break;
      case 1:
          cout << "Drive does not exist\n";
          break;
      case DRIVE_REMOVABLE:
          cout << "Media removable\n";
          break;
      case DRIVE_FIXED:
          cout << "Fixed disk\n";
          break;
      case DRIVE_REMOTE:
          cout << "Network drive\n";
          break;
      case DRIVE_CDROM:
          cout << "CD-ROM drive\n";
          break;
      case DRIVE_RAMDISK:
          cout << "RAM disk\n";
          break;
    }
cout << endl;
```

GetDriveType   *Returns information about a type of drive*

```
UINT GetDriveType
    (LPTSTR rootName)
```

rootName   The name of the logical drive

Returns a bit mask that should be compared against the DRIVE_constants

---

The **GetDriveType** function accepts a string that represents the logical drive. In Listing 3.2, drive C has been requested. The function returns an integer that can be matched against a set of predefined constants, as shown in the code and described next:

0	Unknown drive type
1	No root directory found on the drive
DRIVE_REMOVABLE	Disks can be removed from the drive, as in a floppy disk or cartridge disk
DRIVE_FIXED	Disk is permanently fixed in the drive
DRIVE_REMOTE	The drive is mounted over the network
DRIVE_CDROM	The drive is for CD-ROMs
DRIVE_RAMDISK	The drive is a RAM disk

3.4 Getting Free Space

You can find out the maximum size of any drive, along with its available free space, using the **GetDiskFreeSpace** function. Listing 3.3 demonstrates the use of this function.

Listing 3.3   *Getting the size and free space on a disk*

```
// drvsize.cpp

#include <windows.h>
#include <iostream.h>

void main()
{
   BOOL success;
   unsigned long sectorsPerCluster, bytesPerSector,
      freeClusters, clusters;

   // Get disk space for drive C
   success = GetDiskFreeSpace( "c:\\",
      &sectorsPerCluster,
      &bytesPerSector, &freeClusters, &clusters);
   if (!success)
   {
      cout << "Error number: " << GetLastError()
         << endl;
      return;
   }

   // Output full disk size and free space
   cout << "Disk size: " << sectorsPerCluster *
      bytesPerSector * clusters << endl;
   cout << "Free space: " << sectorsPerCluster *
      bytesPerSector * freeClusters << endl;
   cout << endl;
}
```

GetDiskFreeSpace   *Returns information about the size of a drive and its free space*

```
BOOL GetDiskFreeSpace(
    LPTSTR rootName,
    LPDWORD freeClusters,
    LPDWORD clusters)
```

rootName	The name of the logical drive
sectorsPerCluster	The number of sectors in each cluster
bytesPerSector	The number of bytes per sector
freeClusters	The number of unused clusters on the drive
clusters	The number of clusters per drive

Returns a Boolean indicating success

The **GetDiskFreeSpace** function returns information about the number of *clusters* or *free clusters* on a disk. Clusters are sets of sectors grouped together as a logical unit. The function also returns the number of sectors per cluster and the number of bytes per sector. Using this information, you can calculate the size of the drive and the amount of free space available on it.

There are two ways that you might use this information. The most obvious use is to detect how much free space is available on a drive before writing a file to it. For example, if you know you are about to write 6 megabytes of information to a drive, you might first check to make sure that amount of space is available. This still is no guarantee: In a multi-tasking system, two processes can write to the disk at the same time, so the disk space may get consumed by other processes before you completely write the file. However, if you check and see that only 12K of space is available, you can warn the user. The second way to use the information is to check for cluster size. No file can be smaller than the size of one cluster, so if the cluster size is very large on a drive, you might want to take some steps to avoid writing a large number of very small files.

Note that the product of the sector size, the number of sectors per cluster, and the number of clusters can potentially overflow a 32-bit integer when the NT file system is in use. When checking the disk size, you may want to consider looking only at the free cluster number. The number of free clusters will certainly fall well below 4 billion for the foreseeable future. Alternately, use Microsoft's 64-bit math library found in `largeint.h`.

3.5 Getting Logical Drives and Drive Strings

You can query Windows for the drive letters that are currently in use. Windows returns that information to you either as a bit array or as a set of strings. Listings 3.4 and 3.5 demonstrate the two functions that return this information.

| Listing 3.4 | *Getting the logical drives with GetLogicalDrives (Page of)* |

```cpp
// drvgld.cpp

#include <windows.h>
#include <iostream.h>

void main()
{
   DWORD drives;
   int x;

   drives = GetLogicalDrives();
   cout << "Logical drives on this machine: ";
   for (x=0; x<26; x++)
   {
      if (drives & 1!=0)
         cout << (char) ('A'+x) << ' ';
      drives = drives >> 1;
   }
   cout << endl;
}
```

| Listing 3.5 | *Getting logical drive strings with GetLogicalDriveStrings* |

```cpp
// drvglds.cpp

#include <windows.h>
#include <iostream.h>

void main()
{
   DWORD len;
   char buffer[1000];
   char *p;

   len = GetLogicalDriveStrings(1000, buffer);
   cout << "Logical drives on this machine: \n";
   for (p=buffer; *p != '\0'; p++)
   {
      cout << p << endl;
      while (*p != '\0') p++;
   }
}
```

GetLogicalDrives *Returns a bit array containing drives in use*

```
DWORD GetLogicalDrives(void)
```

Returns a 32-bit bit string

GetLogicalDriveStrings   *Returns all the logical drive strings in use*

```
DWORD GetLogicalDriveStrings(
   DWORD bufferSize,
   LPTSTR buffer)
```

bufferSize   The size of the buffer

buffer   Buffer to hold the strings

Returns 0 on error, or the length of the string in bytes

In Listing 3.4, the **GetLogicalDrives** function returns a 32-bit value that contains one bit for each drive letter currently in use. Bit zero represents drive A. The code looks at each bit up through bit 25 and prints out the corresponding drive letter for each bit that contains a one.

In Listing 3.5, the **GetLogicalDriveStrings** function returns a set of strings, one for each drive letter currently in use. The strings are embedded in a single character array with NULL characters between them. Two NULL characters follow the final string to mark the end of the set. The program simply prints all these strings to stdout.

If the return value from **GetLogicalDriveStrings** is zero, it indicates failure, and you should use GetLastError to determine the problem. If the return value is greater than the size of the buffer, you should resize your buffer and call **GetLogicalDriveStrings** again.

3.6 Setting the Volume Label

You can change the label on a volume, provided your account has sufficient privilege to do so, using the **SetVolumeLabel** function as shown in Listing 3.6.

Listing 3.6   *Setting the volume label*

```cpp
// drvsvl.cpp

#include <windows.h>
#include <iostream.h>

void main()
{
   BOOL success;
   char volumeName[MAX_PATH];

   cout << "Enter new volume label for drive C: ";
   cin >> volumeName;
```

```
    success = SetVolumeLabel("c:\\", volumeName);
    if (success)
        cout << "success\n";
    else
        cout << "Error code: " << GetLastError()
            << endl;
}
```

SetVolumeLabel	*Changes the label on a volume*

```
BOOL SetVolumeLabel(
    LPTSTR rootName,
    LPTSTR volumeName)
```

rootName	The name of the logical drive
volumeName	New name for the volume

Returns TRUE on success

The volume name is typically first set when the administrator or user formats the drive. For example, if you format a new floppy disk with the File Manager, you can set its volume label at that time. You can also change a volume label from the File Manager or with the `label` command from the command line. The **SetVolumeLabel** function simply provides a programmatic mechanism for doing the same thing. If the function does not succeed, **GetLastError** contains the appropriate error code.

3.7 WNet Functions

Windows is designed to work with networks. When several Windows machines exist on a network, they can easily share disk drives and printers with one another. Both the File Manager and the Print Manager provide easy ways for users to connect to these shared devices. The 32-bit APIs also gives you mechanisms to connect to these devices from within your applications.

Windows sees the network as a tree. Any Windows network is divided into a series of *domains*, each of which contains a set of machines. Each machine can share zero or more drives, directories, or printers on the network. This arrangement is shown in Figure 3.2.

The 32-bit APIs contains a set of functions that allows you to enumerate all the shared drives available throughout the network and then to connect to any one of these drives. The network itself, its domains, and the machines in the domains are called *containers*. Containers are opened with the **WNet OpenEnum** function. A container can contain other containers (for example, domains contain machines), or it can contain actual drive and printer resources,

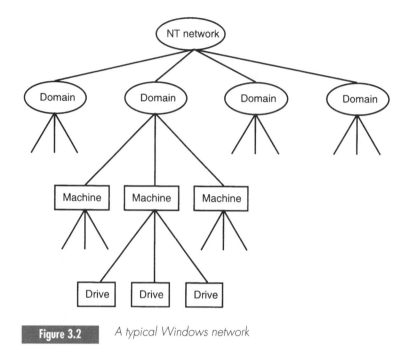

A typical Windows network

called *objects*. You *enumerate* all the items in a container—that is, you request a list of everything that a container holds—using the **WNetEnum Resources** function. Once you get down to the drive level, you can connect to a drive with the **WNetAddConnection2** function.

This section shows you how to walk through the resource tree and also how to gather information about connected resources.

3.7.1 Enumerating Drives

The code shown in Listing 3.7 demonstrates how to recursively walk through all the resources available on your network. It starts with the network itself and opens every container it finds until it reaches actual drives and printers that the machines share on the network. It is these drive and printer objects that receive connections, as demonstrated in Section 3.7.2.

Listing 3.7   *Enumerating all shared resources on a network*

```
// drvenum.cpp

#include <windows.h>
#include <iostream.h>
```

```
/////////////////
// Needs mpr.lib
/////////////////

// This function handles WNet errors
void ErrorHandler(DWORD errorNum, char *s)
{
   DWORD result, error;
   char errorString[1000];
   char name[1000];

   if (errorNum != ERROR_EXTENDED_ERROR)
     cout << "Error number " << errorNum
        << " returned by " << s << endl;
   // If its an extended error, get the error.
   else
   {
      result = WNetGetLastError(&error,
         errorString, 1000, name, 1000);
      if (result != NO_ERROR)
         cout << "Failure in WNetGetLastError: "
            << result << endl;
   else
     cout << "Extended Error: " << errorString
        << ". Provider: " << name << endl;
   }
}

// This function displays the information in
// a NETRESOURCE structure
void DisplayStruct(NETRESOURCE l)
{
   cout << "Type: ";
   switch (l.dwType)
   {
      case RESOURCETYPE_DISK:
         cout << "disk\n";
         break;
      case RESOURCETYPE_PRINT:
         cout << "Printer\n";
         break;
   };

   cout << "Display type: ";
   switch (l.dwDisplayType)
   {
      case RESOURCEDISPLAYTYPE_DOMAIN:
         cout << "domain\n";
         break;
      case RESOURCEDISPLAYTYPE_GENERIC:
```

Listing 3.7 *Enumerating all shared resources on a network (continued)*

```
         cout << "generic\n";
         break;
      case RESOURCEDISPLAYTYPE_SERVER:
         cout << "server\n";
         break;
      case RESOURCEDISPLAYTYPE_SHARE:
         cout << "share\n";
         break;
   };

   if (l.lpLocalName)
      cout << "Local name: " << l.lpLocalName
         << endl;
   if (l.lpRemoteName)
      cout << "Remote name: " << l.lpRemoteName
         << endl;
   if (l.lpComment)
      cout << "Comment; " << l.lpComment << endl;
   if (l.lpProvider)
      cout << "Provider: " << l.lpProvider << endl;
   cout << endl;
}

// Recursive function to enumerate resources
BOOL EnumerateResources(
   LPNETRESOURCE startingPoint)
{
   DWORD result, resultEnum;
   HANDLE enumHandle;
   LPNETRESOURCE buffer;
   DWORD bufferSize = 16384;
   DWORD numEntries = 0xFFFFFFFF;
   DWORD i;

   // Open a container
   result = WNetOpenEnum(RESOURCE_GLOBALNET,
      RESOURCETYPE_ANY, 0, startingPoint,
      &enumHandle);

   if (result != NO_ERROR)
   {
      ErrorHandler( result, "WNetOpenEnum");
      return FALSE;
   }

   // allocate a buffer to hold resources
   buffer = (LPNETRESOURCE) GlobalAlloc(GPTR,
      bufferSize);
```

```
// Loop through all the elements in the
// container
do
{
   // reset bufferSize each time thru loop
   bufferSize = 16384;
   numEntries = 0xFFFFFFFF;

   // Get resources
   resultEnum = WNetEnumResource(enumHandle,
      &numEntries, buffer, &bufferSize);
   if (resultEnum == NO_ERROR)
   {
      // Loop through all entries
      for(i = 0' i < numEntries; i++)
      {
         DisplayStruct( buffer[i]);
         // if the entry is a container,
         // recursively open it
         if (buffer[i].dwUsage &
            RESOURCEUSAGE_CONTAINER)
         {
            if (!EnumerateResources(&buffer[i]))
               cout << "Enumeration failed."
                  << endl;
         }
         // else add a connection.
         // See Section 3.7.2
      }
   }
   else if (resultEnum != ERROR_NO_MORE_ITEMS)
   {
      ErrorHandler(resultEnum,
         "WNetEnumResource");
      break;
   }
}
while(resultEnum != ERROR_NO_MORE_ITEMS);

// Clean up
GlobalFree((HGLOBAL) buffer);
result = WNetCloseEnum(enumHandle);
if (result != NO_ERROR)
{
   ErrorHandler(result, "WNetCloseEnum");
   return FALSE;
}
return TRUE;
}
```

Listing 3.7   *Enumerating all shared resources on a network (continued)*

```
void main()
{
   // Start the recursion at the net level
   EnumerateResources(NULL);
}
```

The program in Listing 3.7 starts in its **main** function with a single call to the **EnumerateResources** function, which recursively traverses a container. Since this initial call passes a NULL parameter, the function will begin at the level of the network itself. Inside the **EnumerateResources** function, the program immediately calls **WNetOpenEnum**.

WNetOpenEnum   *Opens a container*

```
DWORD WNetOpenEnum(
   DWORD scope,
   DWORD type,
   DWORD usage,
   LPNETRESOURCE resource,
   LPHANDLE enumHandle)
```

scope	Scope of the search
type	Type of items to enumerate
usage	Type of objects to open
resource	Specifies container to open. NULL for network
enumHandle	Handle returned to the opened container

Returns NO_ERROR on success, or an error code

The **WNetOpenEnum** function opens a container, returning a handle to that container so that you can enumerate its contents. The **resource** parameter specifies the container that you want to open. The **scope**, **type**, and **usage** parameters specify the types of objects that will be enumerated by the **WNetEnumResources** function.

Initially, the **WNetOpenEnum** function receives NULL for its **resource** parameter, indicating that it should start at the top level of the network tree (see Figure 3.2) and open up the network container itself. Once the container is open, Listing 3.7 enters a loop that calls **WNetEnumResources** to get all the objects inside the container.

WNetEnumResources   *Enumerates resources in an open container*

```
DWORD WNetEnumResource
   HANDLE enumHandle,
```

```
    LPDWORD numEntries,
    LPVOID buffer,
    LPDWORD bufferSize)
```

enumHandle	Handle to an open container
numEntries	Number of entries desired/returned
buffer	Buffer to hold returned entries
bufferSize	Original/returned size of buffer

Returns NO_ERROR or ERROR_NO_MORE_ITEMS on success, or an error code

The **WNetEnumResources** function accepts the handle returned by **WNetOpenEnum**, the number of entries desired (or 0xFFFFFFFF if you want them all), a buffer to place the entries in (allocated by **GlobalAlloc**; see Chapter 21 for details), and the size of the buffer (the documentation specifies that 16K is a reasonable value). In the buffer, the function returns an array of NETRESOURCE structures that contains information about each entry in the container.

```
typedef struct _NETRESOURCE {
    DWORD   dwScope;
    DWORD   dwType;
    DWORD   dwDisplayType;
    DWORD   dwUsage;
    LPTSTR  lpLocalName;
    LPTSTR  lpRemoteName;
    LPTSTR  lpComment;
    LPTSTR  lpProvider;
} NETRESOURCE;
```

Much useful information is contained in a NETRESOURCE structure. The **DisplayStruct** function near the top of Listing 3.7 displays most of this information. The **Scope** field tells the status of an enumeration:

RESOURCE_CONNECTED	The device is already connected
RESOURCE_GLOBALNET	The enumeration is not connected
RESOURCE_REMEMBERED	There is a persistent connection to the device

If connected or remembered, the enumeration must be a device, either a printer or a drive, and the **LocalName** field contains the local name of the device. An enumeration marked as USAGE_GLOBALNET gives more information about itself in the **Usage** field, which can have one of the following values:

RESOURCEUSAGE_CONNECTABLE	The enumeration is a connectable device
RESOURCEUSAGE_CONTAINER	The enumeration is a container (a domain or a machine)

In either case, the **RemoteName** field contains the name used to connect to or to open the enumeration. The **Type** field tells whether a connectable object is a disk or a printer:

```
RESOURCETYPE_ANY
RESOURCETYPE_DISK
RESOURCETYPE_PRINT
```

The **DisplayType** field tells how to display the object. This field is used in Windows's connection dialogs to determine the icon placed next to each item:

```
RESOURCEDISPLAYTYPE_DOMAIN
RESOURCEDISPLAYTYPE_GENERIC
RESOURCEDISPLAYTYPE_SERVER
RESOURCEDISPLAYTYPE_SHARE
```

The NETRESOURCE structure also contains the comment and the name of the provider.

Following the call to **WNetEnumResources,** Listing 3.7 loops through all the NETRESOURCE structures in the buffer. First it displays each record's contents. Then it inspects each record to decide whether it is a container. If it is a container, the **EnumerateResources** function recursively calls itself so that it can open and display the container. If it is not a container, it is a drive or a printer, and a connection can be formed with it. See Section 3.7.2 for details on adding connections. Once the code has examined all the entries in **buffer**, it cleans up and returns.

The first time you call **WNetEnumResources** for any container, it should return the error code NO_ERROR, as well as a buffer full of entries. However, there is no guarantee that the function was able to place all the entries for a given container in the buffer on the first call. Therefore, you should call it repeatedly until it returns ERROR_NO_MORE_ITEMS. This is the reason for the **do...while** loop in the code.

If something goes wrong, the **ErrorHandler** function seen in Listing 3.7 handles any **WNet** error. In cases where the network provider reports an error, the **ErrorHandler** function makes use of the special **WNetGetLast Error** function, which returns extended error information.

WNetGetLastError	*Explains extended* **WNet** *errors*

```
DWORD WNetGetLastError(
   LPDWORD errorCode,
   LPTSTR description,
   DWORD descriptionSize,
   LPTSTR name,
   DWORD nameSize)
```

errorCode	The error code returned by the provider
description	The provider's description of the error

descriptionSize	Buffer size for description
name	The name of the provider
nameSize	The size of the name buffer

Returns NO_ERROR on success or ERROR_INVALID_ADDRESS if the buffer address is invalid

The **WNetGetLastError** function talks to the provider and retrieves an error code, an error string describing the problem, and the name of the provider.

3.7.2 Adding and Canceling Connections

In Listing 3.7, the code enumerates all the containers and objects found on the network, but does not really do anything with them except dump the information to stdout. If you look in the **EnumerateResources** function of Listing 3.7, however, it contains a comment that says "else add a connection." At this point in the program, the code has found a connectable object. You can call the function shown in Listing 3.8 to form a connection using the following call:

```
AddConnection(&buffer[i]);
```

This line passes a single NETRESOURCE structure to the function that forms the connection.

Listing 3.8   *Adding a connection to a drive or printer*

```
// drvcpmm.cpp
void AddConnection(LPNETRESOURCE nr)
{
   char localName[100];
   char s[100];
   DWORD result;

   cout << "Do you want to add a connection? ";
   cin.getline(s,100);
   if (s[0]!='y' && s[0]!='Y')
      return;
   cout << "Enter local name (eg 'f:'): ";
   cin.getline(localName, 100);
   nr->lpLocalName = localName;

   result = WNetAddConnection2(nr, 0, 0, 0);
   if (result != NO_ERROR)
      ErrorHandler(result, "WNetAddConnection2");
   else
      cout << "Success.\n";
   cout << endl;
}
```

The **AddConnection** function asks the user if it should form a connection. It then asks for the local name for the resource and adds this name to the NETRESOURCE structure. The connection is formed using the **WNetAdd Connection2** function.

WNetAddConnection2   *Adds a connection to a shared resource*

```
DWORD WNetAddConnection2(
    LPNETRESOURCE netResource,
    LPTSTR password,
    LPTSTR userName,
    DWORD connection)
```

netResource	NETRESOURCE structure holding connection info
password	Password string
userName	User name
connection	Flag controlling persistence of the connection

Returns NO_ERROR on success

Once you insert the local name into it, the NETRESOURCE structure contains all the information needed to form the connection. It lacks the name of the user, as well as the password required for certain network objects shared by systems such as Windows for Workgroups or Netware. In the example code, these values are set to NULL, and this will work properly on homogeneous Windows networks. You will need to query the user for these fields on networks that require this information.

Modify Listing 3.7 so that it contains Listing 3.8 and run the program. Use the program to connect to a drive on the network. Once you connect to a drive, start up the File Manager (if it is already started, quit it and start again). The new connection will appear just like any other. You can cancel connections just as easily with the **WNetCancelConnection2** function.

WNetCancelConnection2   *Cancels a connection to a shared resource*

```
DWORD WNetCancelConnection2(
    LPTSTR name,
    DWORD flag,
    BOOL force)
```

name	Name of the resource (for example, "s:")
flag	Flag controlling persistence
force	Flag that forces disconnection

Returns NO_ERROR on success

For example, if you pass the function a drive letter in the form "s:", the function will eliminate the connection "s" holds and free up the drive letter for another connection.

3.7.3 Getting Connection Names

You can learn the remote name of any connected resource using the **WNetGetConnection** function shown in Listing 3.9.

Listing 3.9　　*Getting a connection's name with WnetGetConnection*

```cpp
// drvgc.cpp

#include <windows.h>
#include <iostream.h>

void main()
{
   DWORD result;
   char name[256];
   DWORD bufferSize = 256;

   result = WNetGetConnection("s:", name,
      &bufferSize);
   if (result == NO_ERROR)
     cout << name << endl;
   else
      cout << "Error: " << result;
}
```

WNetGetConnection	*Gets the remote name for a local connection*
```DWORD WNetGetConnection(LPTSTR localName, LPTSTR remoteName, LPDWORD bufferSize)```	
localName	Name of the resource (for example, "s:")
remoteName	Buffer to hold the remote name
bufferSize	The size of the remoteName buffer
Returns NO_ERROR on success	

The **WNetGetConnection** function accepts the name of the local resource and a buffer to hold the remote name. It returns the remote name in the buffer. If it is unsuccessful, errors come back through the return value or **GetLastError**.

3.7.4 Getting User Names

You can retrieve the current user's name or the name used to connect to any network resource using the **WNetGetUser** function as shown in Listing 3.10.

| Listing 3.10 | *Using the **WNetGetUser** function to get the name of the current user. If you replace the 0 in the first parameter with a string like the one shown in Listing 3.9, it will return the name used to connect to that resource* |

```cpp
// drvgetu.cpp

#include <windows.h>
#include <iostream.h>

void main()
{
    DWORD result;
    char name[256];
    DWORD bufferSize = 256;

    result = WNetGetUser(0, name, &bufferSize);
    if (result == NO_ERROR)
        cout << name << endl;
    else
        cout << "Error: " << result;
}
```

WNetGetUser   *Get the name of the current user or a resource's owner*

```
DWORD WNetGetUser(
    LPTSTR localName,
    LPTSTR userName,
    LPDWORD bufferSize)
```

localName	Name of the resource (for example, "s:") or NULL for user
userName	Buffer to hold the user name
bufferSize	The size of the userName buffer

Returns NO_ERROR on success

If you pass zero or NULL in for the **localName** parameter, the function returns the name of the current user. If you pass in a device name, the function returns the name used to attach to the device when **WNetAddConnection2** was called. The function returns an error code, or you can retrieve the error code with **GetLastError**.

3.8 Conclusion

There are many different and interesting ways to use the **WNet** functions described in this chapter. For example, you might want to make a tape-backup program that scours the entire network and attaches to every shared drive it can find. Or you might want to create a Find program that searches every directory on every drive on every machine on the network. You might also want to create specialized applications that connect to specific drives during a run and then disconnect from them automatically to prevent users from accessing the drives randomly. You can create any of these capabilities using the functions described in this chapter.

Directories

*E*very current modern operating system uses hierarchical, or tree-structured, directories to store its files. In Windows, these directory trees cap off the network-wide tree of domains and machines seen in Section 3.7. The functions used to traverse directory trees, however, bear no resemblance to the network-walking functions seen previously.

A directory tree in Windows has its root at a drive letter, for example, C:\. This means that a Windows machine has multiple root directories, one for each drive letter. Each drive (or partition) can have a file system different from that of the other drives, so individual directory trees can have slightly different characteristics. For example, the old FAT file system has much smaller file names than does the Windows 2000 file system, and a FAT partition has a much smaller potential size than an NTFS partition. None of the three file systems native to Windows 2000 (FAT, NTFS, or HPFS) allow symbolic links, but other file systems may support this capability in the future. You can learn the characteristics for a given directory tree by using the drive information functions presented at the beginning of Chapter 3.

In all file systems, a directory can hold zero or more entries. The entries can be either files, or other directories, as shown in Figure 4.1. Because of this tree-like structure, functions that walk directory trees tend to be recursive.

Compatibility Note: All of the code in this chapter works identically in both Windows 2000 and Windows 98.

Directory

File

C:

Figure 4.1   *Directory trees in a Windows machine*

4.1 The Possibilities

This chapter discusses the methods available in the APIs for manipulating directories, and then turns to the directory-walking functions. You will learn how to do the following:

- Create and delete directories
- Set the current directory or find out the current directory
- Search a directory for a file
- Recursively traverse all of the directories on a drive
- Asynchronously detect changes to files and directories. For example, if you are writing a text-editor application, you can make the program detect when some other process has modified a file that the editor is currently editing, and warn the user of the change.

The asynchronous detection functions in particular are quite unique, and you will find many interesting ways to use them.

4.2 Creating and Deleting Directories

Typically a user creates a directory either with the File Manager or with the mkdir command. There are many reasons that you may do the same thing inside of an application. For example, if you are writing an application that installs another application or a set of data files, you will need to create directories to hold the files that you are installing.

Listing 4.1 uses the **CreateDirectory** function to create a new directory.

| Listing 4.1 | *Creating a new directory (Page of)* |

```
// dircreat.cpp

#include <windows.h>
#include <iostream.h>

void main()
{
    char s[MAX_PATH];
    BOOL success;

    // get name of directory
    cout << "Enter path/name of new directory: ";
    cin >> s;

    success = CreateDirectory(s, 0);
    if (!success)
        cout << "Error code = " << GetLastError()
            << endl;
    else
        cout << "success.\n";
}
```

CreateDirectory   *Creates a new directory*

```
BOOL CreateDirectory(
    LPTSTR dirName,
    LPSECURITY_ATTRIBUTES security)
```

dirName	Name/path of the directory to create
security	Security attributes. See Chapter 10

Returns TRUE on success

The **dirName** parameter accepts either a name or a path. If it receives just a name, it forms the new directory as a child of the current directory. If it receives a path (e.g. "C:\dos\temp\new"), it traverses the path ("c:\dos\temp") and creates the new directory ("new") there. If the path is invalid, it fails. The **GetLastError** function contains a detailed error code following any failure.

It is just as easy to delete a directory, using the **RemoveDirectory** function as shown in Listing 4.2.

| Listing 4.2 | *Removing a directory* |

```
// dirremov.cpp

#include <windows.h>
#include <iostream.h>

void main()
{
    char s[MAX_PATH];
    BOOL success;

    // get name of directory
    cout << "Enter name of directory to remove: ";
    cin >> s;

    success = RemoveDirectory(s);
    if (!success)
        cout << "Error code = " << GetLastError()
            << endl;
    else
        cout << "success.\n";
}
```

RemoveDirectory	*Removes an empty directory*
BOOL RemoveDirectory(LPTSTR dirName)	
dirName	Name/path of the directory to remove
Returns TRUE on success	

The **RemoveDirectory** function can remove a directory only if it is empty. It accepts the same name and/or path information described for **CreateDirectory** above.

4.3 Getting and Setting the Current Directory

It is easy to get and set an application's current directory using the **Get CurrentDirectory** and **SetCurrentDirectory** functions, as demonstrated in Listing 4.3.

| Listing 4.3 | *Getting and setting the current directory* |

```cpp
// dirget.cpp

#include <windows.h>
#include <iostream.h>

void main()
{
    char s[MAX_PATH];
    char buffer[MAX_PATH];
    DWORD len;
    BOOL success;

    // print current directory
    len = GetCurrentDirectory(MAX_PATH, buffer);
    if (len == 0)
        cout << "Get error: " << GetLastError()
            << endl;
    else
        cout << "Current Directory = " << buffer
            << endl;

    // get name of new directory
    cout << "Enter path/name of directory to set: ";
    cin >> s;

    // change directory
    success = SetCurrentDirectory(s);
    if (!success)
        cout << "Set error: " << GetLastError()
            << endl;

    // print current directory
    len = GetCurrentDirectory(MAX_PATH, buffer);
    if (len == 0)
        cout << "Get error: " << GetLastError()
            << endl;
    else
        cout << "Current Directory = " << buffer
            << endl;
}
```

Listing 4.3 starts by retrieving the current directory and printing it to std-out. It then requests a new directory name from the user, and sets the current directory appropriately. It retrieves the current directory again to show that it has been set successfully. Note that the directory change applies only to the application's perspective—the user's current directory in the command shell will not change.

GetCurrentDirectory   *Retrieves the current directory name*

```
DWORD GetCurrentDirectory(
   DWORD bufferSize
   LPTSTR buffer
```

bufferSize   Size of the buffer

buffer   Buffer to hold the current directory string

Returns the number of characters in the buffer or 0 on error

SetCurrentDirectory   *Sets the current directory*

```
BOOL SetCurrentDirectory(
   LPTSTR newDir
```

newDir   String containing the new directory path

Returns TRUE on success

If either of these functions detects an error, **GetLastError** contains the error value.

4.4 Searching for a File

The **SearchPath** function searches for a file, either in the system path or in an arbitrary directory or directory tree. Its use is demonstrated in Listing 4.4.

Listing 4.4   *Using the SearchPath function*

```cpp
// dirsrch.cpp

#include <windows.h>
#include <iostream.h>

void main()
{
   char name[MAX_PATH];
   char pathName[MAX_PATH];
   char *pathPointer;
   char *p;
   char buffer[MAX_PATH];
   DWORD len;
```

| Listing 4.4 | *Using the SearchPath function (continued)*

```
// get name of file
cout << "Enter the name of the file to find: ";
cin >> name;

// get name of directory to start search
cout << "Enter path to start search, or PATH: ";
cin >> pathName;

// Search named path, or system path
if (strcmp(pathName, "PATH") == 0)
   pathPointer = NULL;
else
   pathPointer = pathName;

// do the search. It may take a while
len = SearchPath(pathPointer, name, 0,
   MAX_PATH, buffer, &p);
cout << "The search may take awhile...\n";

if (len == 0)
   cout << "Not found: " << GetLastError()
      << endl;
else
   cout << "Found in " << buffer << endl;
}
```

The program in Listing 4.4 starts by asking for the name of the file to be found. This file name must be specific—it cannot contain wild-card characters. The program then asks for the directory in which it will start the search. If you type "PATH" here, the program understands that command to mean that you want to search the system path. It places the value NULL in the **pathPointer** parameter, which tells the **SearchPath** function to search a specific set of directories in the order given below:

1. The directory containing the application's executable
2. The current directory
3. The Windows system directory
4. The Windows main directory
5. Any directories contained in the PATH environment variable

The function stops on the first match and returns the path to the file if it finds it. If it does not find the file, it returns an error code.

SearchPath *Searches for the specified file*

```
DWORD SearchPath(
    LPCTSTR path,
    LPCTSTR fileName,
    LPCTSTR fileExtension,
    DWORD bufferSize,
    LPTSTR buffer,
    LPTSTR *filePart)
```

path	NULL for system path, or a string indicating the starting directory for the search
fileName	Name of file to find
fileExtension	File extension appended if fileName has none
bufferSize	Size of the buffer
buffer	Buffer for path of found file
filePart	Pointer to start of filename in buffer

Returns the length of the path found, or 0 on error.

The **SearchPath** function accepts in its first parameter either zero or a string indicating the starting directory. Zero implies that the system should search the system path for the file. The **fileName** parameter may or may not contain the file extension. If it does not, you can place an extension in the **fileExtension** parameter and the function will append it to the file name before starting the search. The **bufferSize** and **buffer** parameters specify the buffer into which the function should return the result of the search, which is the path to the found file name. The **filePart** parameter returns a pointer to the first character of the actual file name in the buffer.

If an error occurs during the search, the function returns a zero; the error code can be obtained using the **GetLastError** function. It is also possible that the buffer size is inadequate to hold the entire path name. In this case, the returned value will be greater than the **bufferSize** parameter passed to the function.

The **SearchPath** function is a convenience. It returns the first instance of the file name requested. To do a more thorough search for duplicates, or to search for file names containing wildcards, you have to write code to do the search yourself, as described in the next section.

4.5 Traversing Directory Trees

Directory traversal is a very common activity in many different types of applications, and there are a number of good reasons to use this capability. For example, you might need to accomplish any of the following tasks:

1. Delete a directory and any subdirectories within it
2. Search a drive for the biggest file or 100 biggest files
3. Get all of the file names held in a directory so that you can back them up to tape
4. Search for a file or group of files anywhere on a drive
5. Search through directories to find .obj or .tmp files to delete, to free disk space
6. Find the total disk space consumed by a directory tree
7. Search for a specific word in any .txt file you find on a drive
8. Display the directory tree for a drive as a graphic
9. Check a path to ensure that each directory it contains is valid
10. Count the total number of files on a drive

The 32-bit APIs provides a set of three functions that let you easily traverse a directory. Using these same functions recursively, you can traverse entire directory trees.

Listing 4.5 demonstrates the use of the directory-walking functions in their simplest form. This code lists all of the files and directory names found in a single directory.

Listing 4.5   *Listing the current directories contents (equivalent to the "dir" command)*

```cpp
//dir1.cpp

#include <iostream.h>
#include <windows.h>

// Prints data in findData
void PrintFindData(WIN32_FIND_DATA *findData)
{
  // If it's a directory, print the name
  if( findData->dwFileAttributes &
    FILE_ATTRIBUTE_DIRECTORY )
  {
    cout << "Directory: "
      << findData->cFileName << endl;
  }
  // else if it's a file, print name and size
  else
  {
    cout << findData->cFileName;
    cout << "\t(" << findData->nFileSizeLow
      << ")";
```

```
         cout << endl;
    }
}

// Lists the contents of the current directory
void ListDirectoryContents(char *fileMask)
{
    HANDLE fileHandle;
    WIN32_FIND_DATA findData;

    // get first file
    fileHandle = FindFirstFile( fileMask,
        &findData );
    if( fileHandle != INVALID_HANDLE_VALUE )
    {
        PrintFindData( &findData );

        // loop on all remeaining entries in dir
        while( FindNextFile( fileHandle,
            &findData ) )
        {
            PrintFindData( &findData );
        }
    }

    FindClose( fileHandle );
}

int main(int argc, char *argv[])
{
    // List current directory's contents
    ListDirectoryContents( "*.*" );
    return( 0 );
}
```

In Listing 4.5, the **ListDirectoryContents** function starts by calling the API's **FindFirstFile** function.

FindFirstFile	*Finds the specified file in the current directory*

```
HANDLE FindFirstFile(
    LPTSTR searchFile,
    LPWIN32_FIND_DATA findData)
```

searchFile	The file to search for (wild cards are OK)
findData	Information about the file it finds

Returns a *search handle* to the first matching file found or INVALID_HANDLE_VALUE on failure

---

The **FindFirstFile** function accepts the name of the file to be found, and returns both a HANDLE to the file if it is found, and a structure describing the file. *The file handle is not a normal file handle like the ones produced by **CreateFile*** (see Chapter 2). It is specific to the **Find** functions described in this section. The WIN32_FIND_DATA structure returns the following information (from the API documentation):

```
typedef struct _WIN32_FIND_DATA {
    DWORD dwFileAttributes;
    FILETIME ftCreationTime;
    FILETIME ftLastAccessTime;
    FILETIME ftLastWriteTime;
    DWORD    nFileSizeHigh;
    DWORD    nFileSizeLow;
    DWORD    dwReserved0;
    DWORD    dwReserved1;
    TCHAR    cFileName[ MAX_PATH ];
    TCHAR    cAlternateFileName[ 14 ];
} WIN32_FIND_DATA;
```

A great deal of this information duplicates the information returned by the **GetFileInformationByHandle** function (see Section 2.4.4). It also returns the actual file name, to as well as the alternative FAT file name.

You can pass to the **FindFirstFile** function a specific file name, to a file name containing wild cards, or to a path with or without a file name. If you include a path, the search starts in that directory. If you do not, it starts in the current directory. If it finds a file that matches the file name you have passed, it returns the HANDLE and information about the file. If it cannot find the file, it returns INVALID_FILE_HANDLE for the handle.

In Listing 4.5, the program is searching for every file in the current directory. It passes the structure returned by **FindFileFirst** to **PrintFindData**, which decides whether or not it is a directory name and also prints out some of the information. The program then continues looking for other files in the directory using the **FindNextFile** function.

FindNextFile	*Finds the next file following a **FindFileFirst***

```
BOOL FindNextFile(
   HANDLE findFile,
   LPWIN32_FIND_DATA finData)
```

findFile	File handle returned by FindFileFirst or Next
findData	Information about the file it finds
Returns TRUE on success	

FindNextFile accepts a handle produced either by **FindFirstFile** or by a previous call to **FindNextFile**. It finds the next file in the directory that matches the file name description first passed to **FindFirstFile**, and returns a HANDLE and file information on the match. If no match is found, the returned Boolean value will be false, and the **GetLastError** function will contain the error code. Once no match is found, it means that the code has reached the end of the directory. At this point, the program calls **FindClose** to clean up the file handle used by the previous **Find** functions.

FindClose *Closes the search handle*

```
BOOL FindClose(
    HANDLE findFile
```

findFile   File handle returned by FindFileFirst or Next

Returns TRUE on success

The code in Listing 4.5 is suitable for examining all of the files in any single directory. If you want to look at entire directory trees, then you can make slight modifications to the code to make it recursive. In the recursive version, any directory found must in turn be traversed. Listing 4.6 demonstrates the process.

Listing 4.6   *Recursively traversing a directory tree starting at the current directory (Page of)*

```cpp
// dir2.cpp

#include <iostream.h>
#include <windows.h>

// prints information about a file
void PrintFindData(WIN32_FIND_DATA *findData)
{
   cout << "\t";
   cout << findData->cFileName;
   cout << "\t(" << findData->nFileSizeLow << ")";
   cout << endl;
}

// Recursively lists directories
void ListDirectoryContents(char *dirName,
   char *fileMask)
{
   char *fileName;
   char curDir[ 256 ];
   char fullName[ 256 ];
   HANDLE fileHandle;
   WIN32_FIND_DATA findData;
```

Listing 4.6 *Recursively traversing a directory tree starting at the current directory (Page of) (continued)*

```
// save current dir so it can restore it
if( !GetCurrentDirectory( 256, curDir) )
   return;

// if the directory name is neither . or .. then
// change to it, otherwise ignore it
if( strcmp( dirName, "." ) &&
   strcmp( dirName, ".." ) )
{
   if( !SetCurrentDirectory( dirName ) )
     return;
}
else
   return;

// print out the current directory name
if( !GetFullPathName( fileMask, 256, fullName,
   &fileName ) )
   return;
cout << endl << "Directory - " << fullName
   << endl;

// Loop through all files in the directory
fileHandle = FindFirstFile( fileMask,
   &findData );
while ( fileHandle != INVALID_HANDLE_VALUE )
{
   // If the name is a directory,
   // recursively walk it. Otherwise
   // print the file's data
   if( findData.dwFileAttributes &
     FILE_ATTRIBUTE_DIRECTORY )
   {
     ListDirectoryContents( findData.cFileName,
        fileMask );
   }
   else
     PrintFindData( &findData );

   // loop thru remaining entries in the dir
   if (!FindNextFile( fileHandle, &findData ))
     break;
}

// clean up and restore directory
FindClose( fileHandle );
```

```
SetCurrentDirectory( curDir );
}

int main(int argc, char *argv[])
{
   char curDir[ 256 ];

   if( !GetCurrentDirectory( 256, curDir ) )
   {
     cerr << "Couldn't get the current directory."
        << endl;
     return( 1 );
   }

   // List all files, starting with the
   // current directory
   ListDirectoryContents( curDir, "*.*" );
   return( 0 );
}
```

The main differences between Listings 4.5 and 4.6 lies in the code's treatment of directories. The **ListDirectoryContents** function in Listing 4.6 accepts two parameters, one for the file name and one for the current directory. It changes into the specified directory and begins looking for files using **FindFileFirst** and **FindNextFile**. If it encounters any directories during its search, it recursively calls itself to probe the new directory. This process continues until all of the files in the subtree have been examined.

4.6 Combining Capabilities

It is possible to combine the concepts learned in this chapter with concepts learned in Chapter 3 and concepts from other chapters to create very interesting search capabilities. For example, you might want to use the recursive drive-walking code from Listing 3.7, along with the directory-walking code demonstrated above, to create a program that connects to every drive on the network and searches every directory on each one for a specific file.

The code in Listing 4.7 demonstrates an advanced searching program using capabilities from this chapter as well as from Chapter 3. The program searches all directories on all drives connected to the machine that is looking for the indicated file. When the program starts, it will ask you for the name of the file that you want to find. Wildcards are acceptable. It will then search each connected drive and list every matching file that it finds.

Listing 4.7   *Code that searches for the indicated file on all connected drives (Page of)*

```cpp
// dir3.cpp

#include <iostream.h>
#include <windows.h>

// prints information about a file
void PrintFindData(WIN32_FIND_DATA *findData,
   char *dirName)
{
   cout << dirName << '\\'
      << findData->cFileName;
   cout << endl;
}

// Recursively lists directories
void ListDirectoryContents(char *dirName,
   char *fileMask)
{
   char curDir[ 256 ];
   char printDir[ 256 ];
   HANDLE fileHandle;
   WIN32_FIND_DATA findData;

   // save current dir so it can restore it
   if( !GetCurrentDirectory( 256, curDir) )
      return;

   // if the directory name is neither . or .. then
   // change to it, otherwise ignore it
   if( strcmp( dirName, "." ) &&
      strcmp( dirName, ".." ) )
   {
      if( !SetCurrentDirectory( dirName ) )
         return;
      if( !GetCurrentDirectory( 256, printDir ) )
         return;
   }
   else
      return;

   // Loop through all files in the looking for
   // the file name of interest.
   fileHandle = FindFirstFile( fileMask,
      &findData );
   while ( fileHandle != INVALID_HANDLE_VALUE )
   {
      PrintFindData( &findData, printDir );
```

```
        // loop thru remaining entries in the dir
        if (!FindNextFile( fileHandle, &findData ))
            break;
    }
    FindClose( fileHandle );

    // Loop through all files in the directory
    // looking for other directories
    fileHandle = FindFirstFile( "*.*",
        &findData );
    while ( fileHandle != INVALID_HANDLE_VALUE )
    {
        // If the name is a directory,
        // recursively walk it.
        if( findData.dwFileAttributes &
            FILE_ATTRIBUTE_DIRECTORY )
        {
            ListDirectoryContents( findData.cFileName,
                fileMask );
        }
        // loop thru remaining entries in the dir
        if (!FindNextFile( fileHandle, &findData ))
            break;
    }

    // clean up and restore directory
    FindClose( fileHandle );
    SetCurrentDirectory( curDir );
}

int main(int argc, char *argv[])
{
    char curDir[ 256 ];
    char findName[ 256 ];
    DWORD drives;
    int x;

    cout << "Enter name to find: ";
    cin >> findName;

    drives = GetLogicalDrives();
    // Eliminate drives A and B
    drives = drives >> 2;

    for (x=0; x<24; x++)
    {
        if (drives & 1!=0)
        {
            cout << (char) ('C'+x) << endl;
            curDir[0] = (char) ('C'+x);
            curDir[1] = ':';
```

Listing 4.7   *Code that searches for the indicated file on all connected drives (Page of) (continued)*

```
        curDir[2] = '\\';
        curDir[3] = '\0';
        ListDirectoryContents(curDir,
            findName);
    }
    drives = drives >> 1;
}
cout << endl;

return( 0 );
}
```

The program in Listing 4.7 is structurally similar to that in Listing 4.6. It starts by asking the user for a file name. It then retrieves a bit mask that indicates all of the drive letters currently in use. It skips over drives A and B and starts searching on drive C, if it exists.

The code has to run two separate find loops in order to accomplish its goal. The first find loop looks through one directory for any file names matching the user's requested file name. The code prints the path and name of every appropriate file. The program then uses a second find loop to look for subdirectories of the current directory so that it can recursively traverse them as well.

Two interesting improvements could be made to Listing 4.7. Using the concepts in Chapter 6, you can multi-thread the program. Most of the time used during the search operation is spent waiting for data to arrive over the network from other drives. By extracting data from several drives simultaneously, the delays can be overlapped and therefore minimized. The advantage of this technique is that it speeds up the overall search operation. The disadvantage is that it saturates the network.

An alternative is to place the search engine into an RPC server, and place a copy of that RPC server on each machine on the network that contains a searchable drive. The data needed for the search is handled locally on each machine by the RPC servers, rather than being shipped over the network. The advantage of this approach is an increase in speed along with the minimization of network traffic. Chapter 9 contains an extensive discussion of RPCs and RPC strategies.

4.7 Detecting Changes to Directories and Files

The 32-bit APIs contains a set of functions that allow you to detect changes in files and directories. For example, if you set up a change notification handle on a certain directory and a new file appears in that directory, you can detect it in your application.

Two applications that allow you to see this capability in action are the File Manager and Visual C++ (VC++). In VC++, if someone modifies a file that VC++ has open, then VC++ will recognize the change and advise you of it. For example, another user might attach to your drive over the network, open a file with Notepad, modify it, and write it back to the disk. VC++ will post an error dialog when it detects the change, and ask you what to do. In the File Manager, if the contents of the drive change after a search operation and the search window is still visible, then the File Manager will ask if you want to re-search the drive to update the window.

To use the change-notification functions, you must indicate a directory for the functions to watch, specify whether you want them to watch only the directory or the directory plus all of its sub-trees, and what you want them to watch for. The change notification functions can detect any or all of the following changes to directories:

- FILE_NOTIFY_CHANGE_FILE_NAME: The functions notify you when any file name change occurs due to renaming, creation, or deletion.
- FILE_NOTIFY_CHANGE_DIR_NAME: The functions notify you when any directory name change occurs due to renaming, creation, or deletion.
- FILE_NOTIFY_CHANGE_ATTRIBUTES: The functions notify you when any file attribute changes.
- FILE_NOTIFY_CHANGE_SIZE: The functions notify you when any file changes size due to a file write operation.
- FILE_NOTIFY_CHANGE_LAST_WRITE: The functions notify you when any file's last-write time changes
- FILE_NOTIFY_CHANGE_SECURITY: The functions notify you when any file's security descriptor changes.

Section 7.6 contains an example and shows how to wait for the change notification in both a standard and an MFC program.

4.8 Conclusion

The concepts presented in this chapter allow you to manipulate and traverse all the directory trees of any Windows drive. You can use these techniques to create search engines and installation programs, or to create your own directory-handling tools, like those found in the File Manager.

See Chapter 13 for information on securing directories.

Active Directory

If you work on a large project within a large corporation and need to find a file, but you are not sure exactly where the file is stored or even which server on your network holds it, what can you use to see your network's directory structure? How can you "drill down" on each server if you don't even know the server names? When you manage an enterprise network and you have a set of internal servers for your users, a set of servers for sensitive data, an intranet with restricted and open areas, and a public Internet site, how can you see everything you have from a single view? How can you set restrictions so that others do not have access to sensitive data? How can you replicate data so that it is controlled, yet available? And most importantly: how can you ensure that your directory solution will function across network and operating-system boundaries and will grow as your network grows?

5.1 The Possibilities

Traditionally, directory services have been tools for organizing, managing, and locating "interesting objects in a computing system. "Interesting" objects are things users (and applications) need in order to do their jobs: printers, documents, e-mail addresses, databases, users, distributed components, and other resources.

In their simplest form, directory services are like the white pages of a telephone book. Using specific input (a person's name, for example), a user can receive specific output (a person's address and telephone number). Directory services also provide the functionality of the yellow pages. Using general input (e.g., "where are the printers?"), a user can receive a listing of printer resources that can be browsed.

But directory services must do more, as networked environments become larger and more complex even before connecting to the global environment of the Internet. The Active Directory was created to meet the challenge of unifying and bringing order to diverse server hierarchies, or name spaces.

The Active Directory supports a wide range of well-defined protocols and formats, and provides powerful, flexible, and easy-to-use APIs. Moreover, the Active Directory provides administrators and users with a one-step source for resource and management information. Let's look at a summary of the features and benefits of Active Directory before introducing it.

- Support for standard name formats to ensure ease of migration and ease of use.
- Support for open standards to facilitate cross-platform directory services, including support for the Domain Name Service (DNS) and support for standard protocols, such as Lightweight Directory Access Protocol (LDAP).
- A rich set of APIs, which are easy to use for both the scripted writer and the C/C++ programmer.
- Simple, intuitive administration through a simple hierarchical domain structure and the use of drag-and-drop administration.
- Directory object extensibility via an extensible schema.
- Fast lookup via the global catalog.
- Speedy, convenient updates through multi-master replication.
- Backward compatibility with previous versions of the Windows NT operating system.
- Interoperability with NetWare environments.

5.2 Introduction to Active Directory

Some concepts and terms used to describe the Active Directory may be new to you. Unfortunately, some of the terms that have been around for a while are used to mean more than one particular thing. Before going on, it is important that you understand how the following concepts and terms are defined in the context of the Active Directory.

The scope of the Active Directory is large. It can include every single object (printer, file, or user), every server, and every domain in a single, wide-area network. It can also include several combined wide-area networks.

Some of the following terms apply to more than a single network, so it is important to keep in mind that the Active Directory can scale from a single computer, to a single computer network, to many computer networks combined.

NAMESPACE

The Active Directory is primarily a namespace, as is any directory service, like a telephone directory. A namespace is any bounded area in which a given name can be resolved. Name resolution is the process of translating a name into some object or information that the name represents. A telephone directory forms a namespace in which the names of telephone subscribers can be resolved to telephone numbers. The Windows file system forms a namespace in which the name of a file can be resolved to the file itself. The Active Directory forms a namespace in which the name of an object in the directory can be resolved to the object itself.

OBJECT

An object is a distinct, named set of attributes that represents something concrete, such as a user, a printer, or an application. The attributes hold data describing the subject that is identified by the directory object. Attributes of a user might include the user's given name, surname, and e-mail address.

CONTAINER

A container is like an object in that it has attributes and is part of the Active Directory namespace. However, unlike an object, it does not represent something concrete. It is a container for a group of objects and other containers.

TREE

Tree is used throughout the book to describe a hierarchy of objects and containers. Endpoints on the tree are usually objects. Nodes in the tree (points at which the tree branches) are containers. A tree shows the way in which objects are connected or the path from one object to another. A simple directory is a container. A computer network or domain is also a container. A contiguous sub-tree is any unbroken path in the tree, including all members of any container in that path.

DISTINGUISHED NAME

Every object in the Active Directory has a distinguished name (DN). The distinguished name identifies the domain that holds the object, as well as the complete path through the container hierarchy by which the object is reached. A typical DN might be

/O=Internet/DC=COM/DC=Microsoft/CN=Users/CN=James Smith

The DN identifies the "James Smith" user object in the Microsoft.com domain as follows:

Organization=Internet
Domain Component=COM
Domain Component=Microsoft
Common Name=Users
Common Name=James Smith

RELATIVE DISTINGUISHED NAME

The Relative Distinguished Name (RDN) of an object is the part of the name that is an attribute of the object itself. In the preceding example, the RDN of the "James Smith" user object is CN=James Smith. The RDN of the parent object is CN=Users.

NAMING CONTEXTS AND PARTITIONS

The Active Directory is made up of one or more naming contexts or partitions. A naming context is any contiguous sub-tree of the directory. Naming contexts are the unit of replication. In the Active Directory, a single server always holds at least three naming contexts:

* The schema
* The configuration (replication topology and related metadata)
* One or more user naming contexts (sub-trees containing the actual objects in the directory)

DOMAINS

A domain is a single security boundary of a Windows 2000 computer network. The Active Directory is made up of one or more domains. On a stand-alone workstation, the domain is the computer itself. A domain can span more than one physical location. Every domain has its own security policies and security relationships with other domains. When multiple domains are connected by trust relationships and share a common schema, configuration, and global catalog, you have a domain tree. Multiple domain trees can be connected together into a forest.

FORESTS

A forest is a set of one or more trees that do not form a contiguous namespace. All trees in a forest share a common schema, configuration, and Global Catalog. All trees in a given forest trust each other via transitive hierarchical Kerberos trust relationships. Unlike a tree, a forest does need a distinct name. A forest exists as a set of cross-reference objects and Kerberos trust relationships known to the member trees. Trees in a forest form a hierarchy for the purposes of the Kerberos trust; the tree name at the root of the trust can be used to refer to a given forest.

SITES

A site is a location in a network that contains Active Directory servers. A site is defined as one or more well-connected TCP/IP subnets. "Well-connected" means that network connectivity is highly reliable and fast (for example, LAN speeds of 10 million bits per second or greater). Defining a site as a set of subnets allows administrators to quickly and easily configure the Active Directory access and replication topology to take advantage of the physical network. When a user logs on, the Active Directory client finds Active Directory servers in the site where the user is located. Because machines in the same site are close to each other in network terms, logon time is accomplished easily because the user's workstation already knows what TCP/IP subnet it is on, and subnets translate directly to Active Directory sites.

5.3 Active Directory Architecture

This section introduces some of the primary architectural components of the Active Directory.

DATA MODEL

The Active Directory data model is derived from the X.500 data model. The directory holds objects that represent things of various sorts, which are described by attributes. The universe of objects that can be stored in the directory is defined in the schema. For each object class, the schema defines what attributes an instance of the class must have, what additional attributes it may have, and what object class can be a parent of the current object class.

SCHEMA

The Active Directory schema is implemented as a set of object-class instances stored in the directory. This is very different from many other directories, which have a schema but store it as a text file to be read at startup. Storing the schema in the directory has many advantages. For example, user applications can read the schema to discover what objects and properties are available. Also, the Active Directory schema can be updated dynamically. That is, an application can extend the schema with new attributes and classes, and can use the extensions immediately. Schema updates are accomplished by creating or modifying the schema objects stored in the directory. Like every object in the Active Directory, schema objects are protected by access control lists (ACLs), so only authorized users may alter the schema.

SECURITY MODEL

The directory is part of the Windows 2000 Trusted Computing Base and is a full participant in the Windows 2000 security infrastructure. ACLs protect all objects in the Active Directory. The Windows 2000 access validation routines use the ACL to validate any attempt to access an object or attribute in the Active Directory.

ADMINISTRATION MODEL

Only authorized users may perform administration in the Active Directory. A user is authorized by a higher authority to perform a specified set of actions on a specified set of objects and object classes in some identified sub-tree of the directory. This is called delegated administration. Delegated administration allows for very specific control over who can do what, and enables delegation of authority without granting elevated privileges. The Directory System Agent (DSA) is the process that manages the directory's physical storage. Clients use one of the supported interfaces to connect to the DSA, and then search for, read, and write directory objects and their attributes. The DSA keeps client isolated from the physical storage format of the directory data.

5.4 Frequently Asked Questions

Let's look, at this point, at some of the most frequently asked questions, to get a feel for what people most often inquire about.

HOW DOES A WORKSTATION DISCOVER ITS SITE?

A workstation discovers its site by presenting its subnet to the first Active Directory server contacted. The workstation determines the subnet by applying its subnet mask to its IP address. The subnet mask and IPO address can be either assigned by DHCP or statically configured. The first server contacted uses the presented subnet to locate the site object for the site where the workstation is located. If the current server is not in that site, the server notifies the workstation of a better server to use.

HOW DOES A WORKSTATION FIND A DIRECTORY SERVER?

A workstation finds a directory server by querying DNS. Directory servers for a given domain publish SRV Resource Records in DNS with names in the format

LDAP.TCP.<domain name>

Thus, a workstation logging in to Microsoft.com will query DNS for SRV records for LDAP.TCP.Microsoft.com. A server will be selected from the list and contacted. The contacted server will use the subnet information presented by the workstation to determine the best server, as described in the previous answer.

HOW DO I LOG ON?

A user can use a variety of names in a variety of formats to log on to Windows 2000 Professional. These include the name formats supported by the Win32 application programming interface DSCrackNames, which is used to convert these name forms as necessary.

- Domain NETBIOS name and SAM-Account-Name—This is the Windows NT 4.0 style logon name. The domain NETBIOS name is the name the domain had prior to migration. The SAM-Account-Name is the account name the user had prior to migration.
- User Principal Name—This is the format <friendly name>@dotted-dns-domain-name>. If the name is not unique, the logon attempt will fail with an Unknown User error.

WHAT HAPPENS TO ACCESS CONTROL LISTS ON DOMAIN RESOURCES AFTER MIGRATION?

Access control lists are not affected directly by migration. If all Windows NT 3.51 and Windows NT 4.0 domains are migrated in place, nothing changes, from an ACL perspective. If you move servers from a resource domain into an organizational unit in migrated account domains and then delete the resource domain, you will need to edit any ACLs that hold ACEs referring to the now deleted domain. This is not a function of the Windows 2000 migration; if you delete a domain in any version of Windows NT, security identifiers issued by that domain become invalid.

To reduce the effort involved in reapplying ACL resources, if you have a resource domain in Windows NT 3.51 or 4.0 and you plan to replace it with an OU and delete it in Windows 2000 you should not put groups from the resource domain into ACLs. This does not affect local groups from member servers; it affects only those from Domain Controllers.

WHAT HAPPENS TO ACLS WHEN I DELETE A DOMAIN?

When you create a group in a domain, it has a Security Identifier (SID) issued by that domain. When you put that SID into an ACL, it grants access to users who have that SID that's in their token. Users get the SID in their token by logging on to the domain that issued the SID. This can be a network logon and happens transparently. When you edit an ACL, the LookupAccountName API is called with the SID. If you delete the domain that issued the SID, you will see "Unknown User" in the list of users and groups for the ACL. This happens in Windows 3.51 and Windows NT 4.0 if you delete a domain or remove a trust link.

WHAT HAPPENS TO LOCAL GROUPS?

There are two parts to this answer:

- Part 1: Local Groups on Member Servers—Local groups on a member server stay local; they exist only in the SAM on the member server and are not migrated to the Active Directory. A typical function of a local group on a member server is to hold global groups from account domains. The server administrator puts the local group in the ACLs on the server's resources and adds the global groups to the local group. This does not change in Windows 2000. The only difference is that the global groups become normal groups and are published in the Active Directory.
- Part 2: Local Groups on PDCs and BDCs—Backup Domain Controllers have a read-only SAM. When you create a local group on a BDC, the create operation is remoted to the PDC and replicated back to all BDCs. Semantically, these local groups are identical to the local groups on a member server, but they exist on the PDC and on all BDCs. When you upgrade to Windows 2000, the upgrade process creates a Domain Local group object in the Active Directory for each of these groups.

WHEN IS THE GLOBAL CATALOG SEARCHED?

A search of the global catalog is initiated in one of several ways:

- By a sub-tree or one-level LDAP search rooted at the null DN (the root of the namespace)—this generates a reference to the Global Catalog.
- By a direct reference to the GC port at a GC replica (although client programs are unlikely to take this approach).
- By an explicit reference to the GC ADSI provider (GC://).

DO I HAVE TO USE MICROSOFT'S DNS SERVICE?

No. There are significant advantages to using Microsoft DNS, but any RFC-compliant DNS service will work. Dynamic DNS is recommended because, with a Dynamic DNS Service, Active Directory servers can automatically register the necessary records in DNS. Static DNS service works equally well, but the DNS registration for each Active Directory server must be accomplished manually.

WHAT ARE THE ADVANTAGES OF USING MICROSOFT'S DNS SERVICE?

The DNS Service included with Windows 2000 is an RFC- and BIND-compliant implementation of Dynamic DNS. It is a native implementation for Windows 2000, not a port of the public-domain BIND implementation. The Microsoft DNS Service stores the DNS zones for which it is responsible in the Active Directory. DNS data is replicated among Microsoft DNS Services by Active Directory replication, not by Zone Transfer. The Microsoft DNS Service supports standard DNS Zone Transfer for interoperability with other DNS Services.

WHAT HAPPENS TO DHCP?

The DHCP Service is largely unchanged for Windows 2000. The DHCP client is DNS-aware and uses the services of Dynamic DNS to register addresses issued by DHCP directly in DNS. The DHCP client will continue to register with WINS if DHCP identifies a WINS server.

WHAT HAPPENS TO WINS?

WINS is unchanged for Windows 2000. Windows 2000 clients (and Windows 98 clients with the Active Directory upgrade installed) no longer need to use the NETBIOS namespace. WINS is still required in order for down-level clients to find servers, and vice versa. When there are no more down-level clients in the enterprise, the WINS servers can be turned off.

5.5 Conclusion

With the release of Windows 2000 Server and Advanced Server, Microsoft now offers an integrated solution to directory services via Active Directory services. The Microsoft solution provides tools to allow use of Active Directory for managing networks. Storing network resources in Active Directory lets you manage them across the enterprise. This is perfect for system administrators and engineers, but developers need a solution geared toward specific data-storage problems. In Windows 2000 Server, Microsoft changed the way network domains are handled. Windows NT 4.0 used Primary Domain Controllers (PDCs) and Backup Domain Controllers (BDCs). The domain system information (users, groups, permissions, and so on) could only be changed on the PDC. Eventually the data was replicated to the BDCs, but there was no guarantee that the replication would happen in a timely manner. With Windows 2000, there is no distinction between a server with Active Directory services and a domain controller. There are no longer PDCs and BDCs; either it's a domain controller or it isn't. Each domain controller can belong to a domain tree, and domain trees can also belong to domain forests.

Trees and forests have trust relationships with each other and allow for secure data sharing within these trust relationships. The domain forest also contains a global catalog—the Active Directory services—from which data is replicated (and optionally partitioned) throughout the forest. This allows for the directory services to be as far from the client as necessary. This means that any objects you store in the Active Directory services will be visible from any trusted domain, assuming the security rights are available. This is especially useful for directories that must be shared within an enterprise.

The Active Directory services will not design your systems for you or provide an instant replacement for relational databases, but they do solve a particular problem: long-term storage of fairly static objects in hierarchical storage. Active Directory services provide an enterprise solution for sharing a global catalog of information, and tools to manage that information. The Active Directory Service Interfaces (ADSI) provide a way of managing your directory objects in a simple yet robust way. Using the Microsoft ADSI interfaces simplifies the interaction with directory services. ADSI, which was not covered in this chapter, is a set of COM objects that allows you to administer Active Directory on Windows 2000.

ActiveX Data Objects (ADO), the Microsoft database access layer, uses a provider paradigm to specify how objects will query their data. With this in mind, Microsoft created a provider to fill a gap in ADSI and to provide new functionality at the same time. With ADO, you can query Active Directory using SQL syntax.

```
SELECT cn, AdsPath, description
FROM LDAP://twain.local/cn=users
WHERE objectClass = "user" AND cn = "a*";
```

This is helpful for those who have invested time in learning SQL syntax, and will shorten the learning curve for querying Active Directory.

Processes and Threads

*P*rocesses and threads are two of the most exciting and useful features in Windows. Processes give you the ability to run multiple programs on a Windows machine at one time. Threads allow you to break up a single program into multiple threads of execution. In this chapter you will learn how to create new threads within your applications so that your applications make better use of the system. Threads also let you take advantage of the extra CPU power available in machines that contain multiple processors.

Compatibility Note: All of the code in this chapter works identically in both Windows 2000 and Windows 98. Note, however, that Windows 98 can use only one processor per machine, while Windows 2000 can make use of multiple CPUs.

6.1 The Possibilities

There are a number of ways that you might use threads in your own programs. Here are some ideas:

- If you create an MDI (Multiple Document Interface) application, it is often useful to assign a separate thread to each window. For example, in an MDI communications program that lets you connect to multiple hosts simultaneously via multiple modems, it simplifies things considerably if each window has its own thread that communicates with just one host.
- In a program that takes a long time to refresh its display because of the complexity of the graphics involved (for example, a CAD/CAM

program may have to draw 10,000 line segments to refresh the display in a complicated drawing), it is useful to create a separate thread to handle the redrawing. The user interface, with its own thread, remains active for the user while the redrawing takes place in the background. See Section 6.4 for details.

- In a complicated simulation program (for example, a program that simulates the activity of organisms in an environment), the design of the program is often conceptually simpler if each entity has its own thread. The entities are then fully independent of one another and can respond to their own simulation events individually.

- If you have part of a program that needs to respond to certain high-priority events very quickly, the problem is easily solved using thread priorities. The high-priority portion of the code is placed in its own thread, and that thread is given a higher priority than other threads running on the machine. The high-priority thread then waits for the necessary events. When it senses one, it will awaken and receive almost all of the CPU cycles available until it completes its task. It can then go back to sleep while waiting for the next event to arrive. See Section 6.7.

- If you are using a machine with multiple processors and you want to take full advantage of all of the CPU power available, then you need to break the application into multiple threads. Windows 2000's unit of division across CPUs is the thread, so if you have an application that contains only one thread, it will, by default, use only one CPU out of those available. If the program breaks up its work into multiple threads, however, Windows 2000 can run each thread on a different CPU. See Section 6.5 for details.

- Any task that needs to happen in the background while the user continues to work with the application is easily handled with threads. For example, you might place lengthy recalculations, page formatting operations, file reading and writing, and so forth in separate threads that let the activities proceed in the background without disturbing the user.

As you go through the examples in this chapter and the next, you will come up with many other ideas of your own. The thread concept turns out to be quite useful and flexible once you grasp its capabilities.

6.2 Introduction

If you are moving to Windows 2000 from UNIX, VMS, or a mainframe, then multi-processing is a concept familiar to you. Multi-threading, however, may be new to you. If you are moving from MS-DOS, then both multi-processing and multi-threading are probably new to you. Let's start by looking at what multi-processing and multi-threading actually mean from an operating-system standpoint.

The MS-DOS operating system is a *single-tasking* operating system. It can run one program at a time. You load a program, work with it, quit it, and then run another. TSRs can, in certain situations, give an impression of multi-processing. However, the problems that TSRs normally cause show that they are, at best, an illusion that MS-DOS was never intended to support.

Microsoft Windows 3.1, as well as Apple's Macintosh system, are *cooperative multi-tasking* operating environments. Both can run multiple programs (processes) at the same time. For example, you can run a word processor in one window, run a spreadsheet in another window, and download a file from a BBS in a third window. The word *cooperative* is used because it is up to each program to properly relinquish control at appropriate times so that all of the processes appear to be working simultaneously. Cooperative multi-tasking works to some degree. However, a lengthy disk access or other undividable task performed by one program will tend to monopolize the entire system for a moment, and the cooperation breaks down. This makes cooperative multi-tasking systems seem jerky in many cases. Cooperative systems also have a fatal flaw: if one program locks up, the whole system often dies with it. As soon as one program locks, it cannot relinquish control to the others, so everything stops.

UNIX is a *preemptive multi-tasking* operating system. The operating system, rather than individual applications, is in charge of giving CPU time to all of the running processes, and it does so as it best sees fit. UNIX gives a process a *time slice* of CPU time—perhaps 20 milliseconds or so—and when that amount of time expires the operating system *preempts* the process and gives the next slice of CPU time to another process. A UNIX machine can therefore have literally hundreds of processes running at one time and still feel very smooth to the user. If one process locks it has no effect on the others because the operating system is still in control of delegating CPU time.

Windows 2000 is a *preemptive multi-tasking, multi-threaded* operating system. Because it uses preemptive multi-tasking, it shares with UNIX the same smoothness of operation and process independence. However, multi-threading goes one step further. An individual program, by default, contains one thread, but it can break itself into several independent threads of execution so that, for example, one thread of an application can send a file to the printer while another is responding to user input. This simple change in a program's design can significantly reduce any waiting that the user normally does during lengthy recalculations, screen painting, file reading and writing, and so on.

Windows 2000 multi-threading also lets you take advantage of the multiple CPUs available in some machines. Say, for example, that you purchase an advanced RISC machine capable of using up to ten CPU chips, but initially you purchase only one CPU for it. As part of your learning cycle, you write a simple Mandelbrot set program, and you find that for a window of a certain size it takes 15 seconds to redraw the image of the Mandelbrot set.

Now you add nine more CPU chips to the machine. When you rerun the Mandelbrot program, you will find that it still takes almost 15 seconds to execute. Windows 2000 has the ability to run different threads on different CPUs, but it cannot do anything with a single-threaded program but devote one CPU to it. There is no way for Windows 2000 to divide a single thread across CPUs. Since Windows 2000 is itself multi-threaded, the Mandelbrot program will speed up slightly because it is not competing with Windows 2000's system threads for CPU time. However, any one program cannot harness more than one tenth of the CPU power in a ten-CPU machine unless it is multi-threaded.

If you multi-thread your Mandelbrot program, Windows 2000 can run the separate threads on separate CPUs, thus allowing it to take full advantage of all of the available CPU power. For example, if the Mandelbrot program breaks itself into ten threads, one thread will run on each CPU and the program will run ten times faster. There is no reason, from a performance standpoint, to use more than ten threads on a 10-CPU machine, because each thread incurs a very slight amount of overhead, and it is therefore wasteful to have more than ten. However, you could break the program into 100 threads if you wanted, or use one thread for each scan-line of the drawing, if that makes things conceptually easier. The overhead incurred by a thread is minimal. There are many cases in which breaking an application into multiple threads actually makes the whole program much easier to understand, and threads turn out to be remarkably easy to create.

Processes in Windows are not nearly as interesting as threads. A program can create a separate process, but the new process is completely and totally separate from the original program. Unlike UNIX, where a new process results in a complete copy of the variable space of the original process, a new process in Windows 2000 can inherit copies of, at most, specifically indicated handles. Generally, you use a process when you want to start another independent program from within a running program. For example, if you wanted to write your own version of the Program Manager or File Manager, you would use processes to launch other applications from your program.

When any process starts in Windows, it contains, by default, one thread of execution. For example, when you type "Notepad" on the command line or double-click on the Notepad's icon, Windows creates a process. That process has one thread that "runs" Notepad's code. The process is essentially a container for the global variables, the environment strings, the heap owned by the application, and the thread. The thread is what actually executes the code.

All threads in one process *share* the global variable space of their parent process. Each thread also has its own stack. When you create a new thread within a process, it has access to all of the global variables and the heap of the parent process. (See Figures 6.1 and 6.2.) All of the problems that arise from the careless use of global data in a normal program are therefore compounded in a multi-threaded program, because now several different threads can modify the same global variables independently of one another.

Process

Global variables

Heap

Environment strings

Thread stack

Thread

| Figure 6.1 | *A process just after creation, with one thread. The process holds the global variables, heap, and environment strings, while the thread owns its stack (and therefore any local variables)* |

To solve the problems that tend to arise in such situations, there are *synchronization mechanisms* built into Windows that help you guarantee exclusive access to global values. See Chapter 7 for more information.

6.3 Simple Examples

For many people, the whole idea of creating multiple threads within a single process requires some mental adjustment. Let's start by looking at several extremely simple examples to see how threads work in Windows.

Listing 6.1 contains a very simple program. In this program, the code prints the value of the global variable named **count** each time the user presses the return key. Nothing in the program changes **count**, so the program always prints zero. There is no magic here.

Now let's add a *thread* to Listing 6.1, as shown in Listing 6.2 and Figure 6.3. A thread in Windows is simply a function that executes in the background. The function **CountThread** in Listing 6.2 increments the global variable **count** and then *sleeps* for 100 milliseconds. When you run the program, you will find that each time you press the enter key, **count** has increased. The thread runs in the background, incrementing **count**, while the

Process

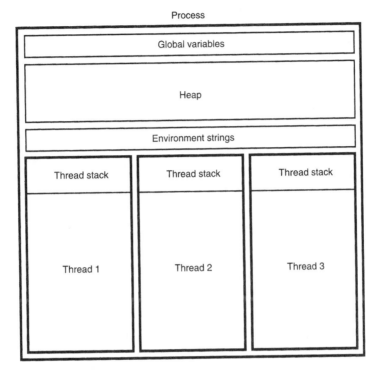

Global variables

Heap

Environment strings

Thread stack	Thread stack	Thread stack
Thread 1	Thread 2	Thread 3

Figure 6.2   *A process holding three threads. The threads share the global data, heap, and environment strings, while each thread has its own stack (and therefore its own local variables)*

original thread is responding to user input. The program is doing two things at once.

Listing 6.1   *A very simple single-threaded program*

```
//nothread.cpp
#include <windows.h>
#include <iostream.h>

UINT count;

void main(void)
{
  CHAR retStr[100];

  count=0;
  while(1)
  {
```

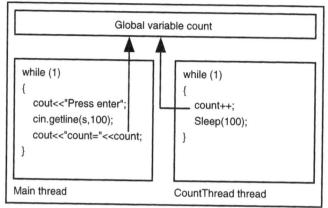

Figure 6.3   *The arrangement of the main thread, the counting thread, and the global variable in Listing 6.2*

Listing 6.1   *A very simple single-threaded program (continued)*

```
cout
  << "Press <ENTER> to display the count... ";
cin.getline(retStr, 100);
cout << "The count is: " << count << endl
  << endl;
  }
}
```

Listing 6.2   *A very simple thread*

```
// thread1a.cpp

#include <windows.h>
#include <iostream.h>

volatile UINT count;

void CountThread()
{
  while(1)
  {
    count++;
    Sleep(100);
  }
}
```

```
void main(void)
{
  HANDLE countHandle;
  DWORD threadID;
  CHAR retStr[100];

  count=0;

  // create a thread which
  // executes the "CountThread" function
  countHandle=CreateThread(0, 0,
    (LPTHREAD_START_ROUTINE) CountThread,
    0, 0, &threadID);
  if (countHandle==0)
    cout << "Cannot create thread: "
      << GetLastError() << endl;

  while(1)
  {
    cout
      << "Press <ENTER> to display the count... ";
    cin.getline(retStr, 100);
    cout << "The count is: " << count << endl
      << endl;
  }
}
```

The code in Listing 6.2 starts by creating the thread using the **Create Thread** function.

CreateThread	*Creates a new thread in the parent process*

```
HANDLE CreateThread(
  LPSECURITY_ATTRIBUTES security,
  DWORD stack,
  LPTHREAD_START_ROUTINE function,
  LPVOID param,
  DWORD flags,
  LPDWORD threadID)
```

security	Security attributes. See Chapter 10
stack	The initial size of the thread's stack
function	The name of the function that the thread starts
param	A four-byte value that the thread function receives at startup
flags	Pass in 0 or CREATE_SUSPENDED
threadID	A pointer to a DWORD to receive the thread's ID

Returns a handle to the new thread, or 0 on error.

The **CreateThread** function accepts the name of the *thread function,* the function to execute in the new thread. Here, the thread function is **CountThread**. The thread function can optionally accept one four-byte parameter. In Listing 6.2 the function uses no parameters, but if it did, the parameter that the thread function receives would be passed to **CreateThread** in the **param** parameter, and **CreateThread** in turn would pass it on to the thread function (see thread2.cpp). **CreateThread** returns both a thread ID and a handle to the thread. The thread ID is used to uniquely identify the thread system-wide, and is also accepted by a few functions such as **AttachThreadInput**.

You can control the initial size of the thread's stack using the **stack** parameter. Setting **stack** to zero causes the thread to start with a stack of the same size as that of its parent thread. The stack will grow as necessary, but growth is a wasteful activity; if you know that the thread will need a certain amount of space in its stack because of the size of its local variables, you should try to accommodate that from the start. It is also possible to start a thread so that it is originally suspended. In this case, the thread will consume no CPU time until some other thread unsuspends it with **ResumeThread**.

The **Sleep** function in Listing 6.2 provides an efficient way for a thread to delay itself. In a previous life you may have used a **for** loop or some similar mechanism to cause a delay, but you know that **for** loops are unreliable and also extremely wasteful. As the **for** loop is spinning, it consumes CPU cycles that could be put to better use. The **Sleep** function lets a thread delay itself without consuming any CPU cycles. A thread is totally suspended during a sleep.

Sleep	*Causes a thread to delay for a fixed number of milliseconds*

```
VOID Sleep(
   DWORD time)
```

time	The amount of time to sleep, in milliseconds

Returns nothing

Note the use of the **volatile** modifier on the **count** global variable. If you comment out the **Sleep** function in the thread and remove the **volatile** modifier, **count** may always be zero when you press the enter key. This phenomenon occurs because of strange side effects resulting from compiler optimizations. The compiler, for example, may use a register to store the **count** variable in the main thread, so changes made to the value by the second thread are ignored. The **volatile** modifier is a way of telling the compiler that you do not want any optimizations applied to the variable, that you do not want it placed in a register, and that the value may change due to outside influences during evaluation. You will find it to be a very important modifier for global variables referenced by multiple threads.

The code shown in Listing 6.3 is another simple example of a background thread that is running separately from the main thread. This thread beeps in the background while the main thread waits for it to finish. The code shows how to pass an integer parameter to a thread, and also how to wait for a thread to complete.

Listing 6.3   *A simple thread that beeps in the background*

```cpp
// thread1.cpp

#include <windows.h>
#include <stdlib.h>
#include <iostream.h>

// The function to run in a thread
void HonkThread(DWORD iter)
{
  DWORD i;

  for (i=0; i<iter; i++)
  {
    Beep(200, 50);
    Sleep(1000);
  }
}

void main(void)
{
  HANDLE honkHandle;
  DWORD threadID;
  DWORD iterations;
  CHAR iterStr[100];

  cout << "Enter the number of beeps to produce: ";
  cin.getline(iterStr, 100);

  // convert string into integer
  iterations=atoi(iterStr);

  // create a thread which
  // executes the "HonkThread" function
  honkHandle=CreateThread(0, 0,
    (LPTHREAD_START_ROUTINE) HonkThread,
    (VOID *) iterations, 0, &threadID);

  // wait until the thread has finished
  int count=0;
  while ( WaitForSingleObject(honkHandle, 0)
    == WAIT_TIMEOUT)
```

Listing 6.3   *A simple thread that beeps in the background (continued)*

```
{
  cout
    << "waiting for the thread to finish "
    << count++
    << endl;
  }
}
```

When you run Listing 6.3, you should enter an integer value, such as five. The main program will start the thread, passing it the value five through the parameter. The thread will run in the background, beep five times, and quit. Meanwhile, the main program is waiting for the thread to quit, using the **WaitForSingleObject** function in a loop. Each time through the loop it increments an integer and prints it to stdout.

WaitForSingleObject   *Causes a thread to wait for a signal*

```
DWORD WaitForSingleObject(
   HANDLE object,
   DWORD timeout)
```

Object   The object to wait for

Timeout   The maximum amount of time to wait, in milliseconds

Returns an error code or the event that caused it to stop waiting.

The **WaitForSingleObject** function is waiting on the thread handle for the thread to terminate. See Section 7.4 for details. The value zero passed in as the timeout value causes **WaitForSingleObject** to return immediately and indicate that the thread either has or has not completed. If the thread has not completed, **WaitForSingleObject** returns the value WAIT_TIMEOUT. See Chapter 7 for more information on this function—it has many different uses. Here, we are using it simply to detect whether or not the background thread has finished.

It is possible to pass structures into a thread function by passing a pointer to the structure through the parameter, as shown in Listing 6.4. The structure should be stable. That is, it should be a global variable, a static local variable, or a block allocated from the heap. The structure should not be a local variable to a function that might cease to exist during the run of the thread.

| Listing 6.4 | *Passing a structure to a thread* |

```cpp
// thread2.cpp

#include <windows.h>
#include <stdlib.h>
#include <iostream.h>

typedef struct
{
  DWORD frequency;
  DWORD duration;
  DWORD iterations;
} honkParams;

void HonkThread(honkParams *params)
{
  DWORD i;

  for (i=0; i<params->iterations; i++)
  {
    Beep(params->frequency, params->duration);
    Sleep(1000);
  }
}

void main(void)
{
  HANDLE honkHandle;
  DWORD threadID;
  honkParams params;
  CHAR freqStr[100];
  CHAR durStr[100];
  CHAR iterStr[100];

  cout << "Enter the beep frequency to produce: ";
  cin.getline(freqStr, 100);
  params.frequency=atoi(freqStr);

  cout << "Enter the beep duration to produce: ";
  cin.getline(durStr, 100);
  params.duration=atoi(durStr);

  cout << "Enter the number of beeps to produce: ";
  cin.getline(iterStr, 100);
  params.iterations=atoi(iterStr);

  // create a thread and pass it the address of
  //the "params" structure
```

| Listing 6.4 | *Passing a structure to a thread (continued)* |

```
honkHandle=CreateThread(0, 0,
  (LPTHREAD_START_ROUTINE) HonkThread,
  &params, 0, &threadID);

WaitForSingleObject(honkHandle, INFINITE);
}
```

In Listing 6.4, the three values entered by the user are placed in a structure that is then passed to the thread. The main function calls **WaitFor SingleObject** to keep from terminating before the thread has completed. Without this call, the main function would return immediately, killing off both the main process and the threads. With it in place, the main function efficiently waits for thread completion. Compare this to Listing 6.3.

Listing 6.5 takes Listing 6.4 a step further, and shows that it is possible to create multiple background threads using either multiple-thread functions or a single-thread function that is called several times.

| Listing 6.5 | *Creating multiple threads* |

```
// thread3.cpp

#include <windows.h>
#include <stdlib.h>
#include <iostream.h>

typedef struct
{
  DWORD frequency;
  DWORD duration;
  DWORD iterations;
} honkParams;

void HonkThread(honkParams *params)
{
  DWORD i;

  for (i=0; i<params->iterations; i++)
  {
    Beep(params->frequency, params->duration);
    Sleep(1000);
  }

  GlobalFree(params);
}

void main(void)
```

```
{
  HANDLE honkHandles[3];
  DWORD threadID;
  honkParams *params;
  DWORD count;
  CHAR freqStr[100];
  CHAR durStr[100];
  CHAR iterStr[100];

  for (count=0; count<3; count++)
  {
    // allocate memory for a "params" structure
    params=(honkParams *) GlobalAlloc(GPTR,
      sizeof(honkParams));

    cout << "Enter the beep frequency: ";
    cin.getline(freqStr, 100);
    params->frequency=atoi(freqStr);

    cout << "Enter the beep duration: ";
    cin.getline(durStr, 100);
    params->duration=atoi(durStr);

    cout << "Enter the number of beeps: ";
    cin.getline(iterStr, 100);
    params->iterations=atoi(iterStr);

    // create a thread and pass it the pointer
    // to its "params" struct
    honkHandles[count]=CreateThread(0, 0,
      (LPTHREAD_START_ROUTINE) HonkThread,
      params, 0, &threadID);
  }

  // wait for all threads to finish execution
  WaitForMultipleObjects(3, honkHandles,
    TRUE, INFINITE);
}
```

When you run Listing 6.5, the program asks you to enter a frequency and duration as well as the number of beeps. You can do this three times, so you will hear beeps from all three threads simultaneously if you set the number of beeps for each thread high enough to cause an overlap.

In Listing 6.5, a wait function is again used to keep the main function, and therefore the process, from completing before all three threads have finished. The **WaitForMultipleObjects** does the same thing that **WaitFor SingleObject** does, but it waits for all of the specified events to occur. **Wait ForMultipleObjects** accepts an array of object handles, in this case handles from the three threads. See Section 7.4 for details.

WaitForMultipleObjects	*Causes a thread to delay waiting for one-of-many or all-of-many signals to occur*

```
DWORD WaitForMultipleObjects(
    DWORD numObjects,
    CONST HANDLE * objectArray,
    BOOL waitForAll,
    DWORD timeout)
```

numObjects	Number of objects in objectArray
objectArray	An array of object handles to wait on
waitForAll	If TRUE, the function waits for all events to occur, otherwise for any one of them
timeout	The maximum amount of time to wait, in milliseconds

Returns an error code or the event that caused it to stop waiting.

You can see from the examples given in this chapter that the use of threads, at least at a simple level, is not much more difficult than calling a normal function. The thread function executes in the way that you expect, but it returns immediately and executes in the background, in parallel with the main thread of the application.

6.4 Using Threads in GUI Applications

The book entitled *Visual C++: Developing Professional Applications for Windows 98 and NT using MFC,* by Marshall Brain and Lance Lovette (ISBN 0-13-085121-3), shows how to use C++ and the Microsoft Foundation Class library to create GUI applications for Windows. In this section we will look at two different ways to use threads in a typical GUI application.

Listing 6.6 contains the code for a simple Mandelbrot set program that does not use threads. See Appendix A for compilation instructions. When you run this program, you can choose the **Draw** option in the **File** menu to cause the window to redraw. Unless you are working with a very zippy machine, do not initially make the window any larger than its default size. Now resize the window so that redrawing takes between 10 and 15 seconds.

Listing 6.6   *A simple Mandelbrot set program created with the MFC class hierarchy and C++*

```
// mandel0.cpp

#include <afxwin.h>
#include "menus.h"
```

```
#define NUM_ITERATIONS 64

const double left = -1.0;
const double right = 1.0;
const double top = -1.0;
const double bottom = 1.0;


DWORD colors[64];

typedef struct
{
   double real;
   double imag;
} complex;

// Define the application object class
class CManApp : public CWinApp
{
public:
   virtual BOOL InitInstance();
};


// Define the edit window class
class CManWindow : public CFrameWnd
{
public:
   CManWindow();
   void RunMandel();
   void SetPix(int x, int y, WORD iter);
   afx_msg void OnPaint();
   afx_msg void OnDoDraw();
   afx_msg void OnExit();
   DECLARE_MESSAGE_MAP()
};


// Create an instance of the application object
CManApp manApp;

// member function used to set pixel colors in
// the window
void CManWindow::SetPix(int x, int y, WORD iter)
{
   CClientDC dc(this);
   dc.SetPixel(x, y, colors[iter]);
}


// member function used to redraw the
// mandelbrot set
void CManWindow::RunMandel()
```

Listing 6.6   *A simple Mandelbrot set program created with the MFC class hierarchy and C++ (continued)*

```cpp
{
   CRect r;
   double xstep, ystep;
   double x, y;
   int i,j;
   WORD iter;
   complex k;
   complex z;
   double real, imag, spread;

   GetClientRect(&r);

   ystep = (double) (bottom - top) / r.Height();
   xstep = (double) (right - left) / r.Width();

   for (y=top, j=0; y <= bottom; y += ystep, j++)
   {
      for (x=left, i=0; x<=right; x += xstep, i++)
      {
         k.real = x;
         k.imag = y;
         z.real=z.imag=0.0;

         for (iter=0; iter<NUM_ITERATIONS-1;
            iter++)
         {
            real = z.real + k.real;
            imag = z.imag + k.imag;
            z.real = real * real -
               imag * imag;
            z.imag = 2 * real * imag;
            spread = z.real * z.real +
               z.imag * z.imag;
            if (spread > 4.0)
               break;
         }
         ((CManWindow *)manApp.m_pMainWnd)->
            SetPix(i, j, iter);
      }
   }
}

// The message map
BEGIN_MESSAGE_MAP(CManWindow, CFrameWnd)
   ON_WM_PAINT()
   ON_COMMAND(IDM_DODRAW, OnDoDraw)
   ON_COMMAND(IDM_EXIT, OnExit)
END_MESSAGE_MAP()
```

```
// Handler for the Draw menu option
void CManWindow::OnDoDraw()
{
    // clear the window
    CClientDC dc(this);
    CRect r;
    GetClientRect(&r);
    dc.PatBlt(0, 0, r.Width(), r.Height(),
        WHITENESS);
    // Redraw the set
    RunMandel();
}

// Handler for WM_PAINT messages
void CManWindow::OnPaint()
{
    // Do not do anything in response to
    // paint events
    ValidateRect(NULL);
}

// Handler for the Exit menu option
void CManWindow::OnExit()
{
    DestroyWindow();
}

// CManWindow constructor
CManWindow::CManWindow()
{
    WORD x;
    BYTE red=0, green=0, blue=0;

    Create( NULL, "Normal Mandel Example",
        WS_OVERLAPPEDWINDOW,
        CRect(0,0,150,150), NULL, "MainMenu" );
    for (x=0; x<64; x++)
    {
        colors[x] = RGB(red, green, blue);
        if (!(red += 64))
            if (!(green += 64))
                blue += 64;
    }
    colors[63] = RGB(255,255,255);
}

// Initialize the CManApp m_pMainWnd data member
BOOL CManApp::InitInstance()
{
    m_pMainWnd = new CManWindow();
```

Listing 6.6   *A simple Mandelbrot set program created with the MFC class hierarchy and C++ (continued)*

```
m_pMainWnd -> ShowWindow( m_nCmdShow );
m_pMainWnd -> UpdateWindow();

    return TRUE;
}
```

Listing 6.7   *The menus.h file used by Listing 6.6*

```
// menus.h

#define IDM_DODRAW         1001
#define IDM_EXIT        1002
```

Listing 6.8   *The menus.rc resource file used to create the menus for Listing 5.6*

```
// mandel.rc

#include <windows.h>
#include <afxres.h>

#include "menus.h"

MainMenu MENU
{
    POPUP "&File"
    {
      MENUITEM "&Draw",  IDM_DODRAW
      MENUITEM "E&xit",  IDM_EXIT
    }
}
```

When you run the code shown in Listing 6.6, you will notice a serious problem with the application. Once the user selects the Draw option from the menu, the user cannot do anything, because the redrawing code prevents the event loop from running. The user cannot use the menu, quit the program, or minimize the program until the redrawing step completes. If the user does happen to click on anything, the event queue stores the clicks and plays them all rapidly once the redraw completes. If the application's window is full-screen and the machine is slow, it may be several minutes before a redraw completes and therefore before the user can do anything with the application.

The situation presented here is common in any program that creates sophisticated displays. For example, a CAD/CAM program may have to extract

10,000 vectors from a database to refresh the screen for a complex drawing. Mapping programs, three-dimensional rendering programs, complex mathematical visualization programs, and others of the sort, all suffer from the same problem.

Threads offer an easy solution to this problem. By placing all redrawing activity in one thread, you allow the user to continue to use the program while redrawing takes place in the background. From the user's standpoint, this is a major improvement over being locked out of the interface. From a programmer's standpoint, the thread solution is significantly easier to work with than the **OnIdle** capability that MFC provides for solving this problem in non-threaded environments.

Listing 6.9 contains a version of the Mandelbrot program that has a separate thread to handle redrawing. It works just like the code in Listing 6.6, except that the menus will function properly during redrawing. You can use the **Exit** option to terminate the program even while redrawing is taking place.

Listing 6.9   *A multi-threaded version of the Mandelbrot program that uses a thread to handle redrawing*

```cpp
// mandel1.cpp

#include <afxwin.h>
#include "menus.h"

#define NUM_ITERATIONS 64

const double left = -1.0;
const double right = 1.0;
const double top = -1.0;
const double bottom = 1.0;

DWORD colors[64];

typedef struct
{
    double real;
    double imag;
} complex;

typedef struct
{
    WORD height;
    WORD width;
} mandelParams;

// Define the application object class
class CManApp : public CWinApp
```

Listing 6.9 *A multi-threaded version of the Mandelbrot program that uses a thread to handle redrawing (continued)*

```
{
public:
   virtual BOOL InitInstance();
};

// Define the edit window class
class CManWindow : public CFrameWnd
{
private:
   HANDLE threadHandle;
   mandelParams params;
public:
   CManWindow();
   void RunMandel();
   void SetPix(int x, int y, WORD iter);
   afx_msg void OnPaint();
   afx_msg void OnDoDraw();
   afx_msg void OnExit();
   DECLARE_MESSAGE_MAP()
};

// Create an instance of the application object
CManApp manApp;

// member function used to set pixel colors
// in the window
void CManWindow::SetPix(int x, int y, WORD iter)
{
   CClientDC dc(this);
   dc.SetPixel(x, y, colors[iter]);
}

// the thread function which does the drawing
DWORD MandelThread(mandelParams *params)
{
   double xstep, ystep;
   double x, y;
   int i,j;
   WORD iter;
   complex k;
   complex z;
   double real, imag, spread;

   ystep = (double) (bottom - top) /
      params->height;
   xstep = (double) (right - left) / params->width;
```

```
    for (y=top, j=0; y <= bottom; y += ystep, j++)
    {
        for (x=left, i=0; x<=right; x += xstep, i++)
        {
           k.real = x;
           k.imag = y;
           z.real=z.imag=0.0;

           for (iter=0; iter<NUM_ITERATIONS-1;
              iter++)
           {
              real = z.real + k.real;
              imag = z.imag + k.imag;
              z.real = real * real -
                 imag * imag;
              z.imag = 2 * real * imag;
              spread = z.real * z.real +
                 z.imag * z.imag;
              if (spread > 4.0)
                 break;
           }
           ((CManWindow *)manApp.m_pMainWnd)->
              SetPix(i, j, iter);
        }
    }
    return(0);
}

// member function used to instigate
// the drawing thread
void CManWindow::RunMandel()
{
    DWORD threadID;
    CRect r;

    GetClientRect(&r);
    params.height=r.Height();
    params.width=r.Width();

    threadHandle=CreateThread(NULL, 0,
        (LPTHREAD_START_ROUTINE) MandelThread,
        &params, 0, &threadID);
}

// The message map
BEGIN_MESSAGE_MAP(CManWindow, CFrameWnd)
    ON_WM_PAINT()
    ON_COMMAND(IDM_DODRAW, OnDoDraw)
    ON_COMMAND(IDM_EXIT, OnExit)
END_MESSAGE_MAP()
```

Listing 6.9 *A multi-threaded version of the Mandelbrot program that uses a thread to handle redrawing (continued)*

```
// Handler for the Start/Stop menu option
void CManWindow::OnDoDraw()
{
   DWORD threadStatus;
   BOOL status;

   status = GetExitCodeThread(threadHandle,
      &threadStatus);
   if (threadStatus == STILL_ACTIVE)
   {
      // stop the existing thread
      TerminateThread(threadHandle, 0);
      CloseHandle(threadHandle);
}
   // clear the window
   CClientDC dc(this);
   CRect r;
   GetClientRect(&r);
   dc.PatBlt(0, 0, r.Width(), r.Height(),
      WHITENESS);
   // redraw
   RunMandel();
}


// Handler for WM_PAINT messages
void CManWindow::OnPaint()
{
   ValidateRect(NULL);
}


// Handler for the Exit menu option
void CManWindow::OnExit()
{
   CloseHandle(threadHandle);
   DestroyWindow();
}


// CManWindow constructor
CManWindow::CManWindow()
{
   WORD x;
   BYTE red=0, green=0, blue=0;

   Create( NULL, "Threaded Mandel Example",
      WS_OVERLAPPEDWINDOW,
      CRect(0,0,150,150), NULL, "MainMenu" );
   for (x=0; x<64; x++)
```

```
        {
            colors[x] = RGB(red, green, blue);
            if (!(red += 64))
                if (!(green += 64))
                    blue += 64;
        }
        colors[63] = RGB(255,255,255);
}

// Initialize the CManApp m_pMainWnd data member
BOOL CManApp::InitInstance()
{
    m_pMainWnd = new CManWindow();
    m_pMainWnd -> ShowWindow( m_nCmdShow );
    m_pMainWnd -> UpdateWindow();

    return TRUE;
}
```

If you compare the code in Listing 6.6 and Listing 6.9, you will find only minor differences. First, the **OnDoDraw** function in Listing 6.9 must check to see if a redrawing thread is active before it starts a new one. The **GetExitCodeThread** function is used here, but the **WaitForSingleObject** function seen in the previous section would work just as well. If the **OnDo-Draw** function finds an active thread, it kills the thread. It then clears the window and calls **RunMandel,** just as Listing 6.6 does.

The **RunMandel** function now has two pieces. The first piece, **Run-Mandel** itself, sets up a parameter structure and calls **CreateThread** to start the thread function. The thread function is called **MandelThread,** and it contains all of the actual redrawing code. The code is not any different from the redrawing code seen in Listing 6.6, except that the threaded version takes its width and height from the parameter structure.

You can see here that the addition of a thread to an MFC program is fairly straightforward. In any application that you create, you can place the redrawing step in the background by following the same pattern seen in this code. It is also easy to place any sort of recalculation code in a thread using the same techniques.

6.5 Matching the Number of Threads to the Number of CPUs

When you run a compute-bound program on a Windows 2000 machine that has multiple CPUs, you should split the computation portion of the program into a set of threads whose number matches the number of CPUs. For example, in the Mandelbrot program seen in the previous section, you would create one redrawing thread for each CPU that is available. Each redrawing thread can handle a portion of the image. Windows 2000 will run each separate thread on a different CPU, so the program will make maximum use of the CPU power available. Listing 6.10 demonstrates how to split the Mandelbrot program into multiple threads.

| Listing 6.10 | *A multi-threaded implementation that will create one thread for each processor found on the machine (if it finds only one processor, it creates four threads by default)* |

```cpp
// mandel2.cpp

#include <afxwin.h>
#include "menus.h"

#define NUM_ITERATIONS 64

const double left = -1.0;
const double right = 1.0;
const double top = -1.0;
const double bottom = 1.0;

DWORD colors[64];
BOOL quit;

typedef struct
{
    double real;
    double imag;
} complex;

typedef struct
{
    double xstep;
    double ystep;
    WORD height;
    double startpoint;
    WORD startpos;
} mandelParams;

// Define the application object class
class CManApp : public CWinApp
{
public:
    virtual BOOL InitInstance();
};

// Define the edit window class
class CManWindow : public CFrameWnd
```

```
{
private:
    DWORD numThreads;
    HANDLE *threadHandles;
    BOOL initialized;
public:
    CManWindow();
    void RunMandel();
    void SetPix(int x, int y, WORD iter);
    afx_msg void OnPaint();
    afx_msg void OnDoDraw();
    afx_msg void OnExit();
    DECLARE_MESSAGE_MAP()
};

// Create an instance of the application object
CManApp manApp;

// member function which sets pixel colors
// in the window
void CManWindow::SetPix(int x, int y, WORD iter)
{
    CClientDC dc(this);
    dc.SetPixel(x, y, colors[iter]);
}

// thread function which draws on the window
DWORD MandelThread(mandelParams *p)
{
    double x, y;
    int i,j;
    WORD iter;
    complex k;
    complex z;
    double real, imag, spread;

    for (y=p->startpoint, j=p->startpos;
        y <= (p->startpoint + p->height*p->ystep);
          y += p->ystep, j++)
    {
        for (x=left, i=0; x<=right; x += p->xstep,
            i++)
        {
            k.real = x;
            k.imag = y;
            z.real=z.imag=0.0;

            for (iter=0; iter<NUM_ITERATIONS-1;
                iter++)
            {
                real = z.real + k.real;
```

| Listing 6.10 | A multi-threaded implementation that will create one thread for each processor found on the machine (if it finds only one processor, it creates four threads by default) (continued) |

```
            imag = z.imag + k.imag;
            z.real = real * real -
                imag * imag;
            z.imag = 2 * real * imag;
            spread = z.real * z.real +
                z.imag * z.imag;
            if (spread > 4.0)
                break;
        }
        ((CManWindow *)manApp.m_pMainWnd)->
            SetPix(i, j, iter);
        if (quit)
        {
            GlobalFree(p);
            return(0);
        }
    }
    }
    return(0);
}

// member function which instigates the thread(s)
void CManWindow::RunMandel()
{
    DWORD threadID;
    SYSTEM_INFO sysInfo;
    CRect r;
    WORD n;
    WORD height;
    double xstep, ystep;
    mandelParams *params;

    GetSystemInfo(&sysInfo);

    numThreads=sysInfo.dwNumberOfProcessors;
    if (numThreads==1) numThreads=4;

    quit=FALSE;

    threadHandles=(HANDLE *) GlobalAlloc(GPTR,
        (sizeof(HANDLE)*numThreads));

    GetClientRect(&r);
    xstep=(right - left)/double(r.Width());
    ystep=(bottom - top)/double(r.Height());
    height=r.Height()/(WORD)numThreads;
```

```
    for(n=0; n<numThreads; n++)
    {
       params=(mandelParams *) GlobalAlloc(GPTR,
          sizeof(mandelParams));
       params->xstep=xstep;
       params->ystep=ystep;
       params->height=height;
       params->startpoint=top + height*ystep*n;
       params->startpos=height*n;
       threadHandles[n]=CreateThread(0, 0,
          (LPTHREAD_START_ROUTINE) MandelThread,
          params, 0, &threadID);
    }
}

// The message map
BEGIN_MESSAGE_MAP(CManWindow, CFrameWnd)
   ON_WM_PAINT()
   ON_COMMAND(IDM_DODRAW, OnDoDraw)
   ON_COMMAND(IDM_EXIT, OnExit)
END_MESSAGE_MAP()

// Handler for the Start/Stop menu option
void CManWindow::OnDoDraw()
{
   if (!initialized)
{
      initialized=TRUE;
      RunMandel();
   }
   else
   {
      WORD n;

      // wait for and stop all existing threads
      quit=TRUE;
      WaitForMultipleObjects(numThreads,
         threadHandles, TRUE,
         INFINITE);
      for (n=0; n<numThreads; n++)
         CloseHandle(threadHandles[n]);
      GlobalFree(threadHandles);
      // clear the window
      CClientDC dc(this);
      CRect r;
      GetClientRect(&r);
      dc.PatBlt(0, 0, r.Width(), r.Height(),
         WHITENESS);
      // start over again
      RunMandel();
   }}
```

Listing 6.10 *A multi-threaded implementation that will create one thread for each processor found on the machine (if it finds only one processor, it creates four threads by default) (continued)*

```
void CManWindow::OnPaint()
{
    ValidateRect(NULL);
}

// Handler for the Exit menu option
void CManWindow::OnExit()
{
    WORD n;

    quit=TRUE;
    WaitForMultipleObjects(numThreads,
        threadHandles,
        TRUE, INFINITE);
    for (n=0; n<numThreads; n++)
        CloseHandle(threadHandles[n]);

    GlobalFree(threadHandles);

    DestroyWindow();
}

// CManWindow constructor
CManWindow::CManWindow()
{
    WORD x;
    BYTE red=0, green=0, blue=0;

    Create( NULL, "Multi-Threaded Mandel Example",
        WS_OVERLAPPEDWINDOW,
        CRect(0,0,150,150), NULL, "MainMenu" );
    for (x=0; x<64; x++)
    {
        colors[x] = RGB(red, green, blue);
        if (!(red += 64))
            if (!(green += 64))
            blue += 64;
    }
    colors[63] = RGB(255,255,255);

    initialized=FALSE;
}

// Initialize the CManApp m_pMainWnd data member
BOOL CManApp::InitInstance()
```

```
{
  m_pMainWnd = new CManWindow();
  m_pMainWnd -> ShowWindow( m_nCmdShow );
  m_pMainWnd -> UpdateWindow();

  return TRUE;
}
```

If you compare Listing 6.10 to Listing 6.9, you will find most of the differences to be within the **RunMandel** and **MandelThread** functions. The **RunMandel** function determines the number of threads to create by calling the **GetSystemInfo** function:

```
GetSystemInfo(&sysInfo);

numThreads=sysInfo.dwNumberOfProcessors;
if (numThreads==1) numThreads=4;
```

See Chapter 16 for more information on this function. One of the things that **GetSystemInfo** returns is the number of processors in the machine. If the program finds only one processor, it arbitrarily chooses to think that it has four processors, simply to create an interesting display.

RunMandel next sets the global variable **quit** to FALSE. This variable will control the threads: if a thread sees **quit** change to TRUE, it cleans up its allocated memory and terminates immediately. This technique lets threads manage their own termination, which greatly simplifies a multi-threaded application like this one.

The **RunMandel** function next allocates a block of memory big enough to hold all of the thread handles it needs to create. This array will hold copies of the handles so that the program can later wait for all of the threads to complete.

```
threadHandles=(HANDLE *) GlobalAlloc(GPTR,
  (sizeof(HANDLE)*numThreads));
```

Next, **RunMandel** determines the area of the picture that each of the threads will manage, and then creates a parameter structure to hold the coordinates. Once it has calculated the area for a thread, it starts the thread and assigns it an area.

```
GetClientRect(&r);
xstep=(right - left)/double(r.Width());
ystep=(bottom - top)/double(r.Height());
height=r.Height()/(WORD)numThreads;

for(n=0; n<numThreads; n++)
{
  params=(mandelParams *) GlobalAlloc(GPTR,
```

```
        sizeof(mandelParams));
    params->xstep=xstep;
    params->ystep=ystep;
    params->height=height;
    params->startpoint=top + height*ystep*n;
    params->startpos=height*n;
    threadHandles[n]=CreateThread(0, 0,
        (LPTHREAD_START_ROUTINE) MandelThread,
        params, 0, &threadID);
    }
}
```

Perhaps a simpler way to implement this portion of the program would be to create a separate thread for each scan line in the image. For example, if the image is 100 pixels high, the program could create 100 threads. The advantage of this approach is simplicity. The disadvantage is a slight inefficiency, which comes from the operating-system overhead of managing the threads and swapping between them. Section 7.2.3 demonstrates how to use semaphores to limit the actual number of threads that are running, while keeping the simplicity of having one thread per scan line.

The **MandelThread** function contains two changes. First, it paints only the indicated portion of the image rather than the entire image. Second, it looks at the global **quit** variable each time it draws a pixel. If it notices **quit** change to TRUE, it cleans up space allocated for the parameters on the heap and kills itself off.

The **OnExit** function is one place where the global **quit** variable gets set:

```
// Handler for the Exit menu option
void CManWindow::OnExit()
{
    WORD n;

    quit=TRUE;
    WaitForMultipleObjects(numThreads,
        threadHandles,
        TRUE, INFINITE);
    for (n=0; n<numThreads; n++)
        CloseHandle(threadHandles[n]);

    GlobalFree(threadHandles);

    DestroyWindow();
}
```

The function sets **quit** and then waits for all of the threads to terminate. Once they have terminated, it closes their handles and frees the memory used to hold all of the thread handles.

The **OnDoDraw** function contains the only other significant modification to the code. It starts by checking to see whether or not the program has redrawn itself once. If not, it redraws immediately. If it has already redrawn once, then it uses the same technique seen in **OnExit** to clean up any running threads.

6.6 Using Thread Local Storage

The 32-bit APIs contains a unique feature called Thread Local Storage (TLS), which you can use in processes and DLLs in a variety of ways. The capability itself is very straightforward, but its extended ramifications are what make it interesting.

The TLS capability consists of four very simple functions: **TlsAlloc**, **TlsFree**, **TlsSetValue**, and **TlsGetValue**. You use TLS by first calling the **TlsAlloc** function, as shown below:

```
DWORD tlsIndex;    // probably a global variable
```

. . .

```
// allocate a thread local storage index
tlsIndex=TlsAlloc();
```

The call to **TlsAlloc** creates a block of memory that contains one 32-bit storage location for each existing thread in a process. Any new threads created after the call to **TlsAlloc** also receive a unique 32-bit storage location. **TlsAlloc** returns an index value that the process uses when referring to this particular set of 32-bit thread storage locations. The process can call **TlsAlloc** as many times as it likes, as long as it uses a different variable each time. See Figure 6.4.

The TLS location contains one 32-bit value for each thread

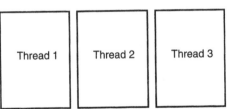

The relationship between TLS and the threads in a process. TlsIndex references a block of storage that contains one 32-bit value for each thread in the process

Inside any thread, a call to the function **TlsGetValue** with the **TlsIndex** value returns the 32-bit value from TLS storage associated with that particular thread. That is, the value returned by **TlsGetValue** is context-sensitive based on whatever thread is calling the function. The same goes for **TlsSetValue**.

The **TlsFree** function frees up the space occupied by all of the storage locations.

The TLS capability is frequently used inside of DLLs to store pointers to blocks of memory associated with the different threads calling the DLL. See Chapter 17 for details.

Listing 6.11 demonstrates TLS in a simple program. You should compare this program with Listing 6.5, because they do approximately the same thing in different ways.

Listing 6.11   *Using Thread Local Storage (TLS). Compare with Listing 6.5*

```cpp
// thread4.cpp

#include <windows.h>
#include <stdlib.h>
#include <iostream.h>

DWORD tlsIndex;

typedef struct
{
  DWORD frequency;
  DWORD duration;
} honkParams;

void ParamsAlloc()
{
  honkParams *params;

  params=(honkParams *) GlobalAlloc(GPTR,
    sizeof(honkParams));

  // generate a randomish value for the frequency
  params->frequency=GetTickCount() & 0x00000FFF;
  cout << "Using frequency: "
    << params->frequency << endl;
  params->duration=100;

  // save the pointer value relevant
  // for the calling thread
  TlsSetValue(tlsIndex, params);
}

void ParamsFree()
```

```
{
  honkParams *params;

  // retrieve the pointer value relevant
  // for the calling thread
  params=(honkParams *) TlsGetValue(tlsIndex);

  GlobalFree(params);
}

void Honk(void)
{
  honkParams *params;

  // retrieve the pointer value relevant
  // for the calling thread
  params=(honkParams *) TlsGetValue(tlsIndex);

  Beep(params->frequency, params->duration);
}

void HonkThread()
{
  DWORD i;

  // use a general purpose "params"
  // allocation function
  ParamsAlloc();

  for (i=0; i<8; i++)
  {
    Honk();
    Sleep(1000);
  }

  // use a general purpose "params" free function
  ParamsFree();
}

void main(void)
{
  HANDLE honkHandles[3];
  DWORD threadID;
  DWORD count;

  // allocate a thread local storage index
  tlsIndex=TlsAlloc();

  for (count=0; count<3; count++)
  {
```

Listing 6.11 *Using Thread Local Storage (TLS). Compare with Listing 6.5 (continued)*

```
    // create a thread which beeps
    honkHandles[count]=CreateThread(NULL, 0,
      (LPTHREAD_START_ROUTINE) HonkThread, 0, 0,
      &threadID);
    Sleep(1500);
  }


  WaitForMultipleObjects(3, honkHandles, TRUE,
    INFINITE);


  // free the thread local storage index
  TlsFree(tlsIndex);
}
```

The code in Listing 6.11 declares a global variable named **TlsIndex**. The program's first action in the main function is to allocate a TLS storage block pointed to by **TlsIndex**. The main function then creates three threads and waits for their completion before freeing the TLS storage space.

TlsAlloc   *Allocates a TLS storage structure*

```
DWORD TlsAlloc(VOID)
```

Returns an index to the TLS storage structure, or 0xFFFFFFFF on failure

---

TlsFree   *Frees a TLS storage structure*

```
BOOL TlsFree(
   DWORD index)
```

Index   The index of an existing TLS structure

Returns TRUE on success

Each thread calls the **ParamsAlloc** function, which allocates a parameter structure on the heap and fills it with values for the thread. The pointer to the parameter block is placed in the TLS area using **TlsSetValue. TlsSetValue** chooses the TLS location in which to place the pointer based on the thread that calls the function. To later free up its parameter storage block, each thread calls **ParamsFree**. This function retrieves the pointer from the TLS and frees the block.

TlsGetValue	*Retrieves a value from a TLS structure based on the thread making the call*

```
LPVOID TlsGetValue(
    DWORD index)
```

index	The index of an existing TLS structure

Returns the value for the thread on success, or 0 on failure

TlsSetValue	*Sets a value into a TLS structure based on the thread making the call*

```
BOOL TlsSetValue(
    DWORD index,
    LPVOID value)
```

index	The index of an existing TLS structure
value	The value to store

Returns TRUE on success

The TLS capability could be used to implement the parameter storage for the multi-threaded Mandelbrot program shown in Listing 6.10, especially since each thread is in charge of cleaning up its own allocated memory in that program. The TLS capability is also frequently used in DLLs to keep memory allocations in the DLL separated on a thread-by-thread basis. See Chapter 17 for details.

6.7 Thread Priorities

Windows 2000 uses a round-robin priority queue structure to schedule CPU time among available threads. In order to understand both thread priorities and how to set them, you need to be familiar with the priority and scheduling mechanisms used by Windows 2000. This section contains a brief overview.

All of the threads in a process have a priority relative to their parent process. The priority of the threads determines the amount of CPU time they receive relative to one another and relative to other threads in other processes. You set a thread's priority using the **SetThreadPriority** function and retrieve it using the **GetThreadPriority** function.

GetThreadPriority	*Retrieves the priority of a thread*

```
int GetThreadPriority(
    HANDLE threadHandle)
```

threadHandle	The handle of the thread

Returns the priority or THREAD_PRIORITY_ERROR_RETURN

SetThreadPriority	*Sets the priority of a thread*

```
BOOL SetThreadPriority(
    HANDLE threadHandle,
    int priority)
```

threadHandle	The handle of the thread
priority	The new priority

Returns TRUE on success

Every process in Windows starts with a base priority determined by its *priority class*. Windows defines six different classes:

Class	Base priority
IDLE_PRIORITY_CLASS	4
BELOW_NORMAL_PRIORITY_CLASS	5
NORMAL_PRIORITY_CLASS	9 foreground, 7 background
ABOVE_NORMAL_PRIORITY_CLASS	11
HIGH_PRIORITY_CLASS	13
REALTIME_PRIORITY_CLASS	24

A regular process, such as one launched from the Program Manager or the command line, is "normal." The threads within a process can then adjust their priority relative to the base priority of the process. The BELOW_NORMAL_PRIORITY_CLASS and ABOVE_NORMAL_PRIORITY_CLASS classes are new in Windows 2000; they are not supported in Windows 98. When you call **SetThreadPriority**, it accepts one of the following values and adds it to the base priority value:

THREAD_PRIORITY_TIME_CRITICAL	+3
THREAD_PRIORITY_HIGHEST	+2
THREAD_PRIORITY_ABOVE_NORMAL	+1
THREAD_PRIORITY_NORMAL	Normal
THREAD_PRIORITY_BELOW_NORMAL	−1
THREAD_PRIORITY_LOWEST	−2
THREAD_PRIORITY_ABOVE_IDLE	−3
THREAD_PRIORITY_IDLE	−4

For example, if a foreground process has a normal priority class and one of its threads sets its priority to THREAD_PRIORITY_LOWEST, then the thread's priority value is 7 (9 − 2 = 7).

Windows's scheduler uses the priority value of all of the threads currently in existence to determine which thread gets the next slice of CPU time. Threads are scheduled in a round-robin fashion at each priority level, and only when there are no executable threads at a higher level does scheduling of threads at a lower level take place.

All threads initially start at THREAD_PRIORITY_NORMAL. You can use the **GetThreadPriority** function to find out the priority value of a thread.

Think about a typical Windows system in the middle of operation on a typical day. It has all sorts of threads running. If you open up the Performance Monitor in Windows 2000 and look at the Threads counter under the Objects object, it will tell you exactly how many threads currently exist on your machine. On my machine, at this particular moment, there are 155. By killing off all of the extraneous windows, I can get it down to 138. These are threads associated with different background services, operating system tasks, and so on.

At any given moment, a thread can be in any of several states. Some threads are *suspended*. For example, you might have called the **Suspend-Thread** function on a thread. Some threads are *sleeping* because they called the **Sleep** function. Some of the threads are *waiting* for something. For example, one thread might need user input from the keyboard to continue, while another is waiting for a network packet, and another is waiting for a sector from the hard disk.

The rest of the threads are *ready*. They have something to do, and the only thing preventing them from doing it is the fact that there is only one CPU and perhaps five threads needing to share it (on a multi-CPU Windows 2000 machine, there might be three CPUs and five threads waiting for one of them).

Like most preemptive operating systems, Windows picks a ready thread and lets it use the CPU for a specified amount of time, a *time slice*, of perhaps 20 milliseconds. The thread will normally end up requesting something that is not available, like a keystroke or a disk sector, before its time slice completes. The operating system will then stop it and let it wait for what it needs. Otherwise, the time slice will elapse and Windows will preempt the thread. It then picks another ready thread and gives it the next time slice.

Windows picks the thread that will receive the next time slice by using a set of ready queues arranged by priority. Figure 6.5 shows a typical arrangement. Each queue works in a round-robin fashion, so a thread that is ready gets put on the end of one of the priority queues. The queue chosen is determined by the priority of the thread. The operating system services all of the threads in a given queue in order. If a thread uses up its time slice and is

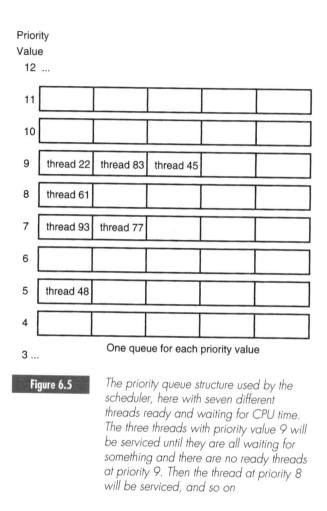

Priority
Value

One queue for each priority value

Figure 6.5 *The priority queue structure used by the scheduler, here with seven different threads ready and waiting for CPU time. The three threads with priority value 9 will be serviced until they are all waiting for something and there are no ready threads at priority 9. Then the thread at priority 8 will be serviced, and so on*

still ready, it gets put onto the end of its ready queue again. All of the ready threads in the highest-priority queue get serviced until that queue is empty. The system then moves down to the next-lower queue and begins servicing its threads, and so on.

Given this description of the Windows priority structure, it is easy to see how one can easily wreak havoc with it. For example, say that you take Listing 6.2, remove the call to **Sleep** in the thread function, and then set the thread's priority just one level up by changing it to THREAD_PRIOR-ITY_ABOVE_NORMAL after you create the thread. This simple act will essentially lock up all of the other normal processes currently running. Once you remove the call to **Sleep**, the thread function in Listing 6.2 contains an endless counting loop, so it never needs to wait for anything. It is always ready. It is compute-bound. Windows therefore services it continually, at the expense of *all* threads below it. The operating system threads that are in higher classes still run, so the whole machine does not lock up, but all of the normal processes appear to die. While there is a safety value—lower priority threads do get an occasional time slice—the frequency of these spurious time slices is so low (perhaps one slice every two seconds) that for all practical purposes they do not occur.

There is an important lesson here. If you have a thread that you know will always be ready—that is, a thread that is compute-bound—you should probably lower its priority so that it does not stall all of the threads below it in the scheduler. Alternatively, you can cause it to sleep occasionally or (frequently) to give the threads below it some time slices. An idle thread with priority value 1 *never* gets a time slice unless *all* threads above it are waiting for something. Therefore, it may be a reasonable practice to set your compute-bound threads to the absolute priority THREAD_PRIORITY_IDLE so that they don't cut off any other processes. If every application did that, things would work well.

You should never give a thread a high priority unless you *know* that it will frequently wait, and that it will not use much CPU time when it becomes ready. For example, you might place a call to **WaitCommEvent** in a high priority thread waiting for a certain communications event such as the arrival of a character. The thread can then quickly process that character and wait again. Design the application so that a normal-priority thread actually does something with the character retrieved, or set the priority of the high-priority thread back to normal during processing so that you do not starve everything else.

6.8 Other Thread Functions

There are several thread functions not demonstrated in the above examples that are useful in certain situations. Each of these functions is briefly described below:

The **SuspendThread** and **ResumeThread** functions let you temporarily stop and restart the execution of a thread. If you start a thread in a suspended state by setting the creation flags in **CreateThread** to CREATE_ SUSPENDED, then **ResumeThread** is the only way to get the thread running at a later time. There are also cases where the use of suspension and resumption is the easiest way to control a thread. See, for example, Chapter 12, where the Pause and Continue features of a service are implemented this way.

Each thread keeps track of a suspend count. Calling **SuspendThread** increments the count, so if several different pieces of code suspend the thread, the count will rise. The **ResumeThread** function looks at the count.

If it is greater than zero, it decrements the count. If the new count equals zero it resumes the thread. The suspend counter ensures that multiple suspend requests are handled properly. It also means that your calls to suspend and resume must match.

SuspendThread	*Suspends a thread's execution*
DWORD SuspendThread(HANDLE threadHandle)	
threadHandle	The handle of the thread to suspend
Returns the suspend count or 0xFFFFFFFF on failure	

ResumeThread	*Resumes a thread's execution*
DWORD ResumeThread(HANDLE threadHandle)	
threadHandle	The handle of the thread to suspend
Returns the suspend count or 0xFFFFFFFF on failure	

Inside of a thread, you can exit immediately using the **ExitThread** function. It accepts an exit code. Calling **ExitThread** is equivalent to calling **return** from within the thread function. If the thread function calls another function, then **ExitThread** lets you terminate the thread that called the function.

ExitThread	*Exits a thread*
VOID ExitThread(DWORD exitCode)	
exitCode	The exit code of the thread, retrievable by **GetExit CodeThread**
Returns nothing	

The **GetCurrentThread** function returns a pseudohandle for the current thread. A pseudohandle is valid when used inside the thread it represents. Otherwise it is invalid. Do not pass copies of pseudohandles off to other threads. To turn a pseudohandle into a real handle, duplicate it with **DuplicateHandle** and then use the duplicate.

GetCurrentThread	*Retrieves a pseudohandle for a thread*
HANDLE GetCurrentThread(VOID)	
Returns a pseudohandle to the current thread	

If you need to retrieve a thread's ID within the thread, call the **Get CurrentThreadID** function. The thread ID is used by the following functions: **GetThreadDesktop**, **AttachThreadInput**, **PostThreadMessage**, and **SetWindowsHookEx**.

GetCurrentThreadId   *Retrieves the ID for a thread*

```
DWORD GetCurrentThreadId(VOID)
```

Returns the current thread's ID

6.9 Processes

Windows' threads give you an extremely easy way to create multiple execution streams within an application. It is also easy for the threads to communicate with one another, because they share the same global variable space. Since the system does not copy any global or environment areas when creating a thread, threads also have a very low creation overhead.

Because of these advantages, you will generally create threads when you need multiple streams of execution. There are situations, however, where it is useful to be able to spawn an entirely new process. For example, if you want to create your own version of the File Manager, you need a way to launch other applications from within your application. The launched applications need to be created as stand-alone processes.

In addition, it is sometimes useful to design a single application as several independent shells. You might do this to make a project more segmentable during construction (several teams work independently on completely separate applications), or because you want to sell different modules to different clients. An application like this often has a "main window" that is able to launch the other applications. The other applications need to be started as independent processes.

Listing 6.12 demonstrates how to start a separate process from within a running application, using the **CreateProcess** function. The program in Listing 6.12 is nearly identical to the `start` command used in the MS-DOS prompt, except that it asks for the name of the application to be started rather than accepting a command-line argument.

Listing 6.12   *Creating a separate process from within an application*

```cpp
// proc1.cpp

#include <windows.h>
#include <iostream.h>
```

```
void main(void)
{
  CHAR cmdStr[100];
  STARTUPINFO startUpInfo;
  PROCESS_INFORMATION procInfo;
  BOOL success;

  // Get the name of the child process to run
  cout << "Enter the command to execute: ";
  cin.getline(cmdStr, 100);

  // Retrieve the STARTUPINFOR structure for
  // the current process
  GetStartupInfo(&startUpInfo);

  // Create the child process
  success=CreateProcess(
    0, cmdStr, 0, 0, FALSE,
    CREATE_NEW_CONSOLE,
    0, 0, &startUpInfo, &procInfo);
  if (!success)
    cout << "Error creating process: "
      << GetLastError() << endl;

  // Wait for the child process to complete
  WaitForSingleObject(procInfo.hProcess,
    INFINITE);
}
```

The program in Listing 6.12 starts by asking for the name of the executable. You can follow the name with command-line arguments. The way that the program calls **CreateProcess** in Listing 6.12 causes the program to search the path, as well as several other directories, for the executable. You can enter any executable command name in response to the program's prompt. Note that you cannot enter shell commands like "dir" unless you say cmd -c dir (in NT) or command /c dir (in Windows 98).

Next, the program retrieves the current process's startup information using the **GetStartupInfo** function. Calling this function is simply a convenient way to shorten the code. There are a number of fields you can set in the startup structure, as seen below in this description copied from the Win32 help file:

```
typedef struct _STARTUPINFO { /* si */
    DWORD   cb; // number of bytes in structure
    LPTSTR  lpReserved;
    LPTSTR  lpDesktop;  // 0 for curr. desktop
    LPTSTR  lpTitle; // title for consoles
    DWORD   dwX; // X,Y offset of new window
    DWORD   dwY;
```

```
    DWORD     dwXSize; // W,H of new window
    DWORD     dwYSize;
    DWORD     dwXCountChars; // size of new consoles
    DWORD     dwYCountChars;
    DWORD     dwFillAttribute; // colors in consoles
    DWORD     dwFlags; // one or more of many flags
    WORD      wShowWindow; SW_ constants
    WORD      cbReserved2;
    LPBYTE    lpReserved2;
    HANDLE    hStdInput; // Stdin handle
    HANDLE    hStdOutput; // stdout handle
    HANDLE    hStdError; // stderr handle
} STARTUPINFO, *LPSTARTUPINFO;
```

Listing 6.12 starts the new process by calling the **CreateProcess** function. The function accepts 10 parameters.

CreateProcess	*Creates a new stand-alone process*

```
BOOL CreateProcess(
    LPCTSTR imageName,
    LPCTSTR commandLine
    LPSECURITY_ATTRIBUTES processSecurity,
    LPSECURITY_ATTRIBUTES threadSecurity,
    DWORD create,
    LPVOID environment,
    LPCTSTR currDir,
    LPSTARTUPINFO startInfo,
    LPPROCESS_INFORMATION procInfo)
```

imageName	An explicit path to the executable
commandLine	Command line parameters, led if desired by an executable name
processSecurity	Security attributes for the process
threadSecurity	Security attributes for the first thread
inherit	If true, inheritable handles in the parent process are inherited by the child
create	Possible values (one or more of): DEBUG_PROCESS, DEBUG_ONLY_THIS_PROCESS, CREATE_SUSPENDED, DETACHED_PROCESS, CREATE_NEW_CONSOLE, CREATE_NEW_PROCESS_GROUP, plus one of IDLE_PRIORITY_CLASS, NORMAL_PRIORITY_CLASS, HIGH_PRIORITY_CLASS, REALTIME_PRIORITY_CLASS
environment	Points to an array of strings containing environment variables
currDir	Starting drive and directory for the process
startInfo	Appearance Information about the process's window when it starts
procInfo	Returned information for a process
Returns TRUE on success	

You can create the new process using **CreateProcess** in one of two ways:

1. You can supply an explicit path to the executable in the first parameter and then supply command-line parameters for it in the second parameter.

2. You can supply the name of the program to be executed along with its command line options, in the second parameter. The function will search the original program's load directory, the current directory, the Windows and Windows system directories, and then all directories in the PATH for the file specified.

The first option is generally faster because it minimizes search times.

Using the parameters, there are eight important things you can know about the way the new process starts:

1. The process will automatically start in a new window if it is a GUI application. If it is a console application, it will either use the current console or create its own, depending on the value of the creation flags. The CREATE_NEW_CONSOLE flag indicates that the system should create a new console for the application.

2. You indicate the priority class in the creation flags.

3. You determine whether the process should start in an active or suspended state by using the CREATE_SUSPENDED flag.

4. The initial security attributes of the new process and its thread are controlled by the security parameter.

5. You can control whether or not the parent's handles are inherited by the child process by using the inherit parameter.

6. The new process can receive new environment variables if desired, through the use of the environment parameter.

7. The default drive and directory for the new process are determined by the currDir parameter.

8. The startup state of the new process is controlled by the startup structure. It controls things like window size and position.

Once the new process starts, it is completely independent of the parent process.

6.10 Inheriting Handles

When a process creates a child process, the child is completely independent of the parent. By default, the parent and the child have absolutely no connection with one another. However, it is possible for the child process to inherit handles from the parent if the parent marks any of its handles as inheritable. For example, if the parent creates a file handle, or a handle to a thread, or an event handle, it is possible for the parent to share those handles with any child processes it creates. Listings 6.13 and 6.14 show a parent and a child process that share a file handle.

| Listing 6.13 | *The parent process that will share a file handle with an appropriately designed child. Listing 6.14 contains the child process* |

```cpp
// parent.cpp

#include <windows.h>
#include <iostream.h>
#include <stdlib.h>

HANDLE sample;

void main(void)
{
  STARTUPINFO startUpInfo;
  PROCESS_INFORMATION procInfo;
  BOOL success;
  char s[100];
  SECURITY_ATTRIBUTES sa;

  // Set up security attributes to allow
  // inheritance of the file handle
  sa.nLength = sizeof(SECURITY_ATTRIBUTES);
  sa.lpSecurityDescriptor = 0;
  sa.bInheritHandle=TRUE;

  // Create a file handle
  sample = CreateFile("parent.cpp", GENERIC_READ,
    FILE_SHARE_READ, &sa, OPEN_EXISTING,
    FILE_ATTRIBUTE_NORMAL, 0);
  if (sample==INVALID_HANDLE_VALUE)
    cout << "In CreateFile" << GetLastError()
      << endl;

  // Init a startup structure
  GetStartupInfo(&startUpInfo);

  // convert the sample handle to a string
  _itoa((DWORD)sample, s, 10);

  // Create the child process, specifying
  // inherited handles. Pass the value of the
  // handle as a command line parameter
  success=CreateProcess("child.exe", s, 0, 0, TRUE,
```

Listing 6.13 *The parent process that will share a file handle with an appropriately designed child. Listing 6.14 contains the child process (continued)*

```
    CREATE_NEW_CONSOLE,
      0, 0, &startUpInfo, &procInfo);
  if (!success)
    cout << "Error creating process: "
      << GetLastError() << endl;

  // wait for the child to return (this
  // is not a requirement since the child
  // is its own independent process)
  WaitForSingleObject(procInfo.hProcess, INFINITE);
}
```

Listing 6.14 *The child process that inherits the file handle from the parent shown is Listing 6.13*

```
// child.cpp

#include <windows.h>
#include <iostream.h>
#include <stdlib.h>

HANDLE sample;

void main(int argc, char *argv[])
{
  char str[200];
  DWORD numRead;
  BOOL success;

  // Get the handle value off of the command line
  sample = (HANDLE) atoi(argv[0]);

  // Now use it like a normal file handle to
  // read the file
  success = ReadFile(sample, str, 100,
    &numRead, 0);
  if (!success)
    cout << "In ReadFile: " << GetLastError()
      << endl;

  // Output the string read from the file
  str[numRead] = '\0';
  cout << str << endl;

  Sleep(2000);
}
```

The parent process in Listing 6.13 has to do three things to allow the child process in Listing 6.14 to share the file handle:

1. When it calls **CreateFile** to create the file handle, it must supply security attributes that indicate that its handle should be inheritable. It does this by setting the **bInheritHandle** field of the security parameter to TRUE.
2. It must communicate the value of the handle to the child. Here, this communication is done by converting the handle value to a string using **_itoa** and then passing the string to the child on the command line.
3. The **inherit** parameter passed to **CreateProcess** must be set to TRUE so that the child process is allowed to inherit handles.

The child process receives a copy of the parent's *handle table*. This handle table contains all of the parent's handles. You can declare a handle in the child as usual:

```
HANDLE sample;
```

When you do this, you are declaring a variable that holds an index that points into the handle table. When the parent passes the value of that index to the child, the child can load the index into a handle variable of its own. Since the child has a copy of the parent's handle table, it can gain access to one of the parent's handles. Listing 6.14 shows the process. The child in Listing 6.14 can read from the file that the parent opened.

In Listings 6.13 and 6.14, the handle value is passed as a string on the command line. It is also possible to pass the handle value using any other interprocess communication method. See Section 6.11 for more information on interprocess communication.

If the handle is not marked as inheritable in the parent, then the child will get an error the first time it tries to use the handle. The child cannot access one of the parent's handles in the handle table unless it was marked as inheritable when the parent created it.

6.11 Interprocess Communication

There are some situations where you want a new process to be able to communicate with other processes on its system, or with other systems on the network. For example, you might want to create a Control Panel applet to control a service (see Chapter 12). Or several processes might want to share information so that they can chop up a problem among themselves. There are three preferred mechanisms that you can use for interprocess communication:

1. Named Pipes: In situations where one process knows that another will probably be there when it starts up, named pipes are useful. For example, if you want to use a Control Panel applet to control a service, then named pipes are appropriate. The applet knows that the service should be there and that it should respond. Therefore, the service can listen for connections on a specific named pipe and the Control Panel applet can automatically try to attach to it. See Chapter 8 for information on named pipes. When you use named pipes, it is just as easy to transmit data across the network to remote processes as it is to transmit data to a local process on the same machine.

2. Mailslots: If several processes need to share information among the group, mailslots are useful. All of the processes can open a known mailslot name and send data to it, or can both listen and send. Mailslots limit you messages to a maximum size, but also work over the network just as well as they do on a single machine. See Chapter 8 for details.

3. File Mapping: File mapping allows a file of a specified name to map itself into a process's address space, as discussed in Section 2.11. It is possible for multiple processes to access the same mapped file by name, and, in that way, to share data with one another. File mapping is faster than either named pipes or mailslots, and it is also as secure as any file is. However, it does not work over the network. It is also possible to share memory without using an interceding file on the hard disk by using the handle 0xFFFFFFFF when first calling the **Create FileMapping** function. This memory is mapped into the normal swap file, and has no real advantage over a mapped file except that it does not require you to create an actual file on the file system to use it.

If you are designing an application or a set of applications in which multiple processes must communicate, you should use shared memory if you will need to transmit a large amount of data between processes on a single machine. Since file mapping is efficient, this is the quickest way to move the data. If you have two processes that need to form a connection, then named pipes are useful. If many processes need to communicate, use mailslots.

6.12 Jobs

How many times, when creating an involved application, have you had many processes that worked together to form an application set? Up until recently, Windows had not maintained any parent/child process relationship between processes. Windows 2000 now has a new job kernel that lets you group processes together to create, in essence, a process set that allows control over what the processes can do. It is also useful to create jobs that contain a single process. This gives you the capability of placing restrictions on the process, which typically you couldn't do. One might view this set of processes as being in a job container.

Windows 98 does not support jobs.

A process is placed in a job by calling the following:

```
BOOL AssignProcessToJobObject(
        HANDLE          hJob,
        HANDLE          hProcess);
```

This API tells the system to treat the process as part of an existing job. One of the most useful capabilities of a job is the ability to kill all processes within it. You call the following to kill the processes within a job:

```
BOOL TerminateJobObject(
        HANDLE          hJob,
        UINT            uExitCode);
```

This is very much like calling TerminateProcess for each process contained in the job. There are several other APIs used to manage the new job functionally, but we will not cover them at this time.

6.13 Conclusion

When you use threads in a program, you make it possible for the application to simultaneously perform two or more tasks. For example, the application can recalculate an equation in the background while servicing user requests in the foreground.

Chapter 8 contains a number of thread examples, because it demonstrates multi-threaded servers and clients using named pipes. The chapter also demonstrates the use of the **_beginthread** function as an alternative for starting threads.

See Chapter 13 for information on securing threads.

Synchronization

The previous chapter discussed threads and processes. Threads in particular tend to be extremely useful because they give your applications the ability to do many things at once. After a little practice, you start to think of a thread function as nothing more than a normal function that returns immediately and executes in the background.

However, there is one minor problem with thread functions. Because you can have several threads running at the same time, it is possible for them to compete with each other, or for them to run into each other, in ways that are often quite unexpected. A single-threaded application is something like a car driving around in a completely empty parking lot. Because the lot is empty, the car cannot run into anything. If you let two cars drive around in the lot, however, they will eventually run into each other, unless you create mechanisms that prevent collisions.

In this chapter you will learn about the problems that can arise when multiple processes and threads compete for resources. You will also learn about the mechanisms that are provided by the 32-bit APIs to eliminate these problems.

Compatibility Note: All of the code in this chapter works identically in both Windows 2000 and Windows 98, with the exception of the overlapped-file demonstrations in Section 7.5.

7.1 Understanding the Problem

If you have never worked in a preemptive multi-threaded environment before, it may be hard to imagine that anything peculiar can happen. If you *have* worked in such an environment, then you know the problems all too well. Let's look at two very simple examples of the problems that can arise when you use multiple threads in Windows.

Listing 7.1 contains a simple program. Upon starting, the program immediately creates four identical threads. Each thread increments the same global variable 250,000 times, so **count** is incremented a total of 1,000,000 times. The main program waits for the four threads to complete, and then prints out the global **count** variable. (See Chapter 6 for an explanation of thread functions and of the volatile keyword.)

Listing 7.1   *A simple program in which four identical threads increment a count variable 250,000 times each*

```
// prob1.cpp

#include <windows.h>
#include <stdlib.h>
#include <iostream.h>

volatile INT count;

void CountThread(INT iterations)
{
  INT i;
  INT x;

  for (i=0; i<iterations; i++)
  {
    x=count;
    x++;
    count=x;
  }
}

const INT numThreads=4;

void main(void)
{
  HANDLE handles[numThreads];
  DWORD threadID;
  INT i;

  for (i=0; i<numThreads; i++)
  {
    // create the threads
    handles[i]=CreateThread(0, 0,
        (LPTHREAD_START_ROUTINE) CountThread,
        (VOID *) 250000, 0, &threadID);
  }
```

Listing 7.1   *A simple program in which four identical threads increment a count variable 250,000 times each (continued)*

```
// wait for all threads to finish execution
WaitForMultipleObjects(numThreads, handles,
   TRUE, INFINITE);

cout << "Global count = " << count << endl;
}
```

Run this program on your own machine and you will immediately see the problem. I ran it 10 times on my machine, and got different output each time. Here are my results:

Global Count = 469459
Global Count = 520484
Global Count = 459216
Global Count = 508529
Global Count = 710670
Global Count = 588914
Global Count = 584157
Global Count = 462185
Global Count = 508553
Global Count = 720819

None of these numbers is close to the expected value. Since the four threads increment the global variable 250,000 times each, the global count should always be 1,000,000 at the end of the run. Instead, we get apparently random output. The output is, in fact, totally and truly random. Try changing the counter to 25,000 or 25,000,000, and note the results.

The random output is occurring because the four threads are running "simultaneously." On a machine with one processor, the operating system is periodically stopping one thread and giving the CPU to another one. On a machine with four or more processors, the four threads are truly running concurrently. We will discuss the single-CPU case here because it is more common.

When the operating system starts thread 1, it gives it a "slice" of CPU time, perhaps 20 milliseconds. When that slice of time runs out, the operating system stops the thread and gives CPU time to another thread on the system, sharing the CPU very rapidly among all of the threads, and giving the impression that they are running simultaneously. (See Section 6.7 for a discussion of thread priorities and how they affect scheduling.) When all four copies of the thread function are running, the CPU is giving each one a time slice in a round-robin fashion.

Let's say that the global **count** value is currently 100, that thread one is running, and that the program has just executed the "x=count" statement in the thread function of Listing 7.1. Thread one places a value of 100 in its local variable **x**. At this moment its time slice runs out and the operating system preempts it to let another thread run.

Thread two gets the next time slice. Let's say it is just starting, so it also copies the value 100 into its local copy of **x**, increments **x**, and stores the result, 101, back in the global **count** variable. Thread two may get through its loop hundreds of times, raising the value of the global count to 400, before its time slice ends and the CPU is given to another thread.

Eventually thread 1 gets another time slice, and it picks up exactly where it left off. It increments its copy of **x**, which happened to be 100 at the end of its previous time slice, and stores 101 into **count**. This obliterates the work of the other threads. When four threads are doing the same thing hundreds of times per second, you get results like those seen in the sample output above. In order to get correct output, something must be done to prevent the threads from stepping on each other like this.

As a second example, say that you have two threads sharing a common, global data structure. In this case, it is a stack. One thread writes to the stack, while the other reads from it. The code in Listing 7.2 illustrates a possible implementation for the push and pop operations using pointers. There is no error-checking in the code, to simplify things.

Listing 7.2   *Sample code demonstrating possible implementations of the push and pop operations*

```
typedef struct _NODE
{
   int data;
   _NODE *next;
} NODE;

NODE *top = 0;

void push(int value)
{
   NODE *temp;

   temp = new NODE;
   temp->data = value;
   temp->next = top;
   top = temp;
}

int pop()
{
   NODE *temp;
   int value;
```

Listing 7.2 *Sample code demonstrating possible implementations of the push and pop operations (continued)*

```
if (top == 0)
  return 0;
temp = top;
value = top->data;
top = top->next;
delete temp;
return value;
}
```

Say that thread one is pushing a value onto the stack. It gets down to the line "top = temp" in the **push** function of Listing 7.2, but is unable to execute the line before it gets preempted. Figure 7.1a illustrates the situation.

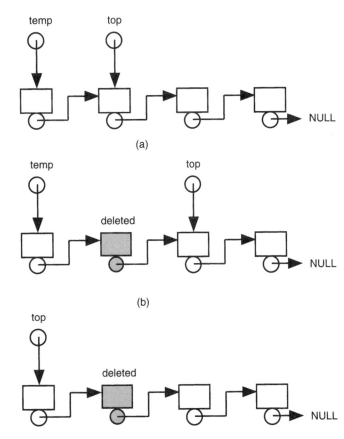

(a)

(b)

Figure 7.1

The state of the stack when preemptive multi-tasking allows the pushing thread to be preempted in the middle of a push operation. See text for a description.

(c)

Now thread two starts, and performs a complete **pop**, as shown in Figure 7.1b. Thread 1 then gets another time slice and completes its push operation. The final result is shown in Figure 7.1c. Because the two threads were working simultaneously in a preemptive environment, the stack is corrupted in a way that is impossible in a single-tasking environment.

What is so sad about this particular stack example is that the code *looks* fine. It may *appear* to work correctly for quite some time as you test it. It is often very difficult to track the problem, because it may manifest itself quite subtly and infrequently. However, the code is clearly wrong unless something is done to prevent separate threads from colliding, as they do here.

These are very simple examples, but they clearly illustrate the problem. You can imagine what might happen when ten threads are competing for 20 global resources. What you need is a way to control access to shared global resources so that threads can access them only in controlled ways. In both cases illustrated on the previous pages, there needs to be a way to prevent multiple accesses to the global resources. People will often use a variety of different ways to speak about this concept:

- "We need to serialize the access to the global **count** variable so that only one thread can access it at a time."
- "We should synchronize the threads so that only one can access the global **count** variable at any given time."
- "Access to the **count** variable should be mutually exclusive—no two threads should be able to use it at the same time."
- "That incrementing code for the global **count** variable is a critical section. We cannot let more than one thread run it at one time."

The terminology differs depending on what book the particular person was using when he or she learned about process synchronization. Different operating-system researchers who studied synchronization came up with different ways to talk about and solve the problem. The 32-bit API tries to accommodate these different ways of thinking.

7.2 Four Different Synchronization Methods

The 32-bit APIs provides four different *synchronization mechanisms:*

1. Critical sections
2. Mutexes
3. Semaphores
4. Events

All four mechanisms may be used to solve the two problems described above, although once you understand them you will see that either critical sections or mutexes would be the logical choices for these particular problems. Semaphores and events have more advanced applications. The following four sections look at each of the techniques and show you how they can be used to solve the simple counting problem demonstrated in Listing 7.1, as well as other more important problems.

One thing that you will notice in the following examples is that all of the synchronization mechanisms implement *efficient waiting*. That is, the synchronization mechanisms built into the 32-bit APIs all suspend a waiting thread so that the thread requires little or no CPU time while it is waiting. Also note that all of the mechanisms are totally under operating system control, and therefore do not compromise the system's reliability in any way. For example, in some environments, you ensure that a thread has mutually-exclusive access to something by turning off interrupts, thereby preventing any type of preemption. Windows does not allow you to do this, for obvious system integrity reasons. In addition, the mechanisms discussed here work regardless of the number of processors the machine uses.

Another thing you will notice is that the mechanisms described here all provide implicit queuing. For example, say that you want to control access to a communication port so that only one thread accesses it at a time. As you will see in the following, you can use a *mutex* to control access. All of the threads "wait on the mutex," and once one owns the mutex it can safely access the communications port. The operating system queues the waiting threads for you, so if five threads are waiting they wait efficiently in a queue and the operating system releases them one at a time based on arrival order.

7.2.1 Critical Sections

The term *critical section* refers to a section of code that should be executed by only one thread at a time. In Listing 7.1, the critical section is the three lines of code that increment the count in the thread function. In the example, both the **push** and the **pop** functions contain critical sections, and they are linked. If the **push** function is executing, other pushes *as well as* other pops should be prevented, because both functions use the same global data structure. You would therefore mark the contents of both the **push** and the **pop** functions with the same critical section variable.

In the 32-bit APIs, four functions implement critical sections. To create a critical section, you declare a variable of type CRITICAL_SECTION. Call the **InitializeCriticalSection** function to initialize that variable. At the beginning of a critical piece of code, use the **EnterCriticalSection** function, and at the end, call **LeaveCriticalSection**. When you are done with the critical section variable call **DeleteCriticalSection.**

InitializeCriticalSection   *Initializes a critical section variable*

```
VOID InitializeCriticalSection(
   LPCRITICAL_SECTION criticalSection)
```

Returns nothing

EnterCriticalSection   *Marks the beginning of a critical section*

```
VOID EnterCriticalSection(
   LPCRITICAL_SECTION criticalSection)
```

Returns nothing

LeaveCriticalSection   *Marks the end of a critical section*

```
VOID LeaveCriticalSection(
   LPCRITICAL_SECTION criticalSection)
```

Returns nothing

DeleteCriticalSection   *Releases any allocation for the critical section*

```
VOID DeleteCriticalSection(
   LPCRITICAL_SECTION criticalSection)
```

Returns nothing

Listing 7.3 demonstrates the use of the critical-section functions to solve the problem with the global **count** variable demonstrated in Listing 6.1. The critical section variable **critSec** appears globally. The main thread initializes it and then later deletes it just before it quits. The thread function marks the three increment lines as the critical section of code in this program. When you run Listing 7.3, it will produce the correct answer but will require quite much longer (perhaps 50 times longer) to execute.

Listing 7.3   *Applying the critical section code to Listing 7.1*

```cpp
// critsec.cpp

#include <windows.h>
#include <stdlib.h>
#include <iostream.h>

volatile INT count;
CRITICAL_SECTION critSec;

void CountThread(INT iterations)
```

Listing 7.3   *Applying the critical section code to Listing 7.1 (continued)*

```
{
  INT i;
  INT x;

  for (i=0; i<iterations; i++)
  {
    EnterCriticalSection(&critSec);
    x=count;
    x++;
    count=x;
    LeaveCriticalSection(&critSec);
  }
}

const INT numThreads=4;

void main(void)
{
  HANDLE handles[numThreads];
  DWORD threadID;
  INT i;

  InitializeCriticalSection(&critSec);

  for (i=0; i<numThreads; i++)
  {
    // create a thread and pass it the pointer
    // to its "params" struct
    handles[i]=CreateThread(0, 0,
      (LPTHREAD_START_ROUTINE) CountThread,
      (VOID *) 25000, 0, &threadID);
  }

  // wait for all threads to finish execution
  WaitForMultipleObjects(numThreads, handles,
    TRUE, INFINITE);

  DeleteCriticalSection(&critSec);

  cout << "Global count = " << count << endl;
}
```

The marking for the **push** and **pop** functions of Listing 7.2 is shown in Listing 7.4. Note that they both use the same critical-section variable.

Listing 7.4	*Marking the push and pop functions with a single critical section*

```c
typedef struct _NODE
{
  int data;
  _NODE *next;
} NODE;

CRITICAL_SECTION critSec;
NODE *top = 0;

void push(int value)
{
  NODE *temp;

  EnterCriticalSection(&critSec);
  temp = new NODE;
  temp->data = value;
  temp->next = top;
  top = temp;
  LeaveCriticalSection(&critSec);
}

int pop()
{
  NODE *temp;
  int value;

  EnterCriticalSection(&critSec);
  if (top == 0)
  {
    LeaveCriticalSection(&critSec);
    return 0;
  }
  temp = top;
  value = top->data;
  top = top->next;
  delete temp;
  LeaveCriticalSection(&critSec);
  return value;
}
```

The **InitializeCriticalSection** function initializes the specified critical-section variable, Do not call this function more than once for the given variable.

A call to **EnterCriticalSection** causes the system to check the specified critical-section variable. If the critical section is not in use, the system marks the variable as in-use and returns. If it is in use, the operating system suspends the thread that is calling **EnterCriticalSection**. Later, when a thread calls **LeaveCriticalSection**, the operating system wakes up the suspended thread and allows it to proceed into the critical section code. Multiple threads can be waiting to enter the critical section at one time. They are allowed to enter on a first-come-first-served basis each time another thread calls **LeaveCriticalSection**.

Here are some points to keep in mind about critical sections:

- A thread can call **EnterCriticalSection** on the same critical-section variable multiple times without harm. The system will not block it, and thus makes it impossible for a thread to deadlock itself. The thread must call **LeaveCriticalSection** an equal number of times.
- A program can have multiple critical sections by declaring multiple critical section variables. You might do this if you have two global variables to increment or two stacks that are active. Two threads should be able to access two independent stacks simultaneously.
- A critical-section variable should not be initialized more than once, nor should it be moved or copied. Declare it as a global or member variable and use it in only that way.
- Critical-section variables are only valid for threads that are in the same process. Use a mutex (Section 7.2.2) to provide mutual exclusion between multiple processes.
- Do not call **LeaveCriticalSection** unless it has been preceded by a call to **EnterCriticalSection**. The results of an unmatched Leave are unpredictable.

With critical sections and all other synchronization techniques, you need to guard against deadlock when there is more than one critical section being used in a single process. See Section 7.3 for details.

Critical sections should be kept short, and should never contain non-deterministic code. For example, a critical section should never contain a read statement that accepts input from the user, because it is impossible to predict how long it will take for the user to respond. In the meantime, all other threads waiting on the critical section are blocked indefinitely.

If you have a large block of code, or a block of code that contains a non-deterministic section, then break up the critical section. For example:

```
EnterCriticalSection
... Deterministic, short-duration code ...
LeaveCriticalSection

... Non-deterministic code ...
EnterCriticalSection
... Deterministic, short-duration code ...
LeaveCriticalSection
```

A critical section should never contain a loop unless you know that the number of iterations is *always* small. It is better to enter and leave the critical section each time through the loop, as shown in Listing 7.3.

Note that it is *extremely* easy to create faulty code by not exactly matching your Enters and Leaves, and this code is extremely hard to debug. For example, forgetting the second Leave in the **if** block of the **Pop** function in Listing 7.4 is an easy mistake to make, but is very hard to debug.

7.2.2 Mutexes

A mutex provides mutually-exclusive access to a piece of code or a variable in a way that is valid across multiple processes. You often think of a mutex differently from the way you think of a critical section. Usually you associate a mutex with a global resource, whereas you think of a critical section as referring to a piece of code.

For example, you might assign a mutex to a global variable, or to a communications port, a printer, or a file, to make sure that only one thread uses that resource at a time. The thread accessing the resource "owns" the mutex until it is done with the resource. Then it "releases" the mutex. Other threads wanting to use the resource are "waiting" for the mutex, and as soon as it is released, it is acquired by one of the waiting threads.

Listing 7.5 demonstrates a simple use of a mutex. It does the same thing that Listing 7.3 does, except that it uses a mutex instead of a critical section to serialize access to the shared global counter.

Listing 7.5   *Using a mutex to provide mutual exclusion. Compare to Listing 7.3*

```
// mutex.cpp

#include <windows.h>
#include <stdlib.h>
#include <iostream.h>

volatile INT count;
HANDLE mutex;

void CountThread(INT iterations)
{
  INT i;
  INT x;

  for (i=0; i<iterations; i++)
  {
    WaitForSingleObject(mutex, INFINITE);
    x=count;
```

| Listing 7.5 | *Using a mutex to provide mutual exclusion. Compare to Listing 7.3 (continued)* |

```
      x++;
      count=x;
      ReleaseMutex(mutex);
   }
}

const INT numThreads=4;

void main(void)
{
  HANDLE handles[numThreads];
  DWORD threadID;
  INT i;

  mutex = CreateMutex(0, FALSE, 0);

  for (i=0; i<numThreads; i++)
  {
    // create the threads
    handles[i]=CreateThread(0, 0,
      (LPTHREAD_START_ROUTINE) CountThread,
      (VOID *) 25000, 0, &threadID);
  }

  // wait for all threads to finish execution
  WaitForMultipleObjects(numThreads, handles,
    TRUE, INFINITE);

  CloseHandle(mutex);

  cout << "Global count = " << count << endl;
}
```

The program in Listing 7.5 starts by creating a mutex using the **Create-Mutex** function. A mutex is an object, so **CreateMutex** returns a handle to it.

CreateMutex   *Creates a mutex and returns a handle to it, or opens a mutex by name if it already exists*

```
HANDLE CreateMutex(
  LPSECURITY_ATTRIBUTES security,
  BOOL initialOwner,
  LPCTSTR name)
```

security   Security attributes. See Chapter 10

initialOwner	Set to TRUE if you want to initially own the mutex
name	The name of the mutex, or 0 if nameless

Returns a handle to the mutex, or 0 on error. If a mutex of the specified name already exists, then **GetLastError** will return ERROR_ALREADY_EXISTS but the handle will be valid.

OpenMutex	*Opens a mutex by name if it already exists*

```
HANDLE OpenMutex(
   DWORD access,
   BOOL inherit,
   LPCTSTR name)
```

access	SYNCHRONIZE and/or MUTEX_ALL_ACCESS
inherit	Set to TRUE if you want the mutex handle to be inheritable
name	The name of the mutex to be opened

Returns a handle to the mutex, or 0 on error

The mutex object can be named or unnamed. In Listing 7.5 it is unnamed because it is used in only one process. If you want to use it in multiple processes, then you can name it and allow other processes to open handles to access it using either **CreateMutex** or **OpenMutex**. When you use **CreateMutex** with the name of a mutex that already exists, then it simply opens the existing mutex and returns a handle, just as **OpenMutex** would.

The main function in Listing 7.5 then creates the four threads. The threads wait for the mutex by calling the **WaitForSingleObject** function. See Section 7.4 for details.

WaitForSingleObject	*Waits for the mutex to be released*

```
DWORD WaitForSingleObject(
   HANDLE object,
   DWORD timeout)
```

object	The mutex to wait for
timeout	0, a number of milliseconds, or INFINITE

Returns WAIT_FAILED, WAIT_ABANDONED, WAIT_TIMEOUT, or WAIT_OBJECT_0

The **WaitForSingleObject** function waits for the specified object to be "signaled." A mutex is initially set to the signaled state (unless **initialOwner** is TRUE), so the first thread to call **WaitForSingleObject** gets the mutex immediately. Multiple threads can efficiently wait on a single mutex, which will remain "unsignaled" until the owning thread releases it. As soon as the mutex is released, the operating system gives it to one of the waiting threads.

If a thread already owns a mutex and calls **WaitForSingleObject** again, then it continues execution so that a thread cannot block itself. The thread must release the mutex an equivalent number of times.

The **WaitForSingleObject** function accepts a timeout value. If the value is 1,000, then the function returns when the mutex is signaled, or when 1,000 milliseconds (one second) elapses, whichever comes first. If the timeout value is 0, then the function returns immediately, regardless of the state of the mutex, and provides an easy way to test the mutex's state. If the timeout value is set to INFINITE, the function does not return until the mutex is signaled.

The **WaitForSingleObject** function returns WAIT_FAILED on an error. It returns WAIT_TIMEOUT if the timeout period elapsed. It returns WAIT_ OBJECT_0 if the mutex is signaled. It returns WAIT_ABANDONED if the thread owning the mutex died before calling the **ReleaseMutex** function to formally release the mutex. Abandonment implies an error, and the thread receiving a mutex in this state should assume that the resource that the mutex guards is in an unstable state. It is a good design practice to provide a function that the thread can call to restabilize the resource whenever it detects an abandoned mutex.

When a thread is done with the resource, it should call the **Release Mutex** function. This allows another thread waiting on the mutex to access the resource.

ReleaseMutex   *Releases a mutex so another thread can use it*

```
BOOL ReleaseMutex(
   HANDLE mutex)
```

mutex   The mutex to be released

Returns TRUE on success

Mutexes are often used when mutual exclusion between multiple processes is needed. By naming the mutex, another process can open a handle to it. Listing 7.6 demonstrates the use of a named mutex.

Listing 7.6   *Creating handles to a named mutex in each thread rather than using a single handle*

```
// mutex2.cpp

#include <windows.h>
#include <stdlib.h>
#include <iostream.h>

volatile INT count;

void CountThread(INT iterations)
```

```
{
  INT i;
  INT x;
  HANDLE mutex;

  mutex = CreateMutex(0, FALSE, "counterMutex");

  for (i=0; i<iterations; i++)
  {
    WaitForSingleObject(mutex, INFINITE);
    x=count;
    x++;
    count=x;
    ReleaseMutex(mutex);
  }

  CloseHandle(mutex);
}

const INT numThreads=4;

void main(void)
{
  HANDLE handles[numThreads];
  DWORD threadID;
  INT i;

  for (i=0; i<numThreads; i++)
  {
    // create the threads
    handles[i]=CreateThread(0, 0,
      (LPTHREAD_START_ROUTINE) CountThread,
      (VOID *) 25000, 0, &threadID);
  }

  // wait for all threads to finish execution
  WaitForMultipleObjects(numThreads, handles,
    TRUE, INFINITE);

  cout << "Global count = " << count << endl;
}
```

In Listing 7.6, each thread calls **CreateMutex** using the name "counter-Mutex." The first thread to call **CreateMutex** actually creates the mutex. All other calls to **CreateMutex** with the same name perform an open operation and return a handle to the existing mutex. Each thread keeps a local handle pointing to the mutex, so four handles point to the same mutex once all four threads have started. If the threads happened to be in different processes, the effect would be the same.

When a thread is through with a mutex, it should close the handle to it with **CloseHandle**. The thread should release the mutex first if it owns it. When all handles pointing to the mutex are closed, the operating system automatically deletes the mutex object.

7.2.3 Semaphores

A semaphore is a superset of a mutex. It works just like a mutex, but it also has a counter associated with it. The counter always has a value between zero and a maximum that you set when you create the semaphore. When the counter is greater than zero, the semaphore is signaled, and any Wait function will proceed (see Section 7.4 for details). When the counter is zero, the semaphore is not signaled, and any Wait function is blocked until the count rises above zero due to another thread releasing the semaphore. When you call the release function, you specify a value to be added to the semaphore's counter, generally one. You set the initial value of the semaphore's counter when you create the semaphore.

By setting a semaphore's maximum value to one and initial value to one, you get behavior that is identical to a mutex. Listing 7.7 duplicates Listing 7.5 using a semaphore in place of a mutex.

Listing 7.7   *A duplication of Listing 7.5, using a semaphore with a maximum value of one in place of the mutex*

```cpp
// sema.cpp

#include <windows.h>
#include <stdlib.h>
#include <iostream.h>

volatile INT count;
HANDLE semaphore;

void CountThread(INT iterations)
{
  INT i;
  INT x;
  LONG semaCount;

  for (i=0; i<iterations; i++)
  {
    WaitForSingleObject(semaphore, INFINITE);
    x=count;
    x++;
    count=x;
    ReleaseSemaphore(semaphore, 1, &semaCount);
  }
}
```

```
const INT numThreads=4;

void main(void)
{
  HANDLE handles[numThreads];
  DWORD threadID;
  INT i;

  semaphore = CreateSemaphore(0, 1, 1, 0);

  for (i=0; i<numThreads; i++)
  {
    // create the threads
    handles[i]=CreateThread(0, 0,
      (LPTHREAD_START_ROUTINE) CountThread,
      (VOID *) 25000, 0, &threadID);
  }

  // wait for all threads to finish execution
  WaitForMultipleObjects(numThreads, handles,
    TRUE, INFINITE);

  CloseHandle(semaphore);

  cout << "Global count = " << count << endl;
}
```

You can see that the functions used when working with a semaphore are nearly identical to those used with mutexes. The **CreateSemaphore** function accepts an initial and maximum count.

CreateSemaphore	*Creates a semaphore, or opens one if the name specified already exists*

```
HANDLE CreateSemaphore(
  LPSECURITY_ATTRIBUTES security,
  LONG initialValue,
  LONG maxValue,
  LPCTSTR name)
```

security	Security attributes. See Chapter 10
initialValue	The initial value of the semaphore's count
maxValue	The maximum value of the semaphore's count
name	The name of the semaphore, or 0 if nameless

Returns a handle to the semaphore, or NULL on error. If a semaphore of the specified name already exists, then GetLastError will return ERROR_ALREADY_EXISTS but the handle will be valid.

OpenSemaphore   *Opens an existing semaphore by name*

```
HANDLE OpenSemaphore(
    DWORD access,
    BOOL inherit,
    LPCTSTR name)
```

access	SEMAPHORE_MODIFY_STATE, SYNCHRONIZE, and/or SEMAPHORE_ALL_ACCESS
inherit	Set to TRUE if handle should be inheritable
name	The name of the semaphore to open

Returns a handle to the named semaphore, or NULL if it does not exist

---

Semaphores, like mutexes, can be named or unnamed. If they are named, processes can share them by opening an existing semaphore.

Threads wait on a semaphore using **WaitForSingleObject**, as shown in the previous section. If the value of the semaphore is zero, the thread blocks when it calls the Wait function. Any non-zero value lets the thread proceed. Because of this, semaphores can allow a limited number of threads to use a resource simultaneously. In Listing 7.7, with the maximum value of the count set to one, only one thread can access the global counter. However, if the maximum value and initial value were set to three, then three threads could access the resource together. As with a mutex, you can specify a timeout value for the Wait function.

To release a semaphore, call the **ReleaseSemaphore** function.

ReleaseSemaphore   *Increments the count of the semaphore by the specified value.*

```
BOOL ReleaseSemaphore(
    HANDLE semaphore,
    LONG incrementValue,
    LPLONG count)
```

semaphore	The semaphore to release
incrementValue	The value to add to the semaphore's counter, generally 1
count	A variable to hold the returned count prior to incrementing. Set to 0 if you don't need the count

Returns TRUE on succe ss

Generally you pass one as the increment value, although other values are possible.

The use of a semaphore in Listing 7.7 is something of a waste. With the maximum value of the semaphore set to 1, the semaphore behaves just like a mutex. The count value associated with semaphores makes them useful in a variety of situations, however. For example, it is easy to solve the "bounded buffer" problem using semaphores.

The bounded-buffer problem assumes that there is a single buffer shared by two threads. One thread is filling the buffer, while the other is emptying it. The buffer might hold messages passed between the two threads, queuing them when the reader cannot keep up with the writer. The buffer, however, is "bounded." It cannot hold more than some fixed number of messages. Once the buffer reaches its maximum size, the writer should stop adding messages until there is room available in the buffer again. If the buffer becomes empty, the reader should stop until something appears in the buffer again.

To solve the bounded-buffer problem with semaphores, assume that you create two of them. One semaphore is called **empty** and starts with the value N, where N is the maximum size of the buffer. The other is called **full** and starts with the value 0.

The writer thread waits on the **empty** semaphore. Since **empty** starts with the value N, the writer proceeds through the wait and puts a value in the buffer. The writer then increments the **full** semaphore to signal that the buffer contains one value. For example:

```
WaitForSingleObject(empty);
... add to the buffer ...
ReleaseSemaphore(full, 1);
```

The reader thread is doing just the opposite, waiting on **full** and then incrementing **empty**. For example:

```
WaitForSingleObject(full);
... remove from the buffer ...
ReleaseSemaphore(empty, 1);
```

As the writer places values in the buffer, it decrements empty toward zero. Once the buffer is full, **empty** will hit zero and the writer will be blocked until the reader removes a value and releases **empty**, thereby incrementing it. On the other hand, the reader decrements **full** each time it reads a value. Since **full** starts at zero, the reader is initially blocked, but becomes unblocked each time the writer increments **full** by releasing it. The value of **full** never rises above the maximum because the writer has to wait on **empty** first.

Listing 7.8 shows an implementation of the bounded-buffer problem using two semaphores. It uses the stack code discussed in Listings 7.2 and 7.4 to add and remove values from the buffer, with a critical section to prevent faulty access to the stack's global variables. A second critical section is also used for the **cout** statements, because they sometimes do odd things when called simultaneously.

Listing 7.8   *A solution to the bounded-buffer problem using semaphores*

```cpp
// buffer.cpp

#include <windows.h>
#include <iostream.h>

typedef struct _NODE
{
  int data;
  _NODE *next;
} NODE;

NODE *top = 0;
HANDLE empty, full;
CRITICAL_SECTION critSec;
CRITICAL_SECTION coutCritSec;
const MAX_BUFFERS = 5;

void push(int value)
{
  NODE *temp;

  EnterCriticalSection(&critSec);
  temp = new NODE;
  temp->data = value;
  temp->next = top;
  top = temp;
  LeaveCriticalSection(&critSec);
}

int pop()
{
  NODE *temp;
  int value;

  EnterCriticalSection(&critSec);
  if (top == 0)
  {
    LeaveCriticalSection(&critSec);
    return 0;
  }
  temp = top;
  value = top->data;
  top = top->next;
  delete temp;
  LeaveCriticalSection(&critSec);
  return value;
}

VOID ReadThread(VOID)
```

```
{
  int x, p;
  LONG count;

  for (x=0; x<10; x++)
  {
    WaitForSingleObject(full, INFINITE);
    p = pop();
    ReleaseSemaphore(empty, 1, &count);
    EnterCriticalSection(&coutCritSec);
    cout << "Read iteration: " << x
      << " value popped: " << p
      << " empty count: " << count << endl;
    LeaveCriticalSection(&coutCritSec);
    Sleep(200);
  }
}

VOID WriteThread(VOID)
{
  int x;
  LONG count;

  for (x=0; x<10; x++)
  {
    WaitForSingleObject(empty, INFINITE);
    push(x);
    ReleaseSemaphore(full, 1, &count);
    EnterCriticalSection(&coutCritSec);
    cout << "Write iteration: " << x
      << " full count: " << count << endl;
    LeaveCriticalSection(&coutCritSec);
    Sleep(100);
  }
}

const INT numThreads=2;

void main(void)
{
  HANDLE handles[numThreads];
  DWORD threadID;

  // Init synchronization
  InitializeCriticalSection(&critSec);
  InitializeCriticalSection(&coutCritSec);
  full = CreateSemaphore(0, 0, MAX_BUFFERS, 0);
  empty = CreateSemaphore(0, MAX_BUFFERS,
    MAX_BUFFERS, 0);
```

Listing 7.8 *A solution to the bounded-buffer problem using semaphores (continued)*

```
// create a thread to read from the buffer
handles[0]=CreateThread(0, 0,
  (LPTHREAD_START_ROUTINE) ReadThread,
  0, 0, &threadID);

// create a thread to write to the buffer
handles[1]=CreateThread(0, 0,
  (LPTHREAD_START_ROUTINE) WriteThread,
  0, 0, &threadID);

// wait for all threads to finish execution
WaitForMultipleObjects(numThreads, handles,
  TRUE, INFINITE);

// Clean up
CloseHandle(empty);
CloseHandle(full);
DeleteCriticalSection(&critSec);
DeleteCriticalSection(&coutCritSec);
}
```

In Listing 7.8, the writer will produce 10 values and push them onto the stack. The reader reads 10 values by popping them off of the stack. You can adjust the sleep times in the reader and writer to let the writer outpace the reader, or to let the reader outpace the writer. With the values shown in Listing 7.8, I received the following output from the program:

```
H:\users\brain\nt\internal\code\sync>buffer
Write iteration: 0 full count: 0
Read iteration: 0 value popped: 0 empty count: 4
Write iteration: 1 full count: 0
Read iteration: 1 value popped: 1 empty count: 4
Write iteration: 2 full count: 0
Write iteration: 3 full count: 1
Read iteration: 2 value popped: 3 empty count: 3
Write iteration: 4 full count: 1
Write iteration: 5 full count: 2
Read iteration: 3 value popped: 5 empty count: 2
Write iteration: 6 full count: 2
Write iteration: 7 full count: 3
Read iteration: 4 value popped: 7 empty count: 1
Write iteration: 8 full count: 3
Write iteration: 9 full count: 4
Read iteration: 5 value popped: 9 empty count: 0
Read iteration: 6 value popped: 8 empty count: 1
Read iteration: 7 value popped: 6 empty count: 2
Read iteration: 8 value popped: 4 empty count: 3
Read iteration: 9 value popped: 2 empty count: 4
```

Here the writer was working twice as fast as the reader, so it filled the buffer quickly and then finished, while the reader emptied the buffer.

Semaphores are useful in many similar situations where you want to limit access to a resource to a fixed number of threads. For example, you might want to create a different thread to calculate each scan line in a Mandelbrot set (see Section 6.4 for details) because this makes the problem conceptually easy to multi-thread. However, you may want to limit the number of threads running simultaneously to the number of available processors for maximum efficiency. Semaphores solve this problem easily using the techniques seen in Listing 7.8.

7.2.4 Events

Events are a general-purpose signaling system that you can use when one process or thread needs to signal another process or thread. Events are also used inside of overlapped structures (see Section 7.5). They come in two flavors: manual and automatic. In automatic mode they have the same functionality as a mutex, as demonstrated in Listing 7.9.

Listing 7.9   *Using events like a mutex. Compare to Listing 7.3*

```
// event.cpp

#include <windows.h>
#include <stdlib.h>
#include <iostream.h>

volatile INT count;
HANDLE event;

void CountThread(INT iterations)
{
  INT i;
  INT x;

  for (i=0; i<iterations; i++)
  {
    WaitForSingleObject(event, INFINITE);
    x=count;
    x++;
    count=x;
    SetEvent(event);
  }
}

const INT numThreads=4;

void main(void)
```

Listing 7.9 *Using events like a mutex. Compare to Listing 7.3 (continued)*

```
{
  HANDLE handles[numThreads];
  DWORD threadID;
  INT i;

  event = CreateEvent(0, FALSE, TRUE, 0);

  for (i=0; i<numThreads; i++)
  {
    // create a thread and pass it the pointer
    // to its "params" struct
    handles[i]=CreateThread(0, 0,
      (LPTHREAD_START_ROUTINE) CountThread,
      (VOID *) 25000, 0, &threadID);
  }
  // wait for all threads to finish execution
  WaitForMultipleObjects(numThreads, handles,
    TRUE, INFINITE);

  CloseHandle(event);

  cout << "Global count = " << count << endl;
}
```

Listing 7.9 starts by creating an event. An event can be thought of as a general-purpose signaling mechanism. You usually use it to cause a thread to wait efficiently for something to happen.

CreateEvent   *Creates an event, or opens one if the name specified already exists*

```
HANDLE CreateEvent(
  LPSECURITY_ATTRIBUTES security,
  BOOL manualReset,
  BOOL initialState,
  LPCTSTR name)
```

security	Security attributes. See Chapter 10
manualReset	TRUE for manual reset, FALSE for automatic reset
initialState	The initial state of the event: TRUE if signaled
name	The name of the event, or 0 if nameless

Returns a handle to the event, or 0 on error. If a event of the specified name already exists, then GetLastError will return ERROR_ALREADY_EXISTS but the handle will be valid.

OpenEvent   *Opens an existing event by name*

```
HANDLE OpenEvent(
    DWORD access,
    BOOL inherit,
    LPCTSTR name)
```

access	EVENT_MODIFY_STATE, SYNCHRONIZE, and/or EVENT_ALL_ACCESS
inherit	Set to TRUE if handle should be inheritable
name	The name of the event to be opened

Returns a handle to the named event, or NULL if it does not exist

---

When you wait for an automatic event using, for example, **WaitFor SingleObject**, the thread blocks until the event is in a signaled state. When the event is signaled the Wait function returns and the thread proceeds. The event becomes unsignaled automatically by the Wait function, and the thread "owns" the event. When the thread is finished with the event it calls **SetEvent**, which signals the event for another thread. As you can see, an automatic event acts just like a mutex.

SetEvent   *Sets an event to the signaled state*

```
BOOL SetEvent
    HANDLE event)
```

event	The event to set

Returns TRUE on success

Events also come in a manual type. In manual mode, each thread must set the event to signaled or reset it to unsignaled on its own. A Wait function has no automatic effect on the event.

ResetEvent   *Resets an event to the unsignaled state*

```
BOOL ResetEvent(
    HANDLE event)
```

event	The event to be reset

Returns TRUE on success

You use manual events when you want to allow one thread to signal another and the other thread needs to wait efficiently until it receives the signal. For example, say that one thread is calculating a result and a second thread needs to wait for the answer. The second thread can wait efficiently on an event, and the first thread can signal the event when it is ready.

In manual mode you can also "pulse" an event. When you pulse an event, the event becomes signaled long enough to release all waiting threads, and then becomes unsignaled again.

PulseEvent	*Sets an event to the signaled state long enough to release all waiting threads, and then resets the event*
`BOOL PulseEvent(` `   HANDLE event)`	
event	The event to pulse
Returns TRUE on success	

Events are also used in overlapped structures. See Section 7.5 for examples and more information.

7.2.5 Interlocked Operations

The 32-bit APIs supplies three low-level functions that can be used in special situations or as primitives for building your own synchronization mechanisms. These are called the *interlocked* functions. The **Interlocked-Increment** function increments a value of type LONG and returns a result that is zero, positive, or negative. If the value of the variable becomes zero as a result of the increment operation, then the returned result is zero. Otherwise, the result has the same sign, but not necessarily the same value, as the variable that was incremented. **InterlockedDecrement** decrements a variable in the same way. The **InterlockedExchange** function replaces one value with another value and returns the replaced value. All three of these functions are atomic: they will not be interrupted once they start.

InterlockedIncrement	*Increments a variable and indicates if it became zero, positive, or negative*
`LONG InterlockedIncrement(` `   LPLONG value)`	
value	The value to increment
Returns 0 if the value became zero, or a value with the appropriate sign	

InterlockedDecrement	*Decrements a variable and indicates if it became zero, positive, or negative*
`LONG InterlockedDecrement(` `   LPLONG value)`	
value	The value to increment
Returns 0 if the value became zero, or a value with the appropriate sign	

InterlockedExchange	*Replaces a variable with the value indicated*

```
LONG InterlockedExchange(
    LPLONG target,
    LONG value)
```

target	The variable to replace
value	The value to use as the replacement

Returns the value of target prior to the exchange

7.3 Deadlocks, Starvation, and Other Synchronization Bugs

The reason you use the synchronization mechanisms described in the preceding sections is to prevent threads from colliding with one another when they access global resources. When used properly, the synchronization mechanisms accomplish this goal. Unfortunately, one of their problems is that they can breed their own special variety of bugs, both simple and complex. Several of these bugs are demonstrated in this section.

One classic synchronization problem is called the "dining philosophers" problem. You will find a solution to this problem in every textbook on operating systems. It may initially seem a bit contrived if this is the first time you have seen it, but it is a good metaphor for general multi-resource allocation problems. Framing the problem as a group of philosophers allows you to easily see and understand the concepts of *deadlock* and *starvation*.

Imagine that you have a square or round table with several people sitting around it. Typically the people are characterized as Chinese philosophers, hence the name of the problem. Each philosopher has a large bowl of food in front of him, one chopstick to his left, and one chopstick to his right. However, there is only one chopstick for each philosopher: the chopstick to the right of one philosopher is the same chopstick that is to the left of the next. (See Figure 7.2.) Ignore the hygiene issues of this arrangement for the moment, and also assume that there will be no cooperation or communication among the philosophers to modify their dilemma.

The philosophers either think or eat. Each philosopher sits back in his chair, thinks for a while, then gets hungry and decides to eat. In order to eat the philosopher must pick up the chopsticks on his left and right side. However, because of the chopstick arrangement, if either chopstick is in use then the philosopher must wait for his neighbor to finish eating. Assume that each philosopher picks up his left chopstick first, and then his right chopstick.

As you can see, the problem is conceptually simple. However, it represents a number of real-life problems in which threads must share global resources. Each philosopher represents a thread, and each chopstick represents a resource. Each thread must have two resources to complete its job, and

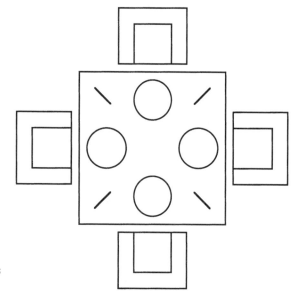

Figure 7.2

The table arrangement for the dining philosophers problem with four philosophers.

different threads are competing for the resources they need. For example, one thread might need the communications port and the printer to complete its task. Another might need the printer and exclusive access to a file. Yet another might need the same file and the communications port. This is exactly the sort of scenario that the dining-philosophers problem portrays.

Listing 7.10 shows an implementation of the dining-philosophers problem using mutexes to represent the chopsticks and threads to represent the philosophers.

Listing 7.10   *An implementation of the dining-philosophers problem*

```cpp
// dinphil.cpp

#include <windows.h>
#include <stdlib.h>
#include <iostream.h>

const INT numPhilosophers=3;
HANDLE chopsticks[numPhilosophers];
CHAR csStat[numPhilosophers+1];
CHAR pStat[numPhilosophers+1];

void PhilosopherThread(INT id)
{
  while (1)
```

```
  {
    //thinking
    Sleep(GetTickCount() % 50);

    // hungry, so picks up chopsticks
    WaitForSingleObject(chopsticks[id],
      INFINITE);
    csStat[id]='1';
    WaitForSingleObject(
      chopsticks[(id+1)%numPhilosophers],
      INFINITE);
    csStat[(id+1)%numPhilosophers]='1';
    pStat[id]='1';

    // eating
    cout << csStat << "  " << pStat << endl;
    Sleep(GetTickCount() % 50);

    pStat[id]='0';
    // done eating
    ReleaseMutex(chopsticks[id]);
    csStat[id]='0';
    ReleaseMutex(
      chopsticks[(id+1)%numPhilosophers]);
    csStat[(id+1)%numPhilosophers]='0';
  }
}

void main(void)
{
  HANDLE handles[numPhilosophers];
  DWORD threadID;
  INT i;

  csStat[numPhilosophers]='\0';
  pStat[numPhilosophers]='\0';

  // Create the chopstick mutexes
  for (i=0; i<numPhilosophers; i++)
    chopsticks[i] = CreateMutex(0, FALSE, 0);

  // Create the philosopher threads
  for (i=0; i<numPhilosophers; i++)
  {
    // create the philosopher threads
    handles[i]=CreateThread(0, 0,
      (LPTHREAD_START_ROUTINE) PhilosopherThread,
      (VOID *) i, 0, &threadID);
  }
```

| Listing 7.10 | *An implementation of the dining-philosophers problem (continued)* |

```
// wait for all threads to finish execution
WaitForMultipleObjects(numPhilosophers, handles,
  TRUE, INFINITE);

for (i=0; i<numPhilosophers; i++)
  CloseHandle(chopsticks[i]);

cout << "Done" << endl;
}
```

In Listing 7.10, the main program starts by initializing the mutexes and then creating the threads. As shown, the code will create three philosophers and three chopsticks. In each thread, the code simulates the philosophers' thinking by sleeping for a random amount of time. The thread then attempts to pick up two chopsticks using **WaitForSingleObject** on the left and right chopstick. As soon as it has both, the thread sleeps for a random amount of time to simulate the philosophers' eating, and then puts down its two chopsticks using **ReleaseMutex**.

The program in Listing 7.10 contains two arrays that help you see what is going on inside the program. When you run the program, it will print out the contents of both arrays. The **chStat** array is the chopstick status array. It shows which chopsticks are currently allocated to a philosopher. That is, **chStat** indicates which chopsticks are currently in somebody's hand because somebody either wants to eat or is in the process of eating. The **pStat** array indicates which philosophers are actually eating. In the three-philosopher case shown in Listing 7.10, only one philosopher can eat at a time.

This program seems simple enough, but when you run it, there is a problem. It will run for a bit and then stop. Run it again and it stops again. It may run for quite some time in certain cases, but eventually it will stop.

What is happening here is called *deadlock*. In this program, a deadlock occurs when every philosopher has one of the chopsticks in his left hand. No one can proceed because there are no right chopsticks to pick up, so everyone waits infinitely, and the program locks up. In the three-philosopher case, the probability of a deadlock is fairly high, so the program locks quickly.

There are two other problems with the code in Listing 7.10. Increase the number of philosophers to 20 and run the program again. The first problem you should notice is that the program probably does not lock up. With this many people eating, the probability of all 20 picking up their left chopsticks at the same time is very small, so the deadlock problem is *hidden*. You could test the program for quite some time and never see anything wrong, but the possibility of deadlock is still there. The fact that the program runs correctly for three days does not prove it to be bug-free—it just proves that you are lucky. It also shows how synchronization problems can lurk in code and avoid detection for quite some time.

You can see another problem by looking at the output, a sample of which is shown below for the 20-philosopher case. The left column shows the number of chopsticks held by philosophers, while the right column, shows how many people are actually eating.

```
11000111110011110111    00001000000000100000
11100111110011110111    01001000000000100000
11111011110011110111    01010000000000100000
11111111110011111111    01010000000001000000
11011111110011111111    10010000000001000000
11111111110011001111    10010000000010000000
11111111110011001111    00010000000010000001
01111111110010001111    00100000000010000001
00111111110010101111    00100000000100000001
00101111110010101111    01000000000100000001
00111111110011101111    01000000000100000010
10111111110101101100    01000000001000000000
10111111111001101100    01000000010000000000
10111111111011101110    01000000010000000100
10111111111111101111    00000000100000000100
11111111111111101111    10000000100000000100
11111111101111101111    10000000100000001000
11111111100111101001    00000000100000001001
11111111100111101011    00000000100000001001
11111111010111101111    00000001000000010001
11111111010111101111    00000010000000010001
01111111010111101111    00000010000000010010
```

Many people are waiting, but only two or three eat at one time, because a lot of mini-deadlocks occur at different points on the table.

Probably the easiest way to solve the deadlock problem here is to require each philosopher to not pick up any chopsticks unless he can pick up both at the same time. There are several ways to implement this behavior, but Windows makes it easy with the **WaitForMultipleObjects** function. **WaitForMultipleObjects**, when configured with its **waitAll** parameter set to TRUE, does not return until all of the requested objects are available. See Listing 7.11.

Listing 7.11   *An improved version of the dining-philosophers problem that eliminates deadlock*

```cpp
// dinphil2.cpp

#include <windows.h>
#include <stdlib.h>
#include <iostream.h>
```

Listing 7.11 *An improved version of the dining-philosophers problem that eliminates deadlock (continued)*

```
const INT numPhilosophers=20;
HANDLE chopsticks[numPhilosophers];
CHAR csStat[numPhilosophers+1];
CHAR pStat[numPhilosophers+1];

void PhilosopherThread(INT id)
{
  HANDLE cs[2];
  while (1)
  {
    //thinking
    Sleep(GetTickCount() % 50);

    // hungry, so picks up chopsticks
    cs[0] = chopsticks[id];
    cs[1] = chopsticks[(id+1)%numPhilosophers];
    WaitForMultipleObjects(2, cs, TRUE, INFINITE);
    csStat[id]='1';
    csStat[(id+1)%numPhilosophers]='1';
    pStat[id]='1';

    // eating
    cout << csStat << "   " << pStat << endl;
    Sleep(GetTickCount() % 50);

    pStat[id]='0';
    // done eating
    ReleaseMutex(chopsticks[id]);
    csStat[id]='0';
    ReleaseMutex(
      chopsticks[(id+1)%numPhilosophers]);
    csStat[(id+1)%numPhilosophers]='0';
  }
}

void main(void)
{
  HANDLE handles[numPhilosophers];
  DWORD threadID;
  INT i;

  csStat[numPhilosophers]='\0';
  pStat[numPhilosophers]='\0';

  // Create the chopstick mutexes
  for (i=0; i<numPhilosophers; i++)
    chopsticks[i] = CreateMutex(0, FALSE, 0);
```

```
// Create the philosopher threads
for (i=0; i<numPhilosophers; i++)
{
  // create the philosopher threads
  handles[i]=CreateThread(0, 0,
    (LPTHREAD_START_ROUTINE) PhilosopherThread,
    (VOID *) i, 0, &threadID);
}

// wait for all threads to finish execution
WaitForMultipleObjects(numPhilosophers, handles,
  TRUE, INFINITE);

for (i=0; i<numPhilosophers; i++)
  CloseHandle(chopsticks[i]);

cout << "Done" << endl;
}
```

In the three-philosopher case (and in all other cases), the code in Listing 7.11 eliminates deadlock. In the 20-philosopher case, it improves
throughput tremendously, as shown in the output sample below:

```
00001101101111110000   00001001001010100000
00001101101111110011   00001001001010100010
00001101101111111111   00001001001010101010
00001101101111110000   00001001001010100000
00001101101111110000   00001001001010100000
00001101101111110000   00001001001010100000
01111001110011111111   01010001010010101010
01111111110011111111   01010101010010101010
01111001110011111111   01010001010010101010
01111111110011111111   01010101010010101010
01111111110111001111   01010101010100001010
01111001110011111111   01010001010010101010
01111111110011111111   01010101010010101010
01111111110111001111   01010101010100001010
01101101101111111111   01001001001010101010
01111111110100001100   01010101010100001000
01111111110100011100   01010101010100010000
01111111110111001111   01010101010100001010
01101101101111111111   01001001001010101010
01101101111111111111   01001001010010101010
01111111110100001100   01010101010100001000
01111111110100001100   01010101010100001000
```

As you can see, about the same number of chopsticks are held by
philosophers, but many more philosophers eat at one time.

This new implementation has the potential for a problem of its own. Imagine that you are looking at a group of three philosophers at the 20-philosopher table. Let's call them A, B, and C for simplicity. Both A and C are eating. B would like to eat but has no utensils. Philosopher A finishes and puts down his chopsticks. Later, A starts eating again. Now C finishes and puts down his chopsticks. Before A finishes, C starts eating again. Now before C finishes, A starts eating again, and so on. If A and C get in a cycle like this, perhaps because they are sharing another resource that synchronizes their behavior, philosopher B starves to death.

There is no particularly simple way to prevent starvation in the dining-philosophers problem. One technique you can use is putting a timeout value in the call to **WaitForMultipleObjects** that represents a tolerable wait time. If B times-out while waiting to eat, he can then revert to picking up his chopsticks one at a time to break the cycle of A and C.

Another problem that you should be aware of when working with synchronized threads is called a *race condition*. Like the problems of deadlocks and starvation, race conditions are subtle and can lie hidden in code for quite some time before they manifest themselves.

Let's say that you have three threads accessing a resource. These three threads can access the resource simultaneously. Perhaps these three threads all want to read a certain data structure, and because they are only reading it, it is acceptable for them to access the data structure simultaneously. Now a fourth thread wants to write to the data structure. Because of the changes it has to make, any readers need to be eliminated so that the writer has exclusive access to the data structure during the write operation. Once the writer finishes, the readers can resume their activity.

The scenario described in the previous paragraph is known as the "readers/writers problem." Let's say that you think about this problem and you come up with code for the reader thread that looks like this:

```
Wait(writerEvent);
numReaders++;
if (numReaders==1)
  Reset(readerEvent);

... read the data structure ...

numReaders—;
if (numReaders==0)
  Set(readerEvent);
```

Each reader checks the **writerEvent** to make sure that the writer is not writing. If not, the reader increments the number of readers, and if it is one, resets the **readerEvent** to advise the writer that readers are working. When the last reader finishes reading, it sets the writer event so that the writer can work if it needs to.

You also create corresponding code for the writer that looks like this:

```
Wait(readerEvent);
Reset(writerEvent);

... write for awhile ...

Set(writerEvent);
```

The writer waits on the **readerEvent** so that it has exclusive access, then locks out readers by resetting the **writerEvent**.

This code looks good, but there are two problems. The first is that if multiple readers arrive continuously, **readerEvent** will never reach zero and the writer will starve. Let's ignore that problem. The second problem involves the way that the incrementing is done in the reader code. Assume that one reader is reading, and that the reader thread is about to finish. A second reader thread has just barely started: it has finished the line that waits on **WriterEvent**, but gets preempted just before the line that increments **numReaders**. Now the first reader thread gets a time slice, decrements **numReaders** to zero, and sets **readerEvent**. At this moment a writer starts and begins writing.

You can see the problem: now the reader just getting started will increment **numReaders**, but it is too late. A reader and a writer are in the data structure at the same time, colliding with each other. This situation is called a *race condition* because the two threads are racing each other for control. One thread usually has a much higher probability of winning, so the code *seems* OK when you test it, but every once in a while conditions line up just wrong and the program dies.

You prevent race conditions by firmly tying together competing threads with the *same* synchronizing mechanism. Listing 7.12 shows a solution to the readers/writers problem that uses a semaphore *shared by the reader and the writer*. This solution completely prevents race conditions because the readers and writers are interlocked with one another through a single synchronization mechanism.

Listing 7.12   *A valid solution to the readers-writers problem*

```
// rw.cpp

#include <windows.h>
#include <stdlib.h>
#include <iostream.h>

volatile INT readerCount=0;
HANDLE mutex;
HANDLE write;
```

Listing 7.12 *A valid solution to the readers-writers problem (continued)*

```
void ReaderThread(INT id)
{
  while (1)
  {
    // Simulate the reader processing
    Sleep(GetTickCount() % 100);

    // The reader needs to read
    WaitForSingleObject(mutex, INFINITE);
    readerCount++;
    if (readerCount==1)
      WaitForSingleObject(write, INFINITE);
    ReleaseMutex(mutex);

    // The reader is reading
    cout << readerCount << " readers"
      << endl;
    Sleep(GetTickCount() % 100);

    // The reader is done reading
    WaitForSingleObject(mutex, INFINITE);
    readerCount—;
    cout << readerCount << " readers"
      << endl;
    if (readerCount==0)
      ReleaseSemaphore(write, 1, 0);
    ReleaseMutex(mutex);
  }
}

void WriterThread(INT id)
{
  while (1)
  {
    // Simulate the write processing
    Sleep(GetTickCount() % 1000);

    // The writer needs to write
    cout << "writer " << id << " waiting"
      << endl;
    WaitForSingleObject(write, INFINITE);

    // The writer is writing
    cout << id << " writing\n";
    Sleep(GetTickCount() % 1000);
    cout << "writer " << id << " done"
      << endl;
```

```
    // The writer is done
    ReleaseSemaphore(write, 1, 0);
  }
}


const INT numReaders=6;
const INT numWriters=3;

void main(void)
{
  HANDLE handles[numReaders+numWriters];
  DWORD threadID;
  INT i;

  mutex = CreateMutex(0, FALSE, 0);
  write = CreateSemaphore(0, 1, 1, 0);

  // start readers
  for (i=0; i<numReaders; i++)
  {
    handles[i]=CreateThread(0, 0,
      (LPTHREAD_START_ROUTINE) ReaderThread,
      (VOID *) i, 0, &threadID);
  }

  // start writers
  for (i=0; i<numWriters; i++)
  {
    handles[i+numReaders]=CreateThread(0, 0,
      (LPTHREAD_START_ROUTINE) WriterThread,
      (VOID *) i, 0, &threadID);
  }

  // wait for all threads to finish execution
  WaitForMultipleObjects(numReaders+numWriters,
    handles, TRUE, INFINITE);

  CloseHandle(mutex);
  CloseHandle(write);
}
```

A good operating system book will discuss deadlocks, starvation, and race conditions in detail, and you might consider getting one if this material is new to you.

7.4 Wait Functions

Windows provides two wait functions, **WaitForSingleObject** and **WaitForMultipleObjects,** that allow you to "wait on handles." See Section 1.5 for a description of objects and handles in the 32-bit API. We have used these two functions extensively in the previous sections to wait on events, mutexes, and semaphores.

All handles have two states: *signaled* and *unsignaled*. The **WaitForSingleObject** function waits efficiently (blocks) until the handle it is waiting on becomes signaled.

WaitForSingleObject   *Causes a thread to wait for a signal*

```
DWORD WaitForSingleObject(
    HANDLE object,
    DWORD timeout)
```

object   The object to wait for

timeout   The maximum amount of time to wait, in milliseconds

Returns an error code or the event that caused it to stop waiting

---

WaitForSingleObject accepts a single object handle and a timeout value, and returns either when the object switches to the signaled state or when the timeout elapses. It returns with one of four values:

1. WAIT_FAILED on an error
2. WAIT_TIMEOUT if the timeout period elapsed
3. WAIT_OBJECT_0 if the object is signaled.
4. WAIT_ABANDONED if the object is a mutex and the thread owning the mutex died before calling the **ReleaseMutex** function to formally release the mutex. See Section 7.2.2.

The **WaitForMultipleObjects** function waits for multiple objects in either a one-of-many way or an all-of-many way.

WaitForMultipleObjects   *Causes a thread to delay waiting for one-of-many or*
                                all-of-many signals to occur

```
DWORD WaitForMultipleObjects(
    DWORD numObjects,
    CONST HANDLE * objectArray,
    BOOL waitForAll,
    DWORD timeout)
```

numObjects	Number of objects in objectArray
objectArray	An array of object handles to wait on
waitForAll	If TRUE, the function waits for all events to occur, otherwise for any one of them
timeout	The maximum amount of time to wait, in milliseconds

Returns an error code or the event that caused it to stop waiting.

The **WaitForMultipleObjects** function accepts an array of object handles, the number of handles in the array, a timeout value, and a boolean that switches it between one-of-many and all-of-many behavior. It returns the same values as **WaitForSingleObject**, but it can also indicate which of the several objects signaled the one-of-many case.

It is possible to wait on many objects in Windows, and each one tells you something different when it changes state. The list below summarizes the different objects and what they mean to the wait functions:

- Change function handle: Section 7.6 describes the **Find-FirstChangeNotification** function. The handle returned by this function changes to signaled when a change occurs in the specified directory.
- Console input: Chapter 14 describes consoles. A console-input handle changes to signaled when there is input available in the console's input buffer.
- Event: An event object is signaled when the event is Set, and unsignaled when it is Reset. An event object can start in a signaled or unsignaled state. An automatic event reverts to unsignaled as soon as a Wait function unblocks as a result of its being in the signaled state. Manual events must be set and reset manually. See Section 7.2.4.
- Mutex: A mutex object is signaled when no thread owns it, and is unsignaled when it is owned. A thread calls **ReleaseMutex** to give up ownership and signal it. See Section 7.2.2.
- Process: A process object is unsignaled while the process is active, and it signals when the process terminates. See Chapter 6.
- Semaphore: A semaphore object is signaled if its count is greater than zero, and unsignaled when the count equals zero. See Section 7.2.3.
- Thread: A thread object is unsignaled while the thread is active, and signaled when the thread terminates. See Chapter 6.

Certain other handles signal in some cases. For example, a file handle returned by **CreateFile** can signal when it is used in overlapped mode and the overlapped structure's event is set to NULL. However, the documentation clearly discourages such use. You should use only the handles listed above with the Wait functions.

The SYNCHRONIZE standard right enables an object to work with a Wait function. See Chapter 13 for information on standard rights.

7.5 Overlapped I/O

*Compatibility Note: The code in this section works properly in Windows 2000 but does not work in Windows 98 because the overlapped concept does not apply to files. See the **ReadFile** and **ReadFileEx** functions in the Win32 help file for further information.*

The APIs supports an asynchronous form of file access that allows you to start an I/O operation and then proceed with other activities. The technique is referred to as *overlapped I/O.* This capability exists in Windows for two reasons:

1. Overlapped I/O lets you create the impression of multi-threading without actually implementing a separate thread. In certain situations, this makes the code more compact, or lets you handle asynchronous file I/O more easily than a second thread would.

2. Overlapped I/O makes it possible for separate threads in a single program to manipulate the same file handle simultaneously. With overlapped I/O, each thread can keep track of its file position independently of other threads, and this lets threads simultaneously access the same pipe, file, and so on.

Asynchronous operations are extremely useful when you want to perform multiple file operations on the same file handle simultaneously. For example, in Section 8.5.2 a single named pipe is read in one thread and written in another. Overlapped I/O is the only way to handle this situation.

Overlapped file operations rely on events. See Section 7.2.4 for details on this object. Events are used with overlapped file operations to let the operation signal that the I/O request has completed.

To implement an asynchronous file operation, you must do the following:

1. Create the file, specifying a FILE_FLAG_OVERLAPPED flag when calling **CreateFile**

2. Create and initialize a synchronizing event (see Section 7.2.4)

3. Create and initialize an OVERLAPPED structure

4. Attempt to read from the file

5. If the read is successful, continue

6. If not, and the I/O operation is pending, continue, and check the event or **GetOverlappedResult** to know when it completes

The key step is step 6. Once you set up everything, you have a non-blocking way to access the file that also allows the operation to complete on its own. Listing 7.13 shows an implementation of the six steps described above.

Listing 7.13   *Overlapped file access*

```cpp
// fileovlp.cpp

#include <windows.h>
#include <iostream.h>

void main()
{
    HANDLE fileHandle;
    BOOL success;
    char s[300000];
    DWORD numRead;
    char filename[1000];
    OVERLAPPED overlappedInfo;
    HANDLE event;
    BOOL waitSuccess;

    // get the file name
    cout << "Enter filename: ";
    cin >> filename;

    // Open the file
    fileHandle = CreateFile(filename,
        GENERIC_READ, FILE_SHARE_WRITE,
        0, OPEN_EXISTING, FILE_FLAG_OVERLAPPED, 0);
    if (fileHandle == INVALID_HANDLE_VALUE)
    {
        cout << "Error number " << GetLastError()
            << endl;
        return;
    }

    // set up the overlapped structure
    overlappedInfo.Offset = 0;
    overlappedInfo.OffsetHigh = 0;
    event = CreateEvent(0, TRUE, FALSE, 0);
    overlappedInfo.hEvent = event;

    // Read from the file
    success = ReadFile(fileHandle, s, 100000,
        &numRead, &overlappedInfo);

    // wait for the operation to finish
```

| Listing 7.13 | *Overlapped file access (continued)* |

```
if (!success &&
    GetLastError() == ERROR_IO_PENDING)
{
    cout << "Error number = " << GetLastError()
        << endl;  //just to see it
    do
    {
        cout << "waiting...\n";
        // check for completion
        waitSuccess =
            WaitForSingleObject(event, 0);
    }
    while (waitSuccess == WAIT_TIMEOUT);
    // find out how many bytes were read
    GetOverlappedResult(fileHandle,
        &overlappedInfo, &numRead, FALSE);
}
// update the file pointer
overlappedInfo.Offset += numRead;
cout << numRead << endl;

// Close the file
CloseHandle(event);
CloseHandle(fileHandle);
}
```

To demonstrate this code, use it to open and read any existing file. Try it on both the hard disk and the floppy disk drive. Since the **ReadFile** statement in Listing 7.13 requests 100,000 bytes, the file needs to be fairly large, but it does not matter what the file contains. The program starts by requesting a file name and opening the file in the normal way. It then reads from the file asynchronously. This means that the program can go off and do whatever it likes while the I/O operation completes. In Listing 7.13, the code loops while waiting for completion, printing a message to stdout each time through the loop to show that it could be doing useful work. When working inside a normal event loop in a GUI application, you can have the event loop check for completion each time through. In an MFC program, you can handle the event in several different ways. See Section 7.7 for details.

Overlapped file access requires the use of an OVERLAPPED structure. This structure contains information about the starting file position for the operation, and also contains the synchronizing event. The OVERLAPPED structure contains the file position because **SetFilePointer** has no meaning for an asynchronous file access. In an asynchronously opened file, each process or thread maintains its own position information in its overlapped structure, and must update the information manually after each read or write operation. Multiple overlapped operations can occur simultaneously in the same file.

The program in Listing 7.13 initializes the **overlapped** structure just after it creates the file. It starts with the file offset at zero (it is permissible to start anywhere), and also creates the synchronizing event using the **CreateEvent** function (see Section 7.2.4). It is important that any synchronizing event used in an overlapped-file operation be a manual event, and start in a reset (FALSE) state, as shown in Listing 7.13.

The program passes the OVERLAPPED structure to the **ReadFile** function, which attempts to read from the file starting at the indicated position. If the read operation can return immediately with the requested data, it does so, but if it cannot, it signals that the I/O operation is pending and then returns. The program is now free to do whatever it wants—the requested operation will complete in the background, and the program can access the results in the buffer whenever it needs to.

The system signals that the I/O operation has finished by setting the synchronizing event in the OVERLAPPED structure. You can check the state of the event with the **GetOverlappedResult** function or by using the **Wait ForSingleObject** function on the event itself (see Section 7.4 for details). The **GetOverlappedResult** function also determines how many bytes the I/O operation transferred. This number indicates the new file position for sequential reads.

GetOverlappedResult   *Gets the result of the overlapped operation*

```
BOOL GetOverlappedResult(
    HANDLE fileHandle,
    LPOVERLAPPED overlapped,
    LPDWORD numTransfered,
    BOOL wait)
```

fileHandle	Handle to the file
overlapped	OVERLAPPED structure
numTransferred	Number of bytes transferred
wait	Whether or not the function should wait for completion

Returns TRUE on success. The function will return FALSE and ERROR_IO_PENDING if the I/O operation has not completed yet.

If you are reading sequentially in a loop, the **numTransferred** parameter returned by **GetOverlappedResult** should be added to the **Offset** field in the OVERLAPPED structure as shown in the example code. If you are reading random records, then this step is not necessary since the next read operation will set the **Offset** field to a new random location anyway.

Chapters 8, 11, and 14 contain good examples of the usefulness of over-lapped I/O. You can gain a better understanding of overlapping by examin-ing these examples closely.

Chapter 8 discusses network communications. Section 8.5.2 discusses a multi-threaded network client for a named pipe server. One thread of the client reads from the pipe while the other one writes to the pipe. The imple-mentation *must* use overlapped I/O because the client process can open only one connection to the named pipe. Overlapped I/O allows two threads to ac-cess the same pipe object simultaneously. In Listing 8.11, the core of the writ-ing thread looks like this:

Listing 7.14   *A code fragment from Listing 8.11 that demonstrates the writing thread of a multi-threaded network client using overlapped I/O*

```
while(1)
{
  cout << "Type text to send: ";
  cin.getline(textToSend, BUFSIZE);

  // Write message to named pipe
  WriteFile(msnpPipe,
    textToSend, strlen(textToSend) + 1,
    &numBytesWritten, &overlappedWrite)
  GetOverlappedResult(msnpPipe,
    &overlappedWrite, &numBytesWritten,
    TRUE);
  overlappedWrite.Offset += numBytesWritten;

} // while
```

It gets a line of text from the user and writes it to the pipe using over-lapped I/O. The core of the reading thread looks like this:

Listing 7.15   *A code fragment from Listing 8.11 that demonstrates the reading thread of a multi-threaded network client using overlapped I/O*

```
while (1)
{
  // Read a message from the server
  ReadFile(msnpPipeDup,
    textBuffer, BUFSIZE,
    &numBytesRead, &overlappedRead)
  GetOverlappedResult(msnpPipeDup,
    &overlappedRead, &numBytesRead,
    TRUE);
  overlappedRead.Offset += numBytesRead;
```

```
// send the message to the screen
cout << textBuffer << endl;
} /* while */
```

Note that the code in both threads calls the **GetOverlappedResult**
function immediately after the read and write operations, so it might as well
use synchronous calls to read and write. The overlapped I/O capability is important here, not because of background operation, but because it allows
both threads to work with a single pipe at the same time. See Section 8.5.2
for details.

Section 11.7 discusses a simple terminal emulator. It uses overlapped
I/O in a completely different way. Here the core of the program needs to be
able to accept characters from either the keyboard or the modem asynchronously. If a character arrives from the modem, the program must post it to
the screen immediately. At the same time, if the user types a character on the
keyboard, then the program must send it to the modem immediately. The
main loop of the program uses overlapped I/O on a communications port,
along with console signaling (see Section 7.4) to implement this behavior.

The program first calls **SetUpCommPort** to initialize the communications port for overlapped I/O. It then sets up read and write OVERLAPPED
structures for the port, as shown in the code fragment from Listing 11.3
below:

Listing 7.16   *A code fragment from Listing 11.3 that shows overlapped I/O being
used to read in the background from a communications port*

```
comHandle = SetupCommPort(portString);

// Set up for overlapped reading and
// writing on the port
overlappedRead.Offset =
   overlappedWrite.Offset = 0;
overlappedRead.OffsetHigh =
   overlappedWrite.OffsetHigh = 0;
readEvent = CreateEvent(0, TRUE, FALSE, 0);
writeEvent = CreateEvent(0, FALSE, FALSE, 0);
overlappedRead.hEvent = readEvent;
overlappedWrite.hEvent = writeEvent;

// Set up handles array
// for WaitForMultipleObjects
handles[0] = consoleStdin;
handles[1] = readEvent;

// Prime the pump by getting the read
// process started
```

Listing 7.16   *A code fragment from Listing 11.3 that shows overlapped I/O being used to read in the background from a communications port (continued)*

```
success = ReadFile(comHandle, &readBuffer, 1,
    &numRead, &overlappedRead);
do
{
    // Wait for either a keystroke or a
    // modem character. Time out after
    // 1000 seconds
    s = WaitForMultipleObjects(2, handles,
        FALSE, 1000000);
    if (s==WAIT_TIMEOUT)
        break;
    // If it is a character from the
    // keyboard then...
    else if (s==WAIT_OBJECT_0)
    {
    ... read from console and write to port ...
    }
    // If the character is coming in from
    // the comm port, then...
    else if (s==WAIT_OBJECT_0 + 1)
    {
        // Get the character from the port
        // and send it to the console
        success = GetOverlappedResult(comHandle,
            &overlappedRead, &numRead, TRUE);
        overlappedRead.Offset += numRead;
        WriteFile(consoleStdout, &readBuffer, 1,
            &numWrite, 0);
        ResetEvent(readEvent);
        // Wait for the next character
        // from the comm. port
        ReadFile(comHandle, &readBuffer, 1,
            &numRead, &overlappedRead);
    }
// Terminate when the user types an 'X'
} while  (writeBuffer != 'X');
```

The code in Listing 7.16 uses the **WaitForMultipleObjects** function to detect an arriving character from either the keyboard or the modem. A character arriving from the keyboard causes the console handle to signal (see Section 14.4 for a discussion of raw input from consoles). A character arriving from the modem triggers the read event in the OVERLAPPED structure. The incoming modem character is counted with the **GetOverlappedResult** function and written to the console. The code then calls another overlapped **ReadFile** operation so that it can wait for the next character from the modem. See Section 11.7 for details.

You can see in these two examples two different ways to use over-lapped I/O. Be certain that you use overlapped I/O whenever two threads need to access the same file or the same pipe simultaneously.

The 32-bit API supports a second and completely separate form of overlapped I/O that uses *completion routines*. Five functions support this facility: **ReadFileEx**, **WriteFileEx**, **WaitForSingleObjectEx**, **WaitForMultipleObjectsEx**, and **SleepEx**. A completion routine is a function called by the **ReadFileEx** or **WriteFileEx** function when an I/O operation completes and the thread enters an *alertable wait* via the **WaitForSingleObjectEx**, the **WaitForMultipleObjectsEx**, or the **SleepEx** function.

Listing 7.17 demonstrates the use of completion routines. When you run this program it will ask you for a file name. Use a file that is at least 10,000 bytes long, because the read statement attempts to read 10,000 bytes. Once the program finishes reading the data you will see output from the completion routine, and then the main function will print a message and terminate.

Listing 7.17   *Using completion routines*

```
// fileovex.cpp

#include <windows.h>
#include <iostream.h>

VOID WINAPI CompletionRoutine(
   DWORD error, DWORD transferred,
   LPOVERLAPPED overlapped)
{
   if (error != 0)
   {
      cout << "Completion Error = "
         << error << endl;
      return;
   }
   // update the file pointer
   overlapped->Offset += transferred;
   cout << "Inside completion routine. \n";
   cout << "Number of bytes read = ";
   cout << transferred << endl;
}

void main()
{
   HANDLE fileHandle;
   BOOL success;
   char s[300000];
   char filename[1000];
   OVERLAPPED overlappedInfo;
   HANDLE event;
```

Listing 7.17   *Using completion routines (continued)*

```
// get the file name
cout << "Enter filename: ";
cin >> filename;

// Open the file
fileHandle = CreateFile(filename, GENERIC_READ,
    0, 0, OPEN_EXISTING,
    FILE_FLAG_OVERLAPPED, 0);
if (fileHandle == INVALID_HANDLE_VALUE)
{
    cout << "Error number " << GetLastError()
       << endl;
    return;
}

// set up the overlapped structure
overlappedInfo.Offset = 0;
overlappedInfo.OffsetHigh = 0;
event = CreateEvent(0, TRUE, FALSE, 0);
overlappedInfo.hEvent = event;

// Read from the file
success = ReadFileEx(fileHandle, s, 10000,
    &overlappedInfo, CompletionRoutine);
if (!success)
{
    cout << "Error number " << GetLastError()
       << endl;
    return;
}

// Sleep until I/O is complete
SleepEx(INFINITE, TRUE);
cout << "\nSleep complete.\n";

// Close the file
CloseHandle(event);
CloseHandle(fileHandle);
}
```

In Listing 7.17, the code uses the **CreateFile** function to open the file in overlapped mode. It then initializes an overlapped structure as described earlier. The call to **ReadFileEx** specifies the completion routine, which you will find at the top of the listing.

ReadFileEx	*Reads bytes from a file and calls a completion routine when the read operation is complete*

```
BOOL ReadFileEx(
    HANDLE file,
    LPVOID buffer,
    DWORD requestedBytes,
    LPOVERLAPPED overlapped,
    LPOVERLAPPED_COMPLETION_ROUTINE compRoutine)
```

file	File handle created with **CreateFile**
buffer	Buffer to hold the read bytes
requestedBytes	The number of bytes desired
overlapped	Pointer to overlapped structure. See Section 6.5
compRoutine	The address of the completion routine to call

Returns TRUE on success

The call to **ReadFileEx** is very similar to a call to **ReadFile** (see Section 2.7). **ReadFileEx** does not return the number of bytes read (this value is instead passed to the completion routine), but it does accept the address of the completion routine it should call when its I/O operation finishes.

After calling **ReadFileEx**, the main function calls **SleepEx**. This function causes the main thread to sleep until the timeout value expires or until the I/O operation completes.

SleepEx	*Causes a thread to delay for a fixed number of milliseconds or until an I/O operation completes*

```
DWORD SleepEx(
    DWORD time,
    BOOL alertable)
```

time	The amount of time to sleep, in milliseconds
alertable	Set to TRUE if the function should return after an I/O completion

Returns 0 on timeout or WAIT_IO_COMPLETION if an I/O operation completed

Since the code in Listing 7.17 passes TRUE to **SleepEx**, the main thread is in an *alertable wait* state. If either a **ReadFileEx** or a **WriteFileEx** operation completes, then the **SleepEx** function will return once the completion routine finishes execution. In Listing 7.17, the call to **SleepEx** returns once **CompletionRoutine** finishes.

Completion routines have a standard format.

FileIOCompletionRoutine   *The standard format for an I/O completion routine*

```
VOID WINAPI FileIOCompletionRoutine(
    DWORD error,
    DWORD transferred,
    LPOVERLAPPED overlapped)
```

error	An error code
transferred	Number of bytes transferred in theI/O operation
overlapped	An overlapped structure
Returns nothing	

As shown in Listing 7.17, the completion routine receives a number of things: an error code from the I/O operation, the number of bytes transferred during the operation, and a pointer to the overlapped structure used in the call to **ReadFileEx** or **WriteFileEx,** so that the completion routine can update the structure.

When do you use completion routines? This facility accomplishes approximately the same thing as normal overlapped I/O. However, in certain situations where many overlapped operations are in process at once, completion routines can simplify your code. For example, imagine that you are designing a server that must talk to several clients simultaneously, and each client can be in one of several states. With completion routines, you can read from the client, specify a completion routine that will handle the client's response appropriately, and then forget about that client. With normal overlapped I/O you would have to build a case statement instead, which can be structurally annoying. However, the two techniques accomplish the same goal, and you should pick the one with which you feel most comfortable.

7.6 Change Functions

The 32-bit APIs supports a facility called *change notification,* which allows an application to detect changes in files and directories. (See Section 4.7 for a description of the facility and its uses.)

The change notification facility uses *change handles* to notify the program of changes. A change handle is initially un-signaled but changes to signaled when the appropriate directory is modified. You use the Wait functions (Section 7.4) in your code to detect when a change handle signals.

Listing 7.18 demonstrates change handles. When you run this program, it will display a line that indicates that it is waiting. If you use the File Manager or a second DOS shell to rename a file in c:\, then the program will indicate that a change occurred and then wait for a second change. Once the second change occurs, the program terminates.

Listing 7.18   *A demonstration of the change-notification facility*

```cpp
//filefind.cpp


#include <iostream.h>
#include <windows.h>


int main(int argc, char *argv[])
{
    HANDLE changeHandle;


    // Wait for a file name change in the
    // current directory
    changeHandle = FindFirstChangeNotification("c:\\",
        FALSE, FILE_NOTIFY_CHANGE_FILE_NAME);
    cout << "Waiting for a change ..."
        << endl;
    WaitForSingleObject(changeHandle, INFINITE);
    cout << "A file name changed." << endl;


    // Wait for a second change
    FindNextChangeNotification(changeHandle);
    cout << "Waiting for a 2nd change ..."
        << endl;
    WaitForSingleObject(changeHandle, INFINITE);
    cout << "A file name changed." << endl;


    // quit
    FindCloseChangeNotification(changeHandle);
    return( 0 );
}
```

The program in Listing 7.18 starts by calling the **FindFirstChange Notification** function.

FindFirstChangeNotification   *Returns a change handle that signals when the specified change occurs in the specified directory*

```
HANDLE FindFirstChangeNotification(
   LPCTSTR path,
   BOOL watchSubTree,
   DWORD flags)
```

path	The path of the directory to watch
watchSubTree	Indicates whether or not to watch all subtrees of the specified directory
flags	Indicates the changes to watch for

Returns a change handle or INVALID_HANDLE_VALUE on error

The **FindFirstChangeNotification** function can detect any or all of the following changes in the specified directory or in the specified directory and all of its subtrees:

- FILE_NOTIFY_CHANGE_FILE_NAME: upon renames, creations, and deletions of files
- FILE_NOTIFY_CHANGE_DIR_NAME: upon renames, creations, and deletions of directories
- FILE_NOTIFY_CHANGE_ATTRIBUTES: upon changes to attribute bits in any file
- FILE_NOTIFY_CHANGE_SIZE: upon changes to file of any file
- FILE_NOTIFY_CHANGE_LAST_WRITE: upon changes to the last-write time of any file
- FILE_NOTIFY_CHANGE_SECURITY: upon changes to the security descriptors of any file or directory

The function returns a *change handle*. You can use this handle in any Wait function. Once one of the specified changes occurs, the change handle is signaled.

The program next calls the **FindNextChangeNotification** function. This function resets the change handle so that it can signal again on the next change.

FindNextChangeNotification   *Resets a change handle so that it signals again when the specified change occurs in the specified directory*

```
BOOL FindNextChangeNotification(
HANDLE changeHandle)
```

changeHandle	Handle created by FindFirstChangeNotification

Returns TRUE on success

When you are finished using a change handle, call the **FindClose ChangeNotification** function.

FindCloseChangeNotification   *Closes a change handle*

```
BOOL FindCloseChangeNotification(
    HANDLE changeHandle)
```

changeHandle   Handle created by FindFirstChangeNotification to
                                      be closed

Returns TRUE on success

The following section demonstrates how to integrate the change functions into a normal MFC program.

7.7 Integrating Synchronization into MFC Programs

All of the sample code in this chapter is in simple text programs designed to demonstrate synchronization. In these examples, the blocking behavior of functions like **WaitForSingleObject** is acceptable. In a GUI application using the 32-bit APIs or MFC, however, blocking is a problem because it shuts down the event loop.

For example, if you want to create an MFC program that waits for a file change as demonstrated in Section 7.6, you cannot simply call **WaitForSingleObject** with an infinite timeout value, and then wait. An MFC program must return to the event loop frequently so that it can continue processing user events. One solution is to use the **OnIdle** member function of **CWinApp** and poll the change handle using a timeout value of zero in **WaitForSingleObject**. However, this misses the whole point of the Wait functions. The **WaitForSingleObject** function waits efficiently if you let it, but polling destroys that efficiency.

The code in Listing 7.19 demonstrates how to wait efficiently using **WaitForSingleObject** in an MFC program. When you run this program, it will display a button that you can push at any time. The application will beep and display a message box in response to a button click. The program also contains a call to **FindFirstChangeNotification**, so if you rename a file in the current directory, a dialog will appear telling you that the program detected the change. The program monitors the change handle returned by **FindFirstChangeNotification** efficiently and recognizes the change immediately.

Listing 7.19   *An MFC program that uses* **WaitForSingleObject** *to efficiently wait on a change handle*

```
// mfc.cpp

#include <afxwin.h>

#define IDB_BUTTON 100
#define FIND_MSG "find change message"

// Declare the application class
class CButtonApp : public CWinApp
{
public:
   virtual BOOL InitInstance();
};

// Create an instance of the application class
CButtonApp ButtonApp;

// Declare the main window class
class CButtonWindow : public CFrameWnd
{
   CButton *button;
   static UINT findMsg;
public:
   CButtonWindow();
   ~CButtonWindow();
   afx_msg void HandleButton();
   afx_msg LONG FindHandler( UINT param1,
      LONG param2 );

   DECLARE_MESSAGE_MAP()
};

// declare the static variable in CButtonWindow
UINT CButtonWindow::findMsg =
   ::RegisterWindowMessage(FIND_MSG);

// The message handler function
void CButtonWindow::HandleButton()
{
   Beep(700,100);
   MessageBox("Button pushed", "Dialog", MB_OK);
}

// The message handler for file changes
LONG CButtonWindow::FindHandler( UINT wParam,
   LONG lParam )
```

```
{
   Beep(500,500);
   MessageBox( "A file changed",
      "Find Dialog", MB_ICONINFORMATION );
   return 0;
}


// The message map
BEGIN_MESSAGE_MAP(CButtonWindow, CFrameWnd)
   ON_COMMAND(IDB_BUTTON, HandleButton)
   ON_REGISTERED_MESSAGE( findMsg, FindHandler )
END_MESSAGE_MAP()


// The InitInstance function is called once
// when the application first executes
BOOL CButtonApp::InitInstance()
{
   m_pMainWnd = new CButtonWindow();
   m_pMainWnd->ShowWindow(m_nCmdShow);
   m_pMainWnd->UpdateWindow();

   return TRUE;
}


// The thread that waits for the file change
// in the background
VOID FindThread(VOID)
{
   HANDLE changeHandle;
   UINT threadMsg;

   Beep(1000, 1000);

   // Register a custom message that the message
   // map will recognize
   threadMsg = RegisterWindowMessage(
      FIND_MSG );
   // wait for the first change
   changeHandle = FindFirstChangeNotification("c:\\",
      TRUE, FILE_NOTIFY_CHANGE_FILE_NAME);
   WaitForSingleObject(changeHandle, INFINITE);
   // inform the main event loop of the change
   ::SendMessage( ButtonApp.m_pMainWnd->m_hWnd,
      threadMsg, 0, 0 );
}


// The constructor for the window class
CButtonWindow::CButtonWindow()
```

Listing 7.19   An MFC program that uses **WaitForSingleObject** to efficiently wait
on a change handle

```
{
   CRect r;
   DWORD threadId;

   // Create the window itself
   Create(NULL,
      "CButton Tests",
      WS_OVERLAPPEDWINDOW,
      CRect(0,0,200,200));

   // Get the size of the client rectangle
   GetClientRect(&r);
   r.InflateRect(-20,-20);

   // Create a button
   button = new CButton();
   button->Create("Push me",
      WS_CHILD|WS_VISIBLE|BS_PUSHBUTTON,
      r,
      this,
      IDB_BUTTON);

   findMsg = RegisterWindowMessage(
      FIND_MSG );
   CreateThread(0, 0,
      (LPTHREAD_START_ROUTINE)FindThread,
      0, 0, &threadId);
}

// The destructor for the window class
CButtonWindow::~CButtonWindow()
{
   delete button;
   CFrameWnd::~CFrameWnd();
}
```

The code in Listing 7.19 creates a separate thread and a custom message to wait efficiently. The program creates the thread in the window's constructor, but you can create it anywhere in your own applications. The thread registers a custom window message, requests a file-change notification in the current directory, and then waits on the change handle. When a change occurs, the thread sends a message to the message map and terminates.

The message map for the **CButtonWindow** class contains an ON_REGISTERED_MESSAGE handler for the custom message generated by the thread.

When the message map sees the thread's message, it calls the **FindHandler** function. This function simply displays a message box.

You can apply the technique demonstrated here to efficiently wait on any object in an MFC program. For example, you might want to wait on the event returned by an overlapped I/O operation, or wait for a mutex to change to signaled. The separate thread shown above allows the event loop to proceed while the Wait function blocks. The custom message lets the thread inject a message into the program's event loop when the object is signaled, so that the program can respond appropriately.

For more information on MFC programming, see the book *Visual C++: Developing Professional Applications for Windows 98 and NT using MFC,* by Marshall Brain and Lance Lovette, ISBN 0-13-085121-3.

7.8 Conclusion

This chapter has covered several diverse but related topics, including Windows synchronization mechanisms, synchronization bugs, the wait functions, and file overlapping.

This chapter also demonstrates how to integrate the Wait functions into normal MFC applications. Chapters 8, 11, and 14 use these concepts extensively and contain further examples.

Network Communications

*W*indows *is meant to be used on a network. It is designed from the ground up to interact with other Windows machines. The 32-bit APIs therefore offers several different software abstractions for communicating over the net, both with other Windows machines and with other TCP/IP machines.*

In this chapter you will learn about the four different techniques that are used for network communications: mailslots, named pipes, UDP, and TCP. Sample code demonstrates both simple connections and more advanced application ideas. The capabilities discussed here can be used in your own applications to provide full network interconnectivity on simple local nets as well as on worldwide TCP/IP networks. You can also use the techniques discussed in Section 7.7 to integrate these concepts into MFC code.

Compatibility Note: All of the code in this chapter works identically in both Windows 2000 and Windows 98, with one exception. At the time of publication, it is not possible to create a named-pipe server in Windows 98.

8.1 The Possibilities

If you have never programmed with a network operating system before, you may have trouble imagining what is possible, or why network programming is so exciting and versatile. The following list describes five different programs and shows how each makes use of the network.

1. A multi-player game: Say that you want to create a multi-player game that runs on a network. For example, you might create a flight simulator that lets several people fly separate airplanes and have dogfights with one another. Or you might want to have several players run a dungeon-type adventure game on their machines, and then link the machines through the network so that the different players can "see" and "talk to" each other in the dungeon. One easy way to implement games like these is to have each copy of the game broadcast packets of information to all other copies of the game running on the network.

2. Finger: All UNIX machines support a program called Finger, which lets you see information about other users on other machines on the network. For example, if you type "finger brain@iftech.com" from a UNIX machine connected to the Internet, you will receive information about the user named "brain" on the specified machine. The Finger program forms a point-to-point connection using TCP packets to a Finger server on the remote machine, and retrieves the data.

3. Chat: The Chat program that comes with Windows 2000 forms a point-to-point connection to the machine that you wish to chat with, and then sends the characters typed by both users back and forth over the network.

4. Client/server applications: Many database engines act as "servers" that allow multiple "clients" to connect to them through the network. The client forms a connection to the server, and then sends a packet requesting information from the database. The server responds to the request by sending the data back over the network. Client/server architectures like this are becoming very popular, not only for databases but also for graphical information, conferencing, information distribution, and so on.

5. Bulletin boards: A network-based bulletin board would also act in a client/server relationship, with the bulletin board itself as the server. A user wanting to access the bulletin board would run a special client that would connect to the server and begin making requests for information from the bulletin board.

You will find that network connections tend to come in three general forms, as shown in Figure 8.1:

1. Two programs that can form a direct connection between one another and send data back and forth, as with the Chat program.

2. Client/server relationships, in which a central server accepts multiple connections and responds to all clients simultaneously.

3. Broadcast mode, in which several or many programs listen on the network simultaneously. When one of the programs wants to signal the

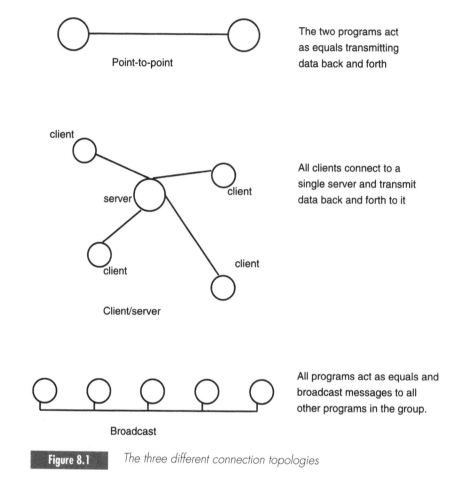

Point-to-point

The two programs act
as equals transmitting
data back and forth

Client/server

All clients connect to a
single server and transmit
data back and forth to it

Broadcast

All programs act as equals and
broadcast messages to all
other programs in the group.

Figure 8.1   *The three different connection topologies*

others, it broadcasts a single packet that is heard by all listeners. Many game programs use this configuration.

Each mode has advantages and disadvantages, but one approach is generally best for any given application.

8.2 Understanding Your Options

There are many different ways for you to access the network from the programs that you write, and one of these techniques involves absolutely no work at all on your part. It is important that you recognize that the trivial technique is a viable way to perform network communications, because it often simplifies program design. More-advanced techniques let you form dedicated network connections between specific programs running on different machines, and therefore give you better control over when and how data flows between the source and destination. This section will help you to understand all of the options that are available.

The word *network* is normally used to mean several different things. For example, you might use the words "the network" to mean a collection of interconnected machines that act together as a single, amorphous system. You might say, "Let me log into the network and print that file for you." On the other hand, the word "network" often refers to the cable and adapter cards that make up the interconnection scheme between all of the individual machines. For example, you might say, "I've installed an Ethernet network," or "The network is down today; you can still use your machine but it cannot talk to anybody else." Another way to think of a network is as a set of specific software protocols used to standardize communications between machines. For example, UNIX machines normally communicate over "TCP/IP networks," while Windows machines natively communicate on "NetBEUI networks." We tend to use these words interchangeably, but it is important to recognize the differences. In this chapter, the word "network" is generally used in the second and third senses, to imply specific interconnections between individual machines at either a wiring or a protocol level.

Figure 8.2 shows a typical small network. Each machine on the net has a network adapter and a cable that connects it to the other machines. Note two things from this diagram. First, each machine has a name, and this name uniquely identifies it on the network. Second, in any small Windows network, each machine can communicate with any other. If you know a machine's name, then you can form an immediate network connection to it.

Data is transmitted on the network in *packets*. For example, if the machine named "klondike" in Figure 8.1 wants to send 100K bytes of data specifically to the machine called "lancaster," it first communicates with

Figure 8.2 *A typical small network. Each machine has a name and can communicate with any other*

lancaster to establish a connection, and then sends the data in packets of perhaps 1K bytes each. Each packet contains a header that identifies the packet and the recipient. The network adapter on klondike waits for an opportunity to access the network cable (in Ethernet systems it waits for the cable to become idle and then transmits, while in token-ring systems it waits for an empty token to arrive and fills it), and then transmits the packet. The recipient receives the packet, recognizes itself as the recipient by examining the packet's header, and uses the data in the packet appropriately. Many machines can access the net simultaneously by interleaving their packets, giving the impression of many simultaneous network conversations happening at once.

Network connections come in two flavors: point-to-point and broadcast. In a point-to-point connection, you indicate a specific recipient machine and communicate with only that machine. This type of connection has two advantages: it is secure, and it is dependable. Once you have established a point-to-point connection, the delivery of the packets is guaranteed. If the connection breaks (for example, because the application on the recipient machine terminates), the transport mechanism responsible for sending the packets realizes the problem and informs you. Client/server systems use multiple point-to-point connections to the server.

Broadcast connections allow you to send packets to many machines at once, but the link is in one direction only. You have no way of knowing which machines actually receive any packet without having them all transmit a packet back. Unfortunately, the network traffic created by such an arrangement makes acknowledgment impractical. You will therefore use point-to-point connections for bi-directional communications in which you need to know that the data actually arrived. You will use broadcast communications when you need to send one packet to many recipients and guaranteed delivery is not important.

There are at least four different ways to communicate over a network in Windows.

1. The simplest way is through a normal file. If you use the File Manager to connect to a hard disk on another system and then copy a file to that hard disk, you have effectively communicated over the network using almost no code at all. If many other machines are also connected to that same hard disk, then you can essentially broadcast the contents of the file to many machines at once. Windows completely abstracts away the network in this case, and all that you have to do is call the **CopyFile** function (discussed in Chapter 2) to use the network. The advantage of this scheme is its simplicity. The disadvantage is the relative slowness that comes from opening a file and writing to a hard disk. If all that you want to do is transmit a few characters, then the overhead of opening, closing, and erasing many small files becomes quite large. However, if you want to move several megabytes of data

around on the network and many machines need to be able to see it, then the file approach is probably best.

2. Remote Procedure Calls also communicate over the network, and they do all the work for you. RPCs use an abstraction based on function calls, so a normal function call that you make in an application ends up getting transmitted over the network and executed on another machine. It is extremely easy to set up client/server systems using RPCs, and this is the preferred way to create such systems, not only because it is easy, but because it allows Windows and UNIX machines to intercommunicate. See Chapter 9 for details on RPCs.

3. Another way to transmit data on the network is through "mailslot." Mailslots are one-directional and are generally used as a broadcast mechanism. One machine sends a message, and the message appears on all other machines on the network. Any machine that is running a program listening to the appropriate mailslot gets the message. The advantages of mailslots are their ease of use and speed. To get a message to 20 different machines, you simply send it once and all recipients receive it. The disadvantage is that you have no way of knowing that the message was received. In network parlance, mailslots form an "unreliable connection," and data delivery is not guaranteed. In many applications, however, reliable delivery is not important, so mailslots are appropriate and easy to use.

4. A named pipe forms point-to-point connections between two programs. Named pipes are also used to implement client/server connections. The advantage of a named pipe is that it forms a reliable connection. You form the connection specifically, and if it breaks, you learn about it as soon as you try to use the pipe. For example, if the server goes down, the client gets official notification of it when it next tries to access the pipe. Therefore, the client knows about the problem immediately. The disadvantage of a named pipe is that the point-to-point nature of the connections can lead to inefficiencies. For example, if a server wants to send the same message to 20 connected clients, it must do so by sending the message 20 times, once down each pipe.

Named pipes and mailslots are the two native and preferred mechanisms for communicating between Windows machines. If you need to communicate on TCP/IP networks, however, particularly networks of UNIX machines, you will want to use the TCP or UDP connection mechanisms. Generally speaking, TCP is a point-to-point scheme similar to a named pipe, while UDP is a connectionless system that works in broadcast mode like a mailslot. You use TCP for the same applications that you would named pipes, while UDP and mailslots perform the same tasks. See Section 8.6 for details.

8.3 Mailslots

One of the simplest ways to perform network communications in Windows is through a mailslot. Mailslots provide a one-directional communication path from the sender to one or more recipients on the same network segment. You use mailslots when you do not particularly care whether or not the data actually arrives, or when you want to send one piece of data to many recipients at once.

For example, say that you want to create a status-board application. You have probably seen a status board in many office environments; they are particularly common in large real-estate or law firms. The board lists everyone in the office and whether each person is currently "in" or "out." If the person is out, the board normally says where the person has gone and when he or she expects to return. This system informs the secretary and other employees of everyone's location.

You can easily create a program with status-board functionality using mailslots. Figure 8.3 shows a view of the application. Each user would run a copy of the program on his or her workstation to see where everyone is.

This application would use mailslots in the following way: Whenever a copy of the program begins execution, it would broadcast a message onto the network using a well-known mailslot name. For example, all copies of the program might automatically broadcast to a mailslot named "status." The startup message would indicate that a new copy of the program is running and needs to be updated. All other copies of the program on the network

Name	In	Out	Reason
Marshall Brain	X		
Kelly Campbell		X	Meeting in Raleigh, back at 2:00
Lance Lovette	X		
Leigh Clarke	X		
Shay Woodard		X	Gone with Kelly

Name: Marshall Brain   Status: ● In   ○ Out

Reason:

Figure 8.3 *A status-board application*

would have *mailslot servers* open on their machines, using the well-known name for the name of the mailslot. Each copy of the program would hear the message from the new copy that has just started, and they would each send back a response containing their user's name and status.

During the day, whenever the user changed his or her status, the application would broadcast a message, indicating the change, onto the net. All other copies of the program would receive the message and update their displays appropriately.

Mailslots are extremely easy to create, and reading and writing are done using the normal **ReadFile** and **WriteFile** file commands discussed in Chapter 2. When creating the mailslot, a special path name passed to the **CreateMailslot** function causes the system to create a mailslot rather than a normal file. The following example demonstrates how to use a mailslot in a very simple program.

Listing 8.1 shows a piece of code that opens and then reads from a mailslot. This piece of code demonstrates a *mailslot server*. Listing 8.2 demonstrates how to create and write to a mailslot as a *mailslot client*. If you run these two programs simultaneously on one workstation, the writer will send a message every five seconds and the reader will receive it. The writer broadcasts to all machines on the network, so if you run multiple copies of the reader on different machines, all of them will see the message produced by the writer. Alternatively, you can run multiple writers on the net, and any copies of the reader will see the messages from all of them.

Listing 8.1	*A program that creates a mailslot server and reads from it*

```
// sms_recv.cpp

// Usage: sms_recv

#include <windows.h>
#include <iostream.h>

int main()
{
  char toDisptxt[80];
  HANDLE hSMS_Slot;
  DWORD nextSize;
  DWORD Msgs;
  DWORD NumBytesRead;
  BOOL Status;

  /* Create a mailslot for receiving messages */
  hSMS_Slot=CreateMailslot("\\\\.\\mailslot\\sms",
    0, 0, (LPSECURITY_ATTRIBUTES) NULL);
```

| Listing 8.1 | *A program that creates a mailslot server and reads from it (continued)* |

```
/* Check and see if the mailslot was created */
if (hSMS_Slot == INVALID_HANDLE_VALUE)
{
  cerr << "ERROR: Unable to create mailslot"
    << endl;
  return (1);
}


/* Repeatedly check for messages until the
   program is terminated */
while(1)
{
  Status=GetMailslotInfo(hSMS_Slot,
    (LPDWORD) NULL, &nextSize, &Msgs,
    (LPDWORD) NULL);
  if (!Status)
  {
    cerr << "ERROR: Unable to get status."
      << endl;
    CloseHandle(hSMS_Slot);
    return (1);
  }

  /* If messages are available, then get them */
  if (Msgs)
  {

    /* Read the message and check to see if
       read was successful */
    if (!ReadFile(hSMS_Slot, toDisptxt, nextSize,
      &NumBytesRead, (LPOVERLAPPED) NULL))
    {
      cerr
        << "ERROR: Unable to get status."
        << endl;
      CloseHandle(hSMS_Slot);
      return (1);
    }

    /* Display the Message */
    cout << toDisptxt << endl;
  }
  else
    /* Check for new messages twice a second */
    Sleep(500);
} /* while */
}
```

Listing 8.2   *A program that writes to a mailslot every five seconds*

```c
// sms_send.c

// Usage: sms_send

#include <windows.h>
#include <iostream.h>
#include <string.h>

int main()
{
  char toSendTxt[100], buffer[100];
  DWORD bufferLen=100;
  HANDLE hSMS_Slot;
  BOOL Status;
  DWORD NumBytesWritten;

  /* Create the mailslot file handle for
     sending messages */
  hSMS_Slot=CreateFile("\\\\*\\mailslot\\sms",
    GENERIC_WRITE, FILE_SHARE_READ,
    (LPSECURITY_ATTRIBUTES) NULL,
    OPEN_EXISTING,
    FILE_ATTRIBUTE_NORMAL,
    (HANDLE) NULL);

  /* Check and see if the mailslot file was
     opened, if not terminate program */
  if (hSMS_Slot == INVALID_HANDLE_VALUE)
  {
    cerr << "ERROR: Unable to create mailslot"
      << endl;
    return (1);
  }

  /* form string to send */
  GetComputerName(buffer, &bufferLen);
  strcpy(toSendTxt, "Test string from ");
  strcat(toSendTxt, buffer);

  /* Repeatedly send message until program
     is terminated */
  while(1)
  {
    cout << "Sending..." << endl;
    /* Write message to mailslot */
    Status=WriteFile(hSMS_Slot,
      toSendTxt, (DWORD) strlen(toSendTxt)+1,
      &NumBytesWritten, (LPOVERLAPPED) NULL);
```

Listing 8.2 *A program that writes to a mailslot every five seconds (continued)*

```
  /* If error occurs when writing to mailslot,
     terminate program */
  if (!Status)
  {
    cerr << "ERROR: Unable to write to mailslot"
      << endl;
    CloseHandle(hSMS_Slot);
    return (1);
  }

  /* Wait sending the message again */
  Sleep(4800);
  } /* while*/
}
```

The programs shown in Listings 8.1 and 8.2 were made as simple as possible so that you can easily see the steps necessary to transmit and receive data through a mailslot. Listing 8.1 shows how to create a mailslot and read from it. This form of mailslot is referred to as a *server*. The **CreateMailslot** function creates the server.

CreateMailslot *Creates a mailslot that you can then read from*

```
HANDLE CreateMailslot(
   LPTSTR name,
   DWORD maxMsg,
   DWORD readTimeout,
   LPSECURITY_ATTRIBUTES security)
```

name	The name of the mailslot
maxMsg	Max message size, or 0 for no max
readTimeout	Zero or MAILSLOT_WAIT_FOREVER
security	Security attributes. See Chapter 10

Returns a handle to the mailslot or INVALID_HANDLE_VALUE

The **CreateMailslot** function creates a mailslot server on the local machine. The server is a queue that holds messages received until you read them using the **ReadFile** function. The queue stores messages in the order of their arrival. You can read from the handle returned by **CreateMailslot.**

If you want to create a group of programs that all communicate through the same mailslot, you must make sure that all of them are using the same name. The name of the mailslot must be of the form "\\.\mailslot\[path] name." This looks like a file name, and it acts like a file name in that the normal **ReadFile** command works to read from the mailslot. Messages that arrive are buffered in a first-in-first-out queue. However, no actual file is created by the function: The mailslot is held in memory. A typical mailslot name is shown in Listing 8.1. It is also possible to add paths to further categorize mailslots, and you will see an example of this below.

When you create the mailslot, you can specify the maximum message length, as well as the readTimeout. Mailslots can send no more than 400 bytes over the network at one time. You can set the timeout value to 0, in which case any read operations will be non-blocking. That is, as soon as you call **ReadFile,** the function will return immediately, regardless of whether there is anything in the buffer. You can set the timeout to a specific number of milliseconds to cause any read operation to fail if that amount of time elapses before a message arrives. You can also create a blocking read by passing the MAILSLOT_WAIT_FOREVER constant.

Listing 8.1 takes the non-blocking approach, and then additionally demonstrates the **GetMailslotInfo** function to make sure that messages exist in the queue before it performs a read. This function returns the maximum length of the messages in the mailslot queue, the length of the next message in the queue, and the number of messages waiting.

GetMailslotInfo	*Gets information about the given mailslot*

```
BOOL GetMailslotInfo(
    HANDLE mailslot,
    LPDWORD maxMsgLen,
    LPDWORD nextMsgLen,
    LPDWORD numMsgs,
    LPDWORD readTimeout)
```

mailslot	Handle to the mailslot
maxMsgLen	Max message size
nextMsgLen	Length of next message
numMsgs	The number of messages in the queue
readTimeout	The timeout value
Returns TRUE on success	

Listing 8.1 uses **GetMailslotInfo** to determine if messages exist in the mailslot. If there are any, then it reads the first one. Reading from a mailslot is just like reading from a file. See Section 2.7 for details. A corresponding **Set MailslotInfo** function lets you change the timeout value of an existing mailslot at any time.

A message sent from any computer on the network to a machine running Listing 8.1 will be received, provided that the mailslot names of the sender and the receiver match. There are two limits on message size, however. Messages sent from a sender to a receiver running on the *same* machine can be no longer than 64K bytes, while messages sent over the network between machines have a 400-byte limit.

Listing 8.2 shows how to send messages to a mailslot. It starts by using the **CreateFile** function discussed in Section 2.7 to open a writeable connection to the mailslot. You use **CreateFile** whenever you want to create a program that writes to a mailslot. The program is referred to as a mailslot *client* because it writes to mailslot servers already running on the network. The **CreateFile** function understands, because of the use of the special mailslot file name, that you are not creating a file but instead wish to communicate with a mailslot. Four different formats for the file name are typically used:

1. \\.\mailslot\[path]name
2. *\mailslot\[path]name
3. \\domain\mailslot\[path]name
4. \\machine\mailslot\[path]name

In the first and last cases, the name specifies the local machine or a specific machine on the net, respectively. The second form specifies a broadcast operation to all machines in the local machine's primary domain. The third form specifies all machines in the indicated domain. See the book *Windows NT Administration: Single Systems to Heterogeneous Networks* for more information on domains and domain controllers. In order for the code in Listing 8.2 to function appropriately, there must be a mailslot with the same name on the specified machine or machines.

After opening the mailslot, Listing 8.2 gets the local computer's name using **GetComputerName** (see Section 16.2), and then proceeds to broadcast the name to all mailslots in the current domain every five seconds. The code uses the normal **WriteFile** function seen in Section 2.7 to perform the write operation.

When you run the programs, note that termination of either the reader or the writer has no effect on the other end of the pair. A mailslot program can broadcast packets on the network even if no machine has created a server to receive them. Conversely, a server can exist in the absence of any clients. You will see that named pipes, discussed in the following section, are much more specific when forming connections. In Listings 8.1 and 8.2, also note the presumption that the program will be terminated externally. You can formally close either a mailslot server or a client using the **CloseHandle** function discussed in Chapter 2.

Listing 8.1 uses a polling technique to check for messages. Everyhalf-second it calls **GetMailslotInfo** and checks to see if any messages are waiting in the slot. This approach works well in certain cases. In general, however, polling is not a good technique to use in a multi-threaded environment because it is inefficient. An efficient way to wait on a mailslot is to *specify a* *timeout value* when you call **CreateMailslot.** You may want the value to be infinite if waiting forever is appropriate, or you may want to make it shorter if, for example, you want the server to time out if it does not receive any messages during a certain period of time. In the **while** loop seen in Listing 8.1, set up code that looks like this in order to eliminate the polling:

```
while (1)
{
  /* Block waiting for input */
  ReadFile(hSMS_Slot, toDisptxt, 0,
    &NumBytesRead, (LPOVERLAPPED) NULL))
  if (GetLastError() !=
      ERROR_INSUFFICIENT_BUFFER)
  {
    ... handle error
    ... it may be a timeout, so check
  }

  Status=GetMailslotInfo(hSMS_Slot,
    (LPDWORD) NULL, &nextSize, &Msgs,
    (LPDWORD) NULL);
  if (!Status)
  {
    ... handle errror
  }

  /* If messages are available, then get them */
  if (Msgs)
  {
    /* Read the message and check to see if
       read was successful */
    if (!ReadFile(hSMS_Slot, toDisptxt, nextSize,
      &NumBytesRead, (LPOVERLAPPED) NULL);
    {
      ... handle error
    }
    ... handle message
  {
```

The first call to **ReadFile** is there simply to wait efficiently. It requests 0 bytes from the mailslot. As soon as anything arrives in the mailslot, **ReadFile** will unblock. You still have to call **GetMailslotInfo** to find out how big the message is, but then you can read it and proceed using the second **ReadFile.**

Listings 8.3, 8.4, and 8.5 present a more involved and realistic use of mailslots in a facility called Ranmon, or the "Run And Notify MONitor" system. This system lets you run a program on one machine and then receive notification of the program's completion on other machines. You might use this facility to run a program on one machine in the lab and to then receive a message indicating its completion on your personal machine in your office. You can run any executable using the Ranmon system.

The "Ran" program, shown in Listing 8.5, is used to run a program. For example, you might type the following command on the command line:

```
ran labtest data1.db
```

The command `ran` is used like the command `start` on the command line: it simply precedes a normal command and its command line options. "lab-test" is the name of an application and "data1.db" is a dataset used by that application. The "ran" program records the start time, and then runs labtest. When the program finishes execution, ran uses a mailslot to broadcast a message on the net indicating this fact.

Ranmon, shown in Listing 8.4, listens to a mailslot, and, when it hears a message from "ran," pops up a dialog indicating that the labtest application has completed. Note that you must use the same login ID on both machines. Ranmon creates separate mailslots for specific users, as described below; the login ID of the current user determines the separation.

Listing 8.3   *The common header file ran.h for ran and ranmon*

```
// ran.h

typedef struct
{
  char AppName[10];
  char WkstnName[MAX_COMPUTERNAME_LENGTH + 1];
  long RunHrs;
  long RunMin;
  long RunSec;
  int stopMonitors;
} RANData;
```

Listing 8.4   *The ranmon program waits for messages produced by ran (Listing 8.5) and pops up a message box when it receives one*

```
// ranmon.cpp

// Usage: ranmon

#include <windows.h>
#include <string.h>
#include "ran.h"

#define TITLE_NAME "Run And Notify MONitor"
#define MAX_USERNAME 15

int WINAPI WinMain(HANDLE ghInstance,
  HANDLE hPrevInstance, LPSTR lpCmdLine,
  int nCmdShow)
```

```
{
  HANDLE RANSlot;
  DWORD NumBytesRead;
  DWORD length;
  RANData randata;
  char slotPath[MAX_PATH];
  char msgString[255];
  char tmp[85];
  char userName[MAX_USERNAME + 1];

  strcpy(slotPath, "\\\\.\\mailslot\\ran\\");
  length=sizeof(userName);
  GetUserName(userName, &length);
  strcat(slotPath, userName);

  /* Create a mailslot for receiving messages */
  RANSlot=CreateMailslot(slotPath, sizeof(RANData),
    MAILSLOT_WAIT_FOREVER,
    (LPSECURITY_ATTRIBUTES) NULL);

  /* Check and see if the mailslot was created */
  if (RANSlot == INVALID_HANDLE_VALUE)
  {
    MessageBox(NULL,
      "ERROR: Unable to create mailslot.",
      TITLE_NAME, MB_OK | MB_ICONHAND);
    return(1);
  }

  /* Repeatedly check for messages until
     the program terminates */
  while(1)
  {
    /* Read a message and check to see if
       read was successful */
    if (!ReadFile(RANSlot, &randata,
      sizeof(RANData),
      &NumBytesRead, (LPOVERLAPPED) NULL))
    {
      MessageBox(NULL,
        "ERROR: Unable to read from mailslot.",
        TITLE_NAME, MB_OK | MB_ICONHAND);
      CloseHandle(RANSlot);
      return(1);
    }

    if (randata.stopMonitors == 1) return(0);

    strcpy(msgString, "The application \"");
    strcat(msgString, randata.AppName);
```

| Listing 8.4 | *The ranmon program waits for messages produced by ran (Listing 8.5) and pops up a message box when it receives one (continued)* |

```
    strcat(msgString, "\" executing on ");
    strcat(msgString, randata.WkstnName);
    strcat(msgString, " has finished.\n\n");
    wsprintf(tmp, "It executed for: %ld hours,\
      %ld minutes, and %ld seconds.",
      randata.RunHrs, randata.RunMin,
      randata.RunSec);
    strcat(msgString, tmp);
    MessageBox(NULL, msgString,
      TITLE_NAME, MB_SETFOREGROUND | MB_OK
      | MB_ICONINFORMATION);
  } /* while */
}
```

| Listing 8.5 | *The ran portion of the ranmon system. This program runs a program and then signals ranmon when it is complete* |

```cpp
// ran.cpp

// Usage: ran <executable|batch file|-stopmon>

#include <windows.h>
#include <process.h>
#include <iostream.h>
#include <stdlib.h>
#include <string.h>
#include <time.h>
#include "ran.h"

#define MAX_USERNAME 15

int main(int argc, char *argv[])
{
  HANDLE RANSlot;
  BOOL Status;
  DWORD NumBytesWritten;
  DWORD length;
  RANData randata;
  char cmdLine[MAX_PATH];
  char slotPath[MAX_PATH];
  char userName[MAX_USERNAME + 1];
  int i;
  long elapsedTime;
  time_t startTime;
  time_t stopTime;
  char *timeString;
```

```
    if (argc < 2)
    {
      cout <<
        "Usage: ran <executable|batch file|-\
stopmon>\n"
        << endl;
      return(1);
    }


    /* If -stopmon, stop ranmon */
    if (!strcmp(argv[1], "-stopmon"))
    {
      randata.stopMonitors=1;
      cout << "Sending Ranmon the stop signal..."
        << endl;
    }
    /* otherwise, run the requested program */
    else
    {
      /* Get the comp name and record it */
      randata.stopMonitors=0;
      strcpy(randata.AppName, argv[1]);
      length=sizeof(randata.WkstnName);
      GetComputerName(randata.WkstnName, &length);
      strcpy(cmdLine, argv[1]);
      for (i=2; i<argc; i++)
      {
        strcat(cmdLine, " ");
        strcat(cmdLine, argv[i]);
      }

      /* Get the start time */
      time(&startTime);
      timeString=ctime(&startTime);
      cout << argv[1] << " started: " << timeString
        << endl;

      /* run the program */
      system(cmdLine);

      /* Record the stop time */
      time(&stopTime);
      timeString=ctime(&stopTime);
      cout << argv[1] << " exited: " << timeString
        << endl;

      elapsedTime=stopTime-startTime;
      randata.RunHrs=elapsedTime / 3600;
      elapsedTime-=(randata.RunHrs * 3600);
```

Listing 8.5 *The ran portion of the ranmon system. This program runs a program and then signals ranmon when it is complete (continued)*

```cpp
    randata.RunMin=elapsedTime / 60;
    elapsedTime-=(randata.RunMin * 60);
    randata.RunSec=elapsedTime;

    cout << argv[1] << " executed: "
      << randata.RunHrs
      << " hours, " <<  randata.RunMin
      << " minutes, and "
      << randata.RunSec << " seconds\n" << endl;
  }

  /* Set up mailslot path */
  strcpy(slotPath, "\\\\*\\mailslot\\ran\\");
  length=sizeof(userName);
  GetUserName(userName, &length);
  strcat(slotPath, userName);
  /* Create the mailslot file handle
     for sending messages */
  RANSlot=CreateFile(slotPath,
    GENERIC_WRITE, FILE_SHARE_READ,
    (LPSECURITY_ATTRIBUTES) NULL,
    OPEN_EXISTING, FILE_ATTRIBUTE_NORMAL,
    (HANDLE) NULL);

  /* Check and see if the mailslot file was opened,
     if not terminate program */
  if (RANSlot == INVALID_HANDLE_VALUE)
  {
    cerr << "ERROR: Unable to create a mailslot"
      << endl;
    return (1);
  }

  /* Send message that program has terminated */
  /* Write message to mailslot */
  Status=WriteFile(RANSlot,
    &randata, sizeof(RANData),
    &NumBytesWritten, (LPOVERLAPPED) NULL);

  /* If error occurs when writing to mailslot,
     terminate program */
  if (!Status)
  {
    cerr << "ERROR: Unable to write message"
      << endl;
    CloseHandle(RANSlot);
    return (1);
  }
```

```
   CloseHandle(RANSlot);
   return(0);
}
```

The ran program in Figure 8.5 is straightforward. It first checks for proper usage, and then for the -stopmon option. If -stopmon is seen, it signals the fact by setting the **stopMonitors** value to 1. Ranmon will interpret this value as a signal to terminate itself. Otherwise, "ran" notes the time, uses the **system** function to execute the requested application, and, when it finishes, notes the stop time. All of the time data, along with the application and machine name, is stored in the **randata** structure (see Listing 8.3 for its definition).

Ran then creates the client side of a mailslot. Note that the mailslot name here includes the path "ran" as well as the user name—for example,

```
\\*\mailslot\ran\smith
```

This allows multiple users to use ranmon on the same network and keep their messages separate. Once the mailslot is created, ran broadcasts the **randata** structure onto the network and exits.

The ranmon application is fairly simple. Its job is to run in the background and wait for messages from copies of the ran program. The messages will contain a **randata** structure, and will always have a fixed size, so you can use **ReadFile** without having to call **GetMailslotInfo** first to determine the message size. When ranmon sees a message, it either terminates itself if **stopMonitors** is 1, or it pops up a message box containing the data.

Note that ranmon creates an infinite loop in its **WinMain** function. The fact that the program uses **WinMain** (see Appendix A) means that you cannot kill it with ctrl-C on the command line, hence the backdoor -stopmon option in ran that allows you to kill off ranmon when necessary. You can start ranmon by placing an icon for it in your startup group in the Program Manager if you want it to run every time you log in.

Note: If you have both the NetBEUI and TCP/IP drivers loaded and active in the Network applet of the Control Panel, you will probably get two copies of every packet sent to a mailslot. If you find that your machine receives multiple copies of mailslot messages, that is probably why. You should therefore design any mailslot protocol that you create to detect duplicates of a message and ignore them.

8.4 Named Pipes

*Compatibility Note: At the time of publication, it is not possible to create a named pipe server in Windows 98 because of a **ConnectNamedPipe** failure.*

While the mailslot facility discussed in the previous section is easy to use, it has one handicap that often makes it unacceptable: it does not guarantee delivery. For example, if two programs on different machines communicate via mailslots, the following problem arises: When machine one sends a message to machine two, it has no way to know that the data actually arrived. You could code the programs so that machine two sends back an acknowledgment, but then you could argue that it has no way of knowing if the acknowledgment arrived. This problem means that if machine one has sent a command to machine two and machine two does not respond, it has no way of knowing what happened. Should it send the packet again, wait for a while, or give up? Guaranteed delivery solves this problem.

Named pipes provide a guaranteed delivery mechanism. Instead of broadcasting the packet onto the network, you form a distinct connection with another machine using a named pipe. If the connection ever breaks, perhaps because a machine goes down or because a portion of the network fails, both parties to the connection find out as soon as they try to send or receive anything. Packets are also guaranteed to arrive in sequence through a named pipe. The only problem with named pipes is that you lose the ability to broadcast packets. To broadcast anything, all of the target machines must have a connection to a central server, and the server must separately transmit the message to each one. This limitation is actually an advantage in large networks, because it forces you to discipline yourself in your use of network bandwidth. You cannot afford to broadcast packets across multiple domains with mailslots: If there were many programs doing this, the network would rapidly be saturated. By forcing the server to converse only with directly-connected machines, you limit network traffic.

You use named pipes to form point-to-point connections between pairs of processes (on the same machine or on separate machines), or to create client/server systems where many machines connect to a single, central server. For example, say that you want to create a conference system, something like a multi-user chat program. Each user can type a message, and sees in a scrolling window the comments of everyone else. See Figure 8.4.

One easy way to implement this program is with mailslots, but if the users are hundreds of miles apart on a giant network, this approach won't work. What you might do instead is set up a conference server at a known location on the network. At the appointed time, everyone starts the conference application and connects to the server. The application connects using a named pipe. Whenever a user types a message and presses the send button, the message gets transmitted to the server. The server then resends the message to each of the connected users, one at a time. Since named pipes are used, the server can monitor and announce connections and disconnections.

Named pipes are only slightly more difficult to create than mailslots. Listings 8.6 and 8.7 show how to create a simple point-to-point connection between two applications using named pipes. If you run the receiving program shown in Listing 8.6 first, and then on the same machine run the sending program in 8.7, the program will query you for the name of the machine

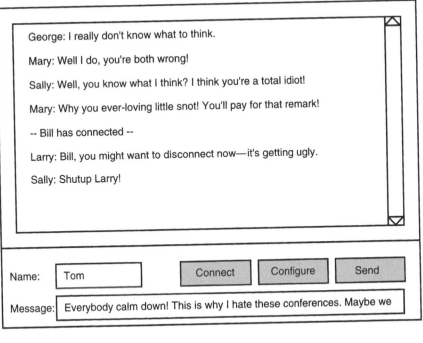

George: I really don't know what to think.

Mary: Well I do, you're both wrong!

Sally: Well, you know what I think? I think you're a total idiot!

Mary: Why you ever-loving little snot! You'll pay for that remark!

-- Bill has connected --

Larry: Bill, you might want to disconnect now—it's getting ugly.

Sally: Shutup Larry!

Name: Tom   Connect   Configure   Send

Message: Everybody calm down! This is why I hate these conferences. Maybe we

Figure 8.4   *A multi-user conferencing system*

to connect to. Since you are running the sender and the receiver on the same machine, type "." or enter your machine name. You will see a message sent from sender to receiver every five seconds or so. When you kill off the sender, notice that you immediately see a message in the receiver indicating that it has detected the break in the pipe. If you try to start up the sender without having the receiver running, the sender will fail immediately because it cannot connect. Unlike mailslots, pipes can tell when the other end is not working properly.

A named-pipe connection can occur across the network as simply as it occurs on one machine. For example, if the server program in Listing 8.6 is running on a machine named "orion," log in to a different machine *using an account with the exact same login ID and password as the one you are using on "orion."* Run the sender in Listing 8.7 on the new machine and enter the name "orion" when it asks for the machine name to connect to. The connection will occur properly. Note that, with named pipes, you *must* know the name of the machine running the server.

Also note that if you have a different user try to connect to the receiver, then the connection fails. For example, if the user "jones" is running the receiver on the machine "orion" and the user "smith" tries to connect using the sender on another machine, the connection fails with an "access denied" error. This is the Windows 2000 security system at work. See Chapter 13, particularly Section 13.9, for explanations and solutions.

Listing 8.6   *A simple program that creates a named pipe server. The server will wait and accept one connection, and then receive messages from it*

```cpp
// ssnprecv.cpp

// Usage: ssnprecv

#include <windows.h>
#include <iostream.h>

int main()
{
  char toDisptxt[80];
  HANDLE ssnpPipe;
  DWORD NumBytesRead;

  /* Create a named pipe for receiving messages */
  ssnpPipe=CreateNamedPipe("\\\\.\\pipe\\ssnp",
    PIPE_ACCESS_INBOUND,
    PIPE_TYPE_MESSAGE | PIPE_WAIT,
    1, 0, 0, 150,
    (LPSECURITY_ATTRIBUTES) NULL);

  /* Check and see if the named pipe was created */
  if (ssnpPipe == INVALID_HANDLE_VALUE)
  {
    cerr << "ERROR: Unable to create a named pipe."
      << endl;
    return (1);
  }

  /* Allow a client to connect to the name pipe,
     terminate if unsuccessful */
  if(!ConnectNamedPipe(ssnpPipe,
    (LPOVERLAPPED) NULL))
  {
    cerr << "ERROR: Unable to connect a named pipe"
      << endl;
    CloseHandle(ssnpPipe);
    return (1);
  }

  /* Repeatedly check for messages until the program
     is terminated */
  while(1)
```

```
{
  /* Read the message and check to see if read
     was successful */
  if (!ReadFile(ssnpPipe, toDisptxt,
    sizeof(toDisptxt),
    &NumBytesRead, (LPOVERLAPPED) NULL))
  {
    cerr
      << "ERROR: Unable to read from named pipe"
      << endl;
    CloseHandle(ssnpPipe);
    return (1);
  }

  /* Display the Message */
  cout << toDisptxt << endl;

} /* while */
}
```

Listing 8.7 A named-pipe client able to connect to Listing 8.6 and send it
messages

```
// ssnpsend.cpp

// Usage: ssnpsend

#include <windows.h>
#include <iostream.h>

int main()
{
  char *toSendtxt="Test String";
  HANDLE ssnpPipe;
  DWORD NumBytesWritten;
  char machineName[80];
  char pipeName[80];

  cout << "Enter name of server machine: ";
  cin >> machineName;
  wsprintf(pipeName, "\\\\%s\\pipe\\ssnp",
    machineName);

  /* Create the named pipe file handle for sending
     messages */
  ssnpPipe=CreateFile(pipeName,
    GENERIC_WRITE, FILE_SHARE_READ,
```

Listing 8.7	*A named-pipe client able to connect to Listing 8.6 and send it messages (continued)*

```
    (LPSECURITY_ATTRIBUTES) NULL,
    OPEN_EXISTING, FILE_ATTRIBUTE_NORMAL,
    (HANDLE) NULL);


    /* Check and see if the named pipe file was
       opened, if not terminate program */
    if (ssnpPipe == INVALID_HANDLE_VALUE)
    {
      cerr << "ERROR: Unable to create a named pipe"
        << endl;
      cerr << GetLastError() << endl;
      return (1);
    }


    /* Repeatedly send message until program is
       terminated */
    while(1)
    {
      cout << "Sending..." << endl;
      /* Write message to the pipe */
      if (!WriteFile(ssnpPipe,
          toSendtxt, (DWORD) strlen(toSendtxt)+1,
          &NumBytesWritten, (LPOVERLAPPED) NULL))
      {
        /* If error occurs when writing to named
           pipe, terminate program */
        cerr << "ERROR: Unable to write to named pipe"
          << endl;
        CloseHandle(ssnpPipe);
        return (1);
      }


      /* Wait before sending the message again */
      Sleep(4800);
    } /* while*/
}
```

In Listing 8.6, the program starts by creating a named-pipe server using the **CreateNamedPipe** function.

CreateNamedPipe   *Creates a named pipe that you can then read from*

```
HANDLE CreateNamedPipe(
    LPCTSTR name,
    DWORD openMode,
    DWORD pipeMode,
    DWORD maxInstances,
    DWORD outBufferSize,
    DWORD inBufferSize,
    DWORD timeOut,
    LPSECURITY_ATTRIBUTES security)
```

name	The name of the named pipe
openMode	Flags specifying pipe access mode
pipeMode	Flags specifying type, read mode, and wait mode of the pipe
maxInstances	Maximum number of instances, 1 through PIPE_UNLIMITED_INSTANCE. Must be the same for all instances
outBufferSize	The output buffer size
inBufferSize	The input buffer size
timeOut	The time out value for the pipe. All instances must have the same value
security	Security attributes. See Chapter 10

Returns a handle to the named pipe or INVALID_HANDLE_VALUE.

The name used with the **CreateNamedPipe** function will always have the same form:

```
\\.\pipe\[path]name
```

As with mailslots, you can specify a path before the name of the pipe to clearly distinguish it from other pipes on the system.

The **openMode** parameter passed to **CreateNamedPipe** lets you determine the direction of the pipe. Named pipes can be one directional or bidirectional, depending on the following constants used with the **openMode** parameter:

PIPE_ACCESS_DUPLEX
PIPE_ACCESS_INBOUND
PIPE_ACCESS_OUTBOUND

You can also specify the buffering and overlap behavior of the pipe with two other constants:

FILE_FLAG_WRITE_THROUGH
FILE_FLAG_OVERLAPPED

On byte-type pipes (described later), write-through causes all bytes sent to a pipe to be transmitted immediately, rather than being held in a buffer. The write function does not return until all bytes are sent. If write-through is not specified, then bytes are placed in a buffer and collected until the system can send a reasonably-sized network packet. The overlapped flag enables overlapped reads on a pipe (see Section 7.5). Overlapped operations on a pipe allow asynchronous operations, just as they do in a file. They also allow simultaneous reading and writing on the same pipe, and this is very important in multi-threaded servers and in clients that use pipes. See the example that follows.

The **pipeMode** parameter of **CreateNamedPipe** determines whether the pipe works with a pure stream of bytes, or with packets of bytes called messages. A stream of bytes has no logical boundaries that group the bytes together, so bytes can be broken up anywhere when forming network packets. Messages contain a group of bytes that must be kept together as a unit. You can declare byte or message behavior in both the read and write directions:

PIPE_TYPE_MESSAGE
PIPE_TYPE_BYTE
PIPE_READMODE_MESSAGE
PIPE_READMODE_BYTE

You also specify the PIPE_WAIT constant as shown, unless you are using overlapped I/O. In Listing 8.6, the different constants in the open and pipe mode parameters are used to create a pipe that is one-directional inbound, message-oriented, and blocking.

A pipe can have more than one instance on a single machine. This capability allows multiple-server threads to service multiple clients, each in different threads. An example appears in Section 8.5. Since the example shown in Listings 8.6 and 8.7 is a simple point-to-point connection, only one instance is necessary, so a maximum of one instance is specified in the call to **CreateNamedPipe** in Listing 8.6. The call to **CreateNamedPipe** also uses zero for the buffer sizes to pick default values, and finally specifies a timeout value of 150 milliseconds. The timeout value is relevant only when the **Wait NamedPipe** function is used.

Listing 8.6 next waits for a connection on the named pipe using the **ConnectNamedPipe** function.

ConnectNamedPipe   *Waits for a connection to the pipe*

```
BOOL ConnectNamedPipe(
   HANDLE pipeHandle,
   LPOVERLAPPED overlapped)
```

pipeHandle	A handle to a pipe created by **CreateNamedPipe**
overlapped	A pointer to an overlapped structure

Returns TRUE on success

A connection is formed in the server when a client program calls **CreateFile** with named pipe specified in the server as its destination. Upon connection, the **ConnectNamedPipe** function returns. Alternatively you can specify an overlapped structure (See Section 7.5) and **ConnectNamedPipe** will return immediately and later signal the event in the overlapped structure upon connection.

Listing 8.6 then enters a loop, waiting for data to arrive with a **ReadFile** function, as described in Chapter 2.7. The **ReadFile** function behaves slightly differently here from the way it does with files, communications ports, and so on. Because this named pipe is in message mode, the **ReadFile** function will return as soon as it receives a complete message, regardless of how many bytes the message contains. It is possible to use a blocking read, as shown, or to use an overlapped read. Overlapped reads are discussed in Section 7.5.

Listing 8.7 is a simple client for Listing 8.6. Listing 8.7 starts by creating a connection to the named pipe with the **CreateFile** function. See Chapter 2.7 for details on **CreateFile.** It is also possible to create a connection to a message-based pipe using the **CallNamedPipe** convenience function, which contains a call to **CreateFile.**

Listing 8.7 then writes messages to the pipe continuously, one every five seconds, using the **WriteFile** function. See Chapter 2 for details on this function. Each individual call to **WriteFile** constitutes a message at the receiving end of the named pipe, so the receiver's **ReadFile** function will unblock when it receives the message. Each time the client writes, the server produces a message on the screen.

If two copies of the client try to connect to the server shown above at the same time, then the server will reject the second client. Only one connection is allowed at a time on a named pipe. The following section shows how to create multiple instances of the same pipe to handle multiple clients in a server.

8.5 Named Pipe Client/Server Systems

If you need to create a client/server system in Windows, where multiple clients connect to a single server somewhere on the network, you have three choices. You can use RPCs, TCP communications, or named pipes. RPCs (see Chapter 9) are easier to use in many cases because they handle all of the connection problems for you. Many of the remote services offered by

Windows 2000 are implemented with RPCs. There are certain cases, however, where named pipes are more appropriate. For example, if you need to stream 10 megabytes of data across the network, then a named pipe is appropriate. It might also be suitable to create a hybrid system, where an RPC server sets up the connection and then a point-to-point named pipe handles the data flow. The advantage of a named pipe is reduced overhead.

In a client/server system using named pipes, the server resides on a known machine on the network, and multiple clients can connect to it. The server machine may respond to each client individually, when the server is managing a database, for example. The clients connect, make requests of the database, and then disconnect. Although many clients may be connected at once, their activities are most likely unrelated. On the other hand, the server may exist to allow intercommunication between clients. The conversation system described earlier is an example of this architecture. Each client connects, and the server broadcasts messages received from the client to all of the other clients currently connected.

This section demonstrates these two different client/server architectures through the use of named pipes. In both systems, multiple clients can connect to the server and send and receive messages. In the first example, the clients are managed independently of one another. In the second example, clients talk to one another through the server, and the clients are multi-threaded to demonstrate the technique of multi-threading a named pipe application to handle reading and writing to the pipe in separate threads.

Please note that when you run these examples, all clients and the server must have the same login ID and password. If they do not, you will get access-denied errors when a client tries to connect to the server. See Chapter 13, particularly Section 13.9, for explanations and solutions.

8.5.1 A Simple Client/Server System

Listings 8.8 and 8.9 contain the code for a typical server and client. The server treats each client independently. You should run the server code on one machine. You can then run multiple copies of the client code on the same machine or on other machines on the network. *When running over the network, be sure all clients have the same login ID and password as the server.* See Chapter 13, particularly Section 13.9, for an explanation of the Windows 2000 security system.

When you run a client, it will connect and then request a line of text from the user. Type something and press return. The server will receive the line, convert it to upper case, and return it to the client, which will display the line received from the server on the screen. The MAX_INSTANCES constant in the server controls how many clients can connect at any one time. Set it to any value you like.

Listing 8.8   *A server that uses named pipes. Multiple clients can connect to the server, and it handles each one separately*

```cpp
// msnpserv.cpp

#include <windows.h>
#include <iostream.h>
#include <string.h>
#include <stddef.h>
#include <process.h>

#define BUFSIZE 128
#define MAX_INSTANCES 3

void msnpClientThread(HANDLE msnpPipe)
{
  CHAR textBuffer[BUFSIZE];
  DWORD numBytesRead;
  DWORD numBytesWritten;

  while (1)
  {
    if (!ReadFile(msnpPipe,
      textBuffer, BUFSIZE,
      &numBytesRead, (LPOVERLAPPED) NULL))
    {
    cerr
      << "ERROR: Unable to read from named pipe"
      << endl;
    break;
    }

    _strupr(textBuffer);

    if (!WriteFile(msnpPipe,
      textBuffer, strlen(textBuffer) + 1,
      &numBytesWritten, (LPOVERLAPPED) NULL))
    {
    cerr
      << "ERROR: Unable to write to named pipe"
      << endl;
    break;
    }

    cout << textBuffer << endl;
  } /* while */

  FlushFileBuffers(msnpPipe);
  DisconnectNamedPipe(msnpPipe);
```

```
        CloseHandle(msnpPipe);
}

INT main(VOID)
{
    HANDLE msnpPipe;
    DWORD msnpThread;

    while (1)
    {
        /* Create a named pipe for receiving
           messages */
        msnpPipe=CreateNamedPipe("\\\\.\\pipe\\msnp",
            PIPE_ACCESS_DUPLEX,
            PIPE_TYPE_BYTE | PIPE_WAIT,
            MAX_INSTANCES, 0, 0, 150,
            (LPSECURITY_ATTRIBUTES) NULL);

        /* Check and see if the named pipe was
           created */
        if (msnpPipe == INVALID_HANDLE_VALUE)
        {
            cerr
                << "ERROR: Unable to create a named pipe"
                << endl;
            continue;
        }

        /* Allow a client to connect to the name pipe,
           terminate if unsuccessful */
        if (!ConnectNamedPipe(msnpPipe,
            (LPOVERLAPPED) NULL))
        {
            cerr
                << "ERROR: Unable to connect a named pipe."
                << endl;
            CloseHandle(msnpPipe);
            return (1);
        }

        msnpThread=_beginthread(msnpClientThread,
            0, (HANDLE) msnpPipe);
        if (msnpThread == -1)
        {
            cerr << "ERROR: Unable to create thread"
                << endl;
            CloseHandle(msnpPipe);
        }
```

```
    } /* while */
}
```

Listing 8.9   *A typical client for Listing 8.8's server*

```cpp
// msnpclnt.cpp

#include <windows.h>
#include <iostream.h>

#define BUFSIZE 128

INT main(VOID)
{
  CHAR textToSend[BUFSIZE];
  CHAR textRecvd[BUFSIZE];
  HANDLE msnpPipe;
  DWORD numBytesRead;
  DWORD numBytesWritten;
  char machineName[80];
  char pipeName[80];

  cout << "Enter name of server machine: ";
  cin >> machineName;
  wsprintf(pipeName, "\\\\%s\\pipe\\msnp",
    machineName);

  /* Create the named pipe file handle for
     sending messages */
  msnpPipe=CreateFile(pipeName,
    GENERIC_READ | GENERIC_WRITE,
    0, (LPSECURITY_ATTRIBUTES) NULL,
    OPEN_EXISTING, FILE_ATTRIBUTE_NORMAL,
    (HANDLE) NULL);

  /* Check and see if the named pipe file was
     opened, if not terminate program */
  if (msnpPipe == INVALID_HANDLE_VALUE)
  {
    cerr << "ERROR: Unable to create a named pipe"
      << endl;
    return (1);
  }

  /* Repeatedly send message until program
     terminates */
  while(1)
  {
    cout << "Type text to send: ";
    cin.getline(textToSend, BUFSIZE);
```

Listing 8.9   *A typical client for Listing 8.8's server (continued)*

```
/* Write message to named pipe */
if (!WriteFile(msnpPipe,
  textToSend, strlen(textToSend) + 1,
  &numBytesWritten, (LPOVERLAPPED) NULL))
{
  cerr << "ERROR: Unable to write to pipe."
    << endl;
  CloseHandle(msnpPipe);
  return (1);
}

if (!ReadFile(msnpPipe,
  textRecvd, BUFSIZE,
  &numBytesRead, (LPOVERLAPPED) NULL))
{
  cerr << "ERROR: Unable to read from pipe"
    << endl;
  CloseHandle(msnpPipe);
  return (1);
}

cout << "Received: " << textRecvd << endl;

} /* while*/
}
```

In the **main** function of Listing 8.8, you will find a loop that starts by creating an instance of the msnp pipe. There will be one instance for each connected client, along with one instance waiting for the next connection. The code then calls **ConnectNamedPipe** to wait for a client to connect. This process is identical to the one described in Section 8.4. After it receives a connection, the server then creates a new thread to handle the new client. The thread receives the instance of the pipe as a parameter. Therefore, the system will contain one independent thread for each connected client, and the thread knows of the pipe instance of its specific client. Once the new thread exists, the server loops to create a new instance of the same pipe so that it can wait for another connection. This is how the server is able to allow several client connections to the "same" pipe.

The code here uses **_beginthread,** from the MSC library (see the Runtime Routines help file), to start the thread. It is used simply for variety. It does the same thing that **CreateThread** does, and **CreateThread** (see Chapter 6) would work just as well here.

The thread, once created, is responsible for all interaction with its client, using the pipe handle that it received as a parameter. Here the interaction is very simple: The thread waits for the client to send it a string, converts the string to upper case, and then sends the new string back to the client.

When the client terminates, the **ReadFile** or **WriteFile** function will fail immediately, breaking out of the thread's loop. At that point the thread cleans up the pipe and disconnects gracefully before terminating. When creating a system of your own, you will probably have a message the client can send to force normal termination, but your server should always handle the unplanned death of a client gracefully, as shown here.

The client program in Listing 8.9 is very simple. It opens a handle to the server's pipe and then enters a loop. The loop requests a string from the user, sends it to the server, waits for the server's response, and then prints the response. See Listing 8.11 for an example of a multi-threaded client.

There is a small but finite chance that the call to **CreateFile** in the client can fail due to the server's being in the middle of creating one client thread but having not yet cycled around to create a new instance of its pipe to handle the next client. In this case, you will receive an ERROR_PIPE_BUSY error code and you may want to cycle through **CreateFile** again to retry the connection.

The code shown in this section is simple because the server can deal with each client independently. Therefore, the client threads in the server do not need to interact with one another. The next section demonstrates the case in which clients interact.

8.5.2 Intercommunicating Clients

Compatibility Note: Be sure that you specify the multi-threaded libraries in the project file when compiling this code. See the diskette for details.

There are many situations in which a server is created to allow multi-client interaction. Mailslots implicitly allow this sort of activity, but are problematic because they are unreliable and insecure. Mailslots also broadcast their messages on the net, so they are inappropriate for inter-segment routing. Named pipes solve all of these problems, and a server that uses named pipes is able to let multiple clients interact in an authenticated way no matter how far apart they are on the network.

Listings 8.10 and 8.11 demonstrate a very simple conversation server. Run the server on one machine. As in Section 8.5.1, clients can run on the server machine or on other machines on the network. *Be sure that you are logged in under the same login ID and password on the server and all client machines,* or the server will reject the client connections. See Chapter 13 and Section 13.9 for explanations and suggestions. The maximum number of clients is controlled by MAX_INSTANCES. See the description at the beginning of Section 8.5.1 for details.

When the server receives a message from any client, it converts the message to upper case and then sends it out to all of the connected clients.

The clients use a multi-threaded design so that they can accept input from the pipe asynchronously, but the same thing can also be accomplished using overlapped I/O (See Section 7.5).

Listing 8.10   *A named pipe server that broadcasts any messages it receives back to all connected clients*

```cpp
// mtnpserv.cpp

#include <windows.h>
#include <iostream.h>
#include <string.h>
#include <stddef.h>
#include <process.h>

#define BUFSIZE 128
#define MAX_INSTANCES 3

// Information needed for each connection
// to a client
typedef struct _CLIENT_INFO
{
  HANDLE h;
  OVERLAPPED overlappedRead;
  OVERLAPPED overlappedWrite;
} CLIENT_INFO;

// The array holds one entry for
// each client
CLIENT_INFO clients[MAX_INSTANCES];
volatile int numClients=0;

// There is one thread for each client
// attached to the server
void mtnpClientThread(HANDLE id)
{
  CHAR textBuffer[BUFSIZE];
  DWORD numBytesRead;
  DWORD numBytesWritten;
  int x;
  int ID = (int) id;

  while (1)
  {
    // Get input from the client
    if (!ReadFile(clients[ID].h,
      textBuffer, BUFSIZE,
      &numBytesRead,
      &(clients[ID].overlappedRead)))
```

```
{
  if (GetLastError() != ERROR_IO_PENDING)
  {
    cerr <<
      "ERROR: Unable to read from named pipe "
      << GetLastError()
      << endl;
    break;
  }
}
GetOverlappedResult(clients[ID].h,
  &(clients[ID].overlappedRead), &numBytesRead,
  TRUE);
clients[ID].overlappedRead.Offset +=
  numBytesRead;

// Convert the client's string to
// upper case to show server is
// doing something
_strupr(textBuffer);

// Send the message to ALL clients
// in the client array
for (x=0; x<numClients; x++)
{
  if (!WriteFile(clients[x].h,
    textBuffer, strlen(textBuffer) + 1,
    &numBytesWritten,
    &(clients[ID].overlappedWrite)))
  {
    if (GetLastError() != ERROR_IO_PENDING)
    {
      cerr
        << "ERROR: Unable to write to pipe "
        << GetLastError()
        << endl;
      break;
    }
  }
  GetOverlappedResult(clients[ID].h,
    &(clients[ID].overlappedWrite),
    &numBytesWritten,
    TRUE);
  clients[ID].overlappedWrite.Offset +=
    numBytesWritten;
}

// Echo the string in the server's window
cout << textBuffer << endl;
} // while
```

Listing 8.10 *A named pipe server that broadcasts any messages it receives back to all connected clients (continued)*

```cpp
  // Clean up the pipe on termination
  // of the thread
  FlushFileBuffers(clients[ID].h);
  DisconnectNamedPipe(clients[ID].h);
  CloseHandle(clients[ID].h);
}

INT main(VOID)
{
  HANDLE mtnpPipe;
  DWORD mtnpThread;

  while (1)
  {
    // Create a named pipe for receiving messages
    mtnpPipe=CreateNamedPipe("\\\\.\\pipe\\mtnp",
      PIPE_ACCESS_DUPLEX | FILE_FLAG_OVERLAPPED,
      PIPE_TYPE_MESSAGE |PIPE_READMODE_MESSAGE|
      PIPE_WAIT,
      MAX_INSTANCES, 0, 0, 150,
      (LPSECURITY_ATTRIBUTES) NULL);

    // Check and see if the named pipe was created
    if (mtnpPipe == INVALID_HANDLE_VALUE)
    {
      cerr << "ERROR: Unable to create pipe"
        << endl;
      return (1);
    }

    // Allow a client to connect to the named pipe,
    // terminate if unsuccessful
    if (!ConnectNamedPipe(mtnpPipe,
      (LPOVERLAPPED) NULL))
    {
      cerr << "ERROR: Unable to connect a pipe."
        << endl;
      CloseHandle(mtnpPipe);
      return (1);
    }

    // Init a client data structure. It contains
    // a handle to the pipe and overlapped structs
    clients[numClients].h = mtnpPipe;
    clients[numClients].overlappedRead.Offset =
      clients[numClients].overlappedWrite.Offset =
        0;
```

```
      clients[numClients].overlappedRead.OffsetHigh =
        clients[numClients].overlappedWrite.
          OffsetHigh = 0;
      clients[numClients].overlappedWrite.hEvent =
        CreateEvent(0, TRUE, FALSE, 0);
      clients[numClients].overlappedRead.hEvent =
        CreateEvent(0, TRUE, FALSE, 0);

      // Create a new thread to accept messages
      // from the new client
      mtnpThread=_beginthread(mtnpClientThread,
        0, (HANDLE) numClients);
      if (mtnpThread == -1)
      {
        cerr << "ERROR: Unable to create thread"
          << endl;
        CloseHandle(mtnpPipe);
      }

      // increment the number of clients
      numClients++;

  } /* while */
}
```

Listing 8.11   *A multi-threaded client for Listing 8.10*

```
// mtnpclnt.cpp

#include <windows.h>
#include <iostream.h>
#include <stddef.h>
#include <process.h>

#define BUFSIZE 128

// The thread receives all messages from
// the server
void mtnpServerThread(HANDLE mtnpPipeDup)
{
  CHAR textBuffer[BUFSIZE];
  DWORD numBytesRead;
  OVERLAPPED overlappedRead;

  // Init the overlapped structure
  overlappedRead.Offset =
    overlappedRead.OffsetHigh = 0;
  overlappedRead.hEvent =
    CreateEvent(0, TRUE, FALSE, 0);
```

Listing 8.11   *A multi-threaded client for Listing 8.10 (continued)*

```
while (1)
{
  // Read a message from the server
  if (!ReadFile(mtnpPipeDup,
    textBuffer, BUFSIZE,
    &numBytesRead, &overlappedRead))
  {
    if (GetLastError() != ERROR_IO_PENDING)
    {
      cerr <<
        "ERROR: Unable to read from named pipe"
        << endl;
      break;
    }
  }
  GetOverlappedResult(mtnpPipeDup,
    &overlappedRead, &numBytesRead,
    TRUE);
  overlappedRead.Offset += numBytesRead;

  // send the message to the screen
  cout << textBuffer << endl;
} /* while */

// clean up the pipe
FlushFileBuffers(mtnpPipeDup);
DisconnectNamedPipe(mtnpPipeDup);
CloseHandle(mtnpPipeDup);
}

// The main function opens a handle
// to the pipe and then writes to it
INT main(VOID)
{
  CHAR textToSend[BUFSIZE];
  HANDLE mtnpPipe;
  DWORD mtnpThread;
  DWORD numBytesWritten;
  BOOL success;
  OVERLAPPED overlappedWrite;
  char pipeName[80];
  char machineName[80];

  cout << "Enter name of server machine: ";
  cin.getline(machineName,80);
  wsprintf(pipeName, "\\\\%s\\pipe\\mtnp",
    machineName);
```

```
// init overlapped structure
overlappedWrite.Offset =
  overlappedWrite.OffsetHigh = 0;
overlappedWrite.hEvent =
  CreateEvent(0, TRUE, FALSE, 0);

// Create the named pipe file handle for
// sending messages
mtnpPipe=CreateFile(pipeName,
  GENERIC_WRITE | GENERIC_READ,
  0,
  (LPSECURITY_ATTRIBUTES) NULL,
  OPEN_EXISTING,
  FILE_ATTRIBUTE_NORMAL|FILE_FLAG_OVERLAPPED,
  (HANDLE) NULL);
// Check and see if the named pipe file was
// opened, if not terminate program
if (mtnpPipe == INVALID_HANDLE_VALUE)
{
  cerr << "ERROR: Unable to create a named pipe "
    << GetLastError()
    << endl;
  return (1);
}

// Set the pipe into message mode
DWORD mode = PIPE_READMODE_MESSAGE | PIPE_WAIT;
success = SetNamedPipeHandleState(mtnpPipe,
  &mode, 0, 0);
if (!success)
{
  cerr << "ERROR: Unable to set pipe mode"
    << endl;
  return (1);
}

// Begin a separate thread to read from
// the pipe
mtnpThread = _beginthread(mtnpServerThread,
  0, (HANDLE) mtnpPipe);
if (mtnpThread == -1)
{
  cerr << "ERROR: Unable to create thread"
    << endl;
  CloseHandle(mtnpPipe);
}

// Repeatedly send messages to the pipe
// until program is terminated
while(1)
```

Listing 8.11   *A multi-threaded client for Listing 8.10 (continued)*

```
{
  cout << "Type text to send: ";
  cin.getline(textToSend, BUFSIZE);

  // Write message to named pipe
  if (!WriteFile(mtnpPipe,
    textToSend, strlen(textToSend) + 1,
    &numBytesWritten, &overlappedWrite))
  {
    if (GetLastError() != ERROR_IO_PENDING)
    {
      cerr
        << "ERROR: Unable to write to pipe "
        << GetLastError() << endl;
      CloseHandle(mtnpPipe);
      return (1);
    }
  }
  GetOverlappedResult(mtnpPipe,
    &overlappedWrite, &numBytesWritten,
    TRUE);
  overlappedWrite.Offset += numBytesWritten;

} // while
return (0);
}
```

You will notice that both the server and client now use overlapped I/O structures (see Section 7.5) even though they do not use asynchronous I/O. The overlapped I/O structures are used here because they are required when multiple threads access the same pipe handle. Since both server and client are multi-threaded, and reading and writing occur in different threads, overlapped I/O is a necessity.

The server's job in Listing 8.10 is to accept connections from multiple clients, just as it is in Listing 8.8. That portion of the code is no different. The server code now contains an array, however, that holds the pipes and overlapped structures for each client connection. The server initializes one element of the array for each connection it receives.

This array allows the different client threads in the server to broadcast all messages received to all of the connected clients. You will see in the **ClientThread** thread function a **for** loop that sends each capitalized string out to all of the clients. The overlapped I/O structures are required because of the **for** loop: Since it is possible for two threads to be reading or writing the same pipe simultaneously, the overlapped structures prevent conflict.

The server shown here does not handle disconnection very well. Ideally, the server should update the array whenever a client disconnects, deleting the client's entry to allow another client to connect. This implementation detail is left as an exercise for the reader. In the current form, expect problems to arise if you kill off one client and try to connect another.

The client side of the system appears in Listing 8.11. The client here is nearly identical to Listing 8.9, except that it is multi-threaded. The main thread interacts with the user and writes to the pipe, while the **ServerThread** function reads from the pipe and writes messages to the screen. Because the two threads use the same pipe, you must use overlapped I/O structures. The program initializes the overlapped structures in the two different threads and then uses **ReadFile** and **WriteFile** normally. Again, the non-blocking behavior of overlapped I/O is not used here: the overlapped structures are necessary because the code is using the same pipe in two separate threads. The code passes the overlapped structures to **ReadFile** and **WriteFile** to make these functions compliant with the cross-thread reading and writing.

Typically, a client program will handle pipe I/O in a more elegant manner than shown here. See Section 7.7 for ideas on integrating asynchronous pipe I/O into an MFC program.

8.6 Connecting with UNIX and Other TCP/IP Machines

In the previous sections, you learned about network communications using Windows' native communication protocol. Mailslots and named pipes work well in cases where you want to communicate with other Windows machines on a homogeneous Windows network.

Windows also supports the TCP/IP protocol. This is the protocol used by UNIX machines and the Internet. If you load the TCP/IP drivers in the Network applet of the Control Panel, a number of TCP/IP commands (ftp, telnet, finger, etc.) become available on the command line. You can also create code that can read and write packets on the network using the TCP/IP protocol. There are at least three reasons for creating code using this protocol:

1. You want to write code that connects to an existing network service on a UNIX machine.
2. You want to create a network service (see Chapter 12) on a Windows 2000 machine that UNIX machines will be able to access.
3. You want to create programs that allow widely-separated Windows machines on the Internet to communicate with one another, and you want to make sure the packets will route correctly on the Internet.

For example, if you want to create a Finger service that allows UNIX users to finger your Windows 2000 machine, you must use the TCP/IP communications functions when you write the code.

Windows supplies a complete library of functions for creating TCP/IP code. The library is called the Windows Sockets API, or "winsock." All winsock functions are documented in the Win32 help file. UNIX programmers will find that the functions are very similar to the functions they are accustomed to for writing socket code on UNIX machines. There is also another API, called the Microsoft Windows Sockets Asynchronous Extensions, that supplies TCP/IP support in a cooperative multi-tasking (non-threaded) environment such as Windows 3.1. These functions work in a manner similar to overlapped I/O. Because Windows 2000 and Windows 98 are multi-threaded, the extension functions are not necessarily needed here, but they can be useful in some situations.

There are several vocabulary words and concepts that you need to understand in order to use the TCP/IP functions:

1. Any machine, whether on the world-wide Internet or on an isolated TCP/IP network, has both an *IP address* and *a fully-qualified domain name*. An IP address is of the form `152.1.45.17`, while a name has the form `server.iftech.com`. Both are unique to a particular machine network-wide. In your code you use IP addresses to connect to a machine, but there are functions that let you convert names to addresses. A typical small TCP/IP network consisting of several Windows machines and a UNIX machine is shown in Figure 8.5.

2. The Berkeley flavor of UNIX popularized the concept of a *socket*. In a sense, a socket is a bi-directional communication device. In a sense a socket is similar to a file handle or a pipe. When you open a file handle to an existing file, you create an entity that you can read from and write to. When you create a socket, you can also read from it and write to it, but it is associated with the network rather than with the file system.

3. You can do one of two things with a socket: You can *bind* it to a *port* on the local machine, or, in TCP mode, you can *connect* it to a port on

Figure 8.5 *A typical small TCP/IP network consisting of three Windows machines and one UNIX machine*

another machine. Ports are referred to by positive integer numbers. When you bind a socket to a port, you are claiming a port with a specific number on the local machine. Programs on other machines can connect to that port. Figure 8.6 shows a simplified representation of the different pieces.

4. A port, when used in TCP mode, has the ability to *accept* connections. First you give it the ability to *listen,* and then you let it start accepting connections. Allowing a port to listen enables the port. Other machines can now start connecting to the port. Each time a program *accepts* a connection, data can start to flow across the network. A port has a queue that holds connections waiting to be accepted. You define the maximum size of the queue at the time you tell the port to start listening.

TCP/IP networks support both mailslot-like (unreliable) communications with the potential for broadcasting and point-to-point connections used in client/server architectures. Point-to-point connections, like named pipes, have guaranteed delivery, error correction, and sequencing. Point-to-point connections are referred to as TCP connections. UDP connections, on the other hand, are unreliable but permit broadcasting. TCP connections are far more common in the UNIX world than UDP connections are.

To be a server using the TCP protocol, a program must create a socket, bind it to a port, let the port begin listening, and then accept connections. Each time it accepts a connection, the server can communicate over the new connection with a different client. A client must create a socket and connect it to a port on another machine. Once it has a connection, it can communicate. See Figure 8.7.

TCP/IP networks support three different types of network packets.

Machine A creates a socket and binds it to a port. Other machines on the network can connect to the port.

Machine B creates a socket and connects it to a specific port on machine A.

Figure 8.6 . *TCP connections using ports and sockets*

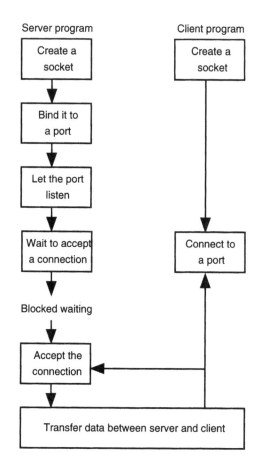

Server program

| Create a socket |

| Bind it to a port |

| Let the port listen |

| Wait to accept a connection |

Blocked waiting

| Accept the connection |

Client program

| Create a socket |

| Connect to a port |

| Transfer data between server and client |

Figure 8.7

The steps involved in connecting a TCP client to a TCP server

1. IP packets are raw packets and are rarely seen. Raw packets are directed to a specific machine or are broadcast, but they bypass the port system and therefore must be handled as generic packets. You will never use IP packets yourself.

2. UDP packets are very similar in concept to mailslot packets. They can be either directed to a port on a machine or broadcast, just like a mailslot. UDP packets are always sent to a specific port number. UDP packets are not very common in the UNIX world because they cannot travel farther than the local network segment and because their use tends to lead to large traffic loads on that segment.

3. TCP packets are similar in concept to named-pipe packets, and are used for point-to-point or client/server communications. They are sent to a specific port on a specific machine. TCP communications are properly-sequenced, reliable, and error corrected, just like named pipes. Almost all UNIX network communications use TCP packets.

One of the most significant advantages of TCP/IP is its routability. A *router* is a device that sits between two separate network *segments,* as shown in Figure 8.8. It examines the TCP/IP header in each packet and decides whether or not a packet on one of the segments should be copied to the other segment. In the diagram below, an administrator has created two separate subnets (128.57.49.xxx and 128.57.50.xxx) and would configure the router to recognize and route packets appropriately. If a machine on network segment one sends a packet to another machine on network segment one, the router ignores it because both machines have the same subnet number. On the other hand, the router would detect a packet on network segment one intended for network segment two because of the difference in the subnet number. It would echo the packet onto network segment two so that the appropriate machine would receive it.

The following sections demonstrate how to write both UDP and TCP code.

8.7 UDP Connections

The most common example of a program using UDP is the rwho command in UNIX. The who command, which you may know, tells you who is logged onto the local UNIX machine. The rwho command does the same thing for all of the machines on the local network segment. The rwho command is made possible by the rwho daemon, which runs on every machine that supports rwho (a daemon is like a Windows 2000 service—it starts at boot time and runs continuously regardless of who is logged in. This daemon periodically broadcasts a UDP packet containing the machine's status information onto the network. The packet includes a list of who is currently logged in, information on the machine's load, the uptime for the machine, and so on.

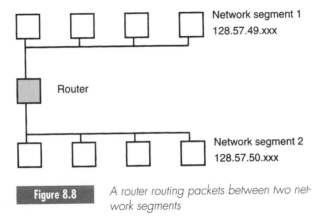

| Figure 8.8 | *A router routing packets between two network segments* |

The daemon also listens for the status messages from other rwho daemons and caches the information it receives.

The rwho command has gone out of favor on most networks because it tends to generate a huge quantity of spurious network traffic. However, it does demonstrate both the pros and the cons of broadcasting packets using UDP. As a side note, it is important to recognize that routers will not pick up broadcast packets, so UDP communications are limited to a single segment.

The programs in Listings 8.12 and 8.13 demonstrate a simple UDP sender and receiver. If you run Listing 8.12, it will wait for UDP packets on port 44,966. The port number used here is arbitrary. Numbers below 1,000 should be avoided because they tend to be pre-defined, but numbers between 1,000 and 64,000 are generally fair game. You will get an error in the server if the port is already in use.

You can run as many senders and receivers as you like on the local machine or on any other machine on the network. They all use port 44,966, and each receiver will print any messages that it receives.

Listing 8.12   *A UDP receiver*

```
// mciprecv.cpp

#include <windows.h>
#include <iostream.h>
#include <winsock.h>

#define NO_FLAGS_SET 0

#define PORT (u_short) 44966
#define MAXBUFLEN 256

INT main(VOID)
{
  WSADATA Data;
  SOCKADDR_IN recvSockAddr;
  SOCKET recvSocket;
  int status;
  int numrcv;
  char buffer[MAXBUFLEN];

  /* initialize the Windows Socket DLL */
  status=WSAStartup(MAKEWORD(1, 1), &Data);
  if (status != 0)
    cerr << "ERROR: WSAStartup unsuccessful"
      << endl;

  /* zero the sockaddr_in structure */
  memset(&recvSockAddr, 0, sizeof(recvSockAddr));
```

```
/* specify the port portion of the address */
recvSockAddr.sin_port=htons(PORT);
/* specify the address family as Internet */
recvSockAddr.sin_family=AF_INET;
/* specify that the address does not matter */
recvSockAddr.sin_addr.s_addr=htonl(INADDR_ANY);

/* create a socket */
recvSocket=socket(AF_INET, SOCK_DGRAM, 0);
if (recvSocket == INVALID_SOCKET)
  cerr << "ERROR: socket unsuccessful" << endl;

/* associate the socket with the address */
status=bind(recvSocket,
  (LPSOCKADDR) &recvSockAddr,
  sizeof(recvSockAddr));
if (status == SOCKET_ERROR)
  cerr << "ERROR: bind unsuccessful" << endl;

while(1)
{
  numrcv=recvfrom(recvSocket, buffer, MAXBUFLEN,
    NO_FLAGS_SET, NULL, NULL);
  if (numrcv == SOCKET_ERROR)
  {
    cerr << "ERROR: recvfrom unsuccessful"
      << endl;
    status=closesocket(recvSocket);
    if (status == SOCKET_ERROR)
      cerr << "ERROR: closesocket unsuccessful"
        << endl;
    status=WSACleanup();
    if (status == SOCKET_ERROR)
      cerr << "ERROR: WSACleanup unsuccessful"
        << endl;
    return(1);
  }
  cout << buffer << endl;
} /* while */
}
```

Listing 8.13   *A UDP sender*

```
// mcipsend.cpp

#include <windows.h>
#include <iostream.h>
#include <winsock.h>
```

Listing 8.13   *A UDP sender (continued)*

```c
#define NO_FLAGS_SET 0

#define PORT (u_short) 44966

INT main(VOID)
{
  WSADATA Data;
  SOCKADDR_IN destSockAddr;
  SOCKET destSocket;
  int status;
  int numsnt;
  int enable=1;
  char *toSendtxt="Test String";

  /* initialize the Windows Socket DLL */
  status=WSAStartup(MAKEWORD(1, 1), &Data);
  if (status != 0)
    cerr << "ERROR: WSAStartup unsuccessful"
      << endl;

  /* specify the IP address */
  destSockAddr.sin_addr.s_addr=
    htonl(INADDR_BROADCAST);
  /* specify the port portion of the address */
  destSockAddr.sin_port=htons(PORT);
  /* specify the address family as Internet */
  destSockAddr.sin_family=AF_INET;

  /* create a socket */
  destSocket=socket(AF_INET, SOCK_DGRAM, 0);
  if (destSocket == INVALID_SOCKET)
  {
    cerr << "ERROR: socket unsuccessful" << endl;
    status=WSACleanup();
    if (status == SOCKET_ERROR)
      cerr << "ERROR: WSACleanup unsuccessful"
        << endl;
    return(1);
  }

  /* permit broadcasting on the socket */
  status=setsockopt(destSocket, SOL_SOCKET,
    SO_BROADCAST, (char *) &enable,
      sizeof(enable));
  if (status != 0)
    cerr << "ERROR: setsockopt unsuccessful"
      << endl;

  while(1)
```

```
  {
    cout << "Sending..." << endl;
    numsnt=sendto(destSocket, toSendtxt,
      strlen(toSendtxt) + 1, NO_FLAGS_SET,
      (LPSOCKADDR) &destSockAddr,
        sizeof(destSockAddr));
    if (numsnt != (int)strlen(toSendtxt) + 1)
    {
      cerr << "ERROR: sendto unsuccessful" << endl;
      status=closesocket(destSocket);
      if (status == SOCKET_ERROR)
        cerr << "ERROR: closesocket unsuccessful"
          << endl;
      status=WSACleanup();
      if (status == SOCKET_ERROR)
        cerr << "ERROR: WSACleanup unsuccessful"
          << endl;
      return(1);
    }

  /* Wait before sending the message again */
  Sleep(4800);
  } /* while */
}
```

The code in Listing 8.12 starts by initializing winsock using the WSAStart-up function (look in the Win32 help file for more information on these functions).

WSAStartup   *Initializes the winsock library*

```
int PASCAL FAR WSAStartup (
  WORD version,
  LPWSADATA data );
```

version   Version number of the winsock library this code uses

data   Pointer to a struct that lets WSAStartup return data

Returns 0 on success.

This step is mandatory. In this call you initialize the winsock DLL for your process, and you make sure that the DLL can support your code by passing in the version number you are using.

Listing 8.12 next initializes a SOCKADDR_IN structure. This structure is required to bind a socket to a port (the following is copied from the Win32 help file):

```
struct sockaddr_in {
        short    sin_family;
```

```
    u_short  sin_port;
    struct   in_addr sin_addr;
    char     sin_zero[8];
};
```

The structure specifies the port that the socket will bind to in **sin_port,** the protocol family in **sin_family,** and the machine it will accept messages from in **sin_addr.** In this case, the receiver will accept messages on the port specified in the PORT constant (44966) and will accept messages from any sender.

The calls to the **htonl** and **htons** functions convert values to *network byte order.* Everything put on the network should always be in network byte order. Individual machines then convert values back to their *host byte order.* This step ensures that machines with different byte orders can communicate without difficulty.

---

htonl   *Converts a u_long from host byte order to network byte order*

```
u_long PASCAL FAR htonl (
   u_long hostlong)
```

hostlong   Host value to convert

Returns value in network byte order.

---

htons   *Converts a u_short from host byte order to network byte order*

```
u_short PASCAL FAR htons (
   u_short hostshort)
```

hostshort   Host value to convert

Returns value in network byte order.

Listing 8.12 creates the socket using the **socket** function. When you create a socket, you specify the address format, the type of socket (UDP or TCP), and the protocol. The library currently supports only one address format, and generally you pass zero for the protocol, so all that this function call does here is choose between UDP and TCP packets. It will create the socket or return an error code.

The next line binds the socket to the specified port using the **bind** function.

---

socket   *Creates a socket*

```
SOCKET PASCAL FAR socket (
   int af,
   int type,
   int protocol)
```

af	Address format
type	Type: SOCK_STREAM (TCP) or SOCK_DGRAM (UDP)
protocol	Network protocol, or 0 if don't care

Returns socket descriptor or INVALID_SOCKET on failure

---

bind	*binds a socket to a port*

```
int PASCAL FAR bind (
   SOCKET socket,
   const struct sockaddr FAR * name,
   int nameLen)
```

socket	The socket to bind
name	The port to bind to
nameLen	Length of the port information

Returns 0 on success or SOCKET_ERROR

The **bind** function accepts the socket to bind as well as the structure containing the port name, and binds the socket to the port.

Listing 8.12 then enters a loop, in which it waits for messages to arrive. The **recvfrom** function blocks until a UDP packet arrives on the port. If there is an error, the code cleans up gracefully, calling **closesocket** and **WSACleanup.** Otherwise, it prints the message received.

---

recvfrom	*Receives a packet from a UDP socket*

```
int PASCAL FAR recvfrom (
   int socket,
   char FAR * buffer,
   int bufferLen,
   int flags,
   struct sockaddr FAR * from,
   int FAR * fromLen)
```

socket	The socket to receive from
buffer	The buffer to place the received message in
bufferLen	Length of the buffer
flags	MSG_PEEK and/or MSG_OOB
from	Sender information
fromLen	Length of sender info

Returns the number of bytes received on success, 0 if the connection was closed, or SOCKET_ERROR

---

closesocket   *Closes a socket*

```
int FAR PASCAL closesocket (
    SOCKET socket)
```

socket   The socket to close

Returns 0 on success or SOCKET_ERROR

WSACleanup   *Terminates the WSA DLL cleanly*

int PASCAL FAR WSACleanup (void)

Returns 0 on success or SOCKET_ERROR

This is all fairly simple: if you were to strip out the error-handling code, the program would be only 11 lines long. It may take a few days to get used to the terminology, but once you do, you do not have to write an immense amount of code to create simple network interactions on heterogeneous networks using UDP packets.

The sender code in Listing 8.13 follows the same general pattern. It initializes WSA, creates a UDP socket, and then sets options on the socket so that it can send things in broadcast mode using the **setsockopt** function.

---

setsockopt   *Sets options on a socket*

```
int PASCAL FAR setsockopt (
    SOCKET socket,
    int level,
    int optName,
    const char FAR * optVal,
    int optLen)
```

socket   The socket

level   SOL_SOCKET or IPPROTO_TCP

optName   The option to set

optVal   The value to set on the option

optLen   The length of the value

Returns 0 on success or SOCKET_ERROR

You can set a wide range of options, as described in the Win32 help file. Here the goal is to tell the socket to permit broadcast transmissions, so the SO_BROADCAST option is set to TRUE (1).

With the socket established and set to broadcast mode, the sender can start transmitting messages to any receivers on the network. It uses the **sendto** function to do this.

sendto	*Sends messages*

```
int PASCAL FAR sendto (
   SOCKET socket,
   const char FAR * buffer,
   int bufferLen,
   int flags,
   const struct sockaddr FAR * to,
   int toLen)
```

socket	The socket
buffer	The message to send
bufferLen	The length of the message
flags	Flags
to	The machine to send it to
toLen	The length of the to buffer

Returns 0 on success or SOCKET_ERROR

The **sendto** function sends the contents of the buffer to the port on the specified machine. The **destSockAddr** structure here specifies a broadcast transmission, so all receivers on the network receive the packet.

Listing 8.14 contains a file named unixsend.c. It is a version of Listing 8.13 for UNIX machines, and you can use it to demonstrate that UNIX machines can talk to Windows machines using UDP packets. Compile Listing 8.14 with a C compiler on a UNIX machine. The UNIX machine needs to be on the same network segment as a Windows machine running the receiver. When we first tested this version of Listing 8.14, it failed on the send-to statement. Our UNIX machine simply will not accept the IP address 255.255.255.255. Our UNIX machine's IP address is 152.1.100.100, however (type hostname -i on the UNIX machine to find its address), and all of our test machines are on the segment 152.1.100.xxx, so by changing the IP address in the sendto statement to 152.1.100.255 we solved the problem. The octet 255 has the meaning "broadcast" in an IP address, here implying "broadcast on the segment 152.1.100.xxx." If the code fails on the sendto statement when you run it, suspect the IP address and work with it.

Listing 8.14   *A UNIX version of the sender in Listing 8.13*

```
/* unixsend.c */

#include <stdio.h>
#include <netinet/in.h>
#include <sys/socket.h>
```

Listing 8.14 *A UNIX version of the sender in Listing 8.13 (continued)*

```c
#define NO_FLAGS_SET 0

#define PORT (unsigned short) 44966

int main()
{
  struct sockaddr_in destSockAddr;
  int destSocket;
  int status;
  int numsnt;
  int enable=1;
  char *toSendtxt="Test String";

  /* specify the IP address */
  destSockAddr.sin_addr.s_addr=
    inet_addr("255.255.255.255");
  /* specify the port portion of the address */
  destSockAddr.sin_port=htons(PORT);
  /* specify the address family as Internet */
  destSockAddr.sin_family=AF_INET;

  /* create a socket */
  destSocket=socket(AF_INET, SOCK_DGRAM, 0);
  if (destSocket == -1)
    printf("Error creating socket\n");

  /* permit broadcasting on the socket */
  status=setsockopt(destSocket, SOL_SOCKET,
    SO_BROADCAST, (char *) &enable,
    sizeof(enable));
  if (status == -1)
    printf("Error setting socket opts\n");

  while(1)
  {
    printf("Sending...\n");
    numsnt=sendto(destSocket, toSendtxt,
      strlen(toSendtxt) + 1, NO_FLAGS_SET,
      &destSockAddr, sizeof(destSockAddr));
    if (numsnt != (int)strlen(toSendtxt) + 1)
    {
      printf("ERROR: sendto unsuccessful\n");
      status=close(destSocket);
      return(1);
    }

  /* Wait before sending the message again */
  sleep(5);
  } /* while */
}
```

Compare the code in Listing 8.14 to the code in Listing 8.13 and you will find that they are nearly identical, except for a few minor declaration changes and the loss of the WSA functions. The winsock library follows the UNIX standards very closely. It would be equally easy to create a UNIX version of Listing 8.12 and have the receiver run on a UNIX machine as well.

8.8 TCP Connections

TCP connections are used almost exclusively for network connections in the UNIX world and in general. TCP packets, unlike UDP packets, are automatically sequenced and error-checked by the network drivers, and the system can detect when the connection terminates automatically. The `telnet`, `ftp`, `finger`, and `talk` commands all rely on point-to-point TCP connections. You can `talk` to someone on a machine in the next room or halfway around the world if you are connected to the Internet.

TCP connections are very similar to Windows' named pipes, but they allow you to connect to a wide variety of machines on heterogeneous networks. This section demonstrates both point-to-point and client/server architectures. Many parts of the code demonstrated here are similar to code demonstrated in the previous section, so you may want to review that code as a starting point. You should also note that the concepts here are very similar to those seen in the named-pipe discussion earlier in this chapter.

Listings 8.15 and 8.16 demonstrate a simple one-directional point-to-point TCP connection. Listing 8.15 contains the receiver, while Listing 8.16 contains the sender. Run the receiver first, and then run the sender on the same machine. You will see a "Test String" message at the receiver every five seconds. Find out the IP address of the receiver machine (use the Network applet in the Control Panel and use the Configure button on the TCP/IP module) and use it to modify the DEST_IP_ADDR constant in the sender. You can then run the sender program on any machine on the network.

| Listing 8.15 | *A single TCP receiver for point-to-point connections* |

```
// ssiprecv.cpp

#include <windows.h>
#include <iostream.h>
#include <winsock.h>

#define NO_FLAGS_SET 0

#define PORT (u_short) 44965
#define MAXBUFLEN 256
```

Listing 8.15 *A single TCP receiver for point-to-point connections (continued)*

```
INT main(VOID)
{
  WSADATA Data;
  SOCKADDR_IN serverSockAddr;
  SOCKADDR_IN clientSockAddr;
  SOCKET serverSocket;
  SOCKET clientSocket;
  int addrLen=sizeof(SOCKADDR_IN);
  int status;
  int numrcv;
  char buffer[MAXBUFLEN];

  /* initialize the Windows Socket DLL */
  status=WSAStartup(MAKEWORD(1, 1), &Data);
  if (status != 0)
    cerr << "ERROR: WSAStartup unsuccessful"
      << endl;

  /* zero the sockaddr_in structure */
  memset(&serverSockAddr, 0,
    sizeof(serverSockAddr));
  /* specify the port portion of the address */
  serverSockAddr.sin_port=htons(PORT);
  /* specify the address family as Internet */
  serverSockAddr.sin_family=AF_INET;
  /* specify that the address does not matter */
  serverSockAddr.sin_addr.s_addr=htonl(INADDR_ANY);

  /* create a socket */
  serverSocket=socket(AF_INET, SOCK_STREAM, 0);
  if (serverSocket == INVALID_SOCKET)
    cerr << "ERROR: socket unsuccessful" << endl;

  /* associate the socket with the address */
  status=bind(serverSocket,
    (LPSOCKADDR) &serverSockAddr,
    sizeof(serverSockAddr));
  if (status == SOCKET_ERROR)
    cerr << "ERROR: bind unsuccessful" << endl;

  /* allow the socket to take connections */
  status=listen(serverSocket, 1);
  if (status == SOCKET_ERROR)
    cerr << "ERROR: listen unsuccessful" << endl;

  /* accept the connection request when one
     is received */
  clientSocket=accept(serverSocket,
```

```
    (LPSOCKADDR) &clientSockAddr,
    &addrLen);

 cout << "Got the connection..." << endl;

 while(1)
 {
   numrcv=recv(clientSocket, buffer,
     MAXBUFLEN, NO_FLAGS_SET);
   if ((numrcv == 0) || (numrcv == SOCKET_ERROR))
   {
     cout << "Connection terminated." << endl;
     status=closesocket(clientSocket);
     if (status == SOCKET_ERROR)
       cerr << "ERROR: closesocket unsuccessful"
         << endl;
     status=WSACleanup();
     if (status == SOCKET_ERROR)
       cerr << "ERROR: WSACleanup unsuccessful"
         << endl;
     return(1);
   }
   cout << buffer << endl;
 } /* while */
}
```

Listing 8.16   *A simple TCP sender for point-to-point connections*

```
// ssipsend.cpp

#include <windows.h>
#include <iostream.h>
#include <winsock.h>

#define NO_FLAGS_SET 0

#define PORT (u_short) 44965
#define DEST_IP_ADDR "127.0.0.1"

INT main(VOID)
{
  WSADATA Data;
  SOCKADDR_IN destSockAddr;
  SOCKET destSocket;
  unsigned long destAddr;
  int status;
  int numsnt;
  char *toSendtxt="Test String";
```

Listing 8.16   *A simple TCP sender for point-to-point connections (continued)*

```
/* initialize the Windows Socket DLL */
status=WSAStartup(MAKEWORD(1, 1), &Data);
if (status != 0)
  cerr << "ERROR: WSAStartup unsuccessful"
    << endl;

/* convert IP address into in_addr form */
destAddr=inet_addr(DEST_IP_ADDR);
/* copy destAddr into sockaddr_in structure */
memcpy(&destSockAddr.sin_addr,
  &destAddr, sizeof(destAddr));
/* specify the port portion of the address */
destSockAddr.sin_port=htons(PORT);
/* specify the address family as Internet */
destSockAddr.sin_family=AF_INET;

/* create a socket */
destSocket=socket(AF_INET, SOCK_STREAM, 0);
if (destSocket == INVALID_SOCKET)
{
  cerr << "ERROR: socket unsuccessful" << endl;
  status=WSACleanup();
  if (status == SOCKET_ERROR)
    cerr << "ERROR: WSACleanup unsuccessful"
      << endl;
  return(1);
}

cout << "Trying to connect to IP Address: "
  << DEST_IP_ADDR << endl;

/* connect to the server */
status=connect(destSocket,
  (LPSOCKADDR) &destSockAddr,
  sizeof(destSockAddr));
if (status == SOCKET_ERROR)
{
  cerr << "ERROR: connect unsuccessful" << endl;
  status=closesocket(destSocket);
  if (status == SOCKET_ERROR)
    cerr << "ERROR: closesocket unsuccessful"
      << endl;
  status=WSACleanup();
  if (status == SOCKET_ERROR)
    cerr << "ERROR: WSACleanup unsuccessful"
      << endl;
  return(1);
}
```

```
cout << "Connected..." << endl;

while(1)
{
  cout << "Sending..." << endl;
  numsnt=send(destSocket, toSendtxt,
    strlen(toSendtxt) + 1, NO_FLAGS_SET);
  if (numsnt != (int)strlen(toSendtxt) + 1)
  {
    cout << "Connection terminated" << endl;
    status=closesocket(destSocket);
    if (status == SOCKET_ERROR)
      cerr << "ERROR: closesocket unsuccessful"
        << endl;
    status=WSACleanup();
    if (status == SOCKET_ERROR)
      cerr << "ERROR: WSACleanup unsuccessful"
        << endl;
    return(1);
  }

  /* Wait before sending the message again */
  Sleep(4800);
  } /* while */
}
```

The TCP receiver program in Listing 8.15 starts the same way that the UDP receiver in Listing 8.12 does. It initializes the library, creates a socket, and binds the socket to a port. The socket here is in SOCK_STREAM mode, which causes it to use TCP rather than UDP packets. Listing 8.15 then calls the **listen** function.

---

listen *Enables a socket to listen for connections*

```
int PASCAL FAR listen(
  SOCKET socket,
  int queue)
```

socket   The socket to enable

queue   The number of pending connections it can hold

Returns 0 on success or SOCKET_ERROR

The **listen** function creates a connection queue on the port attached to the socket. The queue specifies how many *pending connections* the port can support. When another machine tries to connect to the port, its connection request is held in the queue. If the queue is full, or if the port's queue does not exist because the **listen** function has not been called on the port, then the connection request is rejected. If space exists in the queue, then the connection is held in the queue until it is *accepted*. The connecting machine will probably time out if the queued connection is not accepted within 30 seconds or so.

The call to **listen** specifies the size of the queue. In Listing 8.15 the size is set to one, but a typical server program might set it to five to handle multiple incoming requests.

Listing 8.15 next calls the **accept** function. This program is able to accept just one connection. The **accept** function will block until a copy of the send program in Listing 8.16 tries to connect.

---

accept   *Enables a socket to listen for connections*

```
SOCKET PASCAL FAR accept (SOCKET socket,
    struct sockaddr FAR * addr,
    int FAR * addrLen)
```

socket	The socket to accept from
addr	Pointer to a structure that identifies the connector
addrLen	Size of the returned structure

Returns a socket number on success, or INVALID_SOCKET

The **accept** function removes the first connection request from the pending connection queue for the port. It then chooses an unused port number and assigns the connection to that port. The program can then receive on that port, while the space in the queue on the well-known port number is freed up for other connection requests. The **accept** function returns a structure that identifies the connecting machine.

With the connection properly established, Listing 8.15 enters a loop to receive messages from the sender. It uses the **recv** function, which is nearly identical to the **recvfrom** function seen earlier. The **recv** function does not return information about the sender like **recvfrom** does, and this information is not needed here because the connection is point-to-point.

---

recv   *Receives a packet from a socket*

```
int PASCAL FAR recv (
    int socket,
    char FAR * buffer,
    int bufferLen,
    int flags)
```

socket	The socket to receive from
buffer	The buffer to place the received message in

bufferLen	Length of the buffer
flags	MSG_PEEK and/or MSG_OOB

Returns the number of bytes received on success, 0 if the connection was closed, or SOCKET_ERROR

Note that this receiver can accept just one connection because it calls the **accept** function once. If you try to create multiple connections from multiple senders, they will fail. The following example handles multiple connections.

The sender code in Listing 8.16 is nearly identical to that in Listing 8.13, except that it connects to a specific machine rather than broadcasting. TCP connections do not allow broadcast packets—only UDP connections do.

The second example, shown in Listings 8.17 and 8.18, demonstrates a client/server pair like the pair shown for named pipes. The server accepts connections from clients. When a client sends a string, the server converts it to upper case and sends it back to the client. Clients can connect from any machine on the network worldwide, because this system uses TCP packets. This is the same sort of technology you would use to create an FTP or talk server.

Run the server on a Windows 2000 machine. Test the server by running the client on the same machine. The current IP address for the sender, 127.0.0.1 in the DEST_IP_ADDR constant of the client, is a loopback connection to the local machine. The client should connect automatically. Now replace 127.0.0.1 with the actual IP address for the server machine. Recompile the client and you should be able to run multiple copies of it on any machine on the network.

Listing 8.17   *A multi-client server using TCP*

```cpp
// msipserv.cpp

#include <windows.h>
#include <iostream.h>
#include <winsock.h>
#include <process.h>

#define NO_FLAGS_SET 0

#define PORT (u_short) 44965
#define MAXBUFLEN 256

VOID talkToClient(VOID *cs)
{
  char buffer[MAXBUFLEN];
  int status;
```

Listing 8.17   *A multi-client server using TCP (continued)*

```
    int numsnt;
    int numrcv;
    SOCKET clientSocket=(SOCKET)cs;

    while(1)
    {
      numrcv=recv(clientSocket, buffer,
        MAXBUFLEN, NO_FLAGS_SET);
      if ((numrcv == 0) || (numrcv == SOCKET_ERROR))
      {
        cout << "Connection terminated" << endl;
        break;
      }

      _strupr(buffer);

      numsnt=send(clientSocket, buffer,
        strlen(buffer) + 1, NO_FLAGS_SET);
      if (numsnt != (int)strlen(buffer) + 1)
      {
        cout << "Connection terminated." << endl;
        break;
      }

    } /* while */

    /* terminate the connection with the client
       (disable sending/receiving) */
    status=shutdown(clientSocket, 2);
    if (status == SOCKET_ERROR)
      cerr << "ERROR: shutdown unsuccessful" << endl;

    /* close the socket */
    status=closesocket(clientSocket);
    if (status == SOCKET_ERROR)
      cerr << "ERROR: closesocket unsuccessful"
        << endl;
}

INT main(VOID)
{
  WSADATA Data;
  SOCKADDR_IN serverSockAddr;
  SOCKADDR_IN clientSockAddr;
  SOCKET serverSocket;
  SOCKET clientSocket;
  int addrLen=sizeof(SOCKADDR_IN);
  int status;
  DWORD threadID;
```

```
/* initialize the Windows Socket DLL */
status=WSAStartup(MAKEWORD(1, 1), &Data);
if (status != 0)
{
  cerr << "ERROR: WSAStartup unsuccessful"
    << endl;
  return(1);
}

/* zero the sockaddr_in structure */
memset(&serverSockAddr, 0,
  sizeof(serverSockAddr));
/* specify the port portion of the address */
serverSockAddr.sin_port=htons(PORT);
/* specify the address family as Internet */
serverSockAddr.sin_family=AF_INET;
/* specify that the address does not matter */
serverSockAddr.sin_addr.s_addr=htonl(INADDR_ANY);

/* create a socket */
serverSocket=socket(AF_INET, SOCK_STREAM, 0);
if (serverSocket == INVALID_SOCKET)
{
  cerr << "ERROR: socket unsuccessful"
    << endl;
  status=WSACleanup();
  if (status == SOCKET_ERROR)
    cerr << "ERROR: WSACleanup unsuccessful"
      << endl;
  return(1);
}

/* associate the socket with the address */
status=bind(serverSocket,
  (LPSOCKADDR) &serverSockAddr,
  sizeof(serverSockAddr));
if (status == SOCKET_ERROR)
  cerr << "ERROR: bind unsuccessful" << endl;

/* allow the socket to take connections */
status=listen(serverSocket, 1);
if (status == SOCKET_ERROR)
  cerr << "ERROR: listen unsuccessful" << endl;

while(1)
{
  /* accept the connection request when
     one is received */
  clientSocket=accept(serverSocket,
    (LPSOCKADDR) &clientSockAddr,
```

| Listing 8.17 | *A multi-client server using TCP (continued)* |

```
    &addrLen);
  if (clientSocket == INVALID_SOCKET)
  {
    cerr << "ERROR: Unable to accept connection."
      << endl;
    return(1);
  }

  threadID=_beginthread(talkToClient,
    0, (VOID *)clientSocket);
  if (threadID == -1)
  {
    cerr << "ERROR: Unable to create thread"
      << endl;
    /* close the socket */
    status=closesocket(clientSocket);
    if (status == SOCKET_ERROR)
      cerr << "ERROR: closesocket unsuccessful"
        << endl;
  }

  } /* while */
}
```

| Listing 8.18 | *A TCP client for the server in Listing 8.17* |

```
// msipclnt.cpp

#include <windows.h>
#include <iostream.h>
#include <winsock.h>

#define NO_FLAGS_SET 0

#define PORT (u_short) 44965
#define DEST_IP_ADDR "127.0.0.1"
#define MAXBUFLEN 256

INT main(VOID)
{
  WSADATA Data;
  SOCKADDR_IN destSockAddr;
  SOCKET destSocket;
  unsigned long destAddr;
  int status;
  int numsnt;
```

```
int numrcv;
char sendText[MAXBUFLEN];
char recvText[MAXBUFLEN];

/* initialize the Windows Socket DLL */
status=WSAStartup(MAKEWORD(1, 1), &Data);
if (status != 0)
  cerr << "ERROR: WSAStartup unsuccessful"
    << endl;

/* convert IP address into in_addr form*/
destAddr=inet_addr(DEST_IP_ADDR);
/* copy destAddr into sockaddr_in structure */
memcpy(&destSockAddr.sin_addr, &destAddr,
  sizeof(destAddr));
/* specify the port portion of the address */
destSockAddr.sin_port=htons(PORT);
/* specify the address family as Internet */
destSockAddr.sin_family=AF_INET;

/* create a socket */
destSocket=socket(AF_INET, SOCK_STREAM, 0);
if (destSocket == INVALID_SOCKET)
{
  cerr << "ERROR: socket unsuccessful" << endl;
  status=WSACleanup();
  if (status == SOCKET_ERROR)
    cerr << "ERROR: WSACleanup unsuccessful"
      << endl;
  return(1);
}

cout << "Trying to connect to IP Address: "
  << DEST_IP_ADDR << endl;

/* connect to the server */
status=connect(destSocket,
  (LPSOCKADDR) &destSockAddr,
  sizeof(destSockAddr));
if (status == SOCKET_ERROR)
{
  cerr << "ERROR: connect unsuccessful"
    << endl;
  status=closesocket(destSocket);
  if (status == SOCKET_ERROR)
    cerr << "ERROR: closesocket unsuccessful"
      << endl;
  status=WSACleanup();
```

Listing 8.18   *A TCP client for the server in Listing 8.17 (continued)*

```
  if (status == SOCKET_ERROR)
    cerr << "ERROR: WSACleanup unsuccessful"
      << endl;
  return(1);
}

cout << "Connected..." << endl;

while(1)
{
  cout << "Type text to send: ";
  cin.getline(sendText, MAXBUFLEN);

  /* Send the message to the server */
  numsnt=send(destSocket, sendText,
    strlen(sendText) + 1, NO_FLAGS_SET);
  if (numsnt != (int)strlen(sendText) + 1)
  {
    cout << "Connection terminated." << endl;
    status=closesocket(destSocket);
    if (status == SOCKET_ERROR)
      cerr << "ERROR: closesocket unsuccessful"
        << endl;
    status=WSACleanup();
    if (status == SOCKET_ERROR)
      cerr << "ERROR: WSACleanup unsuccessful"
        << endl;
    return(1);
  }

  /* Wait for a response from server */
  numrcv=recv(destSocket, recvText,
    MAXBUFLEN, NO_FLAGS_SET);
  if ((numrcv == 0) || (numrcv == SOCKET_ERROR))
  {
    cout << "Connection terminated.";
    status=closesocket(destSocket);
    if (status == SOCKET_ERROR)
      cerr << "ERROR: closesocket unsuccessful"
        << endl;
    status=WSACleanup();
    if (status == SOCKET_ERROR)
      cerr << "ERROR: WSACleanup unsuccessful"
        << endl;
    return(1);
  }
```

```
cout << "Received: " <<  recvText << endl;

  } /* while */
}
```

The server code in Listing 8.17 bears a strong resemblance to that in Listing 8.15. The main difference occurs around the **accept** function in Listing 8.17. Right after accepting a connection, the program creates a new and independent thread to manage the new client. Each client will have its own thread (see the Run-time Routines Help file for information on **_begin thread**).

Inside the **talkToClient** thread function, the program simply accepts client messages as they arrive, converts them to uppercase, and then sends them back. The client in Listing 8.18, meanwhile, is accepting strings from the user, sending them to the server, and then displaying the upper-case result to the user. If the server dies, the client code correctly detects it and terminates.

In all of the client code demonstrated above, one thing that would improve the code is a way to connect to the server by name rather than by IP address. The function that does the translation from name to IP address is called **gethostbyname**. The following code demonstrates how to use the function:

```
struct hostent *serverHostent;

serverHostent = gethostbyname("itgate.iftech.com");
if (serverHostent == 0)
  ... error
else
{
  memcpy(&destSockAddr.sin_addr,
    serverHostent->h_addr,
    serverHostent->h_length);
}
```

---

gethostbyname   *Converts a machine name to its IP address*

```
struct hostent FAR * PASCAL FAR gethostbyname(
  const char FAR * name)
```

name   The machine name

Returns a pointer to a structure or 0 on failure

The pointer returned by **gethostbyname** points to a single copy of the structure that is maintained by the library. *Do not* modify or delete this structure.

8.9 Conclusion

This chapter contains an example of network communication arrangement possible in Windows 2000. It uses threads in a number of different ways, and you may therefore want to review Chapter 6 for more information on this topic.

Chapter 9 presents Remote Procedure Calls, or RPCs. RPCs automatically work in a client/server fashion and hide most of the network details, so you may want to use them to automate the process of creating client/server applications.

Serial communication over modems is another way for Windows machines to talk to one other. Chapter 11 discusses this topic.

See Chapter 13 for information on security and impersonation in pipes.

Remote Procedure Calls

*R*emote Procedure Calls (RPCs) allow you to call a function
that, instead of being executed on your local machine, is executed
on a machine somewhere else on the network. The RPC concept
gives you tremendous flexibility in using the computing resources
on your network, and allows you to optimize different machines
for specific tasks. In this chapter you will learn how to design and
implement your own RPC servers and clients, and you will also
learn how to create and configure RPC servers and clients properly. DCOM, which will be covered in the next chapter, uses RPCs.
As a programmer, you would never notice the difference between
them except that RPCs are slower.

Compatibility Note: All of the code in this chapter works in Windows 2000. At the
time of publication, you can run both RPC servers and clients on Windows 98
provided that (1) you do not use the ncacn_np (named pipe) protocol, and (2)
you implicitly bind to a specific machine rather than using the name-server features. The code in Section 9.9 is configured to use ncacn_ip_tcp and a specific
machine name so that it will work in Windows 98 without modification.

9.1 The Possibilities

There are many ways to use remote procedure calls to improve the speed of your
applications and to use the network's specialized resources more efficiently.
Listed below are several examples that will help you to see the possibilities.

- Compute servers: Say that your company has purchased a new machine that contains ten high-speed RISC processors, and you want to spread the power of that machine across the network when running certain in-house applications. One easy way to do it is to place RPC servers for CPU-intensive functions onto the new machine. You can then modify your in-house applications slightly so that they call the RPC servers for those functions. For example, if you have a rotation operation in a graphics program and the operation takes a tremendous amount of CPU power to execute, it would be a perfect candidate for an RPC. Or you might build libraries of math-intensive functions (FFTs, fractal calculations, etc.) and make the entire library available to every machine on the network using an RPC server for the library.

- Data management: You might have a machine containing a large and fast hard disk that holds an extremely large data set. Suppose certain operations on the data set require scanning it from one end to the other. You don't want to perform those operations on any other machine on the network because it means transmitting the entire data set over the net. However, you can put an RPC server on the machine that contains the data set, and perform the data-intensive operations locally. When another machine performs the operation, it calls the RPC, and all of the data is handled directly on the machine containing the hard disk. Only the results are transmitted back over the network. A good example of this situation can be found in the Search capability in the File Manager. When you search a hard disk on your local machine, it is fairly quick. However, it slows down significantly when you perform the search on a network drive, because all of the file name information is transmitted over the network and scanned on your machine. If each machine had an RPC server that handled the searching, then your machine could call the RPC server, which would scan the file names on the machine where it resides and return just the result. A system like this would reduce network traffic significantly during search operations.

- Memory-intensive operations: If you have an application that occasionally requires 100 megabytes of physical memory to perform an operation, it might not be practical to give every user on the network 100 megabytes of RAM. However, you can make one machine that possesses the required RAM the RPC server for that operation, and then let other machines perform the operation remotely.

- Combinations: Say that you have a single application that occasionally needs 100 megabytes of physical memory and also uses an extremely large data set and a lot of very CPU-intensive math functions. You want 10 people on the network to be able to run it from inexpensive, low-end machines. If you have RPC servers on suitably optimized high-end machines, then the low-end machines will be able to run the application at an acceptable rate. All of the real work is farmed out to the big machines, and the low-end machines simply pull the pieces together.

You can see from these examples that the RPC mechanism is simply a standardized way to implement client/server architectures. The RPC facility gives you the ability to create your own servers very easily and share them over the network.

9.2 The Basic Idea

Once everything is set up and working properly, a remote procedure call looks very easy. In your code, you simply call a function just like you normally would. Looking at the code, there is no way to distinguish an RPC from a normal function. For example, in a graphics program you might have a function named **CalcPixel** that calculates the value for a pixel in a ray-traced image. In any ray-tracing application, **CalcPixel** would represent a fairly CPU-intensive function call. A typical call might look like this:

```
color = CalcPixel(x,y);
```

In a normal program, when you call the function, the program first branches off to execute the function, then calculates the result, and returns with the answer. In an RPC program, however, the computer instead acts as an *RPC client* and sends a network packet containing the x and y parameters to another machine running the *RPC server* for that function. The function executes on the second machine, and when it is done, that machine sends a network packet containing the function's result back to the caller. See Figure 9.1

Figure 9.1   *Remote procedure calls send parameters to a remote machine, where the function executes. Any results are sent back to the caller through the network as well*

There is nothing magical about RPCs. For example, it is possible for you to implement most of an RPC's functionality yourself using the network commands discussed in Chapter 8. However, it would take a lot of code, and it would not be nearly as clean as the RPC implementation is. The advantage of using RPCs is that the syntax is so delightfully simple. You just call a function like you always do, and everything else is automatic. All of the network details are hidden from view and you can ignore them.

The most important advantage of RPCs is the ability they give you to optimize use of the hardware resources available on your network. For example, if you have a machine that contains a board that is very good at calculating ray-traced pixels, you can put the RPC server for **CalcPixel** on that machine. Now anyone on the network, regardless of the type of machine they are using, can run the ray-tracing program and take advantage of the speed of that special board. RPCs give you an extremely powerful tool for creating client/server applications.

9.3 Design Issues

As with anything else, RPCs have trade-offs. RPCs' disadvantages stem primarily from the fact that the network is being used to transport parameters and results back and forth. This tends to give RPCs high latencies. RPCs also have a fairly significant per-call overhead because of the amount of coordinating the system is doing behind the scenes. It is important for you to understand the overhead and trade-offs involved with RPCs so that you can design effective RPC architectures.

The best way to get a feel for the trade-offs involved with RPCs is to walk through the design of a simple RPC application. For example, let's walk through the design of a simple Mandelbrot-set application and see if RPCs can speed up its execution time. This is a good sample application because it is easy to understand, and because it can be broken down in several different ways.

A Mandelbrot-set program produces an image of the Mandelbrot set as its output (See Section 6.4). It has to perform one independent calculation to produce each pixel in the image. This calculation is a fairly complex floating-point operation. Let's call the calculation function **CalcPixel**. The program has to call this function once for each pixel in the image it creates, so the function has the following prototype:

```
int CalcPixel(double x, double y);
```

The function accepts double-precision floating-point values that represent the pixel's location on a complex number plane. For example, the plane might stretch from −1.0 to 1.0 in both the x and y directions. The program simply divides the real number distance (2.0 in this case) by the number of pixels in the display window and passes those coordinates to the **CalcPixel** function one at a time.

Let's say that you want to run this Mandelbrot program on an inexpensive machine that does not have a floating point co-processor. It will take quite a while to generate an image if you do the floating point calculations locally. Therefore, you want to execute **CalcPixel** using an RPC so that the RPC server can reside on a faster machine that does have floating point capabilities.

The time on your machine will vary, of course, but for comparison purposes a normal function call to **CalcPixel** with a null body (the function does nothing but return immediately) on a 33MHZ machine requires about one microsecond. In other words, an RPC call is roughly 5,000 times more expensive than a normal function call.

When you add in network delay, things get worse. We ran the RPC server on one of the 33MHZ machines and the RPC client on the other. The network is a stock Ethernet (10 Mbits/second) network with no other traffic. The run time for the Mandelbrot program increased to 234 seconds. The time required to transmit the parameters on the network and send the result back was, therefore, 87 seconds, or almost 6 milliseconds per call.

As a final experiment, we ran the RPC server on the 66MHZ machine and the client on a 33MHZ machine. The client completed in 149 seconds, or 85 seconds faster than it did when the server ran on the 33MHZ machine. This is almost exactly what you would expect: The 66MHZ machine was able to complete the RPC version of the program 81 seconds faster than the 33MHZ machine when both were using local RPC servers.

	33MHZ	**66MHZ**	**Difference**
		(Time in seconds)	
Normal function calls	70	15	55
Local RPC servers	147	66	81
33MHZ client with remote server	234	149	85

There is one fundamental conclusion that should be drawn from all of these comparisons: each remote procedure call incurs a penalty of roughly 10 milliseconds. Six milliseconds of that is network delay, and it will increase when network traffic is high. The remaining four or so milliseconds is hardware-dependent, and will decrease when the program is run on faster hardware. However, it will never go away completely.

Given this conclusion, you can formulate a design rule: You should not use an RPC function call for any function unless you expect to get more than a 10-millisecond speedup by running it on a different machine. For example, if you have a function that takes 30 seconds to run on one machine but only five seconds to run on another, then this function call be made into an RPC call with great benefit. The savings of 25 seconds significantly overshadows the

10-millisecond delay of the RPC call. If you are going to save only a few milliseconds on the call, you should not use an RPC.

From the results cited above, we can conclude that RPCs were a dismal failure in the Mandelbrot program *because the design of the program used RPCs incorrectly.* The original program took 70 seconds to execute on the 33MHZ machine, and we wanted to decrease that time. Instead, the current design, which makes an RPC call for each pixel in the image, doubles or triples the execution time. Adding in an RPC call for every single pixel made the program run more slowly because the time savings gained from calculating one pixel on the 66MHZ machine is less than 10 milliseconds.

If the **CalcPixel** function were redesigned, RPCs might still be useful in the Mandelbrot application. For example, if the RPC calculated an entire scan line instead of a single pixel, only 104 RPC calls, instead of 14,768, would be made. 104 RPC calls require only about one second of total CPU and network overhead to execute, but the expected savings is 55 seconds, so the 33MHZ client would take 16 rather than 70 seconds to complete. RPCs would be very worthwhile in this situation.

In designing your own programs, keep this simple design rule in mind: Design your RPC functions so that you gain more time from operating on a faster remote machine than you are losing due to RPC call overhead. You can perform experiments on your own network to determine what the exact RPC overhead is at your site and on your equipment, but the 10-millisecond number is a good rule of thumb.

9.4 Creating RPCs

The steps that you must follow to create an RPC server, as well as an RPC client that can communicate with it, are fairly involved. The first time you see it, the whole sequence can be rather intimidating. In this section we will walk through the steps using a simple example program. This will let you try the process once and get the whole thing working on your network (or on a single machine). The next section explains all of the terminology and steps in detail.

Start by creating the code for the RPC server. In this example, the server will contain one function called **SumUp**. This function accepts an integer, and then calculates the sum of all of the integers between one and that value. Therefore, if you call **SumUp** with the value five it will return 15 (5 + 4 + 3 + 2 + 1 = 15). The server will run continuously on a machine and make the **SumUp** function available to RPC clients which need to execute that function. You create the server in four separate parts:

1. The server's **SumUp** function itself (sum.cpp)

2. The server body (autoserv.cpp)

3. An IDL (Interface Definition Language) file (sum.idl)

4. An ACF (Attribute Control File) (sum.acf)

The same IDL and ACF files are also used by the client program. Listing 9.1 shows the **SumUp** function, Listing 9.2 shows the server body, Listing 9.3 shows the IDL file, and Listing 9.4 shows the ACF.

| Listing 9.1 | *The **SumUp** function (sum.cpp)* |

```cpp
// sum.cpp

#include <windows.h>
#include "sum.h"

long SumUp(short sumVal)
{
  short iter;
  long theSum;

  theSum=0;
  for (iter=1; iter<=sumVal; theSum+=iter, iter++);

  Beep(300, 30);

  return(theSum);
}
```

| Listing 9.2 | *The server body (autoserv.cpp)* |

```cpp
// autoserv.cpp

#include <windows.h>
#include <iostream.h>
#include <rpc.h>
#include "sum.h"
#include "memstub"

INT main(VOID)
{
  RPC_BINDING_VECTOR *bindVector;

  // use the protocols specified in the
  // IDL file for this interface
  if (RpcServerUseAllProtseqsIf(1,
    sumup_v1_0_s_ifspec, NULL))
  {
    cerr << "ERROR: Could not specify protocols"
      << endl;
```

Listing 9.2   *The server body (autoserv.cpp) (continued)*

```
      return(1);
    }


    // register the interface
    if (RpcServerRegisterIf(sumup_v1_0_s_ifspec,
      NULL, NULL))
    {
      cerr <<
        "ERROR: Could not register interface handle"
        << endl;
      return(1);
    }


    // get binding handles for the interface
    if (RpcServerInqBindings(&bindVector))
    {
      cerr
        << "ERROR: Could not inquire about bindings"
        << endl;
      return(1);
    }


    // add an entry in the name service
    // for the interface
    if (RpcNsBindingExport(RPC_C_NS_SYNTAX_DEFAULT,
      (UCHAR *) "/.:/autorpc",
      sumup_v1_0_s_ifspec, bindVector, NULL))
    {
      cerr
        << "ERROR: Could not export binding" << endl;
      return(1);
    }


    // listen for and service RPC requests
    if (RpcServerListen(1, 5, FALSE))
    {
      cerr <<
        "ERROR: Server cant listen for RPC requests"
        << endl;
      return(1);
    }


    return(0);
}
```

| Listing 9.3 | The IDL file (sum.idl) |

```
[
  uuid (22449651-4321-1234-4321-987654321CBA),
  version(1.0),
  endpoint ("ncacn_np:[\\pipe\\autorpc]")
]
interface sumup
{
  long SumUp([in] short sumVal);
}
```

| Listing 9.4 | The ACF file (sum.acf) |

```
[
  auto_handle
]
interface sumup
{
}
```

The client side of things is much simpler. Shown in Listing 8.5 is a simple client that uses the **SumUp** function.

| Listing 9.5 | A simple RPC client that calls SumUp (autoclnt.cpp) |

```
// autoclnt.cpp

/*
This program uses an autobinding RPC call to
calculate a running sum.
*/

#include <windows.h>
#include <iostream.h>
#include <rpc.h>
#include <stdlib.h>
#include "sum.h"
#include "memstub"

INT main(VOID)
{
  CHAR sumUpToStr[10];
  long theSum;
```

Listing 9.5	*A simple RPC client that calls SumUp (autoclnt.cpp) (continued)*

```
cout << "Enter a value to compute running sum: ";
cin.getline(sumUpToStr, 10);

theSum=SumUp((short)atoi(sumUpToStr));

cout << "The running sum is: " << theSum << endl;

return(0);
}
```

Finally, you need a "memstub" file that defines how the RPC runtime libraries will allocate and deallocate memory, as well as a makefile. These are shown in Listings 9.6 and 9.7.

Listing 9.6	*A memstub file. Replace with **malloc** and **free** if you are writing C code (memstub)*

```
void __RPC_FAR * __RPC_API midl_user_allocate(
    size_t len)
{
    return(new(unsigned char [len]));
}

void __RPC_API midl_user_free(void __RPC_FAR * ptr)
{
    delete(ptr);
}
```

Listing 9.7	*A makefile for both client and server (makefile)*

```
NODEBUG=1
CLIENT=autoclnt
SERVER=autoserv
RPCFILE=sum

!include <ntwin32.mak>

.SUFFIXES: .cpp

.c.obj:
    $(cc) -J $(cflags) $(cvars) $(cdebug) $<

.cpp.obj:
    $(cc) -J $(cflags) $(cvars) $(cdebug) $<
```

```
all: $(CLIENT).exe $(SERVER).exe


$(SERVER).exe: $(SERVER).obj $(RPCFILE).obj \
$(RPCFILE)_s.obj
    $(link) $(conlflags) $(ldebug) $(conlibs) \
        rpcrt4.lib rpcns4.lib -out:$(SERVER).exe \
        $(SERVER).obj $(RPCFILE).obj \
        $(RPCFILE)_s.obj


$(CLIENT).exe: $(CLIENT).obj $(RPCFILE)_c.obj
    $(link) $(conlflags) $(ldebug) $(conlibs) \
        rpcrt4.lib rpcns4.lib -out:$(CLIENT).exe \
        $(CLIENT).obj $(RPCFILE)_c.obj


$(SERVER).obj: $(SERVER).cpp $(RPCFILE).h

$(CLIENT).obj: $(CLIENT).cpp $(RPCFILE).h

$(RPCFILE).obj: $(RPCFILE).cpp $(RPCFILE).h

$(RPCFILE)_c.obj: $(RPCFILE)_c.c $(RPCFILE).h
$(RPCFILE)_s.obj: $(RPCFILE)_s.c $(RPCFILE).h

$(RPCFILE).h $(RPCFILE)_c.c \
$(RPCFILE)_s.c: $(RPCFILE).idl \
$(RPCFILE).acf
    midl $(RPCFILE).idl
```

The above code looks rather messy, especially the first time you see it. Here are two things to keep in mind:

1. Note how simple Listing 9.5, the client, is. Once the server is set up and running, creating clients is easy. The only things that tell you that the client even contains an RPC are the rpc.h and memstub include files—the code itself looks absolutely normal.

2. Everything except Listings 9.1, 9.3 and 9.5 is mostly boilerplate, so you won't have to modify it very much for your own applications.

Get all of this code set up on your machine, and then make the makefile (See Appendix A). You will get two useful pieces of output: autoserv.exe, and autoclnt.exe.

To run the RPC server and client on a single machine, first make sure that the RPC services in the Services applet of the Control Panel have started. Both the RPC Locator and the RPC service must be active. Set them for automatic startup if they are not already configured that way. Then run the server on your machine by opening an MS-DOS prompt and typing:

```
autoserv
```

The server will run continuously while waiting for connection attempts from clients. If it fails to run, look at its error messages. They will help you to debug the problem. See the Win32 API help file for help decoding error messages. You should have no problems if you enter the code exactly as shown above.

Now run the client by opening a second MS-DOS window on the same machine and typing:

```
autoclnt
```

When you input a value at the client's prompt, you should experience a several-second pause, followed by a beep from the server and then the result.

RPCs are not really useful unless you are working on a network. If you want to try running the server and client on separate machines, take the following steps:

1. If the server and client machines use different CPU architectures, you will need to recompile the server and the client for their appropriate machines. It is best to compile both server and client on both architectures and try running the pairs on their own machines to make sure they work. As you will learn in the next section, it is safe for a client on one architecture to call a server on another architecture, because the design of RPCs goes to great lengths to ensure cross-architecture compatibility.

2. On Windows 2000, make sure the RPC services (in the Services applet of the Control Panel) are running.

3. Now, on the RPC server machine, start the server by typing:
   ```
   autoserv
   ```

4. Make sure no other copies of the server are running anywhere else on the network.

5. On the client machine, run the client by typing:
   ```
   autoclnt
   ```

You should see a several-second delay once you type in the number, followed by a beep on the server machine and the result on the client machine. If you run the client a second time, its result should appear somewhat more quickly. The first run takes a hit due to network-locator and binding delays.

If your RPC server or client will not run, first make sure that your code exactly matches Listings 9.1 through 9.7. Check the Services applet in the

Control Panel and make sure both RPC services have started. If you experience memory problems, close several applications or add memory to your machine.

Now that you have successfully created and used an RPC server and client, we will examine the details.

9.5 Understanding RPCs at a High Level

Microsoft's RPC mechanism was originally designed by the Open Software Foundation (OSF) as an open standard for RPC functionality on heterogeneous networks. It is the standard for UNIX DCE (Distributed Computing Environment) RPC implementation, and is already in widespread use on the UNIX side because of that. OSF had several goals for its design:

1. Allow machines with different architectures to communicate without the problems that normally arise from differing word sizes, byte sexes, and so on.

2. Allow the use of most normal C types without difficulty. These types include integer and real types, strings, arrays, pointers, structures, and unions.

3. Support multiple network protocols.

4. Hide the underlying network protocols as much as possible through the use of high-level functions.

5. Allow the programmer to have flexibility in determining the amount of control that he/she wants over the network connections. The programmer generally can trade convenience for efficiency.

To a large extent, the OSF specification accomplishes these goals. For example, you can place an RPC server on an Windows 2000 machine and connect to it from an RPC client on a UNIX machine with a completely different CPU architecture, and it will work. It also works in the other direction, with the client on a Windows 2000 machine and the server on the UNIX machine. The RPC server can exist on a Cray computer 200 miles away from any of its clients, and the system will still work.

To meet these goals, the OSF RPC design has to demand certain information from the programmer when creating both servers and clients. For example, in order to eliminate word-size and byte-sex problems, a programmer has to carefully describe how he/she is planning to use parameters in function calls. These descriptions go far beyond the normal prototype descriptions used in C or C++. The IDL file seen in Listing 9.3 contains these parameter specifications. To handle multiple-network protocols, the programmer must specify the protocols desired, and must set up endpoints in the RPC server for RPC clients to attach to. This information can come from the IDL file, or can be hard-coded in the server code. In order to publicize the existence of an RPC server on the network, the programmer must write code that tells the RPC name server about the RPC server. None of these steps is particularly difficult, but they are new and thus require some education before you can work with them.

Let's start by looking at how an RPC client connects to an RPC server at a high level. This will allow you to see some of the options available.

9.5.1 The Server

Compatibility Note: See Section 9.8 for a discussion of RPC name services.

The server must always start first. In the preceding example, you explicitly started the server at an MS-DOS prompt. In a production version of an RPC server, you generally wrap it in a service (Chapter 12) so that it starts automatically when the machine boots.

When the RPC server begins running, it does several things. First, it tells the machine on which it is running what network protocols it will use for communication with clients. It also tells the machine the names of the endpoints for the different protocols. Clients will then connect to these endpoints. Windows 2000 RPCs support eight different protocols (Windows 98 does not support ncacn_np):

Name	Description
ncacn_dnet_nsp	DECnet on DOS and Windows 3.1
ncacn_ip_tcp	TCP/IP
ncacn_nb_nb	NetBIOS over NetBEUI
ncacn_nb_tcp	NetBIOS over TCP
ncacn_np	Named pipes
ncacn_spx	SPX (Novell)
ncalrpc	Local

Each supported protocol has a different sort of name for its endpoint. For example, when using the TCP/IP protocol, you specify a port number. When using the named-pipe protocol, you specify a pipe name such as \pipe\pipename (as shown in Listing 9.3; see also Section 8.4 for general information on named pipes). As you can see, you need to have a little knowledge of how the different protocols work in order to pick appropriate endpoint names. If you are working strictly with Windows 2000 machines on your network, use named pipes for simplicity. If you are using Windows 98, use strictly TCP/IP. See Chapter 8 for information on both TCP/IP and NetBEUI network communications.

With the protocols and endpoints established, the RPC server next registers an *interface* for the functions it supports. The interface defines exactly how parameters will flow through the supported functions, and guarantees compatibility across architectures. The IDL file specifies the interface for all of the functions supported by a server. In this simple example, the server supports just one function named **SumUp**.

The RPC server can optionally register itself with a name server. The name server allows RPC clients to quickly find appropriate servers anywhere on the network. If the RPC server does not publicize itself through a name server, then the client must know the name of the machine running the server, the supported protocol(s), and the name of the endpoint(s). With a name server on the network, the client can obtain all of this information at run time.

On a domain-controlled network, the domain controller normally acts as the name server. In the absence of a domain controller, you can arbitrarily pick a machine on a peer-to-peer network and use it as the name server. If you do not pick a specific name server machine, then the RPC clients will scan a peer-to-peer network looking for servers on a machine-by-machine basis. On a heterogeneous network of Windows and UNIX machines, a UNIX machine can act as a name server. In this case, the UNIX name server is called the cell directory server. We will ignore this heterogeneous case in our examples, but it works just the same way as Windows 2000's locator service. See Section 9.8 for details.

On a Windows 2000 machine, the RPC Locator service acts as the name server. If you are using a name server on your network, only the name-server machine needs to be running the RPC Locator. If you do not have a specific name-server machine, then all machines running RPC servers must run the RPC Locator so that RPC clients can hunt on the network for RPC servers.

Having said all of this, you can see that any RPC server performs the following tasks as it begins running:

1. Specifies the protocols it will use and the endpoint names for those protocols
2. Registers the interfaces for the functions it supports
3. Optionally registers itself with a name server

Once these tasks are complete, the RPC server is ready to accept function calls from RPC clients.

9.5.2 The Client

An RPC client that wants to perform a remote procedure call first needs to *bind* with the appropriate RPC server. It can do this either automatically or manually. In *manual binding*, the RPC client must know the machine name, protocol, and endpoint name for the RPC server it wants to use. It binds to the server and calls the functions it needs, and then unbinds itself. The programmer must write code to perform the binding, and the programmer or the user must know the binding information.

Optionally, an RPC client can manually query the name server (see **RpcNsBindingImportBegin**) and obtain the machine name, protocol, and endpoint name for an RPC server. It can then manually bind to the server. Again, the programmer must write code to perform the binding, but the name server provides the required connection information.

In *automatic binding*, the programmer for the client code does nothing. Each time the client program calls an RPC server function, the RPC runtime library automatically queries the network's RPC name server, finds an appropriate RPC server, binds to it, performs the remote function call, and then unbinds from the server. As you can imagine, this is much easier to implement, but executes slowly if you need to make many remote calls to a server. Manual binding is preferred when the program needs to make numerous remote calls, because the RPC client can bind to the server just once before making all of the calls.

Figures 9.2, 9.3, and 9.4 illustrate the three different binding modes.

9.6 Parameter Passing

During an RPC call between an RPC client and an RPC server, the network acts as a transport mechanism for all parameters to, and all results from, the RPC function in the server. The interface specification for each function in the IDL file describes how parameters and return values get passed. IDL specifications are extremely specific so that you can minimize the amount of network traffic generated by an RPC call.

Windows RPCs support the following basic types:

boolean	TRUE or FALSE
byte	8-bit value
char	8-bit value, unsigned
double	64-bit real number
float	32-bit real number
long	32-bit integer value, signed or unsigned
short	16-bit integer value, signed or unsigned
small	8-bit integer value, signed or unsigned
wchar_t	Wide character type

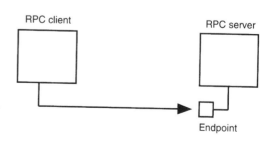

Figure 9.2

A pure manual binding. The RPC client knows the machine, the protocol, and the endpoint for the RPC server, binds to it, and then performs the remote function call(s)

Figure 9.3
An assisted manual binding. The RPC client manually queries the name server to obtain the machine, protocol, and endpoint for the server, and then binds to the server manually as in Figure 9.2

When you declare a function's interface, you declare the type of each parameter as well as the direction that the data flows. For example, the **Calc Pixel** function seen in Section 9.2 accepts two parameters but does not modify them. Therefore, the parameters need to be transmitted to the RPC server, but not back from the server. The interface description in the IDL file in Listing 9.3 therefore looks like this:

```
long CalcPixel([in] double x, [in] double y);
```

Figure 9.4
Automatic binding. The RPC client code automatically queries the name server, binds to the RPC server, makes one remote function call, and then unbinds from the RPC server

Parameters that are modified by the server do need to be transmitted back and are declared as **[out]** parameters. Parameters that need to move in both directions are declared as **[in, out]**.

Arrays pose different problems. With an array, the contents of the array must get passed to, or returned from, the server. You therefore need a way to describe the size of the array and the number of elements to pass. Sometimes you need to pass the entire array, but other times you may need to pass only a few values to complete a computation. Function parameters can specify sizes dynamically. For example:

```
long sumArray([in] long arraySize,
    [in, size_is(arraySize)] long array[]);
```

Here, **arraySize** specifies the number of elements to be transferred. The **first_is**, **last_is**, and **length_is** keywords can additionally let you specify exactly how much of the array needs to be passed on each call.

Strings are handled by passing all characters up to the '\0' over the network, and allocating enough space on the server to handle them. For example:

```
long strlen([in, string] char str[]);
```

In this call, the characters in the string up to the first '\0' are passed to the server and used as **str**.

It is also possible to pass pointers, although this is slightly more difficult because the system must also pass enough of the memory pointed to by the pointer in order for the pointer to work. See the topic "Attributes, Arrays and Pointers" in the RPC help file in the SDK for details, or see the MIDL on-line help file (in win32 helpfile). The following table summarizes different parameter options in the IDL file:

first_is	Specifies the first array element to transfer
in	Specifies that the value should be transmitted when the function is called
last_is	Specifies the last array element to transfer
length_is	Specifies the length of a variable length array
max_is	Specifies the maximum value of an array index
min_is	Specifies the minimum value of an array index
out	Specifies that the value should be transmitted when the function returns
ptr	Designates a full pointer
ref	Designates a reference pointer
size_is	Specifies the amount of memory to allocate for an array
string	Specifies that the parameter is a string and characters up to the first \0 should be copied
unique	Designates a unique pointer

9.7 Understanding the Code

To understand the code in Section 9.4, start with the IDL file shown in Listing 9.3, duplicated here:

```
[
  uuid (22449651-4321-1234-4321-987654321CBA),
  version(1.0),
  endpoint ("ncacn_np:[\\pipe\\autorpc]")
]
interface sumup
{
  long SumUp([in] short sumVal);
}
```

Each RPC server will have a unique IDL file that identifies the server and defines all of the functions it supports. The example file shown here, like all IDL files, contains a *uuid* (universally unique identifier) value that uniquely identifies this server. The uuid number is generated, along with the stub for the IDL file, by a program named `uuidgen`. For example, if you type

```
uuidgen -i
```

you will get a new IDL stub file containing a new uuid number. The ID number is formed from both the current time and the machine ID, so it is unique on the network.

The version number in the IDL file starts at 1.0 but can be changed, allowing you to have multiple versions of the same server running on the network simultaneously without conflict.

The endpoint line defines the protocol and the appropriate name for the endpoint. It is possible for a single server to support multiple protocols—for example,

```
endpoint ("ncacn_np:[\\pipe\\autorpc]",
     "ncacn_ip_tcp:[1050]")
```

This definition specifies that the server should use the named-pipe protocol with the endpoint named `\pipe\autorpc`, as well as the TCP/IP protocol with the endpoint at port number 1050. The interface line names the server, here as "sumup," and is then followed by the parameter descriptions for all of the functions in the server. Here the server supports only one function.

If you look at the last part of the makefile seen in Listing 9.7, you can see a line that resolves to this:

```
midl sum.idl
```

The MIDL program is the *IDL compiler*. It accepts the IDL file, looks at the name of it (here it is "sum" from "sum.idl"), automatically opens a file named "sum.acf" if it exists (in this case, the ACF file tells the MIDL compiler that auto binding should be used), and produces the following files:

sum.h
sum_c.c
sum_s.c

These files contain "behind the scenes" code that make the RPC server and RPC client work correctly. The makefile eventually compiles the code in these files and links them to the code you write. Because this example uses auto binding, this supplemental code contains everything necessary to query the name server and bind the client to the server. You can learn quite a bit about the binding process by looking through the code. The ACF file specifies the binding type and therefore controls how the binding takes place in this code.

Given the three files generated by the MIDL compiler, the normal C++ compiler can compile and link both the server and the client. The client code in Listing 9.5 is trivial. There really is no indication, beyond the header files, that it uses RPCs. All of the details of the network interaction were generated automatically by the MIDL compiler and appear in the sum_c.c file.

On the server side there are two files. The sum.cpp file in Listing 9.1 looks normal, and it contains the code for the **SumUp** function itself. The autoserv.cpp file in Listing 9.2 is a different story, and will look totally foreign to you. The functions called here are described in the 32-bit API help file. If you strip out the error checking, there really are only five lines in this file:

```
RpcServerUseAllProtseqsIf(1,
  sumup_v1_0_s_ifspec, NULL);
RpcServerRegisterIf(sumup_v1_0_s_ifspec,
  NULL, NULL);
RpcServerInqBindings(&bindVector);
RpcNsBindingExport(RPC_C_NS_SYNTAX_DEFAULT,
  (UCHAR *) "/.:/autorpc",
  sumup_v1_0_s_ifspec, bindVector, NULL);
RpcServerListen(1, 5, FALSE);
```

The first function call to **RpcServerUseAllProtseqsIf** tells the server to use all of the protocols specified in the IDL file. It is also possible to use protocols individually.

RpcServerUseAllProtseqsIf   *Obtains all of the protocol and endpoint information generated by the IDL file.*

```
RPC_STATUS RPC_ENTRY RpcServerUseAllProtseqsIf(
    unsigned int MaxCalls,
    RPC_IF_HANDLE IfSpec,
    void * SecurityDescriptor)
```

MaxCalls	The maximum number of concurrent calls the server will accept at one time
IfSpec	The protocol and endpoint information
SecurityDescriptor	Windows 2000 Security descriptor. See Chapter 13

Returns a status code

The **sumup_v1_0_s_ifspec** name comes from sum.h, which the MIDL compiler generated from the IDL file you supplied. The word "sumup" in the variable name is the name you supplied for the interface in the IDL file.

The second function call to **RpcServerRegisterIf** lets the server know about the interfaces that clients can call.

RpcServerRegisterIf   *Registers an interface*

```
RPC_STATUS RPC_ENTRY RpcServerRegisterIf(
    RPC_IF_HANDLE IfSpec,
    UUID * MgrTypeUuid,
    RPC_MGR_EPV * MgrEpv)
```

IfSpec	The interface to register
MgrTypeUuid	UUID or NULL
MgrEpv	Entry-point vector or NULL

Returns a status code

The third call to **RpcServerInqBindings** returns a list enumerating all of the bindings that this server provides. The list is used in the following call so that the name server can publicize these bindings.

RpcServerInqBindings   *Obtains binding handles*

```
RPC_STATUS RPC_ENTRY RpcServerInqBindings(
    RPC_BINDING_VECTOR** BindingVector)
```

BindingVector	The binding vector retrieved

Returns a status code

The fourth call to **RpcNsBindingExport** tells the name server about this RPC server and gives it the name "autorpc" (the name is required, but is irrelevant in the case of auto binding). The name server now starts publicizing this RPC server.

RpcNsBindingExport	*Registers the RPC server with the name server, telling the name server its name and valid bindings*

```
RPC_STATUS RPC_ENTRY RpcNsBindingExport(
    unsigned long EntryNameSyntax,
    unsigned char* EntryName,
    RPC_IF_HANDLE IfSpec,
    RPC_BINDING_VECTOR* BindingVec,
    UUID_VECTOR* ObjectUuidVec)
```

EntryNameSyntax	Use RPC_C_NS_SYNTAX_DEFAULT
EntryName	The name of the RPC server
IfSpec	The interface for the server
BindingVec	The bindings for the server
ObjectUuidVec	Vector of object UUIDs, or NULL

Returns a status code

The last call to **RpcServerListen** causes the server to begin listening for connection requests from RPC clients.

RpcServerListen	*Allows the server to begin listening for requests from clients*

```
RPC_STATUS RPC_ENTRY RpcServerListen(
    unsigned int MinCallThreads,
    unsigned int MaxCalls,
    unsigned int DontWait)
```

MinCallThreads	Minimum number of threads
MaxCalls	Maximum number of concurrent calls the server will accept at one time
DontWait	If TRUE, this function returns immediately. If FALSE, it blocks until shutdown

Returns a status code when the server stops listening

It is helpful to read the descriptions of each of these functions in the RPC help in the SDK file to gain a better understanding of what each function does. On the other hand, if you use auto binding for all of your RPC servers, the code shown in Listing 9.2 is generic and will work in many different situations. You should change the name "autorpc" passed to the **RpcNs BindingExport** function for each different server you create.

The last piece of code shown in Section 9.4 is the stub file in Listing 9.6. These two routines are used by the hidden code generated by the MIDL compiler to allocate and deallocate memory.

All of these pieces work together to form a working RPC server and client. The following sections explore other options through several different example programs and descriptions.

9.8 Setting up a Name Server in the Registry

Compatibility Note: At the time of publication, RPC name services as described in this section do not work in Windows 98.

By default, the Windows 2000 RPC mechanism uses a distributed architecture for name services. When an RPC client starts, it will look first on the local machine for any RPC servers it needs, then on the domain controller if there is one. Then it will begin enumerating machines on the network, talking with their RPC locators, and searching for the appropriate RPC servers. This last process can be time consuming. By declaring one machine on the network to be the RPC name server, you centralize all RPC-server information and make the search process much faster. If you have a domain controller on the network, then it is normally chosen to fulfill the responsibility of being the name server. However, you can arbitrarily choose any machine on the network for this role. The chosen machine is the only one on the network required to run the RPC Locator service.

To specify the name server, go to each machine that will run an RPC client and open the registry (use `regedt32.exe` in Windows 2000 and `regedit.exe` in Windows 98). Find the key named HKEY_LOCAL_MACHINE\Software\Microsoft\RPC\NameService. Change the Network Address and ServerNetworkAddress values to hold the name of the chosen name server machine. For example, if the name server machine is called "nts," then fill the values with "\\nts." Now RPC clients will automatically go to \\NTS when they want to use the name server.

If you are working on a heterogeneous network that uses a UNIX machine as the name server for RPCs, then that UNIX machine is called the cell directory service. You can tell NT to use the cell directory service by opening the Network applet in the Control Panel. Find the RPC Name Service Provider module in the list of installed network software, and click the **Configure** button. Select DCE Cell Directory Server from the list, and enter the IP address of the machine supplying the service in Network Address field. The address will appear in the registry automatically.

If at some point you find that RPC clients that formerly worked begin failing for no apparent reason, you should check on the health of the name-server machine. Also, if somebody randomly changes the name of the name-server machine, it can play havoc with a network using RPCs because all of the registries on the client machines must change. One advantage of not using a centralized name server is that you don't have any dependency on a single machine.

9.9 Manual Binding with Implicit Handles

Compatibility Note: All of the code in this section is configured so that it will work identically in Windows 98, Windows 2000, and any combination of Windows 98 and Windows 2000 pairs on a TCP/IP network. Note that you must change the machine name in conclnt.cpp (Listing 9.12) from "localhost" to a specific machine name and recompile in order for this code to work across the network.

Auto handles, which were used in the example code described previously, are nice because they make the client code extremely simple. However, auto handles are inefficient when you need to make multiple calls to the RPC server. With auto handles, each call to the server means that the RPC client first binds to the RPC server, then calls the remote function it needs, and finally unbinds. The binding and unbinding is expensive. Manual binding allows you to bind once and then make numerous function calls before unbinding.

Listings 9.8 though 9.14 demonstrate the pieces of code necessary to implement manual binding with the **SumUp** function seen previously.

Listing 9.8   *The SumUp function (sum.cpp), identical to Listing 9.1*

```
// sum.cpp

#include <windows.h>
#include "sum.h"

long SumUp(short sumVal)
{
  short iter;
  long theSum;

  theSum=0;
  for (iter=1; iter<=sumVal; theSum+=iter, iter++);

  Beep(300, 30);

  return(theSum);
}
```

| Listing 9.9 | *The server body (conserv.cpp). Because the client uses direct manual binding, there is no need to register with the name server, so that code is left out. Otherwise it is identical to Listing 9.2* |

```cpp
// conserv.cpp


#include <windows.h>
#include <iostream.h>
#include <rpc.h>
#include "sum.h"
#include "memstub"


INT main(VOID)
{
  // use the specified protocol and endpoint
  if (RpcServerUseProtseqEp(
    (UCHAR *) "ncacn_ip_tcp", 1,
    (UCHAR *) "55449", NULL))
  {
    cerr << "ERROR: Could not specify protocol"
      << endl;
    return(1);
  }


  // register the interface
  if (RpcServerRegisterIf(sumup_v1_0_s_ifspec,
    NULL, NULL))
  {
    cerr <<
      "ERROR: Could not register interface handle"
      << endl;
    return(1);
  }


  // listen for and service RPC requests
  if (RpcServerListen(1, 5, FALSE))
  {
    cerr <<
      "ERROR: Server unable to listen for requests"
      << endl;
    return(1);
  }


  return(0);
}
```

Listing 9.10   *The IDL file (sum.idl) is the same as Listing 9.3 but does not contain the protocol or endpoint information because it appears in the client code*

```
[
  uuid (55449658-4321-1234-4321-987654321CBA),
  version(1.0)
]
interface sumup
{
  long SumUp([in] short sumVal);
}
```

Listing 9.11   *The ACF file (sum.acf) declaring an implicit handle*

```
[
  implicit_handle(handle_t SumUpHandle)
]
interface sumup
{
}
```

Listing 9.12   *The RPC client (conclnt.cpp) that calls SumUp. This client contains the code to perform the manual binding*

```
// conclnt.cpp

/*
This program calls an RPC function
using a manual handle.
*/

#include <windows.h>
#include <iostream.h>
#include <rpc.h>
#include <stdlib.h>
#include "sum.h"
#include "memstub"

INT main(VOID)
{
  CHAR sumUpToStr[10];
  long theSum;
  UCHAR *stringBinding;

  cout << "Enter a value to compute running sum: ";
  cin.getline(sumUpToStr, 10);

  // put together string binding
```

```
if (RpcStringBindingCompose(NULL,
  (UCHAR *) "ncacn_ip_tcp",
  (UCHAR *) "localhost", // Change to specific machine
  (UCHAR *) "55449", NULL, &stringBinding))
{
  cerr <<
    "ERROR: Unable to compose string binding"
    << endl;
  return(1);
}

// bind to server using string binding info
if (RpcBindingFromStringBinding(stringBinding,
  &SumUpHandle))
{
  cerr << "ERROR: Unable to bind" << endl;
  return(1);
}

// free the string binding info
if (RpcStringFree(&stringBinding))
{
  cerr
    << "ERROR: Unable to free string binding"
    << endl;
  return(1);
}

theSum=SumUp((short)atoi(sumUpToStr));

cout << "The running sum is: " << theSum << endl;

// release binding to server
if (RpcBindingFree(&SumUpHandle))
{
  cerr
    << "ERROR: Unable to free binding"
    << endl;
  return(1);
}

return(0);
}
```

Listing 9.13   *The memstub file. Replace with malloc and free if you are using C rather than C++*

```
void __RPC_FAR * __RPC_API midl_user_allocate
  (size_t len)
```

| Listing 9.13 | The memstub file. Replace with malloc and free if you are using C rather than C++ (continued) |

```
{
    return(new(unsigned char [len]));
}
void __RPC_API midl_user_free(void __RPC_FAR * ptr)
{
    delete(ptr);
}
```

| Listing 9.14 | A makefile for both client and server |

```
NODEBUG=1
CLIENT=conclnt
SERVER=conserv
RPCFILE=sum

!include <ntwin32.mak>

.SUFFIXES: .cpp

.c.obj:
    $(cc) -J $(cflags) $(cvars) $(cdebug) $<

.cpp.obj:
    $(cc) -J $(cflags) $(cvars) $(cdebug) $<

all: $(CLIENT).exe $(SERVER).exe


$(SERVER).exe: $(SERVER).obj $(RPCFILE).obj \
$(RPCFILE)_s.obj
    $(link) $(conlflags) $(ldebug) $(conlibs) \
    rpcrt4.lib rpcns4.lib -out:$(SERVER).exe \
    $(SERVER).obj $(RPCFILE).obj \
    $(RPCFILE)_s.obj


$(CLIENT).exe: $(CLIENT).obj $(RPCFILE)_c.obj
    $(link) $(conlflags) $(ldebug) $(conlibs) \
    rpcrt4.lib rpcns4.lib -out:$(CLIENT).exe \
    $(CLIENT).obj $(RPCFILE)_c.obj \


$(SERVER).obj: $(SERVER).cpp $(RPCFILE).h

$(CLIENT).obj: $(CLIENT).cpp $(RPCFILE).h
```

```
$(RPCFILE).obj: $(RPCFILE).cpp $(RPCFILE).h

$(RPCFILE)_c.obj: $(RPCFILE)_c.c $(RPCFILE).h
$(RPCFILE)_s.obj: $(RPCFILE)_s.c $(RPCFILE).h

$(RPCFILE).h $(RPCFILE)_c.c \
$(RPCFILE)_s.c: $(RPCFILE).idl \
$(RPCFILE).acf
   midl $(RPCFILE).idl
```

You can see, by comparing the seven listings above with the seven listings from Section 9.3, that there are many similarities between the two. The main difference is the extra code added to the client program in Listing 9.12. The following is a complete list of the similarities and differences:

1. Listing 9.8 (the **SumUp** function) and 9.1 are identical.

2. Listing 9.9 (the server code) is very similar to Listing 9.2, but 9.9 declares the protocol and endpoint within the server itself. It is also missing the two calls (**RpcServerInqBindings** and **RpcNsBindingExport)** seen in Listing 9.2 that register the RPC server with the name server. These changes were made to simplify the work that the client has to do to perform the manual binding. The client in this example will bind to the server directly, rather than requesting server information from the name server, so there is no need for the server to register with the name server. However, you could use the version of the server shown in Listing 9.2 and query the name server in the client if you chose.

3. Listing 9.10 (the IDL file) is the same as Listing 9.3, but is missing the declaration of the protocol and endpoint seen in Listing 9.3. The server and client code in Listings 9.9 and 9.12 both contain this information rather than reading it from the IDL file. Either technique is valid.

4. Listing 9.11 (the ACF file) declares an implicit handle, which implies manual binding, rather than the auto handle seen in Listing 9.4. The name **SumUpHandle** is used by the MIDL compiler as an internal-variable name when calling RPC functions. The client code will initialize this handle.

5. The RPC client seen in Listing 9.12 is significantly more complicated than its counterpart, which is seen in Listing 9.5. The client now contains the code to perform the manual binding. The client contains within it the name of the machine, the protocol, and the endpoint for the RPC server it needs. The client creates first a binding string containing all of the information about the server, and then the actual binding to the server. It calls the RPC function it needs, and then releases the binding. There could be hundreds of RPC function calls between the formation and release of the binding, so this approach is significantly

more efficient than auto binding, which binds and releases individually for every function call it makes.

6. The stub files and makefiles are identical. Change the name of the CLIENT and SERVER in the makefile.

The name "localhost" seen in Listing 9.12 implies that the server and client are running on the same machine (useful for initial testing), but can be changed to any machine on the network provided that that machine is running the RPC server. You could also modify the client code so that the machine name comes in through a command line parameter.

If you strip out the error-handling code in the RPC client program, it is only a few lines long:

```
cout << "Enter a value to compute running sum: ";
cin.getline(sumUpToStr, 10);

// Form the manual binding
RpcStringBindingCompose(NULL,
  (UCHAR *) "ncacn_ip_tcp",
  (UCHAR *) "localhost", // change to machine name
  (UCHAR *) "55449", NULL, &stringBinding)
RpcBindingFromStringBinding(stringBinding,
  &SumUpHandle);
RpcStringFree(&stringBinding);

// Call the RPC function
theSum=SumUp((short)atoi(sumUpToStr));
cout << "The running sum is: " << theSum << endl;

// Release the manual binding
RpcBindingFree(&SumUpHandle);
```

To create a manual binding, the first step is to compose a string containing the binding information from its components. This string specifies the binding. The client needs to know the name of the machine on which the RPC server is running, as well as the protocol the RPC server uses and the name of the endpoint. The **RpcStringBindingCompose** function handles this task, returning a pointer to a block of memory containing the string. This pointer is called a *string-binding handle*. In this example, all binding information appears explicitly in the code. It is also possible to extract it from the IDL file as shown in several other examples that follow.

RpcStringBindingCompose   *Composes a string-binding handle from its components*

```
RPC_STATUS RPC_ENTRY
  RpcStringBindingCompose(
  unsigned char* ObjUuid,
  unsigned char* ProtSeq,
```

```
unsigned char* NetworkAddr,
unsigned char* EndPoint,
unsigned char* Options,
unsigned char** StringBinding)
```

ObjUuid	A UUID, or NULL to use the one from the IDL file
ProtSeq	The network protocol
NetworkAddr	The name of the machine holding the server, or "localhost" for the local machine
EndPoint	The name of the endpoint
Options	Options, or NULL for none
StringBinding	The function returns a pointer to a block containing the binding string

Returns a status code

Given a string-binding handle, the client can bind to the server using the **RpcBindingFromStringBinding** function. The binding is returned in the variable **SumUpHandle**, which the MIDL compiler has created in the sum.h file. The name **SumUpHandle** is user-definable and is specified in the ACF file. The run-time library will use this name implicitly whenever the client code calls **SumUp**.

RpcBindingFromStringBinding   *Binds the client to the RPC server*

```
RPC_STATUS RPC_ENTRY RpcBindingFromStringBinding(
    unsigned char* StringBinding,
    RPC_BINDING_HANDLE* Binding)
```

StringBinding	A string-binding handle
Binding	A binding handle

Returns a status code

If successful, the **RpcBindingFromStringBinding** function returns a binding handle and the client can talk to the RPC server. The client should free up the block of memory pointed to by the string-binding handle using the **RpcStringFree** function.

RpcStringFree   *Frees memory associated with a string-binding handle*

```
RPC_STATUS RPC_ENTRY RpcStringFree(
    unsigned char** String)
```

String	A string-binding handle

Returns a status code

In this example, the client calls the RPC function just once. In a production program you would normally make many RPC function calls after forming the binding. If you need to make just one function call, you should use automatic binding instead, to simplify the client.

Once the client is finished using the RPC server, it should release the binding to the server by calling the **RpcBindingFree** function.

RpcBindingFree   *Releases the binding to the RPC server*

```
RPC_STATUS RPC_ENTRY RpcBindingFree(
    RPC_BINDING_HANDLE* Binding)
```

Binding   The binding to release

Returns a status code

In Listings 9.9 (the RPC server) and 9.12 (the RPC client), both the protocol and the endpoint are declared directly in the code. This information can remain in the IDL file when using manual binding—the choice is yours. For example, if you change the IDL file, the server file, and the client file, then both the server and client will pull the protocol and the endpoint name from the IDL file.

Listing 9.15   *A replacement for Listing 9.9. This code uses the endpoint in the IDL file rather than declaring it explicitly in the code. It is also possible to use RpcServerUseAppProtseqsIf rather than naming the protocol explicitly—see Section 9.10 for an example*

```cpp
// conserv2.cpp

#include <windows.h>
#include <iostream.h>
#include <rpc.h>
#include "sum.h"
#include "memstub"

INT main(VOID)
{
  // use the specified protocol and
  // get endpoint from IDL file
  if (RpcServerUseProtseqIf(
    (UCHAR *) "ncacn_ip_tcp", 1,
    sumup_v1_0_s_ifspec, NULL))
  {
    cerr
      << "ERROR: Could not specify protocol"
      << endl;
    return(1);
  }
```

```
// register the interface
if (RpcServerRegisterIf(sumup_v1_0_s_ifspec,
  NULL, NULL))
{
  cerr
    << "ERROR: Could not register interface"
    << endl;
  return(1);
}

// listen for and service RPC requests
if (RpcServerListen(1, 5, FALSE))
{
  cerr
    << "ERROR: Unable to listen for requests"
    << endl;
  return(1);
}

  return(0);
}
```

Listing 9.16   *A replacement for Listing 9.10 that contains the TCP/IP endpoint*

```
[
  uuid (55449651-4321-1234-4321-987654321CBA),
  version(1.0),
  endpoint ("ncacn_ip_tcp:[55465]")
]
interface sumup
{
  long SumUp([in] short sumVal);
}
```

Listing 9.17   *A replacement for Listing 9.12 that uses the IDL file's endpoint*

```
// conclnt2.cpp

#include <windows.h>
#include <iostream.h>
#include <rpc.h>
#include <stdlib.h>
#include "sum.h"
#include "memstub"

INT main(VOID)
{
  CHAR sumUpToStr[10];
  long theSum;
```

Listing 9.17   *A replacement for Listing 9.12 that uses the IDL file's endpoint (continued)*

```
UCHAR *stringBinding;

cout << "Enter a value to compute running sum: ";
cin.getline(sumUpToStr, 10);

// put together string binding
if (RpcStringBindingCompose(NULL,
  (UCHAR *) "ncacn_ip_tcp",
  (UCHAR *) "localhost",
  NULL, NULL, &stringBinding))
{
  cerr
    << "ERROR: Unable to compose string binding"
    << endl;
  return(1);
}

// bind to server using string binding info
if (RpcBindingFromStringBinding(stringBinding,
  &SumUpHandle))
{
  cerr << "ERROR: Unable to bind" << endl;
  return(1);
}

// free the string binding info
if (RpcStringFree(&stringBinding))
{
  cerr
    << "ERROR: Unable to free string binding"
    << endl;
  return(1);
}

theSum=SumUp((short)atoi(sumUpToStr));

cout << "The running sum is: " << theSum << endl;

// release binding to server
if (RpcBindingFree(&SumUpHandle))
{
  cerr
    << "ERROR: Unable to free binding"
    << endl;
  return(1);
}

return(0);
}
```

9.10 An RPC Server for Mandelbrot Sets

Chapter 6 demonstrates a simple Mandelbrot-set program and shows how to multi-thread it. It is fairly easy to add RPCs to the Mandelbrot program, and this idea was the basis for the discussion of RPC design issues in Section 9.3.

This section presents the Mandelbrot-set code using a single RPC call for each pixel in the image. The following section shows how to significantly improve the speed of the Mandelbrot program by using one RPC call for each scan line of the image rather than for each pixel.

Listings 9.18 through 9.26 contain all of the code and auxiliary files necessary to create the Mandelbrot program's RPC server and client.

Listing 9.18   *The work function of the RPC server (ccrpc.cpp)*

```cpp
// ccrpc.cpp


#include <windows.h>
#include "ccrpc.h"


#define NUM_ITERATIONS 64


short CalcColor(complex k)
{
   complex z;
   double real, imag, spread;
   WORD iter;


   z.real=z.imag=0.0;


   for (iter=0; iter<NUM_ITERATIONS-1; iter++)
   {
      real = z.real + k.real;
      imag = z.imag + k.imag;
      z.real = real * real - imag * imag;
      z.imag = 2 * real * imag;
      spread = z.real * z.real + z.imag * z.imag;
      if (spread > 4.0)
         break;
   }


   return(iter);
}
```

Listing 9.19   *The RPC server body (mandels.cpp). The server uses manual binding and pulls the protocols and endpoints from the IDL file*

```cpp
// mandels.cpp

#include <windows.h>
#include <iostream.h>
#include <rpc.h>
#include "ccrpc.h"
#include "memstub"

INT main(VOID)
{
  // use the protocols specified in
  // the IDL file for this interface
  if (RpcServerUseAllProtseqsIf(1,
    calcclr_v1_0_s_ifspec,
    NULL))
  {
    cerr
      << "ERROR: Could not specify protocols"
      << endl;
    return(1);
  }


  // register the interface
  if (RpcServerRegisterIf(calcclr_v1_0_s_ifspec,
    NULL, NULL))
  {
    cerr <<
      "ERROR: Could not register interface handle"
      << endl;
    return(1);
  }


  // listen for and service RPC requests
  if (RpcServerListen(1, 5, FALSE))
  {
    cerr <<
      "ERROR: Unable to listen for RPC requests"
      << endl;
    return(1);
  }


  return(0);
}
```

Listing 9.20   *The IDL file (ccrpc.idl). Note the use of a structure as a parameter*

```
[
  uuid (87654321-4321-1234-4321-987654321CBA),
  version(1.0),
  endpoint ("ncacn_np:[\\pipe\\ccrpc]")
]
interface calcclr
{
  typedef struct
  {
    double real;
    double imag;
  } complex;

  short CalcColor([in] complex k);
}
```

Listing 9.21   *The ACF file (ccrpc.acf) specifying implicit handles and manual binding*

```
[
  implicit_handle(handle_t calcclrHandle)
]
interface calcclr
{
}
```

Listing 9.22   *The RPC client (mandelc.cpp). Note that the binding occurs once in the window's constructor and is released in OnExit*

```
// mandelc.cpp

#include <afxwin.h>
#include <rpc.h>
#include "ccrpc.h"
#include "menus.h"

const double left = -1.0;
const double right = 1.0;
const double top = -1.0;
const double bottom = 1.0;

DWORD colors[64];

typedef struct
```

Listing 9.22 *The RPC client (mandelc.cpp). Note that the binding occurs once in the window's constructor and is released in OnExit (continued)*

```cpp
{
   WORD height;
   WORD width;
} mandelParams;

// Define the application object class
class CManApp : public CWinApp
{
public:
   virtual BOOL InitInstance();
};

// Define the edit window class
class CManWindow : public CFrameWnd
{
private:
   HANDLE threadHandle;
   BOOL running;
   BOOL initialized;
   mandelParams params;
public:
   CManWindow();
   void RunMandel();
   void SetPix(int x, int y, WORD iter);
   afx_msg void OnPaint();
   afx_msg void OnStartStop();
   afx_msg void OnExit();
   DECLARE_MESSAGE_MAP()
};

// Create an instance of the application object
CManApp manApp;

// member function used to set pixel colors
// in the window
void CManWindow::SetPix(int x, int y, WORD iter)
{
   CClientDC dc(this);
   dc.SetPixel(x, y, colors[iter]);
}

// the thread function which does the drawing
DWORD MandelThread(mandelParams *params)
{
   double xstep, ystep;
   double x, y;
   int i,j;
```

```
   WORD iter;
   complex k;

   ystep = (double) (bottom - top) /
      params->height;
   xstep = (double) (right - left) /
      params->width;

   for (y=top, j=0; y <= bottom; y += ystep, j++)
   {
      for (x=left, i=0; x<=right; x += xstep, i++)
      {
         k.real = x;
         k.imag = y;
         RpcTryExcept
         {
            iter=CalcColor(k);
         }
         RpcExcept(1)
         {
            MessageBox(NULL,
               "Unable to call CalcColor( ).\n\
Click OK and then Exit.",
               "ERROR", MB_SETFOREGROUND |
                  MB_OK | MB_ICONSTOP);
            ExitThread(1);
         }
         RpcEndExcept;

         ((CManWindow *)manApp.m_pMainWnd)->
            SetPix(i, j, iter);
      }
   }
   return(0);
}

// member function used to instigate the
// drawing thread
void CManWindow::RunMandel()
{
   DWORD threadID;
   CRect r;

   GetClientRect(&r);
   params.height=r.Height();
   params.width=r.Width();

   threadHandle=CreateThread(NULL, 0,
      (LPTHREAD_START_ROUTINE) MandelThread,
      &params, 0, &threadID);
```

Listing 9.22   *The RPC client (mandelc.cpp). Note that the binding occurs once in the window's constructor and is released in OnExit (continued)*

```cpp
    running=TRUE;
}


// The message map
BEGIN_MESSAGE_MAP(CManWindow, CFrameWnd)
   ON_WM_PAINT()
   ON_COMMAND(IDM_STARTSTOP, OnStartStop)
   ON_COMMAND(IDM_EXIT, OnExit)
END_MESSAGE_MAP()


// Handler for the Start/Stop menu option
void CManWindow::OnStartStop()
{
   if(running)
      SuspendThread(threadHandle);
   else
      ResumeThread(threadHandle);

   running=!running;
}


// Handler for WM_PAINT messages
void CManWindow::OnPaint()
{
   ValidateRect(NULL);
   if (!initialized)
   {
      initialized=TRUE;
      RunMandel();
   }
   else
   if (running)
   {
      // stop the existing thread
      TerminateThread(threadHandle, 0);
      CloseHandle(threadHandle);
      // clear the window
      CClientDC dc(this);
      CRect r;
      GetClientRect(&r);
      dc.PatBlt(0, 0, r.Width(), r.Height(),
      WHITENESS);
      // start over again
      RunMandel();
   }
}
```

```
// Handler for the Exit menu option
void CManWindow::OnExit()
{
    SuspendThread(threadHandle);
    CloseHandle(threadHandle);
    RpcBindingFree(&calcclrHandle);
    DestroyWindow();
}

// CManWindow constructor
CManWindow::CManWindow()
{
    WORD x;
    BYTE red=0, green=0, blue=0;
    UCHAR *stringBinding;
    CHAR serverName[MAX_PATH];

    Create( NULL, "RPC Mandel Example",
        WS_OVERLAPPEDWINDOW,
        CRect(0,0,150,150), NULL, "MainMenu" );
    // Set up a set of colors
    for (x=0; x<64; x++)
    {
        colors[x] = RGB(red, green, blue);
        if (!(red += 64))
            if (!(green += 64))
        blue += 64;
    }
    colors[63] = RGB(255,255,255);

    if (strlen(manApp.m_lpCmdLine))
        strcpy(serverName, manApp.m_lpCmdLine);
    else
        strcpy(serverName, "\\\\.");

    RpcStringBindingCompose(NULL,
        (UCHAR *) "ncacn_np", (UCHAR *) serverName,
        (UCHAR *) "\\pipe\\ccrpc", NULL,
        &stringBinding);

    RpcBindingFromStringBinding(stringBinding,
        &calcclrHandle);

    RpcStringFree(&stringBinding);

    initialized=FALSE;
}

// Initialize the CManApp m_pMainWnd data member
BOOL CManApp::InitInstance()
```

Listing 9.22   *The RPC client (mandelc.cpp). Note that the binding occurs once in the window's constructor and is released in OnExit (continued)*

```
{
    m_pMainWnd = new CManWindow();
    m_pMainWnd -> ShowWindow( m_nCmdShow );
    m_pMainWnd -> UpdateWindow();

    return TRUE;
}
```

Listing 9.23   *The stub file (memstub)*

```
void __RPC_FAR * __RPC_API
    midl_user_allocate(size_t len)
{
    return(new(unsigned char [len]));
}

void __RPC_API midl_user_free(void __RPC_FAR * ptr)
{
    delete(ptr);
}
```

Listing 9.24   *The makefile*

```
NODEBUG=1
SERVER=mandels
RPCFILE=ccrpc

!include <ntwin32.mak>

.SUFFIXES: .cpp

.c.obj:
    $(cc) -J $(cflags) $(cvars) $(cdebug) $<

.cpp.obj:
    $(cc) -J $(cflags) $(cvars) $(cdebug) $<

all: $(SERVER).exe

$(SERVER).exe: $(SERVER).obj $(RPCFILE).obj \
$(RPCFILE)_s.obj
    $(link) $(conlflags) $(ldebug) $(conlibs) \
    rpcrt4.lib \
      rpcns4.lib -out:$(SERVER).exe \
      $(SERVER).obj $(RPCFILE).obj \
      $(RPCFILE)_s.obj
```

```
$(SERVER).obj: $(SERVER).cpp $(RPCFILE).h

$(RPCFILE).obj: $(RPCFILE).cpp $(RPCFILE).h

$(RPCFILE)_c.obj: $(RPCFILE)_c.c $(RPCFILE).h
$(RPCFILE)_s.obj: $(RPCFILE)_s.c $(RPCFILE).h

$(RPCFILE).h $(RPCFILE)_c.c \
$(RPCFILE)_s.c: $(RPCFILE).idl \
$(RPCFILE).acf
   midl $(RPCFILE).idl
```

Listing 9.25   *The RC file for the menus (mandelc.rc)*

```
// mandelc.rc

#include <afxres.h>

#include "menus.h"

MainMenu MENU
{
    POPUP "&File"
    {
      MENUITEM "&Start/Stop", IDM_STARTSTOP
      MENUITEM "E&xit", IDM_EXIT
    }
}
```

Listing 9.26   *The menu constants (menus.h)*

```
// menus.h

#define IDM_STARTSTOP    1001
#define IDM_EXIT         1002
```

Listings 9.18 through 9.24 have been ordered so that they correspond exactly to Listings 9.1 through 9.7 and 9.8 through 9.14. The Mandelbrot program uses manual binding for efficiency, as duplicated below from Listing 9.22:

```
// CManWindow constructor
CManWindow::CManWindow()
{
    WORD x;
    BYTE red=0, green=0, blue=0;
    UCHAR *stringBinding;
    CHAR serverName[MAX_PATH];
```

```
Create( NULL, "RPC Mandel Example",
    WS_OVERLAPPEDWINDOW,
    CRect(0,0,150,150), NULL, "MainMenu" );
// Set up a set of colors
for (x=0; x<64; x++)
{
    colors[x] = RGB(red, green, blue);
    if (!(red += 64))
        if (!(green += 64))
        blue += 64;
}
colors[63] = RGB(255,255,255);

if (strlen(manApp.m_lpCmdLine))
    strcpy(serverName, manApp.m_lpCmdLine);
else
    strcpy(serverName, "\\\\.");

RpcStringBindingCompose(NULL,
    (UCHAR *) "ncacn_np", (UCHAR *) serverName,
    (UCHAR *) "\\pipe\\ccrpc", NULL,
    &stringBinding);

RpcBindingFromStringBinding(stringBinding,
    &calcclrHandle);

RpcStringFree(&stringBinding);

initialized=FALSE;
}
```

Note that the machine name for the RPC server comes from the command line. As an experiment, you might want to change this code and the RPC server code over to automatic binding and see how badly their performance degrades on your network.

Note that the manual binding code occurs once, unobtrusively, in the main window's constructor. The binding is released in the **OnExit** function. Beyond that, the code is almost identical to the code seen earlier. In the **MandelThread** function in Listing 9.22 you can see the call to the RPC server, duplicated below:

```
RpcTryExcept
{
    iter=CalcColor(k);
}
RpcExcept(1)
{
    MessageBox(NULL,
        "Unable to call CalcColor( ).\n\
Click OK and then Exit.",
            "ERROR", MB_SETFOREGROUND |
                MB_OK | MB_ICONSTOP);
```

```
    ExitThread(1);
}
RpcEndExcept;
```

This code uses RPC exceptions to detect errors in the RPC call (see Chapter 15 for more information on Windows' exception-handling mechanisms). Because the binding occurs early in the program and the computations take a long time (on the order of several minutes), there really is no guarantee that the RPC server and network will remain stable throughout the program's execution. If a problem arises, the RPC runtime library will raise an exception during the call to the RPC server. In the code shown here, the exception generates a message box to tell the user about the problem, and the thread terminates.

To run this RPC client and server at your own site, take the following steps:

1. Compile the client and server initially on a single machine to make sure everything is working. You should simply have to type "nmake" to get everything set up.

2. Run the server in one window by typing:

   ```
   mandels
   ```

3. Run the client in another window by typing:

   ```
   mandelc
   ```

   If you look in the window's constructor function in Listing 9.22, you will find that the RPC client program looks to the local machine for the RPC server if no command-line parameters are given.

4. Now compile and run the server on a different machine on the network.

5. Run the client by typing:

   ```
   mandelc machinename
   ```

   where machinename is the name of the machine running the server.

The mandelc program will run significantly more slowly than the version presented in Chapter 6. As noted in Section 9.3, this occurs because of poor use of RPC functions here. The overhead of the RPC call is not justified by the savings garnered by a single pixel calculation. This problem is remedied in the following section.

9.11 Improving the Mandelbrot RPC Server

As discussed in Section 9.3, the key to an efficient RPC client/server arrangement is to make sure that the overhead inherent in an RPC call is appropriately balanced by the amount of time saved by making the call. The arrangement for the Mandelbrot program shown in Section 9.10 is not really appropriate because one RPC call is made for each pixel in the image. The overhead penalty incurred by these thousands of RPC calls has a devastating effect on the program's overall performance.

To solve this problem and make RPCs useful in the Mandelbrot program, you must somehow create batches of pixels that are calculated in a single function call to the RPC server. The batches need to be broken up so that the returned pixel values form a reasonably sized network packet, but at the same time, you want to minimize the number of calls to the RPC server. One extreme is shown in Section 9.10: network packet size is at a minimum, and the number of RPC calls is at a maximum. This created a problem due to RPC-call overhead.

At the other extreme, you could call the RPC server once for the entire frame, and pass back all of the pixel values at the same time. There are two problems with this approach:

1. On a 1000x1000 image, the two mega-byte network packet returned by the call bogs down the network. Actually, the system would end up transmitting back about two thousand network packs of about 1K bytes each.

2. There is a long (up to several minutes) lag time between the user's request for the image and its appearance on the screen.

What is ideal is some midpoint between these two extremes. An easy solution is to calculate entire lines of pixels in a single RPC call. A line is a good increment to use, because the results returned by a call form a nicely-sized network packet, and the user is informed of progress in reasonable time increments.

The program shown in Section 9.10 must be modified in several different ways to complete the conversion:

1. The server function `ccrpc.cpp` shown in Listing 9.18 must be modified to handle lines of pixels rather than single pixels. See Listing 9.27.

2. The IDL file shown in Listing 9.20 must be changed to reflect the change in Listing 9.18. See Listing 9.28.

3. The MandelThread function in Listing 9.22 needs to change slightly to reflect the change in Listing 9.18 as well. Several other minor naming and declaration changes are also required. See Listing 9.29.

After you make these modifications, you will find that the performance of the Mandelbrot program is only degraded by about one second per 100 scan lines due to RPC-call overhead.

Listing 9.27	*The new server function ccrpc2.cpp, modified to handle pixels one line of the image at a time. Compare with Listing 9.18*

```cpp
// ccrpc2.cpp

#include <windows.h>
#include "ccrpc2.h"

#define NUM_ITERATIONS 64

void CalcLine(double left, double right, double y,
   long width, short line[])
{
   complex k, z;
   double x, xstep, real, imag, spread;
   WORD i, iter;

   xstep = (double) (right - left) / width;

   for (x=left, i=0; x<=right; x += xstep, i++)
   {
      k.real = x;
      k.imag = y;
      z.real=z.imag=0.0;

      for (iter=0; iter<NUM_ITERATIONS-1; iter++)
      {
         real = z.real + k.real;
         imag = z.imag + k.imag;
         z.real = real * real - imag * imag;
         z.imag = 2 * real * imag;
         spread = z.real * z.real + z.imag *
            z.imag;
         if (spread > 4.0)
            break;
      }
      line[i]=iter;
   }
   return;
}
```

Listing 9.28	*The new IDL file, reflecting the changes seen in Listing 9.27. Compare with Listing 9.20*

```
[
  uuid (87654329-4321-1234-4321-987654321CBA),
  version(1.0),
  endpoint ("ncacn_np:[\\pipe\\ccrpc2]")
]
```

| Listing 9.28 | *The new IDL file, reflecting the changes seen in Listing 9.27. Compare with Listing 9.20 (continued)* |

```
interface calcline
{
  typedef struct
  {
    double real;
    double imag;
  } complex;

  void CalcLine([in] double left,
    [in] double right,
    [in] double y, [in] long width,
    [out, size_is(width)] short line[]);
}
```

| Listing 9.29 | *The new client program. All important changes appear in the MandelThread function. Compare with Listing 9.22* |

```
// mandelc2.cpp

#include <afxwin.h>
#include <rpc.h>
#include "ccrpc2.h"
#include "menus.h"

const double left = -1.0;
const double right = 1.0;
const double top = -1.0;
const double bottom = 1.0;

DWORD colors[64];

typedef struct
{
    WORD height;
    WORD width;
} mandelParams;

// Define the application object class
class CManApp : public CWinApp
{
public:
    virtual BOOL InitInstance();
};
```

```
// Define the edit window class
class CManWindow : public CFrameWnd
{
private:
    HANDLE threadHandle;
    BOOL running;
    BOOL initialized;
    mandelParams params;
public:
    CManWindow();
    void RunMandel();
    void SetPix(int x, int y, WORD iter);
    afx_msg void OnPaint();
    afx_msg void OnStartStop();
    afx_msg void OnExit();
    DECLARE_MESSAGE_MAP()
};

// Create an instance of the application object
CManApp manApp;

// member function used to set pixel colors
// in the window
void CManWindow::SetPix(int x, int y, WORD iter)
{
    CClientDC dc(this);
    dc.SetPixel(x, y, colors[iter]);
}

// the thread function which does the drawing
DWORD MandelThread(mandelParams *params)
{
    double ystep;
    double y;
    int i,j;
    short line[150];

    ystep = (double) (bottom - top) /
        params->height;

    for (y=top, j=0; y <= bottom; y += ystep, j++)
    {
        RpcTryExcept
        {
            CalcLine(left, right, y,
                params->width, line);
        }
        RpcExcept(1)
```

*The new client program. All important changes appear in the
MandelThread function. Compare with Listing 9.22 (continued)*

```
        {
            MessageBox(NULL,
                "Unable to call CalcLine( ).\n\
Click OK and then Exit.",
                "ERROR", MB_SETFOREGROUND |
                MB_OK | MB_ICONSTOP);
            ExitThread(1);
        }
        RpcEndExcept;

        for (i=0; i<params->width; i++)
            ((CManWindow *)manApp.m_pMainWnd)->
                SetPix(i, j, line[i]);
    }
    return(0);
}

// member function used to instigate
// the drawing thread
void CManWindow::RunMandel()
{
    DWORD threadID;
    CRect r;

    GetClientRect(&r);
    params.height=r.Height();
    params.width=r.Width();

    threadHandle=CreateThread(NULL, 0,
        (LPTHREAD_START_ROUTINE) MandelThread,
        &params, 0, &threadID);

    running=TRUE;
}

// The message map
BEGIN_MESSAGE_MAP(CManWindow, CFrameWnd)
    ON_WM_PAINT()
    ON_COMMAND(IDM_STARTSTOP, OnStartStop)
    ON_COMMAND(IDM_EXIT, OnExit)
END_MESSAGE_MAP()

// Handler for the Start/Stop menu option
void CManWindow::OnStartStop()
{
    if(running)
        SuspendThread(threadHandle);
```

```
    else
        ResumeThread(threadHandle);

    running=!running;
}


// Handler for WM_PAINT messages
void CManWindow::OnPaint()
{
    ValidateRect(NULL);
    if (!initialized)
    {
        initialized=TRUE;
        RunMandel();
    }
    else
    if (running)
    {
        // stop the existing thread
        TerminateThread(threadHandle, 0);
        CloseHandle(threadHandle);
        // clear the window
        CClientDC dc(this);
        CRect r;
        GetClientRect(&r);
        dc.PatBlt(0, 0, r.Width(), r.Height(),
            WHITENESS);
        // start over again
        RunMandel();
    }
}


// Handler for the Exit menu option
void CManWindow::OnExit()
{
    SuspendThread(threadHandle);
    CloseHandle(threadHandle);
    RpcBindingFree(&calclineHandle);
    DestroyWindow();
}


// CManWindow constructor
CManWindow::CManWindow()
{
    WORD x;
    BYTE red=0, green=0, blue=0;
    UCHAR *stringBinding;
    CHAR serverName[MAX_PATH];
```

| Listing 9.29 | *The new client program. All important changes appear in the MandelThread function. Compare with Listing 9.22 (continued)* |

```
Create( NULL, "RPC Mandel Example 2",
    WS_OVERLAPPED,
    CRect(0,0,150,150), NULL, "MainMenu" );
for (x=0; x<64; x++)
{
    colors[x] = RGB(red, green, blue);
    if (!(red += 64))
        if (!(green += 64))
            blue += 64;
}
colors[63] = RGB(255,255,255);

if (strlen(manApp.m_lpCmdLine))
    strcpy(serverName, manApp.m_lpCmdLine);
else
    strcpy(serverName, "\\\\.");

RpcStringBindingCompose(NULL,
    (UCHAR *) "ncacn_np", (UCHAR *) serverName,
    (UCHAR *) "\\pipe\\ccrpc2", NULL,
        &stringBinding);

RpcBindingFromStringBinding(stringBinding,
    &calclineHandle);

RpcStringFree(&stringBinding);

initialized=FALSE;
}


// Initialize the CManApp m_pMainWnd data member
BOOL CManApp::InitInstance()
{
    m_pMainWnd = new CManWindow();
    m_pMainWnd -> ShowWindow( m_nCmdShow );
    m_pMainWnd -> UpdateWindow();

    return TRUE;
}
```

You can see in the IDL file shown in Listing 9.28 that the RPC server now accepts the x,y coordinate of the start of a line of pixels, the x coordinate of the end of the line of pixels, and the number of pixels in the line, and then returns an array that contains all of the desired pixels.

It is very interesting to compare the performance of the single-line version with the single-pixel version in a quantitative way. You can do this with a stopwatch, or you can use the Performance Meter found in the Administrative Tools group of the Program Manager. On the server machine, get out the Performance Meter and look at the Processor Time item in the Processor object, the Packets/sec item in the NetBEUI object, and the Frame Bytes/sec item in the NetBEUI object. Run each server (single pixel and single line) independently, using a client on a different machine. When you run the single-pixel version, you can see that the number of bytes per packet (divide frame bytes/sec by packets/sec) hovers right at 100 bytes or so per packet. Most of those 100 bytes are wasted packet overhead, because the code sends 16 bytes per packet at most. You will also notice that the total frame bytes/sec remains fairly low, because of all of the network-processing overhead involved with sending a packet.

You will see a very different picture when you run the second implementation using scan lines. The packet-overhead bytes remain constant no matter the size of a packet, so their percentage declines. The number of packets per second declines noticeably as well. The network is working much more efficiently in the second case.

9.12 Explicit Handles

The previous examples have used either *auto-binding* or *implicit manual binding* to bind the RPC client to the RPC server. In auto-binding, the MIDL compiler generates code that lets the client bind to the server automatically. In implicit manual binding, the client code creates the binding to the server, but stores the binding handle in a variable that the MIDL compiler generated using the ACF file. Once the initialization of the binding handle is complete, the client can call RPC functions implicitly.

Auto binding is the easiest to implement. The client code looks exactly like normal code. However, auto binding is slow if the client needs to make a large number of function calls to the RPC server. The client binds to the server and releases for each function call it makes. Implicit manual binding is more efficient, but it requires slightly more work in the client code to manually bind to the server and then release.

In *explicit manual binding*, the RPC client goes one step further. Now in each function call, the client code specifies explicitly which server it wants to talk to. You use explicit handles when you want to open the same RPC server on several different machines and call all of them simultaneously. For example, a Mandelbrot RPC client program might open the same Mandelbrot RPC server on four different machines, and then multi-thread itself (see Chapter 6) so that it can call all four servers simultaneously. In this situation, each of the four threads must explicitly state which server it wants to talk to when it makes RPC calls.

Listings 9.30 through 9.34 show how to modify the **SumUp** RPC server and client demonstrated previously so that they use explicit handles. You will notice the following changes in the code when you compare Listings 9.30 through 9.34 with Listings 9.8 through 9.12:

- In Listing 9.30, the **SumUp** function accepts an explicit handle as its first parameter. Otherwise, the function is unchanged. The parameter is actually used in sum_c.c (generated by the MIDL compiler) to determine which server gets called when the client uses the **SumUp** function.
- The server body in Listing 9.31 is unchanged from that in previous versions.
- The IDL file in Listing 9.32 is similar to previous IDL files, but contains the extra parameter needed by **SumUp**.
- The ACF file is empty and actually unneeded for explicit handles.
- The client code in Listing 9.34 is very similar to the client code for implicit handles seen in Listing 9.12. The main difference is that the client code now declares its own copy of **SumUpHandle** to hold the binding information. It initializes this handle as it binds to the server and then uses it when it calls **SumUp** to direct the call to a specific server.

The explicit handle should *always* appear as the first parameter in any RPC function that uses explicit manual binding.

The client code could bind to the same RPC server running on several different machines by declaring and initializing multiple binding handles like **SumUpHandle**. Then it could call the same function named **SumUp** but direct it at different servers in each call.

> **Listing 9.30**   *The implementation of the SumUp function using explicit handles (sum.cpp)*

```
// sum.cpp

#include <windows.h>
#include "sum.h"

long SumUp(handle_t SumUpHandle,
  short sumVal)
{
  short iter;
  long theSum;

  theSum=0;
  for (iter=1; iter<=sumVal; theSum+=iter, iter++);
```

```
  Beep(300, 30);

  return(theSum);
}
```

Listing 9.31   *The server body for explicit handles (explserv.cpp)*

```cpp
// explserv.cpp

#include <windows.h>
#include <iostream.h>
#include <rpc.h>
#include "sum.h"
#include "memstub"

INT main(VOID)
{
  // use the protocols specified in the IDL file
  // for this interface
  if (RpcServerUseAllProtseqsIf(1,
    sumup_v1_0_s_ifspec,
    NULL))
  {
    cerr << "ERROR: Could not specify protocols"
      << endl;
    return(1);
  }

  // register the interface
  if (RpcServerRegisterIf(sumup_v1_0_s_ifspec,
    NULL, NULL))
  {
    cerr
      << "ERROR: Could not register intf handle"
      << endl;
    return(1);
  }

  // listen for and service RPC requests
  if (RpcServerListen(1, 5, FALSE))
  {
    cerr
      << "ERROR: nable to listen for RPC requests"
      << endl;
    return(1);
  }

  return(0);
}
```

Listing 9.32 *The IDL file for explicit handles (sum.idl)*

```
[
  uuid (22449651-4321-1234-4321-987654321000),
  version(1.0),
  endpoint ("ncalrpc:[explrpc]")
]
interface sumup
{
  long SumUp([in] handle_t SumUpHandle,
    [in] short sumVal);
}
```

Listing 9.33 *The ACF file for explicit handles (sum.acf)*

```
interface sumup
{
}
```

Listing 9.34 *A client program that calls SumUp using explicit handles (explclnt.cpp)*

```cpp
// explclnt.cpp

#include <windows.h>
#include <iostream.h>
#include <rpc.h>
#include <stdlib.h>
#include "sum.h"
#include "memstub"

INT main(VOID)
{
  CHAR sumUpToStr[10];
  long theSum;
  UCHAR *stringBinding;
  handle_t SumUpHandle;

  cout << "Enter a value to compute running sum: ";
  cin.getline(sumUpToStr, 10);

  // put together string binding
  if (RpcStringBindingCompose(NULL,
    (UCHAR *) "ncalrpc", NULL,
    NULL, NULL, &stringBinding))
  {
    cerr
      << "ERROR: Unable to compose string binding"
      << endl;
```

```
    return(1);
  }

  // bind to server using string binding info
  if (RpcBindingFromStringBinding(stringBinding,
    &SumUpHandle))
  {
    cerr << "ERROR: Unable to bind" << endl;
    return(1);
  }

  // free the string binding info
  if (RpcStringFree(&stringBinding))
  {
    cerr << "ERROR: Unable to free string binding"
      << endl;
    return(1);
  }

  theSum=SumUp(SumUpHandle,
    (short)atoi(sumUpToStr));

  cout << "The running sum is: " << theSum << endl;

  // release binding to server
  if (RpcBindingFree(&SumUpHandle))
  {
    cerr << "ERROR: Unable to free binding"
      << endl;
    return(1);
  }

  return(0);
}
```

The makefile and memstub files for this code are identical to those seen in Listings 9.13 and 9.14.

9.13 Context Handles

There are many situations in which you would like to maintain context information in the RPC server's memory space and then be able to refer to that context from call to call. For example, you might want to build and maintain a linked list on the RPC server using many different calls to the RPC server. If you want all clients to be able to access a single linked list, then you can declare global variables in the server and use appropriate synchronization mechanisms (Chapter 7) so that clients don't collide. However, if you want each client to be able to create and refer to its own linked list, then each client needs its own context on the RPC server.

As another example, say that you would like clients to be able to open a file on the server, and to then read that file line-by-line using RPC calls. The client needs to be able to open a file handle and refer to that handle from call to call.

RPCs allow you to preserve context information in individual clients by using *context handles*. Context handles are an extension of explicit handles. They contain an explicit handle, but they also allow the RPC server and client to pass one 32-bit value back and forth to each other. This value is normally a pointer to a structure. The pointer points to memory *in the server's address space* and is therefore valid only when used by the RPC server.

Listings 9.35 through 9.39 contain a very simple example that uses context handles. In this code, the context handle points to a structure that contains an integer. Each call to the RPC server adds a value to the integer. Because the code uses context handles, multiple clients can maintain their own running sums independently of one another.

If you look at the client code in Listing 9.39 and the server implementation of the **SumUp** and supporting functions in Listing 9.35, you can get a good idea of how context handles work. Here is a summary of the interaction between client and server in the example program:

1. The client program in Listing 9.39 binds to the RPC server.

2. The client program calls **InitSum**. This function's implementation appears in Listing 9.35. Two things happen during this call. The first is made obvious in Listing 9.35: the server allocates memory for a structure. The pointer to this structure is returned in the context handle. The second occurs behind the scenes: the implicit handle **SumUpHandle** is copied into the context handle in code generated by the MIDL compiler. The context handle thus becomes an explicit handle to a specific server. This occurs because the context handle contains a pointer that applies to the address space of a specific RPC server on the network.

3. The client program in Listing 9.39 now calls **SumUp** repeatedly, passing it the context handle. In Listing 9.35, the implementation of **SumUp** uses the pointer in the context handle to refer to the block of memory allocated to its particular client. The server adds a value to the integer in the structure pointed to by the context handle.

4. When the client is done, it calls **UnInitSum**, which frees the context structure in the server's memory space.

The structure that appears in the server can be as big as you like. It can contain integers, file handles, pointers to other blocks of memory allocated in the server, and so on.

Note that the server implementation in Listing 9.35 contains an extra function named **SumUpContext_rundown**. This function does not appear in the IDL file. Instead, it is used by the server if contact is lost with a client. It allows the server to clean up the client's memory allocations. There will be one rundown function for each structure declared in the IDL file; these functions are named by taking each structure name and appending "_rundown" to it.

The IDL file in Listing 9.37 contains the three functions used in the client, along with a declaration for the context structure.

```
[
  uuid (22449651-4321-1234-4321-987654321010),
  version(1.0),
  endpoint ("ncalrpc:[ctxtrpc]")
]
interface sumup
{
  typedef [context_handle] void *SumUpContext;

  void InitSum([out, ref]
    SumUpContext *contextHandle);

  long SumUp([in] SumUpContext contextHandle,
    [in] short sumVal);

  void UnInitSum([in, out, ref]
    SumUpContext *contextHandle);
}
```

The context handle is declared in the IDL file as a **void** pointer marked as a context handle using the [context_handle] key word. The IDL file does not care about what the pointer points to: it cares only about the name and the fact that it is a context handle. The IDL file specifies that the **InitSum** function returns the pointer by marking it as [out,ref]. The **out** key word means that the function returns the pointer value, and the **ref** key word means "pass by reference." Only the pointer's value gets returned. When the RPC client calls **InitSum**, it passes in the address of a pointer (the **SumUp Context** type is a pointer), and the value returned by the RPC server fills this pointer. Each time the client program calls the **SumUp** function, it passes this pointer back to the server. The server can use this pointer to refer to the structure for that client allocated in the server's memory space. The **UnInit Sum** function accepts the pointer so that it can free the memory block, and also returns it so it can set it to NULL in the client.

Note that the implementation of **InitSum** and **UnInitSum** in Listing 9.35 use **midl_user_allocate** and **midl_user_free**. These functions come from the memory stub file seen in Listing 9.6.

An RPC server can have multiple context structures in a single IDL file, and each one should have its own rundown function.

Listing 9.35   *The implementation of the SumUp function using context handles (sum.cpp)*

```cpp
// sum.cpp

#include <windows.h>
#include "sum.h"

typedef struct
{
  long currentSum;
} sumContext;

// function to initialize sum context
void InitSum(SumUpContext *contextHandle)
{
  sumContext *tmpSum;

  tmpSum=(sumContext *)
    midl_user_allocate(sizeof(sumContext));

  tmpSum->currentSum=0;

  *contextHandle=(SumUpContext)tmpSum;
}

long SumUp(SumUpContext contextHandle,
  short sumVal)
{
  short iter;
  long theSum;

  theSum=((sumContext *)contextHandle)->currentSum;

  for (iter=1; iter<=sumVal; theSum+=iter, iter++);

  ((sumContext *)contextHandle)->currentSum=theSum;

  Beep(300, 30);

  return(theSum);
}

// function to uninitialize sum context
void UnInitSum(SumUpContext *contextHandle)
{
  midl_user_free(*contextHandle);

  *contextHandle=NULL;
}
```

```
// function which gets called if client
// looses contact with server
void __RPC_USER SumUpContext_rundown
  (SumUpContext contextHandle)
{
  midl_user_free(contextHandle);
}
```

Listing 9.36   *The server body for context handles (ctxtserv.cpp)*

```
// ctxtserv.cpp

#include <windows.h>
#include <iostream.h>
#include <rpc.h>
#include "sum.h"
#include "memstub"

INT main(VOID)
{
  // use the protocols specified in the IDL file
  // for this interface
  if (RpcServerUseAllProtseqsIf(1,
    sumup_v1_0_s_ifspec,
    NULL))
  {
    cerr << "ERROR: Could not specify protocols"
      << endl;
    return(1);
  }

  // register the interface
  if (RpcServerRegisterIf(sumup_v1_0_s_ifspec,
    NULL, NULL))
  {
    cerr
      << "ERROR: Could not register intf handle"
      << endl;
    return(1);
  }

  // listen for and service RPC requests
  if (RpcServerListen(1, 5, FALSE))
  {
    cerr
      << "ERROR: Unable to listen for RPC requests"
      << endl;
    return(1);
  }
```

Listing 9.36   *The server body for context handles (ctxtserv.cpp) (continued)*

```
  return(0);
}
```

Listing 9.37   *The IDL file for context handles (sum.idl)*

```
[
  uuid (22449651-4321-1234-4321-987654321010),
  version(1.0),
  endpoint ("ncalrpc:[ctxtrpc]")
]
interface sumup
{
  typedef [context_handle] void *SumUpContext;

  void InitSum([out, ref]
    SumUpContext *contextHandle);

  long SumUp([in] SumUpContext contextHandle,
    [in] short sumVal);

  void UnInitSum([in, out, ref]
    SumUpContext *contextHandle);
}
```

Listing 9.38   *The ACF file for context handles (sum.acf)*

```
[
  implicit_handle(handle_t SumUpHandle)
]
interface sumup
{
}
```

Listing 9.38   *A client program that calls SumUp using context handles (ctxtclnt.cpp)*

```
// ctxtclnt.cpp

#include <windows.h>
#include <iostream.h>
#include <rpc.h>
#include <stdlib.h>
#include "sum.h"
#include "memstub"

INT main(VOID)
```

```
{
  long theSum;
  UCHAR *stringBinding;
  SumUpContext sumupContext;

  // put together string binding
  if (RpcStringBindingCompose(NULL,
    (UCHAR *) "ncalrpc", NULL,
    NULL, NULL, &stringBinding))
  {
    cerr
      << "ERROR: Unable to compose string binding"
      << endl;
    return(1);
  }

  // bind to server using string binding info
  if (RpcBindingFromStringBinding(stringBinding,
    &SumUpHandle))
  {
    cerr << "ERROR: Unable to bind" << endl;
    return(1);
  }

  // free the string binding info
  if (RpcStringFree(&stringBinding))
  {
    cerr << "ERROR: Unable to free string binding"
      << endl;
    return(1);
  }

  // establish sum context
  InitSum(&sumupContext);

  // release initial binding to server
  if (RpcBindingFree(&SumUpHandle))
  {
    cerr << "ERROR: Unable to free binding"
      << endl;
    return(1);
  }

  do
  {
    theSum=SumUp(sumupContext, 5);

    cout << "The running sum is: "
      << theSum << endl;
```

Listing 9.39   *A client program that calls SumUp using context handles (ctxtclnt.cpp)*
(continued)

```
    Sleep(1000);
  } while (theSum < 150);

  // release sum context
  UnInitSum(&sumupContext);

  return(0);
}
```

The makefile and memstub files for this code are identical to those seen in Listings 9.13 and 9.14.

9.14 Common Questions

This chapter only scratches the surface of RPCs—one could easily write an entire book on the subject. The RPC help file that comes with the SDK is useful as a reference, as are the MIDL and Win32 API on-line help files. Here are some questions commonly asked about RPCs, along with answers that will help you to find the material you need in the available documentation.

• Can an RPC server handle more than one RPC client at a time?

Yes. An RPC server can accept multiple function calls from multiple clients simultaneously. The number of concurrent clients that an RPC server can accept is controlled by the **RpcServerUseAllProtseqsIf** and **RpcServerListen** functions.

• Can an RPC server contain global variables?

Yes. Declare them as `extern` in the server functions (see Listing 9.1), and then declare their instances in the server itself (see Listing 9.2). See question three also. Since multiple server functions can execute simultaneously, you need to guard global variables with appropriate synchronization calls. See Chapter 7.

• What if I want to implement an operation that needs to retain information across calls to the RPC server? For example, I want to open a file on the server and then read from it with multiple calls, so I need the server's file handle. How do I implement that?

Global variables are a bad solution to this problem because of the number of potential clients and the problem with identifying clients. Instead, you should use a manually bound *context* handle, which can return context information like a file handle in the binding handle. See Section 9.13 for more information and an example.

• Is there a way for a manual handle to retrieve information from the name server so that the client program does not need to know where the server is?

Yes. Use **RpcNsBindingImportBegin**, **RpcNsBindingImportNext**, and **RpcNsBindingImportDone** to enumerate servers in the name server.

• What is the optimal size for a network packet sent to or returned from an RPC server?

1K bytes is a good, optimal packet size to aim for. Ethernet will not accept packets larger than about 1,500 bytes, so if you go above that limit multiple packets will be generated anyway.

• The exception-handling code seen in Section 9.10 seems fairly generic. Is it possible to get more detailed exception information?

Yes. The **RpcExceptionCode** function works somewhat like **Get LastError** to identify the specific cause of the exception.

• Walking over to the server machine and manually starting an RPC server from the command line seems fairly primitive. How do I make an RPC server available all of the time, starting when the machine boots?

Place the RPC server in a service. See Chapter 12.

• Do I have to do anything special to shut down an RPC server?

The code shown in these examples does nothing explicit to shut down the server, but to close a server cleanly you should call **RpcMgmtStop-ServerListening** and **RpcServerUnregisterIf**, as shown below:

```
void ShutdownServer(void)
{
   RPC_STATUS stat;
   status = RpcMgmtStopServerListening(0);
   status = RpcServerUnregisterIf(0, 0, FALSE);
}
```

You can add this function to the available functions for the RPC server and let an RPC client call it to terminate the server, or you can place it in the Stop code for the RPC server's service. The latter is preferred. See the previous question.

• What do I need to give to a programmer who wants to create a client program to access one of my servers?

You need to give the programmer copies of the IDL and ACF files, along with documentation on the RPC server's available functions. The programmer should be able to create the client with just that information.

• Presumably a network will have all sorts of RPC servers running all of the time. How do I find out what all of them do?

Ask people, or find published details on servers at your site. These are the only ways to truly know about the RPC servers that are available on your network. You can enumerate all of the RPC servers registered with the name server (see the question regarding a manual handle retrieving information from the name server) and then try to hunt down their owners, but there is no way to know what the servers do, or how to call them, without some sort of documentation.

• We keep running into name conflicts on endpoints. Two people will pick the same endpoint name or port number and it makes a mess. Is there a way around this problem?

Yes, using *dynamic endpoints* and *partially bound handles.* If you leave endpoint names out of the IDL file and use **RpcServerUseAllProtseqs** instead of **RpcServerUseAllProtseqsIf** in the RPC server, and if you are using a name server, then the name server and RPC server will pick endpoint names dynamically and eliminate these conflicts.

• Can an RPC server handle requests from both Windows and UNIX machines simultaneously?

Yes. Register multiple protocols in the IDL file to handle both. Also, since UNIX machines cannot interrogate NT locators, but Windows 2000 machines *can* interrogate a UNIX cell directory service, you will have to use the cell directory service running on a UNIX machine as the name server. See Section 9.8.

• Is there a way to prevent someone from accessing an RPC server?

Yes. When you specify the protocol sequences for the server (e.g., RpcServerUseAllProtseqsIf), you can pass a security descriptor. See Chapter 13 for details on security descriptors.

• I want to run the same RPC server on ten different machines on the network, and then create a program that splits itself into ten threads and talks to all ten servers at once. Is this possible?

Yes. The client will need to manually bind to all ten machines. You will also have to use *explicit handles*, so that when the client calls the remote function it can pass one of the ten binding handles and in that way specify which of the ten machines it wants to use. See Section 9.12 for an example.

9.15 Conclusion

RPCs are an easy and very effective way to create client/server applications that work on heterogeneous networks. Almost all of the details of the network interactions are hidden from view. When using automatic binding, client programs that use RPCs look no different from normal programs except for the addition of several include files.

If you want to create RPC servers that run all the time, starting when the machine boots, then you need to look at Windows 2000 services. They are described in detail in Chapter 12.

If you want to learn more about the network to get a better understanding of network protocols and endpoints, see Chapter 8.

To learn more about threads and the Mandelbrot program discussed in this chapter, see Chapter 6.

Distributed COM (DCOM)

Microsoft Distributed COM (DCOM) extends the Component Object Model (COM) to support communication among objects on different computers—on a LAN, a WAN, or even the Internet. With DCOM, your application can be distributed at locations that make the most sense to your customer and to the application. I wanted to cover DCOM at this point since the DCOM wire-protocol is based on DCE RPC. As we said in the previous chapter, DCE RPC defines a proven standard for converting in-memory data structures and parameters into network packets. COM and DCOM also borrow the notion of globally unique identifiers (GUIDS) from DCE RPC. GUIDs provide collision-free, unmanaged naming of objects and interfaces and are the basis of COM's robust versioning. DCOM's pluggable security providers enable seamless integration with DCE-based security environments.

Because DCOM is a seamless evolution of COM, you can take advantage of your existing investment in COM-based applications, components, tools, and knowledge to move into the world of standards-based distributed computing. As you do so, DCOM will handle the low-level details of network protocols so that you can focus on your real business. There are several excellent books that cover DCOM in detail, such as those listed below. In this chapter we will try to give a good overview and a functional description of DCOM.

Understanding DCOM
Rubin\Brain   Prentice Hall ISBN 0-13-095966-9
Distributed COM Application Development using Visual C++ 6.0
Maloney   Prentice Hall ISBN 0-13-084874-3
Inside Distributed COM
Eddon/Eddon   Microsoft Press ISBN 1-57231-849
Professional DCOM Programming
Grimes   WROX ISBN 1-861000-60

10.1 The DCOM Architecture

DCOM is an extension of the Component Object Model (COM). COM defines how components and their clients interact. We will be covering COM in Chapter 18. The interactions are defined such that the client and component can connect without the need of any intermediary system component. The client calls methods in the component without any overhead whatsoever. Figure 10.1 illustrates this in the Component Object Model.

In today's operating systems, processes are shielded from each other. A client that needs to communicate with a component in another process cannot call the component directly; it has to use some form of inter-process communication provided by the operating system. COM provides this communication in a completely transparent fashion: it intercepts calls from the client and forwards them to the component in another process. Figure 10.2 illustrates how the COM/DCOM run-time libraries provide the link between client and component.

When client and component reside on different machines, DCOM simply replaces the local inter-process communication with a network protocol. Neither the client nor the component is aware that the wire that connects them has become longer.

Figure 10.3 shows the overall DCOM architecture: The COM run-time provides object-oriented services to clients and components, and uses RPC and the security provider to generate standard network packets that conform to the DCOM wire-protocol standard.

Figure 10.1   *COM components in the same process*

Figure 10.2   *COM components in different processes*

10.2 Components and Reuse

Most distributed applications are not developed from scratch in a vacuum. Existing hardware infrastructure, existing software, and existing components, as well as existing tools, need to be integrated and leveraged to reduce development and deployment time and cost. DCOM directly and transparently takes advantage of all existing investments in COM components and tools. A huge market for off-the-shelf components makes it possible to reduce development time by integrating standardized solutions into a custom application. Many developers are familiar with COM and can easily apply their knowledge to DCOM-based distributed applications.

Any component that is developed as part of a distributed application is a candidate for future reuse. Organizing the development process around the component paradigm lets you continuously raise the level of functionality in new applications and reduce the time-to-market by building on previous work. Designing for COM and DCOM assures that your components are useful now and will be useful in the future.

Figure 10.3   *DCOM : COM components on different machines*

10.3 Location Independence

When you begin to implement a distributed application on a real network, several conflicting design constraints become apparent:

- Components that interact more should be closer to each other.
- Some components can only be run on specific machines or at specific locations.
- Smaller components increase flexibility of deployment, but they also increase network traffic.
- Larger components reduce network traffic, but they also reduce flexibility of deployment.

With DCOM, these critical design constraints are fairly easy to work around, because the details of deployment are not specified in the source code. DCOM completely hides the location of a component, whether it is in the same process as the client or on a machine halfway around the world. In all cases, the way the client connects to a component and calls the component's method is identical. Not only does DCOM not require changes to the source code, it does not even require that the program be recompiled. A simple reconfiguration changes the way components connect to each other.

DCOM's location independence greatly simplifies the task of distributing application components for optimum overall performance. Suppose, for example, that certain components must be placed on a specific machine or at a specific location. If the application has numerous small components, you can reduce network loading by deploying them on the same LAN segment, on the same machine, or even in the same process. If the application is composed of a smaller number of large components, network loading is less of a problem, so you can put the components on the fastest machines available, wherever those machines are.

Figure 10.4 shows how the same "validation component" can be deployed on the client machine when network-bandwidth between "client" machine and "middle-tier" machine is sufficient, and on the server machine when the client is accessing the application through a slow network link.

With DCOM's location independence, the application can combine related components in machines that are "close" to each other onto a single machine or even into the same process. Even if a larger number of small components implement the functionality of a bigger logical module, they can still interact efficiently among each other. Components can run on the machine where it makes the most sense for them to run: user interface and validation will be on or close to the client, and database-intensive business rules on the server close to the database.

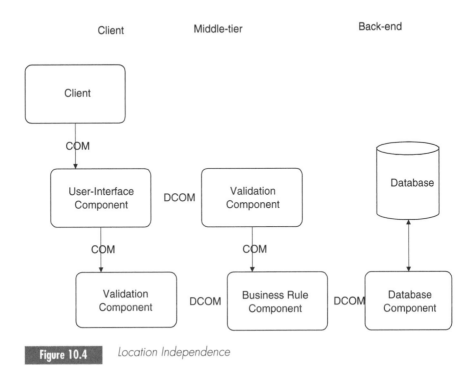

Client   Middle-tier   Back-end

Figure 10.4   *Location Independence*

10.4 Connection Management

Network connections are inherently more fragile than connections inside a machine. Components in a distributed application need to be notified if a client is not active anymore, especially in the case of a network or hardware failure.

DCOM manages connections to components that are dedicated to a single client, as well as to components that are shared by multiple clients, by maintaining a reference count on each component. When a client establishes a connection to a component, DCOM increments the component's reference count. When the client releases its connection, DCOM decrements the component's reference count. If the count reaches zero, the component can free itself. DCOM uses an efficient pinging protocol to detect whether clients are still active. Client machines send a periodic message. DCOM considers a connection to be broken if more than three ping periods pass without the component receiving a ping message. If the connection is broken, DCOM decrements the reference count and releases the component if the count has reached zero. From the point of view of the component, both the benign case of a client disconnecting and the fatal case of a network or client machine crash are handled by the same reference-counting mechanism. Applications can use this distributed garbage-collection mechanism for free.

In many cases, the flow of information between a component and its clients is not unidirectional: The component needs to initiate some operation on the client side, such as a notification that a lengthy process has finished, or the update of data the user is viewing (news ticker or stock ticker), or the next message in a collaborative environment like teleconferencing or a multi-user game. Many protocols make it difficult to implement this kind of symmetric communication. With DCOM, any component can be both a provider and a consumer of functionality. The same mechanism and features manage communication in both directions, making it easy to implement peer-to-peer communication, as well as client/server interactions.

DCOM provides a robust distributed garbage-collection mechanism that is completely transparent to the application. DCOM is an inherently symmetric network protocol and programming model. Not only does it offer the traditional unidirectional client/server interaction, but it also provides rich, interactive communication between clients and servers and among peers.

10.5 Scalability

A critical factor for a distributed application is its ability to grow with the number of users, the amount of data, and the required functionality. The application should be small and fast when the demands are minimal, but it should be able to handle additional demands without sacrificing performance or reliability. DCOM provides a number of features that enhance your application's scalability.

SYMMETRIC MULTIPROCESSING (SMP)

DCOM takes advantage of Windows 2000 support for multiprocessing. For applications that use a free-threading model, DCOM manages a thread pool for incoming requests. On multiprocessor machines, this thread pool is optimized to the number of available processors: Too many threads result in too much context switching, while too few threads can leave some processors idle. DCOM shields the developer from the details of thread management and delivers the optimal performance that only costly hand coding of a thread-pool manager could provide. DCOM applications can easily scale from small, single-processor machines to huge multiprocessor systems by seamlessly taking advantage of Windows 2000 support for symmetric multiprocessing.

FLEXIBLE DEPLOYMENT

As the load on an application grows, it may occur that not even the fastest multiprocessor machine can accommodate demand, even if your budget can accommodate such a machine. DCOM's location independence makes it easy to distribute components over other computers, offering an easier and less expensive route to scalability. Redeployment is easiest for stateless components or for those that do not share their state with other components. For components such as these, it is possible to run multiple copies on different machines. The user load can be evenly distributed among the machines, or criteria like machine capacity or even current load can be taken into consideration. With DCOM, it is easy to change the way clients connect to components and the way that components connect to each other. The same components can be dynamically redeployed, without any rework or even recompilation. All that is necessary is to update the registry, file system, or database where the location of each component is stored.

EXAMPLE

An organization with offices in New York, London, San Francisco, and Sydney can install the components in its servers. Two hundred users simultaneously access 50 components in a server with the expected performance. As new business applications are delivered to users—applications that use some existing business components and some newer ones—the load on the server grows to 600 users, and the number of business components grows to 70. With these additional applications and users, response times become unacceptable during peak hours. The administrator adds a second server and redeploys 30 of the components exclusively on the new machine. Twenty components remain exclusively on the old server, while the remaining twenty are run on both machines. See Figure 10.5.

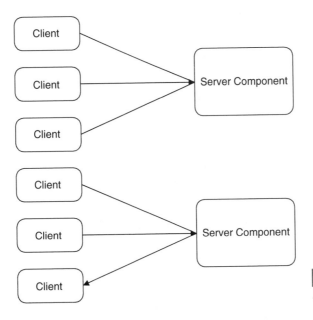

Figure 10.5
Parallel deployment

Most real-world applications have one or more critical components that are involved in most of the operations. These can be database components or business rule components that need to be accessed serially to enforce "first come, first served" policies. These kinds of components cannot be duplicated, since their sole purpose is to provide a single synchronization point among all users of the application. To improve the overall performance of a distributed application, these "bottleneck" components have to be deployed onto a dedicated, powerful server. Again, DCOM helps by letting you isolate these critical components early in the design process, deploying multiple components on a single machine initially and moving the critical components to dedicated machines later. No redesign or even recompilation of the components is needed. See Figure 10.6.

For these critical bottleneck components, DCOM can make the overall task go more quickly. Such bottlenecks are usually part of a processing sequence, such as "buy" or "sell" orders in an electronic trading system: Requests must be processed in the order they are received (first come, first served). One solution is to break the task into smaller components and deploy each component on a different machine. DCOM's location-independent programming model makes it easy to change deployment schemes as the application grows.

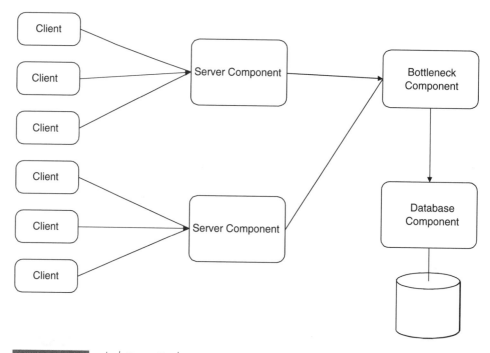

Figure 10.6   *Isolating critical components*

10.6 Conclusion

DCOM makes it easy to write a distributed application, due to these major features:

- Scales from the smallest single computer environment to the biggest pool of server machines.
- Provides rich, symmetric communication between components.
- Can be robustly expanded to meet new functional requirements.
- Takes advantage of existing custom and off-the-shelf components.
- Can be efficiently deployed and administered.
- Can be used with any network protocol and integrated into any hardware platform.
- Can seamlessly take advantage of other Internet standards and protocols.

DCOM is the TCP/IP of objects.

Communications

The communications portion of the Win32 APIs handles both parallel and serial communications through the computer's I/O ports. It also handles an interface to the telnet portion of the TCP/IP package, which you install in the Network applet of the Control Panel. Using the communications capabilities of Windows, you can talk to modems and other serial devices, printers and other parallel devices, and other computers acting as telnet servers on the network.

We will not be covering Serial Device Drivers for Microsoft Windows 2000 in this book. However, be aware that in Microsoft Windows 2000, the serial driver will support both Plug and Play and Power Management. The Windows 2000 serial bus driver, Serial.sys, is now Plug and Play enabled and is a serial device enumeration driver. Serenum.sys has been added to support serial device enumeration from the RS-232 port. To support this functionality, all Windows NT 4.0 serial device drivers should be updated to work with the new serial driver model in Windows 2000.

Compatibility Note: All of the code in this chapter works identically in Windows 2000 and Windows 98.

11.1 The Possibilities

One of the most common ways to use the communications capabilities of the 32-bit APIs is to communicate with a modem. For example, you might want to implement a bulletin board system, or create a terminal emulator:

368

- In a bulletin board system, the program implementing the system runs continuously. It places the modem in auto answer mode, and, when a call comes in, begins a BBS session. The BBS program uses the communications capabilities of Windows for all modem communications.
- In a terminal program, the modem connects with a remote computer system and transfers characters. Most terminal emulators recognize certain *escape sequences* that are interpreted as special terminal commands. For example, on a vt-100 terminal the escape character (ASCII 27) followed by "[;H" followed by another escape character followed by "[2J" means "clear screen." For a vt-100 terminal emulator, the program will recognize perhaps 30 different sequences like this to provide full-screen editing capabilities.

Another way to use the communications capabilities of the 32-bit APIs is to talk with unsupported input and output devices, or devices that use their own human-readable protocols. For example, many high-end digitizing tables use serial lines to communicate pointer positions and keystrokes from the puck. You can easily create a system to read from such a table, using the API's communications facilities.

It is also very easy to communicate with telnet sockets on other computer systems using the \\.\telnet port. Once you open a connection to this port, you get a telnet> prompt and can begin any normal telnet interaction. This capability makes it extremely easy to communicate with other telnet machines on the network. Note that you must load the TCP/IP module in the Network applet of the Control Panel, and start the telnet service, for this capability to work.

11.2 Understanding Serial Communications

In order to fully understand some of the serial communications code described below, it will be helpful to have a good mental image of what is happening when a computer system talks to a modem via an RS-232 communications line. All of the terminology used in RS-232 lingo normally refers to a connection between a terminal and a modem as shown in Figure 11.1. In a normal RS-232 cable, the lines pass straight through from corresponding pin to corresponding pin as shown in Figure 11.1. The following table shows the differences between 9-pin and 25-pin cables:

Signal	DB9 pin	DB25 pin
DCD	1	8
RX	2	3

Signal	DB9 pin	DB25 pin
TX	3	2
DTR	4	20
GND	5	7
DSR	6	6
RTS	7	4
CTS	8	5
RI	9	22

On a null-modem cable, the wiring is set up to transpose all appropriate signals, as shown in Figure 11.2. You use a null modem cable to connect two computers directly together without intervening modems, or to connect a computer to a printer. Because both the computer and the printer are considered to be DTE devices, you cannot connect them together directly.

Figure 11.1   *RS-232 Signaling conventions*

Figure 11.2

Proper null modem cable wiring. In some cases, RTS, CTS, and DCD are all wired together. In extreme cases, only the RX, TX, and GND signals are used

In a typical communication session, the "terminal," which is your computer in this case, raises the DTR line to indicate that it is ready to begin a transmission. The modem will raise the DSR line when it is turned on to indicate that it is ready. Your computer will then raise the RTS line when it wants to transmit and the modem will respond on the CTS line. The computer then begins to transmit. When data is incoming, the modem raises the DCD line.

In the code that follows, you will notice the use of the **EscapeCommFunction** function to raise and lower the DTR line. You will also notice that the DCB structure allows flow control to occur in three different ways. The two hardware techniques rely either on the DTR/DSR lines or on the RTS/CTS lines. These techniques depend on your modem supporting all appropriate signals as well as on your modem cable actually carrying all signals. If you have problems with hardware flow control, check your modem and cable first to make sure they are working as expected.

11.3 A Simple Communications Application

The easiest way to understand how the communications facilities of the 32-bit API work is to look at an extremely simple example of modem communications. While this first example does not accomplish anything particularly useful, it does demonstrate all of the steps that must be followed to create a successful connection.

Listing 11.1 contains a very simple communications program. To use it you will need a Hayes-compatible modem hooked to one of your serial communications ports. With a modem connected, Listing 11.1 sends the command "at" to the modem and receives back the modem's response, which is "ok." Any Hayes-compatible modem understands the characters "at" to be an "attention" command and responds with "ok" to indicate that the modem is functioning properly.

Listing 11.1   *A simple demonstration program*

```
// commtest.cpp

#include <windows.h>
#include <iostream.h>

void ErrorHandler(char *message, DWORD error)
{
   cout << message << endl;
   cout << "Error number = " << error << endl;
   ExitProcess(1);
}

void main()
{
   HANDLE comHandle;
   BOOL success;
   DCB dcb;
   char str[100];
   DWORD numWrite, numRead;
   COMMTIMEOUTS timeouts;

   // Open the comm port. Can open COM, LPT,
   // or \\\\.\\TELNET
   comHandle = CreateFile("COM2",
      GENERIC_READ|GENERIC_WRITE,
      0, 0, OPEN_EXISTING,
      FILE_ATTRIBUTE_NORMAL, 0);
   if (comHandle == INVALID_HANDLE_VALUE)
      ErrorHandler("In CreateFile",
         GetLastError());

   // Get the current settings of the COMM port
   success = GetCommState(comHandle, &dcb);
   if (!success)
      ErrorHandler("In GetCommState",
         GetLastError());

   // Modify the baud rate, etc.
   dcb.BaudRate = 2400;
   dcb.ByteSize = 8;
   dcb.Parity = NOPARITY;
   dcb.StopBits = ONESTOPBIT;

   // Apply the new comm port settings
   success = SetCommState(comHandle, &dcb);
   if (!success)
```

```
        ErrorHandler("In SetCommState",
            GetLastError());

    // Change the ReadIntervalTimeout so that
    // ReadFile will return immediately. See
    // help file
    timeouts.ReadIntervalTimeout = MAXDWORD;
    timeouts.ReadTotalTimeoutMultiplier = 0;
    timeouts.ReadTotalTimeoutConstant = 0;
    timeouts.WriteTotalTimeoutMultiplier = 0;
    timeouts.WriteTotalTimeoutConstant = 0;
    SetCommTimeouts( comHandle, &timeouts );

    // Set the Data Terminal Ready line
    EscapeCommFunction(comHandle, SETDTR);

    // Send an "at" command to the modem
    // Be sure to use \r rather than \n
    strcpy(str, "at\r");
    success = WriteFile(comHandle, str, strlen(str),
            &numWrite, 0);
    if (!success)
        ErrorHandler("In WriteFile", GetLastError());

    // Wait 2 seconds and then retrieve from the
    // modem
    Sleep(2000);
    success = ReadFile(comHandle, str,
            100, &numRead, 0);
    if (!success)
        ErrorHandler("In ReadFile", GetLastError());

    // Print the string received
    cout << numRead << endl;
    str[numRead]='\0';
    cout << str << endl;

    // Clear the DTR line
    EscapeCommFunction(comHandle, CLRDTR);

    CloseHandle(comHandle);
}
```

The code in Listing 11.1 starts by calling the **CreateFile** function to open a handle to the COM2 communication port. Change this port number as necessary for your machine. On a normal Windows workstation, you are likely to have one or two serial communications lines labeled COM1 and COM2, along with one parallel port labeled LPT1.

CreateFile *Opens a file, named pipe, mailslot, or communications port.*

```
HANDLE CreateFile(
    LPCTSTR name,
    DWORD accessMode,
    DWORD shareMode,
    LPSECURITY_ATTRIBUTES securityAttributes,
    DWORD create,
    DWORD attributes,
    HANDLE templateFile)
```

name	Name of the file to open
accessMode	Read/Write mode
shareMode	The way the file should be shared
securityAttributes	Address of a security structure. See Chapter 13
create	The way the file should be created
attributes	Settings for normal file attribute bits
templateFile	File containing extended attributes

Returns a handle on success, or INVALID_HANDLE_VALUE

When you call **CreateFile** on any of these ports, the system checks to make sure that the port is not already in use by some other process, and if it is, it returns the appropriate error code. If the port is available, you are granted exclusive access to it. The parameters and constants used in the call to **CreateFile** here are the same as those used when opening a file, as described in Chapter 2. The following parameters to **CreateFile** must be set as specified:

- Set the **accessMode** function to allow read and write access
- Set **shareMode** to 0 to indicate exclusive access
- Set the **create** parameter to OPEN_EXISTING, since the COM port already exists
- Set **attributes** to FILE_ATTRIBUTES_NORMAL
- Set **templateFile** to 0

Since COM2 is a serial communications port, the next step is to set communications parameters at such a baud rate and parity. Each port retains whatever settings it had from its last use, so it is important to set all relevant parameters to new values to make sure that you are using known settings. The code first calls the **GetCommState** function to retrieve the existing settings.

GetCommState   *Retrieves the current state of the port*

```
BOOL GetCommState(
    HANDLE commHandle,
    LPDCB dcb)
```

commHandle   Handle to a comm port

dcb   A pointer to a DCB structure

Returns TRUE on success

The DCB structure returned by **GetCommState** contains 28 fields, and is best understood through a careful reading of its description in the help file. The following brief summary of the DCB structure is copied from Microsoft's Win32 API help file:

```
typedef struct _DCB {
    DWORD DCBlength; // sizeof(DCB)
    DWORD BaudRate; // current baud rate
    DWORD fBinary: 1; // binary mode, no EOF check
    DWORD fParity: 1; // enable parity checking
    DWORD fOutxCtsFlow:1; // CTS output flow control
    DWORD fOutxDsrFlow:1; // DSR output flow control
    DWORD fDtrControl:2; // DTR flow control type
    DWORD fDsrSensitivity:1; // DSR sensitivity
    DWORD fTXContinueOnXoff:1; // XOFF continues Tx
    DWORD fOutX: 1; // XON/XOFF out flow control
    DWORD fInX: 1; // XON/XOFF in flow control
    DWORD fErrorChar: 1; // enable error replacement
    DWORD fNull: 1; // enable null stripping
    DWORD fRtsControl:2; // RTS flow control
    DWORD fAbortOnError:1; // abort rds/wrs on error
    DWORD fDummy2:17; // reserved
    WORD wReserved; // not currently used
    WORD XonLim; // transmit XON threshold
    WORD XoffLim;// transmit XOFF threshold
    BYTE ByteSize; // number of bits/byte, 4-8
    BYTE Parity; // 0-4=no,odd,even,mark,space
    BYTE StopBits; // 0,1,2 = 1, 1.5, 2
    char XonChar; // Tx and Rx XON character
    char XoffChar; // Tx and Rx XOFF character
    char ErrorChar; // error replacement character
    char EofChar; // end of input character
    char EvtChar; // received event character
} DCB;
```

In Listing 11.1, only the baud rate, the number of bits per character, the parity, and the number of stop bits are modified. The changes are then sent to the COM port using the **SetCommState** function.

SetCommState	*Sets the current state of the port*

```
BOOL SetCommState(
    HANDLE commHandle,
    LPDCB dcb)
```

commHandle	Handle to a comm port
dcb	A pointer to a DCB structure

Returns TRUE on success

It is also possible to set values into a DCB structure using the **Build CommState** function. It accepts a string compatible with the string accepted by the mode command at the command line.

Listing 11.1 next sets timeout values. These values are also retained from use to use, so it is important to set them anew if you are expecting certain behavior. These values give you very subtle control over the timeout behavior of your program during reads and writes, and guarantee that your program does not stall in the event of communication problems. For example, a **ReadFile** operation told to return with 100 bytes will stall until it finds 100 bytes in the input buffer. If there is a communication error, however, 100 bytes will never arrive, and the program gets stuck. Using timeouts, you can instruct the program to return immediately from any **ReadFile** operation regardless of the number of bytes found, or to return after a specified number of milliseconds.

The **ReadIntervalTimeout** value controls timeouts on the interval between characters. For example, you might set it to 1000 to indicate that a **ReadFile** operation should return if two characters are spaced out by more than one second. If you set **ReadIntervalTimeout** to 0, no interval timeouts are used. If you set it to MAXDWORD as shown in the code, and if the other two read intervals are set to 0, then the system returns immediately from any **ReadFile** operation with whatever the input buffer contains.

The **ReadTotalTimeoutMultiplier** and **ReadTotalTimeoutConstant** values let you set a timeout based on the number of bytes specified in the **ReadFile** statement. If you ask to read 100 bytes, for example, the following equation determines the timeout value.

```
Total timeout value = 100 * ReadTotalTimeoutMultiplier
+
          ReadTotalTimeoutConstant
```

After the specified number of milliseconds have elapsed, the **ReadFile** function returns, regardless of how many bytes it has actually read. The same process is used for the Write multiplier and constant in an outgoing direction.

Listing 11.1 uses the timeout values to ensure that a call to the **ReadFile** function returns immediately. Once the timeout structure has been set up, it is passed to the system with the **SetCommTimeouts** function.

SetCommTimeouts   *Sets the timeout values of the port*

```
BOOL SetCommTimeouts(
    HANDLE commHandle,
    LPCOMMTIMEOUTS timeouts)
```

commHandle   Handle to a comm port

timeouts   A pointer to a COMMTIMEOUTS structure

Returns TRUE on success

With all of these preliminaries taken care of, the program is ready to begin communicating with the modem. It sets the DTR line (see Section 11.2) to indicate that it is ready using the **EscapeCommFunction** function.

EscapeCommFunction   *Performs a specified operation*

```
BOOL EscapeCommFunction(
    HANDLE commHandle,
    DWORD operation)
```

commHandle   Handle to a comm port

operation   The operation

Returns TRUE on success

The valid operations for **EscapeCommFunction** are listed below:

SETDTR   Turns on the DTR line
CLRDTR   Turns off the DTR line
SETRTS   Turns on the RTS line
CLRRTS   Turns off the RTS line
SETXON   Turns on XON flow control as though XON were received
SETXOFF   Turns off XON flow control as though XOFF were received
SETBREAK   Stops all transmission until CLRBREAK is received
CLRBREAK   Resumes transmission

The SETBREAK and CLRBREAK operations are also duplicated in the **SetCommBreak** and **ClearCommBreak** functions.

The code in Listing 11.1 uses the SETDTR operation to properly inform the modem that the "terminal" is ready and is about to begin transmission. All of the other signals are handled automatically by the comm port and are not normally manipulated manually. A terminal emulator program will frequently contain a Break option, which you can implement with SETBREAK or **SetCommBreak**.

Listing 11.1 next uses the normal **WriteFile** command (Chapter 2) to send the command "at" to the modem. A Hayes-compatible modem will respond to this command by echoing back the characters and then sending an "ok" response to indicate that it is alive. If the modem is working properly and if it has lights on its front panel, you should see the RX and TX lights glow as the "at" characters are received and echoed, and then half a second later see the TX light glow again when the OK is sent back.

WriteFile   *Writes a block of bytes to a file*

```
BOOL WriteFile(
    HANDLE fileHandle,
    CONST VOID *buffer,
    DWORD bytesToWrite,
    LPDWORD bytesWritten,
    LPOVERLAPPED overlapped)
```

fileHandle	Handle to a file created by **CreateFile**
buffer	Data to write
bytesToWrite	The number of bytes to write
bytesWritten	The number of bytes actually written
overlapped	Overlapped structure. See Section 6.5.
Returns TRUE on success	

The program in Listing 11.1 pauses two seconds to wait for the OK response, and then calls **ReadFile**. Because of the timeout settings, the read operation returns immediately and the output appears on the console. You should see "at" followed by a blank line and then "ok."

ReadFile   *Reads bytes from the specified file*

```
BOOL ReadFile(
    HANDLE file,
    LPVOID buffer,
    DWORD requestedBytes,
    LPDWORD actualBytes,
    LPOVERLAPPED overlapped)
```

file	File handle created with **CreateFile**
buffer	Buffer to hold the read bytes
requestedBytes	The number of bytes desired
actualBytes	The number of bytes actually placed in the buffer
overlapped	Pointer to overlapped structure. See Section 6.5.
Returns TRUE on success	

If you experience problems you should check for the following:

1. Make sure the modem is Hayes compatible. If it is not, look up the equivalent for the "at" command on your modem and use it instead.

2. Make sure that the modem is on.

3. Make sure that the cable is connected properly between computer and modem.

4. Make sure the cable is connected to the proper comm port

5. Make sure that the cable has its wires set up properly. For example, if you connect the computer and modem but do not see the lights glow when the program runs, suspect the cable and try a different one. You may be using a null-modem cable instead of a normal cable.

6. Make sure you are sending a '\r' rather than a '\n' at the end of the "at" command.

11.4 Getting Communications Events

The communications functions provide a way to detect certain communications events, and these events can improve the responsiveness of your programs. We can improve on Listing 11.1 to some degree by using an event character.

The API is able to sense any of the following events:

EV_BREAK	Break was sent in the input
EV_CTS	The CTS line changed
EV_DSR	The DSR line changed
EV_ERR	An error was detected: CE_FRAME, CE_OVERRUN, and CE_RXPARITY are possible
EV_RING	The modem sensed a ring
EV_RLSD	The DCD line changed
EV_RXCHAR	A character was received
EV_RXFLAG	The special event character (as indicated by the EvtChar field in the DCB) was received
EV_TXEMPTY	The last character of the last **WriteFile** operation was sent

The event most easy to trigger, at least when you have an external modem that is properly cabled, is the Data Set Ready (DSR) event. Each time you turn the modem on or off, the DSR line changes state. Another easy event to trigger is the EV_RING. Modems can detect when the phone rings. If in auto-answer mode, the modem picks up and tries to communicate with the caller. If not in auto-answer mode, however, the modem will trigger EV_RING and you can detect it in your code. You might use this in a productivity-manager application to count how many phone calls the user receives each day.

The EV_RXFLAG capability can be extremely useful if you want your code to be sensitive to a special character in the input stream. For example, you might want to make your code sensitive to the newline character. Once you know that a newline character is waiting in the input buffer, it is possible to read a line from the buffer and respond to it.

To demonstrate the EV_RXFLAG capability, add the following line to the code in Listing 11.1 in order to enable the communications event. Place this line with the other lines that set the DCB structure near the top of Listing 11.1 so that the program knows what the event character is:

```
// set the event character
dcb.EvtChar = '\n';
```

Here, the event character is set to the newline character. The following code, which you should use in place of the **Sleep** and **ReadFile** calls in Listing 11.1, then responds to the event character.

```
// Set the mask to wait for the event
// character. Note change to dcb above
SetCommMask(comHandle, EV_RXFLAG);

// Wait for the character, then read a line
WaitCommEvent(comHandle, &mask, 0);
success = ReadFile(comHandle, str, 100,
    &numRead, 0);
if (!success)
    ErrorHandler("In ReadFile", GetLastError());
str[numRead]='\0';
cout << str << "%" << endl;

// Wait for the character, then read a line
WaitCommEvent(comHandle, &mask, 0);
success = ReadFile(comHandle, str, 100,
    &numRead, 0);
if (!success)
    ErrorHandler("In ReadFile", GetLastError());
str[numRead]='\0';
cout << str << "%" << endl;
```

The code starts with a call to **SetCommMask**, which makes the program sensitive to the specified events.

SetCommMask	*Sets the event mask*
```BOOL SetCommMask(HANDLE commHandle, DWORD mask)```	
commHandle	Handle to a comm port
mask	One or more of the mask bits are read together
Returns TRUE on success	

Once you have set the mask, wait for an event using the **WaitComm-Event** function.

WaitCommEvent	*Waits for an event specified by SetCommMask*

```
BOOL WaitCommEvent(
    HANDLE commHandle,
    LPDWORD mask,
    LPOVERLAPPED overlap)
```

commHandle	Handle to a comm port
mask	pointer to a DWORD—will contain the event that released the wait
overlap	An overlapped structure (see Chapter 6)

Returns TRUE on success

The **WaitCommEvent** function will efficiently wait for one of the specified events to occur. Once any of the events occurs, the function will return. You can detect which of the events occurred by looking at the **mask** value and AND-ing it with the different EV_ constants. If an error is detected, you should call the **ClearCommError** function to clear the error. See Section 11.8 for details.

In the code shown above, the program is sensitive to the newline character. It calls the **ReadFile** function to read the input buffer, and then displays the line to the console. The settings in the timeout structure cause the call to **ReadFile** to return immediately with one line.

In the case shown above, the program happens to read a line correctly because of the delay the modem uses before it returns the "ok" response. In more general cases, however, there is nothing to prevent a character from arriving during the interval between the triggering of the event and the call to **ReadFile**. You may, therefore, want to structure your code so that it reads one character at a time up to the event character each time the event is triggered.

11.5 A Simple Bulletin Board System

A bulletin board system normally runs all of the time, and waits for users to call. With the modem in auto-answer mode, it will automatically connect with the user, and send back the string "CONNECT" to indicate that a session has started. The bulletin board system generally asks the user to log in, and then starts processing user commands.

The code in Listing 11.2 demonstrates the basic communications code for a BBS of this type. Normally you would place code like this in a Windows 2000 service (see Chapter 12) so that it runs in the background all of the time. The program places the modem in auto-answer mode and then waits, using a **ReadFile** call, for a character. Once it sees the word "CONNECT" in the input, it returns the string "You're in" to the user and then begins echoing the user's input. When the user types "X," the program quits.

Listing 11.2   *The communications portion of a simple Bulletin Board system*

```
// bbs.cpp

#include <windows.h>
#include <iostream.h>

void ErrorHandler(char *message, DWORD error)
{
    cout << message << endl;
    cout << "Error number = " << error << endl;
    ExitProcess(1);
}

void main()
{
    HANDLE comHandle;
    BOOL success;
    char str[100];
    DCB dcb;
    char c;
    DWORD numWrite, numRead;
    COMMTIMEOUTS timeouts;
    char inputBuffer[1000];
    int inputBufferCntr = 0;
    BOOL connected = FALSE;

    // Open the comm port
    comHandle = CreateFile("COM2",
        GENERIC_READ|GENERIC_WRITE,
        0, 0, OPEN_EXISTING,
        FILE_ATTRIBUTE_NORMAL, 0);
    if (comHandle == INVALID_HANDLE_VALUE)
        ErrorHandler("In CreateFile",
            GetLastError());

    // Get the current COMM settings
    success = GetCommState(comHandle, &dcb);
    if (!success)
        ErrorHandler("In GetCommState",
            GetLastError());
```

```c
// Set the baud rate, etc.
dcb.BaudRate = 2400;
dcb.ByteSize = 8;
dcb.Parity = NOPARITY;
dcb.StopBits = ONESTOPBIT;

// Save the COMM settings
success = SetCommState(comHandle, &dcb);
if (!success)
    ErrorHandler("In SetCommState",
        GetLastError());

// Set the timeouts so ReadFile does
// not return until it has data
timeouts.ReadIntervalTimeout = 0;
timeouts.ReadTotalTimeoutMultiplier = 0 ;
timeouts.ReadTotalTimeoutConstant = 0 ;
timeouts.WriteTotalTimeoutMultiplier = 0 ;
timeouts.WriteTotalTimeoutConstant = 0 ;
SetCommTimeouts( comHandle, &timeouts ) ;

// Set the DTR line
EscapeCommFunction(comHandle, SETDTR);

// Set modem to auto answer mode
strcpy(str, "atq0&d1s0=2\r");
success = WriteFile(comHandle, str, strlen(str),
    &numWrite, 0);
if (!success)
    ErrorHandler("In WriteFile", GetLastError());

// Respond to incoming data
do
{
    // Get a character from the modem
    success = ReadFile(comHandle, &c, 1,
        &numRead, 0);
    if (!success)
        ErrorHandler("In ReadFile",
            GetLastError());

    // if its not alphanumeric, discard it
    if (!isalnum(c) && c != 10 && c != 13)
        continue;

    // if connected, echo it back
    if (connected)
    {
        success = WriteFile(comHandle, &c, 1,
            &numWrite, 0);
```

Listing 11.2   *The communications portion of a simple Bulletin Board system
(continued)*

```
            if (!success)
                ErrorHandler("In WriteFile",
                    GetLastError());
        }
        // if it's CR or LF, then check for
        // the word CONNECT. The word CONNECT
        // means that it is time to start
        // acting like a bulletin board
        else if (c == 10 || c == 13)
        {
            inputBuffer[inputBufferCntr]='\0';
            cout << inputBuffer << endl;
            if (strncmp(inputBuffer, "CONNECT", 7)==0)
            {
                connected = TRUE;
                strcpy(str, "You're in...\r\n");
                cout << "You're in..." << endl;
                success = WriteFile(comHandle, str,
                    strlen(str), &numWrite, 0);
                if (!success)
                    ErrorHandler("In WriteFile",
                        GetLastError());
            }
            inputBufferCntr = 0;
        }
        // otherwise add to buffer
        else
            inputBuffer[inputBufferCntr++] = c;
    } while (c != 'X'); // Once user types 'X', done

    // Clear the DTR line
    EscapeCommFunction(comHandle, CLRDTR);

    CloseHandle(comHandle);
}
```

The first part of Listing 11.2 looks just like Listing 11.1. It opens a connection with the COM port using **CreateFile** and sets up the DCB and timeout structures. Note that the read timeouts in Listing 11.2 are set so that **ReadFile** does not return until it detects data. Once the program has set up everything, it raises DTR and sends a string to the modem telling it to turn on its auto-answer mode.

The code now enters a loop in which it uses a **ReadFile** statement to wait for a character. If the word "CONNECT" has not yet been seen, the code places each character in an input buffer that holds one line of characters. As soon as a return or a line-feed character (ASCII 10 or 13) appears in the input stream, the program recognizes it as an end-of-line indication and looks for the word "CONNECT" in the input buffer. Once it finds it, a session begins. The BBS sends back the string "You're in..." and then simply echoes the user's input. In a real BBS program, you would want to ask the user to log in and then begin to interpret user commands.

The input buffer demonstrated here is one way to buffer lines. The technique described in the previous section using comm events and an event character is another way to do it. With either technique, you end up reading one character at a time from the input stream because you never know how many characters form a line in the input buffer.

In a BBS that handles multiple modems, threads can make the design of the program significantly easier. You can assign one thread to each COM port that you are managing. See Chapter 6 for details.

11.6 Flow Control

The 32-bit APIs supports three different types of flow control:

1. Xon/Xoff (software)
2. RTS/CTS (hardware)
3. DTR/DSR (hardware)

Flow control is used by the comm libraries at both the sending and receiving ends to prevent buffer overflow. When the comm system receives characters, it places them in an input buffer. If the system does not pull characters out of the buffer fast enough to match the rate at which they arrive, then the buffer will fill and eventually overflow. Flow control allows a receiver to send a signal that tells the sender to stop sending characters because of an impending buffer overflow. When the buffer is again clear, the receiver can send another signal to the sender telling it to resume.

Xon/Xoff flow control uses special character values passed in the normal input stream as the signal. Ctrl-S (XOFF) is normally used to halt the flow, while Ctrl-Q (XON) resumes it. Because the characters appear in the normal data stream, they cannot be used while transmitting binary data.

The two hardware flow-control methods use modem control lines to regulate the flow. These lines are discussed at the beginning of the chapter. These control methods both rely on the RS-232 cable and modem correctly supporting the designated lines. For flow control to work properly, the modems at both ends of the connection need to be using the same method.

You can use the **GetCommProperties** function to determine what types of flow control the current comm driver for the specified port supports.

In the case of hardware flow control, this does not necessarily mean that the method will actually work (for example, if the cable is missing the necessary wires, the comm driver will not know about it), but it does indicate whether or not the driver knows how to support the specified protocol.

GetCommProperties   *Returns information about the driver for the specified port*

```
BOOL GetCommProperties(
    HANDLE commHandle,
    LPCOMMPROP properties)
```

commHandle   Handle to a comm port

properties   A pointer to a properties structure

Returns TRUE on success

The COMMPROP structure contains quite a bit of useful information about the comm device. The following summary is copied from the Microsoft API help file and will give you an idea of what is available. See the description in the help file for more information.

```
typedef struct _COMMPROP {
    WORD wPacketLength; // packet size, in bytes
    WORD wPacketVersion; // packet version
    DWORD dwServiceMask; // services implemented
    DWORD dwReserved1; // reserved
    DWORD dwMaxTxQueue; // max Tx bufsize, in bytes
    DWORD dwMaxRxQueue; // max Rx bufsize, in bytes
    DWORD dwMaxBaud; // max baud rate, in bps
    DWORD dwProvSubType; // specific provider type

    DWORD dwProvCapabilities; // caps supported
    DWORD dwSettableParams; // changable parameters
    DWORD dwSettableBaud; // allowable baud rates
    WORD wSettableData; // allowable byte sizes
    WORD wSettableStopParity; // stop bits/parity
    DWORD dwCurrentTxQueue; // Tx buffer size,bytes
    DWORD dwCurrentRxQueue; // Rx buffer size,bytes
    DWORD dwProvSpec1; // provider-specific data
    DWORD dwProvSpec2; // provider-specific data

    WCHAR wcProvChar[1]; // provider-specific data
} COMMPROP;
```

The **dwProvCapabilities** field tells you which of the different flow-control capabilities are available.

You activate the flow-control features using a DCB structure and the **SetCommState** function. To turn on Xon/Xoff flow control, set the following fields:

```
dcb.fInX = dcb.fOutX = TRUE;
dcb.XonLim = 50 ;
dcb.XoffLim = 200 ;
dcb.XonChar = 17;
dcb.XoffChar = 19;
```

These settings turn on XON/XOFF flow control for both sending and receiving, indicate that Ctrl-Q (ASCII 17) and Ctrl-S (ASCII 19) should be used as the XON and XOFF characters, and set the sizes where flow is stopped and resumed. The **fTXContinueOnXoff** field is also relevant.

To turn on RTS/CTS flow control, set the following fields:

```
dcb.fOutxCtsFlow = TRUE ;
dcb.fRtsControl = RTS_CONTROL_HANDSHAKE ;
```

To turn on DTR/DSR flow control, set the following fields:

```
dcb.fOutxDsrFlow = TRUE ;
dcb.fDtrControl = DTR_CONTROL_HANDSHAKE ;
```

11.7 A Simple TTY Terminal Program

Creating a complete terminal emulator program is not an easy task. While the program is conceptually simple, there are a lot of details that make things difficult. For example, any real terminal emulator needs to understand the escape sequences of the one or more terminals it is emulating, and you generally end up building a small-state machine to handle it. In order to demonstrate the communications portion of a terminal emulator, this section presents a very simple TTY-style terminal program that you can use to connect to a remote machine via either a modem or the TELNET facility.

One of the more interesting problems handled by this program is the "two input stream problem." In a terminal program, the user can hit a character on the keyboard at any time and this character must be sent to the modem immediately. At the same time, a character can appear in the modem's input buffer at any moment, and it needs to appear on the screen immediately so the user can see it. You cannot have the code accept a user keystroke and then wait for a modem keystroke, because the two input streams are completely independent of one another. Instead, you have to wait for characters from either stream and respond to them immediately. This program uses NT's **WaitForMultipleObjects** function (see Chapter 6), along with overlapped I/O (see Chapter 7), to solve the problem. You could also use separate threads (see Chapter 6) to monitor the two input sources.

Listing 11.3 contains the code for the terminal-emulator program. It is currently set up to communicate with a modem on COM2. In this mode you should run the program and then type "atdt 555-5555" (use an appropriate

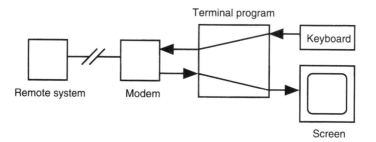

Terminal program

Keyboard

Remote system   Modem

Screen

Figure 11.3

The terminal program must handle two input streams simultaneously and asynchronously

phone number) to dial out to a BBS or remote computer system. If you want to try using the TELNET facility to connect to a telnet server such as a UNIX machine on the network, use "\\\\.\\TELNET" for the **portString** variable in the **main** function. *Make sure you have loaded the TCP/IP facility in the Network applet of the Control Panel, and also make sure you have started the Telnet service in the Services applet of the Control Panel, or else the TELNET port will not work.* You should immediately see a `telnet>` prompt, and you can use it normally. Type "help" if you need help.

Listing 11.3   *A simple TTY terminal emulator*

```
// term.cpp

#include <windows.h>
#include <iostream.h>
#include <stdio.h>
#include <string.h>

void ErrorHandler(char *s, DWORD err)
{
    cout << s << endl;
    cout << "Error number: " << err << endl;
    ExitProcess(err);
}

// Scrolls the console up one line
void ScrollOneLine(HANDLE consoleStdout)
{
    BOOL success;
    CONSOLE_SCREEN_BUFFER_INFO consoleInfo;
    SMALL_RECT scrollRect;
    CHAR_INFO consoleFill;
    COORD coord;
```

```
   // get current console size (may change)
   success = GetConsoleScreenBufferInfo(
      consoleStdout, &consoleInfo);
   if (!success)
      ErrorHandler("In GetConsoleScreenBufferInfo",
         GetLastError());

   // Define the rectangle to scroll
   scrollRect.Top = 0;
   scrollRect.Left = 0;
   scrollRect.Bottom = consoleInfo.dwSize.Y - 1;
   scrollRect.Right = consoleInfo.dwSize.X - 1;

   // Define destination of scrolled rectangle
   coord.X = 0;
   coord.Y = -1;

   // Define how to fill blank line
   consoleFill.Attributes =
      consoleInfo.wAttributes;
   consoleFill.Char.AsciiChar = ";

   // Perform the scroll
   success =
      ScrollConsoleScreenBuffer(consoleStdout,
            &scrollRect, 0,
      coord, &consoleFill);
   if (!success)
      ErrorHandler("In ScrollConsoleScreenBuffer",
         GetLastError());

}

// Handles the newline character
VOID NewLine(HANDLE consoleStdout)
{
   CONSOLE_SCREEN_BUFFER_INFO consoleInfo;
   BOOL success;

   // Find out where cursor is
   success =
      GetConsoleScreenBufferInfo(consoleStdout,
         &consoleInfo);
   if (!success)
      ErrorHandler("In GetConsoleScreenBufferInfo",
         GetLastError());

   // Move cursor to far left
   consoleInfo.dwCursorPosition.X = 0;
```

Listing 11.3   *A simple TTY terminal emulator (continued)*

```
   // If the cursor is on the last line
   // of the console, then scroll the console,
   // else increment position
   if (consoleInfo.dwSize.Y - 1 ==
      consoleInfo.dwCursorPosition.Y)
      ScrollOneLine(consoleStdout);
   else
      consoleInfo.dwCursorPosition.Y += 1;

   // Update the console
   success =
      SetConsoleCursorPosition(consoleStdout,
      consoleInfo.dwCursorPosition);
   if (!success)
      ErrorHandler("In SetConsoleCursorPosition",
         GetLastError());
}

// Initializes the port
HANDLE SetupCommPort(char *port)
{
   HANDLE comHandle;
   BOOL success;
   DCB dcb;
   COMMTIMEOUTS timeouts;

   // Open the file
   comHandle = CreateFile(port,
      GENERIC_READ|GENERIC_WRITE,
      0, 0, OPEN_EXISTING,
      FILE_FLAG_OVERLAPPED, 0);
   if (comHandle == INVALID_HANDLE_VALUE)
      ErrorHandler("In CreateFile",
      GetLastError());

   // Set timeouts so ReadFile does not
   // return until data is available
   timeouts.ReadIntervalTimeout = 0 ;
   timeouts.ReadTotalTimeoutMultiplier = 0 ;
   timeouts.ReadTotalTimeoutConstant = 0 ;
   timeouts.WriteTotalTimeoutMultiplier = 0 ;
   timeouts.WriteTotalTimeoutConstant = 0 ;
   SetCommTimeouts( comHandle, &timeouts ) ;

   // Get current settings and change them
   success = GetCommState(comHandle, &dcb);
   if (!success)
      ErrorHandler("In GetCommState",
      GetLastError());
```

```
      dcb.BaudRate = 2400;
      dcb.ByteSize = 8;
      dcb.Parity = NOPARITY;
      dcb.StopBits = ONESTOPBIT;

      success = SetCommState(comHandle, &dcb);
      if (!success)
         ErrorHandler("In SetCommState",
            GetLastError());

      EscapeCommFunction(comHandle, SETDTR);
      return comHandle;
}

void ProcessIO(HANDLE consoleStdin,
      HANDLE consoleStdout)
{
      char readBuffer, writeBuffer;
      DWORD numRead, numWrite;
      INPUT_RECORD inputEvent;
      DWORD s;
      HANDLE comHandle, readEvent, writeEvent;
      HANDLE handles[2];
      OVERLAPPED overlappedRead, overlappedWrite;
      BOOL success;
      char *portString = "COM2";

      // Set up the comm port. Can setup COM, LPT
      // or \\\\.\\TELNET. If you do TELNET, make sure
      // you have the TCP/IP package loaded and
      // the telnet service started
      comHandle = SetupCommPort(portString);

      // Set up for overlapped reading and
      // writing on the port
      overlappedRead.Offset =
         overlappedWrite.Offset = 0;
      overlappedRead.OffsetHigh =
         overlappedWrite.OffsetHigh = 0;
      readEvent = CreateEvent(0, TRUE, FALSE, 0);
      writeEvent = CreateEvent(0, FALSE, FALSE, 0);
      overlappedRead.hEvent = readEvent;
      overlappedWrite.hEvent = writeEvent;

      // Set up handles array
      // for WaitForMultipleObjects
      handles[0] = consoleStdin;
      handles[1] = readEvent;

      // Prime the pump by getting the read
      // process started
```

Listing 11.3   *A simple TTY terminal emulator (continued)*

```
success = ReadFile(comHandle, &readBuffer, 1,
   &numRead, &overlappedRead);
do
{
   // Wait for either a keystroke or a
   // modem character. Time out after
   // 1000 seconds
   s = WaitForMultipleObjects(2, handles,
      FALSE, 1000000);
   if (s==WAIT_TIMEOUT)
      break;
   // If it is a character from the
   // keyboard then...
   else if (s==WAIT_OBJECT_0)
   {
      // Get a copy of the character but
      // leave it in the queue
      PeekConsoleInput(handles[0], &inputEvent,
         1, &numRead);
      if (numRead>0)
      {
         // If it is a mouse event, or a key up
         // event, or if it is not a valid
         // ASCII character (eg-a shift key),
         // then read and discard the keystroke.
         if (inputEvent.EventType !=
            KEY_EVENT ||
            inputEvent.Event.KeyEvent.bKeyDown
            == FALSE ||
            inputEvent.Event.KeyEvent.
            uChar.AsciiChar==0)
            ReadConsoleInput(handles[0],
               &inputEvent, 1, &numRead);
         // Otherwise, read the keystroke
         // and send it to the comm port.
         else
         {
            ReadFile(handles[0], &writeBuffer,
               1, &numWrite, 0);
            success = WriteFile(comHandle,
               &writeBuffer, 1, &numWrite,
               &overlappedWrite);
            GetOverlappedResult(comHandle,
               &overlappedWrite, &numWrite,
               TRUE);
            overlappedWrite.Offset += numWrite;
         }
      }
   }
```

```
        // If the character is coming in from
        // the comm port, then...
        else if (s==WAIT_OBJECT_0 + 1)
        {
            // Get the character and send it
            // to the console
            success = GetOverlappedResult(comHandle,
                &overlappedRead, &numRead, TRUE);
            overlappedRead.Offset += numRead;
            WriteFile(consoleStdout, &readBuffer, 1,
                &numWrite, 0);
            ResetEvent(readEvent);
            // Wait for the next character
            // from the comm port
            ReadFile(comHandle, &readBuffer, 1,
                &numRead, &overlappedRead);
        }
    // Terminate when the user types an 'X'
    } while  (writeBuffer != 'X');

    // Close all handles
    CloseHandle(readEvent);
    CloseHandle(writeEvent);
    CloseHandle(comHandle);
}

VOID main(void)
{
    DWORD oldMode, newMode;
    BOOL success;
    HANDLE consoleStdout, consoleStdin;

    // Get handles for standard in and out
    consoleStdin = GetStdHandle(STD_INPUT_HANDLE);
    consoleStdout = GetStdHandle(STD_OUTPUT_HANDLE);
    if (consoleStdin == consoleStdout)
        ErrorHandler("In GetStdHandle",
            GetLastError());

    // Get current console mode so can modify it
    success = GetConsoleMode(consoleStdin,
        &oldMode);
    if (!success)
        ErrorHandler("In GetConsoleMode",
            GetLastError());
    newMode = oldMode & ~ENABLE_LINE_INPUT &
        ~ENABLE_ECHO_INPUT;
    success = SetConsoleMode(consoleStdin, newMode);
        if (!success)
        ErrorHandler("In SetConsoleMode",
            GetLastError());
```

Listing 11.3   *A simple TTY terminal emulator (continued)*

```
// Process user I/O
ProcessIO(consoleStdin, consoleStdout);

// put the old mode back
success = SetConsoleMode(consoleStdin, oldMode);
if (!success)
    ErrorHandler("In SetConsoleMode",
        GetLastError());
}
```

The code in Listing 11.3 uses the console code from Listing 14.5 as its basis. The console is in raw mode, so the program can get each individual character typed by the user as it arrives and pass it to the modem.

The **SetupCommPort** function initializes the communications port using the same techniques as in Listing 11.1. The timeouts are set so that the **ReadFile** function does not return until it has input.

The **ProcessIO** function handles all of the input and output for the two streams of data. It uses overlapped reads and writes (see Chapter 7) on the communications port, so the first part of the code creates the overlapped structures and events to make this possible. The event in the overlapped read structure is key to the success of this program: By starting an overlapped read operation on the comm port and then waiting on the overlapped event, the program can detect when the modem has a character in the input buffer ready for processing.

The program actually waits on two events all of the time, using the **WaitForMultipleObjects** function. The array contains the read event from the comm port, along with the input handle for the console. This input handle indicates when the user has typed a key. When **WaitForMultipleObjects** detects that either the modem or the console has a waiting character, it returns. The program then figures out which input source is ready, and processes the character. If the character arrives on the modem, it gets sent to the screen. If a character arrives from the keyboard, the program first peeks at the buffer to make sure that it contains a valid keystroke. If it does, the code sends the character to the modem.

11.8 Other Communications Functions

There are several other communications functions that you may find useful in special situations. The **PurgeComm** function, for example, purges the contents of the input or output buffer.

PurgeComm	*Clears input or output buffers*

```
BOOL PurgeComm(
    HANDLE commHandle,
    DWORD action)
```

commHandle	Handle to a comm port
action	The action(s) to perform

Returns TRUE on success

Four actions are possible, one at a time or in combination with one another:

PURGE_TXABORT	Terminate all write operations
PURGE_RXABORT	Terminate all read operations
PURGE_TXCLEAR	Clear output buffer
PURGE_RXCLEAR	Clear input buffer

The **FileFlushBuffers** function, on the other hand, flushes the output buffer to the receiver, subject to normal flow-control constraints. This function will not return until the buffer is empty.

FlushFileBuffers	*Empties the output buffer*

```
BOOL FlushFileBuffers(
    HANDLE commHandle)
```

commHandle	Handle to a comm port

Returns TRUE on success

The **SetupComm** function lets you change the size of the buffers.

SetupComm	*Sets buffer size*

```
BOOL SetupComm(
    HANDLE commHandle,
    DWORD inputBufferSize,
    DWORD outputBufferSize)
```

commHandle	Handle to a comm port
inputBufferSize	The size of the input buffer
outputBufferSize	The size of the output buffer

Returns TRUE on success

The **TransmitCommChar** function transmits the specified character immediately, ahead of any other characters in the output buffer. It is like placing the character at the very first location in the output buffer—it is still subject to flow control but will be sent next. It is useful for sending Ctrl-C characters to halt commands.

TransmitCommChar	*Transmits a character ahead of buffer contents*

```
BOOL TransmitCommChar(
   commHandle,
   char c)
```

commHandle	Handle to a comm port
c	The character to transmit

Returns TRUE on success

11.9 Conclusion

You will find that the communications portion of the APIs makes it easy to communicate with serial and parallel ports on your Windows workstation. At the same time, the communications API has all of the features necessary to control the many details that make modem communications so complex.

The API and the telnet port make it extremely easy to communicate with other machines supporting telnet servers on a TCP/IP network. For example, if there is a UNIX machine on your network, the telnet port available in the communications API makes communications with it easy.

Windows 2000 Services

Any operating system needs a way to start up processes when the system boots and then leave them running while the system is online. For example, the Messenger service that comes with Windows 2000 monitors the network continuously and displays a dialog box whenever it receives a message. An application that receives faxes needs to start up at boot time and then continuously monitor the fax modem for fax machines dialing in. A home or office-security system needs to continuously monitor sensors and respond to them, regardless of who is currently using the machine.

In UNIX, this functionality is handled by daemons. Daemons are loaded as the system boots and receive CPU time as background tasks. Typical UNIX daemons handle mail coming in over the network, cron jobs (similar to jobs scheduled with the at command in Windows 2000), finger requests, and so on. In DOS, background processing was handled by TSR (Terminate and Stay Resident) programs, which were invoked through the .bat;autoexec.bat file. In Windows 3.1, the Startup group of the Program Manager would start background processes. Windows 3.1 automatically invokes this group as soon as it starts up, unlike Windows 2000, which invokes it only when someone logs in. If you had a FAX board in a normal Windows 3.1 computer, you could place the FAX program's icon in the Startup group and the fax board could start receiving faxes as soon as Windows started.

In Windows 2000, you need a way to create processes that automatically start as the system boots, and then remain running as background processes no matter who is currently logged in. This functionality is handled by *services*. In this chapter you will learn how to create, install, and control your own services.

Compatibility Note: All of the code in this chapter works in Windows 2000, while none of it works in Windows 98.

12.1 The Possibilities

The Service mechanism in Windows 2000 provides an extremely elegant way to create background tasks for Windows 2000 machines. Windows 2000 itself uses services in quite a few ways. At least fifteen services are available after you install the base system, and add-on modules like the Remote Access Server and the FTP server add new services of their own.

Probably the simplest existing service provided by Wndows 2000 is the Messenger service. When it starts, it creates a mailslot and monitors it. When it sees a message in the mailslot's queue, it retrieves it and displays a message box containing the message on the screen. The Schedule service is slightly more advanced. When someone types the `at` command, the requested task is stored in a task list. The Schedule service periodically looks at the list and decides if there are pending jobs that it needs to execute. If it finds one, it executes it and potentially updates the task list.

The FTP server offers a good example of an advanced service. The service automatically starts when Windows 2000 boots (you can also change its behavior so that it starts manually instead). It monitors the network, and when it sees another machine trying to make an FTP connection it accepts the connection and validates the user's login ID. Then it accepts commands from the remote user to get and put files. All of these operations occur in the background.

The FTP server also places an icon in the Control Panel during installation. A service-control process like this one is able to send a signal to the service to tell it to update its current status (see Section 14.5 for an example of how to send a signal to a service). The control process can also use named pipes or other inter-process communication techniques (see Chapter 6) to communicate with the service in a pre-arranged way.

There are many good reasons for you to create your own services. For example:

* If you have a Windows 2000 machine attached to and controlling a piece of manufacturing equipment on the factory floor, you may want the controller software to run all of the time. By implementing the software as a service, you can cause it to start as soon as the machine boots, and it will run no matter who is logged in to the machine. You can set thread priorities (see Section 6.7) on the service's threads so that the service can appropriately respond to high-priority events coming back from the equipment it monitors and controls.

- If you want to create a bulletin board system that runs all of the time, you can implement it as a service. When the machine boots, the BBS will start and begin monitoring the appropriate communications port(s) for incoming calls. When it receives a call, it can process the user's requests without interrupting the person currently logged onto the machine. See Chapter 11 for information on communication ports.
- If you want an RPC server (Chapter 9) to be available all of the time, you can place it inside a service so that it starts when the machine boots. See Section 12.11.
- If you want to create an inventory system that periodically polls a number of separate stores to download their inventory status, you can implement the in-store portion of the system using services. The service in each store runs in the background waiting for a connection request. The central machine at the warehouse can call to each store, and the service there will respond appropriately regardless of who, or whether anyone, is logged in.

Any task that you want to run continuously and in the background, regardless of who is logged in, should be handled using a service.

12.2 Understanding Services

You can learn a great deal about the fundamentals of services simply by working with the Services applet in the Control Panel. If you start up the Control Panel and open the Services applet on your machine now, you will find a number of standard services that come with Windows 2000. For example, the Alerter, Clipbook Server, Computer Browser, and Directory Replicator services are all pre-installed when you load Windows 2000 onto your system. You may also find services that have been loaded by your administrator to handle special tasks, or that came with different applications to handle background processing for them.

Any new service that you create needs to be installed in this applet's list of services. Installation creates an entry for the service in the Registry (specifically in HKEY_LOCAL_MACHINE\System\CurrentControlSet\Services), so that the machine knows about it each time it boots. Windows 2000 provides an installation function that handles the creation of this entry automatically.

Every service must be able to respond to a set of standard events that the Services applet can pass to it. These events are represented in the applet as buttons:

- Start: Starts the service if it is of the manual start variety, if the user stopped it, or if it failed to start at boot time
- Stop: Stops the service

- Pause: Suspends the service temporarily
- Continue: Restarts a suspended service

Using the Services applet, the administrator can select how a given service will start up each time the machine boots. The service can start automatically, can start manually, or can be marked as disabled by the administrator. If a service is disabled, then no one but the administrator or a power user can manipulate the service. The administrator can also assign an account under which the service logs in when it starts. A service normally runs under the LocalSystem account unless another account is specified. An account other than LocalSystem might be used to restrict a service in some way.

If you look at the bottom of the Services applet window, you will see a text area labeled "Startup Parameters." These parameters allow you to pass special values into the service when it manually starts. The parameters come into the service through the **ServiceMain** function in an **argv** list, just as command-line parameters would. Startup parameters apply only to manual start services.

12.3 Service Choreography

All services are managed by a system called the *Service Control Manager*. The SCM maintains the list of known services in the registry and starts them either automatically at boot time or when requested by a user. The SCM keeps a list of services and their start-up status in the registry. New services are added to the list by installation, as described in Section 12.5. It is also possible to remove services.

A program that acts as a service is a normal EXE file, but it must meet special requirements so that it interfaces properly with the Service Control Manager. Microsoft has carefully choreographed the flow of these functions, and you must follow that plan closely or the service will not work. The requirements follow:

- The service's EXE must have a normal **main** or **WinMain** function. This function should immediately (or, in special cases, within 30 seconds—see Section 12.7) call the **StartServiceCrtlDispatcher** function. By calling the function, you register the EXE with the Service Control Manager and give the SCM a pointer to a **ServiceMain** function to call when it wants to start the service. You can name the **ServiceMain** function anything you like, but you will find its description in the documentation under **ServiceMain**. The **main** function should return after registering **ServiceMain** with the SCM.

  You would never run a service's EXE from a command line. Instead, you install it in the services list known to the SCM, and the

SCM starts the EXE itself by calling the **main** function. If you do accidentally execute a service on the command line, it will fail because it cannot connect to the SCM.

- The Service Control Manager will call the **ServiceMain** function when it wants to start the service. For example, if the administrator presses the **Start** button in the Services applet of the Control Panel, the SCM will execute the **ServiceMain** function in a separate thread.

  The **ServiceMain** function has several responsibilities. The main one is to immediately call the **RegisterServiceCtrlHandler** function, which registers a **Handler** function with the SCM for it to call with control requests. See the following section for details on the **Handler** function. You can name the Handler function anything you like, but it is listed in the documentation under **Handler**. The **RegisterServiceCtrlHandler** function will return a handle that the service can use when it wants to send status messages to the SCM.

  The **ServiceMain** function must also start the thread that does the actual work of the service itself. Once this thread has started, the **ServiceMain** function generally waits for an event. The **ServiceMain** function should not return until it is time for the service to stop. When it returns, the service has stopped, and the SCM restarts it by calling **ServiceMain** again.

- The **Handler** function contains a switch statement that parses control requests received from the Service Control Manager. By default, the SCM can send any of the following control constants:
  - SERVICE_CONTROL_STOP: Tells the service to stop.
  - SERVICE_CONTROL_PAUSE: Tells the service to pause.
  - SERVICE_CONTROL_CONTINUE: Tells the service to resume.
  - SERVICE_CONTROL_INTERROGATE: Tells the service to immediately report its status.
  - SERVICE_CONTROL_SHUTDOWN: Tells the service that shutdown is imminent.

It is also possible to create custom constants (with values between 128 and 255) and send them through the SCM to the service. See Section 12.5 for details.

When you create an EXE that contains the **main**, **ServiceMain**, and **Handler** functions described above, as well as a function that contains the thread for the service itself, you have a complete service. Figure 12.1 summarizes the interactions between these different functions and the SCM.

The following section gives an example of the simplest possible service so that you can see how the different pieces shown in the EXE file of Figure 12.1 work together.

12.4 The Simplest Service

Listing 12.1 shows the simplest service possible. This service simply beeps. By default, it beeps every two seconds. Optionally, you can modify the beep interval with startup parameters. This service is complete in that it will appropriately respond to the Service Control Manager for every control signal possible. Because of that, this program can act as a good template for creating your own services. See Appendix A for compilation instructions.

Listing 12.1   *A complete service that beeps at a fixed or user-controlled interval*

```
// beepserv.cpp

#include <windows.h>
#include <stdio.h>
#include <iostream.h>
#include <stdlib.h>

// Global variables

// The name of the service
char *SERVICE_NAME = "BeepService";
// Event used to hold ServiceMain from completing
HANDLE terminateEvent = NULL;
// Handle used to communicate status info with
// the SCM. Created by RegisterServiceCtrlHandler
SERVICE_STATUS_HANDLE serviceStatusHandle;
// The beep interval in ms.
int beepDelay = 2000;
// Flags holding current state of service
BOOL pauseService = FALSE;
BOOL runningService = FALSE;
// Thread for the actual work
HANDLE threadHandle = 0;

void ErrorHandler(char *s, DWORD err)
{
   cout << s << endl;
   cout << "Error number: " << err << endl;
   ExitProcess(err);
}

DWORD ServiceThread(LPDWORD param)
{
   while (1)
   {
     Beep(200,200);
     Sleep(beepDelay);
```

```
    }
    return 0;
}

// Initializes the service by starting its thread
BOOL InitService()
{
    DWORD id;

    // Start the service's thread
    threadHandle = CreateThread(0, 0,
        (LPTHREAD_START_ROUTINE) ServiceThread,
        0, 0, &id);

    if (threadHandle==0)
        return FALSE;
    else
    {
        runningService = TRUE;
        return TRUE;
    }
}

// Resumes a paused service
VOID ResumeService()
{
    pauseService=FALSE;
    ResumeThread(threadHandle);
}

// Pauses the service
VOID PauseService()
{
    pauseService = TRUE;
    SuspendThread(threadHandle);
}

// Stops the service by allowing ServiceMain to
// complete
VOID StopService()
{
    runningService=FALSE;
    // Set the event that is holding ServiceMain
    // so that ServiceMain can return
    SetEvent(terminateEvent);
}

// This function consolidates the activities of
// updating the service status with
// SetServiceStatus
```

Listing 12.1	*A complete service that beeps at a fixed or user-controlled interval (continued)*

```
BOOL SendStatusToSCM (DWORD dwCurrentState,
    DWORD dwWin32ExitCode,
    DWORD dwServiceSpecificExitCode,
    DWORD dwCheckPoint,
    DWORD dwWaitHint)
{
    BOOL success;
    SERVICE_STATUS serviceStatus;

    // Fill in all of the SERVICE_STATUS fields
    serviceStatus.dwServiceType =
        SERVICE_WIN32_OWN_PROCESS;
    serviceStatus.dwCurrentState = dwCurrentState;

    // If in the process of something, then accept
    // no control events, else accept anything
    if (dwCurrentState == SERVICE_START_PENDING)
        serviceStatus.dwControlsAccepted = 0;
    else
        serviceStatus.dwControlsAccepted =
            SERVICE_ACCEPT_STOP |
            SERVICE_ACCEPT_PAUSE_CONTINUE |
            SERVICE_ACCEPT_SHUTDOWN;

    // if a specific exit code is defined, set up
    // the win32 exit code properly
    if (dwServiceSpecificExitCode == 0)
        serviceStatus.dwWin32ExitCode =
            dwWin32ExitCode;
    else
        serviceStatus.dwWin32ExitCode =
            ERROR_SERVICE_SPECIFIC_ERROR;
    serviceStatus.dwServiceSpecificExitCode =
        dwServiceSpecificExitCode;

    serviceStatus.dwCheckPoint = dwCheckPoint;
    serviceStatus.dwWaitHint = dwWaitHint;

    // Pass the status record to the SCM
    success = SetServiceStatus (serviceStatusHandle,
        &serviceStatus);
    if (!success)
        StopService();

    return success;
}

// Dispatches events received from the service
```

```
// control manager
VOID ServiceCtrlHandler (DWORD controlCode)
{
    DWORD   currentState = 0;
    BOOL success;

    switch(controlCode)
    {
        // There is no START option because
        // ServiceMain gets called on a start

        // Stop the service
        case SERVICE_CONTROL_STOP:
            currentState = SERVICE_STOP_PENDING;
            // Tell the SCM what's happening
            success = SendStatusToSCM(
                SERVICE_STOP_PENDING,
                NO_ERROR, 0, 1, 5000);
            // Not much to do if not successful

            // Stop the service
            StopService();
            return;

        // Pause the service
        case SERVICE_CONTROL_PAUSE:
            if (runningService && !pauseService)
            {
                // Tell the SCM what's happening
                success = SendStatusToSCM(
                    SERVICE_PAUSE_PENDING,
                    NO_ERROR, 0, 1, 1000);
                PauseService();
                currentState = SERVICE_PAUSED;
            }
            break;

        // Resume from a pause
        case SERVICE_CONTROL_CONTINUE:
            if (runningService && pauseService)
            {
                // Tell the SCM what's happening
                success = SendStatusToSCM(
                    SERVICE_CONTINUE_PENDING,
                    NO_ERROR, 0, 1, 1000);
                ResumeService();
                currentState = SERVICE_RUNNING;
            }
            break;

        // Update current status
```

Listing 12.1   *A complete service that beeps at a fixed or user-controlled interval (continued)*

```
        case SERVICE_CONTROL_INTERROGATE:
            // it will fall to bottom and send status
            break;

            // Do nothing in a shutdown. Could do cleanup
            // here but it must be very quick.
        case SERVICE_CONTROL_SHUTDOWN:
            // Do nothing on shutdown
            return;
        default:
            break;
    }
    SendStatusToSCM(currentState, NO_ERROR,
        0, 0, 0);
}

// Handle an error from ServiceMain by cleaning up
// and telling SCM that the service didn't start.
VOID terminate(DWORD error)
{
    // if terminateEvent has been created, close it.
    if (terminateEvent)
        CloseHandle(terminateEvent);

    // Send a message to the scm to tell about
    // stopage
    if (serviceStatusHandle)
        SendStatusToSCM(SERVICE_STOPPED, error,
            0, 0, 0);

    // If the thread has started kill it off
    if (threadHandle)
        CloseHandle(threadHandle);

    // Do not need to close serviceStatusHandle
}

// ServiceMain is called when the SCM wants to
// start the service. When it returns, the service
// has stopped. It therefore waits on an event
// just before the end of the function, and
// that event gets set when it is time to stop.
// It also returns on any error because the
// service cannot start if there is an error.
VOID ServiceMain(DWORD argc, LPTSTR *argv)
{
    BOOL success;
```

```
// immediately call Registration function
serviceStatusHandle =
    RegisterServiceCtrlHandler(
        SERVICE_NAME,
        (LPHANDLER_FUNCTION)ServiceCtrlHandler);
if (!serviceStatusHandle)
{
    terminate(GetLastError());
    return;
}

// Notify SCM of progress
success = SendStatusToSCM(
    SERVICE_START_PENDING,
    NO_ERROR, 0, 1, 5000);
if (!success)
{
    terminate(GetLastError());
    return;
}

// create the termination event
terminateEvent = CreateEvent (0, TRUE, FALSE,
    0);
if (!terminateEvent)
{
    terminate(GetLastError());
    return;
}

// Notify SCM of progress
success = SendStatusToSCM(
    SERVICE_START_PENDING,
    NO_ERROR, 0, 2, 1000);
if (!success)
{
    terminate(GetLastError());
    return;
}

// Check for startup params
if (argc == 2)
{
    int temp = atoi(argv[1]);
    if (temp < 1000)
        beepDelay = 2000;
    else
        beepDelay = temp;
}
```

Listing 12.1 *A complete service that beeps at a fixed or user-controlled interval (continued)*

```
    // Notify SCM of progress
    success = SendStatusToSCM(
        SERVICE_START_PENDING,
        NO_ERROR, 0, 3, 5000);
    if (!success)
    {
        terminate(GetLastError());
        return;
    }

    // Start the service itself
    success = InitService();
    if (!success)
    {
        terminate(GetLastError());
        return;
    }

    // The service is now running.
    // Notify SCM of progress
    success = SendStatusToSCM(
        SERVICE_RUNNING,
        NO_ERROR, 0, 0, 0);
    if (!success)
    {
        terminate(GetLastError());
        return;
    }

    // Wait for stop signal, and then terminate
    WaitForSingleObject (terminateEvent, INFINITE);

    terminate(0);
}

VOID main(VOID)
{
    SERVICE_TABLE_ENTRY serviceTable[] =
    {
    { SERVICE_NAME,
        (LPSERVICE_MAIN_FUNCTION) ServiceMain},
    { NULL, NULL }
    };
    BOOL success;

    // Register with the SCM
    success =
```

```
        StartServiceCtrlDispatcher(serviceTable);
    if (!success)
        ErrorHandler("In StartServiceCtrlDispatcher",
            GetLastError());
}
```

The following sections describe what each of the functions in Listing 9.1 does.

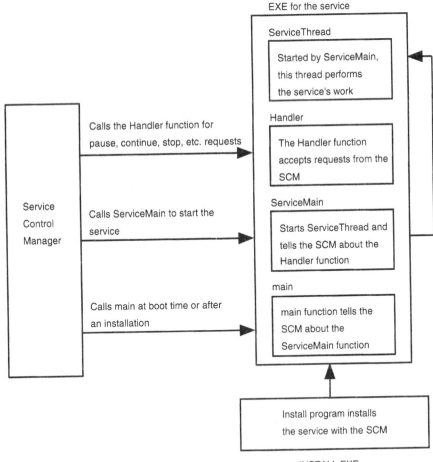

Figure 12.1   *The relationship between the SCM, the service's EXE, and the Install program*

12.4.1 Main

The main function calls **StartServiceCtrlDispatcher** to register the **Service Main** function for this service with the SCM. The registration is performed using an array of SERVICE_TABLE_ENTRY structures. In this case, the program contains just one service, so there is only one entry in the table. However, it is possible for there to be several services contained in a single EXE file, and in that case, the table identifies the appropriate **ServiceMain** function that the SCM should use to start each of the services. See Section 12.7 for details. In the case of a single-service EXE like this one, the SERVICE_NAME constant is irrelevant, and the service picks up its name during the installation process, as described in the next section.

StartServiceCtrlDispatcher	*Tells the SCM about the ServiceMain function for each of the services in the EXE*

```
BOOL StartServiceCtrlDispatcher(
   LPSERVICE_TABLE_ENTRY serviceMainTable;
```

serviceMainTable	A table of ServiceMain entry points for each service in the EXE

returns TRUE on success

If the call to **StartServiceCtrlDispatcher** fails, it will return an error code, and the program prints it to stdout. The user will see this only if the program is accidentally executed from the command line. If properly started by the SCM, there is no way to output the failure except to create an entry in the event log, as described in Chapter 21.

It is possible to put initialization code in the **main** function prior to the call to **StartServiceCtrlDispatcher**, but this code must complete in less than 30 seconds. If it takes longer than 30 seconds, the SCM times out and aborts the service on the assumption that something went wrong. If there is only one service in the EXE, as shown in Listing 12.1, there is no reason to do the initialization in **main**, and the initialization code should be placed in **ServiceMain** instead. If the EXE contains multiple services and you need to perform global initializations for all services, place them in **main**.

12.4.2 ServiceMain

The SCM calls the **ServiceMain** function when it wants to start the service either during the boot process or because of a manual start. **ServiceMain** will always contain the following steps:

1. It immediately calls **RegisterServiceCtrlHandler** to register the **Service CtrlHandler** function with the SCM as this service's Handler function.

The Handler function handles requests from the SCM to stop, pause, resume, or interrogate the service. The **RegisterServiceCtrlHandler** function also returns a handle that the service uses to send status information back to the SCM.

2. The **ServiceMain** function then calls the **SendStatusToSCM** function (created in Listing 12.1). It does this to notify the SCM of progress. The fourth parameter to SendStatusToSCM is a click count value, which increments each time the program updates the status. The SCM and other programs can look at the click count and see that progress is being made during initialization. The last parameter passed to **SendStatusToSCM** is a wait hint, which tells the SCM how long it should expect to wait before the click count next gets updated. This number is rather subjective—someone running the service on a 20MHZ 386 with 8 megabytes or RAM will experience a somewhat longer delay than someone running on an Alpha, so it is better to err on the high side. The five seconds shown in this example is adequate for most situations.

3. The **ServiceMain** function next creates an event (Chapter 7) that it will use at the bottom of the function to prevent it from returning until the SCM issues a STOP request. After it creates the event, the function again updates the SCM on progress by calling **SendStatusToSCM** with an incremented click count.

4. Next, **ServiceMain** checks for startup parameters. These parameters can be passed in by the user, during a manual start, using the Startup Parameters line in the Service applet of the Control Panel. Any parameters typed on the Startup Parameters line in the Services applet come into the **ServiceMain** function exactly like they would come in to the main function of a normal program from the command line. In this example, the program checks to make sure that the user has typed just one parameter. If so, the program converts it to an integer, validates it, and then uses it if appropriate. You can use startup parameters in your own services in any way that you like. The code then updates its status with the SCM.

5. If your service needs to perform other initialization tasks, they should go here just prior to the call to **InitService**.

6. The **ServiceMain** function now, finally, gets to the heart of the matter and calls the **InitService** function, which will start the thread that does the actual work of the service. If this call succeeds, then **ServiceMain** lets the SCM know that the service has successfully started.

7. **ServiceMain** now calls **WaitForSingleObject**, which waits efficiently for the **terminateEvent** event object to be set. This object gets set in the **StopService** function. Once it does get set, **ServiceMain** calls the **terminate** function to clean up, and then returns to stop the service.

As you can see, there is not a lot of flexibility in this function. With the exception of step 5, you must perform each of the tasks mentioned in the order mentioned for the service to start properly.

ServiceMain	*The standard form for any **ServiceMain** function*

`VOID ServiceMain(`
   `DWORD argc,`
   `LPTSTR *argv)`	

argc	A count of the number of startup parameters, plus 1
argv	An array of pointers to strings containing the parameters
No return value	

RegisterServiceCtrlHandler	*Registers the control handler for the service with the SCM*

`SERVICE_STATUS_HANDLE RegisterServiceCtrlHandler(`
   `LPCTSTR serviceName,`
   `LPHANDLER_FUNCTION handler)`	

serviceName	The name of the service for the SCM
handler	A pointer to the handler function
Returns the handle used to send status info back to the SCM	

12.4.3 Terminate

The **terminate** function is called by **ServiceMain** if the service fails to start, or when the service is to be stopped. The **terminate** function cleans up any open handles, and sends a status message to the SCM to tell it that the service is stopped. This function should also place an entry in the event log to notify the administrator of any error. The event log is really the only way that a service has to emit an error message. See Chapter 21 for details on event logging.

12.4.4 ServiceCtrlHandler

The SCM calls the **ServiceCtrlHandler** function whenever it wants to pause, resume, interrogate, or stop the service. This function accepts integer control codes and uses a switch statement to parse them. Five standard control constants are recognized in this implementation:

- SERVICE_CONTROL_STOP: Tells the service to stop.
- SERVICE_CONTROL_PAUSE: Tells the service to pause.
- SERVICE_CONTROL_CONTINUE: Tells the service to resume.
- SERVICE_CONTROL_INTERROGATE: Tells the service to immediately report its status.

- SERVICE_CONTROL_SHUTDOWN: Tells the service that shutdown is imminent.

It is also possible to create new constants, as described in Section 9.5.

To stop the service, the handler tells the SCM that the stop is pending, and then sets **terminateEvent**. By doing this, it causes **ServiceMain**, which is executing as a separate thread, to terminate and return. Once **ServiceMain** returns, the service is stopped, and the only way to restart it is for the SCM to call **ServiceMain** again.

To pause or continue the service, the handler tells the SCM that the operation is pending, and then calls the appropriate function.

An interrogation request simply asks the service to update its status immediately with the SCM.

During a shutdown, each service gets a signal telling it that the shutdown is imminent. Any file cleanup or variable storage can be performed at this point, provided that it occurs very quickly.

Handler   *The standard form for any service **Handler** function*

```
VOID Handler(
    DWORD control)
```

control   A constant indicating the action to perform

No return value

12.4.5 SendStatusToSCM

The **SendStatusToSCM** function consolidates all of the statements necessary to send the service's current status to the SCM. To send a status message, this function takes seven values and places them in a SERVICE_STATUS structure. It then passes that structure to the **SetServiceStatus** function. In Listing 12.1, five of the seven fields in the SERVICE_STATUS structure vary from call to call, while two are constant:

- **serviceType**: Indicates the type of service. Possible values: SERVICE_WIN32_OWN_PROCESS, SERVICE_WIN32_SHARE_PROCESS, SERVICE_KERNEL_DRIVER, SERVICE_FILE_SYSTEM_DRIVER
- **currentState**: Indicates the current state of the service. Possible values: SERVICE_STOP_PENDING, SERVICE_RUNNING, SERVICE_CONTINUE_PENDING, SERVICE_PAUSE_PENDING, SERVICE_PAUSED
- **controlsAccepted**: Indicates which control signals another process can send with the **ControlService** function. Possible values are any or all of the following: SERVICE_ACCEPT_STOP, SERVICE_ACCEPT_PAUSE_CONTINUE, SERVICE_ACCEPT_SHUTDOWN. A service always accepts an

"interrogate" request. There is no way to block service-defined codes except in your own code.

- **win32ExitCode**: If an error occurs while the service is starting or stopping, the service can pass the value retrieved from **GetLast-Error** back through this field. If there is no error, set this field to NO_ERROR. If you want to create your own specific error constants for your service, set this field to ERROR_SERVER_SPECIFIC_ERROR and pass the service-defined code back in the following field.
- **serviceSpecificExitCode**: If the previous field is appropriately marked, then you can send back a service-defined error constant in this field.
- **checkPoint**: During a start, stop, or continue operation, the SCM needs to be able to tell if the service is making progress. You signal progress by incrementing this field and updating the status of the service to the SCM.
- **waitHint**: This field tells the SCM an amount of time, in milliseconds, that it should expect to wait before seeing **checkPoint** increment.

12.4.6 StopService

The **StopService** function gets called by **ServiceCtrlHandler** whenever the SCM requests the service to stop. It sets the event that allows **ServiceMain** to return. **ServiceMain** thus returns, killing off the service's thread in the process and stopping the service.

12.4.7 PauseService

The **PauseService** function gets called by **ServiceCtrlHandler** whenever the SCM requests the service to pause. It simply pauses the thread that does the work of the service, by calling **SuspendService**.

12.4.8 ResumeService

The **ResumeService** function gets called by **ServiceCtrlHandler** whenever the SCM requests the service to resume. It resumes the service's thread by calling **ResumeThread**.

12.4.9 InitService

The **InitService** function gets called by **ServiceMain** when it needs to start the service's thread. This function calls **CreateThread** (Chapter 6) to create a new thread for the service.

It is also possible to start a new process instead of a thread in **InitService**. The process might be a stand-alone application or command-line program that you want to run in the service. For example, if you have a normal application that you need to start running as soon as the machine boots, you can start it by calling **CreateProcess** here.

12.4.10 ServiceThread

The **ServiceThread** function contains the actual work that is to be performed by the service. In this case, the thread consists of an infinite loop that beeps and then sleeps for a predetermined interval. When creating your own services, you can place any normal function call in this thread, either to Win32 functions or to your own functions.

This thread works independently of all of the other code in Listing 12.1, although any changes made to global variables can affect the thread if the thread's code is written that way.

12.4.11 ErrorHandler

The **ErrorHandler** function prints error messages.

12.5 Installing and Removing a Service

In order to use the beep service described in the previous section, you have to install it. Installation makes the SCM aware of the service and causes the SCM to add it to the list of services that appears in the Services Applet of the Control Panel. The code shown in Listing 12.2 demonstrates how to install a service.

Listing 12.2   *Installing a service*

```
// install.cpp

#include <windows.h>
#include <iostream.h>

void ErrorHandler(char *s, DWORD err)
{
    cout << s << endl;
    cout << "Error number: " << err << endl;
    ExitProcess(err);
}

void main(int argc, char *argv[])
{
    SC_HANDLE newService, scm;
```

| Listing 12.2 | *Installing a service (continued)* |

```
    if (argc != 4)
    {
        cout << "Usage:\n";
        cout << "   install service_name \
service_label executable\n";
        cout << "            service_name is the \
name used internally by the SCM\n";
        cout << "            service_label is the \
name that appears in the Services applet\n";
        cout << "               (for multiple \
words, put them in double quotes)\n";
        cout << "            executable is the \
full path to the EXE\n";
        cout << endl;
        return;
    }

    cout << "Starting...\n";
    // open a connection to the SCM
    scm = OpenSCManager(0, 0,
        SC_MANAGER_CREATE_SERVICE);
    if (!scm)
        ErrorHandler("In OpenScManager",
            GetLastError());

    // Install the new service
    newService = CreateService(
        scm, argv[1], // eg "beep_srv"
        argv[2],       // eg "Beep Service"
        SERVICE_ALL_ACCESS,
        SERVICE_WIN32_OWN_PROCESS,
        SERVICE_DEMAND_START,
        SERVICE_ERROR_NORMAL,
        argv[3],       // eg "c:\winnt\xxx.exe"
        0, 0, 0, 0, 0);
    if (!newService)
        ErrorHandler("In CreateService",
            GetLastError());
    else
        cout << "Service installed\n";

    // clean up
    CloseServiceHandle(newService);
    CloseServiceHandle(scm);
    cout << "Ending...\n";
}
```

Listing 12.2 starts by opening a connection to the service control manager using the **OpenSCManager** function.

OpenSCManager	*Opens a connection to the SCM*

```
SC_HANDLE OpenSCManager(
    LPCTSTR machine,
    LPCTSTR database,
    DWORD access)
```

machine	The name of the machine, NULL for the current machine
database	The name of the database to open. Set to NULL
access	Specifies the desired access

Returns a handle to the SCM or NULL on error

In Listing 12.2, the call to the **OpenSCManager** function specifies that the database on the current machine be opened so that the program can create a new service. In the call to **OpenSCManager**, you must also specify what you want to do, so that it can validate that activity. If the account you are logged in under when you execute Listing 12.2 does not have sufficient privilege to perform the requested activity, then the call will return NULL.

The call to **CreateService** actually installs the new service.

CreateService	*Installs a service in the SCM database*

```
SC_HANDLE CreateService(
    SC_HANDLE scm,
    LPCTSTR name,
    LPCTSTR displayName,
    DWORD access,
    DWORD serviceType,
    DWORD start,
    DWORD errorSeverity,
    LPCTSTR exePath,
    LPCTSTR loadOrderGroup,
    LPDWORD ID,
    LPCTSTR dependencies,
    LPCTSTR serviceAccount,
    LPCTSTR password)
```

scm	A handle to the SCM from **OpenSCManager**
name	The name of the service used internally
displayName	The name of the service displayed in the Service applet

access	Desired access to the service
serviceType	The type of service, i.e., process or driver
start	The start type: auto or manual
errorSeverity	Specifies the severity of a failure to start
exePath	The full path to the executable containing the service
loadOrderGroup	A string containing NULL or one of the load-ordering groups from the registry
ID	An ID value for the ordering group used
dependencies	A pointer to an array of strings containing the names of services that must start before this one
account	The account the service uses when it starts. If NULL, LocalSystem is used. Otherwise use "domain\account"
password	Password of the account. Pass NULL for no password

Returns a handle to the new service, or NULL on an error.

In the case shown in Listing 12.2, the call to **CreateService** uses the pointer to the SCM returned by **OpenSCManager**, the name, the label, and the EXE file specified on the command line, along with a set of standard parameters to fill in all of the other values. The use of SERVICE_WIN32_OWN_PROCESS indicates that the service's EXE file contains just one service, and SERVICE_DEMAND_START indicates that the service is initially tagged as manual start rather than automatic start.

A typical invocation of the install program at the command line is shown below:

```
install BeepService "Beeper" c:\winnt\beep.exe
```

The first parameter specifies the name of the service used internally by the SCM. This name is later used to remove the service. The second parameter specifies the label used to display the service in the Services Applet of the Control Panel. The third parameter gives the fully qualified path to the service's executable. When you run the install program, it will either succeed or print an error number that you can look up in the on-line help file for the Win32 API.

To remove a service, you follow the steps shown in Listing 12.3.

Listing 12.3   *Removing a service from the SCM*

```
// remove.cpp

#include <windows.h>
#include <iostream.h>
```

```
void ErrorHandler(char *s, DWORD err)
{
   cout << s << endl;
   cout << "Error number: " << err << endl;
   ExitProcess(err);
}

void main(int argc, char *argv[])
{
   SC_HANDLE service, scm;
   BOOL success;
   SERVICE_STATUS status;

   if (argc != 2)
   {
      cout << "Usage:\n";
      cout << "   remove service_name\n";
      return;
   }

   cout << "Starting...\n";
   // Open a connection to the SCM
   scm = OpenSCManager(0, 0,
      SC_MANAGER_CREATE_SERVICE);
   if (!scm)
      ErrorHandler("In OpenScManager",
         GetLastError());

   // Get the service's handle
   service = OpenService(
      scm, argv[1],
      SERVICE_ALL_ACCESS | DELETE);
   if (!service)
      ErrorHandler("In OpenService",
         GetLastError());

   // Stop the service if necessary
   success = QueryServiceStatus(service, &status);
   if (!success)
      ErrorHandler("In QueryServiceStatus",
         GetLastError());
   if (status.dwCurrentState != SERVICE_STOPPED)
   {
      cout << "Stopping service...\n";
      success = ControlService(service,
         SERVICE_CONTROL_STOP,
         &status);
      if (!success)
         ErrorHandler("In ControlService",
            GetLastError());
      Sleep(500);
   }
```

Listing 12.3 *Removing a service from the SCM (continued)*

```
// Remove the service
success = DeleteService(service);
if (success)
    cout << "Service removed\n";
else
    ErrorHandler("In DeleteService",
        GetLastError());

// Clean up
CloseServiceHandle(service);
CloseServiceHandle(scm);
cout << "Ending...\n";
}
```

Listing 12.3 starts by opening a connection to the service control manager, as described in Listing 12.2. It then opens a connection to the service using the **OpenService** function.

OpenService	*Opens a connection to the specified service*

```
SC_HANDLE OpenService(
    SC_HANDLE scm,
    LPCTSTR name,
    DWORD access)
```

scm	A handle to the SCM from **OpenSCManager**
name	The name of the service used internally
access	The desired access
Returns a handle to the service or NULL on error	

The **OpenService** function accepts a handle to the SCM and the name of the service to open, along with a set of flags representing the requested level of access. If the user running the remove program has sufficient privilege to gain that access to the service in question, then the function returns a pointer that can be used to communicate with the service. Otherwise it returns NULL.

Next, Listing 12.3 queries the service to find out if it is currently stopped. If it is not, it stops it. This is a courtesy to the user removing the service: If the service is running at the time of the removal, then the Services applet will retain a link to the service and the service will, in fact, remain running. When someone tries to stop the orphaned service, the Services applet sometimes complains. By stopping the service first, these problems are avoided.

The **QueryServiceStatus** function gets the current SERVICE_STATUS record from the SCM. To guarantee freshness, you might first send an interrogation request to the service (using **ControlService)**, but that is not necessary in this case. **QueryServiceStatus** fills a status record.

QueryServiceStatus	*Retrieves the current status from the service*

```
BOOL QueryServiceStatus(
    SC_HANDLE service,
    LPSERVICE_STATUS status)
```

service	A handle to the service
status	A pointer to a SERVICE_STATUS structure

Returns TRUE on success

The **dwCurrentState** field of the structure contains the state of the service, and the program in Listing 12.3 checks this field to make sure the service is stopped. If it is not, the program uses the **ControlService** function to attempt to stop the service.

ControlService	*Sends a control constant to the specified service*

```
BOOL ControlService(
    SC_HANDLE service,
    DWORD control,
    LPSERVICE_STATUS status)
```

service	A handle to the service
control	Control constant telling the service what to do
status	A pointer to a SERVICE_STATUS structure

Returns TRUE on success

The call to the **ControlService** function accepts a handle to the service, a control constant, and a pointer to a SERVICE_STATUS record so that it can return the current status after the requested action. If the service was opened using SERVICE_ALL_ACCESS or SERVICE_USER_DEFINED_CONTROL access, then it is possible to send a user-defined control constant (between 128 and 255) to the service. Otherwise, the following constants are understood:

```
SERVICE_CONTROL_STOP
SERVICE_CONTROL_PAUSE
SERVICE_CONTROL_CONTINUE
SERVICE_CONTROL_INTERROGATE
SERVICE_CONTROL_SHUTDOWN
```

Now that the service has stopped, the program deletes it using the **Delete-Service** function.

DeleteService	*Deletes the specified service*

```
BOOL DeleteService(
    SC_HANDLE service)
```

service	A handle to the service to delete

Returns TRUE on success

The **DeleteService** function removes the service from the **Services** applet in the Control Panel. A typical invocation of the removal program shown in Listing 12.3 would look like this:

```
remove BeepService
```

If you like, you can immediately reinstall the service.

12.6 Displaying Dialogs from within a Service

Frequently it is useful to display simple message boxes from within a service. For example, the Messenger service listens on the network for messages sent with the `net send` command and displays a message box for any messages that arrive. It is easy to modify the beep service shown in Section 12.4 to emulate this behavior. Any more advanced user interface to a service requires that you write a separate GUI front end and hook it to the service with something like a named pipe. Note the use of MB_DEFAULT_DESKTOP_ONLY.

As an example, you might want to create a "logon announcement" service that announces people when they log onto an NT machine on your network. In order to do this, the service will want to create a mailslot (Chapter 8) with a specific name just to listen for logon messages. When a logon message arrives at the mailslot, the service can display a message box. Users who want to announce themselves would place a command in their logon script that announces them (or the service could be made smart enough to sense when people log in and announce it automatically—see Section 12.7 for an example).

Listing 12.4 contains a simple console program that performs the announcement operation needed by the logon announcement service. Compile it and call it any time:

```
announce "John has logged in"
```

If you place this command in your logon script, it will send the announcement as soon as you log on.

Listing 12.4   *A console program to send a logon announcement to the logon announcing service*

```cpp
// announce.cpp

#include <windows.h>
#include <stdio.h>
#include <iostream.h>
#include <stdlib.h>

void ErrorHandler(char *s, DWORD err)
{
   cout << s << endl;
   cout << "Error number: " << err << endl;
   ExitProcess(err);
}

VOID main(int argc, char *argv[])
{
   HANDLE mailslot;
   DWORD numWrite;
   BOOL success;

   if (argc != 2)
   {
      cout << "Usage: announce message\n";
      cout << "  if message > 1 word, put it \
in quotes\n";
      return;
   }

   // create a mailslot to write to
   mailslot = CreateFile(
      "\\\\*\\mailslot\\logonann",
      GENERIC_WRITE, FILE_SHARE_READ, 0,
      OPEN_EXISTING, FILE_ATTRIBUTE_NORMAL, 0);
   if (mailslot == INVALID_HANDLE_VALUE)
      ErrorHandler("In CreateFile",
         GetLastError());

   // Write the message to the new slot
   success = WriteFile(mailslot, argv[1],
      strlen(argv[1]), &numWrite, 0);
   if (!success)
      ErrorHandler("In WriteFile", GetLastError());
   else
      cout << "success\n";

   CloseHandle(mailslot);
}
```

The service that receives the messages from Listing 12.4 needs to create a mailslot server (Chapter 8) so that it receives the logon messages. It then needs to produce the message boxes that announce each logon message. To do that, you need to change only three functions in the beepserver program (shown in Listing 12.1). The **main** function needs to turn into a **WinMain** function so that message boxes can appear. The **ServiceThread** function needs to change so that it creates the mailslot server and reads from it properly. The **terminate** function needs to change so that it properly closes the **mailslot** handle. The modified **main** function is shown in Listing 12.5, and the modified **ServiceThread** function appears in Listing 12.6.

| Listing 12.5 | *The main function in Listing 12.1 should be replaced by this WinMain function* |

```
int WINAPI WinMain(HANDLE ghInstance,
   HANDLE hPrevInstance, LPSTR lpCmdLine,
   int nCmdShow)
{
   SERVICE_TABLE_ENTRY serviceTable[] =
   {
   { SERVICE_NAME,
      (LPSERVICE_MAIN_FUNCTION) ServiceMain},
   { NULL, NULL }
   };
   BOOL success;

   // Create the mailslot
   // Another place for this is in ServiceMain
   mailslot = CreateMailslot(
      "\\\\.\\mailslot\\logonann",
      200, MAILSLOT_WAIT_FOREVER, 0);

   // Connect to the SCM
   success = StartServiceCtrlDispatcher(
      serviceTable);
   if (!success)
      ErrorHandler("In StartServiceCtrlDispatcher",
         GetLastError());

   return 0;
}
```

The code in the **WinMain** function shown in Listing 12.5 contains two modifications to the original **main** function:

1. It is a **WinMain** function rather than a **main** function, which means that **MessageBox** calls will work. It needs to be compiled differently, however. See Appendix A for compilation instructions.

2. Listing 12.5 contains a call to **CreateMailslot**, where **mailslot** is a new global variable. A better place to put the initialization code in this particular example is in the **ServiceMain** function, the advantage being that it is possible to detect and then report errors through the SCM from inside of **ServiceMain**.

The new **ServiceThread** function in Listing 12.6 continuously checks the mailslot for new messages and displays them in a message box if any are found, or waits a second before checking again. See Chapter 8 for more information on mailslots.

Listing 12.6   *The* **ServiceThread** *function in Listing 12.1 should be replaced by this* **ServiceThread** *function*

```
DWORD ServiceThread(LPDWORD param)
{
    char buffer[2000];
    DWORD numRead;
    DWORD maxMsg, nextMsg, numMsg, timeout;

    Beep(200,200); // Announce success
    while (1)
    {
        // Check for waiting messages
        GetMailslotInfo(mailslot, &maxMsg,
            &nextMsg, &numMsg, &timeout);
        // if messages are available, read them
        // and display in a message box.
        // Otherwise wait 1 second.
        if (numMsg > 0)
        {
            Beep(200,200);
            ReadFile(mailslot, buffer, nextMsg,
                &numRead, 0);
            buffer[numRead]='\0';
            MessageBox(0, buffer,
                "Logon Announcement", MB_OK |
                MB_SETFOREGROUND | MB_DEFAULT_DESKTOP_ONLY);
        }
        else
            Sleep(1000);
    }
    return 0;
}
```

Once these two functions are in place in Listing 12.1 and the service is compiled and installed as described in Section 12.5, you will see nothing until someone on the network uses the announce command shown at the beginning of this section. Then you will see a message box containing the announcement message. You can test the service by typing announce commands on your own workstation.

12.7 Multiple Services in an Executable

It is possible, and sometimes useful, to put more than one service into a single executable. Generally you do this so that the separate service threads can communicate with one another through shared global variables. Because each of the services is a separate thread that shares the same data space, you can create global variables that are accessible by all of the services. The only requirement is that you use proper synchronization methods (see Chapter 7) to ensure valid access to the shared data.

When you create a multi-service EXE, you have to duplicate everything seen in Listing 12.1 except the **main** function. (See Figure 12.2.) During installation and when reporting status with **SendStatusToSCM**, you must indicate that multiple services are sharing the same process using the SERVICE_WIN32_SHARE_PROCESS flag (an EXE that contains just one service marks itself as SERVICE_WIN32_OWN_PROCESS during installation and when reporting status information). As shown in Listing 12.7, the **main** or **WinMain** function must also change. The service entry table must contain the name of the service and the name of the **ServiceMain** function for each of the services in the EXE.

Listing 12.7   *A typical* **WinMain** *function for a service EXE containing two services. The table indicates the name of each service and the* **ServiceMain** *function for each*

```
int WINAPI WinMain(HANDLE ghInstance,
    HANDLE hPrevInstance, LPSTR lpCmdLine,
    int nCmdShow)
{
    SERVICE_TABLE_ENTRY serviceTable[] =
    {
    { "Service1",
        (LPSERVICE_MAIN_FUNCTION) ServiceMain1},
    { "Service2",
        (LPSERVICE_MAIN_FUNCTION) ServiceMain2},
    { NULL, NULL }
    };
    BOOL success;

    success =
        StartServiceCtrlDispatcher(serviceTable);
```

```
    if (!success)
      ErrorHandler("In StartServiceCtrlDispatcher",
         GetLastError());
    return 0;
}
```

One EXE file contains two services

Global variables shared by both services

Service Thread1

Service Thread2

Handler1

Handler2

Service Main1

Service Main2

Single main function
contains entry table

Figure 12.2   *A typical EXE containing two services. Most of the code for each service is duplicated, but they share a single main function and global variables*

The Service Entry Table in Listing 12.7 is much more important in a multi-service EXE than it is in a single-service EXE like the beep service shown in Listing 12.1. In Listing 12.1, the system ignores the service name in the entry table. You can install the service under any name using the install code shown in Section 12.5, and the service will still start properly. It works because the SCM defaults to using the first **ServiceMain** function in the table if it cannot find a name match or if the EXE is marked as SERVICE_WIN32_OWN_PROCESS during installation. In a multi-service EXE, the SCM looks for the name of the service in the table when it tries to start it, and uses the **ServiceMain** function indicated in the table.

As a very simple example of multiple services in a single-service EXE, say that you want to modify the beep service code shown in Listing 12.1. For example, you might want to have one service beep, and another one increment a global counter than controls the beep frequency. Change the **main** function to contain an entry table like the one shown in Listing 12.7. Duplicate the **ServiceMain** function and name the two versions **ServiceMain1** and **ServiceMain2**. Duplicate the **Handler** function and name the two versions **Handler1** and **Handler2**. Duplicate the other peripheral pieces of code and the necessary global variables such as **terminateEvent**, **service StatusHandle**, and so on, and rename all of them appropriately. Then create two threads and a shared integer variable, as shown in Listing 12.8.

Listing 12.8   *The two service threads for a simple two-service EXE*

```
int frequency = 100;

DWORD ServiceThread1(LPDWORD param)
{
   while (1)
   {
      Beep(frequency,200);
      Sleep(beepDelay);
   }
   return 0;
}

DWORD ServiceThread2(LPDWORD param)
{
   while (1)
   {
      frequency += 50;
      Sleep(5000);
   }
   return 0;
}
```

Compile the program to an EXE named `multbeep.exe`. Place this EXE in `c:\winnt` or an other suitable directory. Then use the install command seen in Listing 12.2, *modified so that it contains SERVICE_WIN32_SHARE_PROCESS rather than SERVICE_WIN32_OWN_PROCESS.* Type the following two commands on the command line:

```
install Service1 "Beeper" c:\winnt\multbeep.exe
install Service2 "Beepfreq" c:\winnt\multbeep.exe
```

Note that the same EXE file is specified for both installs, but the two service names, Service1 and Service2, are different. In the Services applet of the Control Panel, you will find the two services. Start "Beeper" first. The SCM will execute the **main** function, and the entry table tells it to run **Service-Main1** because the service name of "Beeper" is Service1. Now start "Beepfreq." The SCM will *not* execute **main** this time because the process is already running, but it will start the **ServiceMain2** thread in that process. You will hear the beep's frequency rise every five seconds.

Three things can prevent this from working:

1. If you forget to specify SERVICE_WIN32_SHARE_PROCESS in the install program and in the **SendStatusToSCM** function, then it will not be possible to start Service2.

2. If, during the installation of the service, you use service names that do not appear in the entry table, then the misnamed service will not start.

3. If you have an existing service named "Beeper" service from the previous examples, you will not be allowed to install this version of the beeper. Remove the previous instance using the code in Section 12.5.

In more complicated services that share a single EXE, you commonly need to initialize shared global variables or perform other initialization tasks used by all of the services in the EXE. If shared initializations need to take place in a multi-service EXE file, you can do the following things:

1. Place global initialization code in the main function prior to the call to **StartServiceCtrlDispatcher,** as long as it takes less than 30 seconds to complete.

2. Place a **CreateThread** call prior to the call to **StartServiceCtrlDispatcher** and do initializations taking longer than 30 seconds in the thread. You then need to make sure that none of the services start working prior to the completion of that initialization thread by using synchronization mechanisms (see Chapter 7).

3. Place a call to the initialization code in one of the services and make sure that only one service executes it using a semaphore or other control

mechanism. Also make sure that none of the other services tries to start before the initialization is complete.

As another example of a multi-service EXE, we use a logon service similar to the one described previously on our own network at the office. The only difference between our service and the one shown in Listing 12.4 is the fact that the EXE contains two services. The first senses when someone logs on, and the second performs the normal announcement activity seen in Listing 12.4. There is no advantage or disadvantage to placing these two services in a single EXE because they do not share any global variables, but they are related and it is nice to have them copied as a pair when the EXE file gets copied. Listing 12.9 shows the code for the two threads.

Listing 12.9 *Multiple threads in a single service to announce and sense logins*

```
DWORD AnnounceThread(LPDWORD param)
{
    char buffer[2000];
    DWORD numRead;
    DWORD maxMsg, nextMsg, numMsg, timeout;
    HANDLE mailslot;

    mailslot = CreateMailslot(
        "\\\\.\\mailslot\\logonann", 200,
        MAILSLOT_WAIT_FOREVER, 0);

    while (1)
    {
        GetMailslotInfo(mailslot, &maxMsg,
            &nextMsg, &numMsg, &timeout);
        if (numMsg > 0)
        {
            ReadFile(mailslot, buffer, nextMsg,
                &numRead, 0);
            buffer[numRead]='\0';
            MessageBox(0, buffer,
                "Logon Announcement", MB_OK |
                MB_SETFOREGROUND | MB_DEFAULT_DESKTOP_ONLY);
        }
        else
            Sleep(1000);
    }
    return 0;
}


BOOL CALLBACK EnumWindowsProc(HANDLE win,
    LPARAM param)
```

```
{
    char buffer[100];
    DWORD numWrite;

    GetWindowText(win, buffer, 100);
    if (strncmp(buffer, "Program Manager", 15)==0 &&
        strcmp((buffer+18),currentUser) != 0)
    {
        HANDLE writeMailslot = CreateFile(
            "\\\\*\\mailslot\\logonann",
            GENERIC_WRITE, FILE_SHARE_READ, 0,
            OPEN_EXISTING, FILE_ATTRIBUTE_NORMAL, 0);
        WriteFile(writeMailslot, (buffer+18),
            strlen(buffer+18), &numWrite, 0);
        CloseHandle(writeMailslot);
        strcpy(currentUser, (buffer+18));
        return FALSE;
    }
    else
        return TRUE;
}


DWORD SenseThread(LPDWORD param)
{
    BOOL success;

    while (1)
    {
        success = EnumWindows(
            (WNDENUMPROC) EnumWindowsProc, 0);
        Sleep(10000);
    }
    return 0;
}
```

12.8 Getting and Setting Configuration Information

The information passed in the call to **CreateService** in Section 12.5 gets stored in the registry when the SCM creates the service. You can view the information directly using the normal registry viewer, regedt32.exe, or you can run the winmsd command and view all service information there. Inside a program, it is possible both to retrieve a copy of this information and to modify it. The **QueryServiceConfig** function lets you obtain a copy of the configuration information.

QueryServiceConfig	*Retrieves configuration information in the registry for the specified service*

```
BOOL QueryServiceConfig(
   SC_HANDLE service,
   LPQUERY_SERVICE_CONFIG config,
   DWORD bufSize,
   LPDWORD sizeNeeded)
```

service	A handle to the service to query
config	A pointer to a buffer for the returned information
bufSize	The size of the buffer
sizeNeeded	The amount of space needed for the buffer

Returns TRUE on success

You must first open the service using the **OpenService** function as seen in Section 12.5. Listing 12.10 demonstrates the process.

Listing 12.10   *Using the QueryServiceConfig function*

```cpp
// getcon.cpp

#include <windows.h>
#include <iostream.h>

void ErrorHandler(char *s, DWORD err)
{
   cout << s << endl;
   cout << "Error number: " << err << endl;
   ExitProcess(err);
}

void main(int argc, char *argv[])
{
   SC_HANDLE service, scm;
   BOOL success;
   LPQUERY_SERVICE_CONFIG buffer;
   DWORD sizeNeeded;

   if (argc != 2)
   {
      cout << "Usage:\n";
      cout << "   getcon service_name\n";
      return;
   }

   // Open a connection to the SCM
```

```
scm = OpenSCManager(0, 0,
    SC_MANAGER_ALL_ACCESS);
if (!scm)
    ErrorHandler("In OpenScManager",
        GetLastError());

// Get the service's handle
service = OpenService(
    scm, argv[1],
    SERVICE_QUERY_CONFIG);
if (!service)
    ErrorHandler("In OpenService",
        GetLastError());

// Find out how big the buffer needs to be
success = QueryServiceConfig(service, 0, 0,
    &sizeNeeded);

// Allocate space for the buffer
buffer = (LPQUERY_SERVICE_CONFIG)
    LocalAlloc (LPTR, sizeNeeded);

// Get the buffer
success = QueryServiceConfig(service, buffer,
    sizeNeeded, &sizeNeeded);
if (!success)
    ErrorHandler("In QueryServiceConfig",
        GetLastError());

// Print the contents of the buffer
cout << "Service type: "
    << buffer->dwServiceType << endl;
cout << "Start type: "
    << buffer->dwStartType << endl;
// and so on

// Clean up
LocalFree(buffer);
CloseServiceHandle(service);
CloseServiceHandle(scm);
}
```

The code in Listing 12.10 opens a connection first to the SCM and then to a specific service. It then calls **QueryServiceConfig** once to get the size of the buffer it needs. This buffer size changes because of many things: variable-size strings that hold the EXE path, dependencies, and so on. Once the size is known, the appropriate amount of space is allocated and the function is called again to retrieve the data.

Changing configuration information in the registry using **Change-ServiceConfig** follows a similar path, but you must lock the database before you modify it to ensure that no other process tries to use the database during modification. Generally, you would do one of the following: get the current configuration values for a service using the code shown in Listing 12.10 and then modify that information, or specify field values in the call to **Change ServiceConfig** that cause them to remain unchanged. The parameters for **ChangeServiceConfig** follow those of **CreateService** almost exactly.

ChangeServiceConfig   *Changes the service's configuration information*

```
BOOL ChangeServiceConfig(
    SC_HANDLE service,
    DWORD serviceType,
    DWORD start,
    DWORD errorSeverity,
    LPCTSTR exePath,
    LPCTSTR loadOrderGroup,
    LPDWORD ID,
    LPCTSTR dependencies,
    LPCTSTR serviceAccount,
    LPCTSTR password,
    LPCTSTR displayName)
```

service	A handle to the service to change
serviceType	The type of service, i.e., process or driver
start	The start type: auto or manual
errorSeverity	Specifies the severity of a failure to start
exePath	The full path to the executable containing the service
loadOrderGroup	A string containing NULL or one of the load-ordering groups from the registry
ID	An ID value for the ordering group used
dependencies	A pointer to an array of strings containing the names of services that must start before this one
account	The account the service uses when it starts. If NULL, LocalSystem is used. Otherwise use "domain\account"
password	Password of the account. Pass NULL for no password
displayName	The name of the service displayed in the Service applet

Returns TRUE on success

On the **serviceType**, **start**, and **errorSeverity** fields, the SERVICE_ NO_ CHANGE value indicates that you want to make no change to the field. A zero in any other field indicates no change. Listing 12.11 demonstrates the use of this function.

Listing 12.11   *Changing a service's configuration*

```cpp
// setcon.cpp

#include <windows.h>
#include <iostream.h>

void ErrorHandler(char *s, DWORD err)
{
   cout << s << endl;
   cout << "Error number: " << err << endl;
   ExitProcess(err);
}

void main(int argc, char *argv[])
{
   SC_HANDLE service, scm;
   BOOL success;
   SC_LOCK lock;

   if (argc != 2)
   {
      cout << "Usage:\n";
      cout << "   setcon service_name\n";
      return;
   }

   // Open a connection to the SCM
   scm = OpenSCManager(0, 0,
      SC_MANAGER_ALL_ACCESS | GENERIC_WRITE);
   if (!scm)
      ErrorHandler("In OpenScManager",
         GetLastError());

   lock = LockServiceDatabase(scm);
   if (lock == 0)
      ErrorHandler("In LockServiceDatabase",
         GetLastError());

   // Get the service's handle
   service = OpenService(
      scm, argv[1],
      SERVICE_ALL_ACCESS);
   if (!service)
   {
      DWORD err = GetLastError();
      UnlockServiceDatabase(lock);
      ErrorHandler("In ChangeServiceConfig", err);
   }
```

Listing 12.11   *Changing a service's configuration (continued)*

```
// Change the service to automatic start mode
success = ChangeServiceConfig(
   service,
   SERVICE_NO_CHANGE,
   SERVICE_AUTO_START,
   SERVICE_NO_CHANGE,
   0, 0, 0, 0, 0, 0, 0);
if (!success)
{
   DWORD err = GetLastError();
   UnlockServiceDatabase(lock);
   ErrorHandler("In ChangeServiceConfig", err);
}

// unlock the database
success = UnlockServiceDatabase(lock);
if (!success)
   ErrorHandler("In UnlockServiceDatabase",
      GetLastError());

// Clean up
CloseServiceHandle(service);
CloseServiceHandle(scm);
}
```

The code in Listing 12.11 starts by opening a connection to the Service Control Manager and then locks the database using **LockServiceDatabase**. If this function fails, it is either because the database is already locked by someone else or because the call to **OpenSCManager** did not request access to lock the database.

LockServiceDatabase	*Locks the service database to guarantee exclusive access during a configuration change*

```
SC_LOCK LockServiceDatabase(
   SC_HANDLE scm)
```

scm	A handle to the scm

Returns a lock or 0 on error

The function then proceeds to open a specific service and to change its configuration. In this case, it sets the service to start automatically. The code then unlocks the database.

UnlockServiceDatabase   *Unlocks the service database*

```
BOOL UnlockServiceDatabase(
   SC_LOCK lock)
```

lock   A lock created by LockServiceDatabase

Returns TRUE on success

You can also use the **QueryServiceLockStatus** function to check on a lock's current status. Call it using the technique shown in Listing 12.10 for the call to **QueryServiceConfig**.

12.9 Controlling Services

Generally you control a service using the Services applet in the Control Panel. This service allows you to start, stop, pause, or resume any service. There are some cases, however, in which it is useful to be able to control a service either from a separate program or from another service. The **ControlService** and **StartService** functions allow you to control services in your code.

ControlService   *Sends a control constant to the specified service*

```
BOOL ControlService(
   SC_HANDLE service,
   DWORD control,
   LPSERVICE_STATUS status)
```

service   A handle to the service

control   Control constant telling the service what to do

status   A pointer to a SERVICE_STATUS structure

Returns TRUE on success

The **ControlService** function accepts a handle to the service, a control constant, and a pointer to a SERVICE_STATUS record so that it can return the current status after the requested action. If the service was opened using SERVICE_ALL_ACCESS or SERVICE_USER_DEFINED_CONTROL access, then it is possible to send a user-defined control constant (between 128 and 255) to the service. Otherwise, the following constants are understood:

SERVICE_CONTROL_STOP
SERVICE_CONTROL_PAUSE
SERVICE_CONTROL_CONTINUE
SERVICE_CONTROL_INTERROGATE
SERVICE_CONTROL_SHUTDOWN

The user-defined constants provide a very limited communication path between outside programs and a service. For example, one program might send in the special value 132, and the service could respond by sending back a special, service-defined error code. More complicated forms of communication are normally accomplished using named pipes.

Starting a service is different from stopping, pausing, or resuming a service as shown in Listing 12.12. The latter three work through the **Handler** function in the service, while a start operation requires that the SCM start a thread that executes the **ServiceMain** function for the service. A separate call to the **StartService** function tells the SCM to perform a start operation.

StartService	*Starts the indicated service*

```
BOOL StartService(
    SC_HANDLE service,
    DWORD argc,
    LPCTSTR *argv)
```

service	A handle to the service created by **OpenService**
argc	The number of strings in argv
argv	A standard argv array of pointers to character

Returns TRUE on success

The **argc** and **argv** values allow you to pass startup parameters to the service as you can from the Services applet in the Control Panel. Pass zero in both parameters if you do not wish to pass any parameters.

Listing 12.12 *Starting a service*

```
// startsvc.cpp

#include <windows.h>
#include <iostream.h>

void ErrorHandler(char *s, DWORD err)
{
    cout << s << endl;
    cout << "Error number: " << err << endl;
    ExitProcess(err);
}

void main(int argc, const char *argv[])
{
    SC_HANDLE service, scm;
    BOOL success;
```

```
    if (argc < 2)
    {
        cout << "Usage:\n";
        cout << "   start service_name arguments\n";
        cout << "   the arguments are passed as \
startup arguments to the service\n";
        return;
    }

    // Open a connection to the SCM
    scm = OpenSCManager(0, 0,
        SC_MANAGER_ALL_ACCESS | GENERIC_WRITE);
    if (!scm)
        ErrorHandler("In OpenScManager",
            GetLastError());


    // Get the service's handle
    service = OpenService(
        scm, argv[1],
        SERVICE_ALL_ACCESS);
    if (!service)
        ErrorHandler("In OpenService",
            GetLastError());


    // Start the service, passing
    // it startup parameters
    success = StartService(service,
        argc-2, &argv[2]);
    if (!success)
        ErrorHandler("In StartService",
            GetLastError());

    // Clean up
    CloseServiceHandle(service);
    CloseServiceHandle(scm);
}
```

12.10 Enumerating Services

Windows 2000 offers two ways to enumerate services. Using the **Enum ServicesStatus** function, you can enumerate all of the available services. Using **EnumDependentServices,** you can enumerate the services that a specific service expects to have started before it starts. Listing 12.13 demonstrates the **EnumServicesStatus** function.

Listing 12.13 *Enumerating available services*

```cpp
// enum.cpp

#include <windows.h>
#include <iostream.h>

void ErrorHandler(char *s, DWORD err)
{
   cout << s << endl;
   cout << "Error number: " << err << endl;
   ExitProcess(err);
}

void main(int argc, const char *argv[])
{
   SC_HANDLE scm;
   BOOL success;
   LPENUM_SERVICE_STATUS status;
   DWORD numServices=0, sizeNeeded=0, resume=0;

   // Open a connection to the SCM
   scm = OpenSCManager(0, 0,
      SC_MANAGER_ALL_ACCESS);
   if (!scm)
      ErrorHandler("In OpenScManager",
         GetLastError());

   // get the number of bytes to allocate
   // MAKE SURE resume starts at 0
   resume = 0;
   success = EnumServicesStatus(scm,
      SERVICE_WIN32 | SERVICE_DRIVER,
      SERVICE_ACTIVE | SERVICE_INACTIVE,
      0, 0, &sizeNeeded, &numServices, &resume);
   if (GetLastError() != ERROR_MORE_DATA)
      ErrorHandler("In EnumServicesStatus1",
         GetLastError());
   // Allocate space
   status = (LPENUM_SERVICE_STATUS)
      LocalAlloc(LPTR, sizeNeeded);

   // Get the status records. Making an assumption
   // here that no new services get added during
   // the allocation (could lock the database to
   // guarantee that...)
   resume = 0;
   success = EnumServicesStatus(scm,
      SERVICE_WIN32 | SERVICE_DRIVER,
      SERVICE_ACTIVE | SERVICE_INACTIVE,
```

```
        status, sizeNeeded, &sizeNeeded,
            &numServices, &resume);
    if (!success)
        ErrorHandler("In EnumServicesStatus",
            GetLastError());

    DWORD i;
    for (i=0; i < numServices; i++)
        cout << i << " "
            << status[i].lpServiceName << " "
            << status[i].lpDisplayName << endl;

    // Clean up
    LocalFree(status);
    CloseServiceHandle(scm);
}
```

The code in Listing 12.13 starts by opening a connection to the SCM. It then calls **EnumServicesStatus** once to get the amount of memory needed to store all of the service entries in the database. Here it requests all services in existence by requesting SERVICE_WIN32 and SERVICE_DRIVER in the **serviceType** field and SERVICE_ACTIVE and SERVICE_INACTIVE in the **serviceState** field.

EnumServicesStatus	*Retrieves the names and status records of all requested services*

```
BOOL EnumServicesStatus(
    SC_HANDLE scm,
    DWORD serviceType,
    DWORD serviceState,
    LPENUM_SERVICE_STATUS buffer,
    DWORD bufferSize,
    LPDWORD sizeNeeded,
    LPDWORD numServices,
    LPDWORD resume)
```

scm	A handle to the scm
serviceType	The types of services to retrieve (normal and/or drivers)
serviceState	The service state to filter on (active and/or inactive)
buffer	A buffer to hold the retrieved information
bufferSize	Number of bytes available in the buffer
sizeNeeded	Amount of space needed to complete
numServices	Number of services placed in buffer
resume	A pointer to the next service to retrieve on multiple retrievals. Must start at zero

Returns TRUE on success. If FALSE and GetLastError returns ERROR_MORE_DATA then the buffer was not big enough and a second call should be made

In this particular program, all of the required space is allocated at once, but it is also possible to use a fixed-size buffer and call **EnumServicesStatus** multiple times. The program then walks through the returned array and prints out both the name and the display name of each service. By passing different flags into the **serviceType** and **serviceState** parameters, you can control the types of services returned in the array.

The **EnumDependentServices** function works in the same way, but you open a specific service and the function returns a status array for all of the services it is dependent on. You set the dependent services by passing an array of service names to **CreateService** or to **ChangeServiceConfig**.

12.11 Placing an RPC Server in a Service

Chapter 9 describes RPCs and RPC servers. Once you have created and de-bugged an RPC server, you will often want to place it in a service so that it is always available on the network.

Listings 12.14 through 12.19 demonstrate the files necessary to create an RPC server service. These listings combine the simple service shown in Listing 12.1 with the auto-binding RPC server for **SumUp** demonstrated in Listings 9.1 through 9.4. You can use the RPC client in Listing 9.5 to test the new service. *Use the installation program in Section 12.5 to install the RPC server service in the Services Applet of the Control Panel.* See Chapter 9 for a complete description of this process.

Listing 12.14   *The implementation of SumUp, identical to Listing 9.1*

```
// sum.cpp

#include <windows.h>
#include "sum.h"

long SumUp(short sumVal)
{
  short iter;
  long theSum;

  theSum=0;
  for (iter=1; iter<=sumVal; theSum+=iter, iter++);

  Beep(300, 30);

  return(theSum);
}
```

| Listing 12.15 | *The Service implementing the RPC server. Compare to Listings 12.1 and 9.2* |

```cpp
// sumserv.cpp

#include <windows.h>
#include <iostream.h>
#include <rpc.h>
#include "sum.h"
#include "memstub"

// Global variables

// The name of the service
char *SERVICE_NAME = "SumService";
// Event used to hold ServiceMain from completing
HANDLE terminateEvent = NULL;
// Handle used to communicate status info with
// the SCM. Created by RegisterServiceCtrlHandler
SERVICE_STATUS_HANDLE serviceStatusHandle;
// Flags holding current state of service
BOOL pauseService = FALSE;
BOOL runningService = FALSE;

// Initializes the service
BOOL InitService()
{
    RPC_BINDING_VECTOR *bindVector;

    runningService = TRUE;

    // use protocols specified by interface
    if (RpcServerUseAllProtseqsIf(1,
        sumup_v1_1_s_ifspec,
        NULL))
        return FALSE;

    // register the interface
    if (RpcServerRegisterIf(sumup_v1_1_s_ifspec,
        NULL, NULL))
        return FALSE;

    // get binding handles available
    if (RpcServerInqBindings(&bindVector))
        return FALSE;

    // export binding info
    if (RpcNsBindingExport(RPC_C_NS_SYNTAX_DEFAULT,
        (UCHAR *) "/.:/autorpc",
```

Listing 12.15 *The Service implementing the RPC server. Compare to Listings 12.1 and 9.2 (continued)*

```
        sumup_v1_1_s_ifspec,
        bindVector, NULL))
    {
        // release memory used by binding vectors
        RpcBindingVectorFree(&bindVector);
        return FALSE;
    }

    // release memory used by binding vectors
    if (RpcBindingVectorFree(&bindVector))
        return FALSE;

    // activate this server
    if (RpcServerListen(1, 5, TRUE))
        return FALSE;

    return TRUE;
}


// Resumes a paused service
VOID ResumeService()
{
    pauseService=FALSE;
    // reactivate this server
    RpcServerListen(1, 5, TRUE);
}


// Pauses the service
VOID PauseService()
{
    pauseService = TRUE;
    // stop accepting new calls
    RpcMgmtStopServerListening(NULL);
    // wait for existing calls to finish
    RpcMgmtWaitServerListen();
}


// Stops the service by allowing ServiceMain
// to complete
VOID StopService()
{
    runningService=FALSE;
    // Set the event that is holding ServiceMain
    // so that ServiceMain can return
    SetEvent(terminateEvent);
}
```

```
// This function consolidates the activities of
// updating the service status
// with SetServiceStatus
BOOL SendStatusToSCM (DWORD dwCurrentState,
    DWORD dwWin32ExitCode,
    DWORD dwServiceSpecificExitCode,
    DWORD dwCheckPoint,
    DWORD dwWaitHint)
{
    BOOL success;
    SERVICE_STATUS serviceStatus;

    // Fill in all of the SERVICE_STATUS fields
    serviceStatus.dwServiceType =
        SERVICE_WIN32_OWN_PROCESS;
    serviceStatus.dwCurrentState = dwCurrentState;

    // If in the process of starting, then accept
    // no control events, else accept anything
    if (dwCurrentState == SERVICE_START_PENDING)
        serviceStatus.dwControlsAccepted = 0;
    else
        serviceStatus.dwControlsAccepted =
            SERVICE_ACCEPT_STOP |
            SERVICE_ACCEPT_PAUSE_CONTINUE |
            SERVICE_ACCEPT_SHUTDOWN;

    // if a specific exit code is defines, set up
    // the win32 exit code properly
    if (dwServiceSpecificExitCode == 0)
        serviceStatus.dwWin32ExitCode =
        dwWin32ExitCode;
    else
        serviceStatus.dwWin32ExitCode =
            ERROR_SERVICE_SPECIFIC_ERROR;
    serviceStatus.dwServiceSpecificExitCode =
        dwServiceSpecificExitCode;

    serviceStatus.dwCheckPoint = dwCheckPoint;
    serviceStatus.dwWaitHint = dwWaitHint;

    // Pass the status record to the SCM
    success = SetServiceStatus (serviceStatusHandle,
        &serviceStatus);
    if (!success)
        StopService();

    return success;
}
```

Listing 12.15 *The Service implementing the RPC server. Compare to Listings 12.1 and 9.2 (continued)*

```
// Dispatches events received from the service
// control manager
VOID ServiceCtrlHandler (DWORD controlCode)
{
    DWORD   currentState = 0;
    BOOL success;

    switch(controlCode)
    {
        // There is no START option because
        // ServiceMain gets called on a start

        // Stop the service
        case SERVICE_CONTROL_STOP:
            currentState = SERVICE_STOP_PENDING;
            // Tell the SCM what's happening
            success = SendStatusToSCM(
                SERVICE_STOP_PENDING,
                NO_ERROR, 0, 1, 5000);
            // Not much to do if not successful

            // Allow ServiceMain to return
            SetEvent(terminateEvent);
            return;

        // Pause the service
        case SERVICE_CONTROL_PAUSE:
            if (runningService && !pauseService)
            {
                // Tell the SCM what's happening
                success = SendStatusToSCM(
                    SERVICE_PAUSE_PENDING,
                    NO_ERROR, 0, 1, 1000);
                PauseService();
                currentState = SERVICE_PAUSED;
            }
            break;

        // Resume from a pause
        case SERVICE_CONTROL_CONTINUE:
            if (runningService && pauseService)
            {
                ResumeService();
                // Tell the SCM what's happening
                success = SendStatusToSCM(
                    SERVICE_CONTINUE_PENDING,
                    NO_ERROR, 0, 1, 1000);
```

```
                currentState = SERVICE_RUNNING;
            }
            break;

        // Update current status
        case SERVICE_CONTROL_INTERROGATE:
            // it will fall to bottom and send status
            break;

        // Do nothing in a shutdown. Could do cleanup
        // here, but it must be very quick.
        case SERVICE_CONTROL_SHUTDOWN:
            // Do nothing on shutdown
            return;
        default:
            break;
    }
    SendStatusToSCM(currentState, NO_ERROR,
        0, 0, 0);
}

// Handle an error from ServiceMain by cleaning up
// and telling SCM that the service didn't start.
VOID terminate(DWORD error)
{
    if (!error)
    {
        // stop accepting new calls
        RpcMgmtStopServerListening(NULL);

        // remove binding info
        RpcNsBindingUnexport(RPC_C_NS_SYNTAX_DEFAULT,
            (UCHAR *) "/.:/autorpc",
            sumup_v1_1_s_ifspec,
            NULL);

        // unregister interface and wait
        // for existing calls to finish
        RpcServerUnregisterIf(NULL, NULL, TRUE);
    }

    // if terminateEvent has been created, close it.
    if (terminateEvent)
        CloseHandle(terminateEvent);

    // Send a message to the SCM to tell about
    //stoppage
    if (serviceStatusHandle)
        SendStatusToSCM(SERVICE_STOPPED, error,
            0, 0, 0);
```

Listing 12.15   *The Service implementing the RPC server. Compare to Listings 12.1 and 9.2 (continued)*

```
    // Do not need to close serviceStatusHandle
}

// ServiceMain is called when the SCM wants
// to start the service. When it returns,
// the service has stopped. It
// Therefore waits on an event just before the end
// of the function, and that event gets set
// when it is time to stop. It also returns
// on any error because the
// service cannot start if there is an error.
VOID ServiceMain(DWORD argc, LPTSTR *argv)
{
    BOOL success;

    // immediately call Registration function
    serviceStatusHandle =
        RegisterServiceCtrlHandler(SERVICE_NAME,
            (LPHANDLER_FUNCTION)ServiceCtrlHandler);
    if (!serviceStatusHandle)
    {
        terminate(GetLastError());
        return;
    }

    // Notify SCM of progress
    success = SendStatusToSCM(
        SERVICE_START_PENDING,
        NO_ERROR, 0, 1, 5000);
    if (!success)
    {
        terminate(GetLastError());
        return;
    }

    // create the termination event
    terminateEvent = CreateEvent (0, TRUE,
        FALSE, 0);
    if (!terminateEvent)
    {
        terminate(GetLastError());
        return;
    }

    // Notify SCM of progress
    success = SendStatusToSCM(
```

```
      SERVICE_START_PENDING,
      NO_ERROR, 0, 2, 1000);
   if (!success)
   {
      terminate(GetLastError());
      return;
   }

   // Start the service itself
   success = InitService();
   if (!success)
   {
      terminate(GetLastError());
      return;
   }

   // The service is now running.
   // Notify SCM of progress
   success = SendStatusToSCM(
      SERVICE_RUNNING,
      NO_ERROR, 0, 0, 0);
   if (!success)
   {
      terminate(GetLastError());
      return;
   }

   // Wait for stop signal, and then terminate
   WaitForSingleObject (terminateEvent, INFINITE);

   terminate(0);
}

VOID main(VOID)
{
   SERVICE_TABLE_ENTRY serviceTable[] =
   {
   { SERVICE_NAME,
      (LPSERVICE_MAIN_FUNCTION) ServiceMain},
   { NULL, NULL }
   };
   BOOL success;

   // Register with the SCM
   success =
      StartServiceCtrlDispatcher(serviceTable);
   if (!success)
      ExitProcess(GetLastError());
}
```

Listing 12.16   *The IDL file, identical to Listing 9.3*

```
[
  uuid (22449651-4321-1234-4321-987654321CBA),
  version(1.1),
  endpoint ("ncacn_np:[\\pipe\\autorpc]")
]
interface sumup
{
  long SumUp([in] short sumVal);
}
```

Listing 12.17   *The ACF file, identical to Listing 9.4*

```
[
  auto_handle
]
interface sumup
{
}
```

Listing 12.18   *The memstub file*

```
void __RPC_FAR * __RPC_API
  midl_user_allocate(size_t len)
{
  return(new(unsigned char [len]));
}

void __RPC_API midl_user_free(void __RPC_FAR * ptr)
{
  delete(ptr);
}
```

Listing 12.19   *The makefile*

```
NODEBUG=1
SERVER=sumserv
RPCFILE=sum

!include <ntwin32.mak>

.SUFFIXES: .cpp

.c.obj:
  $(cc) -J $(cflags) $(cvars) $(cdebug) $<
```

```
.cpp.obj:
    $(cc) -J $(cflags) $(cvars) $(cdebug) $<

all: $(SERVER).exe


$(SERVER).exe: $(SERVER).obj $(RPCFILE).obj \
$(RPCFILE)_s.obj
    $(link) $(conlflags) $(ldebug) $(conlibs) \
    rpcrt4.lib \
    rpcns4.lib advapi32.lib -out:$(SERVER).exe \
    $(SERVER).obj $(RPCFILE).obj \
    $(RPCFILE)_s.obj


$(SERVER).obj: $(SERVER).cpp $(RPCFILE).h

$(RPCFILE).obj: $(RPCFILE).cpp $(RPCFILE).h

$(RPCFILE)_s.obj: $(RPCFILE)_s.c $(RPCFILE).h

$(RPCFILE).h $(RPCFILE)_s.c: \
$(RPCFILE).idl $(RPCFILE).acf
    midl -client none $(RPCFILE).idl
```

The RPC server demonstrated here uses auto handles. In Listing 12.15, the **InitService** function starts the RPC server and registers with the name server. Once it calls **RpcServerListen**, the RPC server is available (note that **RpcServerListen**'s last parameter is TRUE so the function returns). The **PauseService** function in Listing 12.15 causes the RPC server to stop listening. The server waits for all pending function calls to clear, and then **Pause Service** returns. The **ResumeService** function resumes the RPC server by letting it listen for connections again.

The service formally stops the RPC server in the **terminate** function by first calling **RpcMgmtStopServerListening** and then unregistering the server with the name server and unregistering the interface. The service can then proceed with its normal termination activities.

Compile the RPC server service code to create the service's EXE file. Install the service using the installation program in Section 12.5. You should then be able to start the service using the Services applet in the Control Panel. Once started, run the client in Listing 9.5 to test the server.

You may want to modify the installation program so that this service is dependent on the RPC locator or on other services that it needs to execute properly.

By following the pattern shown above, you can successfully adapt any RPC server so that it runs as a service.

12.12 Conclusion

As discussed in the first section of this chapter, you can use services in a variety of ways to create programs that run constantly on a Windows 2000 machine. By using the beep service in Listing 12.1 as a template, you can easily add your own code and quickly create a wide variety of services.

Services depend heavily on threads. See Chapters 6 and 7 for information on threads and thread synchronization. Services also rely on the registry, which is described in Chapter 21.

Security

*O*ne of the most fascinating parts of Windows 2000 is its security system. As demonstrated in the last 12 chapters, it is possible to almost completely ignore this part of the 32-bit API if you don't care to secure things. However, there are many situations in which the security features built into Windows 2000 can help solve some very interesting problems. In this chapter you will learn about the intent of the Windows 2000 security system, the concepts that help you to understand what is going on, and the techniques used to manipulate it.

Please note that some of the code in this chapter will not work as described unless you log in as the administrator. Only administrators have the rights that are necessary to perform some of the system security tasks demonstrated here.

Compatibility Note: All of the code in this chapter works in Windows 2000. None of it works in Windows 98 at the time of publication, due to unimplemented functions.

13.1 The Possibilities

Most people have never seen or worked with a security system as complete and intricate as Windows 2000. Experienced UNIX programmers are familiar with UNIX's file security system, and with the idea of root privileges, but these systems are primitive compared to Windows 2000. There are many

454

Chapter 13 • **Security**

areas in which Windows 2000 security is adapting to support the Internet-based enterprise. Some of the changes reflect advances in supporting large organizations through the use of the hierarchical Windows 2000 Active Directory. Other changes take advantage of the flexibility of the Windows security architecture to integrate authentication using Internet public-key certificates. The following list introduces the new Windows 2000 security features:

- The Active Directory provides the store for all domain-security policy and account information. The Active Directory, which provides replication and availability of account information to multiple Domain Controllers, is available for remote administration (See Chapter 5).

- The Active Directory supports a hierarchical name space for user, group, and computer-account information. Accounts can be grouped by organizational units, rather than in the flat-domain account-name space provided by earlier versions of Windows NT.

- Administrator rights to create and manage user or group accounts can be delegated to the level of organizational units. Access rights can be granted to individual properties on user objects to allow, for example, a specific individual or group to have the right to reset passwords, but not to modify other account information.

- Active Directory replication allows account updates at any domain controller, not just at the primary domain controller (PDC). Multiple master replicas of the Active Directory at other domain controllers, which used to be known as backup domain controllers (BDCs), are updated and synchronized automatically.

- Windows 2000 employs a new domain model that uses the Active Directory to support a multilevel hierarchy tree of domains. Management of trust relationships between domains is simplified through tree-wide transitive trust throughout the domain tree.

- Windows security includes new authentication based on Internet standard security protocols, including Kerberos Version 5 and Transport Layer Security (TLS) for distributed-security protocols.

- The implementation of secure-channel security protocols (SSL 3.0/TLS) supports strong client authentication by mapping user credentials in the form of public-key certificates to existing Windows NT accounts. Common administration tools are used to manage account information and access control, whether through shared secret authentication or public-key security.

- Windows 2000 supports the optional use of smart cards for interactive logon, in addition to passwords. Smart cards support cryptography and secure storage for private keys and certificates, enabling strong authentication from the desktop to the domain.

- Windows 2000 provides the Microsoft Certificate Services for organizations to issue X.509 version 3 certificates to their employees or business partners. This includes the introduction of the CryptoAPI for certificate management and modules to handle public-key certificates, including standard-format certificates issued by either a commercial Certificate Authority (CA), third-party CA, or the Microsoft Certificate Service included in Windows 2000. System administrators define which CAs are trusted in their environment, and therefore which certificates are accepted for client authentication and access to resources.

- External users who do not have Windows 2000 accounts can be authenticated using public-key certificates and mapped to an existing Windows 2000 account. Access rights defined for the Windows 2000 account determine the resources that the external users can use on the system. Client authentication, using public-key certificates, allows Windows 2000 to authenticate external users, based on certificates issued by trusted Certificate Authorities.

- Windows 2000 users have easy-to-use tools and common interface dialogs for managing the private/public-key pairs and the certificates that they use to access Internet-based resources. Storage of personal-security credentials, which uses secure disk-based storage, is easily transported with the proposed industry-standard protocol, Personal Information Exchange. The operating system also has integrated support for smart card devices.

- Encryption technology is engineered into the operating system in many ways to take advantage of the use of digital signatures for providing authenticated data streams. In addition to signed ActiveX controls and Java Classes for Internet Explorer, Windows 2000 uses digital signatures to ensure image integrity in a variety of program components. In-house developers can also create signed software for distribution and virus protection.

The above information should give you some feeling for the scope and preciseness of the new additions to the Windows 2000 security system. The following gives you some idea of things you can do:

- People using the Windows 2000 File System can see the security features built into it because of the Security menu and security editor in the File Manager. You can write your own code that modifies the security information in a Windows 2000 File System volume at that same level of detail. From programs that you write, you can control who has what type of access to any file on an NTFS volume, just as the File Manager does.

- You can create a named pipe server on one system that, for example, can be accessed only by administrators on other systems. When people try to connect to the server, the security system will check to make sure they have the proper access authority and will reject users who do not have administrative privileges. You might do this so that administrators on different machines can send information to one another in a way that guarantees authenticity. You can write code so that it selectively allows or denies access to any user or group of users, or to all users.

- You can create a mutex with security attributes that allow only certain users or groups to access it. This capability applies to any object in the system: files, semaphores, threads, events, shared memory in file mappings, and so on. In the case of a mutex, you can use this facility to guard against unauthorized access to the synchronization mechanism of an application.
- You can give any object (for example, a thread, mutex, pipe, file, or registry key) the ability to create an entry in the event log whenever it is accessed. You can specify individual types of access, and individual users that generate an event-log entry. For example, you can cause a specific file to generate an event-log entry whenever the user "smith" successfully reads that file.

The above examples show that Windows 2000 allows you to give precise security access to specific objects in the system, and it also allows you to monitor and record how objects are used.

13.2 Understanding the Terminology and Concepts of the Windows 2000 Security System

One of the most interesting and frustrating parts of the Windows 2000 security system is the huge number of new concepts it contains, along with the vocabulary that describes these concepts. The goal of this section is to put those concepts into simple terms so that you can understand them.

By now you are already familiar with the most visible part of the security system: passwords. You can think of the password system as the lock on the front door of a building. The password system keeps people out of a Windows 2000 system, just as a lock on a building keeps people from wandering around in the lobby. Your password gives you a key to the building that is a Windows 2000 system.

If one of your hard disks is formatted with the NT File System, then you know that there is a second layer of security in Windows 2000 as well. You can think of this second layer as locks on individual rooms inside of the building. Some rooms are wide open and allow anyone to walk in, while others have locks on them. The locks on an individual room can be *very* specific in Windows 2000. For example, you can create a file on a volume formatted with the NT File System and you can let any combination of people access it:

- You can let no one but the owner access it
- You can let a single user access it

- You can let several individual users access it
- You can name a Windows 2000 group and let any member of that group access it
- You can name a Windows 2000 group and let members of that group access it, but deny access to specific members of the group
- You can name multiple groups that can access it
- You can let anyone access it

Think of a secured file as a room. The security permissions you put on the file are like a lock that determines who is allowed into the room. You can also control what a person is allowed to do once that person gets into a room. For example, with a file, you can give one user read access, another user write access, and so on. See the Permissions dialog in the Security menu of the File Manager for examples.

You can also put a sentry at the door of any of the rooms. The sentry's job is to monitor who uses the room, and how they use it. This is called *auditing* in Windows 2000. When you attach an auditing request to a Windows 2000 object, the object writes entries in the security portion of the event log whenever certain users access the object in specified ways. For example, if you have access to a Windows 2000 file system volume and have administrative privileges, open the File Manager and select a file that you own. Then select the Auditing option in the Security menu. For any individual user or

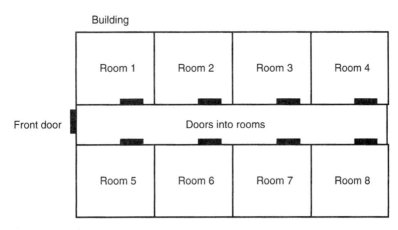

Figure 13.1   *Think of Windows 2000 as a building full of rooms. Your password gives you a key that lets you into the building. Once inside, you can then use your key to enter individual rooms. Some rooms have no locks, while others are locked but will let you in, and still others will refuse you entry. The rooms are individual objects in the Windows 2000 system: files, registry keys, thread and mutex objects, and so on*

group, you can detect when they successfully or unsuccessfully (or both) read the file, write to the file, execute the file, and so on.

The most obvious place to see these security features is in the NT File System. The security editor in the File Manager lets you easily and graphically manipulate all of the different security features available for files. This same level of security detail applies to many different objects in Windows 2000. For example, you can secure items in the Registry with this level of detail, and in fact the registry editor contains the same sort of visual-security editor that the File Manager contains. You can also specify security attributes on many internal system objects. For example, you can limit access to a named pipe (see Section 13.9) in this way.

Here is a brief summary of these concepts:

- A Windows 2000 system is like a building. Your password gives you a key into the building.
- Once you are inside, you find potentially thousands of rooms. A file is like a room, and so are, registry entries, named pipes, threads, and so on.
- Each room can be secured by its owner with a lock that is keyed for user and group IDs. That is, the owner of the room can let just one person use the room, or a selection of users and groups, or everyone.
- Each room can also be manned with a sentry that detects and records who enters the room and what each person does once they are inside.

Now that you understand the general concepts, let's look at some of the Windows 2000 specific vocabulary for discussing security.

13.3 Windows 2000 Security Vocabulary

When you log in to a Windows 2000 system, the system gives you an *access token*. The access token is your key to all of the locks found in a Windows 2000 system. Your key will turn some locks, but it will not work in all of them unless you log in as the administrator. Each process that you create contains a copy of your access token.

The access token does two things. First, it identifies *who you are*. For example, if you logged in as the user "smith," then your access token contains your identity as that user. The access token also identifies you by all of the groups you belong to. For example, in the User Manager you may be a member of the Power User group, the Backup Operator group, and a custom group named Programmers. Your access token identifies you as a member of all of these groups.

Your access token also contains all of your *user rights*. Each group you belong to can have user rights, or *privileges*, associated with it. If you open the User Manager you can look at the list of rights with the User Rights menu option. For example, power users and administrators have the right to set the system time, while normal users do not. Some users can shut down the system while others cannot, and so on. The system builds the list of rights in your access token by combining all of the individual rights found in each group you belong to. Individual users can also have special rights granted to them specifically by the administrator with the User Manager.

Most of the objects in the system can have locks on them. In Windows 2000, a lock is called a *security descriptor*. If the **Create** function for an object contains a security parameter, you can lock it. The following objects can have locks:

- Files (if they exist on a Windows 2000 File System volume)
- Directories (if they exist on a Windows 2000 File System volume)
- Registry keys
- Processes
- Threads
- Mutexes
- Semaphores
- Events
- Named pipes (on the system *and* over the network)
- Anonymous pipes (on the system only)
- Mailslots (on the system only)
- Console screen buffers
- File mappings

Access token

User ID	User rights
Smith	Shut down system
Groups	Traverse directories
Power user	Set system time
Backup operator	Create new accounts
Programmer	etc.

Figure 13.2 *An access token contains a user ID, the names of the groups the user belongs to, and the combined user rights from all of those groups*

- Services
- Private objects

To lock an object, you create a security descriptor and pass it to the object when you create it. In all of the previous sections in this book, the example code has passed a zero in for the security-attributes parameter to functions such as CreateFile or CreateThread. The zero indicates to the system that it should create a default security descriptor that allows you to access the object. See Section 13.8 for a description of default security descriptors.

A security descriptor contains four things:

1. An owner identifier that identifies the current owner of the object
2. A primary group identifier
3. A *system access control list*, or SACL, that contains auditing information
4. A discretionary access control list, or DACL, that determines which users and groups can and cannot access the object

The owner of a Windows 2000 object can always set its security information. For example, if you own a file and accidentally set it so that no one can access it, you can still go back and change its security, because you are the owner. It is like breaking the lock to your house: Even though the lock is broken, you can always replace it with a new one, because you own the house.

The DACL (Discretionary Access Control List) is the heart of the actual lock. It controls who can and cannot access the object. It is an *access-control list*, or ACL, that contains *access-control entries*, or ACEs. Each ACE indicates one user or group, along with what they can or cannot do to the object. For example, if the object is a file and the user "smith" is allowed to read from the file, then there will be an ACE that indicates that user "smith" has read access. This is called an *access-allowed ACE* because it allows a user or group to do something. There is one access-allowed ACE for each person or group

Figure 13.3

The security descriptor for any object contains the owner and group IDs, the discretionary access control list that determines who can and cannot access the object, and the system access control list that controls who gets audited when they use the object

Owner identifier	Group identifier
Sacl	Dacl

allowed to access the object. Similarly, there are *access-denied ACEs,* which deny access to specific users or groups. For example, if you have given the Power Users group access to an object, but "smith" is a power user and you don't want him to have access, an access-denied ACE keeps him out.

The SACL (System Access Control List) also contains ACEs, but these ACEs determine who will be audited and why. An ACE in a SACL is called an *audit-access ACE.* For example, if the system is supposed to create an audit entry whenever the user "smith" successfully reads a file, one ACE in the SACL states that.

To convey its information, each ACE in an ACL consists of three parts: a *Security Identifier* (or SID), an *access mask*, and an *ACE header*. The SID is a value stored in the registry (and also available through function calls) that uniquely identifies each user or group that exists in the User Manager. The ACE header determines the type of ACE: access allowed, access denied, or any of the others. An access mask is a 32-bit mask that determines what the user can do with the object. There are standard rights that apply to all objects on the system. Some objects also have a variety of special access rights that apply only to them. For example, you can apply the following specific and standard access rights to a file object:

specific:
FILE_READ_DATA
FILE_WRITE_DATA
FILE_APPEND_DATA
FILE_READ_EA
FILE_WRITE_EA
FILE_EXECUTE
FILE_READ_ATTRIBUTES
FILE_WRITE_ATTRIBUTES
FILE_ALL_ACCESS

standard:
DELETE
READ_CONTROL
STANDARD_RIGHTS_ALL

Figure 13.4 *An Access Control Entry (ACE) specifies one user or group (the SID identifies the user or group) and the type of access allowed. ACEs are stored in ACLs (see Figure 13.3)*

STANDARD_RIGHTS_EXECUTE
STANDARD_RIGHTS_READ
STANDARD_RIGHTS_REQUIRED
STANDARD_RIGHTS_WRITE
SYNCHRONIZE
WRITE_DAC
WRITE_OWNER

generic:
GENERIC_ALL
GENERIC_EXECUTE
GENERIC_READ
GENERIC_WRITE

The generic rights are pre-defined combinations of standard and specific rights, and they change from object to object. See Section 13.5 for more information on securable objects and their access rights.

An access mask is simply a 32-bit bit-mask. Each of the standard, specific, and generic rights has a bit associated with it in the access mask. The first 16 bits hold specific rights and are keyed to the object that the access mask refers to (for example, the FILE_ constants above). The next eight bits hold standard rights. The high-order four bits hold generic rights.

As you can see, there is a whole cornucopia of new terminology used to describe Windows 2000 security features. However, you will become intimately familiar with all of these words as you work through the sample code, and all of the concepts are easy to understand. Here is a quick summary:

- When users log in, they receive *access tokens*. An access token contains the user's ID, the user's groups, and the user's privileges according to the groups.
- Each object has a *security descriptor,* which acts as its lock. A security descriptor contains an owner and group identifier, a *System ACL,* and a *Discretionary ACL.*
- A *DACL* controls who is allowed to do what to the object.
- A *SACL* controls who is audited for doing what to an object.
- *ACLs* consist of *ACEs.* Each ACE contains a *SID,* which identifies the user or group, an *access mask,* which determines the actions allowed to the user or group, and an ACE header, which determines the type of ACE.

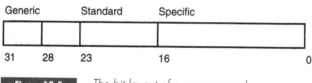

Figure 13.5   *The bit layout of an access mask*

The following section presents three simple examples to show how the security functions and all of this vocabulary fit together.

13.4 Simple Examples

The purpose of this section is to walk through the creation and application of a security descriptor for a file object. A file object is chosen for this example because it is common and easily understood, and also because it is easy to view the results with the security editor in the File Manager to prove that the code works. However, if your hard disk is not formatted with the NT File System, this code will not do anything, and the security editor is disabled. You have three options if this is the case:

1. Convert your hard disk to NTFS
2. Install a new hard disk and format it with the NT File System
3. Partition off a small section (say 10 megabytes) of your existing hard disk and format it with NTFS. This means that you will have to reformat and reload the original partition as well

Alternatively, you can wait a moment and we will apply this same security code to a registry key. You will be able to see the security editor in the registry editor regardless of the file system that you are using.

Listing 13.1 contains a program that creates a new file. The security descriptor for the new file is set up so that only the user "guest" can use the file, and the user can do nothing but read it. The program contains absolutely no error checking, so the essentials are easy to see. When you run Listing 13.1, it should create a file on `c:\` named `testfile`. Select the file in the File Manager and then choose the **Permissions** option in the **Security** menu. You will find that there is one entry in the list: The user "guest" can read the file. Feel free to change the name of the file or the name of the user when you run the code yourself.

Listing 13.1	*A simple security program (without any error checking) that creates a file that only the user "guest" can read. This code will not work unless you have formatted your hard disk with the NT File System*

```
// filesec.cpp

#include <windows.h>
#include <iostream.h>

SECURITY_ATTRIBUTES sa;
SECURITY_DESCRIPTOR sd;
```

Listing 13.1	*A simple security program (without any error checking) that creates a file that only the user "guest" can read. This code will not work unless you have formatted your hard disk with the NT File System (continued)*

```
BYTE aclBuffer[1024];
PACL pacl=(PACL)&aclBuffer;
BYTE sidBuffer[100];
PSID psid=(PSID) &sidBuffer;
DWORD sidBufferSize = 100;
char domainBuffer[80];
DWORD domainBufferSize = 80;
SID_NAME_USE snu;
HANDLE file;

void main(void)
{
  InitializeSecurityDescriptor(&sd,
    SECURITY_DESCRIPTOR_REVISION);
  InitializeAcl(pacl, 1024, ACL_REVISION);
  LookupAccountName(0, "guest", psid,
    &sidBufferSize, domainBuffer,
    &domainBufferSize, &snu);
  AddAccessAllowedAce(pacl, ACL_REVISION,
    GENERIC_READ, psid);
  SetSecurityDescriptorDacl(&sd, TRUE, pacl,
    FALSE);

  sa.nLength= sizeof(SECURITY_ATTRIBUTES);
  sa.bInheritHandle = FALSE;
  sa.lpSecurityDescriptor = &sd;

  file = CreateFile("c:\\testfile",
    GENERIC_READ | GENERIC_WRITE,
    0, &sa, CREATE_NEW,
    FILE_ATTRIBUTE_NORMAL, 0);
  CloseHandle(file);
}
```

Start by looking at the bottom of the program. Here you will find a call to **CreateFile** that creates a file named c:\testfile. However, this call to **CreateFile**, unlike all of the previous calls that you have seen in this book, has a security parameter at location four in the parameter list. In all previous code, we have used a zero in this location. The zero tells the operating system to use a default security descriptor when it creates the object (see Section 13.8). The zero value also disables inheritance (see Chapter 6). In Listing 13.1, the code instead creates a SECURITY_ATTRIBUTES structure that contains a valid security descriptor.

The creation of a security descriptor starts with a call to the **Initialize SecurityDescriptor** function seen at the first line of Listing 13.1.

InitializeSecurityDescriptor	*Initializes a security descriptor*

```
BOOL InitializeSecurityDescriptor(
    PSECURITY_DESCRIPTOR psd,
    DWORD revision)
```

psd	A pointer to a security descriptor
revision	Revision level. Must be SECURITY_ DESCRIPTOR_REVISION

Returns TRUE on success

This step creates a security descriptor in absolute format (there is also a second format called the self-relative format, and the differences are described in Section 13.6). The new security descriptor initially contains no information besides the revision level: no owner identifier, no group identifier, no SACL, and no DACL.

The next line calls **InitializeAcl** to create the ACL that will become the DACL for the security descriptor.

InitializeAcl	*Initializes an ACL*

```
BOOL InitializeAcl(
    PACL pacl,
    DWORD bufferLen,
    DWORD revision)
```

pacl	A pointer to an ACL
bufferLen	The length of the ACL buffer supplied
revision	Revision level. Must be ACL_REVISION

Returns TRUE on success

When the **InitializeAcl** function returns, **pacl** points to an empty ACL. That is, the ACL contains no ACEs. If you were to comment out the next two lines so that this empty ACL was placed into the security descriptor, and that security descriptor was then applied to the file, no one would be able to access the file. In the absence of any ACEs in the discretionary ACL, no one has access. Alternatively, if you were to create no DACL at all and pass NULL during the DACL installation step below, then everyone could access the file. The total absence of a DACL gives access to everyone.

The next two lines of Listing 13.1 create an ACE and add it to the ACL. The **LookupAccountName** function returns a SID for the specified account name.

LookupAccountName	*Returns a SID for the specified account*

```
BOOL LookupAccountName(
   LPCTSTR system,
   LPCTSTR accountName,
   PSID psid,
   LPDWORD sidBufferSize,
   LPTSTR domainName,
   LPDWORD domainNameLen,
   PSID_NAME_USE psnu)
```

system	Name of a remote system, or 0 for local
accountName	The name of the account to look up
psid	A pointer to a buffer for the returned SID
sidBufferSize	The size of the psid buffer
domainName	A pointer to a buffer for the returned domain name
domainNameLen	Size of the domain name buffer
psnu	Returned enumerated type indicating the type of account

Returns TRUE on success

The **LookupAccountName** function looks up the account name specified on the system specified or on the local system. If it is not found locally the function looks on the domain controller, or on trusted domain controllers, if appropriate. The function returns a SID for the account, the domain where it was found if the SID came from a domain controller, and an enumerated value that indicates the type of account:

SidTypeUser
SidTypeGroup
SidTypeDomain
SidTypeAlias
SidTypeWellKnownGroup
SidTypeDeletedAccount
SidTypeInvalid
SidTypeUnknown

A SID is a *security identifier*. It uniquely identifies a user or a group to the system.

The SID returned by the **LookupAccountName** function is used in a call to the **AddAccessAllowedAce** function to create an access-allowed (as opposed to access-denied) ACE and add it to the currently-empty ACL.

AddAccessAllowedAce	*Creates an access allowed ACE and adds it to the specified ACL*

```
BOOL AddAccessAllowedAce(
    PACL pacl,
    DWORD revision,
    DWORD accessMask,
    PSID psid)
```

pacl	A pointer to an ACL
revision	Revision level. Must be ACL_REVISION
accessMask	Access mask bits
Psid	A SID
Returns TRUE on success	

The **AddAccessAllowedAce** function creates the ACE with the SID and access mask specified and adds it to the ACL specified. The GENERIC_READ access mask grants read access to the file and its attributes. See Section 13.5 for a list of the specific and standard rights that GENERIC_READ adds to the access mask.

Now the code in Listing 13.1 has an ACL containing one ACE that specifies that the user "guest" should have read access. This ACL needs to be placed into the Discretionary ACL of the security descriptor using the **Set SecurityDescriptorDacl** function.

SetSecurityDescriptorDacl	*Sets the DACL in a security descriptor*

```
BOOL SetSecurityDescriptorDacl(
    PSECURITY_DESCRIPTOR psd,
    BOOL daclPresent,
    PACL pacl,
    BOOL daclDefaulted)
```

psd	A pointer to a security descriptor
daclPresent	A boolean that if TRUE says pacl contains an ACL. If it is FALSE, the function ignores anything in pacl and sets the DACL in the security descriptor to NULL
pacl	A pointer to the ACL to add
daclDefaulted	A boolean indicating the source of the DACL
Returns TRUE on success	

Now the security descriptor contains a valid DACL with one ACE in it. Listing 13.1 places this security descriptor in a security attributes structure and then passes it to the **CreateFile** function (see Chapter 2).

Compile and run Listing 13.1. Make sure that the file name specified in the program does not already exist when you run it. When you look at the new file with the File Manager's security editor, you will find that its permissions are set as specified in the code.

You can easily modify Listing 13.1 to experiment with security descriptors. For example, try giving write access to a certain group, or add several ACEs to the DACL, or create an access-denied ACE using **AddAccessDenied-Ace**. *Be sure that access-denied ACEs precede access-allowed ACEs.* Use the **SetSecurityDescriptorOwner** function to modify the owner in the security descriptor.

This exact same security descriptor code can be applied to any other securable NT object, because the security system is uniform across all objects. For example, you can use it to create a key in the registry, as demonstrated in Listing 13.2. (See Chapter 21 for information on the registry and registry keys.) If you compare Listing 13.2 with Listing 13.1, you will find that they are exactly the same except that Listing 13.2 uses **RegCreateKeyEx** to create a registry key instead of a file.

Listing 13.2   *Code to create a registry key that only the user "guest" can access*

```cpp
// regsec.cpp

#include <windows.h>
#include <iostream.h>

SECURITY_ATTRIBUTES sa;
SECURITY_DESCRIPTOR sd;
BYTE aclBuffer[1024];
PACL pacl=(PACL)&aclBuffer;
BYTE sidBuffer[100];
PSID psid=(PSID) &sidBuffer;
DWORD sidBufferSize = 100;
char domainBuffer[80];
DWORD domainBufferSize = 80;
SID_NAME_USE snu;
LONG result;
HKEY regKey;
DWORD disposition;

void main(void)
{
  InitializeSecurityDescriptor(&sd,
    SECURITY_DESCRIPTOR_REVISION);
  InitializeAcl(pacl, 1024, ACL_REVISION);
```

```
LookupAccountName(0, "guest", psid,
    &sidBufferSize, domainBuffer,
    &domainBufferSize, &snu);
AddAccessAllowedAce(pacl, ACL_REVISION,
    GENERIC_READ, psid);
SetSecurityDescriptorDacl(&sd, TRUE, pacl,
    FALSE);

sa.nLength= sizeof(SECURITY_ATTRIBUTES);
sa.bInheritHandle = FALSE;
sa.lpSecurityDescriptor = &sd;

result = RegCreateKeyEx(HKEY_CURRENT_USER,
    "junk", 0, 0, REG_OPTION_VOLATILE,
    KEY_ALL_ACCESS, &sa, &regKey,
    &disposition);
cout << result << endl;
RegCloseKey(regKey);
}
```

Before running Listing 13.2, run the registry editor (regedt32.exe) and look at the HKEY_CURRENT_USER window to make sure HKEY_CURRENT_ USER does not already contain a key named "junk." If it does, delete it, or modify the code in Listing 13.2 to create a different key. Now run Listing 13.2. Refresh the registry-editor display if it is not set to automatically refresh, and you will see a new key named "junk." When you check its permissions using the Permissions option in the Security menu, you will find that you or "administrator" owns the key and that "guest" is the only user who has access to it. Change the name of the key or the user, as you desire. Since the code in Listing 13.2 creates volatile keys, they will disappear when you log off or reboot the system.

You can apply the same security-descriptor code to a named pipe to control who can access the pipe, as shown in Listing 13.3. The code in Listing 13.3 is a modification of the simple named pipe receiver seen in Listing 11.4. When applied to a named pipe like this, the security code causes the pipe to reject connections from any user other than "guest." Change "guest" to any user that you prefer. It is probably wise to use your own user ID in this code. See Section 13.9 for a complete description of how named pipes use security descriptors.

Listing 13.3   *Code demonstrating how to secure a named pipe. Only the user "guest" running a program such as Listing 11.7 can connect to this pipe*

```
// pipesec.cpp

#include <windows.h>
#include <iostream.h>
```

Listing 13.3	*Code demonstrating how to secure a named pipe. Only the user "guest" running a program such as Listing 11.7 can connect to this pipe (continued)*

```
SECURITY_ATTRIBUTES sa;
SECURITY_DESCRIPTOR sd;
BYTE aclBuffer[1024];
PACL pacl=(PACL)&aclBuffer;
BYTE sidBuffer[100];
PSID psid=(PSID) &sidBuffer;
DWORD sidBufferSize = 100;
char domainBuffer[80];
DWORD domainBufferSize = 80;
SID_NAME_USE snu;
HANDLE file;

int main(void)
{
  InitializeSecurityDescriptor(&sd,
    SECURITY_DESCRIPTOR_REVISION);
  InitializeAcl(pacl, 1024, ACL_REVISION);
  LookupAccountName(0, "guest", psid,
    &sidBufferSize, domainBuffer,
    &domainBufferSize, &snu);
  AddAccessAllowedAce(pacl, ACL_REVISION,
    GENERIC_READ|GENERIC_WRITE, psid);
  SetSecurityDescriptorDacl(&sd, TRUE, pacl,
    FALSE);

  sa.nLength= sizeof(SECURITY_ATTRIBUTES);
  sa.bInheritHandle = FALSE;
  sa.lpSecurityDescriptor = &sd;

  // Print out the allowed connector
  char domainBuffer[80];
  DWORD domainBufferSize = 80;
  char name[80];
  DWORD nameSize= 80;
  LookupAccountSid(0, psid, name, &nameSize,
    domainBuffer, &domainBufferSize, &snu);
  cout << "allowing " << domainBuffer
    << "\\" << name
    << " to access pipe" << endl;

  char toDisptxt[80];
  HANDLE ssnpPipe;
  DWORD NumBytesRead;

  /* Create a named pipe for receiving messages */
  ssnpPipe=CreateNamedPipe("\\\\.\\pipe\\ssnp",
```

```
PIPE_ACCESS_INBOUND,
PIPE_TYPE_MESSAGE | PIPE_WAIT,
1, 0, 0, 150, &sa);

/* Check and see if the named pipe was created */
if (ssnpPipe == INVALID_HANDLE_VALUE)
{
  cerr << "ERROR: Unable to create a named pipe."
    << endl;
  return (1);
}

/* Allow a client to connect to the name pipe,
   terminate if unsuccessful */
if(!ConnectNamedPipe(ssnpPipe,
  (LPOVERLAPPED) NULL))
{
  cerr << "ERROR: Unable to connect a named pipe"
    << endl;
  CloseHandle(ssnpPipe);
  return (1);
}

/* Repeatedly check for messages
   until the program is terminated */
while(1)
{
  /* Read the message and check to see if read
     was successful */
  if (!ReadFile(ssnpPipe, toDisptxt,
    sizeof(toDisptxt),
    &NumBytesRead, (LPOVERLAPPED) NULL))
  {
    cerr << "ERROR: Unable to read from pipe"
      << endl;
    CloseHandle(ssnpPipe);
    return (1);
  }

  /* Display the Message */
  cout << toDisptxt << endl;

} /* while */
}
```

Run Listing 13.3 in one command window. The program will output the identity of the user allowed to connect to the pipe. As shown in Listing 13.3, only "guest" can connect, but you can change that if you like. Now open another command window and run Listing 11.7, which will connect to the pipe and send messages to it. If you are logged in as "guest" when you run Listing 11.7, the two programs will connect. If not, Listing 11.7 will receive an "Access Denied" error code via **GetLastError**. You will see this same behavior if you try to connect over the network. See Section 11.4 for details on network connections with named pipes. See Section 13.9 for further information on namedpipe security.

13.5 Securable Objects and Access Rights

When you create an access mask in an ACE you can specify standard rights, which apply to any Windows 2000 object, and you can also pick extremely specific rights that apply to individual objects. For example, if you want to give the user "smith" the right to delete an object, then create an ACE giving "smith" the standard right DELETE. If, on the other hand, you want the user "jones" to be able to modify the state of a semaphore object, create an ACE giving "jones" the semaphore-specific right SEMAPHORE_MODIFY_STATE.

All of the different access rights are simply bit definitions that get ORed into the 32-bit access mask. The first 16 bits hold specific rights and are keyed to the object that the access mask refers to (for example, the FILE_ constants). The next eight bits hold standard rights. The high-order four bits hold generic rights.

The standard rights available on all objects, along with their bit definitions, are as follows:

DELETE	(0x00010000) Can delete the object
READ_CONTROL	(0x00020000) Can read the security descriptor except the SACL
WRITE_DAC	(0x00040000) Can write to the DACL in a security descriptor
WRITE_OWNER	(0x00080000) Can write to the owner in a security descriptor
SYNCHRONIZE	(0x00100000) A thread can wait for the object using a Wait function. Not supported for all objects. See Section 10.4.
STANDARD_RIGHTS_ALL	DELETE | READ_CONTROL |

Figure 13.6   *The bit layout of an access mask*

	WRITE_DAC |
	WRITE_OWNER |
	SYNCHRONIZE
STANDARD_RIGHTS_EXECUTE	READ_CONTROL
STANDARD_RIGHTS_READ	READ_CONTROL
STANDARD_RIGHTS_REQUIRED	DELETE |
	READ_CONTROL |
	WRITE_DAC |
	WRITE_OWNER
STANDARD_RIGHTS_WRITE	READ_CONTROL

The specific rights that apply to the different securable-system objects available in Windows 2000 are listed in the following sections, along with the names of the functions that let you create or modify the security descriptor for the objects.

The "Security Overview" section of the Win32 help file contains complete descriptions of all of the specific rights listed in the following sections:

13.5.1 Files

CreateFile: The handle returned has SYNCHRONIZE, FILE_READ_ ATTRIBUTES, and the requested combination of GENERIC_READ and/or GENERIC_WRITE
    GetFileSecurity
    SetFileSecurity

Specific:

FILE_READ_DATA	(0x0001)
FILE_WRITE_DATA	(0x0002)
FILE_APPEND_DATA	(0x0004)
FILE_READ_EA	(0x0008)
FILE_WRITE_EA	(0x0010)
FILE_EXECUTE	(0x0020)
FILE_READ_ATTRIBUTES	(0x0080)
FILE_WRITE_ATTRIBUTES	(0x0100)
FILE_ALL_ACCESS	(0x1FF |
	STANDARD_RIGHTS_REQUIRED |
	SYNCHRONIZE)

Generic:

FILE_GENERIC_READ	(STANDARD_RIGHTS_READ |
	FILE_READ_DATA |
	FILE_READ_ATTRIBUTES |
	FILE_READ_EA |
	SYNCHRONIZE)
FILE_GENERIC_WRITE	(STANDARD_RIGHTS_WRITE |
	FILE_WRITE_DATA |
	FILE_WRITE_ATTRIBUTES |

```
                              FILE_WRITE_EA |
                              FILE_APPEND_DATA |
                              SYNCHRONIZE)

FILE_GENERIC_EXECUTE          (STANDARD_RIGHTS_EXECUTE |
                              FILE_READ_ATTRIBUTES |
                              FILE_EXECUTE |
                              SYNCHRONIZE)
```

13.5.2 Directories

CreateDirectory: The handle returned has SYNCHRONIZE and FILE_ LIST_ DIRECTORY

> CreateDirectoryEx
> GetFileSecurity
> SetFileSecurity

Specific:

```
FILE_LIST_DIRECTORY           ( 0x0001 )
FILE_ADD_FILE                 ( 0x0002 )
FILE_ADD_SUBDIRECTORY         ( 0x0004 )
FILE_READ_EA                  ( 0x0008 )
FILE_WRITE_EA                 ( 0x0010 )
FILE_TRAVERSE                 ( 0x0020 )
FILE_DELETE_CHILD             ( 0x0040 )
FILE_READ_ATTRIBUTES          ( 0x0080)
FILE_WRITE_ATTRIBUTES         ( 0x0100 )
FILE_ALL_ACCESS               (0x1FF |
                              STANDARD_RIGHTS_REQUIRED |
                              SYNCHRONIZE )
```

Generic:

```
FILE_GENERIC_READ             (STANDARD_RIGHTS_READ |
                              FILE_READ_DATA |
                              FILE_READ_ATTRIBUTES |
                              FILE_READ_EA |
                              SYNCHRONIZE)

FILE_GENERIC_WRITE            (STANDARD_RIGHTS_WRITE |
                              FILE_WRITE_DATA |
                              FILE_WRITE_ATTRIBUTES |
                              FILE_WRITE_EA |
                              FILE_APPEND_DATA |
                              SYNCHRONIZE)

FILE_GENERIC_EXECUTE          (STANDARD_RIGHTS_EXECUTE |
                              FILE_READ_ATTRIBUTES |
```

FILE_EXECUTE |
SYNCHRONIZE)

13.5.3 Pipes

CreateNamedPipe: The rights of the handle returned depend on the access requested:

PIPE_ACCESS_DUPLEX	GENERIC_READ | GENERIC_WRITE | SYNCHRONIZE
PIPE_ACCESS_INBOUND	GENERIC_READ | SYNCHRONIZE
PIPE_ACCESS_OUTBOUND	GENERIC_WRITE | SYNCHRONIZE

    CreatePipe
    GetFileSecurity
    SetFileSecurity

Specific:

FILE_READ_DATA	(0x0001)
FILE_WRITE_DATA	(0x0002)
FILE_CREATE_PIPE_INSTANCE	(0x0004)
FILE_READ_ATTRIBUTES	(0x0080)
FILE_WRITE_ATTRIBUTES	(0x0100)
FILE_ALL_ACCESS	(0x1FF | STANDARD_RIGHTS_REQUIRED | SYNCHRONIZE)

Generic:

FILE_GENERIC_READ	(STANDARD_RIGHTS_READ | FILE_READ_DATA | FILE_READ_ATTRIBUTES | SYNCHRONIZE)
FILE_GENERIC_WRITE	(STANDARD_RIGHTS_WRITE | FILE_WRITE_DATA | FILE_WRITE_ATTRIBUTES | SYNCHRONIZE)

13.5.4 Mailslots

CreateMailslot: The handle returned has SYNCHRONIZE, GENERIC_ READ, and WRITE_DAC
    GetFileSecurity
    SetFileSecurity
    Same rights as files. Only GENERIC_READ applies

13.5.5 Consoles

CreateConsoleScreenBuffer

13.5.6 Processes

CreateProcess: The handle returned has PROCESS_ALL_ACCESS rights
  SetKernelObjectSecurity
  GetKernelObjectSecurity

Specific:

PROCESS_TERMINATE	(0x0001)
PROCESS_CREATE_THREAD	(0x0002)
PROCESS_VM_OPERATION	(0x0008)
PROCESS_VM_READ	(0x0010)
PROCESS_VM_WRITE	(0x0020)
PROCESS_DUP_HANDLE	(0x0040)
PROCESS_CREATE_PROCESS	(0x0080)
PROCESS_SET- (0x0200) INFORMATION	
PROCESS_QUERY_ INFORMATION	(0x0400)
PROCESS_ALL_ACCESS	(STANDARD_RIGHTS_REQUIRED | SYNCHRONIZE | 0xFFF)

13.5.7 Threads

CreateThread: The handle returned has THREAD_ALL_ACCESS rights
  SetKernelObjectSecurity
  GetKernelObjectSecurity

Specific:

THREAD_TERMINATE	(0x0001)
THREAD_SUSPEND_RESUME	(0x0002)
THREAD_GET_CONTEXT	(0x0008)
THREAD_SET_CONTEXT	(0x0010)
THREAD_SET_INFORMATION	(0x0020)
THREAD_QUERY_ INFORMATION	(0x0040)
THREAD_SET_THREAD_ TOKEN	(0x0080)
THREAD_IMPERSONATE	(0x0100)
THREAD_DIRECT_(0x0200) IMPERSONATION	
THREAD_ALL_ACCESS	(STANDARD_RIGHTS_REQUIRED |

SYNCHRONIZE |
0x3FF)

13.5.8 File Mappings

CreateFileMapping: The rights of the handle returned depends on the access requested:

PAGE_READWRITE   SECTION_QUERY |
SECTION_MAP_READ |
SECTION_MAP_WRITE

PAGE_READONLY   SECTION_QUERY |
SECTION_MAP_READ

      SetKernelObjectSecurity
      GetKernelObjectSecurity

Specific:

SECTION_QUERY	0x0001
SECTION_MAP_WRITE	0x0002
SECTION_MAP_READ	0x0004
SECTION_MAP_EXECUTE	0x0008
SECTION_EXTEND_SIZE	0x0010

SECTION_ALL_ACCESS   (STANDARD_RIGHTS_REQUIRED |
SECTION_QUERY |
SECTION_MAP_WRITE |
SECTION_MAP_READ |
SECTION_MAP_EXECUTE |
SECTION_EXTEND_SIZE)

13.5.9 Access Tokens

OpenProcessToken
      OpenThreadToken
      SetKernelObjectSecurity
      GetKernelObjectSecurity

Specific:

TOKEN_ASSIGN_PRIMARY	(0x0001)
TOKEN_DUPLICATE	(0x0002)
TOKEN_IMPERSONATE	(0x0004)
TOKEN_QUERY	(0x0008)
TOKEN_QUERY_SOURCE	(0x0010)
TOKEN_ADJUST_PRIVILEGES	(0x0020)
TOKEN_ADJUST_GROUPS	(0x0040)
TOKEN_ADJUST_DEFAULT	(0x0080)

TOKEN_ALL_ACCESS	(STANDARD_RIGHTS_REQUIRED | TOKEN_ASSIGN_PRIMARY | TOKEN_DUPLICATE | TOKEN_IMPERSONATE | TOKEN_QUERY | TOKEN_QUERY_SOURCE | TOKEN_ADJUST_PRIVILEGES | TOKEN_ADJUST_GROUPS | TOKEN_ADJUST_DEFAULT)
TOKEN_READ	(STANDARD_RIGHTS_READ | TOKEN_QUERY)
TOKEN_WRITE	(STANDARD_RIGHTS_WRITE | TOKEN_ADJUST_PRIVILEGES | TOKEN_ADJUST_GROUPS | TOKEN_ADJUST_DEFAULT)
TOKEN_EXECUTE	

13.5.10 Registry Objects

RegCreateKeyEx: The handle returned has the access rights requested in the call
    RegSaveKey
    RegGetKeySecurity
    RegSetKeySecurity

Specific:

KEY_QUERY_VALUE	(0x0001)
KEY_SET_VALUE	(0x0002)
KEY_CREATE_SUB_KEY	(0x0004)
KEY_ENUMERATE_SUB_KEYS	(0x0008)
KEY_NOTIFY	(0x0010)
KEY_CREATE_LINK	(0x0020)
KEY_READ	((STANDARD_RIGHTS_READ | KEY_QUERY_VALUE | KEY_ENUMERATE_SUB_KEYS | KEY_NOTIFY) & (~SYNCHRONIZE))
KEY_WRITE	((STANDARD_RIGHTS_WRITE | KEY_SET_VALUE | KEY_CREATE_SUB_KEY) & (~SYNCHRONIZE))
KEY_EXECUTE	((KEY_READ) & (~SYNCHRONIZE))

KEY_ALL_ACCESS	((STANDARD_RIGHTS_ALL | KEY_QUERY_VALUE | KEY_SET_VALUE | KEY_CREATE_SUB_KEY | KEY_ENUMERATE_SUB_KEYS | KEY_NOTIFY | KEY_CREATE_LINK) & (~SYNCHRONIZE))

13.5.11 Service Objects

OpenService
    OpenSCManager
    QueryServiceObjectSecurity
    SetServiceObjectSecurity

Specific:

SC_MANAGER_CONNECT	(0x0001)
SC_MANAGER_CREATE_ SERVICE	(0x0002)
SC_MANAGER_ ENUMERATE_SERVICE	(0x0004)
SC_MANAGER_LOCK	(0x0008)
SC_MANAGER_QUERY_ LOCK_STATUS	(0x0010)
SC_MANAGER_MODIFY_ BOOT_CONFIG	(0x0020)
SC_MANAGER_ALL_ACCESS	(STANDARD_RIGHTS_REQUIRED | SC_MANAGER_CONNECT | SC_MANAGER_CREATE_SERVICE | SC_MANAGER_ENUMERATE_SERVICE | SC_MANAGER_LOCK | SC_MANAGER_QUERY_LOCK_STATUS | SC_MANAGER_MODIFY_BOOT_CONFIG)
SERVICE_QUERY_CONFIG	(0x0001)
SERVICE_CHANGE_CONFIG	(0x0002)
SERVICE_QUERY_STATUS	(0x0004)
SERVICE_ENUMERATE_ DEPENDENTS	(0x0008)
SERVICE_START	(0x0010)
SERVICE_STOP	(0x0020)
SERVICE_PAUSE_CONTINUE	(0x0040)
SERVICE_INTERROGATE	(0x0080)
SERVICE_USER_DEFINED_ CONTROL	(0x0100)

SERVICE_ALL_ACCESS	(STANDARD_RIGHTS_REQUIRED |
	SERVICE_QUERY_CONFIG |
	SERVICE_CHANGE_CONFIG |
	SERVICE_QUERY_STATUS |
	SERVICE_ENUMERATE_DEPENDENTS |
	SERVICE_START |
	SERVICE_STOP |
	SERVICE_PAUSE_CONTINUE |
	SERVICE_INTERROGATE |
	SERVICE_USER_DEFINED_CONTROL)

13.5.12 Events

CreateEvent: The handle returned has EVENT_ALL_ACCESS rights
   SetKernelObjectSecurity
   GetKernelObjectSecurity

Specific:

EVENT_MODIFY_STATE	0x0002
EVENT_ALL_ACCESS	(STANDARD_RIGHTS_REQUIRED |
	SYNCHRONIZE |
	0x3)

13.5.13 Mutexes

CreateMutex: The handle returned has MUTEX_ALL_ACCESS rights
   SetKernelObjectSecurity
   GetKernelObjectSecurity

Specific:

MUTEX_MODIFY_STATE	0x0002
MUTEX_ALL_ACCESS	(STANDARD_RIGHTS_REQUIRED |
	SYNCHRONIZE |
	0x3)

13.5.14 Semaphores

CreateSemaphore: The handle returned has SEMAPHORE_ALL_ ACCESS rights
   SetKernelObjectSecurity
   GetKernelObjectSecurity

Specific:

SEMAPHORE_MODIFY_ STATE	0x0002
SEMAPHORE_ALL_ACCESS	(STANDARD_RIGHTS_REQUIRED|
	SYNCHRONIZE|
	0x3)

13.5.15 Private Objects

CreatePrivateObjectSecurity
    DestroyPrivateObjectSecurity
    GetPrivateObjectSecurity
    SetPrivateObjectSecurity

13.6 Examining Existing Access Tokens and Security Descriptors

You can learn quite a bit about access tokens and security descriptors by writing and running code that dumps the contents of existing tokens and descriptors. This section contains two different dumping programs. The first dumps an existing process's security descriptor. The second examines the access token of any existing process.

    Processes (along with files and registry keys) are one of the few Windows 2000 objects that you can access without creating the code that creates the object. The process viewer (pview.exe) will give you a list of processes, along with their IDs.

13.6.1 Dumping a Process's Security Descriptor

The code in Listing 13.4 requests a process ID and then obtains and dumps the security descriptor for that process. A process, like any other Windows 2000 object, has a security descriptor, which controls who can access it.

Listing 13.4   *Code that dumps the security descriptor of a process*

```
// psdidump.cpp

#include <windows.h>
#include <iostream.h>
#include <iomanip.h>

VOID main(VOID)
{
  BOOL ret;
  HANDLE procHandle;
  DWORD procID;
  SECURITY_DESCRIPTOR *sdData;
  PSID psid;
  PACL pacl;
  BOOL byDef;
  BOOL haveDACL;
  DWORD sizeRqd;
  CHAR str[80];
```

| Listing 13.4 | *Code that dumps the security descriptor of a process (continued)* |

```
DWORD strSize;
CHAR str2[80];
DWORD str2Size;
SID_NAME_USE sidType;
UINT x;
ACL_SIZE_INFORMATION aclSize;
ACCESS_ALLOWED_ACE *pace;

cout << "Enter process ID to query: ";
cin >> procID;

// get a handle for the process
procHandle=OpenProcess(READ_CONTROL,
  FALSE, procID);
if (procHandle == NULL)
{
  cerr << "Unable to open the process for query."
    << endl;
  return;
}

// find out how much mem is needed
ret=GetKernelObjectSecurity(procHandle,
  OWNER_SECURITY_INFORMATION |
  GROUP_SECURITY_INFORMATION |
  DACL_SECURITY_INFORMATION,
  NULL, 0,
  &sizeRqd);

// allocate that memory
sdData=(SECURITY_DESCRIPTOR *)
  GlobalAlloc(GPTR, sizeRqd);
if (sdData == NULL)
{
  cerr << "Unable to allocate memory." << endl;
  return;
}

// actually get the SD info
ret=GetKernelObjectSecurity(procHandle,
  OWNER_SECURITY_INFORMATION |
  GROUP_SECURITY_INFORMATION |
  DACL_SECURITY_INFORMATION,
  sdData, sizeRqd,
  &sizeRqd);
if (!ret)
{
  cerr << "Unable to get SD info." << endl;
```

```
  return;
}

// close process handle
CloseHandle(procHandle);

// get the owner info
ret=GetSecurityDescriptorOwner(sdData, &psid,
  &byDef);
if (!ret)
{
  cerr << "Unable to get owner info." << endl;
  return;
}

if (psid == NULL)
{
  cout << "SD Owner: NULL"
    << " (No owner)" << endl;
}
else
{
  // specify size of string buffers
  strSize=str2Size=80;

  // convert owner SID into a name and domain
  ret=LookupAccountSid(NULL, psid,
    str, &strSize, str2, &str2Size, &sidType);
  if (!ret)
  {
    cerr << "Unable to look up SID." << endl;
    return;
  }

  cout << "SD owner: \"" << str << "\" from \""
    << str2 << "\"." << endl;
}

// get the group info
ret=GetSecurityDescriptorGroup(sdData, &psid,
  &byDef);
if (!ret)
{
  cerr << "Unable to get group info." << endl;
  return;
}

if (psid == NULL)
{
  cout << "SD Group: NULL"
```

Listing 13.4   *Code that dumps the security descriptor of a process (continued)*

```
    << " (No group)" << endl;
}
else
{
  // specify size of string buffers
  strSize=str2Size=80;

  // convert group SID into a name and domain
  ret=LookupAccountSid(NULL, psid,
    str, &strSize, str2, &str2Size, &sidType);
  if (!ret)
  {
    cerr << "Unable to look up SID." << endl;
    return;
  }

  cout << "SD group: \"" << str << "\" from \""
    << str2 << "\"." << endl;
}

// get the DACL info
ret=GetSecurityDescriptorDacl(sdData,
  &haveDACL, &pacl, &byDef);
if (!ret)
{
  cerr << "Unable to get DACL info." << endl;
  return;
}

if (!haveDACL)
{
  cout << "SD DACL: NULL"
    << " (Unrestricted Access)" << endl;
}
else
{
  // get size info about this DACL
  ret=GetAclInformation(
    pacl, &aclSize, sizeof(ACL_SIZE_INFORMATION),
    AclSizeInformation);
  if (!ret)
  {
    cerr << "Unable to get ACL size info."
      << endl;
    return;
  }

  for (x=0; x<aclSize.AceCount; x++)
```

```
{
  // get ACE info
  ret=GetAce(
    pacl, x, (LPVOID *) &pace);

  // specify size of string buffers
  strSize=str2Size=80;

  // convert ACE SID into a name and domain
  ret=LookupAccountSid(NULL,
    &pace->SidStart,
    str, &strSize, str2, &str2Size, &sidType);
  if (!ret)
  {
    strcpy(str, "       !UNKNOWN!");
    strcpy(str2, "");
  }

  cout << "SD DACL ACE: Type 0x"
    << setiosflags(ios::internal)
    << hex << setw(2) << setfill('0')
    << pace->Header.AceType
    << ", Mask 0x" << setw(8) << pace->Mask
    << resetiosflags(ios::internal)
    << setfill(' ')
    << endl << "                              for \""
    << setw(18) << setiosflags(ios::left)
    << str << "\" from \""
    << setw(12) << str2 << "\"." << endl;
  }
}

// release memory
if(GlobalFree(sdData))
{
  cerr << "Unable to free memory." << endl;
  return;
}

}
```

To run Listing 13.4, first start a copy of the pview application by opening a command window and typing "pview." In the Process list, you will see the names of processes followed by process IDs as hex values in parentheses. Pick a process and note its ID (for example, I picked WINLOGON with an ID of 0x11. If you are not logged in as an administrator, pick a process that you own, such as your program manager). Now run Listing 13.4 and enter the process ID when the program prompts for it. We received the following output for WINLOGON:

```
SD owner: "Administrators" from "BUILTIN".
SD group: "SYSTEM" from "NT AUTHORITY".
SD DACL ACE: Type 0x00, Mask 0x001f0fff
                       for "SYSTEM" from "NT AUTHORITY".
SD DACL ACE: Type 0x00, Mask 0x00120410
                       for "Administrators" from "BUILTIN".
```

Listing 13.4 retrieves the security descriptor from the specified process and dumps the owner, the group, and the ACEs in the DACL. Each ACE contains a header that specifies the type of ACE (access allowed, access denied, audit access), the user it applies to, and the access mask. You can see from the mask of the first ACE in the sample shown just now that the SYSTEM user has full access to the process, while in the second ACE administrators have only partial access.

You can determine exactly what administrators are able to do by looking at the access mask and comparing it with the mask bits in Sections 13.5 and 13.5.6. The access mask contains the 32-bit mask value 0x00120410. The administrator, therefore, has the specific right to read the memory of the process (PROCESS_ VM_READ, 0x0010) and can also query the process (PROCESS_ QUERY_INFORMATION, 0x0400). The administrator can, from the standard rights, read the security descriptor for the process (READ_CONTROL, 0x00020000) and use Wait functions on the process (SYNCHRONIZE, 0x00010000).

From the DACL shown above, you can see that unless you log in as the administrator you will not be able to view the security descriptor for the WINLOGON process, because the security descriptor does not contain an ACE for anyone other than administrators and SYSTEM. However, you will be able to view security descriptors for any process that you own, such as your Program Manager.

The code in Listing 13.4 is straightforward, and demonstrates several security functions that are useful for examining security descriptors. The program first asks the user for the ID of a process to dump, and uses it to open the process. It can then obtain a copy of the process's security descriptor using the **GetKernelObjectSecurity** function. The code uses a two-step process: it calls the function once to figure out how big the security descriptor is, and then allocates the needed memory and calls the function again.

GetKernelObjectSecurity   *Obtains the security descriptor for a kernel object (process, thread, file mapping or token)*

```
BOOL GetKernelObjectSecurity(
   HANDLE objectHandle,
   SECURITY_INFORMATION security,
   PSECURITY_DESCRIPTOR buffer,
   DWORD bufferSize,
   LPDWORD requiredBufferSize)
```

objectHandle   A handle to the kernel object

security	Mask identifying the desired information
buffer	Buffer to hold the returned self-relative security descriptor
bufferSize	The size of buffer
requiredBufferSize	The size of a buffer needed to hold the security descriptor

Returns TRUE on success

The program next retrieves the owner from the security descriptor returned by **GetKernalObjectSecurity**. The **GetSecurityDescriptorOwner** function extracts the SID of the owner from the security descriptor, and the **LookupAccountSid** function converts the SID into a user name.

GetSecurityDescriptorOwner	*Obtains the owner SID from a security descriptor*

```
BOOL GetSecurityDescriptorOwner(
    PSECURITY_DESCRIPTOR psd,
    PSID *sid,
    LPBOOL ownerDefaulted)
```

psd	A pointer to the security descriptor
sid	A pointer to a pointer to a SID structure
ownerDefaulted	Returns a copy of the SE_OWNER_DEFAULTED flag in the boolean pointed to.

Returns TRUE on success

LookupAccountSid	*Looks up the account name of a SID*

```
BOOL LookupAccountSid(
    LPCTSTR system,
    PSID psid,
    LPTSTR accountName,
    LPDWORD accountNameLen,
    LPTSTR domain,
    LPDWORD domainLen,
    PSID_NAME_USE psnu)
```

system	Name of system to look up SID on
psid	A pointer to a SID structure
accountName	A buffer to hold the account name
accountNameLen	The size of the account name buffer
domain	A buffer to hold the name of the domain
domainLen	The size of the domain buffer
psnu	A buffer to hold the SID type

Returns TRUE on success

The **LookupAccountSid** function accepts a system name (or NULL for the local system) and a SID. It returns the name of the account that the SID refers to and the length of the name. It also returns the name of the domain and its length. Finally, it returns a constant identifying the type of SID it is.

Once Listing 13.4 has printed the security descriptor's owner's name, it does the same thing for the security descriptor's group. It calls the **GetSecurityDescriptorGroup** function and then **LookupAccountSid** again.

GetSecurityDescriptorGroup	*Obtains the primary group SID from a security descriptor*

BOOL GetSecurityDescriptorOwner(
    PSECURITY_DESCRIPTOR psd,
    PSID *sid,
    LPBOOL groupDefaulted)	

psd	A pointer to the security descriptor
sid	A pointer to a pointer to a SID structure
groupDefaulted	Returns a copy of the SE_GROUP_DEFAULTED flag in the boolean pointed to.
Returns TRUE on success	

Finally, the program retrieves the DACL and loops through each ACE in it, printing its contents. It starts by calling the **GetSecurityDescriptorDacl** function to get a pointer to the DACL.

GetSecurityDescriptorDacl	*Obtains a pointer to the DACL*

BOOL GetSecurityDescriptorDacl(
    PSECURITY_DESCRIPTOR psd,
    LPBOOL daclPresent,
    PACL *pacl,
    LPBOOL daclDefaulted)	

psd	A pointer to the security descriptor
daclPresent	Returns a boolean indicating that the security descriptor contains a DACL.
pacl	The returned pointer to the DACL
daclDefaulted	Returns a copy of the SE_DACL_DEFAULTED flag in the boolean pointed to.
Returns TRUE on success	

It then gets the number of entries in the DACL by calling the **GetAcl Information** function.

GetAclInformation   *Obtains information about the ACL*

```
BOOL GetAclInformation(
    PACL pacl,
    LPVOID buffer,
    DWORD bufferLen,
    ACL_INFORMATION_CLASS aclClass)
```

pacl	A pointer to the ACL
buffer	The buffer to hold the returned ACL information
bufferLen	The size of the buffer
aclClass	The class of information requested: AclRevisionInformation or AclSize-Information are valid values.

Returns TRUE on success

The **GetAce** function returns the information in each ACE: A type, a SID, and an access mask. The **for** loop calls **GetAce** once for each ACE in the ACL. The program looks up the SID in each ACE as described above.

GetAce   *Retrieves the information in one ACE in the ACL*

```
BOOL GetAce(
    PACL pacl,
    DWORD aceIndex,
    LPVOID *ace)
```

pacl	A pointer to the ACL
aceIndex	The ACE to retrieve
ace	A pointer to a pointer: The function points the pointer to the ace

Returns TRUE on success

Once it has a pointer to the ACE, Listing 13.4 prints out all of the information contained in the ACE and loops back for the next one.

13.6.2 Dumping a Process's Access Token

Listing 13.5 dumps the access token of a process. All of your processes (see Chapter 6 for information on processes) contain a copy of your access token, so this is a way to look at your own access token.

Before you log in, a process called WINLOGON has control of the machine. The WINLOGON process is a SYSTEM process: it runs under the well-known identity SYSTEM, which gives it access to all resources on the machine. Most services run under this same identity. When you log in, the

WINLOGON process authenticates you, creates your access token, and creates your Program Manager window.

Each process running on the system contains an access token, which gives it the right to access certain resources. When WINLOGON creates your Program Manager, it gives it your access token. Every process that you create while you are logged in will be a child of your Program Manager in some way, and every process inherits its copy of the access token from its parent. Therefore, every one of your processes contains a copy of your access token. When you run Listing 13.5 on one of your processes, you are dumping a copy of your access token. Follow the same procedure listed in the previous section for obtaining a process ID from pview, and use it when you run Listing 13.5.

Listing 13.5   *Code that dumps the access token associated with a process*

```
// patidump.cpp

#include <windows.h>
#include <iostream.h>
#include <iomanip.h>

VOID main(VOID)
{
  BOOL ret;
  HANDLE procToken;
  HANDLE procHandle;
  DWORD procID;
  TOKEN_INFORMATION_CLASS tic;
  VOID *tokenData;
  DWORD sizeRqd;
  CHAR str[80];
  DWORD strSize;
  CHAR str2[80];
  DWORD str2Size;
  SID_NAME_USE sidType;
  UINT x;
  DWORD langID;
  ACL_SIZE_INFORMATION aclSize;
  ACCESS_ALLOWED_ACE *pace;

  cout << "Enter process ID to query: ";
  cin >> procID;

  // get a handle for the process
  procHandle=OpenProcess(PROCESS_QUERY_INFORMATION,
    FALSE, procID);
  if (procHandle == NULL)
```

```
{
  cerr << "Unable to open the process for query."
    << endl;
  return;
}

// get a handle for the access token used
// by the process
ret=OpenProcessToken(procHandle,
  TOKEN_QUERY, &procToken);
if (!ret)
{
  cerr
    << "Unable to open the access token."
    << endl;
  return;
}

// close process handle
CloseHandle(procHandle);

// ----- Get user information ----

// specify to return user info
tic=TokenUser;

// find out how much mem is needed
ret=GetTokenInformation(procToken, tic, NULL, 0,
  &sizeRqd);

// allocate that memory
tokenData=(TOKEN_USER *) GlobalAlloc(GPTR,
  sizeRqd);
if (tokenData == NULL)
{
  cerr << "Unable to allocate memory." << endl;
  return;
}

// actually get the user info
ret=GetTokenInformation(procToken, tic,
  tokenData, sizeRqd, &sizeRqd);
if (!ret)
{
  cerr << "Unable to get user info." << endl;
  return;
}

// specify size of string buffers
strSize=str2Size=80;
```

Listing 13.5	*Code that dumps the access token associated with a process (continued)*

```
// convert user SID into a name and domain
ret=LookupAccountSid(NULL,
  ((TOKEN_USER *)tokenData)->User.Sid,
  str, &strSize, str2, &str2Size, &sidType);
if (!ret)
{
  cerr << "Unable to look up SID." << endl;
  return;
}

// release memory
if(GlobalFree(tokenData))
{
  cerr << "Unable to free memory." << endl;
  return;
}

cout << "Token user: \"" << str << "\" from \""
  << str2 << "\"." << endl;

// ----- Get group information -----

// specify to return group info
tic=TokenGroups;

// find out how much mem is needed
ret=GetTokenInformation(procToken, tic, NULL, 0,
  &sizeRqd);

// allocate that memory
tokenData=(TOKEN_GROUPS *) GlobalAlloc(GPTR,
  sizeRqd);
if (tokenData == NULL)
{
  cerr << "Unable to allocate memory." << endl;
  return;
}

// actually get the group info
ret=GetTokenInformation(procToken, tic,
  tokenData, sizeRqd, &sizeRqd);
if (!ret)
{
  cerr << "Unable to get group info." << endl;
  return;
}
```

```
for (x=0;
  x<((TOKEN_GROUPS *)tokenData)->GroupCount;
  x++)
{
  // specify size of string buffers
  strSize=str2Size=80;

  // convert group SID into a name and domain
  ret=LookupAccountSid(NULL,
    ((TOKEN_GROUPS *)tokenData)->Groups[x].Sid,
    str, &strSize, str2, &str2Size, &sidType);
  if (!ret)
  {
    if (((TOKEN_GROUPS *)
      tokenData)->Groups[x].Attributes &
      SE_GROUP_LOGON_ID)
    {
      strcpy(str, "Logon Identifier");
      strcpy(str2, "");
    }
    else
    {
      strcpy(str, "     !UNKNOWN!");
      strcpy(str2, "");
    }
  }

  cout << "Token group: \"" << setw(18)
    << setiosflags(ios::left) << str
    << "\" from \""
    << setw(12) << str2 << "\" w/ attributes 0x"
    << setiosflags(ios::internal)
    << hex << setw(8) << setfill('0')
    << ((TOKEN_GROUPS *)
         tokenData)->Groups[x].Attributes
    << resetiosflags(ios::internal)
    << setfill(' ') << endl;
}

// release memory
if(GlobalFree(tokenData))
{
  cerr << "Unable to free memory." << endl;
  return;
}

// ----- Get privilege information -----

// specify to return privilege info
tic=TokenPrivileges;
```

Listing 13.5   *Code that dumps the access token associated with a process (continued)*

```
// find out how much mem is needed
ret=GetTokenInformation(procToken, tic, NULL, 0,
  &sizeRqd);

// allocate that memory
tokenData=(TOKEN_PRIVILEGES *)
  GlobalAlloc(GPTR, sizeRqd);
if (tokenData == NULL)
{
  cerr << "Unable to allocate memory." << endl;
  return;
}

// actually get the privilege info
ret=GetTokenInformation(procToken, tic,
  tokenData, sizeRqd, &sizeRqd);
if (!ret)
{
  cerr << "Unable to get privilege info."
    << endl;
  return;
}

for (x=0;
  x<((TOKEN_PRIVILEGES *)
     tokenData)->PrivilegeCount;
  x++)
{
  // specify size of string buffers
  strSize=str2Size=80;

  // convert privilege LUID into a name and desc
  ret=LookupPrivilegeName(NULL,
    &((TOKEN_PRIVILEGES *)
    tokenData)->Privileges[x].Luid,
    str, &strSize);
  if (!ret)
  {
    cerr << "Unable to look up LUID." << endl;
    return;
  }

  ret=LookupPrivilegeDisplayName(NULL, str,
    str2, &str2Size, &langID);
  if (!ret)
  {
    cerr << "Unable to look up desc." << endl;
```

```
      return;
    }

    cout << setiosflags(ios::left)
      << "Token privilege: \""
      << setw(26) << str << "\" w/ attributes 0x"
      << setiosflags(ios::internal)
      << hex << setw(8) << setfill('0')
      << ((TOKEN_PRIVILEGES *)
         tokenData)->Privileges[x].Attributes
      << setfill(' ')
      << resetiosflags(ios::internal)
      << endl << "                 Desc: \"" << str2
      << "\""
      << endl;
}

// release memory
if(GlobalFree(tokenData))
{
  cerr << "Unable to free memory." << endl;
  return;
}

// ----- Get default user information -----

// specify to return owner info
tic=TokenOwner;

// find out how much mem is needed
ret=GetTokenInformation(procToken, tic, NULL, 0,
  &sizeRqd);

// allocate that memory
tokenData=(TOKEN_OWNER *) GlobalAlloc(GPTR,
  sizeRqd);
if (tokenData == NULL)
{
  cerr << "Unable to allocate memory." << endl;
  return;
}

// actually get the owner info
ret=GetTokenInformation(procToken, tic,
  tokenData, sizeRqd, &sizeRqd);
if (!ret)
{
  cerr << "Unable to get owner info." << endl;
  return;
}
```

Listing 13.5   *Code that dumps the access token associated with a process (continued)*

```
// specify size of string buffers
strSize=str2Size=80;

// convert owner SID into a name and domain
ret=LookupAccountSid(NULL,
  ((TOKEN_OWNER *)tokenData)->Owner,
  str, &strSize, str2, &str2Size, &sidType);
if (!ret)
{
  cerr << "Unable to look up SID." << endl;
  return;
}

// release memory
if(GlobalFree(tokenData))
{
  cerr << "Unable to free memory." << endl;
  return;
}

cout << "Token default owner: \""
  << str << "\" from \""
  << str2 << "\"." << endl;

// ----- Get default group information -----

// specify to return def DACL info
tic=TokenDefaultDacl;

// find out how much mem is needed
ret=GetTokenInformation(procToken, tic, NULL, 0,
  &sizeRqd);

// allocate that memory
tokenData=(TOKEN_DEFAULT_DACL *)
  GlobalAlloc(GPTR, sizeRqd);
if (tokenData == NULL)
{
  cerr << "Unable to allocate memory." << endl;
  return;
}

// actually get the def DACL info
ret=GetTokenInformation(procToken, tic,
  tokenData, sizeRqd, &sizeRqd);
if (!ret)
```

```
{
  cerr << "Unable to get default DACL info."
    << endl;
  return;
}

if (((TOKEN_DEFAULT_DACL *)tokenData)->
  DefaultDacl == NULL)
{
  cout << "Token default DACL: NULL"
    << " (Unrestricted Access)" << endl;
}
else
{
  // get size info about this DACL
  ret=GetAclInformation(
    ((TOKEN_DEFAULT_DACL *)tokenData)->
      DefaultDacl,
    &aclSize, sizeof(ACL_SIZE_INFORMATION),
    AclSizeInformation);
  if (!ret)
  {
    cerr << "Unable to get ACL size info."
      << endl;
    return;
  }

  for (x=0; x<aclSize.AceCount; x++)
  {
    // get ACE info
    ret=GetAce(
      ((TOKEN_DEFAULT_DACL *)tokenData)->
        DefaultDacl,
      x, (LPVOID *) &pace);

    // specify size of string buffers
    strSize=str2Size=80;

    // convert ACE SID into a name and domain
    ret=LookupAccountSid(NULL, &pace->SidStart,
      str, &strSize, str2, &str2Size, &sidType);
    if (!ret)
    {
      strcpy(str, "     !UNKNOWN!");
      strcpy(str2, "");
    }

    cout << "Token default DACL ACE: Type 0x"
      << setiosflags(ios::internal)
      << hex << setw(2) << setfill('0')
```

Listing 13.5   *Code that dumps the access token associated with a process (continued)*

```
            << pace->Header.AceType
            << ", Mask 0x" << setw(8) << pace->Mask
            << resetiosflags(ios::internal)
            << setfill(' ')
            << endl << "                          for\""
            << setw(18) << setiosflags(ios::left)
            << str << "\" from \""
            << setw(12) << str2 << "\"." << endl;
  }
}

// release memory
if(GlobalFree(tokenData))
{
  cerr << "Unable to free memory." << endl;
  return;
}

// close handle to access token
CloseHandle(procToken);
}
```

When we ran Listing 13.5 on our Program Manager process, we received the following information:

```
Enter process ID to query: 0xa3
Token user: "brain" from "IT".
Token group: "Domain Users      " from "IT           "
        w/ attributes 0x00000007
Token group: "Everyone          " from "             "
        w/ attributes 0x00000007
Token group: "Users             " from "BUILTIN      "
        w/ attributes 0x00000007
Token group: "Administrators    " from "BUILTIN      "
        w/ attributes 0x0000000f
Token group: "Domain Admins     " from "IT           "
        w/ attributes 0x00000007
Token group: "Logon Identifier  " from "             "
        w/ attributes 0xc0000007
Token group: "LOCAL             " from "             "
        w/ attributes 0x00000007
Token group: "INTERACTIVE       " from "NT AUTHORITY"
        w/ attributes 0x00000007
Token privilege: "SeChangeNotifyPrivilege    "
          w/ attributes 0x00000003
          Desc: "Bypass traverse checking"
```

```
Token privilege: "SeShutdownPrivilege          "
          w/ attributes 0x00000000
          Desc: "Shut down the system"
Token privilege: "SeSecurityPrivilege          "
          w/ attributes 0x00000000
          Desc: "Manage auditing and security log"
Token privilege: "SeBackupPrivilege            "
          w/ attributes 0x00000000
          Desc: "Back up files and directories"
Token privilege: "SeRestorePrivilege           "
          w/ attributes 0x00000000
          Desc: "Restore files and directories"
Token privilege: "SeSystemtimePrivilege        "
          w/ attributes 0x00000000
          Desc: "Change the system time"
Token privilege: "SeRemoteShutdownPrivilege "
          w/ attributes 0x00000000
          Desc: "Force shutdown from a remote system"
Token privilege: "SeTakeOwnershipPrivilege  "
          w/ attributes 0x00000000
          Desc: "Take ownership of files or other objects"
Token privilege: "SeDebugPrivilege             "
          w/ attributes 0x00000000
          Desc: "Debug programs"
Token privilege: "SeSystemEnvironmentPrivilege"
          w/ attributes 0x00000000
          Desc: "Modify firmware environment values"
Token privilege: "SeSystemProfilePrivilege  "
          w/ attributes 0x00000000
          Desc: "Profile system performance"
Token privilege: "SeProfileSingleProcessPrivilege"
          w/ attributes 0x00000000
          Desc: "Profile single process"
Token privilege: "SeIncreaseBasePriorityPrivilege"
          w/ attributes 0x00000000
          Desc: "Increase scheduling priority"
Token default owner: "Administrators" from "BUILTIN".
Token default DACL ACE: Type 0x00, Mask 0x10000000
                              for "Administrators" from
"BUILTIN      ".
Token default DACL ACE: Type 0x00, Mask 0x10000000
                              for "SYSTEM       " from
"NT AUTHORITY".
```

An access token, as described in Section 13.3, contains a user ID, a list of groups that the user belongs to, and a set of privileges collected from those groups. The user "brain" is fairly well endowed in terms of privileges and groups, but if you login as "guest" and dump its Program Manager access token, you will find that it is much more sparse.

Listing 13.5 also dumps the default owner and default DACL. These are used when the process creates an object with a default security descriptor. For example, if this user were to run a program that called **CreateFile** and pass it a NULL security attributes structure, then the default owner and DACL are used to create a default security descriptor for the new file.

You can see in the sample output that both the groups and the privileges have *attributes* associated with them. Group attributes are defined as follows:

SE_GROUP_MANDATORY	(0x01) Cannot disable the group
SE_GROUP_ENABLED_BY_ DEFAULT	(0x02) Group enabled by default
SE_GROUP_ENABLED	(0x04) Group enabled
SE_GROUP_OWNER	(0x08) Group is owned by user
SE_GROUP_LOGON_ID	(0xC0000000) Group is logon identifier

Privilege attributes are as follows, and are explained in greater detail in the following section:

SE_PRIVILEGE_ENABLED_BY_DEFAULT	(0x01)
SE_PRIVILEGE_ENABLED	(0x02)
SE_PRIVILEGE_USED_FOR_ACCESS	(0x80000000)

The code in Listing 13.5 is long but straightforward, and follows the same pattern seen in Listing 13.4. For example, to list the groups in the access token, the code in Listing 13.5 does the following (the error-handling code has been removed for clarity):

```
// specify to return group info
tic=TokenGroups;

// find out how much mem is needed
ret=GetTokenInformation(procToken, tic, NULL, 0,
  &sizeRqd);

// allocate that memory
tokenData=(TOKEN_GROUPS *) GlobalAlloc(GPTR,
  sizeRqd);

// actually get the group info
ret=GetTokenInformation(procToken, tic,
  tokenData, sizeRqd, &sizeRqd);

for (x=0;
  x<((TOKEN_GROUPS *)tokenData)->GroupCount;
  x++)
{
  // specify size of string buffers
  strSize=str2Size=80;
```

```
// convert group SID into a name and domain
ret=LookupAccountSid(NULL,
    ((TOKEN_GROUPS *)tokenData)->Groups[x].Sid,
    str, &strSize, str2, &str2Size, &sidType);

cout << "Token group: \"" << setw(18)
    << setiosflags(ios::left) << str
    << "\" from \""
    << setw(12) << str2 << "\" w/ attributes 0x"
    << setiosflags(ios::internal)
    << hex << setw(8) << setfill('0')
    << ((TOKEN_GROUPS *)
            tokenData)->Groups[x].Attributes
    << resetiosflags(ios::internal)
    << setfill(' ') << endl;
}

// release memory
if(GlobalFree(tokenData))
```

The code determines how much space is required to store the group information, allocates that much space, and retrieves the information. It then calls **GetTokenInformation** to find out how many groups exist in the list. The **for** loop cycles through the list, getting the group name of each group with the **LookupAccountSid** function and then printing all of the information for that group.

13.7 Privileges

Access to certain capabilities of the Windows 2000 system is limited by *privileges*. For example, in order to shut down the system, your access token must contain the SE_SHUTDOWN_NAME privilege. To set the system time it must contain the SE_SYSTEMTIME_NAME privilege. The following list shows all of the privileges available in Windows NT:

SE_ASSIGNPRIMARYTOKEN_NAME	Can assign a process's primary token
SE_AUDIT_NAME	Can create audit-log entries
SE_BACKUP_NAME	Can perform backups
SE_CHANGE_NOTIFY_NAME	Can receive file and directory change notifications. Enabled by default for all users
SE_CREATE_PAGEFILE_NAME	Can create a paging file
SE_CREATE_PERMANENT_NAME	Can create a permanent object
SE_CREATE_TOKEN_NAME	Can create a primary token
SE_DEBUG_NAME	Enables process debugging
SE_INC_BASE_PRIORITY_NAME	Can change the priority of a process
SE_INCREASE_QUOTA_NAME	Can change a process's quota

SE_LOAD_DRIVER_NAME	Can load and unload device drivers
SE_LOCK_MEMORY_NAME	Can lock physical memory pages
SE_PROF_SINGLE_PROCESS_NAME	Can obtain profiling data
SE_REMOTE_SHUTDOWN_NAME	Can shut down a system over the network
SE_RESTORE_NAME	Can restore data
SE_SECURITY_NAME	Owner is the security operator Can view security logs, etc.
SE_SHUTDOWN_NAME	Can shut down the system
SE_SYSTEM_ENVIRONMENT_NAME	Can modify configuration information in non-volatile RAM
SE_SYSTEM_PROFILE_NAME	Can profile the entire system
SE_SYSTEMTIME_NAME	Can modify the system time
SE_TAKE_OWNERSHIP_NAME	Can take ownership of an object
SE_TCB_NAME	Owner is part of the trusted computer base
SE_UNSOLICITED_INPUT_NAME	Can read unsolicited input from a terminal

You can see the privileges contained in your access token using the access token dump program in Listing 13.5. You acquire privileges through the User Rights menu option in the User Manager. Generally, rights are associated with groups, and by being a member of a group you acquire its privileges. The administrator can also assign specific rights to specific users.

In a program, you must enable a privilege before you can use it. For example, say that you dump your access token using the code in Listing 13.5, and you see that the SE_SHUTDOWN_NAME privilege is in your list of privileges. You think that you should be able to write a one-line program that reboots your machine using the following line:

```
success = ExitWindowsEx(EWX_REBOOT, 0);
```

When you run this line of code, however, it will fail. Look at the attributes associated with the SE_SHUTDOWN_NAME privilege in the output of the dump program. Privileges have three attribute bits:

SE_PRIVILEGE_ENABLED_BY_DEFAULT	(0x01)
SE_PRIVILEGE_ENABLED	(0x02)
SE_PRIVILEGE_USED_FOR_ACCESS	(0x80000000)

Right now, bit 1 (the SE_PRIVILEGE_ENABLED bit) is set to zero, indicating that the privilege is not enabled. You must enable any privilege before you can use it. Certain privileges are enabled by default, a fact that you can also detect from the attributes of the privilege, but SE_SHUTDOWN_NAME does not happen to be one of them.

Listing 13.6 shows the proper way to enable a privilege before using it. When you run the program, it will reboot your machine. If you prefer to experiment with something more benign than rebooting, see the time-changing code in Chapter 15 for another example. See Chapter 16 for more information on shutting down the system and logging off.

| Listing 13.6 | *Enabling the SE_SHUTDOWN_NAME privilege allows you to reboot the system* |

```
// sireboot.cpp

#include <windows.h>
#include <iostream.h>
#include <process.h>

void HandleError(char *s)
{
    cout << "Error in " << s << endl;
    cout << "Error code = " << GetLastError()
        << endl;
    exit(1);
}

BOOL EnablePrivilege(LPTSTR privilege)
{
    BOOL success;
    HANDLE token;
    LUID luid;
    TOKEN_PRIVILEGES tokenPrivileges;

    // Get token for this process
    success = OpenProcessToken(GetCurrentProcess(),
        TOKEN_ADJUST_PRIVILEGES | TOKEN_QUERY,
        &token);
    if (!success)
    {
        HandleError("OpenProcessToken");
        return FALSE;
    }

    // Gets the value for a privilege
    success = LookupPrivilegeValue(0, privilege,
        &luid);
    if (!success)
    {
        HandleError("LookupPrivilegeValue");
        return FALSE;
    }

    // Enable the privilege
    tokenPrivileges.PrivilegeCount = 1;
    tokenPrivileges.Privileges[0].Luid = luid;
    tokenPrivileges.Privileges[0].Attributes =
        SE_PRIVILEGE_ENABLED;
    success = AdjustTokenPrivileges(token, FALSE,
        &tokenPrivileges, 0, 0, 0);
```

| Listing 13.6 | *Enabling the SE_SHUTDOWN_NAME privilege allows you to reboot the system (continued)* |

```
   // Always returns true, so check GetLastError
   if (GetLastError() != ERROR_SUCCESS)
   {
      HandleError("AdjustTokenPrivileges");
      return FALSE;
   }
   return TRUE;
}


BOOL DisablePrivilege(LPTSTR privilege)
{
   BOOL success;
   HANDLE token;
   LUID luid;
   TOKEN_PRIVILEGES tokenPrivileges;

   // Get tokens for this process
   success = OpenProcessToken(GetCurrentProcess(),
      TOKEN_ADJUST_PRIVILEGES | TOKEN_QUERY,
      &token);
   if (!success)
   {
      HandleError("OpenProcessToken");
      return FALSE;
   }


   // Gets the value for a privilege
   success = LookupPrivilegeValue(0, privilege,
      &luid);
   if (!success)
   {
      HandleError("LookupPrivilegeValue");
      return FALSE;
   }


   // Disable the privilege
   tokenPrivileges.PrivilegeCount = 1;
   tokenPrivileges.Privileges[0].Luid = luid;
   // disable the privilege
   tokenPrivileges.Privileges[0].Attributes = 0;
   success = AdjustTokenPrivileges(token, FALSE,
      &tokenPrivileges, 0, 0, 0);
   // Always returns true, so...
   if (GetLastError() != ERROR_SUCCESS)
   {
      HandleError("AdjustTokenPrivileges");
```

```
        return FALSE;
    }
    return TRUE;
}


void main()
{
    BOOL success;

    if (EnablePrivilege(SE_SHUTDOWN_NAME))
    {
        success = ExitWindowsEx(EWX_REBOOT, 0);
        if (success)
            cout << "Success. Shutting down shortly."
                << endl;
        else
            HandleError("Shutting down");
    }
    DisablePrivilege(SE_SHUTDOWN_NAME);
}
```

The heart of Listing 13.6 is the **EnablePrivilege** function. Given a privilege, this function enables it. Note that it accepts one privilege name as an input parameter. This name must be specified as a string pointer as shown: If you look in the help file, you will find that all privilege constants like SE_SHUTDOWN_NAME are defined as strings.

The goal of the **EnablePrivilege** function is to open the processes token and enable the privilege. It starts by calling **OpenProcessToken**.

OpenProcessToken   *Opens a process's access token so that it can be modified*

```
BOOL OpenProcessToken(
    HANDLE process,
    DWORD accessMask,
    PHANDLE tokenHandle)
```

process	A handle to the process to open
accessMask	The actions that need to be performed on the open token
tokenHandle	A pointer to the token returned by the function

Returns TRUE on success

GetCurrentProcess   *Returns a handle to the current process*

HANDLE GetCurrentProcess(VOID)

Returns a handle to the current process

The access mask passed to **OpenProcessToken** specifies what you plan to do with the access token once you have it open. You can specify any or all of the specific rights shown in Section 13.5.9 for access tokens. Here, the code requests TOKEN_QUERY so that it can get the current value of a privilege and TOKEN_ADJUST_PRIVILEGES so that it can modify a privilege. The **OpenProcessToken** function makes sure that you have the proper authority to perform the requested actions (by looking at the security descriptor on the access token), and if you do, it returns a handle to the token for the process. If you request an access right that you are not allowed to perform on the token, then the function fails. Alternatively, if you do not request the right and later try to perform the action, the later call will fail.

The **EnablePrivilege** function in Listing 13.6 next tries to look up the LUID (Locally Unique Identifier) value of the requested privilege using a call to the **LookupPrivilegeValue** function.

LookupPrivilegeValue   *Retrieves a locally unique identifier for the privilege*

```
BOOL LookupPrivilegeValue(
   LPCTSTR systemName,
   LPCTSTR privilege,
   PLUID pluid)
```

systemName	The name of the system. Pass 0 for the local system
privilege	The privilege to look up
pluid	A pointer that points to the location where the function should return the LUID

Returns TRUE on success

Once it has the LUID value, the program uses it in a TOKEN_ PRIVILEGES structure to modify the privilege:

```
tokenPrivileges.PrivilegeCount = 1;
tokenPrivileges.Privileges[0].Luid = luid;
tokenPrivileges.Privileges[0].Attributes =
   SE_PRIVILEGE_ENABLED;
success = AdjustTokenPrivileges(token, FALSE,
   &tokenPrivileges, 0, 0, 0);
// Always returns true, so check GetLastError
```

A TOKEN_PRIVILEGES structure is defined in the winnt.h file to contain the following fields:

```
typedef struct _TOKEN_PRIVILEGES {
   DWORD PrivilegeCount;
   LUID_AND_ATTRIBUTES Privileges[ANYSIZE_ARRAY];
} TOKEN_PRIVILEGES;
```

The ANYSIZE_ARRAY constant is defined as one, so as declared in this program, you can only change one privilege at a time. When the system returns structures of this type, however, or when you build your own structures of this type, then the array can contain more than one structure.

The LUID_AND_ATTRIBUTES type is also a structure, and it is defined like this in winnt.h:

```
typedef struct LUID_AND_ATTRIBUTES {
    LUID  Luid;
    DWORD Attributes;
} LUID_AND_ATTRIBUTES;
```

The attributes in the LUID_AND_ATTRIBUTES structure are a bit mask that can contain any or all of the following values:

SE_PRIVILEGE_ENABLED_BY_DEFAULT
SE_PRIVILEGE_ENABLED
SE_PRIVILEGE_USED_FOR_ACCESS

In the code in Listing 13.6, the program places the LUID for the SE_SHUTDOWN_NAME privilege, as well as a request to enable it, into the **tokenPrivileges** variable and then passes the variable to the **AdjustToken Privileges** function to enable it.

AdjustTokenPrivileges   *Modifies token privileges as specified, and optionally returns their prior value*

```
BOOL AdjustTokenPrivileges(
    HANDLE tokenHandle,
    BOOL disableAll,
    PTOKEN_PRIVILEGES new,
    DWORD previousSize,
    PTOKEN_PRIVILEGES previous,
    PDWORD previousRequired)
```

tokenHandle	A handle to the token to adjust
disableAll	If TRUE, all privileges in the token are disabled
new	Pointer to TOKEN_PRIVILEGES structure that contains the changes
previousSize	The size of the buffer in previous
previous	Points to a buffer. The function fills this buffer with the previous values of changed privileges
previousRequired	Can be used to find out how much space is needed for the previous buffer

Returns TRUE on success

The code in Listing 13.6 does not request or need the previous value of the privilege, so these values are zero in the call to **AdjustTokenPrivileges**.

At the completion of the **EnablePrivilege** function in Listing 13.6, the requested privilege is enabled. In this case, the requested privilege is SE_SHUTDOWN_NAME, so the program can then proceed to reboot the system. See Chapter 16 for more information on rebooting.

The **DisablePrivilege** function in Listing 13.6 is somewhat superfluous, but shows that disabling privileges involves the exact same process as in **Enable Privilege,** with different attributes. In most cases you will simply enable a privilege in a process and leave it enabled.

You will need to use the principles described here whenever you want to perform any action that requires you to enable a privilege. These actions include such things as shutting down the system, setting the system time, taking ownership of an object, and so on.

13.8 Adding and Deleting ACEs

Listing 13.1 demonstrated how easy it is to create a new security descriptor for any object. Adding ACEs to a new security descriptor that you are creating from scratch is trivial. But what if you want to modify an existing security descriptor by adding or removing ACEs? While conceptually simple, performing additions and deletions to an existing security descriptor takes quite a bit of code because of the difference between *absolute* and *self-relative* security descriptors.

Listing 13.1 at the beginning of the chapter creates a security descriptor in absolute format. It creates a variable of type SECURITY_DESCRIPTOR:

```
SECURITY_DESCRIPTOR sd;
```

The current declaration for the SECURITY_DESCRIPTOR is shown in the following structure declaration copied from winnt.h:

```
typedef struct _SECURITY_DESCRIPTOR {
    BYTE   Revision;
    BYTE   Sbz1;
    SECURITY_DESCRIPTOR_CONTROL Control;
    PSID Owner;
    PSID Group;
    PACL Sacl;
    PACL Dacl;
    } SECURITY_DESCRIPTOR,  *PISECURITY_DESCRIPTOR;
```

In actuality, we are not supposed to look at this structure because it is supposed to be *opaque*. That is, you should only manipulate it using functions supplied in the API, rather than trying to manipulate it directly. Doing it with API functions guarantees that your code will work in the future as the security system matures. However, looking at the structure here doesn't cause any harm, and it allows you to see that a security descriptor is actually made up of five 32-bit values. The first value is a header containing the revision level, a reserved location named Sbz1, and a control value. The next four values are pointers to the four pieces of a security descriptor seen in Figure 13.2.

In Listing 13.1, the program creates the security descriptor by declaring areas of memory, filling them, and then pointing the different pointers in the security descriptor to those areas. The areas might also have been declared on the heap. This is called an *absolute* security descriptor and is pictured in Figure 13.7.

A self-relative security descriptor, on the other hand, is self-contained. This is the sort of security descriptor you obtain when you ask the system to give you a copy of a security descriptor, as in the dump programs in Listings 13.4 and 13.5. The system creates a single block of memory that contains the five words of the security descriptor itself along with all of the elements the four pointers reference. Figure 13.8 shows a self-relative security descriptor.

Looking at Figure 13.8, you can begin to see the problem that arises when you try to change a security descriptor. You request from the system a copy of an existing security descriptor. When it comes back, it is in a self-relative format. If you try to add an ACE into the DACL, you have a problem because there is no room for the new ACE. What you end up having to do, to add an ACE, is turn the entire security descriptor into absolute format, increase the size of the DACL, and add the new ACE to it. You can then pass the absolute security descriptor back to the system to change the security descriptor.

Listing 13.7 demonstrates the process. When you run the program in Listing 13.7, it will obtain the security descriptor for the well-known HKEY_CURRENT_USER key in the registry and add a new ACE to it. Before

Figure 13.7   *An absolute security descriptor points to its different elements*

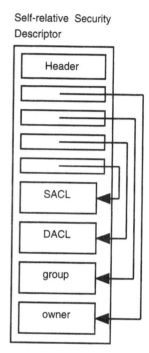

Self-relative Security
Descriptor

Header

SACL

DACL

group

owner

Figure 13.8

An self-relative security descriptor is self-contained

running Listing 13.7, run the Registry Editor (regedt32.exe) and examine the
security permissions for the HKEY_CURRENT_USERS key. Run Listing 13.7,
and then refresh the display to examine the descriptor again. You will find
that it contains a new group called "Administrators" (or you can modify the
code to add any other user or group). The registry is used in this example
simply because all Windows 2000 machines have the registry editor and it
contains a visual security editor. However, if you have an NTFS partition on
your machine you can modify the code slightly to add a new ACE to a file's
DACL instead. This same code will work on the security descriptor of any
Windows 2000 object.

Listing 13.7   *Adding an ACE to an existing ACL*

```
// addace.cpp

#include <windows.h>
#include <iostream.h>

VOID main(VOID)
{
  BOOL ret;
  LONG err;
```

```
SECURITY_DESCRIPTOR *sdData;
SECURITY_DESCRIPTOR absSD;
PSID psid;
PACL pacl;
PACL pNewACL;
DWORD newACLSize;
BOOL byDef;
BOOL haveDACL;
DWORD sizeRqd;
SID_NAME_USE sidType;
DWORD sidSize;
UINT x;
ACL_SIZE_INFORMATION aclSize;
ACCESS_ALLOWED_ACE *pace;
CHAR str[80];
DWORD strSize;

cout << "Adding \"Administrators\" "
  << "to HKEY_CURRENT_USER..."
  << endl;

// ----- Get new group's SID -----

// lookup SID from name
sidSize=0;
strSize=80;
ret=LookupAccountName(NULL, "Administrators", NULL,
  &sidSize, str, &strSize, &sidType);

if (sidSize)
{
  // allocate memory for SID
  psid=(PSID) GlobalAlloc(GPTR, sidSize);
  // actually get SID
  strSize=80;
  ret=LookupAccountName(NULL, "Administrators",
    psid, &sidSize, str, &strSize, &sidType);
  if (!ret)
  {
    cerr << "Unable to get Administrators SID."
      << endl;
    return;
  }
}
else
{
  cerr << "Administrators SID not available. "
    << GetLastError()

    << endl;
```

Listing 13.7   *Adding an ACE to an existing ACL (continued)*

```
    return;
  }


  // ----- Get a copy of the SD/DACL -----

  // find out how much mem is needed
  // to hold existing SD w/DACL
  sizeRqd=0;
  err=RegGetKeySecurity(HKEY_CURRENT_USER,
    DACL_SECURITY_INFORMATION,
    NULL, &sizeRqd);
  if (err != ERROR_INSUFFICIENT_BUFFER)
  {
    cerr << "Unable to get SD size."
      << endl;
    return;
  }


  // allocate that memory
  sdData=(SECURITY_DESCRIPTOR *)
    GlobalAlloc(GPTR, sizeRqd);
  if (sdData == NULL)
  {
    cerr << "Unable to allocate memory." << endl;
    return;
  }


  // actually get the SD info
  err=RegGetKeySecurity(HKEY_CURRENT_USER,
    DACL_SECURITY_INFORMATION,
    sdData, &sizeRqd);
  if (err != ERROR_SUCCESS)
  {
    cerr << "Unable to get SD info." << endl;
    return;
  }


  // ----- Create a new absolute SD and DACL -----

  // initialize absolute SD
  ret=InitializeSecurityDescriptor(&absSD,
    SECURITY_DESCRIPTOR_REVISION);
  if (!ret)
  {
    cerr << "Unable to init new SD."
      << endl;
    return;
  }
```

```
// get the DACL info
ret=GetSecurityDescriptorDacl(sdData,
  &haveDACL, &pacl, &byDef);
if (!ret)
{
  cerr << "Unable to get DACL info." << endl;
  return;
}

if (!haveDACL)
{
  // compute size of new DACL
  newACLSize= sizeof(ACCESS_ALLOWED_ACE) +
    GetLengthSid(psid) - sizeof(DWORD);
}
else
{
  // get size info about existing DACL
  ret=GetAclInformation(pacl, &aclSize,
    sizeof(ACL_SIZE_INFORMATION),
    AclSizeInformation);

  // compute size of new DACL
  newACLSize=aclSize.AclBytesInUse +
    sizeof(ACCESS_ALLOWED_ACE) +
    GetLengthSid(psid) -
    sizeof(DWORD);
}

// allocate memory
pNewACL=(PACL) GlobalAlloc(GPTR, newACLSize);
if (pNewACL == NULL)
{
  cerr << "Unable to allocate memory." << endl;
  return;
}

// initialize the new DACL
ret=InitializeAcl(pNewACL, newACLSize,
  ACL_REVISION);
if (!ret)
{
  cerr << "Unable to init new DACL."
    << endl;
  return;
}

// ----- Copy existing DACL into new DACL -----

if (haveDACL)
```

Listing 13.7   *Adding an ACE to an existing ACL (continued)*

```
{
  // copy ACEs from existing DACL
  // to new DACL
  for (x=0; x<aclSize.AceCount; x++)
  {
    ret=GetAce(pacl, x, (LPVOID *) &pace);
    if (!ret)
    {
      cerr << "Unable to get ACE."
        << endl;
      return;
    }

    ret=AddAce(pNewACL, ACL_REVISION, MAXDWORD,
      pace, pace->Header.AceSize);
    if (!ret)
    {
      cerr << "Unable to add ACE."
        << endl;
      return;
    }
  }
}

// ----- Add the new ACE to the new DACL -----

// add access allowed ACE to new
// DACL
ret=AddAccessAllowedAce(pNewACL,
  ACL_REVISION, GENERIC_ALL, psid);
if (!ret)
{
  cerr << "Unable to add ACE."
    << endl;
  return;
}

// set the new DACL
// in the absolute SD
ret=SetSecurityDescriptorDacl(&absSD,
  TRUE, pNewACL, FALSE);
if (!ret)
{
  cerr << "Unable to install DACL."
    << endl;
  return;
}
```

```
// check the new SD
ret=IsValidSecurityDescriptor(&absSD);
if (!ret)
{
  cerr << "SD invalid."
    << endl;
  return;
}


// ----- Install the new DACL -----


// install the updated SD
err=RegSetKeySecurity(HKEY_CURRENT_USER,
  DACL_SECURITY_INFORMATION,
  &absSD);
if (err != ERROR_SUCCESS)
{
  cerr << "Unable to set registry key SD."
    << endl;
}


// ensure that SD has been updated
RegCloseKey(HKEY_CURRENT_USER);


// release memory
if(GlobalFree(pNewACL))
{
  cerr << "Unable to free memory." << endl;
  return;
}


// release memory
if(GlobalFree(psid))
{
  cerr << "Unable to free memory." << endl;
  return;
}


// release memory
if(GlobalFree(sdData))
{
  cerr << "Unable to free memory." << endl;
  return;
}


  cout << "Done." << endl;
}
```

The code in Listing 13.7 goes through six distinct phases in order to add a new ACE to an existing DACL:

1. Create a SID for the new group to be added to the DACL.
2. Get a copy of the existing DACL for the HKEY_CURRENT_USER key in the registry
3. Create a new absolute security descriptor and a new DACL big enough to hold the old DACL plus one new ACE
4. Copy the old DACL to the new one
5. Add the new ACE to the new DACL
6. Replace the old security descriptor's DACL for HKEY_CURRENT_ USER with the new one

Phase one uses the **LookupAccountName** function to retrieve the SID for the group named "Administrators." If your machine does not support this group, or if you want to use a different user or group, replace "Administrators" with any group you like.

LookupAccountName   *Returns a SID for the specified account*

```
BOOL LookupAccountName(
    LPCTSTR system,
    LPCTSTR accountName,
    PSID psid,
    LPDWORD sidBufferSize,
    LPTSTR domainName,
    LPDWORD domainNameLen,
    PSID_NAME_USE psnu)
```

system	Name of a remote system or 0 for local
accountName	The name of the account to look up
psid	A pointer to a buffer for the returned SID
sidBufferSize	The size of the psid buffer
domainName	A pointer to a buffer for the returned domain name
domainNameLen	Size of the domain name buffer
psnu	Returned enumerated type indicating the type of account

Returns TRUE on success

Phase two uses the **RegGetKeySecurity** function to obtain the existing DACL for the HKEY_CURRENT_USER key in the registry. It would be just as easy to use **GetFileSecurity** to obtain the DACL for a file. The function returns a self-relative security descriptor containing a copy of the key's DACL. As usual, it goes through the two-step process of getting the buffer size required for the copy of the security descriptor and allocating the buffer, and then it actually gets the copy of the security descriptor.

RegGetKeySecurity   *Gets the security descriptor for a registry key*

```
LONG RegGetKeySecurity(
    HKEY keyHandle,
    SECURITY_INFORMATION si,
    PSECURITY_DESCRIPTOR psd,
    LPDWORD secDescLen)
```

keyHandle	Handle to the registry key
si	Flags indicating the desired information from the security descriptor
psd	Pointer to the security descriptor buffer
secDescLen	The size of the buffer

Returns ERROR_SUCCESS on success

You can request any or all of the following pieces of the security descriptor in the **si** parameter:

OWNER_SECURITY_INFORMATION	object's owner
GROUP_SECURITY_INFORMATION	object's group
DACL_SECURITY_INFORMATION	object's DACL
SACL_SECURITY_INFORMATION	object's SACL

If you request all four together, you receive a complete copy of the object's security descriptor. The data always comes back in self-relative format.

Phase three creates a new absolute-format security descriptor. It then looks at the existing DACL and calculates the size required for a new DACL that will hold the existing ACEs plus one new one. If the existing DACL is NULL, then the size of the new DACL is the size of one access-allowed ACE plus the size of the SID that the ACE will contain. The code subtracts the size of one DWORD because the ACE size by default contains one word for the SID, but that space is already accounted for when the code gets the SID's actual size (SIDs are variably-sized objects). If the existing DACL is not NULL, then **GetAclInformation** returns the size of the existing DACL, and this is added to the size of the new ACE and its SID.

GetAclInformation   *Returns information about the specified ACL*

```
BOOL GetAclInformation(
    PACL pacl,
    LPVOID aclInfo,
    DWORD aclInfoSize,
    ACL_INFORMATION_CLASS aic)
```

pacl	A pointer to the ACL
aclInfo	Pointer to a buffer to hold the info
psd	The size of the buffer
aic	ACL_RVISION_INFORMATION or ACL_SIZE_INFORMATION

Returns TRUE on success

Phase four copies the old DACL into the new DACL. Inside a **for** loop, it gets each existing ACE, using **GetAce,** and then adds the ACE to the new DACL with **AddAce**. Phase five then adds the new ACE to the new DACL with **AddAccessAllowedAce**.

GetAce   *Gets the specified ACE from the specified ACL*

```
BOOL GetAce(
    PACL pacl,
    DWORD aceIndex
    LPVOID *ace)
```

pacl	Pointer to the ACL
aceIndex	The ACE to get
ace	Pointer to set with buffer address

Returns TRUE on success

AddAce   *Gets the specified ACE from the specified ACL*

```
BOOL AddAce(
    PACL pacl,
    DWORD revision,
    DWORD index,
    LPVOID aceBuffer,
    DWORD aceBufferLen)
```

pacl	Pointer to the ACL
revision	Must be ACL_REVISION
index	Index pointing to insertion point. 0 for beginning, MAXDWORD for end, or location

| aceBuffer | Buffer holding new ACE(s) |
| aceBufferLen | Size of aceBuffer |

Returns TRUE on success

Phase six completes the process by replacing the old DACL for HKEY_CURRENT_USERS with the new one, using the **RegSetKeySecurity** function. The remainder of the program cleans up allocated memory.

RegSetKeySecurity   *Sets the security descriptor for a registry key*

```
LONG RegSetKeySecurity(
   HKEY keyHandle,
   SECURITY_INFORMATION si,
   PSECURITY_DESCRIPTOR psd)
```

keyHandle	Handle to the registry key
si	Flags indicating the information being set
psd	Pointer to the security descriptor buffer

Returns ERROR_SUCCESS on success

Removing an ACE from an existing security descriptor follows the same pattern as shown in Listing 13.8. After you run Listing 13.7, you can run Listing 13.8 to remove the ACE that 13.7 added.

Listing 13.8   *Removing an ACE from an existing ACL*

```cpp
// remvace.cpp

#include <windows.h>
#include <iostream.h>

VOID main(VOID)
{
  BOOL ret;
  LONG err;
  SECURITY_DESCRIPTOR *sdData;
  SECURITY_DESCRIPTOR absSD;
  PSID psid;
  PACL pacl;
  BOOL byDef;
  BOOL haveDACL;
  DWORD sizeRqd;
  SID_NAME_USE sidType;
  DWORD sidSize;
```

Listing 13.8   *Removing an ACE from an existing ACL (continued)*

```
UINT x;
ACL_SIZE_INFORMATION aclSize;
ACCESS_ALLOWED_ACE *pace;
CHAR str[80];
DWORD strSize;

cout << "Removing \"Administrators\" "
  << "from HKEY_CURRENT_USER..."
  << endl;

// ----- Get SID of group to remove -----

// lookup SID from name
sidSize=0;
strSize=80;
ret=LookupAccountName(NULL, "Administrators", NULL,
  &sidSize, str, &strSize, &sidType);

if (sidSize)
{
  // allocate memory for SID
  psid=(PSID) GlobalAlloc(GPTR, sidSize);
  // actually get SID
  strSize=80;
  ret=LookupAccountName(NULL, "Administrators",
    psid, &sidSize, str, &strSize, &sidType);
  if (!ret)
  {
    cerr << "Unable to get Administrators SID."
      << endl;
    return;
  }
}
else
{
  cerr << "Administrators SID not available."
    << endl;
  return;
}

// ----- Get the existing DACL -----

// find out how much mem is needed
// to hold existing SD w/DACL
sizeRqd=0;
err=RegGetKeySecurity(HKEY_CURRENT_USER,
  DACL_SECURITY_INFORMATION,
  NULL, &sizeRqd);
```

```
if (err != ERROR_INSUFFICIENT_BUFFER)
{
  cerr << "Unable to get SD size."
    << endl;
  return;
}

// allocate that memory
sdData=(SECURITY_DESCRIPTOR *)
  GlobalAlloc(GPTR, sizeRqd);
if (sdData == NULL)
{
  cerr << "Unable to allocate memory." << endl;
  return;
}

// actually get the SD info
err=RegGetKeySecurity(HKEY_CURRENT_USER,
  DACL_SECURITY_INFORMATION,
  sdData, &sizeRqd);
if (err != ERROR_SUCCESS)
{
  cerr << "Unable to get SD info." << endl;
  return;
}

// ----- Create a new absolute SD -----

// initialize absolute SD
ret=InitializeSecurityDescriptor(&absSD,
  SECURITY_DESCRIPTOR_REVISION);
if (!ret)
{
  cerr << "Unable to init new SD."
    << endl;
  return;
}

// get the DACL info
ret=GetSecurityDescriptorDacl(sdData,
  &haveDACL, &pacl, &byDef);
if (!ret)
{
  cerr << "Unable to get DACL info." << endl;
  return;
}

// ----- Search the DACL and delete ACE -----

if (!haveDACL)
```

| Listing 13.8 | *Removing an ACE from an existing ACL (continued)*   { |

```
    cout << "Security Descriptor DACL is NULL."
      << endl;
}
else
{
  // get size info about existing DACL
  ret=GetAclInformation(pacl, &aclSize,
    sizeof(ACL_SIZE_INFORMATION),
    AclSizeInformation);

  // remove Domain Users from DACL
  for (x=aclSize.AceCount; x>0; x--)
  {
    ret=GetAce(pacl, x - 1, (LPVOID *) &pace);
    if (!ret)
    {
      cerr << "Unable to get ACE."
        << endl;
      return;
    }

    ret=EqualSid(&pace->SidStart, psid);
    if (ret)
    {
      cout << "Deleting an ACE..."
        << endl;
      ret=DeleteAce(pacl, x - 1);
      if (!ret)
      {
        cerr << "Unable to delete ACE."
          << endl;
        return;
      }
    }
  }
}

// ----- Add the DACL to absolute SD and install

  // set the new DACL
  // in the absolute SD
  ret=SetSecurityDescriptorDacl(&absSD,
    TRUE, pacl, FALSE);
  if (!ret)
  {
    cerr << "Unable to install DACL."
      << endl;
    return;
  }
```

```
   // check the new SD
   ret=IsValidSecurityDescriptor(&absSD);
   if (!ret)
   {
     cerr << "SD invalid."
       << endl;
     return;
   }

   // install the updated SD
   err=RegSetKeySecurity(HKEY_CURRENT_USER,
     DACL_SECURITY_INFORMATION,
     &absSD);
   if (err != ERROR_SUCCESS)
   {
     cerr << "Unable to set registry key SD."
       << endl;
   }

   // ensure that SD has been updated
   RegCloseKey(HKEY_CURRENT_USER);
 }

// release memory
if(GlobalFree(psid))
{
  cerr << "Unable to free memory." << endl;
  return;
}

// release memory
if(GlobalFree(sdData))
{
  cerr << "Unable to free memory." << endl;
  return;
}

cout << "Done." << endl;
}
```

To delete an ACE in an existing security descriptor, Listing 13.8 goes through six phases. Its first three phases mirror those of Listing 13.7:

1. Create a SID for the group to be deleted from the DACL

2. Get a copy of the existing DACL for the HKEY_CURRENT_USER key in the registry

3. Create a new absolute security descriptor

4. Scan the self-relative DACL for the ACE to delete and delete it if found

5. Install the modified DACL in the absolute security descriptor
6. Install the new DACL in HKEY_CURRENT_USER using the new absolute security descriptor

Phase one uses the **LookupAccountName** function to retrieve the SID for the group named "Administrators." If you want to use a different user or group, replace "Administrators" with anything you like.

Phase two uses the **RegGetKeySecurity** function to obtain the existing DACL for the HKEY_CURRENT_USER key in the registry. It would be just as easy to use **GetFileSecurity** to obtain the DACL for a file. The function returns a self-relative security descriptor containing a copy of the key's DACL. As usual, it goes through the two-step process of getting the buffer size required for the copy of the security descriptor and allocating the buffer, and then it actually gets the copy of the security descriptor.

Phase three creates a new absolute-format security descriptor. Unlike in Listing 13.7, it does not create a new DACL. Instead, Listing 13.8 will delete the ACE from the DACL returned in Phase two.

Phase four uses **GetAclInformation** to get the number of ACEs in the DACL. It then uses a **for** loop to look at each ACE in the DACL until it finds one containing the SID it is looking for. The **EqualSid** function compares SIDs for equality. Once it finds an appropriate ACE, it deletes it with **DeleteAce**.

EqualSid	*Compares two SIDs*

BOOL EqualSid(
    PSID psid1,
    PSID psid2)	

psid1	The first SID
psid2	The second SID
Returns TRUE on success	

DeleteAce	*Deletes the specified ACE from the specified ACL*

BOOL DeleteAce(
    PACL pacl,
    DWORD aceIndex)	

pacl	Pointer to the ACL
aceIndex	The ACE to delete
Returns TRUE on success	

Phase five sets the newly modified DACL into the absolute security descriptor using the **SetSecurityDescriptorDacl** function. It then verifies the

new security descriptor with **IsValidSecurityDescriptor** before installing it
with **RegSetKeySecurity** in Phase six.

SetSecurityDescriptorDacl　　　*Sets a DACL into an absolute security descriptor*

```
BOOL SetSecurityDescriptorDacl(
    PSECURITY_DESCRIPTOR psd,
    BOOL daclPresent,
    PACL pacl,
    BOOL daclDefaulted)
```

psd	Pointer to the security descriptor
daclPresent	Pass FALSE to create a NULL DACL
pacl	Pointer to the ACL
daclDefaulted	Pass TRUE if you got the DACL from somewhere else, or FALSE if you created or modified it yourself

Returns TRUE on success

IsValidSecurityDescriptor　　　*Checks a security descriptor for validity*

```
BOOL IsValidSecurityDescriptor(
    PSECURITY_DESCRIPTOR psd)
```

psd	Pointer to the security descriptor

Returns TRUE on success

You can apply the principles described above for adding and removing
ACEs to any ACL in a Windows 2000 system. The amount of code required is
a bit bothersome, but the process is straightforward.

13.9 Impersonation

Sections 11.4 and 11.5 deal with named pipes. In all of the code samples in
those sections, a named pipe server runs on one machine, and a named pipe
client connects to the server and sends it messages. The client can run on the
same machine as the server, or it can run on a different machine and connect
over the network. You may recall that all through those sections you were
warned that if you run the client on a different machine, *you should make
sure that the logon ID and password used on the server and client machine
are the same.* The reason for this admonition stems from the way that the security system handles default security descriptors.

　　The named pipe code in Chapter 11 creates all of its pipes with the following sort of call:

```
/* Create a named pipe for receiving messages */
ssnpPipe=CreateNamedPipe("\\\\.\\pipe\\ssnp",
  PIPE_ACCESS_INBOUND,
  PIPE_TYPE_MESSAGE | PIPE_WAIT,
  1, 0, 0, 150, 0);
```

The last parameter in the list is the security-attributes parameter, and it is set to 0. This tells Windows 2000 to create a *default security descriptor* for the new pipe. The default security descriptor contains a default DACL. If you go back to Section 13.6 and run the access token dumping program in Listing 13.5, you can see what your default DACL contains.

You will notice that your default DACL is specific to you. It allows only you or the Windows 2000 system itself to access the object. This is fine for normal objects like processes, threads, and semaphores, because you are the only one logged into the Windows 2000 machine. However, when this default DACL is applied to the server end of a named pipe, it restricts the users who can connect to the pipe: Only you can connect. Therefore, when you try to connect from another machine, the account that you logon with must have the exact same name and password as the account on the server machine. If the network has a domain controller, then this is guaranteed as long as you use the same account on both machines.

If you want to create a server that *any* user can connect to, then you need to create a security descriptor with a NULL DACL. As discussed earlier, a NULL DACL is understood by the system to mean "any user can access this object." You would therefore use the following code to create a pipe that any user can access:

```
InitializeSecurityDescriptor(&sd,
  SECURITY_DESCRIPTOR_REVISION);
SetSecurityDescriptorDacl(&sd, TRUE, NULL,
  FALSE);
sa.nLength= sizeof(SECURITY_ATTRIBUTES);
sa.bInheritHandle = FALSE;
sa.lpSecurityDescriptor = &sd;

/* Create a named pipe for receiving messages */
ssnpPipe=CreateNamedPipe("\\\\.\\pipe\\ssnp",
  PIPE_ACCESS_INBOUND,
  PIPE_TYPE_MESSAGE | PIPE_WAIT,
  1, 0, 0, 150, &sa);
```

Try this in Listing 13.3 to prove that it works correctly and that anyone can connect to the resulting pipe.

Letting anyone connect to a named pipe server creates a potential problem, however. Let's say that the goal of the server is to let the user execute certain commands remotely. Let's say that one of those commands is a file-delete command. Once the user connects, the user has the user ID *of the server process on the remote machine.* If the server is implemented as a Windows 2000 service (see Chapter 12), then the server has SYSTEM privileges, and therefore so does the remote user. The remote user can therefore delete any file on the system.

What you would like instead is for the server to take on the identity of the client user while the user is connected. That way the client user can access only those files that are appropriate to him or her. Windows 2000 provides a function that does this, called **ImpersonateNamedPipeClient**, as demonstrated in Listing 13.9.

Listing 13.9   *Impersonating another user in a named pipe server*

```cpp
// imprecv.cpp

#include <windows.h>
#include <iostream.h>

int main(void)
{
  char toDisptxt[80];
  HANDLE ssnpPipe;
  DWORD NumBytesRead;
  char buffer[80];
  DWORD bufferLen;
  SECURITY_ATTRIBUTES sa;
  SECURITY_DESCRIPTOR sd;

  InitializeSecurityDescriptor(&sd,
    SECURITY_DESCRIPTOR_REVISION);
  SetSecurityDescriptorDacl(&sd, TRUE, NULL,
    FALSE);
  sa.nLength= sizeof(SECURITY_ATTRIBUTES);
  sa.bInheritHandle = FALSE;
  sa.lpSecurityDescriptor = &sd;

  /* Create a named pipe for receiving messages */
  ssnpPipe=CreateNamedPipe("\\\\.\\pipe\\ssnp",
    PIPE_ACCESS_INBOUND,
    PIPE_TYPE_MESSAGE | PIPE_WAIT,
    1, 0, 0, 150, &sa);

  /* Check and see if the named pipe was created */
  if (ssnpPipe == INVALID_HANDLE_VALUE)
  {
    cerr << "ERROR: Unable to create a named pipe."
      << endl;
    return (1);
  }
```

Listing 13.9   *Impersonating another user in a named pipe server (continued)*

```
bufferLen = 80;
GetUserName(buffer, &bufferLen);
cout << "Right now my user is: "
  << buffer
  << endl;
cout << "Waiting for connection..." << endl;

/* Allow a client to connect to the name pipe,
   terminate if unsuccessful */
if(!ConnectNamedPipe(ssnpPipe,
  (LPOVERLAPPED) NULL))
{
  cerr << "ERROR: Unable to connect a pipe "
    << GetLastError() << endl;
  CloseHandle(ssnpPipe);
  return (1);
}

cout << "Beginning impersonation...\n";

if (!ImpersonateNamedPipeClient(ssnpPipe))
{
  cerr << "ERROR: Cannot impersonate, "
    << GetLastError() << endl;
  CloseHandle(ssnpPipe);
  return(1);
}

bufferLen = 80;
GetUserName(buffer, &bufferLen);
cout << "Now my user is: "
  << buffer << endl;

/* Repeatedly check for messages until
   the program is terminated */
while(1)
{
  /* Read the message and check to see if read
     was successful */
  if (!ReadFile(ssnpPipe, toDisptxt,
    sizeof(toDisptxt),
    &NumBytesRead, (LPOVERLAPPED) NULL))
  {
    cerr << "ERROR: Unable to read from pipe"
      << endl;
    CloseHandle(ssnpPipe);
    break;
  }
```

```
        /* Display the Message */
        cout << toDisptxt << endl;

    } /* while */

    cout << "Reverting back to original user.\n";
    RevertToSelf();

    bufferLen = 80;
    GetUserName(buffer, &bufferLen);
    cout << "Now my user is: "
        << buffer
        << endl;
}
```

To test Listing 13.9, follow the same procedure used to test Listing 13.3. Compile and execute Listing 13.9 on one machine. It will display a message that indicates its current user ID. Logon to another machine with a different ID, and use the code in Listing 11.7 to connect to the server. Listing 13.9 will recognize the connection, and then immediately copy the access token of the connected client into its thread. It will display its new identity. When you kill off the client, the server will revert back to its former identity using **RevertToSelf**. You should be able to connect to the server using any logon ID.

The call to **ImpersonateNamedPipeClient** causes the calling thread to take on the access token of the thread connected to the other end of the named pipe specified.

ImpersonateNamedPipeClient   *Causes the calling thread to take on the access token of a connected client thread*

```
BOOL ImpersonateNamedPipeClient(
    HANDLE namedPipe)
```

namedPipe   The server end of a named pipe

Returns TRUE on success

The **RevertToSelf** function causes the calling thread to revert back to the access token of its parent process.

RevertToSelf   *Causes a thread to revert to the access token of its parent process*

```
BOOL RevertToSelf(VOID)
```

Returns TRUE on success

In a multiple-client server like the ones shown in Section 8.5, each separate client thread can take on a different identity using the same technique. You can create extremely robust and secure servers using impersonation.

13.10 Conclusion

The Windows 2000 security system is quite extensive. This chapter covers all of the basic concepts, and shows you the techniques you will need in order to handle the vast majority of common security situations. You can learn more by reading through the function descriptions in the security portion of the Win32 help file (start at Security Overview and branch out from there), and by creating simple experiments to test out the different concepts.

Consoles

There are many situations in which an application does not require a full-blown graphical user interface. For example, most of the programs presented in this book are strictly text programs that produce text output in the command window. The terminal emulator presented in Chapter 11 is another example of this. The 32-bit API provides a facility called consoles *that is useful in these situations.*

Consoles are a convenience: They manage a two-dimensional array of characters for you and automatically handle input and display. Thus they make it very easy to create character-mode applications. If you write a text program that runs on the command line and uses **cin** and **cout**, you are using the API's console capabilities implicitly. In other situations, you use them explicitly. In this chapter you will learn how to take advantage of both the "raw" and the "cooked" console modes in your applications.

Compatibility Note: All of the code in this chapter works identically in Windows 2000 and Windows 98.

14.1 The Possibilities

The MS-DOS prompt window is built around a console, and in that form it is immediately recognizable. The console API provides a two-dimensional array of characters that scroll upward when the cursor hits the bottom of the window. The four most common ways to use a console are as follows:

1. If you want to create your own custom command interpreter to replace the MS-DOS prompt, you should use the console library.

2. If you want to add console input or output to a normal GUI or MFC program, you do that using consoles. For example, while debugging an MFC program, you might want to stream a set of coordinates out to a console as you are painting lines on a screen so that you can check the coordinates.

3. If you want to port a full-screen text program over to Windows, probably the easiest way to do it is through a console.

4. Any character-mode program in which you need raw character-by-character access to the input stream is a good candidate for a console. If you run a program from the MS-DOS window as is, you can only access input a line at a time. The console commands let you switch over to a raw character-by-character mode. The terminal program demonstrated in Chapter 11 is a good example of this technique.

If you write any text-based program using either the stdio or iostream libraries and then run it in an MS-DOS window, you are using the console mode without even realizing it. You can use the console functions to add some interesting capabilities. For example, you can add color to the display and accept mouse input.

14.2 Raw versus Cooked Input

UNIX systems have long used the words *raw* and *cooked* to define the two different modes of character input. The same terminology applies to console input in the 32-bit API.

Cooked input is the normal input mode for console windows. It is what you get when you use **cout** and **cin,** or **printf** and **gets**, in a normal MS-DOS window. Cooked input is line-at-a-time input. The user types characters, but you do not receive any of the input until the user presses the Enter key. At that point, the entire line of characters gets placed into the input buffer, and you can access characters one at a time with **getc** or a line at a time with **gets**. The **getc** function, however, will not return anything *until* the user presses the return key.

Cooked-mode input is nice for most command-driven programs, because all that the program cares about is a complete command line. Cooked-mode input also allows the input functions to handle the backspace key automatically. Since no input appears in the input buffer until the user hits return, the system can delete characters when the user hits the backspace key.

If you are trying to create a text editor, however, cooked-mode input is infuriating. In a text editor, you want to receive each character *as it is typed,* and cooked-mode input does not allow that. Raw-input mode places each character into the input buffer when it is received, and lets you use it immediately in your code. In Windows, the raw input mode also gives you access to mouse input, so you can let the user use the mouse in a variety of ways. For example, you might use the mouse to let the user select areas of text. When retrieving characters, in the raw input mode, you can either retrieve the characters, by waiting for them with a normal **ReadFile** statement that retrieves one character, or you can use overlapped input that allows you to do other processing until a character arrives.

14.3 Simple Examples

To get a feel for the console's capabilities, let's start with two simple examples. The first one, shown in Listing 14.1, demonstrates the simplest possible use of a console in cooked mode. When you run the program, it will echo input line by line until you type the word "exit."

Listing 14.1   *A simple console program*

```
// cooked.cpp

#include <windows.h>
#include <iostream.h>
#include <string.h>

void ErrorHandler(char *s, DWORD err)
{
   cout << s << endl;
   cout << "Error number: " << err << endl;
   ExitProcess(err);
}

void ProcessIO(HANDLE consoleStdin,
   HANDLE consoleStdout)
{
   char buffer[1000];
   DWORD numRead, numWrite;

   do
   {
      ReadFile(consoleStdin, buffer,
         1000, &numRead, 0);
      buffer[numRead]='\0'; // will have CR/LF
      WriteFile(consoleStdout,
         buffer, strlen(buffer),
```

Listing 14.1   *A simple console program (continued)*

```
            &numWrite, 0);
    } while  (strncmp(buffer, "exit", 4) != 0);
}


VOID main(void)
{
    HANDLE consoleStdout, consoleStdin;

    // Get handles for standard in and out
    consoleStdin = GetStdHandle(STD_INPUT_HANDLE);
    consoleStdout = GetStdHandle(STD_OUTPUT_HANDLE);
    // they must be invalid if equal
    if (consoleStdin == consoleStdout)
        ErrorHandler("In GetStdHandle",
            GetLastError());

    // Process user I/O
    ProcessIO(consoleStdin, consoleStdout);
}
```

The program starts by retrieving the standard input and standard output handles for the process. Every process, even those using graphical user interfaces, have standard input, output, and error handles that you can access using the **GetStdHandle** function.

GetStdHandle	*Retrieves a process's handle to stdin, stdout or stderr*

```
HANDLE GetStdHandle(
  DWORD device)
```

Device	Possible values: STD_INPUT_HANDLE, STD_OUTPUT_HANDLE, STD_ERROR_HANDLE

Returns a handle to the requested device or INVALID_HANDLE_VALUE

Once you have the handles, you can read and write using the normal **ReadFile** and **WriteFile** commands seen in Chapter 2. Each time the user presses the return key, the **ReadFile** statement retrieves one line of input from the buffer.

If you run Listing 14.1 from a normal MS-DOS window, the program will make use of the existing window's input and output buffers. The program *inherits* the console of the process that spawned it, if that process has a console. If the originating process does not have a console—for example, if you launch the executable for Listing 14.1 from the File Manager—then a new console is created automatically. The system recognizes that it is a console mode program and creates the console it needs for its input and output.

It is also possible to detach from the originating process's console and create a new one, as demonstrated in Listing 14.2. This listing also shows how to detach from the console of the launching program and create a new console. If you run Listing 14.1 from an MS-DOS prompt it will use the MS-DOS window as its console. On the other hand, if you run Listing 14.2 from the same MS-DOS window, it will create its own, separate console window for its input and output.

Listing 14.2   *Creating a separate console*

```cpp
// cooked2.cpp

#include <windows.h>
#include <iostream.h>
#include <string.h>

void ErrorHandler(char *s, DWORD err)
{
   cout << s << endl;
   cout << "Error number: " << err << endl;
   ExitProcess(err);
}

void ProcessIO(HANDLE consoleStdin,
   HANDLE consoleStdout)
{
   char buffer[1000];
   DWORD numRead, numWrite;

   do
   {
      ReadFile(consoleStdin, buffer,
         1000, &numRead, 0);
      buffer[numRead]='\0';
      WriteFile(consoleStdout, buffer,
         strlen(buffer), &numWrite, 0);
   } while  (strncmp(buffer, "exit", 4) != 0);
}

VOID main(void)
{
   HANDLE consoleStdout, consoleStdin;
   BOOL success;

   success = FreeConsole();
   if (!success)
```

Listing 14.2   *Creating a separate console (continued)*

```
        ErrorHandler("In FreeConsole",
            GetLastError());
    success = AllocConsole();
    if (!success)
        ErrorHandler("In AllocConsole",
            GetLastError());

    // Get handles for standard in and out
    consoleStdin = GetStdHandle(STD_INPUT_HANDLE);
    consoleStdout = GetStdHandle(STD_OUTPUT_HANDLE);
    // they must be invalid if equal
    if (consoleStdin == consoleStdout)
        ErrorHandler("In GetStdHandle",
            GetLastError());

    // Process user I/O
    ProcessIO(consoleStdin, consoleStdout);

    success = FreeConsole();
    if (!success)
        ErrorHandler("In FreeConsole",
            GetLastError());
}
```

The program in Listing 14.2 starts with a call to **FreeConsole**.

FreeConsole   *Detaches the process from its spawning console*

```
BOOL FreeConsole(VOID)
```

Returns TRUE on success

The call to **FreeConsole** in Listing 14.2 detaches the new process from the console it inherited when it started. If it starts from an MS-DOS prompt, the call to **FreeConsole** detaches it from the MS-DOS window and leaves the process "floating" for a moment, with no way to communicate. If a process calls **FreeConsole** and no other process is using that console, the existing console closes.

The subsequent call to **AllocConsole** in Listing 14.2 creates a new console.

AllocConsole   *Creates a new console for the process calling the function*

```
BOOL AllocConsole(VOID)
```

Returns TRUE on success

Once it has created a console, Listing 14.2 gets the input and output handles for it, and begins reading and writing.

You can use the **AllocConsole** function to allocate a console for your GUI applications as well. For example, if you create an application using MFC, as described in the book Visual C++: Developing Professional Applications for Windows 98 and NT using MFC, by Marshall Brain and Lance Lovette (ISBN 0-13-085121-3), then the program lacks a console by default. There are many situations in which a console for such a program would be useful, however, especially during debugging. For example, you can stream pixel coordinates and other variables out to the console during the run, and examine them while the program is on the screen. You can send this sort of output to a console using a normal **cout** statement. Listing 14.3 shows how to create a console inside an MFC program.

Listing 14.3   *Allocating a console inside an MFC program*

```
// button.cpp

#include <afxwin.h>
#include <iostream.h>

#define IDB_BUTTON 100

// Declare the handles for the console
HANDLE consoleStdout, consoleStdin;

// Declare the application class
class CButtonApp : public CWinApp
{
public:
   virtual BOOL InitInstance();
};

// Create an instance of the application class
CButtonApp ButtonApp;

// Declare the main window class
class CButtonWindow : public CFrameWnd
{
   CButton *button;
public:
   CButtonWindow();
   ~CButtonWindow();
   afx_msg void HandleButton();

   DECLARE_MESSAGE_MAP()
};
```

Listing 14.3 *Allocating a console inside an MFC program (continued)*

```
// The message handler function
void CButtonWindow::HandleButton()
{
   DWORD n;

   Beep(700,100);
   // Two different ways to write to the console
   WriteFile(consoleStdout, "hello\n", 6, &n, 0);
   cout << "test string" << endl;
}

// The message map
BEGIN_MESSAGE_MAP(CButtonWindow, CFrameWnd)
   ON_COMMAND(IDB_BUTTON, HandleButton)
END_MESSAGE_MAP()

// The InitInstance function is called once
// when the application first executes
BOOL CButtonApp::InitInstance()
{
   // Create an auxiliary console for cout to use.
   // As soon as this function returns you
   // can write to it.
   AllocConsole();

   // Get handles for standard in and out
   consoleStdin = GetStdHandle(STD_INPUT_HANDLE);
   consoleStdout = GetStdHandle(STD_OUTPUT_HANDLE);
   // they must be invalid if equal
   if (consoleStdin == consoleStdout)
      return FALSE;

   m_pMainWnd = new CButtonWindow();
   m_pMainWnd->ShowWindow(m_nCmdShow);
   m_pMainWnd->UpdateWindow();

   return TRUE;
}

// The constructor for the window class
CButtonWindow::CButtonWindow()
{
   CRect r;

   // Create the window itself
   Create(NULL,
      "CButton Tests",
      WS_OVERLAPPEDWINDOW,
      CRect(0,0,200,200));
```

```
    // Get the size of the client rectangle
    GetClientRect(&r);
    r.InflateRect(-20,-20);

    // Create a button
    button = new CButton();
    button->Create("Push me",
        WS_CHILD|WS_VISIBLE|BS_PUSHBUTTON,
        r,
        this,
        IDB_BUTTON);
}


// The destructor for the window class
CButtonWindow::~CbuttonWindow()
{
    delete button;
    CFrameWnd::~CFrameWnd();
}
```

When you run the program shown in Listing 14.3, you will see a button as well as a new console associated with the program. When you click the button, output will appear in the console. As the program demonstrates, you can use either the **WriteFile** function or the **cout** function to write to the console. In the **InitInstance** function for the application, the calls to **AllocConsole** and **GetStdHandle** create and attach the console.

14.4 Raw Input

One of the nicest things about the examples in the previous section is that they are so simple. In Listing 14.1, for example, the program allocates a console, gets its handles, and begins writing to it. The console automatically handles backspacing, scrolling, and so on.

There are many situations, however, where you would like more control over the input and output streams. For example, you may want to retrieve characters one at a time as the user enters them. To do this, you need to get raw input from the console. Alternatively, you can create a GUI program and retrieve characters in the normal event-driven manner from the event queue. Using raw input from consoles is generally easier because it ensures that the console continues to manage the two-dimensional output array for you, and this simplifies text output considerably.

Listing 14.4 demonstrates how to get one character at a time from the input stream, using the raw input mode.

Listing 14.4   *Retrieving one character at a time from the input stream using the raw input mode*

```cpp
// raw.cpp

#include <windows.h>
#include <iostream.h>

void ErrorHandler(char *s, DWORD err)
{
   cout << s << endl;
   cout << "Error number: " << err << endl;
   ExitProcess(err);
}

void ScrollOneLine(HANDLE stdout)
{
   BOOL success;
   CONSOLE_SCREEN_BUFFER_INFO consoleInfo;
   SMALL_RECT scrollRect;
   CHAR_INFO consoleFill;
   COORD coord;

   // get current console size (may change)
   success = GetConsoleScreenBufferInfo(stdout,
      &consoleInfo);
   if (!success)
         ErrorHandler(
            "In GetConsoleScreenBufferInfo",
            GetLastError());

   // Define the rectangle to scroll
   scrollRect.Top = 0;
   scrollRect.Left = 0;
   scrollRect.Bottom = consoleInfo.dwSize.Y - 1;
   scrollRect.Right = consoleInfo.dwSize.X - 1;

   // Define destination of scrolled rectangle
   coord.X = 0;
   coord.Y = -1;

   // Define how to fill blank line
   consoleFill.Attributes =
      consoleInfo.wAttributes;
   consoleFill.Char.AsciiChar = ' ';

   // Perform the scroll
   success = ScrollConsoleScreenBuffer(stdout,
      &scrollRect, 0,
      coord, &consoleFill);
   if (!success)
```

```
         ErrorHandler("In ScrollConsoleScreenBuffer",
            GetLastError());

}

VOID HandleCR(HANDLE stdout)
{
    CONSOLE_SCREEN_BUFFER_INFO consoleInfo;
    BOOL success;

    success = GetConsoleScreenBufferInfo(stdout,
        &consoleInfo);
    if (!success)
        ErrorHandler("In GetConsoleScreenBufferInfo",
            GetLastError());

    // Move cursor to far left
    consoleInfo.dwCursorPosition.X = 0;

    // If the cursor is on the last line of
    // the console, then scroll the console,
    // else increment position
    if (consoleInfo.dwSize.Y - 1 ==
        consoleInfo.dwCursorPosition.Y)
        ScrollOneLine(stdout);
    else
        consoleInfo.dwCursorPosition.Y += 1;

    // Update the console
    success = SetConsoleCursorPosition(stdout,
        consoleInfo.dwCursorPosition);
    if (!success)
        ErrorHandler("In SetConsoleCursorPosition",
            GetLastError());
}

void ProcessIO(HANDLE stdin, HANDLE stdout)
{
    char buffer;
    DWORD numRead, numWrite;

    do
    {
        ReadFile(stdin, &buffer, 1, &numRead, NULL);
        if (buffer == '\r')
            HandleCR(stdout);
        else
            WriteFile(stdout, &buffer, 1,
                            &numWrite, NULL);
    } while  (buffer != 'X');
}
```

Listing 14.4   *Retrieving one character at a time from the input stream using the raw input mode (continued)*

```
VOID main(void)
{
   DWORD oldMode, newMode;
   BOOL success;
   HANDLE stdout, stdin;

   // Get handles for standard in and out
   stdin = GetStdHandle(STD_INPUT_HANDLE);
   stdout = GetStdHandle(STD_OUTPUT_HANDLE);
   if (stdin == stdout) //they must be invalid
      ErrorHandler("In GetStdHandle",
         GetLastError());

   // Get current console mode so can modify it
   success = GetConsoleMode(stdin, &oldMode);
   if (!success)
      ErrorHandler("In GetConsoleMode",
         GetLastError());
   newMode = oldMode & ~ENABLE_LINE_INPUT &
      ~ENABLE_ECHO_INPUT;
   success = SetConsoleMode(stdin, newMode);
      if (!success)
      ErrorHandler("In SetConsoleMode",
         GetLastError());

   // Process user I/O
   ProcessIO(stdin, stdout);

   // put the old mode back
   success = SetConsoleMode(stdin, oldMode);
   if (!success)
      ErrorHandler("In SetConsoleMode",
         GetLastError());
}
```

The program in Listing 14.4 starts by getting the handles for stdin and stdout. It then proceeds to put the console into raw-input mode using the **GetConsoleMode** and **SetConsoleMode** functions.

GetConsoleMode   *Gets the mode bits for the specified console*

```
BOOL GetConsoleMode(
   HANDLE consoleHandle,
   LPDWORD mode)
```

consoleHandle	A handle to a console
mode	A pointer to a DWORD to hold the mode bits

Returns TRUE on success

SetConsoleMode   *Sets the mode bits for the specified console*

```
BOOL SetConsoleMode(
    HANDLE consoleHandle,
    DWORD mode)
```

consoleHandle	A handle to a console
mode	A pointer to a DWORD holding the new mode bits

Returns TRUE on success

The call to **GetConsoleMode** gets the current mode of the console. This mode is then modified to remove the line input and echo capabilities, and sent back to the console using **SetConsoleMode**. The console understands the following mode bits for input:

ENABLE_LINE_INPUT	Input returned only after CR
ENABLE_ECHO_INPUT	Keystrokes are echoed to stdout
ENABLE_PROCESSED_INPUT	Ctrl-C, backspace, and line feeds are handled by console
ENABLE_WINDOW_INPUT	Window size changes are reported in the event queue
ENABLE_MOUSE_INPUT	Mouse motion is reported in the event queue

In Listing 14.4, the removal of the LINE_INPUT and ECHO_INPUT bits causes characters to be reported as they are typed, rather than at the end of a line, and also does not echo them to the output.

Listing 14.4 enters a while loop in the **ProcessIO** function. The while loop reads each character and echoes it to the output until the user types an 'X'. The function must also detect and handle newline characters properly. When it sees a newline character, the program must move the cursor over to the left and down one line. In addition, if the cursor is at the bottom of the window, the program must scroll the console. In cooked mode, all of this happens automatically, but in raw mode you have to handle it yourself.

The **GetConsoleScreenBufferInfo** function returns all of the information necessary to reposition the buffer during scrolling.

| **GetConsoleScreenBufferInfo** | *Gets all screen buffer information for the console* |

```
BOOL GetConsoleScreenBufferInfo(
   HANDLE consoleHandle,
   PCONSOLE_SCREEN_BUFFER_INFO info)
```

| consoleHandle | A handle to a console |
| info | A pointer to a record to contain the console information |

Returns TRUE on success

The **GetConsoleScreenBufferInfo** function returns a CONSOLE_SCREEN_BUFFER_INFO structure, which contains the following information:

```
typedef struct _CONSOLE_SCREEN_BUFFER_INFO {
   COORD      dwSize; // Size of the console
   COORD      dwCursorPosition;
   WORD       wAttributes; // Color attributes
   SMALL_RECT srWindow; // Area currently seen
   COORD      dwMaximumWindowSize;
} CONSOLE_SCREEN_BUFFER_INFO ;
```

Alternatively, the functions **GetConsoleCursorInfo** and **GetLargestConsoleWindowSize** return cursor and window-size fields of this structure individually.

| **GetConsoleCursoInfo** | *Gets cursor information for the console* |

```
BOOL GetConsoleCursorInfo(
   HANDLE consoleHandle,
   PCONSOLE_CURSOR_INFO cursorInfo)
```

| consoleHandle | A handle to the console output |
| cursorInfo | A pointer to a record to contain the console cursor information |

Returns TRUE on success

| **GetLargestConsoleWindowSize** | *Gets window size information for the console* |

```
COORD GetLargestConsoleWindowSize(
   HANDLE consoleHandle)
```

| consoleHandle | A handle to the console output |

Returns a COORD structure holding width and height

```
typedef struct _COORD {
   SHORT X;
   SHORT Y;
} COORD;
```

The console consists of a fixed-size window on the screen, as well as a same-size or larger buffer area off-screen. If the buffer is larger than the window, the window will display scroll bars so that the user can move around and view the entire buffer.

The **dwSize** field contains the size of the buffer. The **dwCursor Position** field indicates where the cursor is in the buffer. The **wAttributes** field indicates the foreground and background colors that will be applied to any character written to the buffer. (See Section 14.6 for details on color). The **srWindow** field is a rectangle that defines what the current window is displaying from the screen buffer. The **dwMaximumWindowSize** field contains the maximum size of a console window that can appear on the screen, given the screen's size.

Using this information, the code in Listing 14.4 moves the cursor to the far left and down one line, and then sets the new position into the buffer using the **SetConsoleCursorPosition** function.

SetConsoleCursorPosition	*Sets the cursor position in the screen buffer*

```
BOOL GetConsoleScreenBufferInfo(
    HANDLE consoleHandle,
    COORD coord)
```

consoleHandle	A handle to a console
coord	The new cursor position

Returns TRUE on success

If the cursor happens to be on the last line of the screen buffer, then the buffer must scroll. It does it in the **ScrollOneLine** function using the following code:

```
success = GetConsoleScreenBufferInfo(stdout,
    &consoleInfo);

// Define the rectangle to scroll
scrollRect.Top = 0;
scrollRect.Left = 0;
scrollRect.Bottom = consoleInfo.dwSize.Y - 1;
scrollRect.Right = consoleInfo.dwSize.X - 1;

// Define destination of scrolled rectangle
coord.X = 0;
coord.Y = -1;

// Define how to fill blank line
consoleFill.Attributes =
    consoleInfo.wAttributes;
consoleFill.Char.AsciiChar = ' ';
```

```
// Perform the scroll
success = ScrollConsoleScreenBuffer(stdout,
        &scrollRect, 0,
    coord, &consoleFill);
```

First, the code gets the buffer information. Using that, it defines the rectangle to scroll. Here it picks the entire buffer, but you can choose smaller parts of it if you like. It then defines the position the buffer should be scrolled to. Here the buffer is moved up one line. The top line of the buffer will be lost during this operation. You must also define how the console should fill the new blank line created at the bottom of the window during the scroll. Here the new line is filled with blanks, and the colors in the rest of the buffer are used as the fill colors.

Having set up everything for the scroll operation, the code can actually scroll the window using the **ScrollConsoleScreenBuffer** function

---

ScrollConsoleScreenBuffer	*Scrolls the console buffer as specified*

```
BOOL ScrollConsoleScreenBuffer(
    HANDLE consoleHandle,
    PSMALL_RECT sourceRect,
    PSMALL_RECT clipRect,
    COORD destination,
    PCHAR_INFO fillStruct)
```

consoleHandle	A handle to a console
sourceRect	The rectangle of characters to move
clipRect	Rectangle defining area affected
destination	The point where the upper left corner of the source rectangle should move to
fillStruct	The character and colors to use for filling

Returns TRUE on success

As you can see, the **ScrollConsoleScreenBuffer** function has a great deal of flexibility in how it scrolls the buffer. If you are creating a complete vt-100 terminal emulator, for example, it would be very easy to emulate any possible rectangular movement code for the terminal using these built-in scrolling capabilities.

The scrolling code makes the program a bit longer, but as you can see, the code is straightforward. Once you've typed the code in, you will use it the same way in every console program that you create.

Let's say that you want to use the raw input mode with the **WaitForSingleObject** function (see Section 7.4 for more information on **Wait** functions). For example, in Chapter 11, the terminal emulator program uses this capability. That program actually uses **WaitForMultipleObject** so that it can wait for either a character from the keyboard or a character from the modem. In order to use either of the **Wait** functions, however, the **ProcessIO** function needs some modification, as shown in Listing 14.5.

| **Listing 14.5** | *Replace the **ProcessIO** function in Listing 14.4 with this new version* |

```cpp
// raw2.cpp

void ProcessIO(HANDLE consoleStdin,
    HANDLE consoleStdout)
{
    char buffer;
    DWORD numRead, numWrite;
    INPUT_RECORD inputEvent;
    DWORD s;
    char *t="waiting\n";

    do
    {
        // wait for the user to do something
        do
        {
            s = WaitForSingleObject(consoleStdin, 0);
        } while (s==WAIT_TIMEOUT);
        // look into the input queue
        PeekConsoleInput(consoleStdin, &inputEvent,
            1, &numRead);
        if (numRead>0)
        {
            // Check the event. If it is unworthy,
            // then discard the event. Otherwise read
            // it and handle it normally.
            if (inputEvent.EventType != KEY_EVENT ||
                inputEvent.Event.
                KeyEvent.bKeyDown==FALSE ||
                inputEvent.Event.KeyEvent.
                uChar.AsciiChar==0)
            {
                ReadConsoleInput(consoleStdin,
                    &inputEvent, 1, &numRead);
            }
            else
            {
                ReadFile(consoleStdin, &buffer, 1,
                    &numRead, NULL);
                if (buffer == '\r')
                    HandleCR(consoleStdout);
                else
                    WriteFile(consoleStdout, &buffer, 1,
```

| Listing 14.5 | *Replace the **ProcessIO** function in Listing 14.4 with this new version (continued)* |

```
                    &numWrite, NULL);
        }
      }
   } while  (buffer != 'X');
}
```

Here is the problem that Listing 14.5 is trying to solve: The input buffer for the console actually receives very low-level events from the keyboard. For example, each time the user presses down a key, the console's input buffer gets an event. It gets another event when the user releases the key. This holds true even for the Shift and Alt keys. If the user presses and releases the Shift key or Alt key, events appear in the input buffer. The **ReadFile** function has no problem with this. It simply waits until a real "the user has entered a valid keystroke" event arrives, and then it retrieves the key. The **WaitFor SingleObject** function, however, releases its wait on *any* of these low-level events. So, for example, if the user presses down the Shift key and then releases it, the **WaitForSingleObject** function will release, but the **ReadFile** function will hang up while waiting for a real keystroke.

The code in Listing 14.5 shows how to solve this problem. Each time the **WaitForSingleObject** function returns, the code examines the event to see if it is interesting or not. It uses **PeekConsoleInput** to look at the event without removing it from the queue.

PeekConsoleInput	*Get a copy of the first event in the event queue*

```
BOOL PeekConsoleInput(
   HANDLE consoleHandle,
   PINPUT_RECORD buffer,
   DWORD bufferSize,
LPDWORD numRead)
```

consoleHandle	A handle to a console
buffer	Pointer to a buffer to hold the event(s)
bufferSize	Number of events buffer can hold
numRead	A pointer to a DWORD to hold the number of records read

Returns TRUE on success

In Listing 14.5, the code is set up to copy one record from the input queue. It examines it with the following if statement:

```
if (inputEvent.EventType != KEY_EVENT ||
   inputEvent.Event.KeyEvent.bKeyDown==FALSE ||
   inputEvent.Event.KeyEvent.uChar.AsciiChar==0)
```

This statement checks the event to make sure that it contains a key-stroke, that it is a "key up" event (the user is releasing the key rather than pressing it down), and that it contains a valid ASCII character (for example, a KeyDown event on the Shift key alone will not return an ASCII character). If the event does not pass these three tests, the code discards it by making a call to **ReadConsoleInput**, which reads a low-level event from the console input queue. The code then loops back to the **Wait** function again to wait for the next event. Otherwise the code can call **ReadFile** because it knows the buffer contains an event that **ReadFile** will accept immediately.

ReadConsoleInput   *Reads a low-level event from the console's event queue*

```
BOOL ReadConsoleInput(
    HANDLE consoleHandle,
    PINPUT_RECORD buffer,
    DWORD bufferSize,
    LPDWORD numRead)
```

consoleHandle	A handle to a console
buffer	Pointer to a buffer to hold the event(s)
bufferSize	Number of events buffer can hold
numRead	A pointer to a DWORD to hold the number of records read

Returns TRUE on success

If you run the code in Listing 14.5 by replacing the **ProcessIO** function in Listing 14.4 with it, you will find that it works exactly the same way. However, the inner **do...while** loop in Listing 14.5 can run continuously because the program can accurately detect keystrokes. (See Chapter 11 for an example of a practical use for this capability in a terminal-emulator program.)

14.5 Other Input Events

As demonstrated in Listing 14.5, the programmer can view a console input stream at two different levels. The **ReadFile** function accesses the input queue at a high level, returning one key at a time. There is also low-level access to the queue, however, using the **PeekConsoleInput**, **ReadConsole Input**, and **WriteConsoleInput** functions. Three types of events appear in the buffer:

- Keyboard events
- Mouse events
- Window re-size events

Listing 14.6 demonstrates how to access these low-level events.

Listing 14.6   *Accessing low-level input from a console (continued)*

```cpp
// events.cpp

#include <windows.h>
#include <iostream.h>

void ErrorHandler(char *s, DWORD err)
{
   cout << s << endl;
   cout << "Error number: " << err << endl;
   ExitProcess(err);
}

void ProcessIO(HANDLE consoleStdin,
   HANDLE consoleStdout)
{
   DWORD numRead, numWrite;
   int x=0;
   INPUT_RECORD inputRecord;
   char s[100];
   DWORD oldMode, newMode;

   GetConsoleMode(consoleStdin, &oldMode);
   newMode = oldMode | ENABLE_WINDOW_INPUT
      | ENABLE_MOUSE_INPUT;
   SetConsoleMode(consoleStdin, newMode);
   do
   {
      ReadConsoleInput(consoleStdin, &inputRecord,
         1, &numRead);
      switch (inputRecord.EventType)
      {
         case KEY_EVENT:
            strcpy(s, "keyboard event\n");
            break;
         case MOUSE_EVENT:
            strcpy(s, "mouse event\n");
            break;
         case WINDOW_BUFFER_SIZE_EVENT:
            strcpy(s, "resize event\n");
            break;
         default:
            strcpy(s, "other event\n");
            break;
      }
      WriteFile(consoleStdout, s, strlen(s),
         &numWrite, 0);
   } while  (x++ < 100);
```

```
      SetConsoleMode(consoleStdin, oldMode);

}

VOID main(void)
{
   DWORD oldMode, newMode;
   BOOL success;
   HANDLE consoleStdout, consoleStdin;

   // Get handles for standard in and out
   consoleStdin = GetStdHandle(STD_INPUT_HANDLE);
   consoleStdout = GetStdHandle(STD_OUTPUT_HANDLE);
   if (consoleStdin == consoleStdout)
      ErrorHandler("In GetStdHandle",
         GetLastError());

   // Get current console mode so can modify it
   success = GetConsoleMode(consoleStdin,
      &oldMode);
   if (!success)
      ErrorHandler("In GetConsoleMode",
         GetLastError());
   newMode = oldMode & ~ENABLE_LINE_INPUT &
      ~ENABLE_ECHO_INPUT;
   success = SetConsoleMode(consoleStdin, newMode);
       if (!success)
      ErrorHandler("In SetConsoleMode",
         GetLastError());

   // Process user I/O
   ProcessIO(consoleStdin, consoleStdout);

   // put the old mode back
   success = SetConsoleMode(consoleStdin, oldMode);
   if (!success)
      ErrorHandler("In SetConsoleMode",
         GetLastError());
}
```

When you run Listing 14.6, you will find that keyboard events, any mouse motion in the console, and resizing events all create output. The mouse and resizing events are enabled at the beginning of the **ProcessIO** function with a call to **SetConsoleMode**. The call to **ReadConsoleInput** reads each event as it arrives and the **switch** statement parses the events to display the appropriate strings. The **inputRecord** structure that **Read ConsoleInput** returns also contains all of the relevant information about each event.

SetConsoleMode   *Sets the mode bits for the specified console*

```
BOOL SetConsoleMode(
    HANDLE consoleHandle,
    DWORD mode)
```

consoleHandle   A handle to a console

mode   A pointer to a DWORD holding the new mode bits

Returns TRUE on success

The most common way to use the mouse is to create a copy-and-paste facility for a command prompt window. For example, an XTerm window on a UNIX workstation lets you use the mouse to select an area of text and then later paste it into another or the same XTerm window. You could implement this capability using the mouse events shown here, along with the coloring capability shown in Section 14.6 and the **ReadConsole** and **WriteConsole** functions to access the output buffer.

Related functions of interest are **GetNumberOfConsoleInputEvents**, which tells you how many events are waiting in the queue, and **Get NumberOfConsoleMouseButtons**, which returns the number of buttons on the console's mouse.

GetNumberOfConsole InputEvents   *Returns the number of waiting input events*

```
BOOL GetNumberOfConsoleInputEvents(
    HANDLE consoleInput,
    LPDWORD mumEvents)
```

consoleHandle   A handle to a console input

numEvents   The number of waiting events

Returns TRUE on success

GetNumberOfConsole MouseButtons   *Returns the number of mouse buttons*

```
BOOL GetNumberOfConsoleMouseButtons(
    LPDWORD numMouseButtons)
```

numMouseButtons   The number of mouse buttons

Returns TRUE on success

As demonstrated in Listing 14.7, it is also possible to register a handler function to trap Ctrl-C, Ctrl-Break, Close, Logoff, and Shutdown events.

Listing 14.7   *Code that demonstrates a console control handler*

```cpp
// handler.cpp

#include <windows.h>
#include <iostream.h>
#include <string.h>

void ErrorHandler(char *s, DWORD err)
{
   cout << s << endl;
   cout << "Error number: " << err << endl;
   ExitProcess(err);
}

void ProcessIO(HANDLE consoleStdin, HANDLE stdout)
{
   char buffer[1000];
   DWORD numRead, numWrite;

   do
   {
      ReadFile(consoleStdin, buffer, 1000,
         &numRead, 0);
      buffer[numRead]='\0'; // will have CR/LF
      WriteFile(stdout, buffer, strlen(buffer),
         &numWrite, 0);
   } while  (strncmp(buffer, "exit", 4) != 0);
}

BOOL HandlerFunc(DWORD ctrlChar)
{
   switch (ctrlChar)
   {
      case CTRL_C_EVENT:
         Beep(100, 100);
         return FALSE;
      case CTRL_CLOSE_EVENT:
         Beep(200, 200);
         return FALSE;
      case CTRL_BREAK_EVENT:
         Beep(300, 300);
         return FALSE;
      case CTRL_LOGOFF_EVENT:
         Beep(400, 400);
         return FALSE;
      case CTRL_SHUTDOWN_EVENT:
         Beep(500, 500);
         return FALSE;
```

Listing 14.7   *Code that demonstrates a console control handler (continued)*

```
    default:
        Beep(2000, 2000);
        return FALSE;
    }
}


VOID main(void)
{
    HANDLE consoleStdout, consoleStdin;
    BOOL success;


    // Get handles for standard in and out
    consoleStdin = GetStdHandle(STD_INPUT_HANDLE);
    consoleStdout = GetStdHandle(STD_OUTPUT_HANDLE);
    // they must be invalid if equal
    if (consoleStdin == consoleStdout)
        ErrorHandler("In GetStdHandle",
            GetLastError());


    success = SetConsoleCtrlHandler(
        (PHANDLER_ROUTINE)HandlerFunc, TRUE);
    if (!success)
        ErrorHandler("In SetConsoleCtrlHandler",
            GetLastError());


    // Process user I/O
    ProcessIO(consoleStdin, consoleStdout);
}
```

If you run the code in Listing 14.7 and then press Ctrl-C, it will beep before quitting, because the handler function executes every time you press Ctrl-C. In the **HandlerFunc** function, you can also change the return value for CTRL_C_EVENT to TRUE, and the program will not quit in response to Ctrl-C. It will simply beep. When the return value is FALSE, the API passes the event to the next function in the handler chain. If it is TRUE, the API assumes that this handler function has completed all necessary processing on the event.

The call to **SetConsoleCtrlHandler** in the main function causes the program to begin detecting the five control events.

SetConsoleCtrlHandler   *Enables the program to monitor control events*

```
BOOL SetConsoleCtrlHandler(
   PHANDLER_ROUTINE handlerRoutine,
   BOOL add)
```

handlerRoutine   A pointer to the handler function

add   TRUE if adding the handler or FALSE if removing it

Returns TRUE on success

The handler routine accepts a DWORD specifying the signal that the console has received, and can then switch off of the signal. The handler can return TRUE or FALSE.

In the case of Ctrl-C and Ctrl-Break, a TRUE value implies that the handler has handled the key and desires no further processing. In the case of the close, logoff and shutdown signals, the signals arrive during the closing operation so that you can do any necessary cleanup. Do not attempt to read or write from the console within the handler function, because the console is already on its way down and may not respond properly.

14.6 Other Capabilities

Several other functions in the console API make it easy to implement advanced capabilities in your consoles. For example, consoles support the concept of an *active* buffer, and allow you to change the active buffer at any time. Listing 14.8 demonstrates the process.

Listing 14.8   *Switching between two buffers*

```
// 2buff.cpp

#include <windows.h>
#include <iostream.h>
#include <string.h>

void ErrorHandler(char *s, DWORD err)
{
   cout << s << endl;
   cout << "Error number: " << err << endl;
   ExitProcess(err);
}
```

Listing 14.8   *Switching between two buffers (continued)*

```
void ShowBuffers(HANDLE consoleStdin,
   HANDLE consoleStdout, HANDLE newBuffer)
{
   char buffer[1000];
   DWORD numRead, numWrite;
   BOOL flag=TRUE;
   int x;

   for (x=0; x<10; x++)
   {
      WriteFile(consoleStdout, "Black\n", 6,
         &numWrite, 0);
       WriteFile(newBuffer, "White\n", 6, &numWrite,
         0);
   }
   do
   {
      ReadFile(consoleStdin, buffer, 1000,
         &numRead, 0);
      if (flag)
         SetConsoleActiveScreenBuffer(newBuffer);
      else
         SetConsoleActiveScreenBuffer(
            consoleStdout);
      flag = !flag;
      WriteFile(consoleStdout, buffer, numRead,
         &numWrite, 0);

   } while  (strncmp(buffer, "quit", 4) != 0);
}

VOID main(void)
{
   HANDLE consoleStdout, consoleStdin;
   HANDLE newBuffer;

   // Get handles for standard in and out
   consoleStdin = GetStdHandle(STD_INPUT_HANDLE);
   consoleStdout = GetStdHandle(STD_OUTPUT_HANDLE);
   // they must be invalid if equal
   if (consoleStdin == consoleStdout)
      ErrorHandler("In GetStdHandle",
         GetLastError());

   // Create second buffer
   newBuffer = CreateConsoleScreenBuffer(
      GENERIC_READ | GENERIC_WRITE,
```

```
      0, 0, CONSOLE_TEXTMODE_BUFFER, 0);

   // Show the two different buffers
   ShowBuffers(consoleStdin, consoleStdout,
      newBuffer);
}
```

The code in Listing 14.8 starts by getting the input and output handles for the console. It then creates a new screen buffer using the **CreateConsole ScreenBuffer** function.

CreateConsoleScreenBuffer   *Creates a new screen buffer*

```
HANDLE CreateConsoleScreenBuffer(
   DWORD accessFlags,
   DWORD shareMode,
   LPSECURITY_ATTRIBUTES security,
   DWORD type,
   PVOID reserved)
```

accessFlags	GENERIC_READ and/or GENERIC_WRITE
shareMode	FILE_SHARE_READ and/or FILE_SHARE_WRITE
security	Security attributes. See Chapter 10
type`	Must currently be CONSOLE_TEXTMODE_BUFFER
reserved	Reserved. Set to 0.

Returns a handle to the new buffer or INVALID_HANDLE_VALUE on error

---

The new buffer initially has the same size as the existing console window. You can change it (or any console's buffer size) using the **SetConsole-ScreenBufferSize** function.

SetConsoleScreenBufferSize   *Sets the specified buffer to a new size*

```
BOOL SetConsoleScreenBufferSize(
   HANDLE consoleHandle,
   COORD size)
```

consoleHandle	Handle to the console to change
size	The new console size

Returns TRUE on success

Listing 14.8 simply uses the default size. It then calls the **ShowBuffers** function. This function demonstrates how to use two separate buffers. The function starts by placing 10 lines of information into the two buffers. Then, each time the user presses the Enter key, the program sets the active buffer using the **SetConsoleActiveScreenBuffer** function.

SetConsoleActiveScreenBuffer   *Sets the active output buffer for the process's console to the buffer specified*

```
BOOL SetConsoleActiveScreenBuffer(
   HANDLE consoleHandle)
```

consoleHandle   Handle to the console

Returns TRUE on success

Processes can have just one console window, and just one console input stream, but can also have many different output buffers. The **Set ConsoleActiveScreenBuffer** function lets you choose among them. As soon as the function is called, the new buffer will appear and the scroll bars will change as necessary to accommodate the new buffer.

Another interesting capability involves coloring the output buffer, or placing characters directly into it. Listing 14.9 demonstrates coloring.

Listing 14.9   *Changing the color of the output buffer*

```cpp
// color.cpp

#include <windows.h>
#include <iostream.h>

void ErrorHandler(char *s, DWORD err)
{
   cout << s << endl;
   cout << "Error number: " << err << endl;
   ExitProcess(err);
}


// Changes the colors of a range of cells.
// Make sure that the console you are
// using is not so big that the area
// colored is not off the screen.
void ChangeColors(HANDLE consoleStdin,
   HANDLE consoleStdout)
{
   COORD c;
   WORD color;
   DWORD numWrite;
```

```
    BOOL success;


    // Fill in the color of a range of 200 cells.
    color = BACKGROUND_RED | FOREGROUND_GREEN;
    c.X = 20;
    c.Y = 10;
    success = FillConsoleOutputAttribute(
       consoleStdout, color, 200, c, &numWrite);
    cout << numWrite << endl;
    if (!success)
       ErrorHandler("In FillConsoleOutputAttribute",
          GetLastError());
}


VOID main(void)
{
    HANDLE consoleStdout, consoleStdin;


    // Get handles for standard in and out
    consoleStdin = GetStdHandle(STD_INPUT_HANDLE);
    consoleStdout = GetStdHandle(STD_OUTPUT_HANDLE);
    if (consoleStdin == consoleStdout)
       ErrorHandler("In GetStdHandle",
          GetLastError());


    // Process user I/O
    ChangeColors(consoleStdin, consoleStdout);
}
```

Every cell in the output buffer has an X-Y coordinate, a character, and a color-attribute byte. The code in Listing 14.9 simply modifies the attribute bytes of a set of 200 characters:

```
    color = BACKGROUND_RED | FOREGROUND_GREEN;
    c.X = 20;
    c.Y = 10;
    success = FillConsoleOutputAttribute(
       consoleStdout, color, 200, c, &numWrite);
```

The **FillConsoleOutputAttribute** function (like the nearly identical **WriteConsoleOutputAttribute** function) accepts a color byte, a starting position, and the number of characters to apply the color to. It changes their color attributes.

| **FillConsoleOutputAttribute** | *Fills in the color attribute bytes of a range of character positions in the buffer* |

```
BOOL FillConsoleOutputAttribute(
    HANDLE consoleHandle,
    WORD color,
    DWORD numberOfCells,
    COORD startingCoord,
    LPDWORD numWritten)
```

consoleHandle	Handle to the console
color	The new attribute byte
numberOfCells	Number of cells to change
startingCoord	The coordinates of the starting character
numWritten	Number of cells actually changed
Returns TRUE on success	

The color byte can contain combinations of red, green, and blue or black for both the foreground and background colors. The **FillConsole OutputAttribute** function fills runs of cells line by line, starting at the indicated position.

The **SetConsoleTextAttribute** function sets the color attribute byte and applies it to all characters that subsequently appear in the text output buffer.

| **SetConsoleTextAttribute** | *Sets the color attribute byte for all subsequent output* |

```
BOOL SetConsoleTextAttribute(
    HANDLE consoleHandle,
    WORD attribute)
```

consoleHandle	Output console handle
attribute	The attribute byte
Returns TRUE on success	

Two other useful convenience functions are **GetConsoleTitle** and **Set-ConsoleTitle**, which get and set the verbiage in the title bar of the console's window.

| **SetConsoleTitle** | *Sets the console's title* |

```
BOOL SetConsoleTitle(
    LPTSTR title)
```

title	The new title
Returns TRUE on success	

GetConsoleTitle	*Gets the console's title*

```
DWORD GetConsoleTitle(
    LPTSTR buffer,
    DWORD numRead)
```

buffer	The buffer in which to place the title
numRead	The size of the buffer

Returns the number of characters copied to the buffer, or 0 on error

---

14.7 Conclusion

You will find that you use consoles whenever you need to create programs that have pure text input and/or output and you do not want or need to create a full graphical application to handle them. You can also use consoles to provide a pure text output stream for an MFC program.

Chapter 11 contains a simple terminal program that uses the raw console input modes described in this chapter.

Microsoft Management Console (MMC)

MMC is designed to centralize and unify the experience of any-one trying to configure or monitor computers and applications, whether they are responsible for a single workstation or an entire network of computers. MMC is a set of application programming interfaces (APIs), a user interface shell (the console), and a set of guidelines. MMC is a tool host—it provides no management func-tionality of its own. Individual components, called snap-ins, pro-vide all of the functionality. Independent software vendors (ISVs) design most of the snap-ins. However, Microsoft will continue to add to the set of snap-ins delivered with Windows 2000. The MMC console is a Windows-based multiple document interface (MDI) application. Both Microsoft and ISVs extend the console by writ-ing MMC snap-ins, which are responsible for actually performing management tasks.

The MMC environment provides for seamless integration between snap-ins, even those provided by different vendors. Administrators will create tools from various snap-ins, from various vendors. Administrators can then save the tools they have created, for later use or for sharing with other administrators, This model provides the administrator with efficient tool customization and the ability to create multiple tools of different levels of complexity for task delegation, among other benefits.

15.1 The Possibilities

MMC provides a way to build better administration tools—tools that scale up and down, tools that integrate seamlessly into the operating system, and tools that can be repackaged and customized to a high degree. In this case, a tool is more than a single application. A tool can be made up of one or more snap-ins and, in turn, each snap-in can be made up of additional extension snap-ins. The modular structure allows the system administrator to significantly reduce costs associated with systems management by grouping snap-ins into custom tools that provide only the desired view and set of options. The administrator can then save each custom tool as an MMC saved console (.msc) file and send it to whoever is delegated to perform the administrative tasks associated with that console. This functionality allows administrators to create special tools for end users and to delegate specific administrative tasks to specific administrative groups.

MMC and the Windows 2000 administration model represent a shift in focus from earlier models. MMC does have some new and helpful features, but its primary value is in its overall design, how easily it fits into the operating system, how simple it appears to a user, how easy it is to repackage for building solutions to specific administration problems, and how well it scales. It is somewhat challenging to design a tool that looks and feels like it's an integral part of the operating system. MMC, however, greatly simplifies this effort. If designed carefully, your administration tool should fit right in, and its use should be fairly intuitive. It should also be able to leverage existing tools, helping you avoid reinventing the wheel.

15.2 MMC Interfaces and Methods

One of the things that is always a problem, when one starts to work with a new capability of an operating system, is knowing what programmatic interfaces are available. So we have summarized the MMC interfaces and given a sample of an interface call. Table 15.1 shows the COM Interfaces Implemented by MMC and the COM Interfaces Implemented by the snap-in; Table 15.2 shows the COM IComponent Interfaces, and Table 15.3 shows a function call construct. As these tables clearly show, a snap-in is nothing but a COM component.

Table 1 — MMC Interfaces and Methods

COM Interfaces Implemented by MMC

- IColumnData—The IColumnData interface allows a snap-in to set and retrieve the persisted view data of list view columns to use for column customization. It provides methods for programmatically providing the same functionality that MMC provides in the Modify Columns dialog box. In addition, the IColumnData interface provides methods for setting and retrieving the sorted column and sort direction of a particular column set.

- IConsole2—The Iconsole2 interface enables communication with the console.

- IConsoleNameSpace2—The IConsoleNameSpace2 interface enables snap-ins to enumerate dynamic subcontainers in the scope pane. The particular snap-in determines what qualifies as a subcontainer. For example, a snap-in that features a domain object might enumerate individual groups or organizations within the domain.

- IConsoleVerb—The IConsoleVerb interface allows snap-ins to enable standard verbs, including cut, copy, paste, delete, rename, refresh, and print. Whenever an item is selected, the snap-in can update the state of these verbs.

- IContextMenuCallback—The IContextMenuCallback interface is used to add menu items to a context menu.

- IContextMenuProvider—The IContextMenuProvider interface implements methods that create new context menus, for the purpose of adding items to those menus, enabling extensions to extend those menus, and displaying the resultant context menus.

- IControlbar—The Icontrolbar interface provides a way to create toolbars and other controls.

- IDisplayHelp—The IDisplayHelp interface enables a snap-in to display a specific HTML Help topic within the merged MMC HTML Help collection file for the console.

- IHeaderCtrl2—The IHeaderCtrl2 interface enables the manipulation of columns and indicates the kind of information that is to be presented in the result pane of the console.

- IImageList—The IImageList interface enables the snap-in to insert images to be used as icons for items in the result or scope pane of the console.

- IMenuButton—The IMenuButton interface enables the snap-in to add and manage menu buttons.

- IMessageView—The IMessageView interface provides support for specifying the text and icons for error messages displayed using the MMC message OCX control. MMC provides a message OCX control the snap-ins can use for displaying error messages in the result pane.

- IPropertySheetCallback—The IPropertySheetCallback interface is used by a snap-in to add its property pages to a property sheet.
- IPropertySheetProvider—The IPropertySheetProvider interface implements Win32 property sheets as COM objects. snap-ins can use the IPropertySheetProvider interface for adding wizard pages to a snap-in. IPropertySheetProvider is also used when a snap-in adds a feature that has a property sheet as the interface but identifies it as something else.
- IRequiredExtensions—The IRequiredExtensions interface enables a snap-in to add some or all of the extension snap-ins that extend it.
- IResultData—The IResultData interface enables a snap-in to add, remove, find, and modify items associated with the result pane. It also enables the manipulation of the view style of the result pane.
- IStringTable—The IStringTable interface provides a means of storing string data with a snap-in. A string table is created in the console file as needed for each snap-in by MMC.
- IToolbar—The IToolbar interface is used to create new toolbars, to add items to them, to extend the toolbars, and to display the resultant new toolbars.

COM Interfaces Implemented by the Snap-In

- IComponent—The IComponent interface enables MMC to communicate with snap-ins. Similar to the IComponentData interface, IComponent is typically implemented at the view level and is closely associated with items being displayed in the result pane.
- IComponentData—The IComponentData interface enables MMC to communicate with snap-ins. Similar to the IComponent interface, IComponentData is typically implemented at the document level and is closely associated with items (folders) being displayed in the scope pane.
- IEnumTASK—The IEnumTASK interface enables a snap-in to enumerate the tasks to add to a task pad.
- IExtendContextMenu—The IExtendContextMenu interface enables snap-ins to add items to an existing context menu.
- IExtendControlbar—The ExtendControlbar interface enables a snap-in to add control bars to the console. This provides a way to improve the functionality and appearance of your snap-in by adding toolbars or other user-interface enhancements.
- IExtendPropertySheet2—The IExtendPropertySheet2 interface enables a snap-in to add pages to the property sheet of an item.
- IExtendTaskpad—The IExtendTaskpad interface enables a snap-in to set up a taskpad and receive notification from the taskpad.

- IResultDataCompare—The IResultDataCompare interface allows primary snap-ins to compare result items, which are displayed in a sorted order in the result pane.
- IResultDataCompareEx—The IResultDataCompareEx interface allows primary snap-ins to compare both scope and result items that are displayed in a sorted order in the result pane.
- IResultOwnerData—The IresultOwnerData interface allows snap-ins to use virtual lists.
- ISnapinAbout—The ISnapinAbout interface enables the console to get copyright and version information from a snap-in. The console also uses this interface to obtain images for the static folder from the snap-in.
- ISnapinHelp2—The ISnapinHelp2 interface enables the console to get the location of a snap-in's compiled HTML Help file. The console merges the HTML Help files of all snap-ins with the MMC console HTML Help collection file.

As you know, a COM interface is a collection of functions. So Table 2 shows one of the above COM interfaces, IComponent, and its collection of functions. When using Visual C++, one can use the Help menu item to get the functions associated with any given interface.

Table 2—COM IComponent Interface

The IComponent interface enables MMC to communicate with snap-ins. Similar to IComponentData interface, IComponent is typically implemented at the view level and is closely associated with items being displayed in the result pane.

Implement the IComponent interface in your in-process server DLL to communicate with the console, which displays the result pane and enumerates the items it contains. All snap-ins that add result items to the namespace implement this interface. They should also implement IComponentData.

IComponent enumerates result items. It also provides display information for scope items when they appear in the result pane. Extension snap-ins that do not extend the namespace (but extend other features like context menus, toolbars, and so on) need not implement IComponent.

METHODS IN Vtable ORDER

• QueryInterface	Returns pointers to supported interfaces.
• AddRef	Increments reference count.
• Release	Decrements reference count.
• Initialize	Provides an entry point to the console.
• Notify	Called by the console to notify the snap-in of actions taken by a user.

- Destroy   Releases all references to the console.
- QueryDataObject   Returns a data object that can be used to retrieve context information for the specified cookie.
- GetResultViewType   Determines what the result pane view should be.
- GetDisplayInfo   Retrieves display information about an item in the result pane.
- CompareObjects   Enables a snap-in to compare two data objects acquired through QuerDataObject. Note that data objects can be acquired from two different instances of IComponent.

Table 3 shows one of the constructs for a call to one of the above functions, IComponent::GetResultViewType.

Table 3 — Function Call Construct

The IComponent::GetResultViewType method determines what the result pane view should be.

```
HRESULT GetResultViewType (
    long        cookie,          // unique identifier
    LPOLESTR    *ppViewType,     // pointer to address of the view
    long        *pViewOptions    // pointer to view options
);
```

Parameters:
cookie
[in] Specifies the snap-in-provided cookie for the scope item. The cookie is a unique identifier associated with the scope item for which the result-view type is required.

ppViewType
[out] Pointer to the address of a string that specifies the view to display for the specified cookie. The callee (snap-in) allocates the view type string using the COM API function CoTaskMemAlloc and the caller (MMC) frees it using CoTaskMemFree. The string that is returned depends on the view type.
Standard list views MMC does not use this value. If the snap-in uses only standard list views, the snap-in can set ppViewType to NULL. MMC uses standard list views as the default view type.
Taskpad view that uses MMC's taskpad templates: ppViewType should point to the address of a string containing the resource path to the taskpad template and a group name that identifies the task.

Custom OCX view provided by an OLE custom control (OCX): ppViewType should point to the address of a string containing the string representation of the custom control's CLSID.

Custom Web view provided by a Web page: ppViewType should point to the address of a string containing the URL for the page.

pViewOptions

[out] Pointer to the value that provides the console with options specified by the owning snap-in. This value can be a combination of the following:

Value	Meaning
MMC_VIEW_OPTIONS_NONE = 0	No view options selected. This is the default view option.
MMC_VIEW_OPTIONS_NOLISTVIEWS = 0x0001	Tells the console to refrain from presenting standard list view choices in the View menu. Allows the snap-in to display only its own custom views in the result pane.

Note: We didn't list all values, but just showed a couple of samples for use with this parameter.

Return Values

S_OK

The returned view type was either an OLE custom control (OCX) CLSID string or a URL.

S_FALSE

A standard list view should be used.

E_UNEXPECTED

An unexpected error occurred.

E_OUTOFMEMORY

Not enough memory to complete the operation.

Remarks

MMC calls GetResultViewType whenever a snap-in scope item is selected.

Note: this is just part of the remarks for the method.

As the preceding material shows, there is a very rich set of APIs that aid in creating MMC snap-ins. As we will show in the next section, there is an ATL snap-in Wizard that makes our life much easier by creating MMC snap-ins. Also, as part of the Microsoft Platform SDK there are sample snap-in programs that show how to create the various functionalities for MMC. Currently, the location has a path similar to the following (here, it is assumed that D: is the Platform SDK installation drive):

```
D:\Platform SDK\Samples\SysMgmt\MMC\
```

15.3 ATL Snap-In Wizard

MMC provides a single programming model for writing management and administrative applications. By specifying the interaction between MMC applications (snap-ins) and MMC itself through well-defined COM interfaces, the programming model becomes clear and easier to understand. ATL 3.0 adds a layer of abstraction to that model, greatly simplifying MMC snap-in programming. Windows 2000 has its management/administrative applications run inside MMC.

To use the ATL snap-in Wizard, one would go to the Visual C++ project toolbar and choose "Insert", and then "New ATL Object". You will get the ATL Object Wizard dialog box. Choose Object for your category and MMC snap-in for the object type. When the dialog box appears, fill in the desired class names, and the Wizard will create four classes. The names clearly represent the purpose of each.

Looking at this generated code for your project, you can get a feel for what type of basic information the Wizard will supply for you. Then, if you visit the various samples, as mentioned above, you can get a feel for what you need to do to create your custom snap-in. The ATL programming model for snap-ins alleviates the problems of trying to write MMC snap-ins at the SDK level.

15.4 Conclusion

As we have seen, the MMC architecture is in some ways rather similar to something we're already familiar with: the Document/View architecture of MFC. A snap-in can offer multiple views of the same data. IComponentData is to Document as IComponent is to View. Every snap-in instance can have any number of IComponent components, usually one for each MDI child window (MMC is an MFC MDI application, and it hosts snap-ins in its child windows), but only one IComponentData (every time you add a snap-in from Add/Remove dialog box, you get an instance of that snap-in). IComponentData methods deal with items in the scope pane, enumerate them, and provide information about them, and so on. IComponent methods handle the result pane. They determine what kind of view should be presented to the user, enumerate items in the result pane, and so forth.

Microsoft has created a very sophisticated and yet very easy-to-use architecture to create custom management/administration tools. Thus administrators can create the kinds of custom controls they need to optimize the use of their configuration by users. The creators of snap-ins can use the familiar Document/View architecture, along with familiar wizard support, to create new snap-ins.

System Information

The system-information functions let you gather information about the system you are currently using. For example, you can examine the number of processors in use on a Windows 2000 machine and then use this information to dynamically decide on the number of threads to create in a multi-threaded application. The system information functions also include a pair function that allows you to initiate a system shutdown or to cancel that shutdown once it has begun.

Compatibility Note: All of the code in this chapter, up to section 16.4, works identically in Windows 2000 and Windows 98. The code in Section 16.4 will not work in Windows 98.

16.1 The GetSystemInfo Function

The **GetSystemInfo** function returns information about the hardware of the system on which your program is running. This information is useful when you want to tune your application's behavior to the hardware that is available.

GetSystemInfo	*Returns information about the current hardware*

```
VOID GetSystemInfo(
    LPSYSTEM_INFO info)
```

info   a SYSTEM_INFO structure

Returns nothing

The function returns a SYSTEM_INFO structure that contains several pieces of immediately obvious information, along with other pieces of information that are more obscure, as follows:

```
typedef struct _SYSTEM_INFO {
    DWORD   dwOemId;
    DWORD   dwPageSize;
    LPVOID  lpMinimumApplicationAddress;
    LPVOID  lpMaximumApplicationAddress;
    DWORD   dwActiveProcessorMask;
    DWORD   dwNumberOfProcessors;
    DWORD   dwProcessorType;
    DWORD   dwAllocationGranularity;
    DWORD   dwReserved;
} SYSTEM_INFO;
```

Listing 16.1 demonstrates the use of this function and prints out all of the data it returns.

Listing 16.1   *Code demonstrating the GetSystemInfo function*

```
// sigsi.cpp

#include <windows.h>
#include <iostream.h>
#include <iomanip.h>

void main()
{
    SYSTEM_INFO si;

    GetSystemInfo(&si);
    cout << "OEM: " << si.dwOemId << endl;
    cout << "PageSize: " << si.dwPageSize << endl;
    cout << "Minimum app address: "
        << si.lpMinimumApplicationAddress << endl;
    cout << "Maximum app address: "
        << si.lpMaximumApplicationAddress << endl;
    cout << "Active processor mask: " << hex
        << si.dwActiveProcessorMask << endl;
```

Listing 16.1   *Code demonstrating the GetSystemInfo function (continued)*

```
    cout << "Number of processors: "
        << si.dwNumberOfProcessors << endl;
    cout << "Processor type: "
        << si.dwProcessorType << endl;
}
```

Some of the more obvious pieces of information contained in the structure include the number of processors, the type of processor used (it returns a constant that you can match against predefined constants in the API's header file), and the OEM string. Other values specify memory-addressing boundaries and virtual-memory parameters. See the description of the SYSTEM_INFO structure in the 32-bit API help file for more information on the individual fields.

16.2 Other System Information Functions

In addition to the **GetSystemInfo** function described in the previous section, there are a number of other information functions scattered throughout the API. Each of them is exercised in the code shown in Listing 16.2.

Listing 16.2   *Code demonstrating the GetComputerName, GetKeyboardType, Get-SysColor, GetSystemDirectory, GetWindowsDirectory, GetSystem Metrics, GetVersion, and GetUserName functions*

```
// siinfo.cpp

#include <windows.h>
#include <iostream.h>
#include <iomanip.h>


/////////
// needs user32.lib
/////////


void main()
{
    BOOL success;
    int result;
    char s[1000];
    int bufferSize = 1000;
    char computerName[MAX_COMPUTERNAME_LENGTH + 1];
```

```
DWORD computerNameLen = MAX_COMPUTERNAME_LENGTH
    + 1;

success = GetComputerName(computerName,
    &computerNameLen);
if (success)
    cout << "Computer name: " << computerName
        << endl;

cout << "Keyboard type: " << GetKeyboardType(0)
    << endl;
cout << "Keyboard subtype: "
    << GetKeyboardType(1) << endl;
cout << "Number of function keys: "
    << GetKeyboardType(2) << endl;

cout << "Border color: " << hex
    << GetSysColor(COLOR_ACTIVEBORDER) << endl;

result = GetSystemDirectory(s, 1000);
cout << "System directory: " << s << endl;

result = GetWindowsDirectory(s, 1000);
cout << "Windows directory: " << s << endl;

cout << "Number of mouse buttons: "
    << GetSystemMetrics(SM_CMOUSEBUTTONS)
    << endl;

DWORD version;
version = GetVersion();
if ((version & 0x80000000) == 0)
    cout << "This is NT \n";
else
    cout << "This is not NT\n";
cout << "Version number: "
    << (version & 0x000000FF) << endl;
cout << "Revision number: "
    << ((version & 0x0000FF00) >> 8) << endl;

char userName[100];
DWORD userNameLen = 100;
success = GetUserName(userName, &userNameLen);
cout << "User name: " << userName << endl;
}
```

Each of the functions demonstrated in Listing 16.2 is straightforward. The **GetComputerName** function returns the network name of the current machine.

GetComputerName   *Returns the network name of the computer*

```
BOOL GetComputerName(
    LPTSTR buffer,
    LPDWORD bufferLen)
```

buffer   Contains the network name of the computer upon return

bufferLen   The length of the name

Returns TRUE on success

You pass into the function a buffer and the buffer's length. The function fills the buffer and returns the length of the name.

The **GetKeyboardType** function returns three different pieces of information, which depend on the integer constant passed in when you call the function.

GetKeyboardType   *Returns information about the keyboard*

```
int GetKeyboardType(
    int info)
```

info   An integer constant that controls the information returned

Returns keyboard information

When you pass a 0, 1, or 2 to **GetKeyboardType**, the function returns the keyboard type, the subtype, and the number of function keys, respectively. The value returned is an integer that decodes to various pieces of information. (See the help file to decode information.)

The **GetSysColor** function lets you determine the currently-chosen color for all of the differentiated objects in the Windows user interface. These are the same objects you see in the Colors applet of the Control Panel when you create your own color schemes.

GetSysColor   *Returns color values for user interface objects*

```
DWORD GetSysColor(
    int index)
```

index   A constant indicating the object color desired.

Returns a 32-bit color word

The API defines 21 different constant values that specify the pieces of the user interface for which colors are defined:

COLOR_ACTIVEBORDER
COLOR_ACTIVECAPTION

COLOR_APPWORKSPACE
COLOR_BACKGROUND
COLOR_BTNFACE
COLOR_BTNSHADOW
COLOR_BTNTEXT
COLOR_CAPTIONTEXT
COLOR_GRAYTEXT
COLOR_HIGHLIGHT
COLOR_HIGHLIGHTTEXT
COLOR_INACTIVEBORDER
COLOR_INACTIVECAPTION
COLOR_INACTIVECAPTIONTEXT
COLOR_MENU
COLOR_MENUTEXT
COLOR_SCROLLBAR
COLOR_SHADOW
COLOR_WINDOW
COLOR_WINDOWFRAME
COLOR_WINDOWTEXT

The function returns a DWORD value that indicates the RGB value for the color of the item requested. You can use the **SetSysColor** function to set colors.

SetSysColor   *Sets color values for user interface objects*

```
BOOL SetSysColors(
    int numElements,
    CONST INT *displayElements,
    CONST COLORREF *rgbValues)
```

numElements	The number of elements being set
displayElements	An array of constants indicating which elements to set
rgbValues	An array of RGB values, one for each element

Returns TRUE on success

The **GetSystemDirectory** and **GetWindowsDirectory** functions return the system and Windows directory for the machine. Knowing the location of these directories is useful in some installation programs, as well as when looking for certain standard files and DLLs. Both functions accept a buffer and an integer indicating the maximum length. Both return the directory path in the buffer and the length of the path in the integer value.

GetWindowsDirectory	*Retrieves the path of the windows directory*
GetSystemDirectory	*Retrieves the path of the system directory*

```
UINT GetWindowsDirectory(
    LPTSTR buffer,
    UINT bufferLen)
```

buffer	Character buffer used to return the path
bufferLen	Length of the buffer

Returns the number of characters copied to the buffer. If the number is greater than bufferLen use a buffer of that size.

The **GetSystemMetrics** function retrieves a wide variety of minutiae about the current machine. It can return information as obscure as the width and height of the cursor, or something as important as the number of buttons on the mouse. Forty different values are available from this function:

SM_CXBORDER	Non-resizable window frame width
SM_CYBORDER	Non-resizable window frame height
SM_CYCAPTION	Window caption height
SM_CXCURSOR	Cursor width
SM_CYCURSOR	Cursor height
SM_CXDLGFRAME	Dialog window frame width
SM_CYDLGFRAME	Dialog window frame height
SM_CXDOUBLECLK	Double-click rectangle width
SM_CYDOUBLECLK	Double-click rectangle height
SM_CXFRAME	Resizable window frame width
SM_CYFRAME	Resizable window frame height
SM_CXFULLSCREEN	Full-screen client area width
SM_CYFULLSCREEN	Full-screen Client area height
SM_CYHSCROLL	Arrow height on HScrollbar
SM_CXICON	Icon width
SM_CYICON	Icon height
SM_CXICONSPACING	ProgMan icon tiling width
SM_CYICONSPACING	ProgMan icon tiling height
SM_CYKANJIWINDOW	Kanji window height
SM_CYMENU	Single-line menu bar height
SM_CXMIN	Window minimum width
SM_CYMIN	Window minimum height
SM_CXMINTRACK	Window minimum tracking width
SM_CYMINTRACK	Window minimum tracking height
SM_CMOUSEBUTTONS	Number of mouse buttons
SM_CXSCREEN	Screen width
SM_CYSCREEN	Screen height

SM_CXSIZE	Title bar bitmap width
SM_CYSIZE	Title bar bitmap height
SM_CXVSCROLL	Arrow width on VScrollbar
SM_CYVSCROLL	Arrow height on VScrollbar
SM_CXHTHUMB	Thumb width on HScrollbar
SM_CYVTHUMB	Thumb height on VScrollbar
SM_DBCSENABLED	Double-byte charset status
SM_DEBUG	Debug version
SM_MENUDROPALIGNMENT	Pop-up menu alignment
SM_MOUSEPRESENT	Zero if no mouse installed
SM_PENWINDOWS	Handle to Pen Windows DLL
SM_SWAPBUTTON	Zero if mouse buttons not swapped

See the help file for complete descriptions. You should look through the list at least once so that you know what is possible.

GetSystemMetrics   *Returns a wide variety of system information*

```
int GetSystemMetrics(
    int index)
```

index   A constant indicating the piece of information desired.

Returns the requested value

The **GetVersion** function returns information about the operating system currently running on the system. Most significantly, it can tell you whether the operating system is Windows 2000 or not, and what the version number and revision number are.

GetVersion   *Returns NT status and version number*

```
DWORD GetVersion(VOID)
```

Returns version and status encoded in a DWORD

An encoding scheme is used to pack three pieces of data into the DWORD value returned by the function. The high-order bit, if it is 1, indicates that the system is running Windows 2000. The low-order byte contains the version number, for example, version three. The byte above it indicates the revision number.

The final function that is demonstrated in Listing 16.2 is the **GetUser-Name** function. This function returns the login name of the user that owns the process. This function is useful whenever you need to know or display the current user ID.

GetUserName	*Returns the user name*

```
BOOL GetUserName
  LPTSTR buffer,
  LPDWORD bufferLen)
```

buffer	The buffer that will hold the returned name
bufferLen	The length of the buffer

Returns TRUE on success

You pass in a character array and the length of the array. The function returns the name and the length of the name. If the function fails, it is because the buffer is too short.

To get information about the memory system, use the **GlobalMemory-Status** function. See Chapter 21.

16.3 Getting and Setting Environment Strings

Environment variables often contain information that is useful during the execution of a program. For example, you might want to retrieve the current path so that you can search it for a specific directory name. To retrieve environment variables, use the **ExpandEnvironmentString** function, as shown in Listing 16.3.

Listing 16.3   *Using the ExpandEnvironmentString function*

```
// siees.cpp

#include <windows.h>
#include <iostream.h>

void main()
{
   char s[1000];
   DWORD result;

   result = ExpandEnvironmentStrings("%path%",
      s, 1000);
   if (result == 0)
   {
      cout << "Error: " << GetLastError() << endl;
      return;
   }
   cout << s << endl;
}
```

The function accepts a string containing one or more environment variable names wrapped in "%" characters, in the same way as when you reference the variable in a batch file. When the function returns, the buffer is filled with all of the values for the variables requested.

ExpandEnvironmentStrings   *Retrieves environment variable values*

```
DWORD ExpandEnvironmentStrings(
    LPCTSTR envVars,
    LPTSTR buffer,
    DWORD bufferLen)
```

envVars	String containing the environment values to expand.
buffer	The buffer that will hold the returned values.
bufferLen	The length of the buffer.

Returns the size of the returned string, or zero on error.

If an environment variable is not found, it is not expanded. It is copied into the buffer in its original form. Otherwise, the buffer contains the value of the requested environment variable. The DWORD value returned by the function will be zero if an error occurred during execution.

The **GetEnvironmentVariable** function is equivalent to the **ExpandEnvironmentStrings** function, but expands only one variable at a time.

GetEnvironmentVariable   *Retrieves an environment variable value*

```
DWORD GetEnvironmentVariable(
    LPCTSTR name,
    LPTSTR buffer,
    DWORD bufferLen)
```

name	String containing the environment variable to get.
buffer	The buffer that will hold the returned value.
bufferLen	The length of the buffer.

Returns the size of the returned string, or zero on error.

It is also possible to set environment strings using the **SetEnvironmentVariable** function.

SetEnvironmentVariable   *Creates or modifies an environment variable*

```
BOOL SetEnvironmentVariable(
   LPTSTR variableName,
   LPTSTR newValue)
```

variableName   The name of the variable to create or change

newValue   The new value for the variable

Returns TRUE on success and FALSE on failure, and sets GetLastError.

Pass a new or existing variable name into the **variableName** parameter. Pass the new value into the **newValue** parameter. A NULL value for **newValue** will delete an existing variable.

16.4 Shutting Down the System

It is possible to log the current user off, reboot the system, or shut down the system from within a program. There are many special situations in which these capabilities prove useful. For example, you might want a program to run and then log off the current user when it is done. Then, by locking the screen, one can walk away from the machine and know that it will make itself available to other users upon completion of the program. Listing 16.4 demonstrates how to log off the current user.

Listing 16.4   *Logging off the system*

```
// silogoff.cpp

#include <windows.h>
#include <iostream.h>

void main()
{
   BOOL success;

   success = ExitWindowsEx(EWX_LOGOFF, 0);
   if (success)
      cout << "Success. Logging off.\n" << endl;
   else
      cout << "Error logging off: "
         << GetLastError() << endl;
}
```

ExitWindowsEx	*Logs off or reboots the system*

```
BOOL ExitWindowsEx(
   UINT options,
   DWORD reserved)
```

options	Tells the function what to do.
reserved	Ignored

Returns TRUE on success

By passing different constants into **ExitWindowsEx**, you can cause it to shut down, and to reboot the system as well. Listing 16.5 shows how to reboot the system.

Listing 16.5   *Rebooting the system*

```
// sireboot.cpp

#include <windows.h>
#include <iostream.h>
#include <process.h>

void HandleError(char *s)
{
   cout << "Error in " << s << endl;
   cout << "Error code = " << GetLastError()
      << endl;
   exit(1);
}

BOOL EnablePrivilege(LPTSTR privilege)
{
   BOOL success;
   HANDLE token;
   LUID luid;
   TOKEN_PRIVILEGES tokenPrivileges;

   // Get token for this process
   success = OpenProcessToken(GetCurrentProcess(),
      TOKEN_ADJUST_PRIVILEGES | TOKEN_QUERY,
      &token);
   if (!success)
   {
      HandleError("OpenProcessToken");
      return FALSE;
   }
```

Listing 16.5   *Rebooting the system (continued)*

```
   // Gets the value for a privilege
   success = LookupPrivilegeValue(0, privilege,
      &luid);
   if (!success)
   {
      HandleError("LookupPrivilegeValue");
      return FALSE;
   }


   // Enable the privilege
   tokenPrivileges.PrivilegeCount = 1;
   tokenPrivileges.Privileges[0].Luid = luid;
   tokenPrivileges.Privileges[0].Attributes =
      SE_PRIVILEGE_ENABLED;
   success = AdjustTokenPrivileges(token, FALSE,
      &tokenPrivileges, 0, 0, 0);
   // Always returns true, so check GetLastError
   if (GetLastError() != ERROR_SUCCESS)
   {
      HandleError("AdjustTokenPrivileges");
      return FALSE;
   }
   return TRUE;
}


BOOL DisablePrivilege(LPTSTR privilege)
{
   BOOL success;
   HANDLE token;
   LUID luid;
   TOKEN_PRIVILEGES tokenPrivileges;

   // Get tokens for this process
   success = OpenProcessToken(GetCurrentProcess(),
      TOKEN_ADJUST_PRIVILEGES | TOKEN_QUERY,
      &token);
   if (!success)
   {
      HandleError("OpenProcessToken");
      return FALSE;
   }


   // Gets the value for a privilege
   success = LookupPrivilegeValue(0, privilege,
      &luid);
   if (!success)
   {
```

```
        HandleError("LookupPrivilegeValue");
        return FALSE;
    }

    // Disable the privilege
    tokenPrivileges.PrivilegeCount = 1;
    tokenPrivileges.Privileges[0].Luid = luid;
    // disable the privilege
    tokenPrivileges.Privileges[0].Attributes = 0;
    success = AdjustTokenPrivileges(token, FALSE,
        &tokenPrivileges, 0, 0, 0);
    // Always returns true, so...
    if (GetLastError() != ERROR_SUCCESS)
    {
        HandleError("AdjustTokenPrivileges");
        return FALSE;
    }
    return TRUE;
}

void main()
{
    BOOL success;

    if (EnablePrivilege(SE_SHUTDOWN_NAME))
    {
        success = ExitWindowsEx(EWX_REBOOT, 0);
        if (success)
            cout << "Success. Shutting down shortly."
                << endl;
        else
            HandleError("Shutting down");
    }
    DisablePrivilege(SE_SHUTDOWN_NAME);
}
```

To reboot the system, you must enable the shutdown privilege. The **EnablePrivilege** and **DisablePrivilege** functions handle the enabling and disabling of the SE_SHUTDOWN_NAME privilege required to reboot the system. See Section 16.7 for details. If the user running the code is able to gain the shutdown privilege, then the **ExitWindowsEx** function will succeed and the system will reboot. It is also possible to shut down the system, rather than reboot it, using the EWX_SHUTDOWN constant.

The **InitiateSystemShutdown** function performs a system shutdown as well, but uses an intermediate dialog that warns the current user of the impending loss of service. This function can be revoked using the **AbortSystemShutdown** function. If you call the abort function before the shutdown timer has expired, then the shutdown operation will be canceled.

Listings 16.6 and 16.7 demonstrate the use of these two functions. These are code fragments; use them in place of the **main** function in Listing 16.5.

Listing 16.6   *Initiating a system shutdown. Replace the main function in Listing 16.5 with this code*

```
void main()
{
   BOOL success;

   if (EnablePrivilege(SE_SHUTDOWN_NAME))
   {
      success = InitiateSystemShutdown(0,
         "Shutting Down", 30, FALSE, FALSE);
      if (success)
         cout << "Success. Shutting down shortly."
            << endl;
      else
         HandleError("InitiateSystemShutdown");
   }
   DisablePrivilege(SE_SHUTDOWN_NAME);
}
```

Listing 16.7   *Aborting a system shutdown. Replace the main function in Listing 16.5 with this code*

```
void main()
{
   BOOL success;

   if (EnablePrivilege(SE_SHUTDOWN_NAME))
   {
      success = AbortSystemShutdown(0);
      if (success)
         cout << "Success. Shut down canceled."
            << endl;
      else
         HandleError("AbortSystemShutdown");
   }
   DisablePrivilege(SE_SHUTDOWN_NAME);
}
```

The **InitiateSystemShutdown** function accepts several parameters. The **machineName** parameter indicates the name of the machine to be shut down. If you want to shut down the current machine, pass a null string and enable the SE_SHUTDOWN_NAME privilege. If you want to shut down a remote machine, pass the network name of the machine into this parameter and enable the SE_REMOTE_SHUTDOWN_NAME privilege. See Section 16.7 for details on privileges.

Dynamic Link Libraries

Dynamic Link Libraries, or DLLs, give your applications an extra level of modularity. They also make the operating system extensible to some degree. Many of Windows' operating-system features are supplied in DLLs rather than being embedded in the system. You can extend the operating system yourself by creating your own DLLs including their advantages and disadvantages.

In this chapter, you will learn about the design and implementation of dynamic link libraries. You will also learn about the two different ways to link DLL code to an application including their advantages and disadvantages.

Compatibility Note: All of the code in this chapter works identically in Windows 2000 and Windows 98.

17.1 The Possibilities

Dynamic Link Libraries give you a way to break up an application into separate modules. An application designed using DLLs contains the normal EXE file, but the executable finds and links to one or more external binary object files at runtime. This architecture opens up several possibilities:

- Since the DLL is a separate and completely stand-alone entity, you can have one group of programmers independently develop a DLL while another group works on the application. The only connection needed between the two groups is a header file that defines the function prototypes for the DLL functions. If the DLL needs to change, you do not have to recompile the application. Just swap the old DLL file for a new one.

- You can extend the operating system by creating and publishing a DLL and a header file that describes it. Other programmers can use the DLL without having access to the source code. For example, the compressed-file-handling capabilities described in Chapter 2 come from their own DLL, called LZ32.DLL.

- You can make certain portions of an application replaceable. For example, you might put language-dependent features of a program in a DLL so that you can swap DLLs to create multi-language distributions. Or you might put device-dependent features in a DLL so that you can ship different DLLs to different clients without changing the entire application.

DLLs are extremely easy to create. You will find yourself using them frequently to modularize your code once you understand them.

17.2 Overview

Figure 17.1 shows the difference between a normal executable and an executable that uses dynamic link libraries.

Any application that you write in Windows actually uses DLLs without your really being aware of it. For example, a normal MFC program of any size links to, among other things, KERNEL32.DLL, USER32.DLL, ADVAPI32.DLL, COMDLG32.DLL, GDI32.DLL, WINSPOOL.DLL, OLE32.DLL, SHELL32.DLL, and so on. As you can see, Windows uses DLLs quite extensively. You can find all of Windows' DLLs in the `system32` directory.

DLLs are popular because they have a number of important advantages:

1. You can change a DLL without recompiling applications. For example, suppose it was decided that NETAPI32.DLL contained a serious flaw. You could obtain and load a new DLL for it onto your machine, and nothing else would have to change. The next time you run an application, the application would use the new DLL.

2. DLLs save a tremendous amount of disk space. For example, NETAPI 32.DLL consumes 250K of disk space. However, it only consumes that disk space once. There might be 20 applications on your hard disk that use NETAPI32.DLL, and if it weren't for DLLs, they would all have to contain their own personal copy of that object code at a cost of about five megs of disk space. When you consider that the `system32` directory contains over 150 DLL files used by potentially hundreds of applications, that is a lot of disk space being saved.

Normal Application
Executable

Main application code
Data structure code
Special calculation code

Application Executable
Using DLLs

Main application code

DLLs

Data structure code

Special calculation code

Figure 17.1 *A normal executable compared to an executable that uses DLLs. The normal application contains all object code in its EXE. The DLL application links to the DLLs at run-time*

3. The same savings seen in disk space also apply to memory when an application is running. If two running applications use NETAPI32.DLL, only one copy of the DLL needs to exist in memory.

4. DLLs let you add capabilities to the operating system. For example, the email capability of Windows 2000 exists in MAPI.DLL. Any application (for example, Microsoft Word) that wants to include an email interface uses MAPI to do it. Anyone can develop and distribute their own DLLs.

5. As a programmer, you might want to create a graphics library, an advanced matrix manipulation library, or a statistics library, and sell it. DLLs give you the ideal way to do that. You ship the DLL, as well as a header file that describes the interface to the functions. You also supply a LIB file that lets new programs link to the DLL when they are compiled. Programmers can then use the DLL seamlessly just as they use any other DLL.

There really are not any disadvantages to using a DLL. There is no noticeable overhead involved in calling a DLL function, compared to calling an internal function.

A DLL typically contains a suite of related functions. For example, the MAPI.DLL file contains a set of functions that form the messaging APIs for Windows 2000. If you place a statistical library in a DLL, then all of the functions have to do with statistics. The functions can be independent of one another, or they can work together by sharing global variables to get fast intercommunication. You can get a good feeling for DLL design by looking at DLL header files in the `mstools\h` or the `msvc\include` directory.

17.3 Creating a Simple DLL

Both DLLs and RPCs (see Chapter 9) have a certain amount of startup complexity. That is, the first time you see them, it all seems complicated because there are several different and unfamiliar pieces needed to make the system work. The goal of this section is to show you how easy it is to compile and run the simplest possible DLL. The next section explains how the program and the DLL work together.

The goal of the DLL presented in this section and the next is simple: The DLL contains one function called **MultiHonk** that accepts one integer parameter. The function beeps. If you pass it a 3 it beeps three times. It takes seven files to build the DLL and a test application for it, as shown in Listings 17.1 through 17.7.

Listing 17.1   *The implementation of the MultiHonk function contained in the DLL (snd.cpp)*

```cpp
// snd.cpp
#include <windows.h>

#include "snd.h"

void MultiHonk(DWORD iterations)
{
  UINT i;

  for (i=0; i<iterations; i++)
  {
    Beep(200, 50);
    Sleep(1000);
  }
}
```

Listing 17.2   *The header file for the DLL (snd.h)*

```cpp
// snd.h

extern "C"
```

```
{
void MultiHonk(DWORD iterations);
}
```

| Listing 17.3 | The def file for the DLL, identifying the name and exported function (snd.def) |

```
; snd.def

LIBRARY snd

EXPORTS
    MultiHonk
```

| Listing 17.4 | The makefile needed to compile Listings 17.1 through 17.3 and produce the snd.dll and snd.lib files required by an application that wants to use the DLL |

```
DLL=snd
NODEBUG=1

!include <ntwin32.mak>

$(DLL).dll: $(DLL).obj $(DLL).exp
    $(link) -dll $(ldebug) $(conlibs) \
        $(DLL).obj $(DLL).exp -out:$(DLL).dll

$(DLL).lib $(DLL).exp: $(DLL).def
    $(implib) -def:$(DLL).def \
        -machine:$(CPU) -out:$(DLL).lib

$(DLL).obj: $(DLL).cpp $(DLL).h
    $(cc) $(cflags) $(cdebug) \
        $(cvars) $(DLL).cpp
```

| Listing 17.5 | A simple application that uses the DLL (honker1.cpp) |

```
// honker1.cpp

#include <windows.h>
#include <stdlib.h>
#include <iostream.h>

#include "sndlt.h"

VOID main(VOID)
```

Listing 17.5   *A simple application that uses the DLL (honker1.cpp)*

```
{
  DWORD iterations;
  CHAR iterStr[100];

  cout << "Enter the number of beeps to produce: ";
  cin.getline(iterStr, 100);

  iterations=atoi(iterStr);

  // make the beeps
  MultiHonk(iterations);
}
```

Listing 17.6   *The header file that lets Listing 17.5 use the DLL (sndlt.h)*

```
// sndlt.h

extern "C"
{
void MultiHonk(DWORD iterations);
}
```

Listing 17.7   *A makefile for the application*

```
APP=honker1
NODEBUG=1

!include <ntwin32.mak>

$(APP).exe: $(APP).obj
    $(link) $(conlflags) $(ldebug) \
        $(conlibs) snd.lib $(APP).obj \
        -out:$(APP).exe

$(APP).obj: $(APP).cpp sndlt.h
    $(cc) $(cflags) $(cdebug) $(cvars) \
        $(APP).cpp
```

The DLL files consist of the code for the DLL function (Listing 17.1), the header file for the DLL (Listing 17.2), and a DEF file that describes to the library manager which functions this DLL is going to export to the applications that use it (Listing 17.3). DLLs do not necessarily export all of the functions they contain. A DLL can contain internal "helper" functions that are not made available to applications.

The makefile in Listing 17.4 (or the VC++ project file on the diskette) compiles and creates the DLL. It forms a normal OBJ file from snd.cpp using the normal compiler. The "library manager" ($(implib)) takes the DEF file and uses it to produce a LIB file and an EXP file. The normal linker uses the EXP file and the OBJ file to produce the DLL file.

Normally, you place Listings 17.1 through 17.4 in their own directory. Use nmake or VC++ to create the DLL. You can then put the DLL file either in the application's directory or somewhere in the PATH. You can copy the LIB file to the application's directory or to a standard LIB directory known to the compiler. The application also needs to be able to access sndlt.h, the header file that describes the DLL, either by copying it or by placing it in a standard header directory that the compiler knows about. Note that right now snd.h and sndlt.h are the same, but they will generally differ, as described in later sections.

Listing 17.5 contains an application that uses the DLL. It includes the DLL's header file and then calls the DLL function as it would any other function. The makefile in Listing 17.7 compiles the application and links it to snd.lib. When you run the application, it will automatically look for the file snd.dll in the normal PATH and use it. If it cannot find snd.dll, the program will not execute.

Normally you would place Listings 17.5, 17.6, and 17.7 in their own application directory. For this simple experiment, it is probably easiest to then copy into that directory the files snd.dll and snd.lib from the DLL directory.

Figure 17.2 shows a diagram that explains the interrelationships among Listings 17.1 through 17.7.

When you run the application, it will look for the DLL file. If you hide snd.dll (by either moving, deleting, or renaming it), the program will fail and display a dialog advising you of the problem. If you copy snd.dll into the application's directory or your path so that the application can find it, then the application will ask you for a number and then it will call **Multi-Honk** so that it beeps that many times.

17.4 Understanding a Simple DLL

Looking at Listings 17.1 through 17.7, you can see that two of the files are completely normal. Listing 17.1 is the implementation of the DLL function, and it contains no surprises. Listing 17.5 contains the code for the application, and it is normal as well.

The header file in Listing 17.2 is easy to understand. It contains a standard prototype for **MultiHonk**. The prototype is wrapped in the extern "C" statement to tell the C++ compiler to turn off its name mangling. DLL files as shown here contain normal C functions.

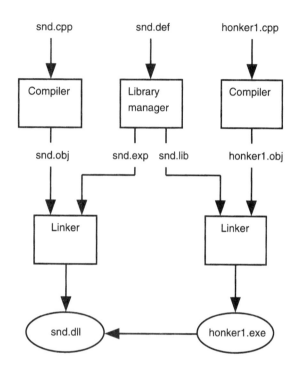

Figure 17.2
How Listings 17.1 through 17.7 work together to form a working DLL and application

The DEF file in Listing 17.3 is new. DLLs rely on the *Library Manager* to build the LIB file that the application needs in order to link to the DLL. The DEF file declares for the Library Manager the name of the library (snd) and the names of all of the functions that the DLL exports. The DLL file here exports one function named **MultiHonk**. Larger DLLs may export as many functions as they need. DLLs do not have to export all of the functions they contain. These unexported "helper" functions can be used by other functions in the DLL as usual. For each exported function in the DLL, create one line containing the function's name in the EXPORTS section of the DEF file.

The makefile in Listing 17.4 compiles Listing 17.1 normally to produce an OBJ file. Next, the make file executes the Library Manager on the DEF file to produce an EXP file and a LIB file. The linker uses the EXP file when creating the actual DLL. The LIB file gets used by the linker for any application that wants to link to the DLL.

The makefile in Listing 17.7 compiles Listing 17.5 to produce the application's OBJ file. The linker takes this OBJ along with the DLL's LIB file to create the application.

When you run the application, the operating system will hunt for any DLLs it needs. The OS looks in the application's load directory, the current directory, the winnt system32 directory, the winnt directory, and the PATH directories for DLLs. If it doesn't find a DLL it needs, the application displays a dialog box indicating the problem and terminates.

When you want to create a DLL of your own, take the following steps:

1. Create a header file that prototypes and describes all of the functions in the DLL. *Make sure* you wrap all functions in this header file with extern "C" as seen in Listing 17.2. If you are using *load-time* linking without an entry-point function, as is done here, then you can use this same header file in the application. If you are using *run-time* linking, you need to create a different header file for the application. See Section 17.5 for details.

2. Create the implementations for the DLL functions in a CPP file. This file should include the header file from step one.

3. Create a DEF file. It needs a LIBRARY line to name the library and an EXPORTS section. Place the name of every function in the header file, one per line, in the EXPORTS section.

4. Create a makefile modeled after Listing 17.4.

Place all four of these files in their own directory and use nmake or VC++ to create the DLL. Make the DLL and LIB files available to any applications that need to use the DLL, either by copying the files to the application's source directories or by copying them to standard directories known to the compiler and linker.

To create an application that uses the DLL, all that you need to do is include the DLL's header file in the application and link the application to the LIB file for the DLL. When the application runs, it will automatically load and use the DLL file.

17.5 Load-time versus Run-time Linking

The above example uses what is called *load-time linking* to connect the DLL to the application. In load-time linking, the operating system automatically loads the DLL for the application as soon as the application starts. If the OS cannot find the necessary DLL, the application cannot run. You access almost all DLLs using load-time linking, because it is easy and transparent. The application programmer needs to put nothing in the application's code to use the DLL.

Run-time linking gives the application a little more control. In run-time linking, the application tells the operating system when to load the DLL. The operating system then tells the application whether the DLL is available. If it is not, the application can decide how to deal with the problem.

Probably the best-known example of the use of run-time linking is the way Microsoft Word loads MAPI.DLL. MAPI is the messaging API and allows Word to support email features. If MAPI.DLL is missing, Word simply advises the user of the problem with a dialog box, disables its email menu options, and continues. If Word were written so that it used load-time linking with MAPI.DLL, then the user would be unable to run Word on machines that did not have MAPI.DLL.

Listings 17.8 through 17.10 show how to write and compile an application so that it uses run-time linking. Listing 17.8 does the same thing as Listing 17.5, but contains the code to perform the run-time linking. *The DLL file and directory do not have to change in any way to use run-time linking.* The DLL itself does not care whether the application uses load-time or run-time linking. Once you create a DLL, any application can use load-time or run-time linking on it interchangeably.

Listing 17.8   *An simple application that uses the DLL with run-time linking (honker2.cpp). Compare with Listing 17.5*

```cpp
// honker2.cpp

#include <windows.h>
#include <stdlib.h>
#include <iostream.h>

#include "sndrt.h"

VOID main(VOID)
{
    DWORD iterations;
    CHAR iterStr[100];
    CHAR modName[MAX_PATH];
    HINSTANCE sndHandle;

    cout << "Enter the number of beeps to produce: ";
    cin.getline(iterStr, 100);

    iterations=atoi(iterStr);

    // map snd.dll into process
    sndHandle=LoadLibraryEx("snd", NULL,
        0);

    if (sndHandle == NULL)
    {
        cerr << "Sorry, unable to use DLL." << endl;
        return;
    }
```

```
    else
    {
      // load function name with address mapped from
      // snd.dll
      MultiHonk=(void (*)(DWORD))GetProcAddress(
        sndHandle, "MultiHonk");

      if (MultiHonk == NULL)
      {
        cerr
          << "Sorry, MultiHonk function not in DLL."
          << endl;
        // release the DLL
        FreeLibrary(sndHandle);
        return;
      }
      else
      {
        GetModuleFileName(sndHandle, modName,
          MAX_PATH);
        cout << "Using DLL: " << modName
          << endl;

        // make the beeps
        MultiHonk(iterations);
        // release the DLL
        FreeLibrary(sndHandle);
      }
    }
}
```

Listing 17.9   *The header file needed for the application to use the DLL with run-time linking (sndrt.h)*

```
// sndrt.h

void (*MultiHonk)(DWORD iterations);
```

Listing 17.10   *A makefile for the application using run-time linking*

```
APP=honker2
NODEBUG=1

!include <ntwin32.mak>

$(APP).exe: $(APP).obj
    $(link) $(conlflags) $(ldebug) \
      $(conlibs) $(APP).obj -out:$(APP).exe
```

```
$(APP).obj: $(APP).cpp sndrt.h
    $(cc) $(cflags) $(cdebug) $(cvars) \
      $(APP).cpp
```

Listing 17.8 is somewhat longer than Listing 17.5, because an application that uses run-time linking must load the DLL itself. Listing 17.8 starts the process by calling the **LoadLibraryEx** function.

LoadLibraryEx	*Loads the object code for a DLL and maps it into the application's address space*

```
HINSTANCE LoadLibraryEx(
    LPCTSTR libraryFile,
    HANDLE file,
    DWORD flags)
```

libraryFile	The DLL to load. The function will automatically append ".dll"
file	Reserved. Must be NULL
flags	Indicates whether the entry point function should be called

Returns a handle to the DLL or 0 on error

The **LoadLibraryEx** function loads the DLL. It accepts "snd" as the name of the DLL and appends ".dll" to it. It will search the directory from which the application loaded, the current directory, the winnt system32 and winnt directory, and all of the directories in the PATH in its attempt to find the DLL. If it cannot find the DLL file, it returns NULL. Listing 17.8 prints an error message and dies if the DLL is missing, but you will probably want to do something more elaborate in a production application.

The application's next step is to load the addresses of all of the functions needed in the DLL. Note that the header file in Listing 17.9 is very different from the header file in Listing 17.6. In Listing 17.9, the functions in the DLL are declared as pointers to functions. The application must initialize these pointers before it can call any of the DLL's functions. There will be one pointer for each function in the DLL, and a line to initialize each pointer in the application. The **GetProcAddress** function returns the address of one function.

GetProcAddress	*Gets the address of one function from the DLL*

```
FARPROC GetProcAddress(
    HMODULE module,
    LPCSTR funcName)
```

module	The handle to the DLL returned by **LoadLibraryEx**
funcName	The name of the function to look up

Returns the address of the function or 0 on error

If the function does not exist in the DLL, then Listing 17.8 quits. Otherwise, the program calls **GetModuleFileName** simply to demonstrate it. The **GetModuleFileName** returns the name of the DLL file.

GetModuleFileName	*Gets the name of the DLL file*

```
DWORD GetModuleFileName(
    HMODULE module,
    LPTSTR buffer,
    DWORD bufferLen)
```

module	The handle to the DLL returned by **LoadLibraryEx**
buffer	The buffer it will return the name in
bufferLen	The length of the buffer

Returns the length of the name in the buffer or 0 one error

The call to **MultiHonk** in Listing 17.8 is anticlimactic. It looks just like a normal function call. The program then calls **FreeLibrary** to clean up, and quits.

FreeLibrary	*Unmaps the DLL if nothing else is using it*

```
BOOL FreeLibrary(
    HINSTANCE module)
```

module	The handle to the DLL returned by **LoadLibraryEx**

Returns TRUE on success

As you can see, run-time linking is not particularly difficult. It simply requires you to load the DLL and map its functions manually, rather than letting the operating system do it for you. Compiling the run-time linked version is identical to compiling the load-time linked version, except that in the run-time version you do not have to link the code to the LIB file for the DLL.

You can run-time link to any existing or new DLL, because a DLL does not care whether it is load-time or run-time linked to the application. If you want to run-time link a DLL to one of your own applications, take the following steps:

1. Create a header file that declares each function in the DLL as a pointer to the function. You can normally look at the standard DLL header file and convert it to this form.
2. Modify the application so that it loads the DLL file manually and gets the address of each function in the DLL.
3. Free the DLL when it is no longer needed.

17.6 DLL Entry Points

A DLL can optionally contain a special function called the *entry-point function*. This function is called automatically each time a new process loads or unloads the DLL and each time an attached process creates or destroys a thread. Applications do not care whether or not a DLL contains an entry-point function. You do not have to modify either load-time or run-time linked applications to accommodate an entry point.

Entry-point functions exist primarily so that DLLs can properly initialize variables or data structures that are private to the processes or threads using the DLL. For example, if the DLL needs to maintain a separate copy of a certain data structure for each process that attaches, the entry point function is the place to perform the initialization. It is a bit like the constructor and destructor in a C++ class.

Listings 17.11 through 17.14 demonstrate the creation of an entry-point function.

Listing 17.11 *The implementation of a DLL containing an entry-point function (snd.cpp)*

```cpp
// snd.cpp

#include <windows.h>

#include "snd.h"

BOOL WINAPI SndEntryPoint(HINSTANCE dllHandle,
  DWORD reason, LPVOID situation)
{
  CHAR buf[80];
```

```
  switch(reason)
  {
    case DLL_PROCESS_ATTACH:
      if (situation)
        wsprintf(buf, "DLL statically loaded.");
      else
        wsprintf(buf, "DLL dynamically loaded.");
      break;

    case DLL_THREAD_ATTACH:
      wsprintf(buf, "New thread starting.");
      break;

    case DLL_PROCESS_DETACH:
      if (situation)
        wsprintf(buf, "DLL released by system.");
      else
        wsprintf(buf, "DLL released by program.");
      break;

    case DLL_THREAD_DETACH:
      wsprintf(buf, "Thread terminating.");
      break;

    default:
      return FALSE;
  }

  MessageBox(NULL, buf, "DLL Info",
    MB_OK | MB_ICONINFORMATION);
  return TRUE;
}

void MultiHonk(DWORD iterations)
{
  UINT i;

  for (i=0; i<iterations; i++)
  {
    Beep(200, 50);
    Sleep(1000);
  }
}
```

Listing 17.12 *The header file for the DLL in Listing 17.11 (snd.h)*

```
// snd.h

extern "C"
```

Listing 17.12   *The header file for the DLL in Listing 17.11 (snd.h) (continued)*

```
{
BOOL WINAPI SndEntryPoint(HINSTANCE dllHandle,
  DWORD reason, LPVOID situation);
void MultiHonk(DWORD iterations);
}
```

Listing 17.13   *The DEF file for the DLL in Listing 17.11 (snd.def)*

```
LIBRARY snd

EXPORTS
    MultiHonk
```

Listing 17.14   *The makefile to create a DLL containing an entry point*

```
DLL=snd
ENTRY=SndEntryPoint
NODEBUG=1

!include <ntwin32.mak>

$(DLL).dll: $(DLL).obj $(DLL).exp
    $(link) -dll -entry:$(ENTRY)$(DLLENTRY) \
        $(ldebug) $(guilibs) $(DLL).obj \
        $(DLL).exp -out:$(DLL).dll

$(DLL).lib $(DLL).exp: $(DLL).def
    $(implib) -def:$(DLL).def \
        -machine:$(CPU) -out:$(DLL).lib

$(DLL).obj: $(DLL).cpp $(DLL).h
    $(cc) $(cflags) $(cdebug) $(cvars) \
        $(DLL).cpp
```

If you create a new directory and compile the DLL file in Listings 17.11 through 17.14, you can use the file snd.dll with either honker1.exe or honker2.exe. You do not even have to re-compile these applications. When you run them, however, you will find that the DLLs display message boxes when the processes attach and detach the DLL, to show that the entry-point function is working. If you modify the applications so that they create and destroy threads, you will find that dialogs also appear when threads come and go.

Listing 17.11 contains the new function **SndEntryPoint**. This function can have any name, but it must follow the parameter prototype and internal structure shown in the example.

| **DLLEntryPoint** | *Standard prototype for a DLL entry point function* |

```
BOOL WINAPI DllEntryPoint(
    HINSTANCE module,
    DWORD reason
    LPVOID situation)
```

module	A handle to the DLL module
reason	Enumerated type indicating why the function was called (process attachment, thread creation, etc.)
situation	Specifies whether the DLL was run-time (dynamically) or load-time (statically) loaded

You can return TRUE or FALSE through the function. If you return FALSE then the process attached to the DLL is told that the DLL failed

The entry-point function in Listing 17.11 takes a standard approach and switches off of the **reason** parameter. It handles all four possible reasons:

DLL_PROCESS_ATTACH
DLL_THREAD_ATTACH
DLL_PROCESS_DETACH
DLL_THREAD_DETACH

In Listing 17.11, the code uses the **reason** and **situation** values to form a message that appears in a message box. In a real application you can do anything you like.

The value returned by the entry-point function controls how the application calling the DLL responds. If you return FALSE, a load-time linked application will die. A run-time-linked application will believe that the DLL loading failed, just as it would if the DLL file did not exist.

Note that the header file for the DLL in Listing 17.12 contains a prototype for the DLL function. The DLL header file that the application uses, should not contain this function. Use the same header files seen in Listing 17.6 and 17.9 for the application. Also note that the makefile for the DLL has to declare the name of the entry-point function for the linker (see the diskette).

17.7 Memory Models

The simple DLL above uses no variables at all, either local or global. That makes the DLL simple and easy to understand, but it is not very realistic. A typical DLL needs to use memory. Local variables inside of functions are easy, because they work as expected. However, you have to think a little bit and plan carefully before you use global static or dynamic variables in a DLL, because variables inside of DLLs work in slightly unexpected ways.

Let's say that you want to create a DLL that implements a stack data structure. The stack is to be created dynamically on the heap. This *sounds* simple, but DLLs allow you to create at least four different memory models for your simple stack DLL, as shown in Figure 17.3.

The implementation for the first configuration, where many processes can have zero or more stacks that are private to the process, is standard and is the most easily created. Listings 17.15 through 17.18 show the files needed to implement this sort of stack DLL.

Listing 17.15   *The implementation of the stack DLL*

```
// stack.cpp

#include <windows.h>
#include "stack.h"

void init(stack *top)
{
   *top=0;
}

void push(stack *top, int value)
{
   stacknode *temp;

   temp = (stacknode *) GlobalAlloc(GPTR,
     sizeof stacknode);
   temp->data = value;
   temp->next = *top;
   *top = temp;
}

int pop(stack *top)
{
   stacknode *temp;
   int value;

   if (*top == 0)
     return 0;
   temp = *top;
   value = (*top)->data;
   *top = (*top)->next;
   delete temp;
   return value;
}
```

```
void destroy(stack *top)
{
  while (*top != 0);
    pop(top);
}
```

Listing 17.16   *The header file for the stack DLL*

```
// stack.h

typedef struct _stacknode
{
    int data;
    struct _stacknode *next;
} stacknode, *stack;

extern "C"
{
    void init(stack *s);
    void push(stack *s, int i);
    int pop (stack *s);
    void destroy(stack *s);
}
```

Listing 17.17   *The DEF file for the stack DLL*

```
LIBRARY stack

EXPORTS
    init
    push
    pop
    destroy
```

Listing 17.18   *The makefile for the stack DLL*

```
DLL=stack
NODEBUG=1

!include <ntwin32.mak>

$(DLL).dll: $(DLL).obj $(DLL).exp
    $(link) -dll $(ldebug) $(conlibs) \
        $(DLL).obj $(DLL).exp -out:$(DLL).dll

$(DLL).lib $(DLL).exp: $(DLL).def
    $(implib) -def:$(DLL).def \
        -machine:$(CPU) -out:$(DLL).lib
```

Listing 17.18	*The makefile for the stack DLL (continued)*

```
$(DLL).obj: $(DLL).cpp $(DLL).h
    $(cc) $(cflags) $(cdebug) \
        $(cvars) $(DLL).cpp
```

Given this structure for the DLL, each process can declare one or more stacks and call the **push** and **pop** functions as needed. Each process must call **init** before using the stack and call **destroy** to clean up. The **push** and **pop** functions will allocate and deallocate memory on the heap. Any memory allocated by **GlobalAlloc** (see Chapter 15) will belong to the process that called **push**, so all of the stacks are completely independent and isolated.

If you want the DLL to manage just one stack for each process that attaches to it, as shown in part 2 of Figure 17.3, then you should create a single global variable in the DLL itself. The DLL will create a new instance of that global variable for each process that attaches. Then you can use explicit **init** and **destroy** functions, as shown previously, or you can use the entry-point function in the DLL to do the initialization and destruction when the processes attach and detach. See Section 17.6 for information on entry-point functions. It would also be possible to create an array or linked list of stack pointers in the DLL to give each process multiple stacks.

If you want to give each thread its own stack, then you can use the thread-local-storage feature described in Chapter 6. When the process attaches, you let the entry-point function create a new TLS location for it, and then whenever the process creates a new thread, you let the DLL_THREAD_ATTACH case of the entry-point function initialize the stack and place a pointer to it in the TLS location for the thread.

Creating the last structure shown in Figure 17.3 is not easy if you want to use dynamic memory. Whenever you call **GlobalAlloc** in the DLL, the memory allocated is owned by the process that called the DLL. This is troublesome for a global stack because the different threads cannot point into each other's address spaces. The only possible solution is to create shared memory with a File Mapping (see Chapter 2), and then use that shared memory for the stack nodes. Unfortunately, shared memory is treated as an array of elements, so you will have to implement your own memory-allocation functions *and* embed synchronization mechanisms (see Chapter 7) in them and in the stack code to prevent the different processes from stepping on each other.

If you want to create normal global variables that are shared by all processes, and if you are willing to forget about sharing dynamic variables, your job is easy. Add the following to your DEF file:

```
SECTIONS
    .bss READ WRITE SHARED ; unitialized globals
    .data READ WRITE SHARED ; initialized globals
```

1. Each process using the DLL can create zero or more stacks for its own, private use

2. Each process automatically receives one private stack when it attaches to the DLL.

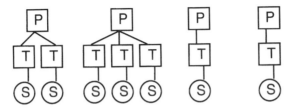

3. Each thread of each process automatically receives one private stack.

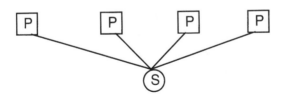

4. All processes share one global stack owned by the DLL.

Figure 17.3   *Four possible memory configurations for stacks implemented in a DLL*

The first line handles uninitialized globals and makes them shared among all processes. The second line does the same for initialized globals.

17.8 Conclusion

DLLs give you an extremely effective modularization tool that has no significant disadvantages. You will find yourself using them frequently once you get used to them.

If you want your DLL to be able to emulate the **GetLastError** behavior of API calls, see Section 21.6. See also exception handling in Section 21.5.

Component Object Model (COM)

*T*he discussion in Chapter 15 showed how the COM Components are being used in the new approach to Windows 2000 administration and management. The distributed program-to-program communications that we showed in Chapter 10, can be handled nicely with Distributed COM (DCOM). The Component Object Model (COM) is a component software architecture that allows applications and systems to be built from components supplied by different software vendors. As we pointed out in Chapter 15, it is expected that a great many of the snap-ins will be produced by ISVs.

The most fundamental question addressed by COM is, how can a system be designed so that binary executables from different vendors, written in different parts of the world and at different times, are able to interoperate? To solve this problem, we have to find solutions to four specific problems:

- *Basic interoperability.* How can developers create their own unique components, yet be assured that these components will interoperate with other components built by different developers?
- *Versioning.* How can one system component be upgraded without forcing all the system components to be upgraded?
- *Language independence.* How can components written in different languages communicate?
- *Transparent cross-process interoperability.* How can we give developers the flexibility to write components to run in-process or cross-process (and eventually cross-network), using one simple programming model?

Additionally, high performance is a requirement for component software architecture. While cross-process and cross-network transparency are laudable goals, it is critical for the commercial success of a binary-component marketplace that components interacting within the same address space be able to utilize each other's services without any undue "system" overhead. Otherwise the components will not realistically be scalable down to very small, lightweight pieces of software equivalent to C++ classes or graphical user-interface (GUI) controls.

18.1 COM Fundamentals

The Component Object Model defines several fundamental concepts that provide the model's structural underpinnings:

- A binary standard for function calling between components.
- A provision for strongly typed groupings of functions into interfaces.
- A base interface providing

   1. A way for components to dynamically discover the interfaces implemented by other components.

   2. Reference counting, to allow components to track their own lifetimes and delete themselves when appropriate.

- A mechanism to uniquely identify components and their interfaces.
- A "component loader" to set up component interactions and, additionally, in the cross-process and cross-network cases, to help manage component interactions.

BINARY STANDARD

John VonNeumann was a brilliant mathematician and computer scientist who is credited with defining the stored-program concept. He realized, as he programmed the binary bits from console switches, that he could store an algorithm and data in the binary-bit memory string. This combination is what we call the stored-program concept. It was then realized that a program could be written which let the programmer specify the program with symbols, rather than enter information via console switches; thus, the assembler was created. We have gone on from there to add significant meta-layers on top of this binary bit string. But as we have done this, the problems mentioned earlier became more significant.

The creation of the COM took us back to our binary roots. We defined what we called a Binary Large Object, or BLOB. The BLOB is simply a sequence of binary numbers stored in the binary bit memory of the computer. Figure 18.1 shows what a BLOB would look like in memory.

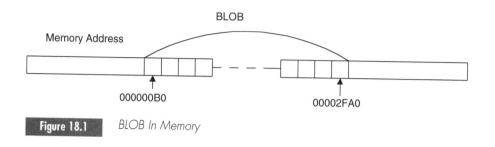

Figure 18.1   *BLOB In Memory*

If we wanted to, we could go to the first address of the BLOB and start execution. This is the way DLLs typically work. However, COM has a different set of specifications for use of this BLOB. COM has specific offset locations in the BLOB that the component user would use. For example, one location would tell the user, if he or she jumped there, what the BLOB could do. Another location would tell the BLOB you were using it. The third location would tell the BLOB that you were finished with it. If we then put the three locations in consecutive sequence in memory, we only have to specify one single offset instead of three. In our case, specifying that 0000000B6 is the offset is enough for the calling program.

Address	Meaning
000000B6	Read the pointer at this location and jump to 000000C0 to find out what the BLOB does.
000000BB	Read the pointer at this location and jump to 000000D3 to let the BLOB know that you are using it.
000000BE	Read the pointer at this location and jump to 000001B8 to let the BLOB know that you are finished using it.

The offset that lets the BLOB tell you what it does is the QueryInterface() method. The offset that lets you tell the BLOB that you are going to be using it is the AddRef() method. The offset that lets you tell the BLOB that you are finished using it is the Release() method. When we combine them into consecutive memory locations, as we mentioned, they become the IUnknown interface. An interface, then, is a table of functions identified by its BLOB address. Since we are dealing with a pointer to an interface in the BLOB, which points to a table of functions, we are dealing with a pointer to a pointer in, for example, C++. Thus, this grouping implies that the first three offsets in any offset table must be pointing to the following functions. The double colons indicate methods in an interface, similar to member functions of a C++ class.

These tables of offsets are frequently called vtables. The compiler-generated structure in the code image produced by the C++ linker has the same type of layout. This is way the C++ compilers for Microsoft create and handle tables of virtual functions for abstract classes. However, COM defines a

IUnknown::QueryInterface()
IUnknown::AddRef()
IUnknown::Release()

Other Methods Of Interface

IUnknown Interface

IMyComInterface

QueryInterface   AddRef   Release

Figure 18.2   *COM BLOB*

standard way to lay out virtual function tables (vtables) in memory, and a standard way to call functions through the vtable. Thus, any language that can call functions via pointers (C, C++, Small Talk, Ada, and Visual Basic) can be used to write components that can interoperate with other components written to the same binary standard. The double indirection (the client holds a pointer to a pointer to a vtable) allows for vtable sharing among multiple instances of the same object class. On a system with hundreds of object instances, vtable sharing can reduce memory requirements considerably. If we put the BLOB diagram in a more language-like diagram it would look like Figure 18.3.

18.2 Component Object Library

Naturally, nowadays we don't have to put software into the machine using console switches and enter 11011....etc to load our programs. So even through COM is a BLOB, we have COM APIs that let us build and use the BLOB components. The Component Object Library is a system component that provides the mechanics of COM. The Component Object Library provides

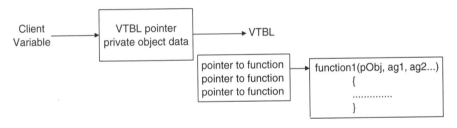

Client
Variable

VTBL pointer
private object data

VTBL

pointer to function
pointer to function
pointer to function

function1(pObj, ag1, ag2...)
{
....
}

Figure 18.3   *Diagram of a vtable*

the ability to use IUnknown calls across processes; it also encapsulates all the "legwork" associated with launching components and establishing connections between components. Typically, when an application creates a component object, it passes the CLSID of that component-object class to the Component Object Library. The Universally Unique Identifier (UUID) for object naming is called CLSID (Class IDs). The Component Object Library uses the CLSID to look up the associated COM server code in the Windows 2000 registration database. If the COM server is an executable, COM launches the .EXE file and waits for it to register its class factory through a call to CoRegisterClassFactory (a class factory is the mechanism in COM used to instantiate new component objects). If that code happens to be a dynamic-link library (DLL), COM loads the DLL and calls DllGetClassFactory. COM uses the object's IClassFactory to ask the class factory to create an instance of the component object and returns a pointer to the requested interface back to the calling application. The calling application neither knows nor cares where the server application is run; it simply uses the returned interface pointer to communicate with the newly created component object.

To summarize, COM defines several basic fundamentals that provide the underpinnings of the object model. The binary standard allows components written in different languages to call each other's functions. Interfaces are logical groups of related functions - functions that together provide some well-defined capability. IUnknown is the interface that COM defines to allow components to control their own life span and to dynamically determine another component's capabilities. A component object implements IUnknown to control its life span and to provide access to the interfaces it supports. A component object does not provide direct access to its data. The Component Object Library is implemented as part of the Windows 2000 operating system and provides the "legwork" associated with finding and launching component objects.

18.3 Summary

We have barely touched upon the ins and outs of COM. However, there are several good books devoted to COM, COM+, and DNA, which we will touch upon in the next couple of chapters. One just-published book that covers the details of COM, COM+, and Windows Distributed Network Architecture (DNA) is Robert Oberg's book "Understanding & Programming COM+", ISBN 0-13-023114-2. He does a great deal of work on the fundamentals of COM and COM+, and then shows how these are used in DNA to create multi-tier applications.

As we have seen, the core of the Component Object Model is a specification for how components and their clients interact. As a specification, it defines a number of other standards for interoperability of software components:

- A binary standard for function calling between components.
- A provision for turning strongly typed groupings of functions into interfaces.
- A base IUnknown interface providing

  - A way for components to dynamically discover the interfaces supported by other components (QueryInterface).
  - Reference counting to encapsulate component lifetime (AddRef and Release).
  - A mechanism to uniquely identify components and their interfaces.

In addition to being a specification, COM is also an implementation contained in the Component Object Library. The implementation is provided through a library, such as a DLL. The DLL includes the following:

- A small number of fundamental API functions that facilitate the creation of COM applications, both clients and servers. For clients, COM supplies basic component-object creation functions; for servers, it supplies facilities to expose their component objects.
- Implementation locator services through which COM determines from a class identifier which server implements that class and where that server is located. This includes support for a level of indirection, usually a system registry, between the identity of an component-object class and the packaging of the implementation such that clients are independent of the packaging (so packaging can change in the future).
- Transparent remote procedure calls when a component object is running in a local or remote server.

In general, only one vendor needs to—or should—implement a COM Library for any particular operating system. All in all, only with a binary standard on a given platform and a wire-level protocol for cross-machine component interaction can an object model provide the type of structure necessary for full interoperability between all applications, and among all different machines, in a network.

COM+

COM+, which is a part of Windows 2000, has been created to make the software developer's life easier. As we all know, systems are getting more complex, especially as we move more heavily into the distributed network application area. COM+ has the MTS (Microsoft Transaction Server) now integrated into COM, and it also provides a messaging alternative for COM calls, based on MSMQ (Microsoft Message Queue). This results in a seamless system in which it becomes almost as easy to implement server applications as to implement client applications. The Component Services, which use snap-ins, provide for highly scalable applications to be built. In this chapter we will just touch the tip of the iceberg as far as capabilities of COM+. But it should give you a feel for what is happening, and for some of the design and application considerations.

19.1 COM+ Programming Overview

COM+ provides a single vision for creating component-based, distributed applications. It provides you with the tools to create transactional, multi-tier applications. COM+ combines enhancements to the Microsoft Component Object Model (COM) with a new version of the technology called Microsoft Transaction Server (MTS), along with many new services.

The COM enhancements include improvements in both threading and security, along with the introduction of Asynchronous COM. The new services include synchronization, object pooling, and Queued Components, as

612

well as a new distributed application administration and packaging service (Component Services). For those familiar with COM programming, the COM+ improvements are significant. COM+ implements a new threading model called neutral apartment threading, which allows a component to have serialized access but also to execute on any thread. In addition to the threading model, COM+ provides role-based security, asynchronous object execution, and a new built-in moniker that represents a reference to an object instant running on an out-of-process server.

ROLE-BASED SECURITY

COM+ now supports both role-based security and process access permissions security. In the role-based security model, access to parts of an application is granted or denied based on the logical group or role to which the caller has been assigned (examples of roles include administrator, developer, and clerk). Also in role-based security is the ability to have security at the method level as well as at the component and interface levels.

THREADING

COM+ includes a new threading model called neutral threading. The neutral model supports execution of objects on any thread type. The benefit of neutral apartment threading is that it does not require the developer of objects to be running a neutral apartment to make the object thread safe.

OBJECT POOLING

Object pooling allows an application to create objects that can be created and pooled according to application needs. Reusing the elements in a pool of deactivated objects can save on system resources. You can pool almost any kind of object, and object pooling is easy to implement.

QUEUED COMPONENTS

Queued Components allow you to create components that can execute immediately if the client and server are connected; or, if the client and server are not connected, the components can defer execution until a connection is made. Queued Components is key functionality for line-of-business applications built for enterprises. It augments "real-time" transactions with the infrastructure necessary to process asynchronous, queued transactions. This technology is effective for creating applications used by clients "in the field" and disconnected from a network; the client can enter transactions that will be executed when the client is again connected to the network. This asynchronous message queuing uses Windows 2000 Messaging Services.

COM+ EVENTS

COM+ events is a component-based event system that uses publishers and subscribers. Publishers send events to subscribers. The publisher identifies the subscribers through subscriptions. A publisher can be any COM+ object that calls an event object. Subscribers can be simple COM+ objects that implement the methods on the event interface.

AUTOMATIC TRANSACTIONS

COM+ supports all Microsoft Transaction Server (MTS) semantics and adds "Auto-done," which allows the system to automatically call either SetAbort (if an exception is triggered) or SetComplete (if not). In addition, COM+ supports components with a special environment called a context, which provides an extensible set of properties that define the execution environment for the component.

APPLICATION AND COMPONENT ADMINISTRATION

In COM+, a new registration database called RegDB stores the metadata that describes components. This database is highly optimized for the type of information that COM+ needs for activation of components and is used in place of the system registry. In addition, COM+ exposes a transactional, scriptable interface called the COM+ catalog, which accesses information in the RegDB. Finally, the Component Services administrative tool provides a fully scriptable user interface for both developers and administrators to administer components as well as to deploy both client-side and server-side multi-tier applications.

19.2 COM+ Application Overview

A COM+ application is the primary unit of administration and security for Component Services. The application is a group of COM components that generally perform related functions. These components further consists of interfaces and methods, as shown in Figure 19.1.

You can use the Component Services administrative tool to create new COM+ applications, add components to applications, and set the attributes for an application and its components. By creating logical groups of COM components as COM+ applications, you can take advantage of the following benefits of COM+:

- A deployment scope for COM components
- A common configuration scope for COM components, including security boundaries and queuing

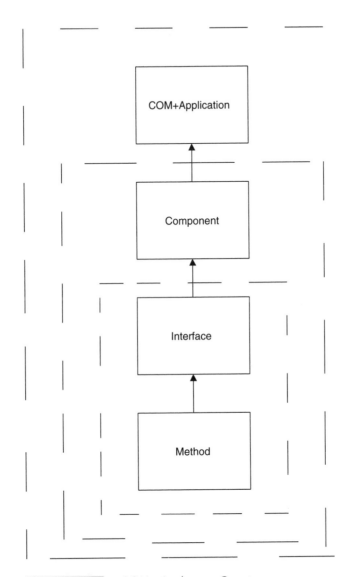

Figure 19.1   *COM+ Application Overview*

- Storage of component attributes not provided by the component developer (for example, transactions and synchronization)
- Component dynamic-link libraries (DLLs) loaded into processes (DLLHost.exe) on demand
- Managed-server processes to host components

- Creation and managements of threads used by components
- Access to the context object for resource dispensers, allowing acquired resources to be automatically associated with the context

19.3 Developing COM+ Applications

Tasks in the development of COM+ applications include designing COM components to encapsulate application logic, integrating these components into a COM+ application, and administering the application through deployment and maintenance.

DESIGNING COM COMPONENTS

The following steps describe a general procedure for good component design:

1. Define the COM classes and implementation classes.
2. Group the classes into components.
3. Integrate the components into a COM+ application. It is a good practice at this stage to select the set of COM+ services for your component, even if you do not specify all of them when developing the component. These services can later be specified using the Component Services administrative tool or the COM+ administration object model.

CREATING THE COM+ APPLICATION

After designing the COM components, the developer integrates the components into a COM+ application and configures the application. The following steps describe the process:

1. Integrate the components into a COM+ application. You can integrate the components into an existing COM+ application, or you can create a new (empty) application for the components.
2. Specify the correct set of attributes for each of the classes (if any, and if not specified in the development tool). These attributes express the component's dependencies on any services its implementation might reply on (for example, transactions, Queued Components, security, object pooling, and JIT activation).
3. Set up the security framework (roles and association of roles to classes, interfaces, and methods).

4. Configure environment-specific attributes on classes and applications (the default pool size, for example). These environment-specific attributes can later be set (or modified) by the system administrator.

5. Export the application for redistribution and/or deployment.

ADMINISTERING COM+ APPLICATIONS

A developer will typically deliver a partially configured COM+ application to the system administrator. The administrator can then customize the application for one or more specific environments (for example, by adding user accounts in roles and server names in an application cluster). The administrator's tasks include the following:

- Installing the partially-configured COM+ application on an administrative machine.
- Providing environment-specific attributes, such as role members and object pool size.
- Re-exporting the fully configured COM+ application.
- Creating an application proxy (if the application is to be accessed remotely).

Once an application is fully configured for a specific environment, the administrator can then deploy it on test and/or production machines. This involves installing the fully configured COM+ application on one or more machines.

19.4 COM+ Design Assumptions and Principles

The Microsoft WinDNA (Windows Distributed interNet Applications) model consists of several technologies, including MSMQ, IIS, DCOM, and COM+. All of these services were designed for use by distributed applications. COM+ was developed to facilitate the creation of distributed applications. The overall architecture is based on a set of assumptions and principles. The three assumptions are as follows:

- The COM+ application will support multiple users across multiple servers. In other words, you are building a distributed application. These multiple users are going to be on different host machines from that on which the code runs. Users are going to access the code via the Internet or via a private network. The user interface is going to be presented via browser or maybe via custom applications, such as a form-based application written with Microsoft Visual Basic or MFC. That user interface is going to be located on the client machine.

- The COM+ application can be made scalable and can provide greater availability and reliability through the deployment of the application across multiple-server machines. By doing this, you can balance the workload of the application and provide fault tolerance using Windows Clustering.
- The state of the persisted data from a COM+ application stored in a database, if things go wrong, will be maintained if you are using transactions. The application state must survive accidents that can occur, such as application errors, system crashes, or network failures.

In addition to these three assumptions, there are three principles that pervade the COM+ programming model. These principles are as follows:

- The application logic will reside on server machines, not on client machines. There are many reasons for this. One reason is that the client machine may not have the processing power or features needed to run the application logic. In addition, keeping the application logic on the server simplifies deployment. Second, the server machines are often closer to the data, and the data are most often in a database. Because your application is accessing databases, you should be very sensitive to the cost of database connections. By putting most of the logic on the server machine, you can share database connections and get a significant performance improvement. There are other resources on the server machines that can be shared as well, also with a performance benefit. Finally, having application logic reside on server machines keeps control of the security context with the application. You have more control over security if you maintain that security on application components running on server machines instead of on client machines.
- Transactions are the core. Transactions so permeate the programming model that you need to understand them thoroughly. You can, however, make use of many of the services of COM+ without using transactions, though if you choose not to use transactions, you really are not taking full advantage of the COM+ services available to you. Transactions are a reasonable solution for the problem of concurrency management. Also, transactions give protection against crashes and have a good error-recovery mode. Furthermore, transactions turn out to be a great way to manage tasks across multiple systems. You can design a transaction-based COM+ application to work with a resource manager and a database so that most state information is protected. By keeping state inside a database or some other storage managed by a resource manager, you don't have to keep much state inside the actual objects your application creates. While this is a departure from a pure object-oriented model, it

works well for creating distributed applications with error recovery. The whole idea of programming transactions and having transactions permeate the application is how COM+ is designed. You do yourself a great favor by using transactions in a COM+ application.

- Build your application functionality as COM objects and wrap the protocols used to communicate with other systems or technologies. Since you are probably building components that are going to stitch together several technologies or legacy systems, plan on using a variety of communication protocols. Use HTTP for client/server communication or application-to-application communication over the Internet. Use DCOM for application-to-application or component-to-component communication on the server.

19.5 Conclusion

The COM+ programming model makes creating COM+ applications fairly straightforward. It maps somewhat naturally to the modern object-based programming model. In Windows 2000 COM+ is a part of the operating system and the Microsoft Transaction Service has been integrated into the COM programming model. There are great many features of COM+ and Windows 2000, but in this chapter we have merely highlighted some important features and specifications. Probably one of the most profound changes in the programming model is the integration of component configuration and interception into the core model and runtime.

Windows Distributed Network Architecture (DNA)

Microsoft developed the Windows Distributed interNet Application Architecture (Windows DNA) as a way to fully integrate the Web with the n-tier model of development. Windows DNA defines a framework for delivering solutions that meet the demanding requirements of corporate computing, the Internet, intranets, and global electronic commerce, while reducing overall development and deployment costs.

Windows DNA architecture employs standard Windows-based services to address the requirements of each tier in the multi-tiered solution: user interface and navigation, business logic, and data storage. The services used in Windows DNA, which are integrated through the Component Object Model (COM), include the following

- Dynamic HTML (DHTML)
- Active Server Pages (ASP)
- COM components
- Component Services
- Active Directory Services
- Windows security services
- Microsoft Message Queuing
- Microsoft Data Access Components

To introduce Windows DNA, we will cover the most frequently asked questions about it.

20.1 Frequently Asked Questions about Windows DNA

WHAT IS WINDOWS DNA?

Microsoft Windows Distributed interNet Applications Architecture (Windows DNA) is the application development model for the Windows platform. Windows DNA specifies how to do many things: develop robust, scalable, distributed applications using the Windows platform, extend existing data and external applications to support the Internet, and support a wide range of client devices to maximize the reach of an application. Because Windows DNA relies on a comprehensive and integrated set of services provided by the Windows platform, developers are free from the burden of building or assembling the required infrastructure for distributed application and can therefore focus on delivering business solutions.

Windows DNA addresses requirements at all tiers of modern distributed applications: presentation, business logic, and data. Like the familiar PC environment, Windows DNA enables developers to build tightly integrated applications by accessing a rich set of application services in the Windows platform using a wide range of familiar tools. These services are exposed in a unified way through the Component Object Model (COM). Windows DNA provides customers with a roadmap for creating successful solutions that build on their existing computing investments and will take them into the future. Using Windows DNA, any developer will be able to build or extend existing applications to combine the power and richness of the PC, the robustness of client/server computing, and the universal reach and global communications capabilities of the Internet.

WHAT PROBLEMS DOES WINDOWS DNA SOLVE?

Windows DNA provides customers with the flexibility to build or buy software solutions that can be easily integrated with existing PC and mainframe computing investments, while taking advantage of the new Internet technologies, such as the Web. By providing a unified approach to integrating the Web and client/server models of computing, Windows DNA makes it easier for customers to build robust distributed computing solutions. Because Windows DNA is based on a richly integrated set of Windows platform services that work together, customers can focus on solving business problems instead of being systems integrators.

WHAT NEW TYPES OF APPLICATIONS WILL WINDOWS DNA MAKE POSSIBLE?

Windows DNA enables organizations to build modern, scalable business solutions that improve the flow of information within and without the organization, that are dynamic and that flexibly change as business needs evolve, that can be centrally managed and maintained, and that can be easily integrated with existing systems and data.

WHAT ARE THE CORE ELEMENTS OF THE WINDOWS DNA ARCHITECTURE?

The Windows DNA architecture consists of a rich set of system services and component-based application services that support open technology standards, all exposed in a unified way through the Component Object Model (COM):

- Presentation services (HTML, DHTML, scripting, components, Win32 API)
- Application services (Internet Information Server, MSMQ, MTS, COM+)
- Data services (ADO, OLE DB)
- System services (directory, security, management, networking and communications)

WHAT ARE THE KEY BENEFITS OF WINDOWS DNA?

- Windows DNA provides the most comprehensive and integrated platform for building distributed applications. This frees developer from the burden of building or assembling commonly-needed middle-tier services, such as asynchronous message queuing, transactions, component services, data access, and web publishing.
- Applications can be built faster and more easily through the use of the common service infrastructure of the Windows platform.
- Window DNA supports a wide choice of programming languages and integrated development tools, thus allowing developers to choose the tool that best fits their needs.
- Windows DNA is designed to provide a high level of interoperability with existing enterprise applications and legacy systems, making it easy to protect and extend current investments.

WHAT SHOULD DEVELOPERS DO TO USE THE WINDOWS DNA ARCHITECTURE AND SERVICES?

Partition your application into 3 logical tiers: Presentation, Business Logic, and Data.

- For Presentation, choose the appropriate Windows components and technologies to provide broad client reach and the richest possible interface.
- For Business Logic, write COM components that use the rich application services of Windows 2000.
- For Data, use ADO to access data, and use OLE DB to expose data.

HOW IS WINDOWS DNA ARCHITECTURE INTEGRATED THROUGH COM?

The heart of Windows DNA is the integration of Web and client/server application development models through the Component Object Model (COM). Windows DNA defines a common set of services, including components, Dynamic HTML, Web browser and server, scripting, transactions, message queuing, security, directory, database and data access, systems management, and user interface. These services are exposed in a unified way through COM, enabling applications to take advantage of them easily.

IS WINDOWS DNA AN OPEN ARCHITECTURE?

Yes. Like the Internet environment, Windows DNA fully embraces an open approach to Web computing by building on the many important industry-specification efforts approved by bodies such as the World Wide Web Consortium (W3C) and the Internet Engineering Task Force (IETF). Windows DNA adheres to open-protocol specifications and published interfaces to enable customers to easily integrate third-party products and platforms. In addition, Microsoft is porting key elements of Windows DNA architecture (COM, Microsoft Internet Explorer browser) to non-Microsoft platforms to provide a framework for interoperability and integration throughout an organization's computing environment.

WHAT CLIENT PLATFORMS DOES WINDOWS DNA SUPPORT?

Windows DNA architecture supports all client environments that adhere to accepted W3C HTML standards. In addition, Microsoft is working with partners to make COM available on UNIX, MVS, and Macintosh platforms, and has ported Internet Explorer to a variety of UNIX platforms and the Macintosh to support a richer cross-platform client than vanilla HTML allows. Unlike other Internet application architectures, Windows DNA supports client solutions that take advantage of the full richness of native Win32 user interface and presentation services, including multimedia, streaming audio and video, help-system technology, and many others.

HOW IS WINDOWS DNA DIFFERENT FROM OTHER VENDORS' APPLICATION ARCHITECTURES?

Windows DNA builds on customers' existing investments in Windows and PC platform technologies, applications, tools, and hardware. With Windows DNA, customers can build distributed, network-aware computing solutions that fully leverage their existing client/server development expertise while enabling them to take advantage of new technologies such as the Web and the Internet. Other vendors' Internet application architectures have studiously ignored these investments.

WHAT APPLICATION DEVELOPMENT TOOLS ARE SUPPORTED WITHIN WINDOWS DNA?

Because Windows DNA builds on customers' existing investments in Windows and COM, all of the industry's leading Rapid Application Development (RAD) tools are supported today, such as the Microsoft Visual Basic programming system, Microsoft Visual J++ development software, Borland's Delphi, PowerSoft's PowerBuilder. In addition, standard-based HTML and Web authoring tools are fully supported within Windows DNA, including the Microsoft Visual InterDev Web development software and Microsoft FrontPage Website creation and management tool.

WHAT APPLICATION SERVER ENVIRONMENT DOES WINDOWS DNA SUPPORT?

The Windows DNA application server model supports scalable connectivity and services built into the underlying operating system platform and tightly integrated through COM. Microsoft's approach is to integrate the capabilities of a high-performance Web server (Internet Information Server), scalable object request broker (COM), robust distributed transaction manager (Microsoft Transaction Server), messaging-oriented middleware server (Microsoft Message Queue Server), and other application services directly into the Windows 2000 Server operating system. These application services work with a common infrastructure in Windows 2000, including distributed security (Windows 2000-based and Kerberos), scalable directory service (X.500 and LDAP), and built-in networking support for TCP/IP and other protocols. All services are available to clients running Windows and other operating systems through open protocols and published interfaces.

Microsoft's model of deeply integrating the application services with the underling OS is in direct contrast to the "layered middleware" approach commonly seen on UNIX platforms. In this approach, the need for portability across various implementations requires that application services sit "on top" of the operating system and offer a completely separate set of services for security, etc. This leads to increased complexity, higher development and deployment costs, and greater integration challenges for developers and customers.

WHAT BACK-END SERVER ENVIRONMENT DOES WINDOWS DNA SUPPORT?

The Microsoft BackOffice platform enables Windows DNA applications to take advantage of scalable back-end services for database management (Microsoft SQL Server), electronic mail and groupware (Microsoft Exchange Server), host integration and connectivity (Microsoft SNA Server), application management (Microsoft Systems Management Server), and Internet/intranet (Microsoft Site Server). In addition, Windows DNA-based applications can access other vendors' back-end services, such as Oracle databases or Lotus Notes groupware servers, through open protocols and common interfaces defined by the Windows Open Services Architecture (WOSA). For example, the Microsoft Universal Data Access model (which integrates OLE DB and ODBC technologies) provides a unified way for Windows DNA applications to access data anywhere in the enterprise.

HOW ARE WINDOWS DNA-BASED APPLICATIONS MANAGED AND DEPLOYED IN A DISTRIBUTED ENVIRONMENT?

Windows DNA supports a variety of mechanisms facilitate the deployment and management of distributed applications. Windows DNA supports a modern multi-tier application architecture, code, and business logic that can be centrally maintained on servers and automatically downloaded to the client on an as-needed basis. Integration with the Windows 2000 directory service (Active Directory) will enable the automated tracking of distributed components and application resources.

The Microsoft Zero Administration Windows initiative (ZAW) specifies additional capabilities for simplifying the management of the desktop environment, including the Windows installation service and IntelliMirror PC management technology, which keeps synchronized copies of critical information on a network server so they can be rapidly restored at the desktop. In addition, Microsoft provides a comprehensive set of Windows-based services for managing the distributed environment, including Web-Based Enterprise Management, Microsoft Management Console (MMC), and Windows Management Interface. Together with the existing facilities provided by Microsoft Systems Management Server and a wide-range of third-party products, these efforts give organizations the tools necessary for managing a distributed Windows DNA application environment.

HOW IS JAVA INTEGRATED INTO WINDOWS DNA?

Today, developers can build Java components that are exposed as COM objects so they can be easily integrated into any tier of the application architecture. Microsoft delivers a high-performance, compatible Java virtual machine (VM) for the Windows 2000 operating system that is tightly integrated into its Internet Explorer browser. In addition, Microsoft's Java VM is integrated with Microsoft Internet Information Server for executing server-side Java code on a Windows 2000 Server. Microsoft is porting its Java VM technology to non-Windows platforms, where it will be delivered with Internet Explorer.

HOW CAN CORBA APPLICATIONS BE INTEGRATED INTO WINDOWS DNA?

Microsoft endorses open approaches to COM/CORBA bridging. COM/CORBA bridging products are available from CORBA vendors, and provide mechanisms that enable Windows DNA-based applications to be integrated with CORBA solutions running on UNIX and other platforms. However, the lack of standard CORBA implementations may make it necessary for customers to carefully match their bridging solution with a specific ORB. Beyond this approach, Microsoft is making COM available on UNIX and other platforms to facilitate the integration of existing systems with new Windows DNA-based applications.

HOW WILL WINDOWS DNA ENABLE EXISTING CLIENT/SERVER APPLICATIONS TO EMBRACE THE INTERNET?

Because Windows DNA Web client/server application services and tools are based on COM and they leverage common Internet protocols, there are many ways to integrate existing applications with the Internet. For example, in Microsoft SQL Server, built-in wizards provide automated conversion of query results into HTML that can be integrated with Internet Information Server, and existing database stored procedures are able to make external callouts to COM components that are hooked into Internet Information Server. This could allow an order-entry application, implemented in SQL Server via Transact-SQL stored procedures, to interface to a component-based electronic commerce solution for processing transactions electronically over the Web. In addition, forms created using Microsoft visual development tools such as Visual Basic can be converted automatically to Web-based forms, simplifying the steps needed to develop a Web-based user interface to an existing client/server application.

HOW WILL WINDOWS DNA PROVIDE INTEGRATION WITH MAINFRAME SYSTEMS AND DATA SOURCES?

In addition to existing Microsoft SNA Server and SQL Server gateway options for providing access to legacy data and systems, Microsoft's COM Transaction Integrator (COMTI) will provide automated object-based encapsulation of legacy applications and data through COM components. COMTI will enable bi-directional access to transaction systems such as CICS, as well as legacy data sources including DB2/MVS, IMS, and VSAM. COMTI will allow existing mainframe application systems to be easily projected over the Web through integration with Internet Information Server. In addition, Microsoft Transaction Server will integrate with COMTI to support heterogeneous distributed transactions between the network and mainframe environments.

HOW CAN CUSTOMERS INTEGRATE WINDOWS DNA-BASED APPLICATIONS WITH DESKTOP PRODUCTIVITY SOFTWARE?

The Microsoft Office application suite provides a standard set of personal productivity applications to users throughout an organization. All Microsoft Office applications are COM and Web-enabled, and can be fully integrated with Windows DNA-based applications. In addition, Microsoft Office supports the same scripting model and open component architecture as Microsoft's Internet Explorer Web browser, which ensures seamless integration of the Web and personal-productivity environment.

WHAT OFFERINGS ARE AVAILABLE TO SUPPORT DEVELOPERS FOR WINDOWS DNA?

The Microsoft Developer Network offers easy access to a wealth of technical information for developers. Membership provides access to quarterly technical CDs, product CDs, and a comprehensive developer Web site containing up-to-the-minute technical information on Microsoft products. Microsoft hosts worldwide developer conferences, where developers learn about the latest technology and future technology directions

20.2 Microsoft Windows Distributed Internet Application Architecture

Windows DNA architecture is Microsoft's framework for building a new generation of *n*-tier computing solutions. Windows DNA provides a framework for delivering solutions that meet the requirements of corporate computing, the Internet and intranets, and global electronic commerce, while reducing overall development costs.

The heart of Windows DNA is COM. Windows DNA architecture makes use of a common set of services, including Hypertext Markup Language (HTML and Dynamic HTML (DHTML), Microsoft ActiveX controls, COM components, client-side and server-side scripting, transactions, security and directory services, database and data access, systems management and HTML, and component authoring environments. These services are exposed in a unified way through COM, which enables applications to interoperate and share components easily. Figure 20.1 shows these various elements.

Windows DNA builds on the client-side services of the Microsoft Windows 2000 operating system and Microsoft Internet Explorer, on the distributed infrastructure of Microsoft Windows 2000 Server and the Microsoft BackOffice family, and on the company's integrated tools, such as the Microsoft Visual Studio development system.

A three-tier architecture based upon the development environment above would look like Figure 20.2.

20.3 The Presentation Tier

In an *n*-tier application built to the Windows DNA model, the user-services tier handles presentation of information and interaction with the users. The first tier is referred to as "presentation services" because some of the services performed in the middle (business) tier of an application, such as authenticating users, are using services as well. It is probably best to think of the presentation

Tools

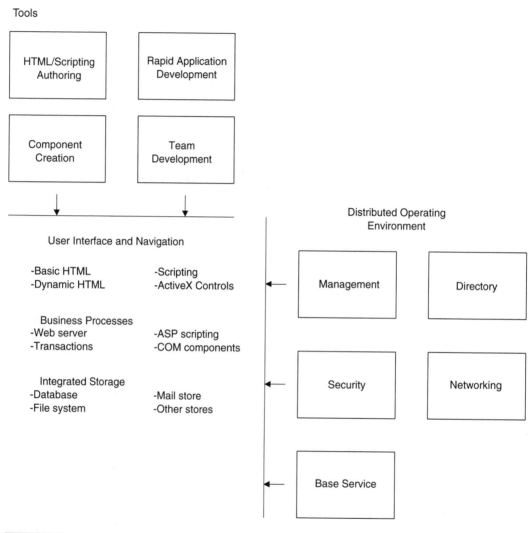

Figure 20.1   *Distributed interNet Application Architecture Development*

Figure 20.2   *Tree-tier Architecture*

tier as the client that you will deploy on a user's desktop. In Windows DNA, you build and deploy clients along a continuum, from thin clients to rich (or thick) clients. This continuum classifies clients in terms of the functionality they present and their dependencies in a given environment.

Figure 20.3 shows how these clients become richer as they support increasingly advanced environments, from simple page-based HTML to more full-featured Win32 executable programs. Windows DNA permits developers to choose the appropriate Windows components and Internet technologies to support the richest possible interface and range of client environments, from handheld wireless devices to high-end workstations.

The following topics discuss the four general types of clients, and describe some of the circumstances for which each is appropriate:

Figure 20.3   *User Client Models*

BROWSER-NEUTRAL CLIENT

A browser-neutral client relies on page-based, simple HTML to present data to the user and enable interaction. This approach maintains the broadest reach of an application because it achieves the greatest compatibility with available browsers. Microsoft tools and application services support the current generation of HTML. The compromise in using simple HTML is the reduced functionality and richness in an application's user interface.

BROWSER-ENHANCED CLIENT

Browser-enhanced clients enable applications to take advantage of the technologies inherent in a particular browser to gain maximum functionality and richness. The reality is that many corporations and organizations standardize to a single browser. Developers who write applications for a corporation's intranet can thus program to a particular browser's features. With technologies like dynamic HTML (DHTML) and scripting languages, developers can create applications with functional Web-based interfaces for data entry or reporting without using custom controls or applets.

DHTML is based on the W3C-standard Document Object Model, which makes all Web-page elements programmable objects. Think of DHTML as a "programmable" HTML. Contents of the HTML document, including style and positioning information, can be modified dynamically by script code embedded in the page. Thus, scripts can change the style, content, and structure of a Web page without having to refresh the Web page from the Web server. This means that the client does not have to repeatedly return to the Web server for changes in display, which would result in increased network performance. Unlike Java applets or Microsoft ActiveX controls, DHTML has no dependencies on the underlying virtual machine or operating system. For clients without DHTML support, the content appears in a gracefully degraded form.

INTERNET-RELIANT CLIENT

Many applications call for greater functionality than HTML, DHTML, and scripting languages can offer. Segments of applications need to access the operating system of the client machine while still maintaining an active connection to the Internet for data or additional services. Under such circumstances, developers can take advantage of the components and Internet services provided by Windows 2000 to build Internet-reliant applications. Unlike page-based applications, which are run within the context of a browser, an Internet-reliant application is a full-fledged Windows 2000 executable program that has full access to the broad range of services provided by the Windows 2000 client. These applications generally use a combination of HTML, DHTML, scripting, and ActiveX controls to provide rich integration with the client system as well as full connectivity to remote services on the Internet.

Financial software suites, such as Microsoft Money 99, represent this type of application. Users save local files that contain information about their stock accounts, which receive live updates when users are connected to the Internet. The bulk of the processing takes place on the client machine as various tables and charts are displayed using Windows 2000 services, while raw data is continually accessed over the Internet.

INTERNET-ENHANCED CLIENT

Applications written using the Microsoft Win32 Application Programming Interface (API), offer the most functionality to developers. These applications are, of course, limited to platforms that support the Win32 API. Through the use of component technology, developers can access the Internet technologies in the Windows 2000 application platform from within a Win32 application. Applications written to the Win32 API that take advantage of system features and utilize Internet connectivity are called Internet-enhanced applications. Some common examples are the Microsoft Office 2000 and Microsoft Visual Studio development systems. These applications support unified browsing by embedding hyperlinks within an application, host the browser for the display of documentation written in DHTML, and provide the capability to seamlessly download updates to the products over the Internet.

The above covers the four types of clients, and we can see that the Windows DNA architecture presents a range of possible clients. Selecting these clients, however, is a critical design choice that has as much to do with maintenance costs as with the functionality your application requires. A Win32 client that makes DCOM calls into the business-services tier provides the richest user interface. A Win32 client can be quite easy to develop, too. A simple client built in Visual Basic can take advantage of the rich array of system services the Win32 API accesses.

20.4 Business Services Tier

In n-tier application development, the business-services tier provides most of an application's functionality. This tier handles the bulk of application-specific processing and enforces an application's business rules. Business logic built into custom components bridge the client environments and the data-services tier. The business-services tier is implemented as both a set of server applications and a run-time environment for COM components. This tier includes Microsoft BackOffice Server products, such as Microsoft Transaction Server, Microsoft Internet Information Server, and Microsoft Message Queue Server. In addition, this tier hosts the Active Server Pages (ASP) pages that the client calls. ASP pages contain a robust mixture of HTML, DHTML, and scripting languages; calls to custom business objects are mode from the ASP environment.

The business objects in turn call the data access components such as ActiveX Data Objects (ADO) that cross the boundary into the data-services tier and return requests to the client. As you use the BackOffice Developer's Guide, you will learn how to program to this n-tier development model and write variations that suit your particular needs. The Windows DNA programming model locates the following application services at the business-services tier.

WEB SERVICES

Microsoft Internet Information Server (IIS) provides a gateway between business services and user services in an n-tier application. IIS extends your application to the Web, over either a corporate intranet or the Internet. IIS can be programmed through the Internet Server Application Programming Interface (ISAPI). Active Server Pages (ASP), the environment that hosts much functionality in the BackOffice Developer's Guide samples, is an example of an ISAPI application. ASP is the language-neutral, interpreted, server-side scripting environment you can use to create and run dynamic interactive Web-server applications. ASP allows you to combine DHTML, scripting, and components. IIS also works closely with Microsoft Transaction Server (MTS), which provides a number of services to applications. This conjunction of MTS and IIS, along with the business objects you create and the data access objects you call from them, make up the bulk of the business-services tier in the n-tier programming model of Windows DNA.

TRANSACTIONS AND COMPONENT SERVICES

Microsoft Transaction Server (MTS) is a component-based transaction-processing system for building, deploying, and administering server applications. MTS is a set of extensions to the Component Object Model (COM). In Windows 2000, MTS and COM converge into COM+, also know as component services. As its name implies, MTS enables you to build applications that can perform transactions that conform to the ACID (Atomic, Consistent, Isolated, Durable) properties. This feature adds a dimension to the Windows 2000 operating system that greatly enhances it as an enterprise platform. Yet MTS is perhaps most important as a run-time environment that allows for greater scalability and enhanced security in multi-tier applications. Building an application to take advantage of the services that MTS offers is the key to scaling it to an increasing number of users.

MTS provides a number of services to the custom COM components in which developers encapsulate an application's business rules:

- Distributed transactions
- A Microsoft Management Console (MMC) snap-in for administering MTS components and applications
- Security services to control object creation and use
- Automatic management of processes and threads

- Object instance management to improve scalability
- Management of database connections

MESSAGING SERVICES

Microsoft Message Queue Server provides asynchronous communication services for applications that run under Windows 2000 Server. Message queuing is an integral part of Windows DNA, because it enables reliable messaging when a user is disconnected from the network. It also allows for greater fault tolerance over unreliable networks. After an MSMQ message is sent, the sender can go on to other work without waiting for the recipient to respond. The message goes into a queue, located on the server, until it receives a request from the recipient indicating that it is ready to receive the message. MSMQ bridges the business-services tier and the data-services tier of a distributed application, because the message queues are considered unstructured storage, like the Microsoft Exchange Server database.

MSMQ provides automatic integration with Microsoft Transaction Server (MTS). This feature enables you to develop applications for portable computers that can, for example, participate in transaction processing without being connected to a network. An application can wrap an MSMQ message in MTS transactions, send it into a local queue on a user's portable computer, and then update a database, such as a customer account or a product inventory, when the network becomes available. When applications use MSMQ's transactional delivery mode, MSMQ makes sure that messages are delivered exactly one time, and that messages are delivered in the order in which they were sent.

MSMQ differs from Microsoft Exchange Server in that Exchange enables person-to-person messaging, whereas MSMQ provides application-to-application messaging. MSMQ can act as a MAPI transport provider to allow MAPI-enabled application to communicate with other applications using MSMQ. The MSMQ Exchange Connector enables MSMQ to act as a communications transport between computers running Microsoft Exchange Server, and to MSMQ-enable applications. For example, Microsoft Exchange Server users can receive e-mail messages through MSMQ or send Microsoft Exchange forms that are received as messages by processing applications.

UNIVERSAL DATA ACCESS

Universal Data Access is Microsoft's strategy for providing access to information across the enterprise. In a Windows DNA *n*-tier application, data-access components cross the boundary between the business-services tier and the data-services tier. These components, such as ActiveX Data Objects (ADO), are called from the custom business objects that run in the Microsoft Transaction Server environment. The Universal Data Access-based framework operates at two levels within an application. At the systems level, OLE DB defines an architecture specified as a set of COM-based interfaces that encapsulates various database management system services. The OLE DB architecture does not constrain the nature of the data source. At the application level, ADO provides a high-level interface to enable developers to access data from any programming language.

The Microsoft Open Database Connectivity (ODBC) interface is an industry standard. The ODBC interface enables applications to access data from a variety of database management systems. ODBC permits maximum interoperability—an application can access data in diverse database management systems through a single interface. Furthermore, that application will be independent of any database-management system from which it accesses data. Users of the application can add software components, called drivers, that create an interface between an application and a specific database management system.

ADO, OLE DB, and ODBC together make up the Microsoft Data Access Component (MDAC). MDAC is part of the Microsoft Data Access SDK, which is integrated into the Platform SDK.

INTEROPERABILITY WITH MAINFRAME ENVIRONMENTS

You can build n-tier applications that access mainframe and AS/400 data using the features of Microsoft SNA Server. SNA Server is a comprehensive gateway and application integration platform that provides a way to embrace Internet, intranet, and client/server technologies while preserving investments in existing AS/400 and mainframe system.

SNA Server ships with COM Transaction Integrator (COMTI), which includes both a run-time environment and a development tool. The run-time environment integrates Microsoft Transaction Server (MTS) with Customer Information Control System and Information Management System. The development too imports COBOL code and automatically generates an MTS-compatible object and method. As a result, application developers can program in the visual, object-oriented environments to which they are accustomed, and can have access to host transactions without needing to learn host-applications programming or communication protocols.

20.5 Data Services Tier

The data-services tier in a Windows DNA n-tier application can consist of data residing in several different kinds of stores. The two most prominent products that provide data services in BackOffice are Microsoft SQL Server databases and Microsoft Exchange Server directories and information stores. The following discussion briefly introduces the structural differences between them and how they are accessed.

MICROSOFT EXCHANGE SERVER DATA SERVICES

Microsoft Exchange implements the Messaging Application Programming Interface (MAPI) and directory-access functions for much of its functionality, though newer technologies such as Collaboration Data Objects (CDO) and Active Directory Service Interface (ADSI) are more easily integrated into the architecture of n-tier applications. The Microsoft Exchange Server architecture includes two primary data stores: the directory and the information store.

The directory serves as the central repository of user information for Microsoft Exchange Server within an organization. The directory consists of a directory information tree, which holds the actual information, and a directory schema, which describes the relationships between directory elements. Information is stored in the directory using a hierarchical object model. The Microsoft Exchange Server directory contains objects that are the principal means for applications to find and access services, mailboxes, recipients, public folders, and other addressable objects within the messaging system. For example, if a directory object represents a public folder with its own destination address, users and applications can send messages directly to the public folder through the messaging system.

The information store is the default message store provided for Microsoft Exchange Server. The information store consists of four implementations of MAPI message stores: the public information store, the private information store, the offline information store, and the personal folder store. The information store's organization of public folders, private folders, and messages is referred to as the organization hierarchy. Another implementation of a MAPI message store is configured when a user works offline. It is called the offline folder store and mirrors the structure of the mailbox while offline.

Programmers can use ADSI to access information in the Microsoft Exchange Server directory and information store. Both the directory and the information store are hierarchical and object-oriented, allowing for easy programmatic access.

MICROSOFT SQL SERVER 7.0 DATA SERVICES

Microsoft SQL Server is a relational database-management system ideally suited for use in Windows DNA. It uses the same code base to scale database applications ranging from laptops running Windows 98 to terabyte symmetric multiprocessor clusters running Windows 2000 server, Enterprise Edition. N-tier applications discussed in the BackOffice Developer's Guide tend to access SQL Server using the high-level Automation Interface, ActiveX Data Objects, which calls into OLE DB, the system-level data interface.

SQL Server does far more than simply warehouse data. For example, SQL Server provides stored procedures, precompiled Transact-SQL statements that are executed as a unit. It also provides extended stored procedures, which dynamically load and execute functions within a dynamic-line library

(DLL). Stored procedures and extended stored procedures provide a great deal of SQL Server's functionality, often making calls outside SQL Server itself and into other applications. One group of stored procedures, for example, allows SQL Server to operate as a workgroup post office for a MAPI-enabled e-mail system.

In addition to stored procedures, SQL Server implements a number of features designed to make data more useful and meaningful. Online Transaction Processing (OLTP) and Online Analytical Processing (OLAP) track and analyze data to reveal trends that users can interpret. Microsoft Repository, which consists of a set of ActiveX interfaces, enables the sharing of metadata among different products and components in a system or application. SQL Server can participate in transactions that include multiple SQL Server databases as well as third-party databases. SQL Server includes a Web Assistant Wizard that quickly guides users through the process of generating HTML pages from SQL Server data and posting SQL Server data to HTTP and FTP locations. Full-text search capabilities increase the usefulness of SQL Server.

Fully integrated with the Windows 2000 Security Model and performing all updates to databases transaction ally, SQL Server protects the integrity of its databases, and functions as a robust and reliable component of large-scale distributed applications.

20.6 Conclusion

In this chapter, we have discussed the overall services and capabilities to create an n-tier computer system. As you can tell, we have just provided a road map to the many functions that can be used. Obviously, a whole book could be written, and many probably will be, on the Windows DNA architecture and its utilization. But this chapter should give you good insight, from the top level, into n-tier Windows DNA systems.

Miscellaneous

*T*his chapter describes six more system services that are important to any application developer working in Windows:

1. The registry
2. The event log
3. Memory management
4. Time
5. The error handler
6. Structured exception handling

All of these topics are small, straightforward, and easy to understand.

Compatibility Note: All of the code in this chapter, with the exception of Section 21.2, works identically in Windows 2000 and Windows 98. Section 21.2 will not work in Windows 98.

21.1 Registry

The registry is a single, well-organized location that stores *all* system, application, and user-configuration information. If you are a former Windows 3.1 programmer, then you are familiar with INI files. All of that information is now in the registry. If you are a UNIX programmer, you are familiar with the use of "dot files" to store application and user information, along with a variety of different text files to store system information. In Windows, all of this information is centralized in the registry.

Normally a user or administrator does not manipulate the registry directly, although this sort of manipulation is possible using the Registry Editor. Instead, applications act as editors for certain sections of the registry, or they use the registry as a storage area for configuration information they need to save from run to run. For example, the User Manager is nothing but a large editor for the user information section in the registry.

The registry will initially seem confusing because it already contains thousands of entries, most of which have cryptic names. The overall structure is easy to understand, however: The registry works just like a directory tree. A directory *tree* consists of *directories,* which can contain other directories or *files.* Files have a name and their contents. A registry tree is called a *hive.* It contains *keys.* Keys can hold other keys or *values.* Values emulate variables more than they do files: they have a name and contain data of some specific type. See Figure 21.1. You reference specific keys and values using paths that look just like file paths, using the "\" character as a separator.

You can view the registry directly using the Registry Editor (regedt32 .exe in Windows 2000, regedit.exe in Windows 98). You will see a display that looks remarkably similar to that of the File Manager, right down to many of the menus and options. The Registry Editor always lets you view four main hives (think of them as you do drives in the File Manager):

- HKEY_CURRENT_USER: Profile information for the current user, such as Program Manager groups and screen colors
- HKEY_USERS: Profile information for all users with accounts on this machine
- HKEY_LOCAL_MACHINE: Information about this machine and its applications

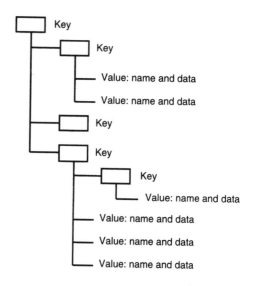

Figure 21.1

Registry hives mirror the structure of directory trees exactly

- HKEY_CLASSES_ROOT: Information used by the File Manager and OLE to open applications. For example, this section associates different file extensions with applications.

The registry overview in the Win32 help file contains a good description of what these hives contain, and what the main sections inside of them do. The file regentry.hlp in the Resource Kit contains detailed explanations of common registry keys and values.

When you are creating an application, there are typically only three things that it will need to do with the registry:

1. Add keys and values to the registry
2. Modify values
3. Read values previously stored

Some keys and values that the application creates will be static. For example, when you install an application, you will typically have the installation program create a key in the registry for the application itself. This key is static in that it never changes. Under this key will go other application keys and values. The installation program will typically create static values like the version number, installation date, owner's name, and so on, inside the application key. All of this information normally goes in HKEY_LOCAL_MACHINE.

Other values that the application places in the registry will change frequently. For example, you might store the current workspace configuration in the registry each time a user quits the application. To do this properly, you will create appropriate keys and values in each user's hive, typically by working through the HKEY_CURRENT_USER hive.

You can store just about anything you like anywhere you like in the registry. However, you *should* store any permanent application information in the HKEY_LOCAL_MACHINE\Software key. Any user-specific configuration information for the application should appear in the HKEY_CURRENT_USER\Software key. Create a new key for your application. Or even better, create a new key that contains your company's name, and then create different application keys inside of it, as Microsoft does. Then build whatever structure you like within that key.

Depending on what you listen to, a value can have five (as far as the Registry Editor is concerned) or 10 (as far as the **RegSetValueEx** API function is concerned) different types. The Registry Editor will let you create the following five types through its Add Value option:

REG_BINARY	Binary data
REG_DWORD	32-bit value
REG_EXPAND_SZ	Environment variable references such as %PATH%
REG_MULTI_SZ	Null-terminated string array like argv
REG_SZ	Null-terminated string

The **RegSetValueEx** function allows the following ten types:

REG_BINARY	Binary data
REG_DWORD	32-bit value
REG_DWORD_LITTLE_ENDIAN	DWORD MSB last, same as DWORD
REG_DWORD_BIG_ENDIAN	DWORD MSB first
REG_EXPAND_SZ	Environment variable references such as %PATH%
REG_LINK	A Unicode symbolic link
REG_MULTI_SZ	Null-terminated string array like argv
REG_NONE	Undefined
REG_RESOURCE_LIST	Resource list for a device driver
REG_SZ	Null-terminated string

You should reserve the registry for short values. Anything big (large chunks of text, bitmaps, etc.) should be stored in a separate file. Use the registry to store the names of those files.

Listing 21.1 shows how to create a new key in the registry. Start up the Registry Editor (regedt32.exe in Windows 2000, regedit.exe in Windows 98) and look in the "HKEY_CURRENT_USER\Software" key. Compile and run Listing 21.1, and refresh the registry display if the editor is not in auto-refresh mode. You will see that it contains a new key named "Interface Technologies."

Listing 21.1   *Adding a key to the registry*

```
// addkey.cpp

#include <windows.h>
#include <iostream.h>

VOID main(VOID)
{
  LONG ret;
  HKEY keyHandle;
  DWORD disposition;

  // add a key for the new vendor
  ret=RegCreateKeyEx(HKEY_CURRENT_USER,
    "Software\\Interface Technologies",
    0, NULL, REG_OPTION_VOLATILE,
    KEY_ALL_ACCESS, NULL, &keyHandle,
    &disposition);
  if (ret != ERROR_SUCCESS)
  {
    cerr << "Unable to create key"
      << endl;
    return;
  }

  switch (disposition)
```

```
{
  case REG_CREATED_NEW_KEY:
    cout << "New key added to registry."
      << endl;
    break;

  case REG_OPENED_EXISTING_KEY:
    cout << "Existing key opened."
      << endl;
    break;

  default:
    cout << "Key disposition unknown."
      << endl;
}

// close the new key
ret=RegCloseKey(keyHandle);
if (ret != ERROR_SUCCESS)
{
  cerr << "Unable to close new key"
    << endl;
  return;
}
}
```

Listing 21.1 starts by calling the **RegCreateKeyEx** function to create a new key.

RegCreateKeyEx   *Creates or opens a key in the registry*

```
LONG RegCreateKeyEx(
  HKEY keyHandle,
  LPCTSTR keyName,
  DWORD reserved,
  LPTSTR className,
  DWORD options,
  REGSAM sam,
  LPSECURITY_ATTRIBUTES security,
  PHKEY resultHandle,
  LPDWORD disposition)
```

keyHandle	Handle to an open key or one of the four HKEYs
keyName	The key to create
reserved	Reserved. Pass 0.
className	The class of the key. Any string
options	Specify REG_OPTION_VOLATILE or REG_OPTION_NON_VOLATILE

sam	Access mask. See Section 10.5.10 for values
security	Security descriptor for the key. See Chapter 10
resultHandle	Handle to the new or opened key
disposition	Returns REG_CREATED_NEW_KEY or REG_OPENED_EXISTING_KEY

Returns ERROR_SUCCESS on success

The call to **RegCreateKeyEx** in Listing 21.1 creates the key "HKEY_CURRENT_USER\Software\Interface Technologies," or opens a handle to it if it already exists. The code creates it as a volatile key, which means that the next time you reboot your machine the key will disappear (a great way to test things). If you want to create a permanent key, create it as nonvolatile. The call to **RegCreateKeyEx** also specifies KEY_ALL_ACCESS. If you as a user do not have sufficient privilege in Windows 2000 to create keys on your machine, the call will fail here. See Chapter 13 for details on security. When the function finishes, it returns a handle to the new or existing key, along with a disposition flag that tells you whether the key is new or old.

Having created the key, the program closes the handle and quits.

RegCloseKey   *Closes a key handle*

```
LONG RegCloseKey(
    HKEY keyHandle)
```

keyHandle   Handle to an open key

Returns ERROR_SUCCESS on success

Listing 21.2 shows how to add a value to a key. Any key can hold values and other keys, just as any directory can hold files and other directories. When you run Listing 21.2 and refresh the Registry Editor, you will find that the Registry contains a new key called "HKEY_CURRENT_USER\Software\Interface Technologies\Sample Application," and inside of it is a value named "sampval" of type REG_SZ (a string) with the value "This is a sample string value." You change a value simply by setting it again.

Listing 21.2   *Adding a value to the registry*

```cpp
// addvalue.cpp

#include <windows.h>
#include <iostream.h>
#include <string.h>

VOID main(VOID)
```

```
{
  LONG ret;
  HKEY keyHandle1, keyHandle2;
  DWORD disposition;

  // add or open a key for the vendor
  ret=RegCreateKeyEx(HKEY_CURRENT_USER,
    "Software\\Interface Technologies",
    0, NULL, REG_OPTION_VOLATILE,
    KEY_ALL_ACCESS, NULL, &keyHandle1,
    &disposition);
  if (ret != ERROR_SUCCESS)
  {
    cerr << "Unable to create key 1"
      << endl;
    return;
  }

  // add or open a key for the app
  ret=RegCreateKeyEx(keyHandle1,
    "Sample Application",
    0, NULL, REG_OPTION_VOLATILE,
    KEY_ALL_ACCESS, NULL, &keyHandle2,
    &disposition);
  if (ret != ERROR_SUCCESS)
  {
    cerr << "Unable to create key 1"
      << endl;
    return;
  }

  // Add a new value to the registry
  char *val = "This is a sample string value";
  ret=RegSetValueEx(keyHandle2, "sampval",
    0, REG_SZ, (CONST BYTE *) val,
    strlen(val)+1);

  // close the keys
  ret=RegCloseKey(keyHandle1);
  ret=RegCloseKey(keyHandle2);
}
```

Listing 21.2 starts in the same way as Listing 21.1. It calls **Reg CreateKeyEx** to create or open keys (you can use **RegOpenKeyEx** to open a key if you know it exists or want to test for existence). It then calls **Reg SetValueEx** to set the value. If the value does not exist, the function creates it. If it does, it changes it.

RegSetValueEx	*Sets a value*

```
LONG RegSetValueEx(
    HKEY hkey,
    LPCTSTR valueName,
    DWORD reserved,
    DWORD type,
    CONST BYTE * data,
    DWORD dataLen)
```

keyHandle	Handle to an open key
valueName	The name of the value
reserved	Reserved. Pass 0
type	The type of the value
data	The data for the value
dataLen	The length of the data. Be sure to include the null character in strings

Returns ERROR_SUCCESS on success

In Listing 21.2, the code creates a value of type REG_SZ with a string value.

You can read values from the registry using the **RegQueryValueEx** function.

RegQueryValueEx	*Gets a value*

```
LONG RegQueryValueEx(
    HKEY keyHandle,
    LPTSTR valueName,
    LPDWORD lpdwReserved,
    LPDWORD type,
    LPBYTE data,
    LPDWORD lpcbData)
```

keyHandle	Handle to an open key
valueName	The name of the value to query
reserved	Reserved. Pass 0
type	Returned type of the value. Pass address
data	Returned data for the value. Pass array or buffer address
dataLen	Size of the buffer. Pass address.

Returns ERROR_SUCCESS on success

The **RegQueryValueEx** function returns the value and its length along with its type.

Like a directory tree, there are certain cases in which it is useful to traverse the registry tree. For example, you might want to hunt through the registry for a particular value. Listing 21.3 demonstrates the process. It enumerates all the Program Manager's groups stored in the registry under the current user's profile. First it enumerates the subkeys of the "HKEY_CURRENT_USER\Control Panel" key, and then it enumerates the values of the "HKEY_CURRENT_USER\Control Panel\Desktop" key.

Listing 21.3   *A program that traverses a portion of the registry tree and dumps the values it finds there*

```cpp
// showgrps.cpp

#include <windows.h>
#include <iostream.h>

VOID main(VOID)
{
  LONG ret;
  HKEY keyHandle;
  CHAR subKeyName[80];
  DWORD subKeyNameSize;
  CHAR valueName[80];
  DWORD valueNameSize;
  BYTE value[80];
  DWORD valueSize;
  DWORD n;
  FILETIME lastUpdate;

  // open the key to enumerate
  ret=RegOpenKeyEx(HKEY_CURRENT_USER,
    "Control Panel", 0,
    KEY_ENUMERATE_SUB_KEYS,
    &keyHandle);
  if (ret != ERROR_SUCCESS)
  {
    cerr << "Unable to open subkey"
      << endl;
    return;
  }

  cout << "As subkeys:" << endl << endl;

  // show all the subkeys
  n=0;
  do
```

Listing 21.3 *A program that traverses a portion of the registry tree and dumps the values it finds there (continued)*

```
  {
    subKeyNameSize=80;
    ret=RegEnumKeyEx(keyHandle, n,
      subKeyName, &subKeyNameSize,
      NULL, NULL, NULL, &lastUpdate);
    if (ret == ERROR_SUCCESS)
    {
      cout << subKeyName << endl;
      n++;
    }
  } while (ret == ERROR_SUCCESS);

  cout << endl << "There are " << n
    << " groups listed." << endl << endl;

  // close the key
  ret=RegCloseKey(keyHandle);
  if (ret != ERROR_SUCCESS)
  {
    cerr << "Unable to close subkey"
      << endl;
    return;
  }

  // open the key to enumerate
  ret=RegOpenKeyEx(HKEY_CURRENT_USER,
    "Control Panel\\Desktop",
    0, KEY_QUERY_VALUE,
    &keyHandle);
  if (ret != ERROR_SUCCESS)
  {
    cerr << "Unable to open subkey"
      << endl;
    return;
  }

  cout << "As values:" << endl << endl;

  // show all the values
  n=0;
  do
  {
    valueNameSize=80;
    valueSize=80;
    ret=RegEnumValue(keyHandle, n,
      valueName, &valueNameSize,
      NULL, NULL, value, &valueSize);
```

```
  if (ret == ERROR_SUCCESS)
  {
    cout << valueName << " is "
      << value << endl;
    n++;
  }
} while (ret == ERROR_SUCCESS);

cout << endl << "There are " << n
  << " groups listed." << endl;

// close the key
ret=RegCloseKey(keyHandle);
if (ret != ERROR_SUCCESS)
{
  cerr << "Unable to close subkey"
    << endl;
  return;
}
}
```

Typical output from Listing 21.3 looks like this:

```
As subkeys:
Cache
Color Schemes
Colors
Current
Cursors
Custom Colors
Desktop
International
IOProcs
Keyboard
MMCPL
Mouse
Patterns
Screen Saver.3DFlyingObj
Screen Saver.3DPipes
Screen Saver.Bezier
Screen Saver.Marquee
Screen Saver.Mystify
Screen Saver.Stars
Sound
Sounds

There are 21 groups listed.

As values:
```

```
CoolSwitch is 1
CursorBlinkRate is 530
BorderWidth is 3
ScreenSaveTimeOut is 900
ScreenSaveActive is 1
SCRNSAVE.EXE is SSSTARS.SCR
ScreenSaverIsSecure is 1
Pattern is (None)
Wallpaper is (None)
TileWallpaper is 0
GridGranularity is 0
IconSpacing is 75
IconTitleWrap is 1
IconTitleFaceName is MS Sans Serif
IconTitleSize is 9
IconTitleStyle is 0
DragFullWindows is 0

There are 17 groups listed.
```

If you look in these particular portions of the registry with the Registry Editor, you will see that the key names and values are the same as the values produced by Listing 21.3.

Listing 21.3 uses the **RegEnumKeyEx** and **RegEnumValueEx** functions to enumerate keys and values.

RegEnumKeyEx	Enumerates keys

```
LONG RegEnumKeyEx(
    HKEY keyHandle,
    DWORD subkeyNum,
    LPTSTR buffer,
    LPDWORD bufferLen,
    LPDWORD reserved,
    LPTSTR class,
    LPDWORD classLen,
    PFILETIME lastWrite)
```

keyHandle	Handle to an open key
subkeyNum	Index of the key to get
buffer	Buffer for returned key name
bufferLen	Size of the buffer. Pass address
reserved	Reserved. Pass 0
class	Returned data for the class. Pass array or buffer address
classLen	Size of the buffer. Pass address
lastWrite	Time of last write to the key

Returns ERROR_SUCCESS on success

RegEnumKeyEx accepts an open key handle. It treats all of the keys inside as a numbered list starting at index 0. The function returns the information about the specified key, or it returns an appropriate error code. Listing 21.3 prints the name of each key found to stdout.

RegEnumValue	*Enumerates values in a key*

```
LONG RegEnumValue(
    HKEY keyHandle,
    DWORD valueNum,
    LPTSTR buffer,
    LPDWORD bufferLen,
    LPDWORD reserved,
    LPDWORD type,
    LPBYTE data,
    LPDWORD dataLen)
```

keyHandle	Handle to an open key
valueNum	Index of the value to get
buffer	Buffer for returned value name
bufferLen	Size of the buffer. Pass address
reserved	Reserved. Pass 0
type	Returned type of the value. Pass address
data	Returned data for the value. Pass array or buffer address
dataLen	Size of the buffer. Pass address

Returns ERROR_SUCCESS on success

RegEnumValue follows the same pattern as **RegEnumKeyEx**, getting values one by one based on an index. The program prints out each value it finds.

You can use the functions described in this section to create keys and read and write values within your own applications. Other registry functions allow you to save and restore entire hives, which would be useful when designing your own backup programs.

21.2 The Event Log

Compatibility Note: The code in this section does not work in Windows 98 at the time of publication, due to unimplemented functions.

The event log centrally records error, warning, and information messages from the operating system, the security system, and applications. When you are developing your own software, you will want to use the event log to record certain types of error and warning information.

You do not need to throw all application errors into the event log. For example, if the user enters an invalid file name, you should display the appropriate error message to the user. However, if the application tries to allocate memory and cannot, you should advise the user and also insert a message in the event log. The administrator needs to know about this problem so that the machine's physical or virtual memory space can be increased if necessary. Place into the event log information that the administrator of the system needs to see to fix system problems. Here are some examples of valid events to place in the event log:

1. Resource problems: lack of memory, network errors and timeouts, disk errors, problems connecting on the network, communication port problems, and so on

2. Missing or corrupted registry keys (may indicate that the program was installed incorrectly or illegally, or that something corrupted the registry)

3. Missing or disabled services

4. Startup problems due to missing files, DLLs, and so on

You might also have the installation program insert a message to indicate successful installation. The administrator would then know when new applications are loaded.

When creating a service (see Chapter 12), you will want to use the event log to record all error messages. The event log is really the only output channel available to a service, and the administrator is the only one who can fix any problems that arise.

Run the Event Viewer now to get a good mental image of what a typical event contains. Look in the Event Viewer's "application section." Each event in the event list has a date, time, source, category, event number, user, and computer. If you double-click on a specific event, you will find that this information is echoed, and the event also contains an English description and possibly some supplemental data.

The Event Viewer uses a very interesting string-handling technique to manage multiple display languages easily. When you add a message to the event log, you supply integer values for both the event itself and the category of the event. The event log then maps these values into a string table that you create with a message compiler (mc.exe). The string table is attached to either the application's EXE or, more commonly, to one of its DLLs, as a resource.

In order for the event viewer to handle your application's event records correctly and completely, you need to place several entries into the registry. In the absence of these registry entries, the best that the event viewer can do is display the integer error codes. If the registry entries are in place, and if you use the message compiler to set up event-message strings, then your events will display proper error messages in the viewer. Listing 21.4 sets up the registry entries for you.

Listing 21.4 *Code that sets up the proper registry values for an application that wants to write to the Event Viewer. Typically, this functionality goes in an installation program*

```cpp
// instsrc.cpp

#include <windows.h>
#include <iostream.h>
#include <stdlib.h>

VOID ShowUsage(VOID)
{
  cout << "Install an Event Logging Source"
    << endl;
  cout << "Usage: instsrc <sourcename> "
    << "<msg&ctgy file> "
    << "<category count>" << endl << endl;
  cout
    << "sourcename   = name that application uses"
    << endl
    << "            to report events"
    << endl;
  cout
    << "msg&ctgy file= complete pathname to file"
    << endl
    << "            which has the message table"
    << endl
    << "            for event and category ID's"
    << endl;
  cout
    << "catgy count  = number of categories used"
    << endl << "            to classify events"
    << endl
    << endl;
  cout
    << "Example: instsrc TTT C:\\ttt\\ttt.dll 2"
    << endl;
}

VOID main(int argc, char *argv[])
{
  LONG ret;
  HKEY keyHandle;
  DWORD eventTypes;
  CHAR strBuf[80];
  DWORD disposition;
  DWORD categoryCount;
```

Listing 21.4	*Code that sets up the proper registry values for an application that wants to write to the Event Viewer. Typically, this functionality goes in an installation program (continued)*

```cpp
if (argc != 4)
{
  ShowUsage();
  return;
}

// build the path for the new key
strcpy(strBuf, "SYSTEM\\CurrentControlSet\\");
strcat(strBuf,
  "Services\\EventLog\\Application\\");
strcat(strBuf, argv[1]);

// add a key for the new source
ret=RegCreateKeyEx(HKEY_LOCAL_MACHINE,
  strBuf, 0, NULL, REG_OPTION_NON_VOLATILE,
  KEY_SET_VALUE, NULL, &keyHandle, &disposition);
if (ret != ERROR_SUCCESS)
{
  cerr << "Unable to create key: "
    << argv[1] << endl
    << "Check and make sure you"
    << " are a member of Administrators."
    << endl;
  return;
}

if (disposition == REG_OPENED_EXISTING_KEY)
{
  cout << "Updating existing source information."
    << endl;
}

// add the EventMessageFile value to key
ret=RegSetValueEx(keyHandle, "EventMessageFile",
  0, REG_EXPAND_SZ, (LPBYTE) argv[2],
  strlen(argv[2]) + 1);
if (ret != ERROR_SUCCESS)
{
  cerr << "Unable to add value to key"
    << endl;
  return;
}

// specify the event types supported
eventTypes=EVENTLOG_ERROR_TYPE |
  EVENTLOG_WARNING_TYPE |
  EVENTLOG_INFORMATION_TYPE;
```

```
  // add the TypesSupported value to key
  ret=RegSetValueEx(keyHandle, "TypesSupported",
        0, REG_DWORD, (LPBYTE) &eventTypes,
        sizeof(DWORD));
  if (ret != ERROR_SUCCESS)
  {
    cerr << "Unable to add value to key"
      << endl;
    return;
  }

  categoryCount=(DWORD) atoi(argv[3]);

  if (categoryCount)
  {
    // add the CategoryCount value to key
    ret=RegSetValueEx(keyHandle, "CategoryCount",
          0, REG_DWORD, (LPBYTE) &categoryCount,
          sizeof(DWORD));
    if (ret != ERROR_SUCCESS)
    {
      cerr << "Unable to add value to key"
        << endl;
      return;
    }

    // add the CategoryMessageFile value to key
    ret=RegSetValueEx(keyHandle,
      "CategoryMessageFile",
      0, REG_EXPAND_SZ, (LPBYTE) argv[2],
      strlen(argv[2]) + 1);
    if (ret != ERROR_SUCCESS)
    {
      cerr << "Unable to add value to key"
        << endl;
      return;
    }
  }

  // close the key
  RegCloseKey(keyHandle);
}
```

You need to run Listing 21.4 only once for an application. Typically, you would place code like this in the installation program. When you run Listing 21.4, you should pass it the name that the application will use to report events (see below), the full path to the file that contains the message table (normally an EXE or DLL file), and the total number of different categories used by your application. Listing 21.4 creates a registry key for the application in the "HKEY_LOCAL_MACHINE\SYSTEM\CurrentControlSet\ Services\EventLog\Application""HKEY_LOCAL_MACHINE\SYSTEM\Current-ControlSet\ Services\EventLog\" portion of the registry. It then adds four values: EventMessageFile, TypesSupported, CategoryMessageFile, and Category Count. If you look in that same section, you will find the same sorts of values for other applications already on the machine.

Listing 21.5 contains a typical application that places events in the event log. It creates two different types of events. The first one is very simple, while the second one uses substitution strings and has supplemental data. Listing 21.6 contains the message file for the message compiler, and Listing 21.7 contains a makefile that will create the application and link the message file to it.

Listing 21.5 *A typical application that records events in the event log (logevent.cpp)*

```cpp
// logevent.cpp

#include <windows.h>
#include <iostream.h>

#include "msgs.h"

VOID main(VOID)
{
  BOOL ret;
  LPCSTR mergeStrs[] = {"LOGEVENT.EXE"};
  HANDLE logHandle;

  // get a handle to log events with
  logHandle=RegisterEventSource(NULL,
    "LogEvent");
  if (logHandle == NULL)
  {
    cerr << "Unable to get log handle"
      << endl;
    return;
  }

  cout << "Reporting event #1." << endl;

  ret=ReportEvent(logHandle,
    EVENTLOG_INFORMATION_TYPE,
    CAT_ONE, MSG_ONE, NULL, 0, 0,
    NULL, NULL);
  if (!ret)
  {
    cerr << "Unable to log an event"
      << endl;
    return;
  }
```

```
cout << "Reporting event #2." << endl;

ret=ReportEvent(logHandle,
  EVENTLOG_WARNING_TYPE,
  CAT_TWO, MSG_TWO, NULL, 1,
  sizeof(HANDLE), mergeStrs,
  &logHandle);
if (!ret)
{
  cerr << "Unable to log an event"
    << endl;
  return;
}

DeregisterEventSource(logHandle);
}
```

Listing 21.6   *The message file for the application in Listing 21.5 (msgs.mc)*

```
MessageIdTypedef=WORD

MessageId=0x1
SymbolicName=CAT_ONE
Language=English
Category #1
.

MessageId=
SymbolicName=CAT_TWO
Language=English
Category #2
.

MessageIdTypedef=DWORD

MessageId=0x100
Severity=Informational
Facility=Application
SymbolicName=MSG_ONE
Language=English
This is message #1.
.

MessageId=
Severity=Warning
Facility=Application
SymbolicName=MSG_TWO
Language=English
Application %1 is about to exit.
(The event data is the log handle which
is about to be closed.)
```

Listing 21.7 *The makefile that compiles the application and its message file and links the messages to the EXE (makefile)*

```
APP=logevent
MSGS=msgs
NODEBUG=1


!include <ntwin32.mak>


$(APP).exe: $(APP).obj $(MSGS).res
    $(link) $(conlflags) $(ldebug) \
        $(conlibs) $(APP).obj $(MSGS).res \
        advapi32.lib -out:$(APP).exe


$(APP).obj: $(APP).cpp $(MSGS).h
    $(cc) $(cflags) $(cdebug) $(cvars) \
        $(APP).cpp


$(MSGS).rc $(MSGS).h: $(MSGS).mc
    mc $(MSGS).mc


$(MSGS).rbj: $(MSGS).rc
    $(rc) $(rcvars) $(MSGS).rc
```

If you place Listings 21.5 through 21.7 in a directory of their own and run the makefile, it will produce an EXE named `logevent.exe`. This EXE file also contains the message file.

Now run Listing 21.4 to create the proper entries in the registry for this program. A typical run might look like this:

instsrc LogEvent c:\xxx\yyy\logevent.exe 2

Supply the proper path to your executable in place of xxx\yyy.

The message file in Listing 21.6 contains two parts. The first part maps category numbers to category names. The second part maps event numbers to event descriptions. The first line of each part is a header that identifies the type of the message IDs. Category IDs are always of type WORD, while message IDs are always of type DWORD.

A category description in the message file is straightforward, as duplicated here from Listing 21.6:

```
MessageId=
SymbolicName=CAT_TWO
Language=English
Category #2
.
```

The first line identifies the category ID number. This is the integer value that maps an ID to a string. If left blank, it tells the system to increment from the previous value, or allows you to specify a specific value. The second line is the symbolic name for the category ID number. The third line identifies the language. With a bit of extra work (see the help file for the message compiler), you can create strings for a variety of other languages as well. The fourth line is the category name associated with the ID. This is the string that will appear in the category field of the event viewer.

An event description in the message file follows the same format:

```
MessageId=
Severity=Warning
Facility=Application
SymbolicName=MSG_TWO
Language=English
Application %1 is about to exit.
(The event data is the log handle which
is about to be closed.)
.
```

The message ID is an integer value. If left blank, it tells the system to increment from the previous value, or you can specify a specific value. The next line indicates the severity of the event. This value controls the icon that appears next to the event in the viewer. There are three possibilities:

1. Informational
2. Warning
3. Error

The next value identifies the facility. There are two possibilities:

1. Application
2. System (for services)

Then, as with categories, you specify the symbolic name (used in Listing 21.5), the language, and the actual string. The string can contain language-independent substitution strings, as long as you mark them with "%1," "%2," and so on in the string.

The message compiler takes all of this information and produces a resource file for the message table that the linker attaches to the EXE.

The code in Listing 21.5 actually produces events in the event viewer. If you run the EXE, you will see two new events appear for each execution. The code starts this process by connecting to the event log with the **Register EventSource** function.

RegisterEventSource   *Connects an application to the event log*

```
HANDLE RegisterEventSource(
    LPCTSTR server,
    LPCTSTR source)
```

server	Name of machine on network, or 0 for local machine
source	Points to the subkey in the registry containing the event log information

Returns a handle to the event log or 0 on error

You pass **RegisterEventSource** the same string you passed as the first parameter to Listing 21.4.

Listing 21.5 then creates two new events in the log using two calls to the **ReportEvent** function.

ReportEvent   Records an event in the event log

```
BOOL ReportEvent(
    HANDLE eventSource,
    WORD eventType,
    WORD category,
    DWORD event,
    PSID userSid,
    WORD numStrings,
    DWORD dataSize,
    LPCTSTR *stringArray,
    LPVOID data)
```

eventSource	Handle from **RegisterEventSource**
eventType	Type of event
category	A symbolic name for a category from the message file
event	A symbolic name for the event from the message file
userSid	A SID for the user, or NULL if irrelevant
numStrings	The number of substitution strings being passed in stringArray
dataSize	The number of bytes in the supplemental data block
stringArray	An argv style pointer to array of pointers to strings
data	A pointer to a block of supplemental data

Returns TRUE on success

Listing 21.5 creates two events in the log. The first is very simple, while the second one uses substitution strings and supplemental data. Substitution strings are language-independent strings, such as file names, that get substituted into the message string automatically. If there is more than one, you create an array of pointers to the string, as in an argv array, and pass **ReportError** a pointer to that array. Supplemental data can contain anything you like, but it will always be displayed in binary. You pass in the address of the buffer holding the data. Here the value of the **logHandle** variable is passed.

When you are finished reporting events to the event log, deregister as shown using the **DeregisterEventSource** function.

DeregisterEventSource   *Disconnects an application from the event log*

```
BOOL DeregisterEventSource(
    HANDLE eventLog)
```

eventLog   Handle to the event log from **RegisterEventSource**

Returns TRUE on success

21.3 Time

The 32-bit API contains a number of functions for getting and setting times on a Windows system. Listing 21.8 demonstrates all of the different time-retrieval functions.

Listing 21.8   *The time-retrieval functions*

```cpp
// timeshow.cpp

#include <windows.h>
#include <iostream.h>

VOID DumpTimeStruct(LPSYSTEMTIME st)
{
  cout << "Year        : "
    << st->wYear << endl;
  cout << "Month       : "
    << st->wMonth << endl;
  cout << "Day of Week : "
    << st->wDayOfWeek << endl;
  cout << "Day         : "
    << st->wDay << endl;
  cout << "Hour        : "
    << st->wHour << endl;
  cout << "Minute      : "
    << st->wMinute << endl;
```

Listing 21.8 *The time-retrieval functions (continued)*

```
  cout << "Second     : "
    << st->wSecond << endl;
  cout << "Milliseconds: "
    << st->wMilliseconds << endl;
}

VOID main(VOID)
{
  SYSTEMTIME st;
  HANDLE file;
  FILETIME ft;
  DWORD ret;
  TIME_ZONE_INFORMATION tzi;
  CHAR name[32];

  cout << "Tick Count is: "
    << GetTickCount() << endl << endl;

  // get UTC time
  GetSystemTime(&st);

  cout << "Current time (UTC):"
    << endl;
  DumpTimeStruct(&st);

  // get local time
  GetLocalTime(&st);

  cout << endl << "Current time (local):"
    << endl;
  DumpTimeStruct(&st);

  // get a file handle
  file=CreateFile("C:\\AUTOEXEC.BAT",
    GENERIC_READ, 0, NULL, OPEN_EXISTING,
    FILE_ATTRIBUTE_NORMAL, NULL);

  // get last write time
  GetFileTime(file, NULL, NULL, &ft);

  // close file handle
  CloseHandle(file);

  // convert file time to system time
  // structure
  FileTimeToSystemTime(&ft, &st);
```

```
cout << endl
  << "Last write time (UTC) of AUTOEXEC.BAT:"
  << endl;
DumpTimeStruct(&st);

// get time zone info
ret=GetTimeZoneInformation(&tzi);

// report time zone
switch(ret)
{
  case TIME_ZONE_ID_UNKNOWN:
    cout << endl << "Time zone not known."
      << endl;
    break;

  case TIME_ZONE_ID_STANDARD:
    cout << endl
      << "It is currently Standard Time."
      << endl;
    break;

  case TIME_ZONE_ID_DAYLIGHT:
    cout << endl
      << "It is currently Daylight Savings Time."
      << endl;
    break;

  default:
    cerr << "Unable to get time zone "
      << "information." << endl;
    return;
}

// report info from time zone
// structure
cout << endl << "Time Zone Information:"
  << endl;
cout << "Bias: " << tzi.Bias
  << endl << endl;
cout << "Standard Time Data" << endl
  << "-----" << endl;
WideCharToMultiByte(CP_ACP, NULL,
  tzi.StandardName, -1, name, 32,
  NULL, NULL);
cout << "Standard Name: " << name
  << endl;
cout << "Transition Date/Time:" << endl;
DumpTimeStruct(&tzi.StandardDate);
```

Listing 21.8   *The time-retrieval functions (continued)*

```
cout << "Standard Bias: "
  << tzi.StandardBias << endl;
cout << "-----" << endl << endl;
cout << "Daylight Savings Time Data" << endl
  << "-----" << endl;
WideCharToMultiByte(CP_ACP, NULL,
  tzi.DaylightName, -1, name, 32,
  NULL, NULL);
cout << "Daylight Name: " << name
  << endl;
cout << "Transition Date/Time:" << endl;
DumpTimeStruct(&tzi.DaylightDate);
cout << "Daylight Bias: "
  << tzi.DaylightBias << endl;
cout << "-----" << endl;
}
```

Listing 21.8 starts by printing out the value of the **GetTickCount** function. This function indicates how long the system has been running, in milliseconds. After about 50 days, the count cycles back to zero because of the limits of a 32-bit integer. We have used this function at several points in this book to generate a random value. It is also useful for testing elapsed times.

GetTickCount	*Returns elapsed time since startup in milliseconds*

`DWORD GetTickCount(VOID)`

Returns the time

Listing 21.8 next dumps both the system time and the local time using **GetSystemTime** and **GetLocalTime**. These functions each return a structure of time information that the **DumpTimeStructure** function prints.

GetSystemTime	*Returns the system time and date in UTC*
GetLocalTime	*Returns the local time and date*

```
VOID GetSystemTime(
  LPSYSTEMTIME time)
```

time   A pointer to a SYSTEMTIME structure

Returns nothing

System time is GMT (or UCT), while local time is adjusted for the time zone that you have set in the Time and Date applet of the Control Panel. Both return a structure that looks like this (from the winnt.h header file):

```
typedef struct _SYSTEMTIME {
    WORD wYear;
    WORD wMonth;
    WORD wDayOfWeek;
    WORD wDay;
    WORD wHour;
    WORD wMinute;
    WORD wSecond;
    WORD wMilliseconds;
} SYSTEMTIME;
```

The **GetFileTime** function accepts a file handle and retrieves its file times from the disk (see also Section 2.4.1). It returns the creation time, the last access time, and the last write time. The FAT file system records only the last write time, but other file systems hold all three. Listing 21.8 uses the **FileTimeToSystemTime** function to convert the file time to system time.

GetFileTime *Returns the times for a file from the file system*

```
BOOL GetFileTime(
    HANDLE fileHandle,
    LPFILETIME creation,
    LPFILETIME lastAccess,
    LPFILETIME lastWrite)
```

fileHandle	Handle to a file
creation	Time of file creation
lastAccess	Time of last access
lastWrite	Time of last write

Returns TRUE on success

FileTimeToSystemTime *Converts a file time to system time*

```
BOOL FileTimeToSystemTime(
    CONST FILETIME * fileTime,
    LPSYSTEMTIME systemTime)
```

fileTime	A file time value
systemTime	A system time structure

Returns TRUE on success

The **GetTimeZoneInformation** function returns information about the time zone used on the current machine.

GetTimeZoneInformation   *Returns information about the current time zone*

```
DWORD GetTimeZoneInformation(
   LPTIME_ZONE_INFORMATION tzi)
```

tzi   Pointer to a time zone information structure

Returns daylight savings time flag or 0xffffffff on error

The time zone information structure tells you about the current time zone, as shown here (copied from winnt.h):

```
typedef struct _TIME_ZONE_INFORMATION {
    LONG        Bias;
    WCHAR       StandardName[ 32 ];
    SYSTEMTIME  StandardDate;
    LONG        StandardBias;
    WCHAR       DaylightName[ 32 ];
    SYSTEMTIME  DaylightDate;
    LONG        DaylightBias;
} TIME_ZONE_INFORMATION;
```

The return value tells you about the daylight-savings-time status, as shown in the code.

Listing 21.9 demonstrates how to set the system time and date.

Listing 21.9   *Setting the system time*

```
// settime.cpp

#include <windows.h>
#include <iostream.h>

BOOL AdjustPrivilege(LPCTSTR privilege,
  DWORD attribute)
{
  BOOL ret;
  HANDLE procToken;
  LUID luid;
  TOKEN_PRIVILEGES tp;

  // get a handle to the access token used
  // by this process
  ret=OpenProcessToken(GetCurrentProcess(),
    TOKEN_ADJUST_PRIVILEGES, &procToken);
  if (!ret)
    return(FALSE);

  // get LUID for privilege
  ret=LookupPrivilegeValue(NULL, privilege,
    &luid);
```

```
  if (!ret)
  {
    CloseHandle(procToken);
    return(FALSE);
  }

  // fill in token privileges struct
  tp.PrivilegeCount=1;
  tp.Privileges[0].Luid=luid;
  tp.Privileges[0].Attributes=attribute;

  // attempt to enable privilege
  AdjustTokenPrivileges(procToken, FALSE, &tp,
    NULL, NULL, NULL);

  if (GetLastError() != ERROR_SUCCESS)
    ret=FALSE;
  else
    ret=TRUE;

  CloseHandle(procToken);

  return(ret);
}

VOID DumpTimeStruct(LPSYSTEMTIME st)
{
  cout << "Year        : "
    << st->wYear << endl;
  cout << "Month       : "
    << st->wMonth << endl;
  cout << "Day of Week : "
    << st->wDayOfWeek << endl;
  cout << "Day         : "
    << st->wDay << endl;
  cout << "Hour        : "
    << st->wHour << endl;
  cout << "Minute      : "
    << st->wMinute << endl;
  cout << "Second      : "
    << st->wSecond << endl;
  cout << "Milliseconds: "
    << st->wMilliseconds << endl;
}

VOID main(VOID)
{
  SYSTEMTIME st;

  // get local time
  GetLocalTime(&st);
```

Listing 21.9   *Setting the system time (continued)*

```
cout << endl << "Current time (local):"
  << endl;
DumpTimeStruct(&st);

st.wYear++;

// enable set system time privilege (delete in win95)
if (!AdjustPrivilege(SE_SYSTEMTIME_NAME,
  SE_PRIVILEGE_ENABLED))
{
  cerr << "Must have set system time "
    << "privilege." << endl;
  return;
}

// set new time
SetLocalTime(&st);

// get local time
GetLocalTime(&st);

cout << endl << "New current time (local):"
  << endl;
DumpTimeStruct(&st);

st.wYear--;

// reset time
SetLocalTime(&st);

// get local time
GetLocalTime(&st);

cout << endl << "Current time (local):"
  << endl;
DumpTimeStruct(&st);

// disable set system time privilege (delete in win98)
AdjustPrivilege(SE_SYSTEMTIME_NAME, 0);
}
```

In order to set the system time in Windows NT, you must have the SE_SYSTEM-TIME_NAME privilege, and you must enable that privilege (see Chapter 13). In Windows 98, anyone can set the time, and you can delete the call to **AdjustPrivilege** from the code. The code in Listing 21.9 gets the system time, enables the privilege, increments the year (simply to demonstrate a change), sets the time using the **SetLocalTime** function, gets the new time, dumps this time to show that it is in fact different, and then sets it back to its original value. If you want to set the time, it is generally easiest to start with an already-filled SYSTEMTIME structure and modify it, although you can create one from scratch if you like.

| **SetLocalTime** | *Sets the system time* |

```
BOOL SetLocalTime(
    CONST SYSTEMTIME * time)
```

| time | Pointer to a SYSTEMTIME structure |

Returns TRUE on success

21.4 Memory

The 32-bit APIs contains its own memory allocation and deallocation functions. Normally you will use functions like **new** or **malloc** to allocate memory inside an application, but there are cases in which you must use the API calls. Probably the best example of a place where you must use the API allocation functions is inside a DLL, where a call to **new** fails.

The APIs contains two identical sets of memory allocation functions. One starts with **Local** (e.g. **LocalAlloc**), while the other starts with **Global** (e.g. **GlobalAlloc**). In older versions of Windows, the two sets had different uses, but in Windows they are identical and completely interchangeable.

Use the **GlobalAlloc** and **GlobalFree** functions to allocate or deallocate a block of memory from the heap.

| **GlobalAlloc** | *Allocates memory from the heap* |

```
HGLOBAL GlobalAlloc(
    UINT flags,
    DWORD numBytes)
```

| flags | Allocation flags |
| numBytes | Number of bytes to allocate |

Returns a pointer or handle to the block allocated, or 0 on error

---

| **GlobalFree** | *Frees a block of memory* |

```
HGLOBAL GlobalFree(
    HGLOBAL memHandle)
```

| memHandle | The block to free |

Returns 0 on success or the handle on error

The **GlobalAlloc** function accepts a number of flags that control the behavior of the function or its resulting block of memory, as listed below. Many of these flags are carried over for compatibility reasons from earlier versions of Windows and are meaningless in newer versions. The normal flag to use for standard allocations is GPTR:

GMEM_FIXED	The memory block resides at a fixed location in memory
GMEM_MOVEABLE	Meaningless in Windows 2000 and 98
GPTR	Combines GMEM_FIXED and GMEM_ZEROINIT. The standard flag to use when allocating memory
GHND	Meaningless in Windows 2000 and 98
GMEM_DDESHARE	Meaningless in Windows 2000, but should be specified if the memory is being used for DDE
GMEM_DISCARDABLE	Allocates a discardable block of memory. Ignored by some implementations
GMEM_LOWER	Meaningless in Windows 2000 and 98
GMEM_NOCOMPACT	Must satisfy the memory request without compacting or discarding memory
GMEM_NODISCARD	Must satisfy the memory request without compacting or discarding memory
GMEM_NOT_BANKED	Meaningless in Windows 2000 and 98
GMEM_NOTIFY	Meaningless in Windows 2000 and 98
GMEM_SHARE	Same as GMEM_DDESHARE
GMEM_ZEROINIT	All bytes in block are initially set to zero. This takes time, so you can speed up an application by not zeroing the block

A typical memory allocation looks like this in a program, here from Listing 17.15 in the DLL chapter:

```
stacknode *temp;
temp = (stacknode *) GlobalAlloc(GPTR,
  sizeof stacknode);
```

With the exception of the flag parameter, this call looks identical to a normal **malloc** call. The HGLOBAL type returned by **GlobalAlloc** acts just like a pointer once you cast it and assign the value to a pointer.

Note that because this code uses the GPTR flag, it returns zeroed memory. If you do not require initialized memory, then use GMEM_FIXED instead and save a little CPU time. For example, Listing 17.10 allocates memory using the GPTR flag. On my machine, it takes the code about 12 seconds to execute. By changing the flag to GMEM_FIXED, the run time drops to 10 seconds.

Listing 21.10 *A simple memory-allocation program that allocates a 1 million-byte block 200 times*

```
// zero.cpp

#include <windows.h>
#include <iostream.h>

HGLOBAL temp;
int x;

void main(void)
{
  for (x=0; x<200; x++)
  {
    temp = GlobalAlloc(GPTR,
      1000000);
    FillMemory(temp,1000000, 0xAA);
    GlobalFree(temp);
  }
}
```

When the system allocates a block of memory, it often rounds the size of the block up. There are times when it is useful to know the actual block size (you can legally access all of the allocated bytes), or to get the size of an unknown block for which you have just received a pointer. Use **GlobalSize** to get a block's size.

GlobalSize   *Returns the actual size of a block given its handle*

```
DWORD GlobalSize(
  HGLOBAL address)
```

address   The address of the block

Returns the size or 0 on error

In other cases, you may receive a handle and want to check it to make sure that you are able to access the memory to which the handle points, before you actually use it. In the 32-bit APIs, four different functions check memory pointers:

IsBadCodePtr   Checks a function pointer for read access
IsBadReadPtr   Checks a pointer for read access
IsBadWritePtr   Checks a pointer for write access
IsBadStringPtr   Checks a string pointer for read access

IsBadCodePtr *Checks a function address to see if the thread can call it*

```
BOOL IsBadCodePtr(
  FARPROC address)
```

address   The address to check

Returns FALSE if memory address is accessible

IsBadReadPtr *Checks a range of bytes to see if the thread can read them*

```
BOOL IsBadReadPtr(
  CONST BYTE *address
  UINT numBytes)
```

address   The address to check

numBytes   The number of bytes in the block

Returns FALSE if all memory is accessible

IsBadWritePtr *Checks a range of bytes to see if the thread can write them*

```
BOOL IsBadWritePtr(
  CONST BYTE *address
  UINT numBytes)
```

address   The address to check

numBytes   The number of bytes in the block

Returns FALSE if all memory is accessible

IsBadStringPtr *Checks a range of bytes to see if the thread can read them, up to EOS or numBytes, whichever is smaller*

```
BOOL IsBadStringPtr(
  LPCTSTR address
  UINT numBytes)
```

address   The address to check

numBytes   The number of bytes in the block

Returns FALSE if all memory is accessible

In all likelihood, you do not want to be checking all of your pointers for validity each time you use them. Structured exception handling (Section 21.5) is a better way to handle memory exceptions.

The APIs provides the **GlobalMemoryStatus** function to get the status of the memory system.

GlobalMemoryStatus   *Returns status information about the memory system*

```
VOID GlobalMemoryStatus(
    LPMEMORYSTATUS status)
```

status   A pointer to a status record

Returns nothing

The **GlobalMemoryStatus** function returns a structure of type MEMO-RYSTATUS, as shown below from the winnt.h file:

```
typedef struct _MEMORYSTATUS {
    DWORD dwLength;
    DWORD dwMemoryLoad;
    DWORD dwTotalPhys;
    DWORD dwAvailPhys;
    DWORD dwTotalPageFile;
    DWORD dwAvailPageFile;
    DWORD dwTotalVirtual;
    DWORD dwAvailVirtual;
} MEMORYSTATUS, *LPMEMORYSTATUS;
```

To use **GlobalMemoryStatus**, declare a structure of type MEMORYS-TATUS. Initialize its **dwLength** field to **sizeof(MEMORYSTATUS)**. Pass the address of the structure to **GlobalMemoryStatus**. When the function returns, the **dwMemoryLoad** field will contain the percentage of memory currently in use. The last two fields tell you how much total memory space is available in the machine's virtual address space and how much is in current use.

The API provides four functions for copying and filling blocks of memory:

CopyMemory   Copies the contents of one block to another, provided that the blocks do not overlap

MoveMemory   Copies the contents of one block to another if they do overlap

FillMemory   Fills a block with the byte specified

ZeroMemory   Fills a block with zeros

CopyMemory   *Copies a block of memory from one address to another non-overlapping address*

```
VOID CopyMemory (
    PVOID destination,
    CONST VOID * source,
    DWORD numBytes)
```

destination   The destination address

source   The source address

numBytes   The number of bytes to copy

Returns nothing

MoveMemory	*Moves a block of memory from one address to another overlapping address*

```
VOID MoveMemory (
    PVOID destination,
    CONST VOID * source,
    DWORD numBytes)
```

destination	The destination address
source	The source address
numBytes	The number of bytes to move
Returns nothing	

FillMemory	*Fills a block of memory with the specified value*

```
VOID FillMemory (
    PVOID destination,
    DWORD numBytes,
    BYTE fill)
```

destination	The destination address
numBytes	The number of bytes to copy
fill	The value to fill with
Returns nothing	

ZeroMemory	*Fills a block of memory with zero*

```
VOID ZeroMemory (
    PVOID destination,
    DWORD numBytes)
```

destination	The destination address
numBytes	The number of bytes to zero
Returns nothing	

The API includes a facility to create a private heap and allocate memory from it. The new heap is private to the process that created it. To use this facility, you can call the **HeapCreate** function and specify the maximum size for the private heap. Windows will allocate all of that memory at once and make it available. You then access it using **HeapAlloc** and **HeapFree** to allocate and free memory on this private heap. You use **HeapAlloc** in the same way you use **GlobalAlloc**.

There are several ways to use private heaps. For example, you might want to give different threads in an application their own private heaps if you expect memory fragmentation to be especially bad when their allocations are mixed. Or, if you know a critical application will need 150 megs of memory and you do not want it to start unless you *know* that much space is available, you can allocate the entire 150 megs in a private heap at startup. Your application is then guaranteed to have all of the memory it needs throughout its run.

21.5 Structured Exception Handling

Compatibility Note: Visual C++ provides a better exception-handling mechanism. You will use structured exception handling (SEH) in your programs in two different ways. First, SEH is Windows' communication channel when hardware and software exceptions occur. A typical exception is an invalid memory access via a pointer. SEH is also useful because you can raise exceptions in your own code and catch and use them just like system exceptions. Both techniques are demonstrated in this section.

Let's say that you create and run a program that offends the computer. For example, you set a pointer **p** to NULL and then say

```
*p=5;
```

When you execute this program, it will die with an application error. What is really happening is that the system generated an exception. Because you did not handle it, the system invoked the default exception handler, which terminates the application.

To instead trap an exception and handle it within your program, you can use structured exception handling, as demonstrated in Listing 21.11.

Listing 21.11   *A simple example of exception handling*

```
// catch.cpp

#include <windows.h>
#include <iostream.h>

VOID main(VOID)
{
  CHAR *ptr;

  // point the pointer to an
  // invalid address
  ptr=NULL;

  __try
  {
    // attempt to assign a value
    // to the location pointed
    // to by the pointer
```

Listing 21.11   *A simple example of exception handling*

```
    *ptr=5;
  }
  __except(EXCEPTION_EXECUTE_HANDLER)
  {
    // report the exception type
    cerr << "Caught exception code: 0x"
      << hex << GetExceptionCode()
      << endl;
  }
}
```

Listing 21.11 contains two new key words: **try** and **except**, both of which use braces to wrap blocks of code. The **try** keyword tells the compiler to monitor any of the code in the try block for exceptions. The block following **try** is called a guarded body of code. The **except** keyword marks a block of code that the system will execute if an exception occurs. This is called the exception handler. The block of code in the **try** block should be sequential. It should not contain any **break**, **continue**, **goto**, or **return** statements, because these are treated and handled like exceptions.

Listing 21.11 contains an invalid instruction, in this case an invalid memory access. When the system executes that instruction, it traps the invalid access. If you execute the code in a normal program, the program simply dies and either the abnormal termination dialog appears or Dr. Watson pops up. But in Listing 21.11, the program executes the code following the **except** keyword.

Immediately following **except** is a set of parentheses that contain the filter expression, which is generally either a constant value as shown here or a function call that returns a constant value. Following the filter expression is the exception handler, a block of code that the system executes if the filter expression indicates EXCEPTON_EXECUTE_HANDLER. Other valid values for the filter expression to indicate are EXCEPTION_CONTINUE_EXECUTION (the code in the try block should continue as though nothing happened) and EXCEPTION_CONTINUE_SEARCH (the system tries to find another exception handler on the stack).

Listing 21.11 presents an extremely simple example. The filter expression for the **except** block indicates that the handler code should always execute, so the handler runs and prints an error to stderr. Part of the output contains the exception code, returned by the **GetExceptionCode** function.

GetExceptionCode   *Returns a constant indicating the cause of the last exception*

`DWORD GetExceptionCode(VOID)`

Returns exception constant.

The constant returned by **GetExceptionCode** is an integer value that matches one of the following constants:

EXCEPTION_ACCESS_ VIOLATION	Cannot access the address specified
EXCEPTION_BREAKPOINT	Breakpoint found
EXCEPTION_DATATYPE_ MISALIGNMENT	System tried to read data not on the proper word boundary for the hardware
EXCEPTION_SINGLE_STEP	One instruction executed in single-step mode
EXCEPTION_ARRAY_ BOUNDS_EXCEEDED	If the hardware supports array bounds checking, then this exception indicates that the bounds were exceeded
EXCEPTION_FLT_ DENORMAL_OPERAND	Floating point value too small
EXCEPTION_FLT_DIVIDE_ BY_ZERO	Divide by zero error
EXCEPTION_FLT_INEXACT_ RESULT	Value cannot be represented exactly (e.g. - 10/3)
EXCEPTION_FLT_INVALID_ OPERATION	Other floating point exceptions
EXCEPTION_FLT_ OVERFLOW	Floating point overflow
EXCEPTION_FLT_STACK_ CHECK	Stack overflow or underflow during floating point operation
EXCEPTION_FLT_ UNDERFLOW	Floating point underflow
EXCEPTION_INT_DIVIDE_ BY_ZERO	Integer divide by zero
EXCEPTION_INT_ OVERFLOW	Integer overflow
EXCEPTION_PRIV_ INSTRUCTION	Privileged instruction executed in user mode
STATUS_ NONCONTINUABLE_ EXCEPTION	The thread tried to continue execution but the exception cannot be continued

Not all hardware will generate all of these codes. Following execution of the handler function, the code drops out the bottom of the handler and continues from that point.

If the filter expression indicates EXCEPTION_CONTINUE_ EXECUTION, then the code in the **try** block continues from the point of the exception as though nothing had happened. Certain exceptions cannot continue, however, and in those cases a STATUS_NONCONTINUABLE_EXCEPTION exception immediately gets raised to indicate that continuation is impossible.

If the filter expression indicates EXECEPTION_CONTINUE_SEARCH, then the system searches for another exception handler. Here it is helpful to understand the implementation of the exception-handling system. When you put a **try** keyword in your code, an exception frame is placed on the stack. The frame is removed at the bottom of the guarded block of code. This is identical to the system's treatment of a local variable on the stack: when you declare the variable, it is placed on the stack, and it is removed from the stack when the bottom of that variable's block is reached.

When an exception occurs, the system scans the stack from the top (in the stack sense of the word top) looking for an exception frame. The frame tells it where to find the **except** statement. The system finds the first one and tries the **except** block. **Try-except** statements can be nested. One inner **try-except** pair might handle a certain exception, but it may want to pass certain more generic exceptions up to a **try-except** pair that it is nested within. When the system sees EXECEPTION_CONTINUE_SEARCH in a filter expression, it returns to the stack and continues searching for the next exception frame. Eventually it will get to the system exception frame at the very bottom of the stack. In this case, the system's exception handler—the default mechanism used normally by programs—executes and terminates the application.

Normally you place a function call in the filter expression. This function decides what action the code wishes to take in response to particular exception codes, and returns the appropriate constant value. In simple cases like the one shown in Listing 21.11, however, the exception handler foregoes the function call and uses a constant instead.

There is a second way to handle exceptions using a **try-finally** pair. The **finally** block is similar to an **except** block, except that it *always* executes at the end of the try block regardless of whether or not an exception occurs. Since it always executes, it does not have a filter expression. Instead, you can use the **AbnormalTermination** function inside the **finally** block to decide whether an exception was generated or not.

AbnormalTermination	*Indicates whether the try block generated an exception or not inside a finally block*

```
BOOL AbnormalTermination(VOID)
```

Returns TRUE on an exception

Listing 21.12 demonstrates the **try-finally** pair. It first uses the **finally** block without generating an exception, and then uses it during an exception.

Listing 21.12   *Demonstration of the try-finally pair*

```
// term.cpp

#include <windows.h>
#include <iostream.h>
```

```
VOID main(VOID)
{
  CHAR *ptr;

  // point the pointer to an
  // invalid address
  ptr=NULL;

  __try
  {
    cout << "No problems." << endl;

  }
  __finally
  {
    if (AbnormalTermination())
      cerr << "Cleaning up after exception."
        << endl;
    else
      cout << "Cleaning up after normal"
        << " execution." << endl;

    // clean up
  }

  __try
  {
    cout << endl << "Make problems." << endl;
    // attempt to assign a value
    // to the location pointed
    // to by the pointer
    *ptr=5;
  }
  __finally
  {
    if (AbnormalTermination())
      cerr << "Cleaning up after exception."
        << endl;
    else
      cout << "Cleaning up after normal"
        << " execution." << endl;

    // clean up
  }
}
```

The try-finally construct allows the programmer to clean up gracefully, regardless of the success of the operation in the try block. This is especially useful when dealing with synchronization mechanisms (see Chapter 7) that must be released to allow other threads to continue.

Although hardware exceptions are right now the most common way to use Windows' exception-handling mechanism, it is also possible for you to design and use your own exceptions. Probably the best current example of this process can be found in the RPC system (see Chapter 9). The RPC facility uses exceptions as an alternate signaling mechanism to indicate RPC system problems. For example, if you create a **CalcPixel** function, as demonstrated in Section 9.2, the return value and parameters for the function are defined by you. There is no way for the RPC system to signal its own errors, such as failed network connections or server communication problems. Therefore, it uses the exception mechanism to signal its problems.

Listing 21.13 demonstrates the process of creating and raising your own exceptions. It also shows how to override the system's default exception handler.

Listing 21.13   *User-defined exception handling*

```cpp
// softexpt.cpp

#include <windows.h>
#include <iostream.h>

#define TYPE_1 0x1  // an ignored exception
#define TYPE_2 0x2  // a handled exception
#define TYPE_3 0x3  // an unhandled exception

VOID MakeException(DWORD type)
{
  switch(type)
  {
    // recoverable exeception
    case TYPE_1:
      RaiseException(TYPE_1, 0, NULL,
        NULL);
      break;

    // exception which must be handled
    case TYPE_2:
      RaiseException(TYPE_2,
        EXCEPTION_NONCONTINUABLE, NULL,
        NULL);
      break;

    // just generate an exception
    case TYPE_3:
      RaiseException(TYPE_3, 0, NULL,
        NULL);
      break;
  }
}
```

```
DWORD Filter(EXCEPTION_POINTERS *ep)
{
  cerr << "Dumping some exception info:" << endl;
  cerr << "Code : 0x" << hex
    << ep->ExceptionRecord->ExceptionCode << endl;
  cerr << "Flags: 0x" << hex
    << ep->ExceptionRecord->ExceptionFlags << endl;
  cerr << "Addr : " << hex
    << ep->ExceptionRecord->ExceptionAddress
    << endl;
  // arguments from RaiseException can also
  // be retrieved from "ep"

  // decide what to do based on type
  switch(ep->ExceptionRecord->ExceptionCode)
  {
    case TYPE_1:
      cerr << "Allow execution to continue."
        << endl;
      return(EXCEPTION_CONTINUE_EXECUTION);
      break;

    case TYPE_2:
      cerr << "Execute exception handler block."
        << endl;
      return(EXCEPTION_EXECUTE_HANDLER);
      break;

    case TYPE_3:
      cerr
        << "Pass exception to debugger or system."
        << endl;
      return(EXCEPTION_CONTINUE_SEARCH);
      break;

    default:
      return(EXCEPTION_EXECUTE_HANDLER);
  }
}

VOID TryExcept(DWORD type)
{
  __try
  {
    MakeException(type);
  }
  __except(Filter(GetExceptionInformation()))
  {
    // report the exception type
    cerr << "Caught exception code: 0x"
```

Listing 21.13   *User-defined exception handling (continued)*

```
            << hex << GetExceptionCode()
            << endl;
    }
}


// User defined exception filter which
// gets dispatched whenever user code
// does not handle an exception
LONG TopLevelExceptionFilter
    (EXCEPTION_POINTERS *ep)
{
    // exception information can be used
    // from "ep" if needed

    cerr << "Exception filtered by user "
        << "defined \"Unhandled Exception "
        << "Filter\"." << endl;
    Beep(300, 100);
    MessageBox(NULL, "Managing Exception",
        "Programmer Defined Filter",
        MB_OK | MB_ICONINFORMATION);

    // allow exception handler to execute which
    // causes program termination
    return(EXCEPTION_EXECUTE_HANDLER);
    // use care when returning
    // EXCEPTION_CONTINUE_EXECUTION
    // because an infinite loop of
    // exceptions may occur
}

VOID main(VOID)
{
    cout << "Generate an exception which "
        << "can be ignored."
        << endl;
    TryExcept(TYPE_1);

    cout << endl
        << "Generate an exception which "
        << "can be handled."
        << endl;
    TryExcept(TYPE_2);

    // Replace system exception filter
    // with a custom filter
    SetUnhandledExceptionFilter(
        (LPTOP_LEVEL_EXCEPTION_FILTER)
```

```
        TopLevelExceptionFilter);

    // generate an exception which
    // gets passed out to the newly
    // defined custom filter
    cout << endl
        << "Generate an exception which "
        << "is not handled."
        << endl;
    TryExcept(TYPE_3);
}
```

For the sake of example, Listing 21.13 generates, or *raises*, three different exceptions (TYPE_1, TYPE_2, and TYPE_3), which are ignored, handled, or not handled, respectively. The main function demonstrates the first two, and then calls the **SetUnhandledExceptionFilter** function to replace the system exception handler with a custom exception handler before generating an unhandled exception.

SetUnhandledExceptionFilter	*Replaces the system's exception handler with a custom handler*

```
LPTOP_LEVEL_EXCEPTION_FILTER
    SetUnhandledExceptionFilter(
        LPTOP_LEVEL_EXCEPTION_FILTER filter)
```

filter	The custom filter function

Returns address of prior filter

When the code wants to generate an exception, it calls the **RaiseException** function. This function accepts an exception code, as well as supplemental exception data if desired.

RaiseException	*Generates a user-defined exception*

```
VOID RaiseException(
    DWORD exceptionCode,
    DWORD exceptionFlags,
    DWORD numArguments,
    CONST DWORD * arguments)
```

exceptionCode	The user-defined exception code
exceptionFlags	Specify EXCEPTION_NONCONTINUABLE if this exception cannot be continued, 0 otherwise
numArguments	The number of DWORD words of supplemental data
arguments	Pointer to a buffer holding supplemental data of DWORDs

Returns nothing

When a function calls **RaiseException**, it stops execution while the system searches for an exception handler. That is, a piece of code has called the function that is raising the exception, and that piece of code may or may not have an exception handler in place to handle the function's new exception. The system searches to see if a handler is in place. If not, the search will eventually arrive at the system exception handler, which terminates the application. However, if it does find an exception handler frame on the stack, it executes it. That frame may handle the exception, or it may allow the function to continue execution.

Exceptions are useful for trapping system errors and terminating the application gracefully. When you are developing your own libraries, you will find that custom exceptions give you an extra channel of communication and can therefore be very useful in special situations.

21.6 Error Handling

The **GetLastError** and **Beep** functions have been used throughout this book. There are several other error-handling functions, however, and you will find them useful for special situations or when trying to polish an application or DLL.

GetLastError   *Returns the error code of the most recent error*

```
DWORD GetLastError(VOID)
```

Returns the error code of the last error

Beep   *Beeps the systems speaker at the specified frequency*
                                     for the specified time

```
BOOL Beep(
    DWORD freq,
    DWORD duration)
```

freq   Frequency of the sound

duration   Time in milliseconds for beep

Returns TRUE on success

For example, in certain cases you want a window that does not currently have focus to be able to get the user's attention. If it beeps it confuses the user because the user does not know where the beep is coming from. However, if the application beeps *and* flashes its title bar or icon, then the user knows which window needs attention. The **FlashWindow** function flashes the title bar for you.

FlashWindow   *Flashes a window's title bar or icon*

```
BOOL FlashWindow(
    HWND window,
    BOOL status)
```

window   Handle of window to flash

status   Whether the title bar should appear enabled or not

Returns TRUE on success

A simple beep generated by **Beep** is fairly mundane in a world of multimedia. There are two ways for you to improve the sound output of your applications. **MessageBeep** lets you play one of the five system-defined error sounds. The user chooses these sounds in the Sound applet of the Control Panel:

MB_ICONASTERISK
MB_ICONEXCLAMATION
MB_ICONHAND
MB_ICONQUESTION
MB_OK

The **PlaySound** function lets you play any WAV file, either on disk or in a resource file. You can pass this function several different flags:

SND_ALIAS	The file name actually specifies an entry in the sounds section of the registry
SND_ASYNC	Play the sound in the background and return immediately
SND_FILENAME	The file name specifies the name of a valid WAV file
SND_NODEFAULT	Do not use default sound if alias not found
SND_NOWAIT	Fail immediately if no WAV device is present
SND_RESOURCE	The file name specifies the name of a resource inside the specified module
SND_SYNC	Play the sound and do not return until it is finished

---

MessageBeep   *Plays one of the system sounds*

```
BOOL MessageBeep(
    UINT type)
```

type   The type of sound to produce

Returns TRUE on success

PlaySound	*Plays a WAV file*

```
BOOL PlaySound(
   LPCTSTR fileName,
   HANDLE module,
   DWORD soundFlags)
```

fileName	The name of the file or resource to play
module	If fileName contains a resource name, a handle to the module containing the resource
soundFlags	Flags controlling the behavior of the function

Returns TRUE on success

The **SetErrorMode** function determines how the application behaves when it receives a system error. The function accepts one of three values:

SEM_FAILCRITICALERRORS	Critical errors are returned to the application rather than being handled by Windows
SEM_NOGPFAULTERRORBOX	Use only if creating a debugger
SEM_NOOPENFILEERRORBOX	If the system cannot find a file, it returns the error to the application, rather than displaying a system error message.

SetErrorMode	*Determines the application's behavior on system errors*

```
UINT SetErrorMode(
   UINT errorMode)
```

errorMode	The new error mode

Returns previous mode

Finally, especially when you are creating your own DLLs, you will want to emulate the **GetLastError** behavior of the API functions in your own functions. The **SetLastError** and **SetLastErrorEx** functions let you set a thread's last error value. Any call to **GetLastError** will return this value until the value is set by some other function. Inside your DLL you can advise the caller of errors by calling this function and then passing back an error indicator.

SetLastError	*Sets the thread's lastError code*

```
VOID SetLastError(
   DWORD error)
```

error	The last error

Returns nothing

SetLastErrorEx   *Sets the thread's lastError code, along with debugger information*

```
VOID SetLastErrorEx(
    DWORD error
    DWORD type)
```

error   The last error

type   Type information for the debugger

Returns nothing

Compiling the Code in this Book

This book contains hundreds of code listings. You will find that these listings break down into four different categories:

1. Pure-console programs that read and write text data (you can compile these either with the SDK or with Visual C^{++})
2. GUI programs using the 32-bit APIs (you can compile these either with the SDK or with Visual C^{++})
3. GUI programs using MFC (you must compile these using Visual C^{++})
4. Other programs: DLL code, RPC code, and others (you can compile these either with the SDK or with Visual C^{++})

This appendix contains information on compiling the first three types of code using the Win32 SDK or Visual C^{++}. The fourth type of code is covered when the code appears. For example, the RPC chapter contains makefiles for compiling RPC programs. You compile these programs using the same techniques that you use to compile the first three categories of code.

The supplied diskette contains appropriately adjusted makefiles for the code in each directory, and also contains Visual C^{++} makefiles. This saves you the trouble of creating your own. ***In addition, README files in each directory on the diskette contain important compilation instructions that you will find extremely helpful.*** This appendix is intended to act as an introduction to compilation.

If you have compilation problems, be sure to contact the information server described in Appendix B to obtain free updates.

A.1 Compiling with the Win32 SDK

The code in Listing A.1 represents a typical console program named textsamp.cpp. The makefile in Listing A.2 will compile it under the SDK. Note that the makefile's first line reads "APP=textsamp." Change the name in this line to compile different programs.

Listing A.1   *A simple console program (textsamp.cpp)*

```
// textsamp.cpp


#include <windows.h>
#include <iostream.h>

void main(void)
{
  int x;

  for (x=0; x<10; x++)
  {
    cout << "Hello" << endl;
    Beep(100, 50);
    Sleep(250);
  }
}
```

Listing A.2   *A makefile for Listing A.1 (textsamp.cpp). Run mstools\setenv.bat before trying to compile, and then type "nmake" to compile. Change the first line to compile a different file*

```
APP=textsamp
NODEBUG=1

!include <ntwin32.mak>

$(APP).exe: $(APP).obj
    $(link) $(conlflags) $(ldebug) \
        $(conlibsmt) $(APP).obj -out:$(APP).exe

$(APP).obj: $(APP).cpp
    $(cc) $(cflags) $(cdebug) \
        $(cvarsmt) $(APP).cpp
```

Before you can compile Listing A.1 with the makefile in Listing A.2, you often must set some environment variables. The easiest way to do this is to run the file setenv.bat in the mstools directory. You might also consider looking at which variables are set by setenv, and then setting them permanently in your account using the System applet in the Control Panel. Once the environment variables are set, create a new directory, place Listings A.1 and A.2 in it, and then type "nmake" to compile the code.

Note that in many cases you will have to add extra libraries to the link line of the makefile. The library advapi32.lib is especially popular. If your program will not link, expect that it is because of missing libraries. For example, to add the advanced API library to the makefile, change the link line in the makefile so that it looks like this:

```
$(APP).exe: $(APP).obj
   $(link) $(conlflags) $(ldebug) advapi32.lib \
     $(conlibsmt) $(APP).obj -out:$(APP).exe
```

Certain programs in Chapters 3 and 4 also want to link to mpr.lib. The mstools\lib directory contains all of the normal system libraries: Use qgrep in the lib directory with the "-l" option to find libraries.

Also note that the makefile uses "convarsmt" and "conlibsmt." These are multi-threaded versions of the libraries, and they guarantee that multi-threaded code will work correctly.

To compile GUI applications created using the 32-bit APIs (as opposed to MFC programs, which are described below), use the makefile shown in Listing A.4. Listing A.3 contains winsamp.cpp, which represents a typical GUI application with a **WinMain** main function. It simply displays a message box and quits. The "ranmon" programs in Chapter 8 need this makefile.

Listing A.3   *A typical Windows GUI program (winsamp.cpp)*

```
// winsamp.cpp

#include <windows.h>
#include <iostream.h>

int WINAPI WinMain(HANDLE ghInstance,
  HANDLE hPrevInstance, LPSTR lpCmdLine,
  int nCmdShow)
{
  Beep (100, 100);
  MessageBox(NULL, "Sample message",
    "Winsamp", MB_OK | MB_ICONHAND);
  return 0;
}
```

Listing A.4   *A makefile for Listing A.3*

```
APP=winsamp
NODEBUG=1
```

```
!include <ntwin32.mak>

$(APP).exe: $(APP).obj
   $(link) $(guilflags) $(ldebug) \
      $(guilibsmt) $(APP).obj -out:$(APP).exe

$(APP).obj: $(APP).cpp
   $(cc) $(cflags) $(cdebug) \
      $(cvarsmt) $(APP).cpp
```

As with the console program, create a new directory. Place in it Listing A.3 with the file name "winsamp.cpp" and Listing A.4 with the file name "makefile." Type "nmake" to compile the code.

This book contains a number of MFC (Microsoft Foundations Class library) programs. These programs require that you use Visual C++ to compile them. Listing A.5 represents a typical MFC program

Listing A.5   *A typical MFC program (mfcsamp.cpp)*

```
// mfcsamp.cpp

#include <afxwin.h>

#define IDB_BUTTON 100

// Declare the application class
class CButtonApp : public CWinApp
{
public:
   virtual BOOL InitInstance();
};

// Create an instance of the application class
CButtonApp ButtonApp;

// Declare the main window class
class CButtonWindow : public CFrameWnd
{
   CButton *button;
public:
   CButtonWindow();
   ~CButtonWindow();
   afx_msg void HandleButton();

   DECLARE_MESSAGE_MAP()
};
```

Listing A.5 *A typical MFC program (mfcsamp.cpp) (continued)*

```
// The message handler function
void CButtonWindow::HandleButton()
{
   Beep(700,500);
}

// The message map
BEGIN_MESSAGE_MAP(CButtonWindow, CFrameWnd)
   ON_COMMAND(IDB_BUTTON, HandleButton)
END_MESSAGE_MAP()

// The InitInstance function is called once
// when the application first executes
BOOL CButtonApp::InitInstance()
{
   m_pMainWnd = new CButtonWindow();
   m_pMainWnd->ShowWindow(m_nCmdShow);
   m_pMainWnd->UpdateWindow();
   return TRUE;
}
```

To compile the code, create a new directory. Copy Listing A.5 into a file named "mfcsamp.cpp." Create a new project file and add the MFC code file to the project as described in Section A.2. Many of the larger MFC programs in this book also use an RC file to handle their menus. Simply add an RC file to the project and it will be compiled automatically.

A.2 Compiling with Visual C++

You can compile the code in this book using Visual C++ either by creating new project files, by loading Visual C++ project files from the diskette, or by loading the makefiles supplied on the diskette as external makefiles. The latter option is required for several of the applications in this book.

To compile a program using a project file supplied on the diskette (they end with a ".mak" extension), simply load the project file by double-clicking on it and Build the project.

To load a normal MAKEFILE into Visual C++, perform the following steps. Listing A.1 in the previous section represents a simple console program. Listing A.2 is its normal makefile. You can either type these two files in or copy them from the diskette that came with the book. To compile this code under Visual C++:

1. Since Visual C++ remembers any previously open project and its files, go into the **File** menu and choose the **Close** option as many times as you are allowed. This clears out the old project and its files.

2. Select the **Open** option in the **File** menu. In this dialog, change to the directory that contains the code contained in Listings A.1 and A.2. Type "makefile." into the **File Name** field (or choose "All Files" from the **File Type** list and double-click on "makefile").

3. The code should compile without error using the **Build** option in the **Project** menu. Run it with the **Execute** option in the **Project** menu.

Follow the same steps for the other example files seen in Section A.1.

To compile multiple files in the same directory, close the current project using the **Close** option in the **File** menu. Change the APP or FILENAME value in the makefile. Load the modified makefile using the **Open** option in the **File** menu.

You should be able to compile all of the code presented in this book using Visual C^{++}, with the possible exception of the RPC code in Chapter 9. Visual C^{++} version 2.x does not contain the MIDL compiler, so there is no way to compile the IDL files. The SDK contains the MIDL compiler, however (midl.exe), and if you borrow it and place it in the VC^{++} BIN directory you can compile RPC code without problems. Also copy WINNT.MAK to the VC^{++} INCLUDE directory, and consider also borrowing the SDK's RPC.HLP file as a reference.

Contacting the Author

Ronald D. Reeves is founder and President of Computer Engineering, Inc. (CEI). CEI is a software development and systems-integration firm that specializes in using the Microsoft tools and technologies to develop custom applications. If you have questions, comments, or suggestions for improving the book, we would like to hear from you. You can contact the author either by U.S. mail or by E-Mail at the following addresses:

Ronald D. Reeves
PO Box 474
Clinton, CT 06413
E-mail ce@ismi.net

Marshall Brain is founder and principal of Interface Technologies, Inc., a nationally recognized software development and enterprise systems design and implementation firm. He is the author of nine books on Windows NT/95 software development.

Error Codes

Whenever you use the **GetLastError** function, you get error codes that do not have any meaning. The following table shows the first 10 such codes:

```
The operation completed successfully.
ERROR_SUCCESS                          0

Incorrect function.
ERROR_INVALID_FUNCTION                 1

The system cannot find the file specified.
ERROR_FILE_NOT_FOUND                   2

The system cannot find the path specified.
ERROR_PATH_NOT_FOUND                   3

The system cannot open the file.
ERROR_TOO_MANY_OPEN_FILES              4

Access is denied.
ERROR_ACCESS_DENIED                    5


The handle is invalid.
ERROR_INVALID_HANDLE                   6

The storage control blocks were destroyed.
ERROR_ARENA_TRASHED                    7

Not enough storage is available to process this command.
ERROR_NOT_ENOUGH_MEMORY                8
```

```
The storage control block address is invalid.
ERROR_INVALID_BLOCK                    9

The environment is incorrect.
ERROR_BAD_ENVIRONMENT                  10
```

To get a complete listing of the several thousand error codes available, look in the WINERROR.H file in the include directory of Visual C++ or the SDK. This file has a complete listing of all codes, along with one-line descriptions like the ones we have shown.

INDEX